The justice of the peace, and parish officer. By Richard Burn, ... to which is added an appendix, ... In four volumes. Vol. I. The fifteenth edition Volume 1 of 4

Richard Burn

PRINT EDITIONS

Eighteenth Century
Collections Online
Print Editions

Gale ECCO Print Editions

Relive history with *Eighteenth Century Collections Online*, now available in print for the independent historian and collector. This series includes the most significant English-language and foreign-language works printed in Great Britain during the eighteenth century, and is organized in seven different subject areas including literature and language; medicine, science, and technology; and religion and philosophy. The collection also includes thousands of important works from the Americas.

The eighteenth century has been called "The Age of Enlightenment." It was a period of rapid advance in print culture and publishing, in world exploration, and in the rapid growth of science and technology – all of which had a profound impact on the political and cultural landscape. At the end of the century the American Revolution, French Revolution and Industrial Revolution, perhaps three of the most significant events in modern history, set in motion developments that eventually dominated world political, economic, and social life.

In a groundbreaking effort, Gale initiated a revolution of its own: digitization of epic proportions to preserve these invaluable works in the largest online archive of its kind. Contributions from major world libraries constitute over 175,000 original printed works. Scanned images of the actual pages, rather than transcriptions, recreate the works *as they first appeared.*

Now for the first time, these high-quality digital scans of original works are available via print-on-demand, making them readily accessible to libraries, students, independent scholars, and readers of all ages.

For our initial release we have created seven robust collections to form one the world's most comprehensive catalogs of 18th century works.

Initial Gale ECCO Print Editions collections include:

History and Geography
Rich in titles on English life and social history, this collection spans the world as it was known to eighteenth-century historians and explorers. Titles include a wealth of travel accounts and diaries, histories of nations from throughout the world, and maps and charts of a world that was still being discovered. Students of the War of American Independence will find fascinating accounts from the British side of conflict.

Social Science

Delve into what it was like to live during the eighteenth century by reading the first-hand accounts of everyday people, including city dwellers and farmers, businessmen and bankers, artisans and merchants, artists and their patrons, politicians and their constituents. Original texts make the American, French, and Industrial revolutions vividly contemporary.

Medicine, Science and Technology

Medical theory and practice of the 1700s developed rapidly, as is evidenced by the extensive collection, which includes descriptions of diseases, their conditions, and treatments. Books on science and technology, agriculture, military technology, natural philosophy, even cookbooks, are all contained here.

Literature and Language

Western literary study flows out of eighteenth-century works by Alexander Pope, Daniel Defoe, Henry Fielding, Frances Burney, Denis Diderot, Johann Gottfried Herder, Johann Wolfgang von Goethe, and others. Experience the birth of the modern novel, or compare the development of language using dictionaries and grammar discourses.

Religion and Philosophy

The Age of Enlightenment profoundly enriched religious and philosophical understanding and continues to influence present-day thinking. Works collected here include masterpieces by David Hume, Immanuel Kant, and Jean-Jacques Rousseau, as well as religious sermons and moral debates on the issues of the day, such as the slave trade. The Age of Reason saw conflict between Protestantism and Catholicism transformed into one between faith and logic -- a debate that continues in the twenty-first century.

Law and Reference

This collection reveals the history of English common law and Empire law in a vastly changing world of British expansion. Dominating the legal field is the *Commentaries of the Law of England* by Sir William Blackstone, which first appeared in 1765. Reference works such as almanacs and catalogues continue to educate us by revealing the day-to-day workings of society.

Fine Arts

The eighteenth-century fascination with Greek and Roman antiquity followed the systematic excavation of the ruins at Pompeii and Herculaneum in southern Italy; and after 1750 a neoclassical style dominated all artistic fields. The titles here trace developments in mostly English-language works on painting, sculpture, architecture, music, theater, and other disciplines. Instructional works on musical instruments, catalogs of art objects, comic operas, and more are also included.

The BiblioLife Network

This project was made possible in part by the BiblioLife Network (BLN), a project aimed at addressing some of the huge challenges facing book preservationists around the world. The BLN includes libraries, library networks, archives, subject matter experts, online communities and library service providers. We believe every book ever published should be available as a high-quality print reproduction; printed on-demand anywhere in the world. This insures the ongoing accessibility of the content and helps generate sustainable revenue for the libraries and organizations that work to preserve these important materials.

The following book is in the "public domain" and represents an authentic reproduction of the text as printed by the original publisher. While we have attempted to accurately maintain the integrity of the original work, there are sometimes problems with the original work or the micro-film from which the books were digitized. This can result in minor errors in reproduction. Possible imperfections include missing and blurred pages, poor pictures, markings and other reproduction issues beyond our control. Because this work is culturally important, we have made it available as part of our commitment to protecting, preserving, and promoting the world's literature.

GUIDE TO FOLD-OUTS MAPS and OVERSIZED IMAGES

The book you are reading was digitized from microfilm captured over the past thirty to forty years. Years after the creation of the original microfilm, the book was converted to digital files and made available in an online database.

In an online database, page images do not need to conform to the size restrictions found in a printed book. When converting these images back into a printed bound book, the page sizes are standardized in ways that maintain the detail of the original. For large images, such as fold-out maps, the original page image is split into two or more pages

Guidelines used to determine how to split the page image follows:

• Some images are split vertically; large images require vertical and horizontal splits.
• For horizontal splits, the content is split left to right.
• For vertical splits, the content is split from top to bottom.
• For both vertical and horizontal splits, the image is processed from top left to bottom right.

THE

JUSTICE of the PEACE,

AND

PARISH OFFICER.

By RICHARD BURN, LL.D.

Chancellor of the Diocese of CARLISLE, and one of his
MAJESTY's Justices of the Peace for the Counties
of WESTMORLAND and CUMBERLAND.

The FIFTEENTH EDITION:
To which is added an APPENDIX, including the
Statutes of the last Session of Parliament (24 G. 3.)

In FOUR VOLUMES.

VOL. I.

LONDON

Printed by W STRAHAN and W. WOODFALL, Law-Printers
to the King's most Excellent Majesty,

For T. CADELL, in the Strand
M.DCC LXXXV.

TO THE RIGHT HONOURABLE

JAMES Earl of LONSDALE, Vifcount Lonfdale of Lonfdale in the county of Weftmorland and county palatine of Lancafter, Vifcount Lowther of Lowther in the faid county of Weftmorland, baron Lowther of Lowther in the county of Weftmorland, Baron Kendal of Kendal in the faid county, Baron Burgh of Burgh in the county of Cumberland, lord lieutenant and cuftos rotulorum of the faid counties of Weftmorland and Cumberland; this book is humbly dedicated, by the author,

RI. BURN.

THE

PREFACE

TO THE

FIRST EDITION.

THE author propofeth in this book to render the laws relating to the fubjects it treats of, a little more intelligible than hath hitherto been done.

The method he makes ufe of is various.

The firſt thing regarded is the order of *time*. Thus in the Poor laws; firſt is fet forth the appointment of *overfeers*, next the feveral branches of their duty, in finding *fettlements* for the poor——in removing them to fuch fettlements ———in making *rates* for their relief——in *relieving* and otherwife ordering them——and laſt of all, in *accounting* at the expiration of their office.——Then again, in treating of *fet-*

tlements,

tlements, it occurs to confider diftinctly, and as near to the faid order as may be, ten different kinds of fettlements——by *birth*——by the *parents* fettlement——by *apprenticefhip*——by *fervice*——by *marriage*——by *inhabiting forty days after notice*——by paying *parifh rates*——by ferving a *parifh office*——by *renting* 10l *a year*——and by a perfon's *own eftate*——In like manner, in treating of the *rates*, firft is fet forth the courfe of *laying the affeffment*—then the *allowance* thereof by the juftices——*publifhing* the fame in the church——*appeal* againft the rates at the feffions——levying the fame by *diftrefs*——and finally, *commitment* where no diftrefs can be had.

Thus to exhibit another inftance——In the article of the *Woollen manufacture*, which makes up a confiderable part of the juftice of the peace his duty, and of the officers fubordinate to him, there is fuch a number and variety of ftatutes, that authors are generally overwhelmed with them. To avoid which perplexity, the laws are here digefted in order, according to the natural progrefs of that bufinefs, from the fhearing of the fheep, to the exportation of the wool manufactured; under the feveral heads of *winding of wool* by the fhearer——laws to prevent its *exportation*——*working* of cloth——*fulling*——*meafuring*——*dying*——*ftretching*——*dreffing*——*exporting*.

Where there is no priority in point of time, the next method is that of Lord *Coke*, to frame

a de-a definition which takes in the whole subject, and then explain the several parts of such definition in their order. Thus *Grand larceny* is defined to be, *A felonious and fraudulent taking and carrying away by any person of the mere personal goods of another, above the value of* 12 *d* In the handling of which, the several branches of the definition are explained in the order as they stand · *viz.* *A felonious and fraudulent taking*————*and carrying away* ———— *by any person*————*of the mere personal goods*————*of another* ———— *above the value of* 12 *d*. Under which heads the general learning relating to that whole title is comprehended.

The like method is pursued in treating of the *commission of the peace*, the form of an *indictment*, the form of an *order of removal*, and other articles.

In general, it is provided, that one thing shall clear the way for another, and the subsequent paragraphs explain the preceding.

Under the influence of which conduct, the author hath attempted to bring together under one general title, divers articles relating to the same subject, which in the common books are broken and detached under various separate titles; hoping thereby, that what hath hitherto been thought introductory of confusion, may tend to render the subject more perspicuous, in exhibiting the whole under one comprehensive view. Thus the laws relating to the *game*, which are above forty in

number,

number, and are interfperfed in the common books under about thirteen different titles, are here digefted under one general title, *Game*, to which the reader fhall have recourfe for the knowledge of whatfoever belongeth to that fubject. For example, if any perfon would be fatisfied, what penalty the law hath provided for *tracing hares in the fnow*; by recurring to the general title concerning the game, he will find the game diftinguifhed into three kinds, the *four-footed* game, the *winged* game, and the game of *fifh*: The *four-footed* game, are diftributed into the feveral fpecies of *deer*, *hares*, and *conies*, under which head concerning *hares*, he will readily find what is defired. In like manner, the *winged* game are fubdivided into feveral branches, concerning *hawks* and *hawking*——*fwans*——*partridges and phiafants* —— *pigeons* —— *wild ducks, wild geefe, and other water fowl* —— *groufe or moor game*—— *herons* —— and *other fowl*, each of which have their peculiar laws.

In thefe large comprehenfive titles, care is likewife taken, to be as particular as may be without injuring the connection in the ftatutes, by inferting the whole law by itfelf, relating to each feparate article. The benefit of which will appear by the following inftance. If a perfon would know, what number of horfes or beafts in a cart or waggon are allowed by the ftatutes for the prefervation of the roads; let him take what treatife at prefent he pleafes concerning the highways, he muft read over the whole, before he fhall be fure that he hath

found

found all which the law hath enacted concerning the fame; and fuch is often the inaccuracy and confufion, that when he hath perufed the whole, perhaps he may be ftill to feek. For as to this inftance before us, there have been regulations made concerning the fame, by ten different acts of parliament, at very different times. Before he can have any competent knowledge thereof, he muft lay all thefe ten acts together, and when he fhall have done this, he will find amongft them fo many repeals, and revivals, and explanations, and amendments, that it will even then be no eafy matter to conclude with certainty how the law doth ftand as to that article. To fpare the reader all which trouble, the author hath in this, and all other the like inftances, laid the whole law together relating thereunto, or at leaft all that hath occurred to him, or which he hath thought it material to infert. So that the reader may receive fatisfaction in a very fmall compafs, as to what he fhall be inquiring about, or at leaft he may be fatisfied in this, that if he doth not find it there, he need not feek for it elfewhere in the book.*

And by this method of bringing together into one general title, all thofe feparate diftinct titles, which have a mutual relation to and dependance upon each other, the author hath

---

* At prefent thefe acts are reduced into two general acts, one for turnpike roads, the other for highways not being turnpike.

avoided

avoided one great inconvenience, of referring the reader from one title to another, and from that other back again to the first, and (which is not unusual in books of the like kind) perhaps losing the thing to be treated of betwixt them.

Upon which account also, where one law occurreth under two different titles, it is usual with him to insert the same under both those titles; so that the reader's attention may not be interrupted, by sending him to search other titles, and from those perhaps others again, which have no principal relation to the matter he hath in hand.

Also, upon another account, he hath sometimes made use of more words than otherwise he would have done, namely to avoid the frequent repetition of the term, *&c.* which is a vague expression, and apt to create an uneasiness in the reader's mind, for that he cannot be satisfied from thence, how much, or how little is intended to be understood.

He hath also been somewhat large in the matter of *precedents* under divers titles; and hath endeavoured to bring them much nearer to the statutes, upon which they ought to be formed, than usually hath been done.

For all which enlargements, he hath the more space allowed to him, for that he hath not thought it necessary (as others have done) to take up near one fourth part of the book, by inserting *Blackerby's* justice at the end of it,

by

by way of index; hoping that the method he hath purſued will render every thing of that kind impertinent and uſeleſs.

THE MATERIALS which the author hath made uſe of, are chiefly of four kinds——The *ſtatutes* at large——the ſeveral treatiſes concerning the *pleas of the crown*——the *reports* of caſes adjudged in the court of king's bench ——and the books concerning the *office of a juſtice of the peace.*

As to the *ſtatutes* at large, or acts of parliament, the author hath not thought himſelf at liberty, as Mr. *Dalton* and others have done, to deliver the import thereof in his own words; but hath conſtantly abridged the act in the words of the act itſelf, leaving out nothing which may ſeem any way material. And to each diſtinct clauſe, he hath annexed the interpretation thereof, where the ſame hath been determined in the court of king's bench, or expounded by other good authority.

The treatiſes concerning the *pleas of the crown*, are thoſe of *Stamford, Coke, Hale,* and *Hawkins.* Of the firſt of theſe, the author hath made little uſe, further than as he is adopted by the other three. As to which three great authorities, where the law hath been declared by Lord *Coke,* and not controverted by any other, nor altered ſince his time by any act of parliament, or judicial determination, the author hath given to him the preference. And where any of theſe differeth

fereth from the other, he hath noted the difference.

In citing of Mr. *Hawkins*, he hath not
thought it allowable, as is usual with others,
to omit the several degrees of caution and afsent, with which he delivereth his opinion;
as, *it seemeth*, or *it hath been said by some*, or
it seemeth to be the better opinion, or *it seemeth
to be agreed*, and the like, which are by no
means arbitrary words without much meaning, but are inserted by him with the utmost
deliberation and judgment.

As to the books of *reports*; where the cases
therein have been considered by Mr. *Hawkins*,
and the other learned persons before mentioned, the author hath judged it very proper to
leave the matter there as settled by them. As
to the rest, he hath by no means thought himself of ability to proceed in Mr. *Hawkins's*
manner, by laying together all the reports on
the same subject, and thereupon extracting an
opinion out of the whole, but hath inserted
the same at large, or what he hath thought
most material thereof, and left the determination thereupon to the reader's better judgment.

And here it may be requisite, that the reader be admonished, not to expect that the
book shall be more perfect, than the materials
of which it is composed. All the books of
reports are not of equal authority. Many of
them are only notes that had been taken for
gentlemens own private use, which doubtless,

would

would have been much more perfect, had they intended them for publication. For thefe, or for any other, the author himfelf voucheth not · And, as he doth not ad† to their credit, fo he doth not detract from it, but leaveth every author (as he needs muft) to anfwer for himfelf. For he hath made it an invariable rule, upon all occafions, to cite his authorities, what fuch foever they be, and, in all material inftances, in the very words of the original authors: that fo, what may be of good authority in itfelf, fhall not be rendered lefs fo by his handling of it. And where no authority is alledged, he defires the reader will look upon it as fuch, namely, as having no authority, the fame being nothing but the author's own private obfervations, which are fubmitted to every reader's judgment, to approve or reject as he fhall fee caufe.

The books of authority concerning the *office of a juftice of the peace*, are thofe of *Fitzherbert, Crompton, Lambard,* and *Dalton*, the laft of which was publifhed in the reign of king *James* the firft: fince which time, no book under that title hath been allowed as fufficiently authentick And even the additions which have been made to *Dalton* fince his death, feem to have no better claim to an uncontroulable authority, than other collections which have not obtained it. And *Dalton* himfelf is much injured in the modern editions, in like manner as was obferved before of Mr *Hawkins*, by delivering that as abfolute, which Mr. *Dalton* publifhed under the

the feveral degrees of affent or doubtfulnefs before mentioned ; and which the author, in juftice to Mr. *Dalton*, hath reftored.

Where *Dalton* hath adopted *Lambard*, *Crompton*, and *Fitzherbert* (which he doth moft frequently in their own words) the author hath thought it fufficient to cite *Dalton*'s fingle authority And generally, in all other cafes, where authors are agreed, he hath judged it unneceffary to alledge more than one or two good vouchers.

Concerning the other books of this kind, which have been publifhed fince *Dalton*'s time, it is unneceffary to inlarge, fince of the moft of them the author hath made no ufe, and of the reft very fparingly ; and he will not feek to recommend his own book, by finding fault with others before him.

Orton, Weftmorland,
Sept. 29 1754.

Advertifement concerning this FIF-
TEENTH EDITION.

WHAT alterations have been neceffary to be made from time to time fince the firft publication of this book, may be eafily conceived from the variety of materials which have been introduced from the Reports of Cafes adjudged in the courts of Weft-

Weftminfter-hall, and the Statutes enacted during that period.

When this book was firft publifhed, in the year 1754, there had been few Reports adjudged in the reign of king George the firft, and almoft none in the reign of king George the fecond. But now this deficiency hath been abundantly fupplied by a greater number of Reports of cafes, determined in matters fubject to the jurifdiction of the juftices of the peace, than had been in the whole period before that time from the firft inftitution of the office of that magiftrate,

The Statutes or acts of parliament which have been made during the faid time, connected more or lefs with the office of a juftice of the peace, are in number above three hundred, befides almoft half as many more that have been repealed, fuperfeded, or permitted to expire.

By the means of which ftatutes, fo many new matters are in every feffion of parliament brought under the jurifdiction of thefe juftices, and fo many alterations are made in fubjects of which they before had cognizance, that every new edition, in order to keep pace with the law is in effect a new book And this is unavoidable. To publifh thofe alterations feparately in an annual appendix, is a work of more difficulty than may be at firft apprehended. For to effect this to any fufficient purpofe, many titles muft be taken in

                                        pieces,

pieces, and wholly new modelled; fometimes one act of parliament breaks into feveral different titles, all of which muft be furveyed, and rendered confiftent with each other; and new titles frequently arife upon new emergencies. Thefe alterations and additions in any one year would increafe to a volume of no inconfiderable dimenfions, and in two or three years time would be productive of infinite confufion, and, notwithftanding all reafonable attention that might be employed, the book and the appendixes, and the feveral appendixes one with another, would be at variance. The beft appendix that the author can imagine is, the ftatutes at large every year, fo far as juftices of the peace are concerned therein, which ftatutes as no acting juftice ought to be without, this would therefore upon that account create unto him no additional expence.

₊ This Edition contains, by way of an Appendix, the ftatutes of the laft feffion of parliament (24 G. 3.)

INTRODUCTION,

Confifting of TWO PARTS;

CONTAINING,

I. *Certain abbreviations made ufe of in this work.*

II. *Some general rules to be obferved, in the conftruction of ftatutes or acts of parliament.*

I. *Certain abbreviations made ufe of in this work.*

IN order to keep the book within a reafonable compafs, the following *abbreviations* are made ufe of.

1. The word *juftice* is always to be underftood to mean *juftice of the peace,* when not otherwife expreffed ^{Juftice}

2. The words *one juftice* fhall be underftood to fignify *one or more juftices,* fo that what is directed to be done by one, fhall not be intended thereby to exclude others from joining with him ^{One juftice}

3. In like manner, *two juftices,* when not otherwife expreffed, fhall be underftood to fignify *two juftices or more.* ^{Two juftices.}

4 So alfo a conviction on the oath of *one witnefs,* fhall be underftood to denote *one witnefs or more.* ^{One witnefs}

Two witnesses　5 And *two witnesses* shall denote *two or more witnesses*

Quorum　6. (1 $\mathcal{Q}$) shall be understood to signify *one whereof is of the* Quorum.

Majority.　7 The *justices in sessions* shall signify the said justices, or *the major part of them*

Sessions.　8. The word *sessions* shall denote *the general quarter sessions*, if not otherwise expressed

Warrant　9 The word *warrant* shall always signify *warrant under hand and seal*, where not expressed otherwise

Judge of assize.　10. Judges or justices of *assize* shall be understood to signify also those of *Nisi Prius, Oyer and Terminer, and General Gaol Delivery*

Mayor　11. The word *mayor* shall always be understood to imply *bailiffs and other chief officers in corporations*, by what appellation soever dignified.

Constable　12 The word *constable* shall always be understood to imply *tythingman, borsholders, headboroughs, and other officers* required to execute the justices warrants.

Overseer　13 The word *overseer* shall be understood to mean *overseer of the poor*, where not expressed otherwise.

Poor　14 Where a penalty, or part thereof is expressed to be given to the *poor*, that shall be always understood to denote *the poor of the parish where the offence was committed*, if not otherwise limited

Penalty.　15. Where a penalty is to be recovered before the justices of the peace, it is thought indispensible to insert particularly the manner of recovering the same, but where it is to be sued for in any of his majesty's court of record at *Westminster*, it is judged not necessary to set forth the special method of procedure there　and generally, where it is expressed, that a person shall do, or not do such a thing, on pain of such a sum, without more, it shall be understood that such penalty is not recoverable before the justices of the peace, but only in the courts at *Westminster*

Overplus　16 In all cases of *distress and sale*, it shall be understood that the *overplus* must be returned to the owner,

owner, after the fum or fums to be thereout deducted, fhall be fatisfied and paid

17. *Lands* fhall be underftood to ftand for *lands*, Lands
tenements, and hereditaments.

18 Where *tranfportation* is directed for any of- Tranfportation.
fence, it fhall always be underftood, *that if the offen-*
der fhall return before the time limited, he fhall be guilty
of felony without benefit of clergy.

19 In the blank fpaces for the names in the pre- Blank fpaces
cedents, inftead of inferting initial letters arbitrarily,
it is thought it may be fome help to the memory,
that *A. O.* fhall fignify the offender, *A. I.* the informer, *A W.* the witnefs, *J P.* the juftice of the
peace, and the like

20 Alfo, for brevity's fake, fums of money and Figures
other numbers are ufually expreffed by figures, and
not in words at length, but it is to be remembered,
that in the forms of warrants, convictions, and other
proceedings before the juftices, they ought to be expreffed in words at length, and not in figures.

21. Where a ftatute is faid to be in force, until Continuance of
fuch a day, month, and year, &c it fhall always be ftatutes.
underftood to imply, *and from thence to the end of the*
then next feffion of parliament.

22 In the ftatutes made in the reign of the late Citing of fta
King *William*, it is thought not neceffary upon all tutes
occafions to fay *William the Third*, fince there are no
printed ftatutes in the reigns of *William the Firft and*
Second

Nor is it thought neceffary in fuch ftatutes to add
the name of Queen *Mary* to that of King *William*,
but it is judged fufficient for the underftanding
thereof, to quote the ftatutes in this manner, *viz.*

1 *W feff* 2. *c* 6 *f* 3 to fignify the ftatute made
in the parliament holden in the firft year of the reign
of King *William* the Third and Queen *Mary*, the
fecond feffion thereof, chapter the fixth, fection the
third.

23 Abbreviations in the names of books cited Citing of books,
as authorities, or elfewhere occafionally noted, con- and abridged
fifting for the moft part of fome of the initial letters cafes.

of the authors names, and other common diſtinctions, need not to be further explained.

So alſo the names of the terms in which the ſeveral caſes were adjudged, to wit, Hilary, Eaſter, Trinity, and Michaelmas, are expreſſed by the initial letters *H. E T* and *M*

II. *Some general rules to be obſerved in the conſtruction of ſtatutes, or acts of parliament.*

To avoid repeating the ſame obſervations ſome hundreds of times, it is thought proper to premiſe the following general rules to be obſerved, in the conſtruction of ſtatutes or acts of parliament.

How far an affirmative repeal eth an affirma tive ſtatute

1. Regularly, a ſtatute in the affirmative doth not repeal a precedent affirmative ſtatute. **11** *Co.* **61.**

But if the latter is contrary to the former, it amounteth to a repeal of the former L. *Raym* o

How far an affirmative ſtatute altereth the common law.

2 A ſtatute made in the affirmative, without any negative expreſſed or implied, doth not take away the common law, and therefore the party may waive his benefit by ſuch ſtatute, and take his remedy by the common law. 2 *Inſt.* 200.

Repealing a repealing ſtatute.

3. By repealing of a repealing ſtatute, the firſt ſtatute is revived *Readings upon the ſtatutes* Parl.

Special power to be purſued.

4 Regularly, where an act of parliament giveth a power or intereſt to one perſon certain, by this expreſs deſignation of one, all others are excluded. 11 *Co* 59, 64

Power to adminiſter an oath.

5. In all caſes, where juſtices may take examinations, or other accuſation or proof, tho' the ſtatute doth not expreſsly ſet down that it ſhall be upon oath, yet it ſhall be intended that it ſhall be upon oath *Dalt c.* 115

In what caſe the ſeſſions may execute the power given to two juſtices

6. Generally, it is holden, that where a ſtatute appoints a thing to be done by one or more juſtices, without giving any appeal to the ſeſſions, there the juſtices in ſeſſions may do that thing. but where

an

an appeal is given to the seffions, the juftices in seffions cannot proceed originally therein, becaufe that method would take away the power of appealing

7 Where a ftatute makes a new offence, which was no way prohibited by the common law, and appoints a particular manner of proceeding againft the offender, as by commitment, or action of debt, or information, without mentioning an indictment, it feems to be fettled at this day, that it will not maintain an indictment, becaufe the mentioning the other methods of proceeding only, feems impliedly to exclude that of indictment Yet it hath been adjudged, that if fuch ftatute give a recovery by action of debt, bill, plaint, information, *or otherwife*, it authorizes a proceeding by way of indictment. 2 *Haw* 211

And if there is a prohibitory claufe in the act, the offender may be indicted upon the prohibitory claufe, notwithftanding the penalty · But otherwife it is, where the act is not prohibitory, but only inflicts the forfeiture, and fpecifies the remedy. 2 *H. H.* 171. *Burrow, Mansfield* 543.

But where the offence was antecedently punifhable by a common law proceeding, and a ftatute prefcribes a particular remedy by a fummary proceeding, there, either method may be purfued, and the profecutor is at liberty to proceed either at common law or in the method prefcribed by the ftatute: becaufe in that cafe the fanction is cumulative, and doth not exclude the common law proceeding. *Bur. Mansf.* 803.

8 But every contempt of a ftatute is indictable, where no other punifhment is limited. 1 *Haw* 60.

9. And wherefoever an act of parliament doth generally prohibit any thing, the party grieved fhall not only have his action for his private relief, but the offender fhall be punifhed at the king's fuit, for the contempt of the law 2 *Inft.* 163.

Marginal notes:

How far an indictment will lie where another method of profecution is appointed

Where no method of profecution is appointed

Where the defendant may be profecuted both by the king, and by the party grieved

10. All

In what time prosecution shall be upon penal statutes.

10. All actions, indictments, or informations, on penal statutes, for any forfeiture limited to the king, shall be brought within two years after the offence committed, if limited to the king and prosecutor, then within one year, and if it is not sued for in that one year, then the king may sue for the same within two years, after the expiration of that one year, and not otherwise 31 *El c* 5 ſ 5 That is to say, unless where it is otherwise specially directed by subsequent statutes.

Statutes not in form or consent of the whole legislature

11. Many ancient statutes are penned in the form of charters, ordinances, commands, or prohibitions from the king, without mentioning the concurrence of either lords or commons, yet inasmuch as they have always been acquiesced in as unquestionably authentick, this establishes and confirms their authority, and the defect is salved by such universal reception *Hawkins's preface to the statutes*

Preamble

12. The preamble or rehearsal of a statute is deemed true, and therefore good arguments may be drawn from the preamble. 1 *Inst.* 11. But the preamble shall not restrain the operation of the enacting part, as where the preamble reciteth only a particular inconvenience, this shall not hinder a subsequent enacting clause from being understood in that more general sense which the words would otherwise and of themselves import, so as to take in other inconveniences of the like kind, altho' not specified in the preamble. 8 *Mod.* 144. 1 *P. Will.* 320.

May do such a thing, how to be understood

13 Where a statute directs the doing of a thing, for the sake of justice, or the publick good, the word *may* is the same as the word *shall.* as where the statute of the 13 & 14 *C.* 2 *c* 12 enacts that the overseers may make a rate to reimburse the constables, this is construed they *shall*, for they are compellable so to do. 2 *Salk* 609

Court of record.

14 Where a statute directs a penalty to be recovered *in any court of record*, this shall not be intended

2   tended

tended of the quarter feffions, unlefs it be fpecially
named in fuch ftatute, but only of the courts of
record at *Weftminfter*.   6 *Co*. 19, 20.   2 *Hale's Hift*
29, 30.

15 It is a general rule in the conftruction of
ftatutes, that where things of an inferior degree are
firft mentioned, thofe of a higher dignity fhall not
be included under general fubfequent words, as
where a ftatute fpeaks of indictments to be taken
before juftices of the peace, or *others having power
to take indictments*, it fhall be underftood only of
other inferior courts, and not of the king's bench,
or other courts at *Weftminfter*   2 *Co*. 46. 2 *Haw*.
305

> Higher courts not intended, where the inferior are firft mentioned.

16. Where a ftatute gives power to the juftices,
to require any perfon to do a thing, as to take the
oaths, the law implicitly gives them power to iffue
their precept to have the body before them, for
when the law granteth any thing to any one, that
alfo is granted, without which the thing itfelf cannot be. And it is againft the office of the juftices,
and the authority given them by the law, that they
fhall go and feek the parties.   12 *Co*. 130, 131.

> Power to convene the parties.

17 Where a ftatute gives power to the juftices of
the peace, to hear and determine an offence in a
fummary way, it is neceffarily implied, and fuppofed, as a part of natural juftice, that the party be
firft cited, and have opportunity to be heard and
anfwer for himfelf.   1 *Haw* 154.

> Neceffity of fummoning the party.

18. Where an act of parliament gives power to
two juftices finally to hear and determine an offence, it is neceffarily fuppofed, that they fhall be
both together, or which is the fame thing in other
words, that they fhall hold a fpecial feffions for that
purpofe   And the like is, when they are to do any
other judicial act, as to make an order of baftardy,
or adjudge the fettlement of a poor perfon.   For it
is unknown to the laws of *England*, that two perfons
fhall act as judges in the fame caufe, when at the
- fame

> Two juftices to be both together.

same time one of them is in one part of the county, and the other in another.

Informer's oath. 19. Where a statute appoints a conviction to be on the *oath of one witness*, this ought not to be by the single oath of the informer, for if the same person should be allowed to be both prosecutor and witness, it would induce profligate persons to commit perjury for the sake of the reward. *L Raym* 1545

Confession 20 Where a statute directeth, that a person shall be convicted of an offence, upon the *oath of one or more witnesses*, and saith nothing of the *confession* of the party, yet if the offender shall before the justice confess the offence, he may be convicted upon such confession · for confession is stronger evidence than the oath of witnesses. *Dalt.* 109, 162 *Str.* 546.

Discretionary power. 21 Where an act of parliament gives power to the justices of the peace, to take order in any matter *according to their discretions*, this shall be understood, according to the rules of reason, law, and justice, and not by private opinion 5 *Co.* 100.

England includes Wales. 22. In all cases where *the kingdom of* England, or *that part of* Great Britain *called* England, hath been or shall be mentioned in any act of parliament, the same shall be deemed to comprehend *the dominion of* Wales, *and town of* Berwick upon Tweed. 20 G. 2. *c.* 42 *s* 3.

Twelve months. 23. It may be laid down as an invariable rule, that *the law favours liberty* So that in the construction of a penal statute, where the interpretation is dubious, that sense must be pursued (all other things being equal) which is more beneficial to the subject, or the party suffering Thus, where an act directs, that the justices shall commit an offender to prison for 12 *months*, the justices may not alter the words, and commit him for *a year*, for in this respect, 12 months and one year are not the same: but the months must be computed at 28

days

days to the month, and not as kalendar months, unless it be so expressed in the act.

24. In all cases wherein, by any act of parliament, an oath shall be allowed or required, the solemn affirmation of quakers shall be allowed instead of such oath, altho' no particular or express provision be made for that purpose in the said act. 22 G. 2. c 46 f. 3^b.

> Quaker's affirmation.

But no quaker shall by virtue hereof be qualified or permitted to give evidence in any criminal cause, or serve on any jury, or bear any office or place of profit in the government. f. 37.

25. To say that a person shall *forfeit* generally, or that he shall *forfeit to the king*, is all one, for the king shall have every forfeiture not otherwise limited. 11 Co. 60.

> Forfeiture.

Except where a forfeiture is *given in lieu of property and interest*, for there it shall go to the party injured. 1 Roll's Rep 90.

For wheresoever a statute giveth a forfeiture or penalty, against him which wrongfully detaineth or dispossesseth another of his duty or interest, in that case, he that hath the wrong shall have the forfeiture or penalty, and shall have an action for the same upon the statute, and the king shall not have the forfeiture in that case 1 Inst 159.

26. Where a statute saith, that such a person shall pay *fine and ransom* to the king, in legal understanding, such fine and ransom are all one for if they were divers, then should the party pay two sums, one for the fine, and another for the ransom, which was never done. 1 Inst 127.

> Fine and ransom.

27. Acts of parliament that speak of fines or ransoms *at the king's pleasure*, are always to be understood of the king in his courts by his justices. 1 H. H 375

> At the king's pleasure.

28. It is said that wheresoever a justice of the peace is impowered, by any statute, to bind a person over, or to cause him to do a certain thing, and such person being in his presence shall refuse to

> Where a power of commitment is implied

be

be bound, or to do such thing, the justice may commit him to the gaol, to remain there till he shall comply. 2 *Haw* 116.

Imprisonment, when.

29. When a statute appoints imprisonment, but limits no time when, it shall be immediately. 8 *Co.* 119

Imprisonment, how long

30 When a statute appoints imprisonment, but limits no time how long, the prisoner in such case must remain at the discretion of the court *Dalt.* 410.

Commitment to the house of correction, for what time

31. Where any offender shall by a justice of the peace be committed to the house of correction, for an offence cognizable before him out of sessions, and the time and manner of punishment is not by law expresly limited, he may commit him to the house of correction, *there to be kept to hard labour, until the next general or quarter sessions, or until discharged by due course of law.* 17 G. 2. c. 5. f. 32.

Statute making an offence felony.

32 Wherever a statute makes any offence *felony;* it incidentally gives it all the properties of felony at common law 1 *Haw* 105

Misprision

33. Therefore an act of parliament that makes an offence felony, doth consequently introduce the punishment of concealing, that is, misprision of felony, and every offence made felony by act of parliament, includeth misprision 1 *H. H* 708.

Infants

34 An act making a new felony, extendeth not to infants under 14 years of age, but if they be of that age it binds them. 1 *H. H* 706.

Life and member

35 Not only those crimes which are made felonies by the express words of any statute, but also those which are decreed to have or undergo *judgment of life and member,* do become felonies thereby, whether the word felony were mentioned or not. 1 *Haw.* 107.

Body and goods.

36 But an offence shall never be made felony, by the construction of any doubtful and ambiguous words of a statute, and therefore if it be only prohibited under pain of *forfeiting body and goods,* or of

being

being *at the king's will for body, lands, and goods,* it shall amount unto no more than a high misdemeanor, punishable by imprisonment or the like. 1 *Haw* 107.

37. All felonies by the common law have the benefit of clergy, therefore where a statute enacts a felony, and says, the offender shall *suffer death,* clergy l es notwithstanding, and is never ousted without exprefs words. 3 *Inst.* 73. 2 *Haw* 342. *Benefit of clergy.*

38 Saving of *dower* in a statute making an offence felony, is superfluous, for by the 1 *Ed* 6. c 12, dower is not loft by the felony of the husband. s 17 *Forfeiture of dower.*

39. Where any complaint shall be made before a justice, and a warrant or summons shall issue in consequence thereof, the justice, upon hearing and determining the matter, may award *costs* to either party. But if the conviction be upon a penal statute, and the penalty amounts to 5 l or upwards, the costs shall be deducted out of the penalty. 18 G 3. c. 19. *Costs.*

40 Upon an indictment or other criminal prosecution, no *damages* can be given to the party grieved: But it is every day's practice in the court of king's bench, to induce defendants to make satisfaction to the prosecutors, by intimating an inclination on that account to mitigate the fine due to the king. 2 *Haw* 210 *Damages.*

41. Where a statute gives *treble damages,* the justices are not to affefs the damages, and then treble them, but the jury ought to find the damages, and then the justices are to treble them *Cro Car.* 449. *Treble damages.*

42 In all cases where a justice is or shall be required by any act of parliament, to iffue a warrant of distrefs for the levying of any penalty inflicted, or any fum of money directed to be paid by such act, it shall be lawful for such justice granting the warrant, therein to order and direct the goods *Distrefs and sale.*

distrained

diftrained to be fold within a certain time to be limited in fuch warrant, fo as fuch time be not lefs than 4 days, nor more than 8 days, unlefs fuch penalty or fum of money, together with reafonable charges of taking and keeping the diftrefs, be fooner paid And the officer making fuch diftrefs, may deduct the reafonable charges of taking, keeping, and felling the faid diftrefs, and the overplus (if any) fhall be returned to the owner on demand. (Except only in cafes of diftrefs for quakers tithes and church rates.) 27 *Geo* 2. *c.* 20.

Second offence. 43. An act inflicting a penalty for a *fecond offence,* muft always be underftood, after conviction and judgment for the firft offence ; and the fecond offence muft be committed after the firft conviction, and judgment thereupon given. for it doth not appear to be an offence, until judgment by proceeding of law be given againft the offender. 2 *Inft.* 468.

And the indictment for a fecond offence, muft recite the record of the firft conviction, and upon the evidence, the record of the firft conviction muft be proved: but the matter of the firft conviction fhall never be re-examined, but muft ftand for granted. 1 *H. H.* 686.

Abjuration.

Abjuration Oath. See 𝔒𝔞𝔱𝔥𝔰.

𝔄𝔠𝔠𝔢𝔰𝔰𝔞𝔯𝔶.

I. Of acceffaries in general.

1. ACCESSARY (*quafi* accedens *ad culpam*) is he
that is not the chief actor, but one that is concerned
in the felony by commandment, aid, or receipt
— *Acceffart, what,*

2 In the higheft capital offence, namely, high treafon,
there are no acceffaries, neither before nor after, for the
confenters, aiders, abettors, and knowing receivers and
comforters of traytors are all principals 1 *Hale's Hift.* 613
— *In the higheft offence, no acceffaries.*

But yet as to the courfe of proceeding, it hath been, and
indeed ought to be the courfe, that thofe who did actually
commit the very fact of treafon, fhould be firft tried, before thofe that are principals in the fecond degree, becaufe
otherwife this inconvenience might follow, that the principals in the fecond degree might be convicted, and yet the
principals in the firft degree may be acquitted, which
would be abfurd. 1 *H. H.* 613. *

3 In cafes that are criminal, but not capital, as in *petit
larceny* and *trefpafs*, there are no acceffaries, for the acceffaries *before* are in the fame degree as principals, and acceffaries *after*, by receiving the offenders, cannot be in law
under any penalties as acceffaries, unlefs the acts of parliament that induce thofe penalties do exprefly extend to
receivers or comforters, as fome do 1 *H H* 613
— *In the loweft offences, no acceffaries.*

4 It remains therefore, that the bufinefs of this title
of acceffaries refers only to *capital felonies*, whether by the
common law, or by act of parliament
— *Acceffaries only in felony*

* The lord chief juftice *Hale* writ a treatife in octavo, enti-
tl d " Pleas of the crown", containing a fketch and plan of his
larger work which was publifhed afterwards in two volumes folio,
intitled " The Hiftory of the pleas of the crown " In quoting
thefe, the former is diftinguifhed thus, *Hale's Pleas*, and the
latter *Hale's Hift* or in a more abbre iated form, *H H*

5 Concerning which, Lord *Coke* obferves generally, that when an offence is felony, either by the common law, or by ftatute, all acceffaries both before and after are incidentally included 3 *Inft* 59

6. But as to felonies by act of parliament, Lord *Hale* diftinguifhes thereupon as follows Regularly (he fays) if an act of parliament enact an offence to be felony, tho' it mention nothing of acceffaries before or after, yet virtually and confequentially thofe that counfel or command the offence are acceffaries before, and thofe that knowingly receive the offender are acceffaries after. 1 *H H* 613

But if the act of parliament that makes the felony, in exprefs terms comprehend acceffaries before, and make no mention of acceffaries after, namely, receivers or comforters, there it feems there can be no acceffaries after, for the expreffion of procurers, counfellors, or abettors, all which import acceffaries before, make it evident, that the law-makers did not intend to include acceffaries after, which is an offence of a lower degree than acceffaries before 1 *H. H* 614

And altho' it be generally true, that an act of parliament creating a felony, renders confequentially acceffaries before and after within the fame penalty, yet the fpecial penning of the act fometimes varies the cafe Thus the ftatute of 3 *H.* 7. *c* 2 for taking away women, makes the taking away, and the procuring and abetting, yea and wittingly receiving alfo, to be all equally *principal* felonies, and excluded of clergy. Again, the ftatute of 27 *Eliz. c.* 2. makes the coming in of a jefuit *treafon*, the receiving or relieving of him *felony*, the contributing of money to his relief a *præmunire*. So that acts of parliament may diverfify the offences of acceffary or principal, according to the various penning thereof, and fo have done in many cafes. 1 *H H* 614, 615.

7. Alfo a ftatute excluding the principals from the benefit of clergy, doth not thereby exclude the acceffaries before or after, neither doth a ftatute, excluding the acceffaries, thereby exclude the principals. 2 *Haw.* 342.

II. *Of acceffaries before the fact*

An acceffary before the fact committed, is he that being abfent at the time of the felony committed, doth yet procure, counfel, command, or abet another to commit a felony.

Being abfent at the time of the felony committed] For if he is prefent, he is not an acceffary, but a principal.

So alſo, if divers come to commit an unlawful act, and be preſent at the time of the felony committed, tho' one of them only doth it, they are *all* principals. *Hale's Pl.* 215

So if one preſent move the other to ſtrike , or if one preſent did nothing, but yet came to aſſiſt the party if needful , or if one hold the party while the felon ſtrikes him; or if one preſent deliver his weapon to the other that ſtrikes for they are *preſent*, aiding, abetting, or comforting. *Id.* 216.

So if ſeveral perſons ſet out together, or in ſmall parties, upon one common deſign, be it murder or other felony, or for any other purpoſe unlawful in itſelf, and each taketh the part aſſigned him; ſome to commit the fact, others to watch at proper diſtances and ſtations to prevent a ſurprize, or to favour (if need be) the eſcape of thoſe who are more immediately engaged ; they are all, provided the fact be committed, in the eye of the law *preſent* at it. For it was made a common cauſe with them , each man operated in his ſtation at one and the ſame inſtant towards the ſame common end , and the part each man took tended to give countenance, encouragement and protection to the whole gang, and to inſure the ſucceſs of their common enterprize *Foſter's Crown Law*, 350.

But if one came caſually, not of the confederacy, tho' he hindred not the felony, he is neither principal nor acceſſary, altho' he apprehend not the felon, but for his negligence he is puniſhable by fine and impriſonment *Hale's Pl.* 216. *2 Haw* 313

Alſo in ſome caſes, even a perſon abſent may be principal, as he that puts poiſon into any thing to poiſon another, and leaves it, tho' not preſent when it is taken And ſo it ſeems all that are preſent when the poiſon is ſo infuſed, and conſenting thereunto *Hale's Pl* 216

Procure, counſel, command, or abet] But here note ſome diverſities As,

(1) *When the principal doth not accompliſh the fact altogether in the ſame ſort, as it was beforehand agreed between him and the acceſſary.* And therefore if one commands another to lay hold upon a third perſon, and he lays hold upon him and robs him, the perſon commanding is not acceſſary to the robbery ; for his command might have been performed without any robbery *Dalt. c* 161

But if the command had been to beat him, and the party commanded doth kill him, or beat him ſo that he dieth thereof, the perſon commanding ſhall be acceſſary to the murder for it is a hazard in beating a man, that he may die thereof *Dalt. c.* 161.

(2) *He that commandeth or counselleth any evil or unlawful act to be done, shall be adjudged accessary to all that shall ensue upon the same evil act, but not to any other distinct thing* As if one command another to steal a horse, and he stealeth an ox, or to rob a man by the highway of his money, and he robs him in his house of his plate, or to burn such a one's house, and he burneth the house of another These are other acts and felonies than he commanded to be done, and therefore he shall not be adjudged accessary to them. *Dalt c 161*

(3) *But if a person commit the same felony, which another did command or counsel to be done, tho' he doth it at another time, or in another place, or in another sort than was commanded or counselled, yet here such person commanding or counselling shall be accessary* As if he doth counsel to kill a man by poison, and he kills him with a dagger, or to kill him by the highway, and he kills him in his house, or to kill him one day, and he kills him on another day, in these and the like cases, he shall be accessary *Dalt c. 161*

(4) *Those offences which in the construction of law are sudden and unpremeditated, cannot have any accessaries before* As killing a man by misadventure, in his own defence, or manslaughter For in such case there can be no procuring, counselling, commanding, or abetting But there may be accessaries after. 1 *H H.* 616

(5) It seems to be generally agreed, that *he who barely conceals a felony, which he knows to be intended, is guilty only of a misprision of felony, and shall not be adjudged an accessary,* for this is not procuring, counselling, or abetting 2 *Haw* 317

(6) Also, if a man counsels or commands another to kill a person, and before he hath killed him, he who counselled or commanded it, repents, and *countermands* it, charging him not to kill him, and yet after he doth kill him, here such person countermanding shall not be adjudged accessary to the murder For, generally, the law adjudgeth no man accessary to a felony before the fact, but such as continue in that mind at the time that the felony is done and executed *Dalt c 161*

(7) But if a person advise a woman to kill her child as soon as it shall be born, and she kill it in pursuance of such advice, he is an accessary to the murder, tho' at the time of the advice, the child not being born, no murder could be committed of it For the influence of the felonious advice continuing till the child was born, makes the adviser as much a felon, as if he had given his advice after the birth 2 *Haw* 315

III *Of*

III Of acceſſaries after the fact.

Acceſſary after the fact is, where a perſon knowing the fe-
lony to be committed by another, relieves, comforts, or aſſiſts the
felon.

Knowing the felony to be committed] There can be no
doubt, but that it is neceſſary that the receiver have notice of the felony, either expreſs or implied, and ſo to
be laid in the indictment, that the receiver *knew* that the
perſon received by him, had committed the principal felony 2 *Haw* 319

The felony] This as hath been ſaid, holds place only in
felonies, and in thoſe felonies, where by the law judgment
of death regularly ought to enſue, and therefore not in
petit larceny 1 *H H* 618

And therefore if a perſon do barely receive, comfort or
conceal an offender guilty of any common treſpaſs, or inferior crime of the like nature, tho' he knew him to have
been guilty, and that there is a warrant out againſt him,
yet he is not an acceſſary to the offence, but perhaps in
ſuch caſe he may be indictable for a contempt of the law,
in hindering the due courſe of juſtice. 2 *Haw.* 311

Relieves, comforts, or aſſiſts the felon] In the explication
of theſe words ſeveral things are conſiderable

(1) Generally, any aſſiſtance whatſoever given to one
known to be a felon, in order to hinder his being apprehended, or tried, or ſuffering the puniſhment to which he is
condemned, is ſufficient to bring a man within this deſcrip-
tion, and make him acceſſary to the felony, as where one
aſſiſts him with a horſe to ride away with, or with money
or victuals to ſupport him in his eſcape. 2 *Haw* 317

(2) But if a man knows that a perſon hath committed
a felony, but doth not diſcover it, this doth not make him
an acceſſary, but it is a miſpriſon of felony, for which
he may be indicted, and upon his conviction fined and
impriſoned 1 *H H* 618

(3) Alſo if a man ſees another commit a felony, but con-
ſents not, nor yet takes care to apprehend him, or to levy hue
and cry after him, or upon hue and cry levied doth not purſue
him, this is a neglect puniſhable by fine and impriſonment,
but it doth not make him an acceſſary 1 *H. H* 618

(4) In like manner, if one commit a felony, and come
to a perſon's houſe before he be arreſted, and ſuch perſon ſuffer him to eſcape without arreſt, knowing him to have committed a felony, this doth not make him acceſſary, but if

he

he take money of the felon to ſuffer him to eſcape, this makes him acceſſary　And ſo it is if he ſhuts the fore door of his houſe, whereby the purſuers are deceived, and the felon hath opportunity to eſcape, this makes him an acceſſary, for here is not a bare omiſſion, but an act done by him to accommodate the felon's eſcape　1 H H 619.

(5) Alſo it ſeems to be ſettled at this day, that whoſoever reſcues a felon from an arreſt for the felony, or voluntarily ſuffers him to eſcape, is an acceſſary to the felony　2 Haw 318.

(6) But if a felon be in priſon, he that relieves him with neceſſary meat, drink, or cloaths, for the ſuſtentation of life, is not acceſſary　1 H H, 620

(7) So if he be bailed out, it is lawful to relieve and maintain him, for he is ſtill in ſome ſort in cuſtody, and is under a certainty of coming to his trial　1 H H 620

(8) But if a felon be in gaol, for a man to convey inſtruments to him to break priſon to make an eſcape, or to bribe the gaoler to let him eſcape, makes the party an acceſſary for tho' common humanity allows every man to afford ſuch perſons neceſſary relief, yet common juſtice prohibits all unlawful attempts to cauſe their eſcapes.　1 H H 621

(9) The ſending a letter in favour of a felon, or adviſing to labour witneſſes not to appear, makes no acceſſary, but it is a high contempt. Hale's Pl 219.

(10) A man may be acceſſary to an acceſſary, by the receiving of him knowing him to be an acceſſary to felony 1 H H 622.

(11) If a man hath goods ſtolen, and he receives his goods again, ſimply, without any contract to favour the felon in his proſecution, this is lawful, but if he receive them upon agreement not to proſecute, or to proſecute faintly, this is theftbote, puniſhable by impriſonment and ranſom, but yet it makes him not an acceſſary, but if he take money of him to favour him, whereby he eſcapes, this makes him acceſſary. 1 H. H 619.

(12) And if any perſon ſhall receive or buy ſtolen goods, knowing them to be ſtolen, or ſhall receive, harbour, or conceal the thieves, he ſhall be deemed an acceſſary, and be tranſported for fourteen years. 3 W. c. 9 ſ. 4. 5 Anr c 31 ſ 5. 4 Geo c 11. And buying the goods at an undervalue, is a preſumptive evidence, that he knew they were ſtolen. 1 H H. 619.

(13) It ſeems agreed, that the law hath ſuch a regard to that duty, love, and tenderneſs, which a wife owes to her huſband, as not to make her an acceſſary to felony by any receipt given to her huſband; yet if ſhe be any way guilty

of procuring her huſband to commit it, it ſeems to make her an acceſſary before the fact, in the ſame manner as if ſhe had been ſole. Alſo it ſeems agreed, that no other relation beſides that of a wife to her huſband, will exempt the receiver of a felon from being an acceſſary to the felony, from whence it follows, that if a maſter receive a ſervant, or a ſervant a maſter, or a brother a brother, or even a huſband a wife, they are acceſſaries in the ſame manner as if they had been mere ſtrangers to one another. 2 *Haw.* 320

(14) But if the wife alone, the huſband being ignorant of it, do receive any other perſon being a felon, the wife is acceſſary, and not the huſband   1 *H. H* 621.

(15) But if the huſband and wife both receive a felon knowingly, it ſhall be adjudged only the act of the huſband, and the wife ſhall be acquitted.   1 *H. H* 621.

IV. *How they are to be proceeded againſt.*

1 By 3 *Ed* 1. *c* 15   Thoſe who are *accuſed of the receipt of felons, or of commandment, or force, or of aid in felony done, ſhall be bailable*, but this ſeemeth to be only where it ſtands indifferent whether the party be guilty or innocent   for if there are ſtrong preſumptions of guilt, it ſeemeth that he is not bailable. 2 *Haw.* 102 — *Acceſſaries how far bailable*

2. Where a perſon is feloniouſly ſtricken or poiſoned in one county, and dies thereof in another county, the acceſſary may be indicted in the county where the death ſhall happen   2 & 3 *Ed.* 6 *c.* 24 ſ 2, 3. — *In what county to be tried*

Alſo, where a murder or felony ſhall be committed in one county, and the perſon ſhall be acceſſary in another county, the acceſſary may be indicted in the county where he was acceſſary   And the judges of aſſize, or two of them, of the county where the offence of the acceſſary ſhall be committed, on ſuit to them made, ſhall write to the keeper of the records where the principal ſhall be convicted, to certify them whether ſuch principal be attainted, convicted, or otherwiſe diſcharged, which he ſhall certify under his ſeal   2 & 3 *Ed* 6. *c.* 24 ſ 4.

3 The acceſſary may be indicted in the ſame indictment with the principal, and that is the beſt and moſt uſual way, but he may be indicted in another indictment, but then ſuch indictment muſt contain the certainty and kind of the principal felony.   1 *H. H* 623 — *Acceſſary and principal in the ſame indictment.*

4 It ſeemeth that the acceſſary may be put to anſwer before the principal hath appeared, but his plea cannot be tried before ſuch appearance, unleſs he deſires it himſelf, but if — *Principal to be firſt tried.*

he will put himself upon his trial, before the principal be tried, he may, and his acquittal or conviction, upon such trial, is good   2 *Haw* 322   1 *H H* 623.

But it seemeth necessary in such case to respite judgment, till the principal be convicted, for if the principal be after acquitted, that conviction or the accessary is annulled, and no judgment ought to be given against him   But if he be acquitted of the accessary, that acquittal is good, and he shall be discharged   1 *H H* 623, 624

Both tried, or one in place

5   It seems to be settled at this day, that if the principal and accessary appear together, and the principal plead the general issue, the accessary shall be put to plead also, and that if he likewise plead the general issue, both may be tried by one inquest, but that the principal must be first convicted, and that the jury shall be charged, that if they find the principal not guilty they shall find the accessary not guilty   But it seems agreed, that if the principal plead a plea in bar, or abatement, or a former acquittal, the accessary shall not be forced to answer, till that plea be determined   for if it be found for the principal, the accessary is discharged, if against the principal, yet he shall after plead over to the felony, and may be acquitted   2 *Haw* 323   1 *H H* 624.

Accessa. may r tried tho' the principal ned attused

6   Anciently the accessary could not be tried, unless the principal were *at ainted* (3 *Ed* 1 *c*. 14) but by the 1 *Ann stat* 2 *c* 9 ʃ 1 if the principal be convicted, or peremptorily challenge above twenty of the jury, the accessary may be tried and punished as if the principal had been attainted, and this, altho' the principal be admitted to his clergy, pardoned, or otherwise delivered before attainder

Receiver of stolen goods, how to be prosecuted if the principal not taken

7   But in the case of stolen goods, if the principal cannot be taken, the buyer or receiver may be prosecuted as for a misdemeanor, to be punished by fine and imprisonment, or other such corporal punishment as the court shall think fit, altho' the principal be not convicted, which shall exempt the offender from being punished as accessary, if the principal be afterwards taken and convicted   1 *Ann stat.* 2 *c* 9 ʃ 2   5 *Ann. c.* 31 ʃ 6. And by the 29 *Geo* 2 *c* 30 the buyer or receiver of stolen lead, iron, copper, brass, bell-metal, or solder, may be convicted, altho' the principal hath not been convicted, and shall be transported for fourteen years

And by the 10 *G* 3 *c* 48 Every person who shall buy or receive any stolen jewel or jewels, or any stolen gold or silver plate, watch or watches, knowing the same to have been stolen, shall, in all cases where such jewel or jewels, or gold or silver plate shall have been feloniously nriouſly ſtolen, accompanied with a burglary actually committed in ſtealing the ſame, or ſhall have been feloniouſly taken by a robbery on the highway,—be triable as well before conviction of the principal felon whether he be in or out of cuſtody, as after his conviction and if ſuch perſon ſo buying or receiving ſhall be convicted thereof, he ſhall be guilty of felony, and tranſported for 14 years

8 It ſeemeth not reaſonable, Mr *Hawkins* ſays, where a perſon is charged as acceſſary to more than one principal, to try him on the conviction of one, before all of them have appeared, becauſe hereby he may be ſubject to the hardſhip and hazard of two trials for his life for the ſame offence, which is contrary to the general courſe of the law 2 *Haw* 323

Caſe where a perſon is charged as acceſſary to more than one.

But if a man be indicted as acceſſary to two or more, and the jury find him acceſſary to one, it is a good verdict, and judgment may paſs upon him *Foſt* 361

And therefore the court in their diſcretion (Sir *Michael Foſter* ſays) may arraign him as acceſſary to ſuch of the principals who are convicted, and if he be found guilty as acceſſary to them or *any* of them, judgment ſhall paſs upon him But on the other hand, if he be acquitted, that acquittal will not diſcharge him as acceſſary to the others, and when they come in and are convicted and attainted, or if judgment of outlawry paſſeth againſt them, he may be arraigned *de novo* as acceſſary likewiſe to them Altho' it is the ſafer courſe (according to lord *Hale*) to reſpite the arraignment of the acceſſary, till all appear or are outlawed *Foſt* 361

9 If the principal be erroneouſly attaint, yet the acceſſary ſhall be put to anſwer, and ſhall not take advantage of the error in that attainder, but the principal reverſing the attainder, reverſeth the attainder of the acceſſary. 1 *H H* 625

Caſe where the principal is erroneouſly attainted.

But upon this, Sir *Michael Foſter* diſtinguiſheth as follows If the principal and acceſſary are joined in one indictment and tried together, which ſeems to be the moſt eligible courſe where both are ameſnable to the court, there is no room to doubt, whether the acceſſary may not enter into the full defence of the principal, and avail himſelf of every matter of fact, and every point of law tending to *his* acquittal For the acceſſary is in this caſe to be conſidered as a partner in the ſuit, and this ſort of defence neceſſarily and directly tendeth to his own acquittal. *Foſt* 365

But when the acceſſary is brought to his trial, *after* the conviction of the principal, it is not neceſſary to enter

into

into a detail of the evidence on which the conviction was founded   Nor doth the indictment aver that the principal was in fact guilty.   It is ſufficient if it reciteth, with proper certainty, the record of the conviction   This is evidence againſt the acceſſary, ſufficient to put him upon his defence.   For it is founded on a legal preſumption, that every thing in the former proceeding was rightly and properly tranſacted.   But a preſumption of this kind muſt, as it ſeemeth, give way to facts manifeſtly and clearly proved   As againſt the acceſſary, the conviction of the principal will not be concluſive, it is as to him *res inter alios acta*.   Id.

And therefore if it ſhall come out in evidence upon the trial of the acceſſary, as it ſometimes hath and frequently may, that the offence of which the principal was convicted did not amount to felony in him, or not to that ſpecies of felony with which he was charged, the acceſſary may avail himſelf of this, and ought to be acquitted *Poſt* 365.

And as in point of *law*, ſo alſo in point of *fact*, if it ſhall manifeſtly appear in the courſe of the acceſſary's trial, that the principal was innocent, common juſtice ſeemeth to require that the acceſſary ſhould be acquitted   As ſuppoſe a man is convicted upon circumſtantial evidence, ſtrong as that ſort of evidence can be, of murder   Another is afterwards indicted as acceſſary to this murder, and it cometh out upon the trial by inconteſtable evidence, that the perſon who was ſuppoſed to be murdered is ſtill living, in this caſe certainly the perſon indicted as acceſſary ſhall be acquitted   Or ſuppoſe the perſon to have been in fact murdered, and that it ſhould come out in evidence to the ſatisfaction of the court and jury, that the witneſſes againſt the principal were miſtaken in his perſon (a caſe of this kind ſir *Michael Foſter* ſays he has known), that the perſon convicted as principal was not nor could poſſibly have oeen preſent at the murder.   *Id* 367, 368

10. If one perſon be indicted as principal, and another as acceſſary, and both be acquit, yet the perſon indicted as acceſſary may be indicted as principal, and the former acquittal as acceſſary is no bar   1 *H H.* 625

11 But if a perſon be indicted as principal and acquitted; lord *Hale* ſays, he ſhall not be indicted as acceſſary before   And if he be, he may plead his former acquittal in bar, for it is in ſubſtance the ſame offence.   1 *H H* 626

But ſir *Michael Foſter* obſerves upon this, that in the eye of the law, the offences of principal and acceſſary do ſpecifically differ, and if a perſon indicted as principal,

cannot

cannot be convicted upon evidence tending barely to prove him to have been acceſſary before the fact, which muſt needs be admitted, it doth not appear how an acquittal upon one indictment can be a bar to a ſecond for an offence ſpecifically different from it. *Foſt.* 362.

12 So if a man be indicted as principal, and acquitted, he may be indicted as acceſſary after, for they are offences of ſeveral natures. 1 *H. H* 626.

Principal acquitted may be indicted as acceſſary after.

13 And ſo it is if he be indicted as acceſſary before, and acquitted; yet for the ſame reaſon he may be indicted as acceſſary after. 1 *H. H.* 626.

Acceſſary before acquitted, may be indicted as acceſſary after.

Indictment of an acceſſary before the fact, taken from *Coke*'s report of Lord *Sanchar*'s caſe, 9 *Co.* 116. which, as the proſecution was by the king's ſpecial command, was probably drawn by good advice, and on which *Robert Creighton*, eſquire, (Lord *Sanchar* of *Scotland*) was convicted and hanged, *viz.*

Middleſex. THE *jurors do preſent for the lord the king upon their oath, That whereas* Robert Carliel *late of* London, *yeoman, and* James Irweng *late of* London *aforeſaid, yeoman, not having God before their eyes, but ſeduced by the inſtigation of the devil, the eleventh day of* May *in the year of the reign of our lord* James *by the grace of God of* England, France, *and* Ireland, *king, defender of the faith, and ſo forth, the tenth, and of* Scotland *the forty-fifth, at* London, *that is to ſay, in the pariſh of St* Dunſtan *in the Weſt, and in the ward of* Farringdon *without* London *aforeſaid, &c. with force and arms, &c. feloniouſly and of their aforethought malice, in and upon one* John Turner *then and there in the peace of God and of the ſaid lord the king being, made an aſſault and affray, and the aforeſaid* Robert Carliel *a certain gun* [termentum] *called a piſtol, of the value of* 5 s. *then and there charged with gunpowder and a leaden bullet, which gun the ſaid* Robert Carliel *in his right hand then and there had and held, in and upon the aforeſaid* John Turner *then and there feloniouſly, voluntarily, and of his malice forethought, did ſhoot off and diſcharge, and the aforeſaid* Robert Carliel, *with the leaden bullet aforeſaid from the gun aforeſaid then and there ſhot and diſcharged, the aforeſaid* John Turner, *in and upon the left part of the breaſt of him the ſaid* John Turner, *near the left pap of him the ſaid* John Turner, *then and there feloniouſly ſtruck, giving to the ſaid* John Turner *then and there with the leaden bullet aforeſaid out of the gun aforeſaid then*

3

and

and there ſhot off and diſcharged, in and upon the left part of the breaſt of him the ſaid John Turner, one mortal wound of the breath of half an inch, and depth of five inches, of which mortal wound the aforeſaid John Turner at London aforeſaid, in the pariſh and ward aforeſaid, inſtantly died And that James Irweng feloniouſly, and of his forethought malice, then and there was preſent, aiding, aſſiſting, abetting, comforting and maintaining the aforeſaid Robert Carliel to the felony and murder aforeſaid in form aforeſaid to be done and committed, and ſo the aforeſaid Robert Carliel and James Irweng the aforeſaid John Turner at London aforeſaid, in the pariſh and ward aforeſaid, in manner and form aforeſaid, feloniouſly, voluntarily, and of their forethought malice, killed and murdered, againſt the peace of the lord the now king his crown and dignity, And that one Robert Creighton, late of the pariſh of St Margaret in Weſtminſter, in the county of Middleſex, eſquire, not having God before his eyes, but being ſeduced by the inſtigation of the devil, before the felony and murder aforeſaid by the aforeſaid Robert Carliel and James Irweng in manner and form aforeſaid done and committed, that is to ſay, the tenth day of May in the year of the reign of our lord James by the grace of God of England, France, and Ireland, king, defender of the faith, and ſo forth, the tenth, and of Scotland the forty-fifth, the aforeſaid Robert Carliel, at the aforeſaid pariſh of St Margaret in Weſtminſter aforeſaid, in the county of Middleſex aforeſaid, to the felony and murder aforeſaid, in manner and form aforeſaid to be done and committed, maliciouſly, feloniouſly, voluntarily and of his forethought malice, did incite, move, abet, counſel and procure, againſt the peace of the ſaid lord the king that now is, his crown and dignity

If after the fact, then the form may be thus,

And that A O late of ———— in the county of ———— yeoman, well knowing the ſaid (offender) to have done and committed the ſaid felony in manner and form aforeſaid, afterwards, to wit, on the ———— day of ———— in the ———— year of the reign of ———— at ———— aforeſaid in the county aforeſaid, with force and arms, him the ſaid ———— did then and there feloniouſly, and of his malice forethought, receive, aid, and comfort, againſt the peace of the ſaid lord the king that now is, his crown and dignity;

Action popular. See **Information.**

Addition.

Addition.

TO prevent the inconvenience of troubling one person for another, it is enacted by 1 *H* 5 *c* 5 that *in every original writ of actions personal, appeals, and indictments, in which the exigent shall be awarded, to the names of the defendants additions shall be made, of their estate or degree or mistery, and of the towns, or hamlets, or places, and counties, of which they were, or be and if by process upon the said original writs, appeals, or indictments, in which the said additions be omitted, any outlawries be pronounced, they shall be void, and before the outlawries pronounced, the said writs and indictments shall be abated by the exception of the party*

In which the exigent shall be awarded] The exigent is a writ whereby the sheriff is commanded to proclaim the party in the county court, in order to his being outlawed And by these words the act extendeth only to cases where process of outlawry may be awarded, and therefore it extendeth not to an indictment for encroaching on a highway, because in that case process of outlawry lieth not, but a distress *Croke Eliz* 148

To the names of the defendants] Regularly by the common law, every natural man, having no name of dignity, ought to be named in all originals and other suits by his christian name, and firname, and that, before this act, sufficed, but if he had a name of inferior dignity (as knight or banneret) he ought to be named by his christian name and firname, and by the addition of his name of dignity 2 *Inst* 665

If there be a corporation of one sole person, that hath a fee simple, and may have a writ of right, he may be named by the common law by his christian name without any firname, as *John* bishop of *P* 2 *Inst* 666

If it be a corporation aggregate of many able persons, as mayor and commonalty, dean and chapter, the mayor or dean need not be named by his christian name, because that such a corporation standeth in lieu both of the christian name and firname 2 *Inst.* 666

A duke, marquis, earl, viscount, or baron might by the common law be named by his christian name, and by the name of his dignity, as *John* duke of *M* 2 *Inst* 666.

Additions shall be made] The addition as well of the estate, degree, or mistery, as the town, hamlet, or place, ought by force of this act to be alledged, in the first name, for an addition after the *alias dictus* is ill As for instance, where the indictment was against *W R* otherwise called *W R.* of *H* for without the *alias dict* is there is no addition of the vill, and if the party is not sufficiently named in the

first

firſt part, the *alias* cannot aid or help it. 2 *Inſt* 669, 3 *Salk.* 20.

Where there are ſeveral defendants of different names, and the ſame addition, it is ſafeſt to repeat the addition after each of their names, applying it particularly to every one of them 2 *Haw.* 187.

Where a father hath the ſame name and the ſame addition with a defendant being his ſon, the action is abateable unleſs it add the addition of *the younger* to the other additions, but where the father is the defendant, it is ſaid that there is no need of the addition of *the elder.* 2 Haw. 187.

Of their eſtate or degree] *Eſquire* is a good addition. And the eldeſt ſons of peers, in the life time of their fathers, tho' frequently titular lords, yet are only eſquires. So alſo the younger ſons of peers, and their eldeſt ſons, in perpetual ſucceſſion Alſo the eldeſt ſons of knights, and their eldeſt ſons There are alſo eſquires by virtue of their office, as juſtices of the peace, and others who bear any office of truſt under the crown. 1 *Blackſt* 405 †

And it ſeems clear, that no one can be well deſcribed by the addition of a temporal dignity of any other nation beſides our own, becauſe no ſuch dignity can give a man an higher title here, than that of an eſquire. 2 *Haw* 187.

Clerk is a good addition of a clergyman, and he that hath taken any degree in either of the univerſities, may be named by that degree. 2 *Inſt.* 668. 1 *Blackſt.* 405.

Gentleman and *gentlewoman* are good additions And as for gentlemen, ſays Sir Thomas Smith, they be made good cheap in this kingdom, for whoſoever ſtudieth the laws of the realm, who ſtudieth in the univerſities, who profeſſeth liberal ſciences, and (to be ſhort) who can live idly, and without manual labour, and will bear the port, charge, and countenance of a gentleman, he ſhall be called Mr ſuch a one, and ſhall be taken for a gentleman. 1 *Blackſt.* 406.

Yeoman is a good addition, under which denomination are comprehended thoſe who have freehold land of 40 s a year, and thereby heretofore could ſerve upon juries, and can yet vote for knights of the ſhire, and do any other act where the law requires one that is *a good and lawful man* Id.

Widow, or *ſinglewoman*, or, (as ſome ſay) *wife* of ſuch a one, are all of them good additions of the eſtate or de-

† Where the abbreviated word *Blackſt* occurs (without more), this is to be underſtood of "Blackſtone's Commentaries on the laws of England" The Reports of that author are diſtinguiſhed by "Blackſt Rep"

gree

gree of a woman, but no such like addition is good, for the estate and degree of a man. Also *spinster* is a good addition of a woman. 2 *Haw* 188.

Or mystery] This includeth all lawful arts, trades and occupations, as taylor, merchant, mercer, parish clerk, schoolmaster, husbandman, labourer, and the like. 2 *Haw* 188.

But servant, groom, or farmer, are not additions within this act, because they are not of any mistery. And chamberer, butler, pantler, or the like, are additions of offices, and not of any mistery or occupation. 2 *Inst* 668.

Neither doth this act extend to unlawful practices, as extortioner, maintainer, thief, vagabond, heretick, and such like. 2 *Haw* 188.

If a man hath divers arts, trades or occupations, he may be named by any of them; but if a gentleman by birth be a tradesman, he shall not be named by his trade, but by the degree of gentleman, because it is worthier than the addition of any mistery. And in general a man shall be named by his worthiest title of addition. 2 *Inst.* 668, 669.

And of the towns or hamlets] If there be two towns in a county of the same principal name, with different additions to distinguish them from one another, as *Great Dale* and *Little Dale*, or *Upper Dale* and *Lower Dale*, and the defendant named only of the principal town without any addition, as of *Dale* only, the defendant may plead that there are two *Dales* in the same county, and none without an addition. But if there be two towns of the same name in a county, without any addition to distinguish them, it may be sufficient in such case to name the defendant generally of either of such towns, without adding any thing to distinguish it from the other. 2 *Hawk* 189.

If the defendant live in a hamlet of a town, it is said to be in the election of the party to name him either of the hamlet or of the town. 2 *Haw.* 189.

But the addition of a parish, if there be two or more towns in it, is not good; but if there be but one town, the addition of parish is good. 2 *Inst* 669.

The addition of the place of habitation of a wife, is sufficiently shewn, by shewing that of the husband, because it shall be intended that the wife lives where the husband does. 2 *Haw* 190.

Or places] If the defendant lives in a place known by a special name, and lying out of any town or hamlet, he may be well named of such place; but if he live in any place known within a town or hamlet, it is said to be safest to name him of the town or hamlet. 2 *Haw* 189, 190.

Of

Of which they were or be] The addition of the estate, degree, or mistery, ought to be as the defendant was of at the day of the indictment brought, and not *late* of such a degree or mistery, but it is a good addition to name the defendant *late* of such a town or place, because men do often remove their habitation. 2 *Inst* 670.

So in the case of lord *Balmerino*, after the rebellion in the year 1745, the indictment charged, that Arthur lord Balmerino *late of the city of Carlisle in the county of Cumberland* did so and so, lord Balmerino objected, that this was no title belonging to him, upon which the lord high steward informed him, that these words were not made part of his title, but only an addition of *place*, which the law for good reasons requires to be inserted by way of description of defendants in all indictments, and it is most commonly taken from that place where the crime is by such indictment charged to have been committed *Lord Balmerino's Trial*, p. 12 *State Trials*, vol. 9.

Shall be void] This being a judgment in law, is interpreted to be made void by a writ of error, or by the plea of the party coming in upon a *capias utlagatum*, for tho' the statute saith they shall be void, yet they are but voidable by a writ of error or plea. 2 *Inst* 670

By the exception of the party] But if the defendant appeareth upon process, and plead, taking no advantage thereof by exception, he hath lost the benefit hereof But it seemeth that the bare appearance of the party, without plea, doth not salve the want of a good addition 2 *Haw* 190.

Adultery.   See **Lewdness.**

Affray.

I What is an affray.
II. How far it may be suppressed by a private person.
III How far by a constable.
IV. How far by a justice of the peace.
V. Punishment of an affray

I. *What is an affray.*

1. **A**N *affray is a publick offence to the terror of the king's subjects, so called* (according to lord Coke) *because it affrighteth and maketh men afraid* 3 Inst 158

2 From whence it seemeth clearly to follow, that there may be an *assault*, which will not amount to an af-

fray, as where it happens in a private place, out of the hearing or seeing of any, except the parties concerned; in which case it cannot be said to be to the terror of the people. 1 *Haw* 134

3 Also it is said, that no quarrelsome or threatning words whatsoever, shall amount to an affray, and that no one can justify laying his hands on those who shall barely quarrel with angry words, without coming to blows, yet it seemeth, that the constable may, at the request of the party threatened, carry the person who threatens to beat him, before a justice in order to find sureties. 1 *Haw.* 135

4. Also, it is certain, that it is a very high offence to challenge another, either by word or letter, to fight a duel, or to be the messenger of such a challenge, or even barely to endeavour to provoke another to send a challenge, or to fight, as by dispersing letters to that purpose, full of reflections, and insinuating a desire to fight. 1 *Haw.* 135

5. But altho' no bare words, in the judgment of law, carry in them so much terror as to amount to an affray, yet it seems certain, that in some cases there may be an affray, where there is no actual violence, as where a man arms himself with dangerous and unusual weapons, in such a manner as will naturally cause a terror to the people, which is said to have been always an offence at the common law, and is strictly prohibited by statute For by 2 *Ed.* 3. *c.* 3. it is enacted, that *no man of what condition soever, except the king's servants in his presence, and his ministers in executing their office, and such as be in their company assisting them, and also upon a cry made for arms to keep the peace, shall come before the king's justices, or other of the king's ministers doing their office, with force and arms, nor bring any force in affray of peace, nor go nor ride armed, by night or day, in fairs or markets, or in the presence of the king's justices, or other ministers, or elsewhere, upon pain to forfeit their armour to the king, and their bodies to prison at the king's pleasure. And the king's justices in their presence, sheriffs and other ministers in their bailiwicks, lords of franchises and their bailiffs in the same, and mayors and bailiffs of cities and boroughs within the same, and borough-holders, constables and wardens of the peace within their wards, shall have power to execute this act And the judges of assize may punish such officers as have not done their duty herein.*

Upon a cry made for arms to keep the peace] It is holden upon these words of exception, that no person is within the intention of this statute, who arms himself to suppress

dangerous

dangerous rioters, rebels, or enemies, and endeavours to suppress or resist such disturbers of the peace and quiet of the realm. 1 *Haw* 136

In affray of peace] *En effrayer de la pees*, Lord *Coke* has it *pais*, of the country, or the people, and so, he observes, that the writ grounded upon this statute saith, In quorundam *de populo* terrorem, and therefore the printed book, *in affray of peace*, ought to be amended. 3 *Inst* 158.

And it is holden upon these words, that no wearing of arms is within the meaning of this statute, unless it be accompanied with such circumstances as are apt to terrify the people, from whence it seems clearly to follow, that persons of quality are in no danger of offending against this statute, by wearing common weapons, or having their usual number of attendants with them, for their ornament or defence, in such places, and upon such occasions, in which it is the common fashion to make use of them, without causing the least suspicion of an intention to commit any act of violence, or disturbance of the peace. 1 *Haw* 136

Nor to go nor ride armed} It is holden, that a man cannot excuse the wearing such armour in publick, by alledging that such a one threatened him, and that he wears it for the safety of his person from his assault, but it hath been resolved, that no one shall incur the penalty of the said statute for assembling his neighbours and friends in his own house against those who threaten to do him any violence therein, because a man's house is his castle. 1 *Haw* 136.

Their bodies to prison} The statute of 20 R. 2. c. 1 adds a fine likewise

Wardens of the peace] It is holden that any justice of the peace, or other person who is impowered to execute this statute, may proceed thereon *ex officio*, and if he find any person in arms, contrary to the form of the statute, he may seize the arms, and commit the offender to prison, and that he ought also to make a record of the whole proceeding, and certify the same into the exchequer. 1 *Haw.* 135.

II. How far it may be suppressed by a private person.

1 It seems agreed, that any one who sees others fighting, may lawfuly part them, and also stay them till the heat be over, and then deliver them to the constable to

be carried before a juſtice; to find ſureties for the peace.
1 *Haw.* 136

2 And the law doth encourage him hereunto, for if
he receive any harm by the affrayers, he ſhall have his remedy by law againſt them ; and if the affrayers receive
hurt, by the endeavouring only to part them, the ſtanders
by may juſtify the ſame, and the affrayers have no remedy
by law. 3 *Inſt.* 158.

3. But if either of the parties be ſlain, or wounded, or
ſo ſtricken that he falleth down for dead, in that caſe the
ſtanders by ought to apprehend the party ſo ſlaying,
wounding, or ſtriking, or to endeavour the ſame by hue
and cry, or elſe for his eſcape, they ſhall be fined and
impriſoned 3 *Inſt.* 158.

III How far by a conſtable.

1 It ſeems agreed, that a conſtable is not only impowered, as all private perſons are, to part an affray which
happens in his preſence, but is alſo bound at his peril to
uſe his beſt endeavours to this purpoſe, and not only to do
his utmoſt himſelf, but alſo to demand the aſſiſtance of
others, which if they refuſe to give him, they are puniſhable with fine and impriſonment. 1 *Haw.* 137

2 And it is ſaid, that if a conſtable ſee perſons either
actually engaged in an affray, as by ſtriking or offering to
ſtrike, or drawing their weapons, or the like, or upon
the very point of entering upon an affray, as where one
ſhall threaten to kill, wound, or beat another, he may
either carry the offender before a juſtice, to find ſureties for
the peace, or he may impriſon him of his own authority
for a reaſonable time, till the heat ſhall be over, and alſo
afterwards detain him till he find ſuch ſurety by obligation.
But it ſeems, that he has no power to impriſon ſuch an offender in any other manner, or for any other purpoſe, for
he cannot juſtify the committing an affrayer to gaol, till he
ſhall be puniſhed for his offence And it is ſaid, that he
ought not to lay hands on thoſe, who barely contend with
hot words, without any threats of perſonal hurt and
that all which he can do in ſuch caſe, is to command
them under pain of impriſonment to avoid fighting.
1 *Haw.* 137

3 But he is ſo far intruſted with a power over all actual affrays, that tho' he himſelf is a ſufferer by them, and
therefore liable to be objected againſt, as likely to be partial
in his own cauſe, yet he may ſuppreſs them, and therefore,
if an aſſault be made upon him, he may not only defend

himſelf,

himfelf, but alfo imprifon the offender, in the fame manner as if he were no way a party   1 *Haw.* 137

4   And if an affray be in an houfe, the conftable may break open the doors to preferve the peace, and if affrayers fly to an houfe, and he follow with frefh fuit, he may break open the doors to take them.   1 *Haw.* 137

5   But it is faid, that a conftable hath no power to arreft a man for an affray done out of his own view, without a warrant from a juftice, unlefs a felony were done, or likely to be done, for it is the proper bufinefs of a conftable to preferve the peace, and not to punifh the breach of it   1 *Haw.* 137.

IV. *How far by a juftice of the peace.*

There is no doubt, but that a juftice of the peace may and muft do all fuch things to the aforefaid purpofe, which a private man or conftable are either enabled or required by the law to do   But it is faid, that he cannot without a warrant authorize the arreft of any perfon for an affray out of his own view, yet it feems clear, that in fuch cafe he may make his warrant to bring the offender before him, in order to compel him to find fureties for the peace. 1 *Haw.* 137.

V. *Punifhment of an affray.*

All affrays in general are punifhable by fine and imprifonment. 1 *Haw.* 138.

And they are inquirable in the leet, as common nufances   3 *Inft* 158.

Warrant to apprehend affrayers.

Weftmorland. } To the conftable of ——

WHEREAS A. I of —— *yeoman, hath this day made oath before me* J P *efquire, one of his majefty's juftices of the peace for the faid county, that on the ——day of —— in the —— year of the reign of —— A O. of —— yeoman, and B O. of —— yeoman, at —— in the faid county, in a tumultuous manner made an affray, wherein the perfon of the faid* A I *was beaten and abufed by them the faid* A O *and* B O *without any lawful or fufficient provocation given to them, or to either of them, by him the faid* A. I   *Thefe are therefore to command you forthwith*

forthwith to apprehend the said A O *and* B O *and bring them before me, or some other of his said majesty's justices of the peace for the said county, to answer the premisses, and to find sureties as well for their personal appearance at the next general quarter-sessions of the peace to be holden for the said county, then and there to answer to an indictment to be preferred against them by the said* A. I *for the said offence, as also for their keeping the peace in the mean time, towards his said majesty and all his liege people, and especially towards him the said* A I. *Hereof fail not, as you will answer the contrary at your peril Given under my hand and seal at ——— in the said county, the ——— day of ——— in the year ———*

Indictment for an affray.

THE *jurors for our lord the king, upon their oath present, that* A. O *of ——— in the county of ——— taylor, and* B. O *of ——— in the said county, blacksmith, with force and arms, on the ——— day of ——— in the ——— year of the reign of our sovereign lord* George *the third, by the grace of God, of* Great Britain, France *and* Ireland, *king, defender of the faith, and so forth, at ——— aforesaid in the county aforesaid, being arrayed and unlawfully assembled together in a warlike manner, did make an affray, to the terror and disturbance of divers of the subjects of our said sovereign lord the king then and there being, and to the evil example of all other the subjects of our said sovereign lord the king, and against the peace of our said lord the king, his crown and dignity.*

Alehouses.

For matters relating to the *excise* on beer and ale,
see title **Excise.**

C 3

X Con-

I *Concerning inns and alehoufes in general.*

Difference between inns and alehoufes

1 EVERY inn is not an alehoufe, nor every alehoufe an inn but if an inn ufes common felling of ale, it is then alfo an alehoufe, and if an alehoufe lodges and entertains travellers, it is alfo an inn

Licence to erect inns

2 It was refolved by all the judges, that any perfon might erect an inn to lodge travellers, without any licence or allowance for fuch erection *Dalt. c* 56 *Blackerby,* 170.

Inn indictable

3 But it feems to be agreed, that the keeper of an inn may by the common law be indicted and fined, as being guilty of a publick nufance, if he ufually harbour thieves, or perfons of fcandalous reputation, or fuffer frequent diforders in his houfe, or take exorbitant prices, or fet up a new inn in a place where there is no manner of need of one, to the hindrance of other ancient and well governed inns, or keep it in a place in refpect of its fituation wholly unfit for fuch a purpofe 1 *Haw* 225.

Innkeeper felling ale

4 And if an inn ufeth the trade of an alehoufe, as almoft all innkeepers do, it fhall be within the ftatutes made about alehoufes *Dalt* 133

Inns to be licenced.

5 It hath been alfo agreed by law, that innkeepers ought to have licence, and be bound by recognizance for keeping good order, as alehoufekeepers are. *Dalt* 24

Power of juftices by the commiffion.

6 By the commiffion of the peace, two juftices (12) may inquire of innholders, and of all and fingular other perfons, who fhall offend in the abufe of weights and meafures, or in the fale of victuals, againft the form of the ordinances in that behalf made

II *Selling ale without licence.*

By the 5 G 3 c 46. Whereas by the law now in force, perfons felling ale or beer, or other excifeable liquors by retail, without licence, are fubject by different

laws

laws to different penalties and punishments, which has occasioned much confusion, and an ill use has been made thereof in many instances, it is therefore enacted, that every person lawfully convicted of selling ale or beer, or other exciseable liquors, by retail, without licence (except in fairs, 5 & 6 *Ed* 6 c 25   3 *G* c 3.   26 G 2 c 31. and except retailers of spirituous liquors without licence, for whom other penalties are provided by law, 9 G 3 c 6) shall for every such offence forfeit and undergo the several penalties and punishments herein after mentioned, instead of the several pecuniary and corporal punishments which they are now subject to by any law now in force, that is to say, for the first offence 40 s, and also the costs and expences of conviction, if not paid within 14 days after conviction, the offender to be imprisoned for one month, unless he shall sooner pay the penalty, and the costs, charges, and expences of the conviction, and of executing the same   for the second offence 4 l, and also the costs and expences of conviction, if not paid within one week after conviction, to be imprisoned two months, unless he shall sooner pay the penalty, and the costs, charges, and expences of such second conviction, and of executing the same   for the third offence 6 l, and also the costs and expences of conviction, if not paid within three days after conviction, to be imprisoned for three months, unless he shall sooner pay the penalty, and the costs, charges, and expences of such third conviction, and of executing the same   and the like penalty for every other offence after the third, as for the third offence   All which costs and expences shall be ascertained by the justice before whom the offender shall be convicted   One moiety of all which penalties and forfeitures shall be to the king, and the other moiety, and all such costs, charges, and expences to the prosecutor   ſ 22

The same to be heard and determined by one justice, who shall, on information (A) exhibited or complaint made to him, summon (B) the party accused, and also the witnesses on either side (if he shall be required to summon any such), and on appearance of the party accused, or contempt in not appearing, shall proceed to hear the matter, and examine witnesses on oath, and give judgment, and if he convict (C) the party accused, and such party shall refuse to pay the penalty within the time above expressed, together with the costs as aforesaid, he shall issue his warrant for apprehending and committing (D) to prison every such offender, for such time, and in such manner, as the nature of the offence shall require. ſ 23

C 4   [Note,

[Note, the *number* of witnesses necessary towards the conviction is not here mentioned, and therefore this seemeth to rest as it was before, on the statute of the 3 C c. 3 which directed the conviction to be on confession of the offender or oath of two witnesses]

Also where any justice shall suspect that any person sells without licence, he may call such person before him, and also any excise officer or gauger to produce his stock book or other account of the charge or survey of such suspected person, and may examine such officer on oath in what manner he charges such person, and how such person pays the duties, and if it shall appear by such stock book or account, or oath of the officer, that such person is surveyed as a victualler or retailer, and is charged with the same duties that victuallers and retailers are charged with and pay for any the liquors aforesaid, and is not intitled to the allowance or abatement given to common brewers, he shall be deemed an alehousekeeper, victualler, retailer, or seller thereof. 26 G 2. c. 31 ſ 9

Witness neglecting or refusing to appear upon summons at the time and place appointed, without a reasonable excuse to be allowed by such justice, or appearing and refusing to be examined on oath and give evidence, shall forfeit 20 s, to be levied in such manner and by such means as is before directed. 5 G. 3 c 46 ſ 24

Note, this penalty is but small, and might defeat the intention of the act, for by the witness paying 20 s, the offender may chance to escape the payment of 2, 4, or 6 l, besides charges. But there is a clause in the statute of the 26 G 2. c 31 which enacts, that if any person summoned as evidence in such case shall refuse to appear, or shall appear and refuse to give evidence upon oath, he shall forfeit 10 l. ſ. 10 †

And

† But how this 10 l shall be levied, is not quite clear By the aforesaid act of the 5 G 3 c 46 it is expressed, that all penalties for offences against the said act, or *against the said former act*, shall be heard and determined as is above set forth. Now there are many acts mentioned before, but what seems to be particularly intended in this place is, such act or acts as did inflict penalties on persons selling ale or beer without licence And there are three acts of this kind, which were the cause as aforesaid of diversity and confusion And therefore it seemeth that this expression should have run [*against this or the said former acts*], that is, against the laws inflicting penalties on persons selling ale or beer without licence. But as it stands, this penalty of 10 l seems to be recoverable

And if any person shall think himself aggrieved by the conviction of such justice, and shall give security to the satisfaction of the said justice for payment of the penalty, costs, and expences, to be expressed in the *warrant of distress* on such conviction, he may appeal to the next quarter sessions, unless such sessions shall be held within six days next after the conviction, and in that case to the next sessions after. And if the sessions adjudge the appeal to be frivolous or vexatious, they may give costs against the appellant, not exceeding 5l. 5 G 3 c 46 f 25

[Note, there seems to be a mistake, in setting forth that the costs shall be expressed in the *warrant of distress*, for no power of distress is given. The meaning seems to have been, that the same shall be expressed in the *conviction*, as is specified in the form prescribed by the act]

The clause excepting *fairs*, in the several acts, is from the necessity of the thing, respecting the accommodation of persons resorting thither. But those who shall brew such ale or beer, to be sold by them in fairs, must take care to give notice to the gaugers, that the same may be surveyed, for tho' they are exempted from taking licence, yet they must nevertheless pay the duties of excise. And this indulgence seemeth to be intended only in the place where the common fair is held, and not in any private house, which may be within the limits of the town where such fair shall be kept, especially wherein there are licensed alehouses sufficient.

BY the statute of the 4 *J* c 4. If any person shall sell or deliver any beer or ale, to any person that shall then sell beer or ale as a common tipler or alehousekeeper, the same person not having licence to sell ale or beer (except it be for the use of his houshold only), he shall forfeit for every barrel 6 s 8 d, and so proportionably for other quantities, half to the poor, and half to him that shall sue in sessions, by action of debt, information, indictment, or presentment.

III. *Licensing alehouses.*

1. By the 5 & 6 *Ed* 6 c 25 any two justices, 1 By two justices at a general meeting. might licence alehouses, but now by the 2 G. 2. c 28 and 26 G 2 c 31, it is enacted, that whereas many inconveniences have arisen from persons being licensed to keep inns

able as it was before, by the said act of the 26 G 2 c 31 that is to say, by distress, by warrant of one justice, and to be paid to the overseers for the use of the poor where the offender dwells

and

and common alehouses, by juſtices who, living remote from the places of abode of ſuch perſons, may not be truly informed as to the occaſion or want of ſuch inns or common alehouſes, or the characters of the perſons applying for licences to keep the ſame, therefore from henceforth no licence ſhall be granted to any perſon to keep a common inn or alehouſe, but at a general meeting of the juſtices acting in the diviſion where the ſaid perſon dwells, to be holden for that purpoſe, on the firſt day of *September* yearly, or within twenty days after, and not at any other time. Excepting, that this ſhall not alter the power or the time of granting licences, in cities and towns corporate. 2 *G.* 2. *c.* 28. *ſ.* 11, 12   26 G. 2 *c* 31 *ſ* 4. 16.

To keep a common inn or alehouſe] In the caſe of *Parker* and *Flint*, M 10 W. it was determined, that houſes at *Epſom*, where they take in lodgers and boarders, coming to drink the waters there during the ſeaſon, and dreſs victuals, and ſell them ale and beer, and entertain their horſes at 8 *d* a day, but ſell to no other perſons, are not inns nor alehouſes within the meaning of theſe acts 12 *Mod* 254

At a general meeting of the juſtices holden for the diviſion] But it is not neceſſary to ſet forth ſpecially in the licence, that it was granted at a general meeting of the juſtices holden for the diviſion, and therefore a conviction for keeping an alehouſe without ſuch licence, is not good upon the evidence of the licence only, but there muſt be other evidence. *M.* 11 *G.* 2. *King* and *Bryan*   2 Seſſ Ca 183. Andr. 81

The meeting how to be aſcertained. 2. And the day and place for granting licences ſhall be appointed by two or more juſtices for the diviſion, by warrant (E) under their hands and ſeals, at leaſt ten days before ſuch meeting, directed to the high conſtables, requiring them to order (F) their petty conſtables, or other peace officers, to give notice to the ſeveral innkeepers and alehouſekeepers within their reſpective conſtablewicks, of the day and place of ſuch meeting   And all licences granted at any other time and place ſhall be void. 26 G. 2, *c* 31 *ſ* 4.

Certificate of perſons to be licenſed. 3 And no licence ſhall be granted to any perſon not licenſed the year preceding (except in cities or towns corporate) unleſs he produce a certificate under the hands of the miniſter and the major part of the churchwardens and overſeers, or elſe of three or four reputable and ſubſtantial houſholders of the place, ſetting forth that ſuch perſon is

of

of good fame and of fober life and converfation; and it fhall be mentioned in fuch licence that fuch certificate was produced, otherwife the licence fhall be void 26 G. 2. *c* 31 *f.* 2. 16

Except in cities and towns corporate] In cities and towns corporate, fuch certificate is fuppofed not to be neceffary, by reafon of the propinquity of the perfons to be licenfed

4 Neverthelefs, altho' a certificate in fuch places is not requifite by this act, yet it is difcretionary in the juftices whom they will licenfe, and a *mandamus* in fuch cafe will not lie to compel the juftices to licenfe any perfon, and on a conviction for felling without licence, the want of fuch licence can only come in queftion, and not the reafon why it was denied *Strange* 881.

Whether a mandamus will lie to compel the juftices to grant a licence.

So in the cafe of the *King* againft the juftices of the peace of *Worcefter*, M. 4 G 2 a *mandamus* was moved for to be directed to them, to grant a licence to a victualler to fell ale Affidavits were offered to be produced, of the juftices declaring that they would grant no licences to any of the inhabitants who figned a petition to the parliament for erecting a workhoufe there, and that the perfon, on whofe behalf the motion was now made, had been a victualler in the town for above thirty-five years. The court faid, that they never knew a motion of this fort granted, but if there was fuch a grievance, as is mentioned, another fort of motion would be more proper. 1 *Barnardift.* 402

5 In the cafe of the *King* againft *Young* and *Pitts*, E. 31 G 2. a motion was made for an information againft thefe two juftices, for arbitrarily, obftinately, and unreafonably refufing to grant a licence to one *Henry Day* to keep an inn at *Everfley*, *Wilts* On fhewing caufe, it was infifted, that the legiflature has made the juftices the fole judges, as being fuch who, from the refidence on the fpot, muft beft know the perfons and their characters, and the circumftances of the place. And the legiflature has even excluded the juftices of other divifions. And the juftices thus intrufted have a right to judge for themfelves No man can judge for another And this power is intrufted to them by the conftitution, by the legiflature It may be very dangerous to them to be obliged to give their reafons publickly, though they may have very fufficient ones to fatisfy their own minds, and to direct their own judgments And if they are thus intrufted, why are they liable to be called to an account by any other jurifdiction, unlefs they act faultily and wilfully

Whether an information will lie

wrong?

wrong? Indeed, if they do wilfully wrong let them be punished, but where they act confcientioufly, they are not accountable to any body By lord Mansfield Ch J. It is certain, this court has no power or claim, to review the reafons of juftices of the peace, upon which they form their judgments in granting licences, by way of appeal from their judgments, or over-ruling the difcretion intruft-ed to them But if it clearly appears, that the juftices have been partially, malicioufly, or corruptly influenced in the exercife of this d ferction, and have confequently abufed the truft repofed in them, they are liable to pro-fecution by indictment or information, or even poffibly by action, if the malice be very grofs and injurious If their judgment is wrong, yet their heart and intention pure, God forbid that they should be punished. And he de-clared, that he should always lean towards favouring them, unlefs partiality, corruption, or malice shall clearly appear And having gone through all the particulars both of the charge and of the defence, he concluded with de-claring it as his opinion, that there was no fufficient ground for a criminal charge againft thefe juftices And by the court unanimoufly, the rule was difcharged with cofts. *Burrow, Mansfield.* 556

M 32 *G.* 2. *K* and *Athay.* On shewing caufe why a rule should not be made abfolute, for an information againft a juftice, for a mifdemeanor in refufing to grant a licence to one *Francis Simes* (who had been licenfed for feveral preceding years) to fell ale, as ufual, and afterwards convicting him, without any previous fummons, for hav-ing fold it without a licence It appeared, that the pre-tended grounds upon which this rule had been applied for and obtained, were either falfe or fallacious The firft was, that the only reafon why the licence was refufed him was, his declining to pay a fum of money (viz 5 *l*), which was claimed of him upon a diftinct and collateral account, and which he denied to be due from him, the payment of which fum of money was (as he alledged) infifted upon by the juftice, as a condition precedent to his granting the man a licence The fecond pretended ground of the motion was, that the juftice had convicted him of the offence, w thout any previous fummons —As to the firft. The court were unanimous, that the allegation ap-peared to be falfe in fact, but, at the fame time, they de-clared explicitly, that the juftices have no fort of autho-rity, to annex any fuch con litions to the grant of thefe licences. As to the fecond They efteemed it to be fal-lacious, as the fact came out upon shewing caufe, for the

man

man was actually prefent before the juftice (who had fent for him), and was fo far from offering at making any defence, that he feemed rather to apply for mercy, declaring, however, that if the juftice did convict him, he would not pay the penalty   Thirdly, the court obferved, that the man had not any where alledged, that he was innocent of the offence, which they thought it incumbent upon him to have done, to entitle himfelf to make this application againft the juftice —And the rule to fhew caufe was difcharged   *Burrow, Mansfield.* 653. *

E 2 G.

* The manner of quoting Sir *James Burrow* is different by different perfons   That author, intending to publifh Reports of cafes determined in the court of king's bench during the times of the four laft lords chief juftices *Hardwicke, Lee, Ryder,* and *Mansfield,* begins with the laft, juftly fuppofing that the lateft would be firft called for by the public expectation, and fo purpofing to continue to advance by a kind of retrograde progreffion; in like manner as was done in the publication of *Croke's* Reports, during the reigns of queen *Elizabeth,* king *James* the firft, and king *Charles* the firft.   Thofe in the reign of *Charles* the firft were firft publifhed, and fo upwards through the times of *James* and *Elizabeth,* and are now commonly diftinguifhed by the titles of *Croke Charles, Croke James,* and *Croke Elizabeth*   But whereas fome authors quote the Reports in the time of king *Charles,* from their having been firft printed, though laft in the courfe of decifion, by the diftinction of 1 *Croke,* and thofe of *Elizabeth* by 3 *Croke,* fo others, by the contrary rule, quote thofe of *Elizabeth* by 1 *Croke,* and thofe of *Charles* by 3 *Croke*   which is fo far the parent of fome confufion.

Sir *James Burrow* intitles his Reports during the time of lord *Mansfield,* the *Fourth Part* of his Reports, and accordingly the fame is quoted by fome, " 4 *Burrow* "   This fourth part, confifting of five volumes in folio, is quoted by others according to the number of volumes comprehending this fourth part, thus " 1, 2, 3, 4, 5, *Burrow* "   But thefe five volumes having the pages numbered uniformly from 1 to 2835, it is thought moft convenient in this book to keep this fourth part diftinct by the appellation of " *Burrow Mansfield,*" and fo referring to the page in which ever of the five volumes the matter fought for may happen to be.   By which method, when the three other parts in procefs of time fhall come to be publifhed (which is a thing much to be defired) they may be denominated in like manner, " *Burrow Ryder,*" " *Burrow Lee,*" and *Burrow Hardwicke,*" which in fome fort may prevent the confufion that happened in the publication of *Croke's* Reports

The faid Sir *James Burrow,* confidering that it muft needs be a confiderable length of time, before his whole collection of cafes can be publifhed, and being defirous in the mean time to

oblige

E. 2 *G* 3 *K* v *Williams* and *Davis*. An information was granted againſt the defendants, as juſtices of the peace for the borough of *Penryn*, for refuſing to grant licences to thoſe alehouſekeepers who voted againſt their recommendation of candidates for members of parliament for that borough It appeared, that they had acted very groſsly in this matter, having previouſly threatened to ruin theſe people, by not granting them licences, in caſe they ſhould vote againſt thoſe candidates whoſe intereſt theſe juſtices themſelves eſpouſed, and afterwards actually refuſing them licences, upon this account only. And lord *Mansfield* declared, that the court granted this information againſt the juſtices, not for the mere refuſing to grant the licences (which they had a diſcretion to grant or refuſe, as they ſhould ſee to be right and proper), but for the corrupt motive of ſuch refuſal, for their oppreſſive and unjuſt refuſing to grant them, becauſe the perſons applying for them would not give their votes for members of parliament as the juſtices would have had them. *Burr. Mansf* 1317.

T. 5 *G* 3. *K* v *Hann* and *Price*, juſtices of the peace for the borough of *Corfe Caſtle* On ſhewing cauſe againſt an information which had been prayed for againſt them, for a miſdemeanor in the execution of their office, in refuſing to grant a licence to ſell ale to one *Ingram*, an innkeeper in that borough, merely from a motive of reſentment againſt him, for having eſpouſed an oppoſite intereſt in the election for members of that borough, the defence was, that they did not act from any reſentment or corrupt motive, but ſolely becauſe *Ingram* was an improper perſon, and had kept a diſorderly houſe, and continued to keep it after full notice to the contrary, and in particular, that he encouraged gaming and cock-fighting at his houſe. By lord *Mansfield* Ch. J. The court ſhould never interpoſe againſt magiſtrates, unleſs they have acted from bad motives and *mala fide*, eſpecially in ſuch a caſe as this, where they are intruſted with an abſolute diſcretion · But for that very reaſon, this is the ſtrongeſt caſe for the interpoſition of the court, if it appears that they

oblige the gentlemen acting in the commiſſion of the peace with (what was exceedingly wanted) a regular courſe of deciſions in Settlement caſes, ſelected out of his whole collection thoſe relating ſolely to the ſettlement of the poor, during the times of the ſaid four laſt lords chief juſtices, a moſt intereſting period, comprehending the ſpace of upwards of forty years, and publiſhed the ſame in two quarto volumes. Theſe are quoted in this book by the title of *Burrow's Settlement Caſes* "

have

have acted upon corrupt motives   If it did appear clearly that this man kept a disorderly house, it would be a reason against the court's interposing against the justices. But this does not clearly appear   And upon the whole he thought, on a full discussion of the affidavits, that the charge upon the justices was not satisfactorily answered by them.   And he declared it to be of very dangerous consequence to permit the due discretion of the justices to be influenced by considerations of this kind.   The court thought it a proper case for an information, and made the rule absolute.

Afterwards, *M* 6 *G* 3 the justices confessing themselves guilty of the information, it was moved for a rule to dispense with their personal appearance, on the undertaking of their clerk in court to answer for their fines. But the court upon full debate were unanimous in refusing the motion   The general doctrine laid down by the court was, that tho' such a motion was subject to the discretion of the court, either to grant or refuse it, where it was clear and certain that the punishment would not be corporal, yet it ought to be denied in every case where it was either probable or possible that the punishment would be corporal.   And this, for the example sake, as the notoriety of their being called up might deter others from the like offences.   And finally, upon their appearance in court, the sentence was, that they should be committed for a month, fined 50 l each, and imprisoned till the fine be paid.   *Burr. Mansf.* 1716, 1786

6. By the 26 *G*. 2. *c*. 13.   No justice of the peace, being a common brewer of ale or beer, innkeeper, or distiller, or a seller of or dealer in ale or spirituous liquors, or interested in any of the said trades, or being a victualler or malster, shall be capable, or have any power to grant licences for selling ale or beer or any other liquors, but the same shall be void   ſ 11.

What justices are prohibited from granting licences.

7. And all mayors, town clerks, and other persons whom it may concern shall make out ale licences (G) duly stamped, before the recognizance be taken, on pain of 10 l, half to the king, and half to the prosecutor, with costs   6 *G* *c* 21   ſ 56.   1 *Ann* stat 2 *c*. 22 ſ 6. Which stamp shall be first of all a 12 d stamp by the 9 *Ann. c* 23.

Stamp

And then moreover a 20 s stamp, by the 29 *G* 2: *c* 12.   And if any person shall write any licence without such stamp, he shall forfeit 10 l with costs, to be recovered as stamp penalties, and the licence shall not be available till the duty shall be paid, and also a penalty of 5 l   29 *G*. 2. *c* 12. ſ 20.

And

And to prevent frauds therein, every victualler or ale-housekeeper shall, on demand by any officer of the stamp duties, produce his licence, and permit him at his own expence to have a copy thereof, on pain of 40s 5 G 3. c 46 f. 20.

And every clerk of the peace, town clerk, common clerk, or person acting as such, shall on demand by any officer of the stamp duties, or within three days next after, deliver to such officer, a true list of the names and places of abode, of all the victuallers, alehouse-keepers and other persons then licensed to sell ale or beer, or other excisable liquors, by retail, within the respective districts, and on delivery thereof, such officer shall pay to him after the rate of one farthing for every licensed person inserted in the list And if he shall refuse or neglect to deliver such list, or not insert therein a full and true account, he shall forfeit 5l f 21

Licence for spirituous liquors   8 And no person shall retail any distilled spirituous liquors, or strong waters, without a licence from the officers of excise taken out ten days before, for which he shall pay 40s yearly. 16 G. 2. c. 8 f 8   24 G 2. c. 40 f 9.

And such person shall be first licensed to sell ale or spirituous liquors by two or more justices of the peace. 2 G 2. c 28 f 11 9 G 2 c 23 f 14. 16 G 2 c. 8. f. 11 29 G 2 c. 12 f 22

And the justices clerk shall have 2 s 6 d, and no more, for such licence 9 G. 2 c. 23. f 14. 24 G. 2. c. 40. f. 28, 29

Which said licence for retailing spirituous liquors, is treated of more at large under the article concerning spirituous liquors in title **Excise**

Note, here is a *double* licence required for retailing of spirituous liquors, first, a licence from the justices to sell ale *or spirituous liquors*, and then a licence by the officers of excise to sell spirituous liquors And therefore the ale licence ought to run so as to include spirituous liquors, or else the law should be altered in this particular The printed alehouse licences from the stamp office endeavour to preserve the jurisdictions distinct, by excepting the several kinds of spirituous liquors by name out of the licence by the justices But this is against the statutes, nor was it intended perhaps by the legislature, that the officers of excise should have the sole jurisdiction in this matter, but rather that the primary judgment concerning the same should be referred to the justices.

Wine licence.   9 By the 9 *Ann* c 23 A wine licence is directed to be on a 4 s stamp And by the 30 *Geo* 2 c 19. a further

ther duty is laid thereon of 5 l, for perfons not having either ale or brandy licence, of 4 l, for perfons having an ale licence, and no brandy licence, and of 40 s, for perfons having both ale and brandy licence   Which is treated of under the title **Wine**.

10. By the 10 G 2 c 17 ∫ 10, 11   No perfon fhall ___Licence for made___ fell made wines, without a licence from two juftices, for ___wines___ which he fhall pay their clerk 2 s 6 d   and none fhall be granted but to keepers of victualling houfes, inns, coffeehoufes, or alehoufes

And by the 31 G. 2 c 31 ∫ 7   The duties impofed upon wine licences by the 30 G 2. c 19 fhall extend to licences for retailing fweets or made wines. As is alfo treated of under the title **Wine**

IV Recognizance, and forfeiture thereof.

1. On granting licences for keeping any common ale- ___Recognizance.___ houfe or tipling houfe, the perfon licenfed fhall enter into a recognizance in 10 l, with two fureties in 5 l each, or one furety in 10 l, (H) as well againft the ufing of unlawful games, as alfo for the ufing and maintainance of good order and rule to be had and ufed within the fame, as by their difcretion fhall be thought neceffary and convenient, and if fuch perfon fhall be hindered thro' ficknefs or infirmity, or other reafonable caufe to be allowed by the juftices, to attend in perfon, they may grant the licence, on two fureties entering into fuch recognizance in 10 l each   5 & 6 Ed. 6 c 25 ∫ 1. 26 G 2 c 31 ∫ 1

As by their difcretion fhall be thought neceffary and convenient] Mr *Dalton* obferves upon thefe words in the ftatute of 5 & 6 *Ed* 6 that the matter of the condition of the recognizance is by the ftatute partly referred to the *difcretion of the juftices* And he fays, in fome fhires the juftices have agreed upon certain articles framed by their difcretion, and generally to be propounded to all common ale fellers, taking their bond for performance of the fame, a copy whereof they ufed to deliver to every of them, which manner (he fays) had been allowed

And amongft articles of this kind, he recommends to the juftices care thefe three efpecially   1 That no alehoufekeeper, upon the Lord's day, fhould receive or fuffer to remain any perfons whatfoever, as their guefts, in any their houfes or other places, to tipple, eat or drink, other than travellers, and fuch as come upon neceffary bufinefs   2 That they fuffer no perfon whatfoever, reforting to their houfes only to eat and drink, to remain there after the hour of nine in the evening in winter, and ten in summer. 3 That they suffer no person, resorting to their houses only to eat and drink, to remain tipling there above one hour, other than travellers. *Dalt. c.* 176

To be filed at the sessions

2 Which said recognizance, with the condition thereof, fairly written or printed, shall forthwith, or at the next sessions at farthest, be sent or returned to the clerk of the peace, under the hands of the justices, to be by him entered or filed among the records 26 G. 2 *c* 31. *f.* 1.

Penalty for licensing otherwise

3 And for every licence granted, without taking such recognizance, and for every such recognizance taken, and not sent or returned, every justice signing such licence, shall forfeit 3 l 6 s 8 d 5 & 6 *Ed.* 6 *c* 25 *f* 2 26 G 2 *c* 31. *f* 1

Which said forfeiture, for granting licences, without taking recognizances, shall be to him who shall sue, together with costs 26 G. 2 *c* 31 *f.* 6 But it is not said who shall have the penalty for not returning the recognizance to the clerk of the peace, therefore that shall go to the king

Recognizances to be calendred.

4 And the clerk of the peace shall keep a register or calendar of all such recognizances, and shall deliver to the justices, at the meeting for granting licences, a true copy of such register or calendar 26 G 2 *c* 31 *f.* 5

Fee for the recognizance.

5. And for every recognizance shall be paid by the clerks of the justices taking such recognizances, to the clerk of the peace, for filing or recording the same, and for making and delivering the copies of the register or calendar 1 s, which shall be paid to the clerks of the said justices, by the persons licensed, over and above the fees payable to the said justices clerks. 26 G 2 *c* 31 *f* 5

Process on the recognizance

6. By the 5 & 6 *Ed* 6 *c.* 25 *f.* 3 The justices shall have power, in their quarter-sessions, by presentment, information, or otherwise by their discretion, to inquire of all such persons as shall be admitted and allowed to keep any alehouse or tipling house, and that be so bound by recognizance, if they have done any act whereby they have forfeited the same recognizance, and they shall upon such presentment or information award process against every such person so presented or complained upon before them, to shew why he should not forfeit his recognizance, and shall have power to hear and determine the same, by all such ways and means, as by their discretion shall be thought good.

And by the 26 G 2 *c* 31 Any justice on complaint or information that such licensed person hath committed any act, whereby in the judgment of such justice the recognizance may be forfeited, or the condition broken, may

by

by summons under hand and seal require such person to appear at the general or quarter sessions, then and there to answer to the matter of such complaint or information , and also may bind the complainant, or any other person in a recognizance to appear and give evidence , and the sessions may direct the jury which shall there attend for the trial of traverses, or some other jury of twelve honest and substantial men, to be then and there impanelled by the sheriff without fee, to inquire thereof, and if the jury find that such person hath done any act whereby the recognizance is broken, such act being specified in such complaint or information, the court may adjudge him guilty , which verdict and adjudication shall be final , and thereupon the court shall order the recognizance to be estreated into the exchequer, to be levied to his majesty's use, and the said person shall be disabled to sell any ale, beer, cyder, perry, or spirituous liquors for three years, and any licence granted to him for such term shall be void § 7 Provided, that the justices, at the request of the prosecutor, or of the party complained of, or either of his sureties, may adjourn the trial to the then next sessions § 8.

And if any person shall be disabled, by conviction, to sell ale, beer, cyder or perry; he shall by the same conviction be disabled to sell any spirituous liquors, any licence before obtained for that purpose notwithstanding, and every licence granted to him for selling ale, beer, cyder, perry, or spirituous liquors, shall be void , and if he shall sell during such disability, he shall be punished as for selling without licence , and a certificate from the clerk of the peace (which he shall grant without fee) of such conviction shall be legal evidence id § 11.

Which conviction shall be in this or the like form

Middlesex. **A.** O. is convicted on his own confession, (or on the oath of ⸺) of having sold ale, beer, or other liquors, in the parish of ⸺ in this county, on the ⸺ day of ⸺ after being disabled to sell the same This is the first, second, or third conviction Given under my hand and seal this ⸺ day of ⸺

Which said conviction shall be certified to the next sessions, to be filed amongst the records § 13.

V. To what places the licence shall extend.

1. No licence shall intitle any person to keep an alehouse *Licence restrained to the place* in any other place, than that in which it was first kept by virtue of such licence , and such licence with regard to all other places shall be void 26 G. 2 c 31 § 3.

2. And

2 'And if any licensed person shall die or remove out of his house so licensed, his executors, administrators, or assigns who shall be possessed of such house, or the occupier thereof, may continue during the residue of the term, without any new licence or certificate. 26 *G.* 2 *c* 31 *ſ* 3 29 *G* 2 *c* 12 *ſ* 23

And if any alehouse or victualling house *shall become empty or unoccupied* after the general day for licensing (the occupier whereof was duly licensed the year preceding), two justices at a petty sessions may grant a licence to any new tenant or occupier till the next general licensing day, obtaining first a certificate as above mentioned. 29 *G* 2 *c* 12 *ſ* 24

Shall become empty or unoccupied] That is, as it seemeth, by the removal of the former tenant, for in many places the tenants change their habitations, not in *September* when the licence is required to be granted, but at some future time, as at *May-day*, or *Whitsuntide* In this case, where the tenant, intending to remove, hath not taken out a licence for that year, his successor may obtain a licence until the next general licensing day, by applying to two justices at a petty sessions, and making it appear to them by certificate that he is a person fit to receive a licence, and also making it appear that the house is proper to be licensed, whereof the proof must be by its having been licensed the year next before

VI How long the licence shall continue in force.

The licence granted at the general licensing day shall be made for one year only, to commence on Sept. 29 26 *G* 2 *c* 31 *ſ* 4

And the licence granted at a petty sessions in the case of a licensed house becoming unoccupied (as hath been said) shall be made until the next general licensing day. 29 *G.* 2 *c.* 12 *ſ* 24

VII. Offences in brewing of ale.

1 By the 1 *W* *ſeſſ* 1. *c* 24. *ſ* 17. No common brewer or retailer of beer or ale, shall use in the brewing or working thereof any melasses, course sugar, honey, or composition or extract of sugar, on pain of forfeiting the liquor, and also 100 *l*, half to the king, and half to him that shall sue in six months

2 And by the 10 & 11 *W* *c* 21 *ſ* 34 If any common brewer or retailer of beer or ale, shall use any melasses,

course

coarfe fugar, honey, or compofition or extract of fugar, in
the brewing, making, or working of any ale or beer, or
if any common brewer fhall receive into his cuftody any
quantity of any the faid materials exceeding ten pounds,
he fhall forfeit 100 *l,* to be recovered and migitated as by
the laws of excife, and the fervant or other affifting therein, fhall forfeit 20 *l* in like manner, and in default of payment fhall be imprifoned three months

3 And by 9 *Ann c.* 12 No common brewer, innkeeper, or victualler, fhall ufe any broom, wormwood, or
any other bitter ingredient (to ferve inftead of hops) in any
beer or ale for fale (except infufing the fame, after it is
brewed and tunned, to make broom or wormwood ale or
beer), on pain of 20 *l,* half to the king, and half to the
profecutor, to be levied as by the laws of excife *f* 24,
26

4 And by 12 *Ann ftat* 1 *c* 2 No common brewer, or
retailer of beer or ale, fhall ufe any fugar, honey, foreign
grains, guinea pepper, effentia bine, coculus india, or any
unwholfome ingredients in the brewing of beer or ale, or
mix any of them therewith, on pain of 20 *l,* to be recovered and mitigated as by the laws of excife, half to the
king, and half to him that fhall fue *f* 32

VIII Innkeepers obliged to receive guefts

If one who keeps a common inn, refufe either to receive a traveller as a gueft into his houfe, or to find him
victuals or lodging, upon his tendring him a reafonable
price for the fame, he is not only liable to render damages for the injury, in an action on the cafe at the fuit
of the party grieved, but may alfo be indicted and fined
at the fuit of the king. 1 *Haw* 225

Alfo it is faid, that he may be compelled by the conftable of the town, or by a juftice of the peace, to receive
and entertain fuch a perfon as his gueft, and that it is no
way material whether he hath a fign before his door or not,
if he make it his common bufinefs to entertain paffengers.
But how the officer may compel him may be a queftion
It feemeth that all the officer can do, is either to caufe fuch
alehoufe to be fuppreffed, or elfe to prefent fuch offence at
the affizes or feffions, that fo fuch offender may be thereupon indicted *Dalt c* 7

IX Soldiers quartered in alehoufes.

By the yearly acts againft mutiny and defertion, the
conftable, and in his default, a juftice of the peace, may

quarter foldiers in inns, livery ftables, alehoufes, and
victualling houfes, as is fet forth more at large in title
Soldiers.

X Concerning ale veffels, and the meafure of ale

Juftices to rate
the price of vef-
fels.

1. The juftices in *Eafter* feffions yearly (and mayors in
corporations) fhall rate the price of all barrels, kilderkins,
firkins, and other veffels to be fold for ale or beer to be
uttered therein. And if any cooper fhall not fell the fame
according to fuch rate, he fhall forfeit 3s 4d, half to the
king, and half to him that fhall fue 8 *El* c 9

Barrel, what.

2. Every barrel of beer, within the bills of mortality,
fhall be 36 gallons, and the barrel of ale 32 gallons, and
in all other places, 34 gallons fhall be reckoned for a barrel of beer or ale. 12 *C* 2 c 24 ʃ 34 1 *W ft.* 1 c
24. ʃ 5

Quarts and pints
to be marked.

3. By 11 & 12 *W* c 15 which is required to be given
in charge at the feffions to the grand jury, it is enacted,
that all innkeepers, alehoufekeepers, futlers, victuallers and
other retailers of ale or beer, and every perfon keeping any
publick houfe, and retailing and felling ale or beer, fhall
retail and fell the fame in and from their houfes, by a full
ale quart or ale pint, according to the ftandard of the exchequer, in a veffel made of wood, earth, glafs, horn, leather, pewter, or of fome other good and wholefome metal,
made and fized to the ftandard, and figned, ftamped, or
marked to be of the content of the faid ale quart or ale pint,
according to the faid ftandard, either from the exchequer,
or from fome city, town corporate, borough, or market
town where a ftandard ale quart or pint, made from the
faid ftandard, fhall be kept for that purpofe, and fhall not
retail and utter any ale or beer, in any other veffel not
figned and marked, on pain of forfeiting not above 40s,
nor under 10s, for every offence, half to the poor, and half
to him that fhall profecute or fue for the fame, to be recovered before one juftice, by the oath of one witnefs, and
to be levied by warrant of diftrefs, rendering the overplus,
deducting thereout the reafonable charges ʃ 1, 6 Inc
profecution to be within thirty days. ʃ 6.

And moreover he fhall not detain any goods for the
reckoning, but fhall be left to his action at law ʃ 2

But it is not neceffary that beer or ale fold to be fpent
out of the houfe, be carried away in ftandard meafure,
but it is fufficient if it be meafured out by the ftandard
ʃ 7

Who fhall mark
them.

4. And every mayor, or chief officer of every city, town
corporate, borough, or market town, fhall on requeft to
him

him made, cause all ale quarts and ale pints, made of wood, earth, glass, horn, leather, pewter, or other good and wholesome metal, which shall be brought to him, to be measured and sized with the standard in his custody, and shall then cause the same, and every of them, to be plainly and apparently signed, stamped, and marked with W R and a crown, for which they shall not receive above one farthing for each measure, on pain of 5 l, to be recovered as aforesaid, and he shall also pay to the party grieved treble damages with costs, by action at law   11 & 12 W c 15 ∫ 5.

Note, Most of the books do set forth that the sub-commissioners or collectors of excise shall procure standard quarts and pints out of the exchequer, for every market town, but this was only required of them before *June* 24, 1700, and not since ∫ 3.

5 An indictment will lie for selling ale in pots un-   Indictment sealed, altho' the statute appoints another method of proceeding, because measures are by common law, and the statutes only direct the manner of ascertaining them. *Blackerby* 10

But in such case the indictment must not be upon the statute, but at the common law, and the offence ought to be laid, not for selling in pots unsealed, but in pots wanting measure.

XI *Enhancing the price of ale.*

By the 2 & 3 *Ed* 6 *c* 15 If any brewers shall conspire to sell their victuals but at certain prices, they shall, on conviction in the sessions or leet, by witness, confession, or otherwise, forfeit 10 l to the king for the first offence, and if not paid in six days, they shall be imprisoned twenty days, for the second offence, 20 l in like manner, or the pillory, for the third offence 40 l in like manner, or the pillory, loss of an ear, and to become infamous   But by the 2 G 3 *c* 14 No brewer, innkeeper, victualler, or other retailer of strong beer or ale, shall be sued or molested by indictment, information, popular action, or otherwise, for advancing the price of strong beer or ale, in a reasonable degree.

XII. *Innkeepers suffering tipling.*

By the 1 *J c* 9 If any innkeeper, victualler, or alehousekeeper, or tavernkeeper keeping an inn or victual-

        ling

ling house, shall suffer any person inhabiting in any city, town corporate, market town, village, or hamlet, where such inn, tipling house, or alehouse shall be [and by 1 C. c 4 wherever he shall inhabit], to continue drinking or tipling therein (except such as shall be invited by any traveller, and shall accompany him only during his necessary abode there, and except labouring and handicraftsmen, in cities, towns corporate, and market towns, upon the usual working days, for one hour at dinner time, to take their diet in an alehouse, and except labourers and workmen, which for the following of their work by the day or by the great, in any city, town corporate, market town or village, shall for the time of their said continuing in work there, sojourn, lodge or victual in any inn, alehouse, or other victualling house, and except for urgent and necessary occasions to be allowed by two justices), he shall, on conviction thereof before the mayor or a justice of the peace, on view or confession, or oath of one witness, forfeit 10s to the poor 1 J c 9 ſ 2 1 C c 4   21 J c 7

The same to be levied by the constables or churchwardens by way of distress, and for default of satisfaction in six days, the distress to be appraised and sold, rendring the overplus, and for want of sufficient distress, the party offending to be by such mayor or justice committed to the common gaol, there to remain until the penalty be truly paid 1 J c 9 ſ 3

And if the constables or churchwardens do neglect their duty in levying, or do not levy the penalties, or in default of distress, do neglect to certify the default, by the space of 20 days, to such mayor or justice, every person so offending shall forfeit 40s to the poor, to be levied by way of distress by warrant from such mayor or justice, the distress to be detained six days, in which time if payment be not made, the goods to be appraised and sold, returning the overplus, for want of sufficient distress, the constable or churchwarden so offending, to be by such mayor or justice committed to the common gaol, there to remain until the penalty be truly paid 1 J c 9 ſ 4

And also, the said offence may be inquired of and presented before justices of assize, justices of the peace in their sessions, mayors in corporations, and in the leet, and thereupon such due proceedings shall be had for the conviction, as in such like cases upon any indictment or presentment is used 4 J c 5 ſ 5

And all constables, churchwardens, aleconners and sidesmen, shall in their several oaths incident to their offices, be charged to present the said offence 4 J c 5 ſ –

And

And moreover, if any alehoufekeeper fhall fuffer any perfon inhabiting in any city, town corporate, market town, village or hamlet, where fuch inn, tipling houfe, or alehoufe fhall be, to continue drinking or tipling therein as aforefaid, he fhall be difabled for the fpace of three years to keep any fuch alehoufe 21 *J* c 7 *f* 4

XIII. *Perfons guilty of tipling.*

Penalty of tip-ling

1 If any perfon (unlefs thofe excepted under the fore-going head, by 1 *J*. c 9) fhall continue drinking or tipling, in any inn, victualling houfe, or alehoufe, or any tavern keeping an inn or victualling houfe, he fhall, on convic-tion thereof before the mayor or a juftice of the peace, on view, confeffion, or oath of one witnefs, forfeit for every offence 3 s 4 d, to be paid within one week next after the conviction, to the churchwardens, who fhall be account-able for the fame to the ufe of the poor And if he fhall refufe or neglect to pay the fame, it fhall be levied by di-ftrefs And if he be not able to pay the forfeiture, then the mayor, juftice, or court where the conviction fhall be, may punifh the offender, by fetting him in the ftocks for every offence by the fpace of four hours 4 *J* c 5. *f* 4 1 *J* c 9 21 *J* c. 7. 1 *C* c 4

The faid offence may alfo be inquired of and prefented, before juftices of affize, juftices of the peace in feffions, mayors, and in the leet, and proceeding fhall be had thereupon for the conviction, as upon indictment or pre-fentment. 4 *J*. c 5 *f*. 5

The offender to be prefented, indicted, or convicted in fix months 4 *J* c 5 *f* 11

And all conftables, churchwardens, aleconners, and fidemen, fhall in their feveral oaths incident to their of-fices, be charged to prefent the faid offence 21 *J* c 7 *f* 5

Alehouf keeper guilty of tipling

2. And if any alehoufekeeper fhall be convicted of the faid offence, he fhall moreover for the fpace of three years be difabled to keep any fuch alehoufe 7 *J*. c. 10. 21 *J* c 7 *f* 4

XIV *Concerning drunkennefs.*

Drunkennefs no excufe

1 Drunkennefs excufeth no crime, but he who is guilty of any crime whatever, though his voluntary drunkennefs, fhall be punifhed for it as much as if he had been fober 1 *Haw* 2

Spiritual cen fure

2 If any offend their brethren by drunkennefs, the churchwardens and fidemen fhall prefent the fame to the ordinary,

ordinary, that they may be punished by the severity of the laws, according to their deserts, and such notorious offenders shall not be admitted to the holy communion, till they be reformed *Can* 109.

And all constables, churchwardens, aleconners, and sidemen, shall be sworn to present the offence of drunkenness 4 *J c.* 5 *J.* 7

Penalty for the first offence.

3. Every person who shall be drunk, and thereof shall be convicted (I K) before one justice, or mayor, on view, confession, or oath of one witness, shall forfeit for the first offence 5 s, to be paid within one week after conviction, to the churchwardens (L), who shall be accountable for the same to the use of the poor, and if he shall refuse or neglect to pay the same as aforesaid, it shall be levied by distress (M), and if the offender be not able (N) to pay the said sum of 5 s, he shall be committed to the stocks (O), there to remain by the space of six hours 4 *J c* 5 *J* 2 21 *J c* 7 *J* 13

And if any constable, or other inferior officer to whom that shall be given in charge by the precept of any mayor or justice, do neglect the due correction of the offender, or the due levying of the penalties where distress may be had, every person so offending shall forfeit 10 s, to be levied by distress, by any other person having warrant from any mayor, justice, or court, where any such conviction shall be, to be paid to the churchwardens, who shall account for the same, to the use of the poor where the offence shall be committed 4 *J c.* 5 *J* 3.

Second offence

4 And if any person once convicted of drunkenness, shall after that be again convicted of the like offence, he shall be bounden with two sureties in a recognizance or obligation of 10 l, with condition to be from henceforth of good behaviour 4 *J c* 5 *J* 6. 21 *J c* 7 *J* 3

To be of good behaviour] Lord *Hale*, speaking of the statute of 34 *L l* 3 *c* 1 which gave justices power to bind malefactors to the good behaviour, generally, without any time limited, says, that it is not meant that the same shall be perpetual, but in the nature of bail, viz. to appear at such a day at their sessions, and in the mean time to be of good behaviour 2 *H H* 136

Who may inquire thereof

5 The said offence may also be inquired of and presented before justices of assize, justices of the peace in their sessions, mayors, and in the leet, and thereupon process shall be had for the conviction, as upon indictment or presentment 4 *J c* 5 *J* 5.

In what time.

6 But the offenders shall be presented, indicted or convicted in six months. 4 *J. c.* 5 *J* 11

7 But

7. It is also provided, that this act shall not abridge the ecclesiastical jurisdiction. 4 J. c. 5 f. 8.

None to be twice punished for the same offence

But when the offender hath been once punished, by any the ways before mentioned, he shall not be punished again by any other ways or means. f. 9.

8. If any alehousekeeper shall be convicted of being drunk, he shall, besides the penalties abovementioned, be utterly disabled to keep any such alehouse, for the space of three years next ensuing the conviction 7 J. c 10.

Alehousekeeper drunk.

9. Every person in his majesty's pay in the navy, being guilty of drunkenness, shall incur such punishment as a court martial shall think fit to impose 22 G. 2. c. 33. Art 2.

Navy

XV. *Detaining goods for the reckoning*

1 An innkeeper may detain the person of the guest who eats, or the horse which eats, till payment And this he may do, without any agreement for that purpose For men that get their livelihood by entertainment of others, cannot annex such disobliging condition, that they shall retain the party's property in case of nonpayment, nor make such disadvantageous and impudent a supposition, that they should not be paid And therefore the law annexes such a condition, without the express agreement of the parties *Bac Abr.* Inns.

General power of detaining.

For it would be hard to oblige him to sue for every little debt, and a greater hardship, that he might not be able to find who was his guest id

2 But an horse committed to an innkeeper, may be detained only for his own meat, and not for the meat of the guest, or of any other horse, for the chattels in such case are only in the custody of the law for the debt that arises from the thing itself, and not for any other debt due from the same party, for the law is open for all such debts, and doth not admit private persons to take reprisals. *Bac. Abr* Inns 1 *Bulst* 207

Horse to be detained only for his own meat.

3 Also, if any innkeeper, alehousekeeper, victualler, or sutler, in giving any account or reckoning in writing, or otherwise, shall refuse or deny to give in the particular number of quarts or pints, or shall sell in measures unmarked, it shall not be lawful for him, for default of payment of such reckoning, to detain any goods or other thing, belonging to the person or persons from whom such reckoning shall be due, but he shall be left to his action at law for the same, any custom or usage to the contrary notwithstanding. 11 & 12 W c. 15 f 2.

Reckoning to be in particulars, and vessels to be sealed

4. In

4. In like manner if the innkeeper gives credit to the
party for that time, and lets him go without payment,
then he hath waived the benefit of the cuftom, and muft
rely on his other agreement. 8 *Mod.* 172.

5 An innkeeper that detains a horfe for his meat, cannot ufe him, becaufe he detains him as in cuftody of the
law and by confequence, the detention muft be in the
nature of a diftrefs, which cannot be ufed by the diftrainer.
Bac Abr Inns

6 But by the cuftom of *London* and *Exeter*, if a man
commit an horfe to an innkeeper, and he eat out his price,
the innkeeper may take him as his own, upon the reafonable appraifement of four of his neighbours, which was,
it feems, a cuftom arifing from the abundance of traffick
with ftrangers, that could not be known, to charge them
with the action. But the innkeeper hath no power to fell
the horfe, by the general cuftom of the realm. *Bac. Abr.*
Inns

So in the cafe of *Jones* and *Pearle*, E 9 G In trover
for three horfes, the defendant pleaded that he kept a publick inn at *Glaftenbury*, and that the plaintiff was a carrier, and ufed to fet up his horfes there, and 36 l being
due to him for keeping the horfes, which was more than
they were worth, he detained and fold them, as well he
might But on demurrer, judgment was given for the
plaintiff, an innkeeper having no power to fell horfes, except by fpecial cuftom, as in the city of *London*. And befides, when the horfes had been once out, the power of
detaining them for what was due before, did not fubfift at
their coming in again. *Sti* 556

XVI. *Goods of a gueft ftolen out of an inn.*

1 Inns were allowed for the benefit of travellers, who
have certain privileges whilft they are in their journeys,
and are in a more peculiar manner protected by the law
it is for this reafon, that the innkeeper fhall anfwer for
thofe things which are ftolen within the inn, though not delivered to him to keep, and tho' he was not acquainted that
the guefts brought the goods to the inn, for it fhall be
intended to be thro' his negligence, or occafioned by the
fault of him or his fervants. 8 Co Caley's cafe

So if he puts a horfe to pafture, without the direction
of his gueft, and the horfe is ftolen, he muft make fatisfaction (But otherwife, if with his direction) *id*

In like manner, if an innkeeper bids his gueft take the
key of his chamber and lock the door, and tells him that

he will not take the charge of the goods , yet if they are stolen he shall be answerable because he is charged by law for all things which come to his inn, and he cannot discharge himself by such or the like words *Dalt c.* 56. *Blackerby* 169.

2. *Holt* C. J doubted whether a man is a guest by setting up his horse at an inn, though he never went into the inn himself, but the other three justices held, that such person is a guest by leaving his horse, as much as if he had staid himself, because the horse must be fed, by which the innkeeper has gain, otherwise if he had left a trunk, or a dead thing   1 *Salk* 388 ^{Who shall be deemed a guest in this respect.}

So if a man comes to an inn with a hamper, in which he hath certain goods (to wit, hats, as the case was), and departs leaving it with the host, and two days after comes again , whereas in the time of his absence this was stolen , he shall not have any action against the host, because he was not a guest at the time of the stealing, and the host had no benefit by the keeping thereof, and therefore shall not be charged for the loss thereof in his absence.   1 *Roll's Abr* 2

If an attorney hires a chamber in an inn for a whole term, the host is not chargeable with any robbery in it, because the party is as it were a lessee   *Mo* 877.

If one comes to an inn, and makes a previous contract for lodging for a set time, and doth not eat or drink there , he is no guest, but a lodger, and so not under the innkeeper's protection but if he eats and drinks, or pays for his diet there, it is otherwise   12 *Mod* 255

Soldiers billeted are guests   *Clayt.* 97

XVII Guests stealing goods

A guest in a common inn, arising in the night time, and carrying goods out of his chamber into another room, and from thence to the stable, intending to ride away with them, is guilty of felony, altho' there was no trespass in the taking of them (which yet is generally required in cases of felony) *Dalt c.* 40

NOTE, The universities are generally excepted out of these acts concerning alehouses

A Information and complaint for selling ale without licence, on the 5 G. 3. c 46.

Westmorland. BE it remembred, that this ——— day of ——— in the ——— year of the reign of his majesty king George the third that now is, A. I. gentleman, in his proper person, as well for his said majesty as for himself, exhibiteth to me J P. esquire, one of his said majesty's justices of the peace in and for the said county, a complaint and information, and thereby informeth me, that on the ——— day of ——— now last past, and at several times between the said ——— day of ——— and the time of exhibiting this information and complaint, one A O of ——— in the county aforesaid, yeoman, at ——— aforesaid in the county aforesaid, did sell ale and beer, and other exciseable liquors by retail, without being duly licensed so to do, whereby the said A. O hath forfeited the sum of 40 s, together with the costs and expences of convicting the said A O for the said offence, and that A. W of ——— in the said county, yeoman, is a material witness to be examined concerning the premisses. And thereupon the said A I who as well for his said majesty as for himself exhibiteth this information, prayeth judgment of me the said justice in the premisses, that he may have one moiety of the said sum of 40 s, and also the costs and expences of such conviction as aforesaid, according to the form of the statute in that case made, and that the said A O may be summoned to answer the premisses, and the said A. W to testify his knowledge therein.

A. I.

Before me the justice
aforesaid,

    J P

B. Summons of a person for selling ale without licence, and also of a witness, on the 5 G. 3. c 46.

Westmorland. { To the constable of ——— in the said county

WHEREAS a complaint and information hath been this day exhibited before me J P. esquire, one of his majesty's justices of the peace in and for the said county, by A I of ——— gentleman, setting forth, that on the ——— day of ——— now last past, and at several times between the said ——— day of ——— and the time of exhibiting the said information and complaint, one A. O of ——— in the county aforesaid,

faid, yeoman, at —— aforefaid in the county aforefaid, did
fell ale and beer, and other exciseable liquors, by retail, without being duly licensed so to do, and that A W. of —— in
the faid county, yeoman, is a material witness to be examined
concerning the premisses. These are therefore to require you forthwith to summon the fame A O to appear before me at ——
in the faid county, on —— the —— day of —— at the
hour of —— to answer to the matter so complained and informed of against him, and to summon also the faid A. W to
appear before me at the fame time and place, to testify his knowledge in the premises. And be you then there to certify what
you shall have done in the execution hereof Herein fail you not.
Given under my hand and feal this —— day of —— in
the —— year ——.

Note, a *feparate* fummons for a witness, in behalf of
either of the parties, may eafily be extracted from the
premifes, *mutatis mutandis*

C. Conviction for felling ale without licence ,
on the 5 G. 3. *c.* 46, fpecially directed by the
ftatute.

Middlefex BE it remembred, that on this —— day of
—— in the year —— A O of ——
was duly convicted before me J P efquire, one of his majefty's
juftices of the peace for the county of M for felling ale or beer,
or other exciseable liquors (as the cafe fhall be) without being
duly licensed so to do, according to the ftatutes in fuch cafe made
and provided, whereby he has forfeited the fum of —— this
being the firft, fecond, or third offence (is the cafe fhall be)
befides the cofts and expences of this conviction , which cofts and
expences I the faid juftice of the peace do hereby afcertain and
affefs at the fum of —— purfuant to the ftatute in fuch cafe
made and provided Given under my hand and feal, the day
and year above written.

D Commitment on non-payment of the penalty
for felling ale without licence, on the 5 G 3.
c 46.

Weftmorland { To the conftable of —— in the faid
county, and to the keeper of his majefty's gaol at —— in the faid county

WHEREAS A.O of —— in the county aforefaid,
yeoman, was on the —— day of —— duly convicted
before me J P efquire, one of his faid majefty's juftices of the
peace

peace in and for the said county, for selling ale [beer, or other exciseable liquors, as the case shall be] without being duly licensed so to do, according to the statutes in such case made and provided, whereby he hath forfeited the sum of forty shillings (this being the first offence,) besides the costs and expences of his conviction, which expences I have ascertained and assessed at the sum of ——— pursuant to the statute in such case made And whereas the said A O on the said ——— day of ——— had notice of the said conviction, and hath refused or neglected to pay, and hath not paid, the said several sums of forty shillings and ——— I do therefore hereby command you the said constable, to apprehend him the said A O. and him to convey to the said gaol at ——— aforesaid, and deliver him to the said keeper thereof, together with this precept And I do hereby command you the said keeper of the said gaol, to receive into your custody in the said gaol him the said A O and him there safely to keep for the space of one month, unless he shall sooner pay the said several sums of forty shillings and ———, and also the costs, charges, and expences of executing the said conviction. Given under my hand and seal, the ——— day of ——— in the year ———.

The like will do for the second, third, or other subsequent offence, *mutatis mutandis.*

E F Precept to the high constable to issue warrants to the petty constables, to summon alehousekeepers to be licensed, on 5 & 6 *Ed.* 6 *c* 25. 2 *G* 2 *c.* 28. and 26 *G.* 2. *c.* 31.

Westmorland { To *John Bowness,* gentleman, high constable of the *East Ward* within the said county

I N *pursuance of the statutes in that case made, these are to require you, on sight hereof, to issue out your warrants to all petty constables belonging to the several constablewicks within your said ward, in the form, or to the effect hereon indorsed. Given under our hands and seals the ——— day of ———.*

J P
K P.

Form of the warrant as above directed :

Weſtmorland, ⎰ To the conſtable of ——
Eaſt Ward. ⎱

BY virtue of a warrant from his majeſty's juſtices of the peace acting within the ſaid ward to me directed, you are hereby required to give notice to all licenſed inn-keepers and alehouſekeepers within your conſtablewick, and alſo to all perſons unlicenſed (ſo far as the ſame ſhall come to your knowledge) who do intend to offer themſelves to be licenſed at the next general meeting of the ſaid juſtices for that purpoſe, that they do perſonally appear before the ſaid juſtices at —— on the —— day of September next, at the hour of —— in the forenoon of the ſame day, to take or renew their licences for the year enſuing, and alſo to give them notice, that every perſon then and there to be licenſed, muſt perſonally enter into a recognizance in the ſum of 10 l, together with two ſureties in 5 l each, or one ſurety in 10 l, that they will not uſe or ſuffer any unlawful games, and that they will keep good order and rule within their reſpective houſes and other places , and if any ſhall be hindred by ſickneſs, or other reaſonable cauſe to be allowed by the ſaid juſtices, that he muſt procure two ſureties then and there to be bound in like manner in 10 l each.

And unto ſuch perſons as have not been licenſed for the year preceding, you are further to give notice, that no licence will be granted to any of them, unleſs he ſhall alſo, at the ſame time and place, produce a certificate under the hands of the miniſter and the major part of the churchwardens and overſeers, or elſe of three or four reputable and ſubſtantial houſeholders of the place where he inhabiteth, ſetting forth that he is of good fame, and of ſober life and converſation.

And you are to make a return to the ſaid juſtices, at the ſame time and place, in writing under your hand, containing the names of all ſuch perſons as you ſhall have ſummoned ſo to appear before them as is aforeſaid, together with their dwelling places, and the ſigns by which their houſes are known

Hereof fail not. Given under my hand at Raiſbeck in the ſaid county the —— day of —— in the year of our Lord ——.

John Bowneſs, high conſtable.

G   Licence to keep an alehouſe; on the 5 & 6 Ed 6 c. 25. 2 G. 2 c. 28. and 26 G 2 c 31.

Weſtmorland, ⎰ AT a general meeting of his majeſty's juſtices of the peace for the ſaid county, acting within the diviſion of the Eaſt Ward aforeſaid in the county aforeſaid,

Eaſt Ward

aforesaid, holden at ———— in and for the said division, for licensing persons to keep common inns and alehouses the ———— day of September in the ———— year of the reign of our sovereign lord George *the third, of* Great Britain, France, *and* Ireland, *king, defender of the faith, and so forth, and in the year of our Lord* ————.

We his majesty's justices of the peace for the said county, whose hands and seals are hereunto set (whereof one is of the quorum) assembled at the said general meeting, do allow and license A. B. *yeoman, at the sign of* ———— *in* ———— *within the division and county aforesaid, to keep a common alehouse or victualling house, and to utter and sell victuals, beer, ale, cyder, and other exciseable liquors, to be drank in the same house wherein he now dwelleth, and not elsewhere, for one whole year from the 29th day of this present month of* September, *and no longer · So as the true assize in bread, beer, ale, and other liquors, hereby allowed to be sold, be duly kept, and no unlawful game or games, drunkenness or any other disorder be suffered in his house, yard, garden, or backside, but that good order and rule be maintained and kept therein, according to the laws of this realm in that behalf made. Given under our hands and seals, the day and year first above written.*

If he hath not been licensed the year before, then these words must be inserted,———— (*A certificate under the hands of* ———— *having been first produced unto us, setting forth that the said* ———— *is of good fame, and of sober life and conversation.*

But if such person hath been licensed the year before, this certificate is not required, and therefore to insert the same in all licences is absurd, and, if executed by the justices in such form, must be in many instances not true.

H. Recognizance of an alehousekeeper, on 5 & 6 *Ed.* 6 *c* 25. and 26 G. 2. *c.* 31.

Westmorland *B*E *it remembred, that on the* ———— *day of* ———— *in the* ———— *year of the reign of* ———— A. P. *of* ———— *in the county aforesaid, innkeeper, and* A S *of* ———— *yeoman, and* B S. *of* ———— *yeoman, personally came before us* ———— *esquires, justices of the peace for the said county, and acknowledged themselves to owe to our said sovereign lord the king, that is to say, the said* A P. *the sum of* 10 l, *and the said* A. S *and* B S *the sum of* 5 l *each, of good and lawful money of* Great Britain, *to be made and levied of their goods and chattels, lands and tenements respectively,*

spectively, to the use of our said sovereign lord the king, his heirs and successors, if the said A P. shall make default in the condition underwritten

THE condition of this recognizance is such, that whereas the above-bounden A. P. is licensed to keep a common inn and ale-house for one year from the 29th day of this present month of September in the house where he now dwelleth at ——— aforesaid, if he the said A. P. shall keep and maintain good order and rule, and shall suffer no disorders or unlawful games to be used in his said house, nor in any outhouse, yard, garden, or backside, thereunto belonging, during the said term, then this recognizance shall be void.

Taken and acknowledged the day and
year above written, before us
$\qquad$ J P.
$\qquad$ K. P.

I. Information of drunkenness, on the 4 J. c. 5. and 21 J. c 7.

Westmorland. {
The information of *A I.* of ——— in the county aforesaid, yeoman, exhibited before me *J P.* esquire, one of his majesty's justices of the peace for the said county, the ——— day of ——— in the year ——— who on his oath saith,

THAT A. O. of ——— in the county aforesaid, labourer, on the ——— day of ——— in the year aforesaid, at the parish of ——— in the said county, was drunk, contrary to the statutes in such case made. And thereupon he the said A I. prayeth that he the said A. O may forfeit the sum of five shillings to the use of the poor of the said parish, as by the said statutes is required.

$\qquad\qquad\qquad\qquad\qquad$ A. I.

Before me
$\qquad$ J P.

K. Summons thereupon.

Westmorland. } To the constable of ———.

FORASMUCH as information upon oath hath been made before me J. P esquire, one of his majesty's justices of the peace for the said county, that A. O of ——— in the

E 2 $\qquad\qquad\qquad$ *county*

county aforesaid, labourer, on the —— day of —— in the year —— at the parish of —— in the county aforesaid, was drunk, contrary to the statutes in such case made These are therefore to require you to summon the said A O. to appear before me at —— in the said county, on —— the —— day of —— to answer unto the said information, and to shew cause why the penalty of five shillings should not be levied on the goods of him the said A O. for the said offence, and be you then there to certify what you shall have done in the premisses. Given under my hand and seal, the —— day of —— in the year ——.

Note, the justice may convict on his own view, and then the information and summons are needless

L. Warrant to the churchwardens (if they are not present at the conviction, or the offender makes default by not appearing) to receive the penalty of drunkenness, by the 4 *J. c.* 5. and 21 *J. c.* 7

Westmorland. { To the churchwardens of the parish of —— in the said county.

FORASMUCH *as A O. of —— in the county aforesaid, labourer, is convicted before me J. P. esquire, one of his majesty's justices of the peace for the said county, for that he the said A O on the —— day of —— in the year —— at the parish of —— in the said county, was drunk, contrary to the statutes in such case made, whereby he hath forfeited the sum of five shillings, to the use of the poor of the said parish These are therefore to require you to demand and receive of and from him the said A O. the said sum of five shillings, to be by you accounted for to the use aforesaid And if he shall refuse or neglect to pay the same, by the space of one week after such demand made, that then you certify to me such refusal and neglect, to the end that such proceedings may be had thereupon, as to justice doth appertain Given under my hand and seal, the —— day of —— in the year ——.*

M. Warrant to levy the penalty of drunkenness, on non-payment, by 4 *J c.* 5. and 21 *J c* 7.

Westmorland. { To the constable of —— in the said county.

WHEREAS *A. O of —— in the parish of —— in the county aforesaid, labourer, was on the —— day of —— convicted before me —— one of his majesty's justice*

juſtices of the peace for the ſaid county, for that he the ſaid
A. O. was on the ———— *day of* ———— *drunk, at* —— *afore-*
ſaid, in the pariſh and county aforeſaid, by which he hath for-
feited the ſum of 5 s *And whereas I the ſaid* ———— *did*
iſſue my warrant on the ———— *day of* ———— *to the church-*
wardens of the pariſh of ———— *aforeſaid, to demand and re-*
ceive the ſaid ſum of 5 s *of and from the ſaid* A O *And*
whereas it duly appears to me, as well on the oath of C W.
churchwarden of the pariſh of ———— *aforeſaid, as otherwiſe,*
that they the ſaid churchwardens did on the ———— *day of* ————
demand the ſaid ſum of 5 s *of and from the ſaid* A O. *but*
that he the ſaid A. O *hath neglected to pay the ſame as afore-*
ſaid, and that the ſame is not yet paid Theſe are therefore to
command you forthwith to levy the ſaid ſum by diſtraining the
goods of him the ſaid A. O *And if within the ſpace of* [ſix]
days next after ſuch diſtreſs by you taken, the ſaid ſum, toge-
ther with reaſonable charges for taking and keeping the ſaid
diſtreſs, ſhall not be paid, that then you do ſell the ſaid goods
ſo by you diſtrained as aforeſaid, and out of the money ariſing
by ſuch ſale, that you do pay the ſaid ſum of 5 s *to the church-*
wardens of the ſaid pariſh, for the uſe of the poor of the ſaid
pariſh, rendring to him the ſaid A. O. *the overplus upon de-*
mand, the neceſſary charges of taking, keeping, and ſelling the
ſaid diſtreſs, being firſt deducted. And if the ſaid A. O. *be*
not able to pay the ſaid ſum of 5 s, *and ſufficient diſtreſs can-*
not be found whereof to levy the ſaid ſum, that you certify the
ſame to me, together with the return of this warrant. Given
under my hand and ſeal this ———— *day of* ————.

N Certificate by the conſtable of want of diſtreſs.

Weſtmorland. **A.** C *conſtable of* ———— *in the ſaid county*
maketh oath this ———— *day of* ———— *in*
the year ———— *before me the juſtice within-mentioned, that he*
hath made diligent ſearch for, but doth not know of, nor can
find, any goods of the within-mentioned A. O. *whereof to levy*
the within ſum of five ſhillings.

A. C.

Before me the ſaid
juſtice,
   J. P.

     O. Com-

O Commitment to the stocks for drunkenness, on inability to pay the penalty, on 4 *J. c* 5. and 21 *J. c* 7

Westmorland } To the constable of ———— in the said county.

WHEREAS A O *of* ———— *in the said county, labourer, was on the* ———— *day of* ———— *convicted before me* ———— *one of his majesty's justices of the peace for the said county, for that he the said A. O was on the* ———— *day of* ———— *drunk at* ———— *aforesaid, in the parish of* ———— *in the said county, whereby he hath forfeited the sum of* 5 s *And whereas it duly appears to me, that the said A O is not able to pay the said sum of* 5 s *These are therefore to require you in his majesty's name, to set him the said A O in the stocks, there to remain for the space of six hours. Given under my hand and seal the* ———— *day of* ————

Almanack.

BY the 9 *Ann c.* 23 & 30 G. 2 *c* 19. For every sheet almanack, for one year or less, printed on one side only, shall be paid a stamp duty of 2 d. For every other almanack for one year, 4 d. If for more than one year, then 2 d for each year, but not so as to charge any for more than if made for three years only.

And by 21 G 3 *c* 56 an additional duty of 2 d is laid on sheet almanacks, whereby to advance the same to the other almanacks not being printed on one side only, reciting that whereas the power of granting a liberty to print almanacks and other books was heretofore supposed to be an inherent right in the crown, and whereas the crown hath by different charters granted to the universities of Oxford and Cambridge, among other things, the privilege of printing almanacks, and whereas the universities did demise to the company of Stationers of the city of London, their privileges of printing and vending almanacks and calendars, and have received an annual sum of 1000 l as a consideration for such privilege, and whereas the money so received by them hath been laid out in promoting different branches of literature and science, to the great increase of religion and learning, and the general benefit and advantage of these realms, and whereas the privilege of printing almanacks has been by a late decision at law found to be

a certain

a common right over which the crown had no controul, and confequently the univerfities had no power to demife the fame to any particular perfon or body of men, whereby the payments fo made to them by the company of Stationers have been difcontinued. therefore out of the additional duties impofed by this act, there fhall be paid to each of the faid univerfities yearly the fum of 500 l clear of all deductions ſ 10.

By the 10 *An. c.* 19 All books and pamphlets ferving chiefly to the purpofe of an almanack, fhall be charged as almanacks

But where an almanack contains more than one fheet, one fheet only need to be ftamped. 9 *An c* 23 ſ 26.

Every almanack fhall be fo printed that fome part of the print be upon the ftamp. 21 *G* 3 *c.* 56 ſ 5

If any perfon fhall expofe to fale any almanack unftamped, he fhall, on conviction before one juftice on the oath of one witnefs, be committed to the houfe of correction not exceeding three months And any perfon may apprehend and carry him before fuch juftice, and on producing a certificate of the conviction under the hand of fuch juftice, he fhall have a reward of 20 s, to be paid by the receiver general of the ftamp duties. 16 *G.* 2. *c* 26. ſ 5 30 *G.* 2. *c.* 19 ſ 26

Annuities.

BY feveral acts, oath of an annuitant's life is to be made before a juftice of the peace, who fhall give a certificate thereof, in order to intitle fuch perfon to receive his annuity.

Apothecary. See **Phyficians.**

Appeal.

1. THIS word has two fignifications in law, the App al, what.
one is, removing a caufe from an interior court, or judge, to a fuperior, as from one or more juftices, to the quarter feffions

The other kind of appeal (which is the fubject of this title) is a profecution againft a fuppofed offender, by the party's own private action, profecuting alfo for the crown, in refpect of the offence againft the publick. 2

Haw 155 E 4 2 And

In what cafes an appeal may be brought.

2. An appeal is brought in three cafes; 1. By a man for a wrong to his anceftor 2 By a wife for the death of her hufband 3 For wrong done to the appellants themfelves, as in the cafe of robbery, rape, or maihem, But appeals are now difufed, on account of the nicety of the pleadings, and the charge of the profecution, and the method of indictment is generally taken. *Wood,* b 4. c 5

When in what time an appeal may be brought.

3. A perfon acquitted on an indictment of murder, fhall not be fet at liberty, but fhall be recommitted, or bailed, till the year and day be paft, within which time an appeal may be brought. 3 *H.* 7 c 1

Appeal brought before the fheriff and coroner.

4 It is certain that an appeal may be commenced before the fheriff and coroner, and removed from them into the king's bench by certiorari. 2 *Haw* 156

Before juftices of the peace.

5 And it feems to be holden in *Fitzherbert's* abridgment, that juftices of the peace have power to receive appeals, but there is much greater authority for the contrary opinion. 2 *Haw.* 156

Perfons acquitted on appeal

6. If the perfon appealed fhall be acquitted, the appellor fhall be imprifoned for a year, and reftore damages to the party, and be grievoufly fined to the king. 13 *Ed* 1 ft 1 c, 12. That is, if the appeal fhall appear to the court to have been malicious 2 *Haw* 198

Pardon

7. Forafmuch as an appeal is the fuit of the party, as well as of the king, hence it is that the king cannot pardon an offender found guilty upon an appeal, as he may when found guilty upon an indictment for in fuch cafe he can only pardon for himfelf, but not for the party. 2 *Haw.* 155

Apples and pears.

WHEREAS apples and pears are frequently fold by meafure, commonly called water-meafure, the contents whereof are very uncertain, therefore for the future, the faid meafure fhall be round, and in diameter eighteen inches and an half within the hoop, and eight inches deep, and fo in proportion. And every meafure, commonly called water-meafure, by which apples and pears are fold, fhall be heaped as ufually And whofoever fhall fell or buy any apples or pears by any other meafure, fhall forfeit 10 s, half to the informer, and half to the poor, on conviction on the oath of one witnefs, before one juftice (or mayor), to be levied by the petty conftable by warrant of the faid juftice, by diftrefs and fale. 1 *Ann.* ft. 1, c. 15 ſ 1.

But

But this shall not extend to any measure sealed and allowed by the fruiterers company in London. *f.* 2

Concerning the robbing of orchards, see title 𝔚𝔬𝔬𝔡.

Apprehending Offenders. See 𝕬𝖗𝖗𝖊𝖋𝖙.

𝕬𝖕𝖕𝖗𝖊𝖓𝖙𝖎𝖈𝖊𝖘.

Concerning the settlement of apprentices. See title 𝕻𝖔𝖔𝖗.

I. Who may take apprentices.

1. EVERY person being an housholder, and having and using half a plough-land in tillage, may take an apprentice above the age of ten years, and under eighteen, to serve in husbandry till twenty-one at the least, or till twenty-four as the parties can agree. 5 *El c* 4. *f.* 25   *In husbandry.*

2 Every person being an housholder, and twenty-four years old at the least, dwelling in any city or town corporate, and exercising any art, mistery, or manual occupation there, may retain the son of a freeman, not occupying husbandry, nor being a labourer, and inhabiting in the same, or in any other city or town corporate, to serve and be bound as an apprentice, after the custom and order of the city of *London*, for seven years at the least, so as such apprenticeship do not expire before the apprentice shall be twenty-four years of age   5 *El. c* 4. *f.* 26.   *In trades in towns corporate.*

But

But no perſon dwelling in any city or town corporate, being a merchant, mercer, draper, goldſmith, ironmonger, imbroiderer, or clothier, ſhall take any apprentice except he be his ſon, or elſe that the father and mother of ſuch apprentices ſhall have an eſtate of inheritance or freehold of 40 s a year, to be certified under the hands and ſeals of three juſtices where the lands lie, to the mayor of that city or town corporate, and to be inrolled among the records there *ſ* 27

And the reaſon of this (Mr *Dalton* ſays) ſeems to be, for that ſuch as are to be bound apprentices in towns corporate, if their parents be of a competent livelihood, then their maſters ſhall be not only better ſecured, but ſuch apprentices alſo in likelihood, ſhall have the better means to ſet up their trades after their times expired And concerning ſuch, whoſe parents have not 40 s a year, they are fitter to be bound apprentices to huſbandry, and the like, in the country *Dalt. c.* 58

But by reaſon of the great alteration in the value of money ſince that time, this proviſion is become of little uſe, for an eſtate of 40 s a year then, was equal to more than 10 l a year now.

But the citizens of *London* and *Norwich* may take and have apprentices, as before this act *ſ* 40.

3 Every perſon being an houſholder, and twenty-four years old at the leaſt, and not occupying huſbandry, nor being a labourer, dwelling in any market town not corporate, and exerciſing any art, miſtery, or manual occupation, may have to apprentice the child or children of any other artificer, not occupying huſbandry, nor being a labourer, inhabiting in the ſame or any other ſuch market town in the ſame ſhire. 5 *El c.* 4. *ſ.* 28

But no perſon dwelling in any ſuch market town, being a merchant, mercer, draper, goldſmith, ironmonger, imbroiderer, or clothier, ſhall take any apprentice except he be his ſon, or elſe that his father and mother ſhall have an eſtate of inheritance or freehold of 3 l a year, to be certified under the hands and ſeals of three juſtices of the ſhire where the lands lie, to the head officer of ſuch market town where ſuch apprentice ſhall be taken, there to be inrolled of record *ſ* 29.

4 Any perſon uſing the art of a ſmith, wheelwright, ploughwright, millwright, carpenter, rough maſon, plaiſterer, ſawyer, limeburner, brickmaker, bricklayer, tyler, ſlater, helier, tyle-maker, linen-weaver, turner, cooper, miller earthen potter, woollen weaver weaving houſhold cloth only, fuller otherwiſe called tucker or walker,

burner of oare and woad afhes, thatcher or fhingler, wherefoever he fhall dwell, may take the fon of any perfon as apprentice, albeit his parents have no land 5 *El.* *c* 4 *f* 30.

5 Every owner of a fhip or veffel, and every houf- *Seamen.* holder exercifing the trade of the feas by fifhing or otherwife, and every gunner commonly called a canoneer, and every fhipwright may take apprentices for ten years or under, and every apprentice fo taken, being above feven years of age, fhall be by the fame covenants bound, ordered and ufed to all intents, according to the cuftom of *London,* fo that the covenant or bond of apprenticefhip be made by writing indented, and inrolled in the town where the apprentice fhall be inhabiting, if it be a town corporate, if not, then in the next town corporate For which inrollment fhall be paid not above 12 d 5 *El. c.* 5 *f* 12

6 Every perfon that fhall have three apprentices in any *Number re-* the crafts of a clothmaker, fuller, fheerman, weaver, tay- *ftrained.* lor, or fhoemaker, fhall keep one journeyman, and for every other apprentice above three, one other journeyman, on pain of 10 l, half to the king, and half to him that fhall fue in the feffions or other court of record, or if it is in a town corporate, then to be applied as by the charter. 5 *El c* 4. *f* 33

No hatmaker fhall have above two apprentices at one time, nor thofe for any lefs term than feven years, on pain of 5 l a month, half to the king, and half to him that fhall fue in any court of record But this not to extend to his own fon, in his own houfe, fo as he bound by indenture for feven years, and his term not to expire before he be twenty-two years of age. 1 *J c.* 17. *f.* 3, 5

Weavers of ftuffs in *Norfoll* and *Norwich,* that fhall employ two apprentices, fhall alfo employ two journeymen, and no mafter fhall have above two apprentices, or any week boy, to weave in the faid trade, on pain of 5 l a month to the king 13 & 14 *C* 2. *c* 5 *f* 18.

II. *Who are compellable to be bound apprentices.*

1. If any perfon fhall be required by any houfholder, *Who fhall be* ufing half a plowland at leaft in tillage, to be an ap- *bound* prentice and to ferve in hufbandry, or in any other art, miftery, or fcience before expreffed, and fhall refufe fo to do, then on complaint of fuch houfekeeper to one juftice (or head officer) he fhall fend for the perfon refufing, and
if

if he fhall think the faid perfon meet to ferve, and fuch perfon refufe to be bound, he may commit him to ward, there to remain until he be contented, and will be bound. 5 *El c* 4. *f.* 35.

2 But no perfon fhall be bound to enter into any apprenticefhip, other than fuch as be under the age of twenty-one years. 5 *El. c* 4 *f* 46.

Upon the whole, the aforefaid directions about the value of the parent's eftate, and fuch like, are become entirely obfolete, and of no ufe, and therefore had better be repealed The reftrictions were originally intended (as appears by the ftatute, 9 *H* 4. *c* 17) for the encouragement of hufbandry, by reafon of the fcarcity of labourers in ancient time And this ftatute of the 5 *Eliz* is only a re-enacting, as it were, of former ftatutes, and expreffeth, that any perfon being an houfholder may take apprentice the fon of any freeman, *not occupying hufbandry, nor being a labourer.*

III. Binding

1 One cannot be bound an apprentice without deed, 1 *Salk.* 68

2 And by the 5 *El. c* 4 it muft be by deed indented *f.* 25

M 1 *G* 2 *Smith* and *Birch* An action was brought againft the defendant, for inticing away and detaining the plaintiff's apprentice, who had agreed by writing to ferve the plaintiff for feven years Upon evidence it appeared, that the ftyle of the writing began, *This indenture,* &c. but in fact the parchment was not indented, but was a deed poll On exception taken to the deed, it was infifted that the young man was not an apprentice, becaufe he was not bound by an indenture An infant can be bound no other way than as the ftatute of 5 *El.* directs, which is by indenture, and nothing can make this good. The deed cannot now be indented, for that would be a forgery. Therefore unlefs the plaintiff fhews the apprentice to be of full age at the time of figning fuch deed, he cannot be accounted his apprentice, and by confequence no action can lie for detaining the apprentice, neither can the plaintiff prove him to be his fervant by his deed, for he has declared for an apprentice, and muft prove him fo to be Therefore the plaintiff was nonfuited. 1 *Seff. Ca.* 222

But

But with respect to settlements, it is enacted by the 31 *G* 2 *c* 11 that the apprentice may gain a settlement under such writing, altho' it shall not be indented.

3 And an apprentice must be retained by the name of an apprentice expressly, otherwise he is no apprentice, tho' he be bound. *Dalt* *c.* 58. — And by the name of an apprentice.

4 And all indentures, covenants, promises, and bargains, for having or taking apprentices otherwise than by the statute of 5 *El.* shall be clearly void in the law to all intents and purposes, and every person that shall take any apprentice contrary to the said act, shall forfeit 10*l*, half to the king, and half to him that shall sue in the sessions, or other court of record, or if it is in a town corporate, then to the use of such town as by the charter. 5 *El* *c* 4. *§* 41. — Binding otherwise, void.

5 By the several stamp acts, the binding (except it be of parish apprentices) shall be on a 5s stamp, and the same shall not be given in evidence in any court till it be stamped, and the duties paid — Stamp.

6 And by the 8 *Ann.* *c* 9 Beside the said stamps and duties, there shall be paid the duty of 6d for every 20s of every sum of 50l or under, and the duty of 1s for every 20s of every sum above 50l given with any apprentice, and proportionably for greater or lesser sums, to be paid by the master *§* 32 — Additional stamp.

And where any thing, not being money, shall be given with such apprentice, the duties shall be answered for the value thereof. *§.* 45.

But this shall not extend to any apprentice, put out at the common charge of any parish or township, or out of any publick charity *§* 40

And the full sum shall be inserted in the indenture in words at length, and shall bear date on the day of the execution thereof, on pain that the master shall forfeit double, half to the king, and half with full costs to him that shall sue. *§* 35

And no such indenture shall be given in evidence in any suit to be brought by any the parties thereunto, unless such party on whose behalf the same shall be given in evidence, do first make oath, that to the best of his knowledge, the sum therein inserted was really and truly all that was directly or indirectly to be given with such apprentice *§* 43

The said indentures, within the bills, shall he brought to the head office to be stamped with a stamp for that purpose, and the duties paid within one month after date *§* 36.

And

And elsewhere shall be brought either to the head office within the bills, or to a collector of the stamp duties out of the said limits, in two months after date, and the duties thereupon shall be paid, and the indenture stamped, if it be at the said head office, otherwise such collector shall indorse on the indenture, a receipt for the duties in words at length, and subscribe his name thereto. ∫ 37

And if it is within 50 miles of the limits of the bills of mortality, the indenture shall within three months after date, and elsewhere within six months, be brought to the head office to be stamped ∫ 38

And all such indentures wherein shall not be inserted the full sum directly or indirectly given, or whereupon the duties shall not be paid, or which shall not be stamped within the time limited, shall be void, and not available in any court or place, or to any purpose whatsoever, and the apprentice shall be incapable of exercising the said trade ∫ 39.

Moreover, by the 9 *Ann. c* 21 If the master shall neglect to pay the duties within the time limited, he shall forfeit 50l, half to the king, and half with full costs to him who shall sue ∫ 66.

And by the 18 *G* 2 *c.* 22. If he shall neglect to pay the same as aforesaid, he shall, besides all other penalties, forfeit double duty. *f.* 23, 24.

And by the 20 *G* 2 *c* 45 If any master, having forfeited the double duty, shall pay the same, and tender the indenture to be stamped, within two years after the determination of the apprenticeship, and before suit hath been commenced for the penalties, the indenture shall be valid, and the penalties discharged *f.* 5.

And if after the master shall have forfeited the double duty, the apprentice shall in the presence of, or by writing under his hand signed in the presence of one witness, require his master to pay the same, and the master shall not do it in three months, and such apprentice shall at any time within two years after the determination of his apprenticeship, pay the double duty, he may in three months after such payment demand of his master double the sum contracted for in the indenture, and if not paid in three months after, may recover the same by action at law, with full costs And the apprentice immediately after payment of the said double duties (if his apprenticeship shall not be then expired) and signifying by writing under his hand, that he desires to be discharged from his apprenticeship, shall be discharged accordingly, and shall have the same benefit of the time he hath served as he would have had in case he had been assigned, or turned over to a new master. *f.* 6, 7

And

And where any profecution fhall be commenced againſt the maſter for the penalties, if the apprentice fhall pay the double duty at any time in two years after the end of his apprenticeſhip, he may thereupon exercife his trade, and the indenture ſhall be valid, and may be given in evidence *ſ* 8

Finally, by the 5 G 3. *c* 46 Every chamberlain and other proper officer of every city and corporate town, and company, where any clerk or apprentice or fervant obtains his freedom by fervitude, fhall enter in a book to be kept for that purpofe, the names of all fuch clerks, apprentices, and fervants, as fhall be put out within the jurifdiction of fuch city or town corporate, and alfo the names and places of abode of the maſters or miſtreſſes, and of the fums of money [but it is not faid, *or other things equivalent*] given or contracted for, and the trade or profeſſion which they are to learn, and the date of the indentures on pain of 20*l*, half to the king, and half to him that ſhall fue in any court of record, with full coſts *ſ.* 18, 41.

And all printed indentures ſhall have the following memorandum printed under the fame , *viz.* "The indenture,
" covenant, article, or contract muſt bear date the day
" it is executed, and what money or other thing is
" given or contracted for with the clerk or apprentice,
" muſt be inferted in words at length, and the duty
" paid to the ſtamp office, if in *London*, or within the
" weekly bills of mortality, within one month after the
" execution, and if in the courtry, and out of the faid
" bills of mortality, within two months, to a diſtributor
" of the ſtamps or his fubſtitute, otherwife the inden-
" ture will be void, the maſter or miſtreſs forfeit 50*l*
" and another penalty, and the apprentice be difabled
" to follow his trade, or to be made free " And if any printer, ſtationer, or other perſon, ſhall ſell or caufe to be fold any fuch indenture, without fuch memorandum being printed under the fame , he ſhall forfeit 10*l* in like manner *ſ.* 19

Note, Until of late years, there was generally an indemnity from time to time, in fome act of parliament, for relief of perfons who had omitted to pay the faid duties, or to infert the faid fums in words at length, provided they paid the duties, and tendred the indentures to be ſtamped, within a time therein limited. The laſt of which acts was the 9 G 3. *c* 37. Since which time, there hath been a claufe in fome act almoſt every year, giving further time to provide admiſſions of officers in corporations duly ſtamped, and to file affidavits of the execution

of

of the indentures of clerks to attorneys and solicitors, but this, concerning the additional stamp for money given with the apprentice, hath (either thro' design or inadvertency) never been revived.

Infant bound tho' under age

7 It seems clearly agreed, that by the common law infants, or persons under the age of 21 years, cannot bind themselves apprentices, in such a manner as to intitle their masters to an action of covenant, or other action, for departing the service, or other breaches of their indentures. which makes it necessary, according the usual practice, to get some of their friends to be bound for the faithful discharge of their offices, according to the terms agreed on. *Bac Abr.* Master and servant.

But by the statute of 5 *El c* 4 Forasmuch as there hath been some doubt, whether any person under 21 years of age, and bound to serve as an apprentice, in any other place than the city of *London,* shall be bound, accepted, and taken as an apprentice, it is enacted, that every such person who shall be bound by indenture, to serve as an apprentice, in any art, science, occupation, or labour, according to this statute, albeit he be within the age of 21 years, shall be bound as amply to every intent, as if he were of full age at the time of making the indentures. *ʃ* 42, 43

But this is to be understood of a compulsion by the means prescribed by the statute, for altho' an infant may voluntarily bind himself apprentice, and if he continue apprentice for seven years, he may have the benefit to use his trade, yet neither at the common law, nor by any words of this statute, a covenant or obligation of an infant for his apprenticeship shall bind him, but if he misbehave himself, the master may correct him in his service, or complain to a justice to have him punished, according to the statute. But no remedy lieth against an infant upon such covenant *Cro Car* 179.

But if his father, or other person, doth covenant for him, such covenant shall bind the father, or such other person as in the case of *Whitley* and *Loftus,* *M* 10 *G* 2. In the indenture of apprenticeship, the father covenants to pay the apprenticeship money, the son covenants to account for his master's goods; and in the conclusion, the father and son each bind themselves for the true performance of all covenants and agreements therein By the court The end of binding the father was to answer wrongs done by the son, and he must answer for any, and the covenant that each did bind himself must be so, where the son is bound to perform the thing for which the

the covenant was made; and this clause is usually inserted, that the covenants may be taken distributively, to wit, that each of the covenantors should perform his part, and this makes the covenant of the son bind the father, who covenanted for him as well as for himself. 8 *Mod* 190.

So in the case of *Brarch* and *Ewington*, M 21 G. 3. On an action of covenant by the master against the father of the apprentice, the indenture was in the common form of the statute, the master covenanting to find the apprentice meat and lodging, the father to find him cloaths and washing, and the apprentice that he would serve faithfully, and for the true performance of all and every the said covenants, each of the said parties bound himself to the other. The breach assigned was, that the apprentice had absented himself from the service —For the father it was contended, that the parties were only bound for the express covenants which they had severally entred into. That it would be absurd to construe the general words so as to render the father liable for breaches of such of the covenants as were to be performed only by the son. The same construction would render the father liable to the son, or the son to the father, for those which the master was to perform. In all covenants the intention is to govern. The master has other remedies besides an action of covenant against the apprentice if he absent himself · He may, by application to the justices, have him punished under the statute of *Elizabeth*, or if he wants compensation for the loss of service, he may compel him to make it up by subsequent service under 6 G 3 *c* 25 ——Lord Mansfield stopped the counsel who was to have argued on the other side, and said, nothing was clearer than that the father was bound for the performance of the covenants by the son. *Douglas.* 500.

And as an infant may be bound by indenture, so the apprenticeship may be *determined* by consent of all the parties concerned, which, in the case of parish poor children, includes the parish officers, in other cases, the father (or guardian), master, and infant. *Burrow's Settlement Cases* 562, 766.

But a covenant between the master and a third person the infant not being party, maketh not an apprenticeship. 2 *Salk* 479

IV. *Binding of poor apprentices.*

1 The churchwardens and overseers, or the greater **Power to bind.** part of them, by the assent of two justices (1 2) may

bind (A) any such children, whose parents they shall judge not able to maintain them, to be apprentices where they shall see convenient, till such man child shall come to the age of 21 (18 G 3. c 47), and such woman child to the age of 21 or marriage, the same to be as effectual to all purposes, as if such child were of full age, and by indenture of covenant bound him or her self. 43 *El.* *c.* 2. *ſ* 5.

Power to take. 2 And all persons, to whom the overseers shall by the 43 *El* bind any children apprentices, may take and keep them as apprentices 21 *J* c 28 3 *C* c 4 *ſ* 22

Indenture to be stamped. 3 By the several stamp acts, the indenture must be on a sixpenny stamped piece of paper or parchment, but is exempted from the additional stamps and duties for money given with the apprentice

Persons refusing to take 4 And where any poor child shall be appointed to be bound apprentice by the 43 *El* the person to whom he is appointed to be bound, shall receive and provide for him, and also execute the other part of the indentures, and if he shall refuse to so do, oath being thereof made by one of the churchwardens or overseers, before two justices, he shall forfeit 10l, by distress and sale, by warrant (B) of such justices, to the use of the poor of the parish or place where the offence was committed, saving always to the person to whom any poor child shall be appointed to be bound apprentice, if he shall think himself aggrieved thereby, his appeal to the next sessions, whose order therein shall be final 8 & 9 *W* c 30 *ſ* 5

And as the churchwardens and overseers have power to place out poor children, therefore they are proper judges of persons who are fit to be their masters, and those are, all persons, who by their profession or manner of living, have occasion to keep servants, but the same are to be approved of by the justices, and if such master is dissatisfied, he may appeal to the sessions *Dalt.* c 58

T 13 *W* *Minchamp*'s case Two justices bound an apprentice to a *merchant* He appealed to the sessions, and the order was discharged And now the court, on consideration of the matter, confirmed the order of sessions, because the act having made persons compellable to take apprentices, and given an appeal to the sessions, it was in the discretion of the justices at sessions to determine, whether it was or was not fitting to put an apprentice upon any one, and therefore the court would not disturb what the sessions had done, but confirmed the order 2 *Salk* 491.

M 12 G 3 *K*. and *Battes*. The parish officers of *Botley* appointed an apprentice to be bound to *Edward Clewerie.*

Clowerley; who appealed to the sessions The sessions discharge the appointment, and state the case specially That it appears to them upon the evidence, that *Edward Clowerly* resides in the parish of *Hound*, but is owner and occupier of an estate in the parish of *Botley*, of the yearly value of 30l, upon which there is an house inhabited by a weekly labourer of the said *Edward* for the better managing the farm That the said *Edward* did not reside or lodge in the said parish of *Botley*, but paid church and poor rates for the premises That a very considerable part of the lands of *Botley* is occupied by persons residing in other parishes —In support of the order of sessions, it was contended, that the sessions have a discretionary power to judge of the fitness or unfitness of binding apprentices to particular persons, and having by their determination declared, that *Clowerly* ought to be relieved from the apprentice, they had determined the question, and the court could not entertain any question of law about it It was suggested, that the only question agitated at the sessions and intended to be referred to this court was, whether occupiers of land, not living within the parish where the land lies, are bound by law to take apprentices —And it not appearing in the state of the case, whether the sessions had determined on the unfitness of that particular person, or on the point of law in general, of his not being liable in respect of his living out of the parish, lord *Mansfield* said that there was no coming at the point on that state of the case by the sessions, but he thought, if they had determined it on the latter ground, they had done very right Mr. Justice *Aston* was of the same opinion, and observed how hard it might be to bind an apprentice on a person occupying lands in one parish, and being a housekeeper in a very distant parish Mr Justice *Willes* assented And the rule for quashing the order of sessions was discharged, and the sessions order confirmed *Bott* 389 *Lofft* 79.

E 13 *Ann.* ℟ and *Wagstaff* It was moved to quash an order to compel a person to take an apprentice, because in the close of the indenture it was said, that the master, at the end of the term, shall give his apprentice two suits of cloaths. Upon debate, the court held this to be ill, for the justices during the term of his apprenticeship cannot order him wages, they must only order him a maintenance as an apprentice, and cannot order him any thing after the term is ended. So the order was quashed *Foley* 205 1 *Seff C* 48

5 In hundreds or other districts incorporated by particular acts of parliament for relief of the poor, where, by such

Binding in incorporated districts.

such acts, power is given to bind poor children apprentices, the respective persons, to whom they shall be appointed to be bound, shall receive and provide for them, according to the indentures to be executed by the directors and acting guardians, and shall execute the counterpart of such indentures And if any person shall refuse to receive such apprentice, or to execute such counterpart of the indenture, he shall, on conviction on the oath of one of the said directors or acting guardians, or other credible witness, before two justices, forfeit 10 l to the poor within such incorporated district, to be levied by distress Saving always to such person his appeal to the next sessions, whose order therein shall be final.——And provided, that nothing herein shall extend to compel any person to take any such poor child apprentice, unless he be an inhabitant and occupier of lands, in the parish to which such child belongs 20 G. 3 c 36

V. Money given to bind out poor apprentices.

By the 7 J. c 3 All money given by any person to be continually employed for the binding out apprentices, shall be employed in manner following, unless otherwise ordered by the givers, v z All corporations of cities, boroughs, and towns corporate, and in places not corporate, the minister, constables, churchwardens, overseers, or the most part of them, shall have the nomination and placing of such apprentices, and ordering of such money, and if they shall not employ the same accordingly, every person offending shall forfeit 3 l 6 s 8 d, half to the poor, and half to him that shall sue ſ 2

And the master that shall receive the money, shall be bound with one or two sureties in double the sum, unto such corporation, or to the other persons appointed by this act in places not corporate, to take care of it, on condition to repay it at the end of seven years, or within three months thereof, and if the apprentice shall happen to die within the seven years, then within one year after such death, and if the master shall die, then within one year after such master's death. ſ 3

And the said money shall always be put forth in three months after it shall come to the said parties hands, and if there are not then fit persons to be bound apprentices, within the places where the money is given to be employed, it shall be disposed of for binding some of the poorest children of any adjoining parish ſ 4.

And choice shall always be made of the poorest children, and no such apprentice shall be above 15 years of age when bound ſ 5.

And

And the faid perfons, in places not corporate, fhall yearly within a month after *Eafter*, account to their fucceffors before two juftices dwelling in or next to the place. ∫ 6

And if any of the truftees fhall break their truft, or commit any offence for which no penalty is given by this act, any perfon may petition the lord chancellor, who may iffue a commiffion to hear and determine the fame, and may levy the money mifemployed upon fuch defaulters, or otherwife upon fuch able inhabitants of the place, as they fhall think fitteft, and perfons aggrieved may appeal to the lord chancellor. ∫ 7

VI. *Binding poor apprentices to the fea-fervice*

1. It fhall be lawful for two juftices, and for the head officers in corporations, and for the churchwardens and overfeers of the feveral parifhes or townfhips, with the confent of fuch juftices or head officers, to bind and put out any boy at the age of ten years or upwards, or who fhall be chargeable, or whofe parents fhall be chargeable, or who fhall beg for alms, to be an apprentice to the feafervice, to any fubject being mafter or owner of any fhip or veffel, until he fhall attain the age of 21 years. 2 & 3 *Ann* c 6 ∫ 1 *(margin: Who may be bound)*

And every perfon to whom any poor parifh boy fhall be put apprentice by the 43 *El.* may, with the confent of two juftices dwelling near the parifh where fuch poor boy was bound, or with the like confent of the chief officer in a corporation, at the requeft of the mafter, his executors, adminiftrators or affigns, by indenture affign over fuch poor boy apprentice, to any mafter or owner of a fhip or veffel, ufing the fea-fervice, during the remaining time of his apprenticefhip ∫ 6.

2 And every mafter or owner of a fhip, from 30 to 50 ton burden, fhall be obliged to take one fuch apprentice, and one more for the next 50 ton, and one more for every hundred ton fuch fhip fhall exceed the burden of an hundred ton, on pain of forfeiting 10 l to the poor of the parifh from whence fuch boy was bound ∫. 8. *(margin: Who fhall take.)*

But no mafter fhall be obliged to take any fuch apprentice, under 13 years of age, or who fhall not appear to be fitly qualified both as to health and ftrength of body for that fervice 4 *An* c 19 ∫ 16

3 The boy's age fhall be inferted in the indenture, being truly taken from a copy of the entry in the regifterbook (where it can be had), which copy fhall be given and *(margin: Age to be inferted in the indenture)*

attefted

F 3

atteſted by the miniſter without fee   And where no ſuch entry can be found, two ſuch juſtices, and ſuch head officers, ſhall as fully as they can inform themſelves of ſuch boy's age, and from ſuch information ſhall inſert the ſame in the indentures. 2 & 3 *An* c 6. ſ 1

What money ſhall be given with him.

4 And the churchwardens and overſeers ſhall pay down to the maſter, at the time of the binding, the ſum of 50 s. for cloathing and bedding, and the charges by this act appointed ſhall be allowed on their accounts   2 & 3 *An*. c 6 ſ 2.

Indentures to be regiſtered

5 The churchwardens and overſeers ſhall ſend the indentures to the collector of the cuſtoms at the port whereunto the maſter belongeth, who ſhall enter the indenture in a book, and make in indorſement upon the indenture of the regiſtry thereof, ſubſcribed by him, without fee And if he ſhall neglect or refuſe to enter ſuch indentures, and indorſe the ſame, or make falſe entries, he ſhall forfeit 5 *l* to the poor of the pariſh from whence ſuch boy was bound 2 & 3 *An* c 6 ſ 5

Apprentice how conveyed to the port,

6 Such apprentice ſhall be conveyed to the port to which his maſter belongeth, by the churchwardens and overſeers, or their agents, and the charges thereof ſhall be paid as by the vagrant act of 11 & 12 *W* 2 & 3 *An*. c 6. ſ 10

That is to ſay, out of the goal and marſhalſea money, which by the 12 G 2. c 29. is directed to be paid out of the general county rate.

Counterpart to be then executed.

7. The counter part of the indenture ſhall be ſealed and executed by the maſter, and atteſted by the collector of the port, and the conſtable or other officer who carries the apprentice, which officer ſhall tranſmit ſuch counterpart to the churchwardens and overſeers of the place from whence the apprentice was bound. 2 & 3 *An* c 6 ſ 11.

Protection from being impreſſed

8 And the collector or his deputy ſhall tranſmit a certificate under his hand, to the commiſſioners of the admiralty, containing the name and age of ſuch apprentice, and to what ſhip he belongs, and on receipt of ſuch certificate, a protection ſhall be made and given *gratis* to ſuch apprentice, till he attain the age of 18 years 2 & 3 *An*. c 6 ſ 5

Alſo every perſon who ſhall voluntarily bind himſelf apprentice to the ſea-ſervice, ſhall not be impreſſed for three years from the date of his indentures, which indentures ſhall be regiſtred, and certificates thereof given and tranſmitted by the collector as aforeſaid, on receipt of which certificates protections ſhall be made and given for the firſt three years, without fee. *id*. ſ. 15.

But

But by 4 *An c* 19 No person of the age of 18 years shall have any protection from being impressed, who shall have been in any sea service, before he bound himself apprentice. ∫ 17

But every person not having before used the sea, who shall bind himself apprentice to serve at sea, shall be exempted from being impressed for three years and the commissioners of the admiralty, on due proof of the circumstances, shall grant a protection accordingly, without fee. 12 *G* 2 *c* 17

9 When such parish or voluntary apprentice shall be impressed, or voluntarily enter into the king's service, the owner or master, his executors, administrators, or assigns, shall be intitled to able seamens wages, for such of the apprentices, as shall upon due examination be found qualified for the same, notwithstanding their indentures of apprenticeship 2 & 3 *An c* 6 ∫ 17

When impressed the master to have the wages

10 Such poor boys bound out, or assigned over, to the sea service, until they shall attain to the age of 18 years, shall be exempted from the payment of 6 d a month to *Greenwich* hospital 2 & 3 *An c* 6 / 17

Exempted from the 6 d a month

11 Every master so obliged to take such apprentice, shall after his arrival into any port aforesaid, and before he clears out of such port, give an account in writing under his hand, to the collector, containing the names and number of such apprentices as are there remaining in his service. 2 & 3 *An c* 6. ∫ 9

Master to enter his apprentices on clearing out

12 And every custom-house officer shall insert at the bottom of their coquets, the number of men and boys on board their respective ships at their going out, describing the apprentices by their names, ages, and dates of their indentures, for which no fee shall be taken 2 & 3 *An • 6 ∫ 14*

The same to be inserted in the coquet

13 And the collector in the port shall keep a register, containing the number and burden of all ships belonging to the port, together with the masters or owners names, and also the names of all such apprentices in such ships, and from what parishes and places they were sent, and shall transmit (gratis) true copies thereof signed by him, to the quarter sessions, or to such towns corporate, parishes, or places, when and so often as he shall be reasonably required so to do, and every collector refusing or neglecting to send such copy, shall forfeit 5 l, to the poor of the parish from whence such boy was bound 2 & 3 *An c* 6 ∫ 13

Register to be kept in the ports.

14 Two justices near the port, and mayors of towns corporate, in or near adjoining to such port to which such ship

Differences between such masters and apprentices.

ship or vessel shall at any time arrive, may determine all
complaints of ill usage from the master to such apprentice,
and also of all such as shall voluntarily put themselves apprentices to the sea service, and make such order therein
as they are now enabled by law to do, in other cases between masters and apprentices 2 & 3 An. c 6 f 12

Penalties

15 All the penalties aforesaid shall, by warrant of two
justices of the county, city, or town corporate, be levied
by distress and sale. 2 & 3 An. c. 6. f 18.

Master dying.

16 If any master who hath been obliged to take such
parish boy an apprentice, shall die, during the term, his
widow, or his executor or administrator, may assign over
such apprentice to any other master who hath not his com-
plement of apprentices 4 An c 19 f 16.

Note, By the 2 G 3 c 15 Masters, apprentices, mariners, and others employed in fishing-vessels upon the
coasts, are exempted, during such their employment, from
being impressed f 22, 23, 24, 25.

VII Differences between the master and apprentice.

**Master may cha-
stise his appren-
tice**

1 A master may by law correct and chastise his apprentice, for neglect or other misbehaviour, so it be done with
moderation though it doth not seem to be lawful for the
master or mistress to beat any other servant of full age
Lamb '27 1 Black. 428. *

**Whether the
master himself
can discharge
his apprentice**

2 The master may not of his own accord discharge his
apprentice, but if they cannot agree, they may proceed
in one of these two ways, either upon the statute of
the 5 El. c. 4. or upon the statute of 20 G. 2 c. 19

**Differences be-
tween the master
and apprentice
by 5 El c 4**

3 By the 5 El. c 4. *If any such master shall misuse or
evil intreat his apprentice, or the said apprentice shall have any
just cause to complain, or the apprentice do not his duty to his
master, then the said master or apprentice being grieved, and
having cause to complain, shall repair unto one justice (C D)
of the county, or to the mayor or other head officer of the city,
town corporate, or market-town, or other place where the master
dwelleth, who shall by his wisdom and discretion take such order*

* In quoting Sir William Blackstone throughout this book, the
following distinction is observed, 1, 2, 3, 4, Black denotes
Blackstone's Commentaries, the first second, third, or fourth
part Black Rep signifies Blackstone's Reports, which tho' in
two volumes, yet the pages being numbered progressively without interruption thro' both volumes, it is judged that it will
create less confusion to mark the page only, and not the number
of the volume.

and

and direction between the master and his apprentice as the equity of the cause shall require and if for want of good conformity in the master, the said justice (or head officer) cannot compound and agree the matter, he shall take bond of the said master to appear at the next sessions, and on his appearance, and hearing of the matter there, if it be thought meet to discharge the said apprentice, then the justices, or four of them at the least (1 Q) or the said mayor or other head officer, with the consent of three other of his brethren, or men of best reputation in such city, town corporate, or market town, shall have power, in writing (E) under their hands and seals, to pronounce and declare, that they have discharged the said apprentice of his apprenticehood, and the cause thereof And the said writing, being inrolled by the clerk of the peace, or town-clerk, amongst the records, shall be a sufficient discharge for the apprentice against his master, his executors and administrators And if the default shall be found to be in the apprentice, then the said justice, or the said mayor or other head officer, with the assistance aforesaid, shall cause such due correction and punishment to be administred unto him, as by their wisdom and discretions shall be thought meet. § 35.

If any such master] That is, any such master as is before mentioned in this statute, in the trades therein specified, and the former resolutions confined the sense of the statute to such trades only, but the latter adjudications seem to extend the equity thereof to other trades not mentioned in the statute, as in the following instances

M 7 W K and *Gately*. On a certiorari it was moved to quash an order of sessions, for the discharge of one *Edward Green* from his apprenticeship to the defendant *Gately*. The fact was, that *Gately* was a mountebank, and being at a place in *Yorkshire*, where he kept a publick stage, *Green* was by indenture bound apprentice to him in this manner, viz. to *Robert Gately*, surgeon, to learn the trade he now useth, and immediately he went upon the stage, and ever since continued in the employ. After which, being with his master *Gately* in *Middlesex*, he complained to the justices, that his master did not teach him the trade Upon which they discharged him This being done, *Green* set up the trade of mountebank himself. It was moved to quash the order, the justices being willing, because they were imposed upon And the exception was, that the statute of the 5 *El* in discharging apprentices is confined, and extends only to apprentices mentioned in that clause, and there neither surgeon nor mountebank is mentioned And tho' a surgeon may be a trade within the statute, which a man cannot exercise without serving an apprenticeship to, because that clause of the statute is general,

neral; yet this part of the statute, relating to the discharge of apprentices, extends only to trades there mentioned. By the court, The clause relating to the discharge of apprentices is general, and goes to all manner of apprentices, even to those of merchants, but afterwards the court were of opinion, that the power of discharging reaches only to the trades mentioned in the statute, among which a surgeon is not mentioned, for that, tho' as to the serving seven years apprenticeship, a surgeon comes under the general term of arts and misteries, yet the power of discharging reaches only to the trades particularly mentioned 2 *Salk.* 471, 2

And *M* 12 *An* 2 and *Furnese* It was held, that the statute extends only to the trades therein mentioned, and therefore not to a glass bottle maker *Caf of S* 29

On the other hand in the case of *K* and *Collingbourn*, *M.* 12 *G.* Exception was taken to an order of discharge, that the justices could not discharge the apprentice, because the trade to which he was bound, viz a glazier, was not within the statute But not allowed, for though formerly it was held, that the trade ought to be a trade within the statute, yet the latter resolutions have been otherwise L. *Raym* 1410 *Str* 663

Shall misuse or evil intreat his apprentice] An apprentice to a surgeon was sent by his master to the *East Indies* It was adjudged, that the master cannot compel his apprentice to go beyond the sea, except the master go with him, but he may send him to any part of *England* 13 *Ja. Coventry* and *Windall.* Brownl 67

But otherwise, if it be expresly agreed, or the nature of the apprenticeship doth import it, as if the master be a merchant adventurer, or sailor *Hobart* 134

Evil entreat] *L* 8 *G* 2 *K* and *Easman* An apprentice was discharged, the master having *used him unkindly*, and refusing to provide for and entertain him But by the court, this is not a good ground for the discharge for there is a power to oblige the master to receive and entertain the apprentice, and *using him unkindly* is too loose *Str* 1014

Or the apprentice do not his duty to his master] *T* 4 *G* *K* and inhabitants of *Hales Owen* An order reciting that *Joseph Higgen* was bound out by indenture, as the statute requires, to *John Parks*, and being lame, and having the king's evil, and in the opinion of surgeons incurable, therefore the justices discharge the master from his apprentice. It was moved to confirm the order, because the master cannot now have the end of the binding, which was, the service of his apprentice. But it was answered, that the

statute

ſtatute only impowers the juſtices to diſcharge for miſbehaviour, and not for ſickneſs   And quaſhed by the court ;
for the maſter takes the apprentice for better and worſe,
and is to provide for him in ſickneſs and in health.   *Str.*
99

Shall repair unto one juſtice] Upon an order made at the
ſeſſions to diſcharge an apprentice, it did not appear, that
he applied himſelf to a juſtice firſt.   And *Holt* Ch J was
of opinion, that the juſtice hath power to make an order,
and if obeyed by the maſter, then the ſeſſions can have no
power , if diſobeyed, then the juſtice upon complaint may
bind the maſter to the ſeſſions, and that the ſeſſions have
no power otherwiſe   1 *Salk* 67

T. 13 *W K* and *Johnſon*   Exception was taken to
an order for diſcharging an apprentice, that the complaint
was made originally at ſeſſions, without any previous application to a ſingle juſtice out of ſeſſions   *Holt* Ch. J delivered the opinion of the court, That the order was good ;
if it had been a new queſtion, he ſhould have held a prior
application to ſome juſtice out of ſeſſions neceſſary , but after ſo many orders affirmed in this court, which have been
otherwiſe, it is too late to unſettle that now.   1 *Salk* 68

So alſo in the caſe of *K* and *Gill,* *H* 5 *G*   It was ſaid
by the court,—It hath been ſo often reſolved, that the ſeſſions hath an original juriſdiction, that we will not ſuffer
it now to be made a queſtion, though it might be doubtful
upon the ſtatute itſelf.   *Str.* 143

And, *T* 12 *G. K* and *Davie*   The court agreed, that
it is a point not now to be diſputed, that the ſeſſions hath
an original juriſdiction to diſcharge apprentices   *Str* 704
And by lord *Hardwicke* Ch J in the caſe of *K & Eaſman,*
E 8 *G.* 2   This determination is right , for the application which the act directs to be made to a private juſtice,
ſeems to mean only to arbitrate and accommodate the diſpute   The ſtatute ſays, if he cannot *compound* the matter,
he is to take bond for the parties appearance at the ſeſſions,
ſo that they are not to take it by appeal   *Caſes in the time
of lord Hardwicke.* 101

Or to the mayor or other head officer] *M* 12 *G. K* and
Collingburne. An order of ſeſſions was made at *Hicks's
Hall,* for the diſcharge of an apprentice to a freeman of
the city of *London,* and who was bound and inrolled there.
And the order being removed into the king's bench, the
queſtion was, whether the court of ſeſſions at *Hicks's Hall*
hath any juriſdiction to diſcharge an apprentice to a freeman of *London* (eſpecially as there is a ſaving in the act,
of the cuſtom of the city of *London*), or whether he
ought

I

ought not to be difcharged by the mayor's court only. It appeared that the apprentice lived with his mafter out of the city of *London*, and within the jurifdiction of the juftices of *Middlefex*. To this exception it was anfwered, that the ftatute doth not regard where the binding or inrolling is, but gives the jurifdiction exprefly to the juftices where the mafter lives, and if this did not belong to the juftices of *Middlefex*, where the mafter lives, there would be a failure of juftice, for neither the chamberlain, nor any other city magiftrate, have power to compel the mafter's appearance before them. The court affirmed the order of difcharge, and faid they would not take away the jurifdiction of the mayor's court, but only give a concurrent jurifdiction to the juftices for the county. And it would be very inconvenient, to have apprentices to a freeman of *London*, who are bound there, and who live in diftant counties, obliged to come up to the mayor's court to get themfelves difcharged. And the words of the ftatute are very plain, for they give the jurifdiction to the juftices *where the mafter dwelleth*. Str 663

Who fhall by his wifdom and difcretion take fuch order and direction between the mafter and his apprentice as the equity of the cafe fhall require] Hereupon the juftice, if he fees caufe, may, by confent of the mafter, difcharge the apprentice from his apprenticefhip; but this muft not be by a verbal difcharge, for the apprentice being by deed, cannot be difcharged but by deed, that is, by order under the hand and feal of the juftice. *Dalt c* 58 6 *Mod* 182

If for want of good conformity in the mafter] If the mafter is diffatisfied, he may have the matter transferred to the feffions; but here is not the like option given to the apprentice, and the reafon feems to be, becaufe the apprentice being moft commonly an infant, the law prefumes that the juftice is more capable of judging what is for the infant's benefit.

On his appearance] E 13 W *Ditton's* cafe. It was moved to quafh an order made for the difcharge of an apprentice. The queftion arofe upon the claufe of the ftatute which directs, that upon appearance of the mafter, the apprentice may be difcharged by four juftices, after one juftice out of feffions hath endeavoured to compofe the matter in difference. And in this cafe it was objected, that *Ditton* the mafter was bound over to appear, and did not, and the juftices have but a limited jurifdiction, and it is exprefly directed by the act, that the difcharge is to be made on the appearance of the mafter, befides, there is another remedy, to proceed on the recognizance which is forfeited

by

by not appearing By the court The act must have a reasonable construction, so as not to permit the master to take advantage of his own obstinacy, and it would be very hard, that supposing the master is profligate, and runs away, the apprentice shall never be discharged. 2 *Salk* 490

H 5 G K and *Gill* An order of sessions for discharging an apprentice was quashed, because it did not set forth, that the master was summoned, or did appear. *Str* 143

So also, E 8 G 2 K and *Eastman* The order was quashed, because it did not appear that the master was present or summoned, which it is plain the act intended he should be. *Str.* 1013

Inrolled by the clerk of the peace] T 4 G K and inhabitants of *Hales Owen* The order of discharge was not inrolled, and by the court for that reason held ill *Str* 99.

Shall be a sufficient discharge for the apprentice against his master] But as the justices may discharge the apprentice from his master, for ill usage, so also they may discharge the master from the apprentice for evil and disorderly behaviour. *Read* Appr

Discharge] T 13 W K and *Johnson* Exception was taken to an order of discharge, that the justices had ordered money to be returned But by the court, the order is good. And *Holt* Ch J. said he never doubted of that matter, for it is a power consequential upon their jurisdiction to discharge 1 *Salk.* 68

But in the case of K and *Vandeleer,* M 4 G The justices at the sessions did order an apprentice to be discharged, and that the master having received 5 l with him, should refund 3 l as a further provision for him. This was moved to be quashed, because the statute which gives the justices power to discharge, gives them no authority to order any money to be returned By the court, it is very hard, that if the master misuseth his apprentice, the next day after he is bound, he should pay back nothing if he is discharged It will be an encouragement to masters to treat their apprentices ill, but the statute being silent, the order must be quashed. *Str* 69

Nevertheless, this doctrine of refunding seemeth now to be established, as founded on great reason, tho' not expresly mentioned in the act, for the justices being authorized to discharge *according to their discretions*, when the end of the apprenticeship cannot be attained with one person, it is but justice the master should return part of the money he has received with his apprentice, to place him out with a new master 2 *Bac Abr* Master and servant

And

And in the cafe of *K* and *Ames*, *T* 7 *G* 2 it was held, that an order of the mafter to return money is good, tho' it is not averred that he had any with the apprentice, for the order being to return money is a necessary proof of the receipt of it, and the justices in their orders are not obliged to set forth all the steps they take in their proceedings, there being nothing in the act which makes it necessary, and there is a known and established distinction between orders and convictions *Id*

In the chancery, Jan 22, 1745. Ex parte *Sandby*. The petitioner, on the tenth of January 1744, was put apprentice to *Ward*, a bookseller at *York*, and the fum of 80 l was given with him as an apprentice for 7 years. In July following, a commission of bankruptcy was taken out against *Ward*, and being declared a bankrupt, assignees were chosen, who fell off the bankrupt's effects, and he is now the supervisor of the prefs to the purchaser, and becomes incapable of performing his part of the contract, nor is the petitioner able to raise any money to put him out an apprentice to another mafter, and the commission being a recent one, probably no dividend may be made in a year, or a year and a half, so that all this time will be loft to the petitioner. Upon these circumstances, the petitioner prayed, that on deducting 10 l out of the 80 l for his board with the bankrupt during the fix months he lived with him, the assignees should be ordered to pay him the fum of 70 l out of the effects of the bankrupt already come to their hands, and not oblige him to prove it as a debt under the commission The lord chancellor *Hardwicke* was at firft doubtful, and feemed inclined to grant the petition, but on ordering fearch to be made for precedents, and feveral being produced wherein it was directed that apprentices should come in as creditors only, after deducting for the time they lived with the bankrupt, upon the remaining fum, it was ordered accordingly in this cafe, and that the petitioner should be admitted a creditor for 70 l only 1 *Atkyns* 149

Shall caufe due correction and punishment to be administred] This being left indefinite, it feemeth moft appofite, that the justice commit the apprentice to the house of correction for a time, to be kept to hard labour, or otherwise corrected as the nature of the offence may require

Differences between the mafter and apprentice by 20 Geo 2 c 19. 4 By the 20 G 2 c 19 On complaint (F) unto two justices, by any parish apprentice, or other apprentice upon whose binding out no larger a fum than 5 l was paid, concerning any misufage, refufal of necessary provifion, cruelty, or other ill treatment, they may fummon (G) the mafter or miftress, to appear

pear before them at a reasonable time to be named in such sum-
mons, and on proof upon oath of the truth of the said complaint
(whether the master or mistress be present or not, if service of
the summons be also upon oath proved) the said justices may dis-
charge (H) the apprentice by warrant or certificate under their
hands and seals, for which warrant or certificate no fee shall
be paid. f. 3.

And such justices on complaint (JK) on oath by any master
or mistress, against any such apprentice, concerning any misde-
meanor, miscarriage, or ill behaviour, may hear and determine
the same, and punish the offender, by commitment (L) to the
house of correction, there to remain and be corrected, and held
to hard labour for a reasonable time, not exceeding one kalen-
dar month, or otherwise by discharging (M) such apprentice.
f. 4

Persons aggrieved by any determination, order or warrant of such justices (except any order of commitment)
may appeal to the next sessions, who may award costs to
either party not exceeding 40 s, to be levied by distress and
sale *f* 5.

And no certiorari shall issue to remove any the said proceedings *f.* 6.

5. If any apprentice of husbandry, or of any art or occupation aforesaid, shall flee into any other shire, the justices, mayors, or other head officers being justices, may
issue writs of capias to the sheriffs of the counties or other
head officers of the places whither he shall so flee, to take
his body, returnable before them at what time shall please
them, so that if he come by such process he may be put
in prison, till he find sufficient surety well and honestly to
serve his master. 5 *El. c.* 4 *f.* 47.

And by the 24 *G* 2 *c* 55. If a justice shall issue a warrant against such person, and he shall escape into another
shire, the constable or other person, on having the warrant indorsed by a justice in such other shire, may arrest
him there, and carry him before a justice in such other
shire, if the offence is bailable, to find bail, or else shall
carry him back before a justice in the shire from whence
the warrant did first issue

6. Feb. 3 1747 *Hill* and *Allen* In chancery The
bill was by an apprentice, who against his master's consent quitted his service of a shipwright, before his time
was out, and went on board a privateer, which took a
very considerable prize, whose share thereof, being 1200 l,
the master claimed By lord Hardwicke In general,
the master is intitled to all that the apprentice shall earn,
consequently, if he runs away, and goes to a different
business,

Margin notes:
Apprentice flee-
ing into another
shire

Apprentice leav-
ing his master's
service, the ma-
ster is entitled to
his earnings

bufinefs, the mafter is intitled at law to all his earnings. And in this cafe, his lordfhip faid, there was nothing in equity to relieve　But he faid he would fend the cafe to be tried at law, unlefs they would agree to compound the matter, which he recommended to them, and thought, as the boy's fhare of the prize was fo very large, the balance ought to be in his favour　And the mafter agreed to accept 450 l　1 *Vezey*, 83

Apprentice to ferve beyond his term, for the time that he abfented

7　By the 6 G 3 c 25　If any apprentice fhall abfent himfelf from his mafter's fervice, before the term of his apprenticefhip fhall be expired, he fhall, at any time thereafter, whenever he fhall be found (fo it be within 7 years after the expiration of his term), he compelled to ferve his faid mafter, for fo long time as he fhall have abfented himfelf, unlefs he fhall make fatisfaction to his mafter for the lofs he fhall have fuftained by fuch abfence　And if he fhall refufe fo to ferve, or to make fatisfaction, the mafter may complain upon oath to one juftice where he fhall refide, who fhall iffue his warrant for apprehending fuch apprentice.　And fuch juftice, on hearing the complaint, may determine what fatisfaction fhall be made to fuch mafter by the apprentice　And if the faid apprentice fhall not give fecurity to make fatisfaction according to fuch determination ; fuch juftice may commit him to the houfe of correction for any time not exceeding three months

Perfons aggrieved by fuch determination, order, or warrant of the juftice (except any order of commitment), may appeal to the next feffions, giving 6 days notice to the juftice and to the parties, and entring into recognizance, within 3 days after fuch notice, before a juftice, with fufficient furety to try the appeal at, and to abide the order or judgment of, and pay fuch cofts as fhall be awarded by the juftices at fuch feffions　Which faid juftices, at their faid feffions, on proof of fuch notice given, and of entring into fuch recognizance, fhall hear and determine the appeal, and give fuch relief and cofts to either party, as they fhall judge reafonable　And their determination fhall be final and conclufive to all parties concerned

Provided, that nothing herein fhall extend to the ftanneries in Devon or Cornwall, or to impeach or leffen the jurifdiction of the chamberlain of London, or of any other court within the faid city, touching apprentices, nor to any apprentice, whofe mafter fhall have received with him the fum of 10 l.

VIII Apprentice stealing his master's goods.

By the 21 *H* 8 *c* 7 Servants going away with their master's goods, with intent to steal them, shall be guilty of felony, but not to extend to apprentices

And by 12 *An. st* 1 *c* 7 Persons stealing to the value of 40 s, being in a dwelling house or outhouse thereto belonging, tho' such house be not broken, and tho' no person be therein, are excluded from the benefit of clergy But this not to extend to apprentices under fifteen years of age

But if they be fifteen years of age, they shall be guilty as other persons

IX Inticing away an apprentice.

The inticing of an apprentice to depart from his master, is not an offence of a public nature, for which an indictment will lie, but the party's remedy is by an action on the case, which he may well maintain 6 *Mod* 182 *Q.* and *Daniel Burrow, Mansfield,* 1306 *Reavely* v. *Mainwaring* and others

X Assigning apprentices (N).

The master assigning, and the apprentice himself consenting, will not make him an apprentice to the assignee within the fifth of *El* But by the custom of *London*, he may be turned over to another *Dalt. c* 58

And an assignment to the sea service is good by act of parliament, as is before mentioned

E 3 *G K* and *Barnes* Order returned on a certiorari It is resolved by the justices at the sessions, where a person was bound an apprentice to *Barnes* by the parish officers, and *Barnes* had assigned him to another, that the assignment is void, and they direct *Barnes* to take his apprentice again. But by the court, The sessions had no power to judge of the validity of a deed, or to hinder a man from assigning his apprentice The covenant to provide for him is well performed, if the person to whom he is bound assigns him to another to provide for him Wherefore the order was quashed *Foley,* 155 *Str* 48

For the jurisdiction of the justices extends no farther, than to compel the master to take care of his apprentice, but in what manner he does it, whether in his own house or otherwise, is nothing to them But if the assignee of the apprentice doth not provide for him, the first master may be compelled to do it, and he may take his remedy over. 1 *S. ff C* 110

XI. *Master dying*

It hath been said, that if the master dies, the apprentices goes to the executor or administrator to be maintained, if there are assets, but the executor or administrator may bind him to another master for the remaining part of his time

And in *M* 10 *W K* and *Peck Eyre* J held, that an apprenticeship is a personal trust between the master and servant, and determines by the death of either of them, and by the death of either of them, the end and design of the apprenticeship cannot be obtained, and it may be the executor is of another trade, he admitted covenant would lie against the executor, but in that there is no inconvenience, because the executor may make his defence by pleading no assets, or debts of a higher nature. *Holt* C J said, that by the custom of *London*, the executor shall put the apprentice to another master of the same trade, and that in other places, it would be very hard to construe the death of the master to be a discharge of the covenants, he said, it had been held, that the covenant for instruction failed, but that he still continues an apprentice with the executor, as to maintenance 1 *Salk* 66

E 20 *G* 2 *Baxter* (widow and executrix) against *Bunfield*. In debt on bond, conditioned for *Matthias Anderson's* performance of the covenants in an indenture of apprenticeship, whereby he was bound to the plaintiff's testator, who was a mariner, the defendant pleaded, that *Anderson* served faithfully to the death of the testator the plaintiff replied, that since the death of the testator, *Anderson* had absented from her service to which there was a demurrer And after argument at bar, *Lee* Ch. J delivered the resolution of the court, viz That they were all of opinion the defendant should have judgment, and that the executrix could maintain no such action The binding was to the *man*, to learn his *art*, and serve *him*, without any mention of executors And as the words are confined, so is the nature of the contract, for it is fiduciary, and the apprentice is bound from a personal knowledge of the integrity and ability of the master *H.* 8 *Ar Horne* and *Blake*, an award that an apprentice should be assigned, was held void, unless there was a custom, or the concurrence of the apprentice. And they held, it

was

was not material, that according to *Cro. Eliz* 553 the
affets were liable on the master's covenant to maintain.
Therefore judgment was given for the defendant *Str.*
1266

Note, the words in *Cro Eliz* 553 are these A covenant lies against an executor in every case, altho' he be
not named, unless it be such a covenant as is to be performed by the person of the testator, which they cannot
perform

But in the case of *East Bridgeford and Orston*, T 13 G 2.
The master of a parish apprentice dying intestate, his
widow, without any administration taken out, assigned
the apprentice to *Edward George*, who, with the consent
of the apprentice, assigned him over, by verbal agreement,
to *Thomas Baggaley* at *East Bridgeford*, for the remainder of
his term of nine years And he accordingly lived with
the said *Thomas Baggaley* at *East Bridgeford*, and served
out his time there, which far exceeded forty days This
was unanimously holden to be a good settlement at *East
Bridgeford*, since to this assignment, tho' only a verbal
one, there was the consent of all the parties concerned,
and he lived and inhabited at *East Bridgeford* under the
terms of the apprenticeship, as an apprentice bound according to the statute *Burrow's Settlem Caf* 133

E 26 G 2 *Eakring and Selson* Two justices make an
order to remove *George Witworth* from *Eakring* to *Selson*.
Upon appeal, the sessions discharge that order. The case
was, the said *George Witworth* was put out a parish apprentice to *Richard Tomlinson* of *Eakring*, till his age of 20
years He served his master under this indenture for several years at *Eakring*. About three years before he attained
20 years of age, he ran away from his master, and loitered
for some time about the country In the mean time his
master died And at Martinmas after, the said *Witworth*
hired himself as a servant to *William Funt* of *Selson* for a
year, and served him that year at *Selson*, and received all
his wages to his own use, the executors of *Tomlinson* taking
no notice of him But he had not, at the expiration of
the said service, attained his age of 20 years And the
sessions being of opinion that the said *George Witworth* did
not, by virtue of such hiring and service at *Selson*, gain a
settlement in the parish of *Selson* aforesaid, reverse the original order But by the court the order of sessions was
quashed, for that after the master's death, the apprentice was at liberty to hire himself, and as he was hired for
a year, and served a year in *Selson*, his legal settlement
was there. Apprenticeship is a personal trust between

the

the master and servant, and is determined by the death of either master or apprentice   The council who were to have shewn cause against quashing the order of sessions, owned that it was not defensible   *Burrow's Set Caf* 320

T 14 G 3 *Wrexham* and *Chirk*   An apprentice bound for three years, without any consideration, to a slater at *Wrexham*, served under the indenture for nine month's   Then his master died, and he continued a fortnight with the widow, to complete the work unfinished by his master   His mistress then told him, having no further employment for him, that he must not stay with her, and he was at liberty to go where he thought proper   On his going away, he told his mistress that he was going to his father, who was a slater   There was no particular agreement between his father and his mistress, nor the indenture delivered up   His father then lived in the parish of *Chirk*, and he continued with him there two or three years.   The court held that his settlement remained at *Wrexham*   The widow does not appear to have had any interest, and no administration appears to have been taken out   *Bur Settl Caf* 782

In the court of chancery   *M* 30 *C* 2   In the case of *Swam* against *Bowden* und *Eyh*   The master received with the apprentice 250*l*, and died within two years, the apprentice having for that time been employed only in inferior affairs   It was decreed, after debts on specialties paid, that the executors repay the 250*l*, as a debt due on simple contract, deducting after the rate of 20*l* a year, for the maintenance of the apprentice, during the time he lived with his master. *Cha Ca Finch* 396

XII Apprentices setting up their trades

By the common law, no man may be prohibited to work in any lawful trade or in more trades than one, at his pleasure   11 *Co* 53

So that without an act of parliament no man may be restrained, either to work in any lawful trade, or to use divers misteries or trades, therefore an act of parliament made to restrain any person herein, must be taken strictly, and not favourably as acts made in affirmance of the common law

The restraining clause in the statute of 5 *El* c 4 is as follows   *It shall not be lawful to any person, to set up, occupy, use or exercise, any craft, mistery or occupation now used or occupied within the realm of England or Wales, except he shall have been brought up therein seven years at the least as an apprentice*

apprentice by this statute, nor to set any person on work therein, except he shall have been apprentice as aforesaid, or else having served as an apprentice will become a journeyman, or hired by the year, on pain of 40 s a month, half to the king, and half to him that shall sue in the sessions, or other court of record, or if it is in a town corporate, then to be disposed of as other fines by the charter ƒ 31

It shall not be lawful] This is a negative clause, and no one shall exercise a trade against it, unless by virtue of a custom as the widows of tradesmen, who by custom carry on the trade of their husbands, which the court held not to be within this statute. 2 *Salk.* 610.

To any person] But by the 15 C 2 c 15. Hemp workers of all kinds, net makers, and makers of tapestry hangings are excepted, who may set up without having served seven years

And by 3 G 3. c 8 All officers, mariners, and soldiers, who have been employed in his majesty's service, and not deserted, may exercise such trades as they are apt for, in any town or place

And by 6 & 7 W c 17 An apprentice discovering two offenders guilty of coining, so as they be convicted, shall be deemed a freeman, and may exercise his trade as if he had served out his time ƒ 12

To set up, occupy, use, or exercise] T 9 G 3 *Beach* and *Turner* On an action brought for exercising a trade, without having served an apprenticeship, it appeared that the defendant was only a journeyman And the question was, whether the statute extends to journeymen, or only to masters? By the court The statute was meant to prevent *masters* only from setting up trades, and did not intend to give a penalty against both There is great difference between setting up a trade and working in it A man may work in it, by doing a very trifling part. A journeyman doth not exercise the trade upon his own account, but for his master *Burn Marsf* 2449

And it is not material, as to the master, that the journeyman hath served seven years, for if the master himself hath not served seven years, he is restrained by the statute to work as a trader, either by himself or others, for the intent of the act is, to annex the benefit of trade to such as underwent the hardship of learning it, thereby to encourage labour in youth And few would undergo the trouble of being apprentices, if they might employ others to work for them. *T.* 3 *W Hobbs* and *Young* 2 *Salk* 610.

If

If a man use the trade of a t llow chandler, baker, brewer, or any other lawful trade, or manual occupation, for his own use, or for the use of his family, without sell ing any for lucre and gain, he may lawfully do it, but he cannot retain an apprentice therein, but he may hire one to be his servant, who is skilful in that trade or oc cupation 8 Co 129

In like manner, a person brought up to the trade may take a *partner*, who hath not served an apprenticeship to the trade, provided the partner share only in the profits or loss of the business, and do not actually exercise the trade As in the case of *Reynard* and *Chase*, M 30 G 2 An action of debt was brought against *Chase*, for a penalty on the act, for exercising the trade of a brewer, without having served an apprenticeship On a special verdict, it was stated, that the defendant *Chase* and one *Coxe* were partners in the trade, that the trade was carried on, and had been for four years carried on, in their joint names, that *Coxe* did serve an apprenticeship to the trade, but *Chase* never did, and that *Coxe* is a working brewer, and was paid a salary for his labour, which salary was always deducted, and allowed to him, previous to a division of the profits, and the entries at the excise office were in their joint names but that the defendant *John Chase* never exercised the trade himself (which was wholly managed and carried on by *Coxe*), but only shared the profits, and stood the risques of the partnership The question was, whether the defendant *John Chase* is within the act, upon this spe cial finding ?——By lord *Mansfeld* Ch J The defendant is to share the profits with *Coxe*, in moieties, and is liable to the debts of the partnership But it is expresly found, that during all the time charged, he never acted in or ex ercised the trade He was not, by the terms of his agree ment, to act in the trade The other partner was to do the whole, and had a particular salary on that account It is not found, that either *Coxe*, or any servant under him, was set to work by *Chase*, nor that *Chase* did any act what ever of exercising the trade, he was only concerned in the profits Now though this may be, to some purposes, ex ercising a trade, in respect of third persons who deal with the partnership as creditors, and within the meaning of the statutes concerning bankrupts, yet the present question is, whether it be exercising a trade, contrary to this act In the argument of this cause it hath been well observed, that this is a penal law, that it is in restraint of natural right, that it is contrary to the general right given by the common law of this kingdom, To which I will add, that

the

the policy on which the act was made, is, from experience, become doubtful   Bad and unskilful workmen are rarely prosecuted   This act was made early in the reign of queen *Elizabeth*   Afterwards, when the great number of manufacturers, who took refuge in *England* from the duke of *Alva*'s persecution, had brought trade and commerce with them, and inlarged our notions , the restraint introduced by this law was thought unfavourable, and the judges by a liberal interpretation, have extended the qualifications for exercising the trade much beyond the letter of it, and confined the penalty and prohibition to cases precisely within the express letter   Let us consider whether the present case be within the letter, or even the meaning of this act. The general policy of the act was, to have trades carried on, by persons who had skill in them   Now here, the personal skill of the defendant makes no real difference in the case   For the person who is skilful acts every thing, and receives no direction from this man   He neither did, nor was to interfere   The case of *Hobbs* and *Young* is not parallel   There, the defendant, a single man, directed the whole trade , was the master, and directed all the servants   As between master and servant, no doubt, it is the master who carries on the trade, and not the servant   But in *Hobbs* and *Young* there was no partnership , nor (what is the distinguishing character of the present case) a mere naked sharing of the profits, and risqueing a proportion of the loss, without his acting or directing at all, in any manner whatsoever   In many considerable undertakings, it is absolutely necessary to take in persons as partners, to share the profits and risque the loss   And the general usage and practice of mankind ought to have weight, in determinations of this sort, affecting trade and commerce, and the manner of carrying them on   It is notorious that many partnerships are entred into, upon the foundation of one partner contributing industry and skill, and the other, money   Many great breweries and other trades have been carried on, for the benefit of infants and residuary legatees, under the direction of the court of chancery   Now if the plaintiff's construction was to hold, the whole direction and decree of the court of chancery was contrary to law, and to an express act of parliament. So it is likewise practised in other great trades The late Mr *Child* directed his business of a banker, to be carried on for the benefit of his children and other persons   Many other instances might be mentioned   It would introduce the utmost confusion in affairs of trade and commerce, if this construction should prevail   On the other hand, I see no inconvenience. It is exactly the

same

fame thing as to trade, in every particular, whether this partner has or has not ferved an apprenticefhip. Therefore I think the defendant not liable to the penalty of the ftatute. The other three juftices concurred. And judgment was given for the defendant. *Burrow Mansfield* 2

Any craft, miftery, or occupation] *T* 3 *G* 3 *French* and *Adams*. An action of debt was brought upon the ftatute againft the defendant for exercifing the trade of a *carpenter*, he not having ferved an apprenticefhip to that trade. It appeared, that the defendant had worked or ferved as a fervant for feven years in the trade of a *glazier*, and for fome time afterwards exercifed that trade as a mafter; that afterwards he exercifed the trade of a *carpenter* for the fpace of nine years, and it was proved that he well underftood that trade. It was objected, that the defendant being originally bred up to the trade of a *glazier*, he could not follow two trades both *glazier* and *carpenter*, and whether he could or not, was the queftion referved for the confideration of the court —By the court. All the judges of England at a meeting lately refolved, that if any man as a mafter had exercifed and followed any trade as a mafter without interruption or impediment for the term of feven years, he was not liable to be fued or profecuted on the ftatute of 5 *El* alfo if a man hath followed two or more different trades for the term of feven years or more, he fhall not be liable to be profecuted on this ftatute. There is no law againft one man's following feveral trades at this day. There was an ancient ftatut, 37 *Ed* 3 *c* 6, that artificers or handicraftfmen fhould ufe but one miftery, and that none fhould ufe any miftery but that which he had before that time chofen and ufed. But this reftraint of trade and traffick was immediately found prejudicial to the public, and therefore at the next parliament it was enacted that all people fhould be as free as they were at any time before the faid ordinance. And lord Coke obferves, that acts of parliament made againft the freedom of trade never live long. Without the leaft doubt, a man may follow twenty trades, if he has worked at or followed each trade feven years. Mr Harrifon of Red Lion Square ferved an apprenticefhip to the trade of a *carpenter*, but for 26 years paft he has been a *watchmaker*, and tho' he never ferved as an apprentice to the trade of a watchmaker, is the beft maker of time pieces in the world, and the parliament has given him a large fum of money towards finding out the longitude by the help of his watches or time-meafurers. And fhall this man be hindred from making watches, and exercifing the trade of a carpenter alfo if he pleafes? And

b/

by the whole court in the prefent cafe, judgment was given for the defendant   2 *Wilfon* 168

Now ufed] That is, on the 12th of *Jan* 1562, when that parliament began, and this reftraint fhall not extend any further than the words do exprefly direct, and therefore not to new arts and mifteries fince invented   1 *Roll. Rep* 10. 1 *Ventr* 326, 346.

Within the realm of England *and* Wales] M 1 G. 2 K. and *Lifter*. Indictment for ufing the trade of a dry falter, being a craft, miftery, or occupation ufed in *this kingdom* on the 12th day of *Jan* in the 5th year of *Eliz.* Which the court held to be ill, for that the words in *this kingdom* tie down the indictment to the kingdom of *Great Britain*, as it is at this day, whereas it fhould have been in *England* or in *England and Wales* Seff. C V 2 160. Str 788

H 3 G 2 K and *Morro* It was moved to quafh an indictment for exercifing the trade of a *baker*, the defendant not having ferved a legal apprenticefhip The exception was, the trade was not laid to be ufed *within the realm of England and Wales* at the time of the act But the court faid, the trade of a *baker* is within the words of the act, and no averment of the trade's being ufed at the time of the act is neceffary, but where the trade only falls within the general conclufion of the claufe at laft   1 *Barnardift* 277.

Except he fhall have been brought up therein feven years] E 11 W K and *Fox* Indictment for ufing the trade of a taylor, not having ferved feven years, was quafhed, becaufe it is faid only, not having ferved as an apprentice within *England* or *Wales*, for it may be he did fo beyond fea, and if it were any where it fufficeth   1 *Salk* 67

As an apprentice] E 5 An Q and *Maddox* By the court, Upon indictment on this ftatute, in evidence we allow following the trade for feven years to be fufficient, without any binding, this being an hard law   2 *Salk* 613

T 3 G 2 K. and *Morrice*. On an indictment for exercifing a trade, without having ferved a legal apprenticefhip, the defendant offered to give evidence of his having exercifed this trade for feven years, as being tantamount to his having ferved an apprenticefhip for that time *Eyre* chief juftice faid, that the cafes indeed had gone fo far, as to allow a wife's living in the fhop with her hufband for feven years to be equivalent to an apprenticefhip, but he thought the prefent cafe not ftrong

I   enough

enough to come up to the meaning of the ſtatute. Accordingly the evidence was diſallowed   1 *Barnard* 367

But in the caſe of *Wallen* and *Holton*, at the aſiſes for *Berkſhire*, T 33 G 2 On an information againſt the defendant for exerciſing the trade of a baker contrary to the ſtatute, it appeared in evidence that he had followed it twelve years, but never had been an apprentice, nor ſerved with any perſon *as ſuch* On a caſe reſerved, Baron *Adams*, before whom it was tried, conſulted the eleven judges, who all joined with him in opinion, that exerciſing a trade ſeven years, without any proſecution with effect, was a ſufficient qualification *Blackſtone's Reports* 233

Nor to ſet any perſon on work therein, except he ſhall have been apprentice as aforeſaid] But by the 17 G 3 c 33 with reſpect to the counties of *Middleſex*, *Eſſex*, *Surry*, and *Kent*, for want of a ſufficient number of perſons who have ſerved apprenticeſhips to the trade of a *dyer*, it ſhall be lawful for any perſon exerciſing that trade within any of the ſaid counties, to employ ſuch number of journeymen, ſervants, and labourers, as he ſhall have occaſion for, without incurring any penalty

Or elſe having ſerved as an apprentice, will become a journeyman] M 26 G 2 K and *Moor* The defendant was indicted for uſing the trade of a weaver, not having ſerved as an apprentice ſeven years, the evidence was, he ſerved ſix as an apprentice, and had ſince as journeyman in the ſame trade worked above that time And by the court, the ſerving of ſeven years is ſufficient either way, and the defendant was found not guilty. 3 *Keb* 400.

A An Indenture of a pariſh apprentice; on 43 El. c. 2. ſ. 1, 5.

THIS indenture made the ———— day of ———— in the year of our Lord ———— Between A B and C D churchwardens, and E F and G H overſeers of the poor of the pariſh of ———— in the county of ———— of the one part, and A M of ———— in the ſaid pariſh, ſhoemaker, of the other part, witneſſeth, that the ſaid churchwardens and overſeers of the poor, by and with the conſent of ———— two of his majeſty's juſtices of the peace for the ſaid county, dwelling near to [or, in] the ſaid pariſh of ———— one whereof is of the quorum, have put, placed and bound, and by theſe preſents do put, place, and bind A P a poor boy, whoſe parents B P, and C P are not able to maintain him, of the age of
———— years

—— years, to be an apprentice with him the said A M. and as an apprentice with him the said A M to dwell, from the date of these presents, until the said A P. shall come to the age of —— years, [or if a female, until the said A P. shall come to the age of —— years, or the time of her marriage, which shall first happen] according to the statutes in such case made and provided By and during all which time and term, the said A P. shall the said A M his said master well and faithfully serve, in all such lawful business as the said A P. shall be put unto by the command of his said master, according to the power, wit and ability of him the said A.P. and honestly and obediently in all things shall behave himself towards his said master, and honestly and orderly towards the rest of the family of the said A. M And the said A. M. for his part, for himself, his executors, and administrators, doth hereby promise and covenant to and with the said churchwardens and overseers of the poor, and every of them, their and every of their executors and administrators, and their and every of their successors for the time being, and to and with the said A P. that he the said A M shall the said A P. in the craft, mystery, and occupation of a shoemaker, which he the said A. M. now useth, after the best manner that he can or may, teach, instruct, and inform, or cause to be taught, instructed, and informed, as much as thereunto belongeth, or in any wise appertaineth, And that the said A M shall also find and allow unto the said apprentice sufficient meat, drink, apparel, washing, lodging, and all other things needful or meet for an apprentice, during the term aforesaid In witness whereof the said parties have hereunto set their hands and seals, the day and year first above written

Where the overseers and master can agree, other covenants may be inserted, according to such agreement, but if the master is to be compelled, it seemeth not safe to require more from him by the indenture than is above expressed

The assent of two justices.

WE —— two of his majesty's justices of the peace for the abovementioned county of —— dwelling near to the abovementioned parish of —— and one of us of the quorum, do hereby declare our assent to the binding the abovenamed A P an apprentice to the abovenamed A M according to the form and effect of the above written indenture. Given under our hands the —— day of, &c.

B. War-

B. Warrant to levy 10 l for not receiving a poor apprentice, on the statute of 8 & 9 *W.*

Westmorland { To the constables of ———.

WHEREAS A B and C D. churchwardens, and E F and G H overseers of the poor of the parish of ——— in the said county, by the assent of [us] ——— two of his majesty's justices of the peace for the said county dwelling near to [or, in] the said parish of ——— one whereof is of the quorum, did endeavour to bind A P a poor male child of the said parish, whose parents are not able to maintain him, apprentice to A M. of ——— in the said parish, taylor, and for that intent did prepare and duly perfect one pair of indentures pursuant to the statute in such case made and provided, which said pair of indentures was signed and confirmed by [us] the said two justices And whereas the said A M is duly convicted before us the justices aforesaid, as well upon the oath of the said A B as otherwise, for that he the said A. M hath refused, and doth refuse to receive and provide for the said A P as an apprentice, and also to execute another part of the said indentures, being duly tendred to him by the said churchwardens and overseers of the poor, whereby the said A M hath forfeited the sum of ten pounds These are therefore, in his said majesty's name, to require and command you, to make distress of the goods and chattels of him the said A M and if within the space of [six] days next after such distress by you made, the said sum of 10 l, together with reasonable charges of taking and keeping the said distress, shall not be paid, that then you do sell the said goods and chattels so by you distrained, and out of the money arising by such sale, pay the said sum of 10 l to the overseers of the poor of the said parish of ——— where the said offence was committed, for the use of the poor of the said parish, returning the overplus upon demand unto him the said A M the reasonable charges of taking, keeping, and selling the said distress being thereout first deducted Herein fail you not Given under our hands and seals the ——— day of ——— in the year ———.

Note, as an appeal is given to the sessions, against the appointment of an apprentice to be bound to any person as aforesaid, it is proper, either not to make out, or not to execute, the warrant of distress, until after the next sessions.

And it is to be observed, that one precedent alone in this case is here inserted, for brevity sake, as being not in

a matter of conſtant practice, but it is to be underſtood, in all ſuch like caſes, that there muſt firſt be a
complaint or information in writing, then a ſummons of
the party accuſed, or warrant as the caſe may be, and
a hearing and determining of the cauſe, and conviction
thereupon if the party ſhall be found to be guilty   But
as the ſpecial fact muſt be the ſame throughout all the
forms of proceedings, it is eaſy from one to frame all
the reſt

C. Summons of the maſter for miſuſing his ap-
     prentice, on 5 *El. c.* 4.

Weſtmorland } To the conſtable of ———.

WHEREAS *complaint and information hath been
        made unto me ——— one of his majeſty's juſtices of
the peace in and for the ſaid county, by* A P *apprentice to*
A M *of———in the ſaid county, ſhoemaker, that the ſaid* A M.
hath miſuſed and evil intreated him the ſaid A P. [*by cruel
puniſhment, and beating him the ſaid* A P. *without juſt cauſe,
and by not allowing unto him ſufficient meat, drink, apparel,
or as the caſe ſhall be*] *Theſe are therefore in his majeſty's
name to command you to ſummon the ſaid* A M *to appear before me at the houſe of——— in the ſaid county, or———the
——— day of ——— at the hour of ——— in the afternoon
of the ſame day, to anſwer unto the ſaid complaint, and to be
further dealt with according to law   Herein fail you not.
Given under my hand and ſeal the ——— day of, &c*

Note, a *ſummons*, rather than a *warrant*, in all ſuch
like caſes, between party and party, is generally moſt
eligible, yet in this caſe it ſeemeth, that a warant is juſtifiable to apprehend the maſter, and bring him before
the juſtice, (eſpecially if he ſhall contemn the ſummons,)
becauſe it is required, that he ſhall give ſecurity to the
juſtice to appear at the ſeſſions, if he ſhall not conform to
the juſtice's order in the premiſſes.

D. Summons of the apprentice on complaint of
     the maſter, on the 5 *El. c.* 4.

Weſtmorland } To the conſtable of ———

WHEREAS *complaint and information hath been made
        unto me ——— one of his majeſty's juſtices of the peace
in and for the ſaid county, by* A. M *of——— in the ſaid
                                                    county,*

county, husbandman, that A P now being an apprentice to him the said A M. is negligent, stubborn, disorderly, [or as the case shall be] and doth not his duty to him the said A M his master, These are therefore to command you to summon the said A. P to appear before me, at——in the said county on—— the——day of——at the hour of——in the afternoon of the same day, to answer to the said complaint, and to be further dwelt with according to law. Herein fail not Given under my hand and seal the——day of, &c

E. Order of discharge by four justices at the sessions, on the 5 *El* c 4. *s* 35.

Westmorland AT a general quarter sessions of the peace holden at ——— in and for the county *aforesaid, the——day of —— in the —— year of the reign of our lord* George *the third, by the grace of God of* Great Britain, France, *and* Ireland, *king, defender of the faith, and so forth, Before ——— justices of our said lord the king assigned to keep the peace in the said county, and also to hear and determine divers felonies, trespasses, and other misdemeanors in the said county committed, and of the quorum, it is ordered as followeth*

Upon the petition of A P apprentice to A M of ——— in the said county, husbandman, to be relieved upon certain neglects of the said master in instructing him in his trade, and in misusing and evil intreating the said apprentice by cruel punishment [or as the case shall be], and the said master having likewise appeared upon his recognizance taken before J P esquire, one of the said justices, to answer to the complaint of the said petition, and having proved nothing whereby to clear himself of the said complaint, but on the contrary, the said A P having given full proof of the truth of the said complaint to the satisfaction of the said court We therefore, whose hands and seals are hereunto set, being four of the said justices, and of the quorum, do hereby order, pronounce, and declare, that the said apprentice shall be, and is hereby discharged and freed from his said apprenticehood And this to be a final order betwixt the said master and apprentice, any thing contained in their indentures of apprenticeship, or otherwise, to the contrary notwithstanding Given under our hands and seals the day and year first above written

F. Com-

F Complaint of an apprentice to two juftices againft his mafter, on 20 G 2. c 19

Weftmorland THE *information and complaint of* A P. *apprentice to* A M *of* —— *in the faid county, hufbandman, exhibit d before us two of his majefty's juftices of the peace in and for the faid county, the* —— *day of* —— *in the year, &c*

Who faith, that he the faid A. P *is an apprentice bound by indenture to* A M. *of* —— *aforefaid, hufbandman., and that he the faid* A M *hath mifufed and ill treated him the faid apprentice, and particularly* [as the cafe fhall be]

A. P.

Before us,

J P
K P

G Summons of the mafter by two juftices, on complaint of the apprentice, on the 20 G. 2 c 19. *f*. 3.

Weftmorland { To the conftable of ——

WHEREAS *information and complaint hath been made unto us* —— *two of his majefty's juftices of the peace in and for the faid county, by* A P. *apprentice to* A.M. *of* —— *in the faid county, hufbandman, that he the faid* A M *hath mifufed and ill treated him the faid* A. P *and particularly* [as the cafe fhall be] *Thefe are therefore to require you to fummon the faid* A. M *to appear before us at* —— *in the faid county, on* —— *the* —— *day of* —— *to anfwer unto the faid information and complaint And be you then there to certify what you fhall have done in the execution hereof Herein fail you not Given under our hands and feals the* —— *day of* —— *in the year* —— .

H Difcharge of an apprentice by two juftices, on the mafter mifufing him, by the 20 G. 2. c. 19. *f* 3.

Weftmorland WHEREAS *complaint hath been made before us* —— *two of his majefty's juftices of the peace in and for the faid county, by* A P. *apprentice to* A M *of* —— *in the faid county, taylor, that he the faid* A M *hath mifufed and evil treated him the faid apprentice, and particularly* [as the cafe fhall be] *And*

whereas

whereas the said A M hath appeared before us in pursuance
of our summons to that purpose, but hath not cleared himself
of and from the said accusation and complaint, but on the con
trary the said A. P hath made full proof of the truth thereof
before us upon oath, We therefore by these presents do discharge
him the said A P of and from his apprenticeship to the said
A. M any thing in the indenture of apprenticeship made be
twixt them, or otherwise howsoever, to the contrary notwith
standing Given under our hands and seals the ——— day
of, &c

[Or, And whereas it hath been duly proved before us, as
well upon the oath of A C. constable of ——— aforesaid, as
otherwise, that he the said A C did duly summon the said
A. M. to appear before us at a reasonable time in the said sum
mons mentioned and specified, but notwithstanding the same, he
the said A M. hath not appeared before us according to such
summons We therefore having duly examined into the matter of
the said complaint, and the truth thereof having been fully
proved before us upon oath, do discharge, &c]

I. Complaint to two justices of the master against
his apprentice; on the 20 G. 2. c 19 f. 4.

Westmorland. THE complaint and information of A M.
of ——— in the said county, husband-
man, taken and made on oath before us ——— two of his ma
jesty's justices of the peace in and for the said county, the ———
day of ——— Who saith, that A P apprentice by indenture to
him the said A. M hath in the service of his apprenticeship
been guilty of several misdemeanours, miscarriages, and ill be
haviour, towards him the said A M and particularly [as the
case shall be]

A M.

Before us,

J P
K. P

K. Warrant for a disorderly apprentice, by two
justices, on the aforesaid complaint by the
20 G 2. c 19. f. 4.

Westmorland } To the constable of———

WHEREAS oath hath been made before us ———
two of his majesty's justices of the peace in and for the
said county, by A. M of——— in the said county, husbandman,

man, that A P. apprentice to the said A M hath committed divers misdemeanours against the said A. M his master, and particularly [as the case shall be] These are therefore to require you forthwith to apprehend the said A. P. and bring him before us, to answer unto the said complaint, and to be dealt with according to law And you are to give notice to the said A. M that he appear before us at the same time, to make good the said complaint. Given under our hands and seals, &c

L. Commitment of an apprentice to the house of correction, on complaint of his master, by two justices, on the 20 G 2. c. 19. f. 4.

Westmorland { To the constable of ———— in the said county, and to the keeper of the house of correction at ———— in the said county

WHEREAS complaint hath been made before us ———— two of his majesty's justices of the peace in and for the said county, upon the oath of A M. of ———— in the said county, husbandman, that A P apprentice of the said A. M hath committed divers misdemeanors against him the said A M. his master, and particularly [as the case shall be] And whereas upon examination thereof, and upon hearing the allegations of both parties, having come before us for that purpose, and upon due consideration had thereof, it manifestly appears to us that he the said A P is guilty of the premisses so charged against him as aforesaid We do therefore hereby command you the said constable, to take and convey the said A. P to the said house of correction, and to deliver him to the said keeper thereof, together with this warrant And we do hereby command you the said keeper of the said house of correction, to receive the said A. P. into your custody in the said house of correction, there to remain and be corrected, and held to hard labour for the space of ————. Given under our hands and seals, the ———— day, &c.

M Discharge of an apprentice by two justices, on complaint of the master, by 20 G. 2. c 19 f 4.

Westmorland. *WHEREAS complaint, &c. (as in the last precedent) ———— We do therefore by these presents discharge the said A. P. from his apprenticeship to the said A. M any thing in any indenture or indentures of apprenticeship betwixt them, or otherwise, to the contrary notwithstanding Given, &c*

N. Assignment of an apprentice.

TO all to whom these presents shall come I A. M of ———— send greeting Whereas my apprentice A P. hath divers years yet to come and unexpired of his apprenticeship, to wit, ———— whole years from the ———— day of ———— now last past, as by his indenture of apprenticeship to me sealed doth appear Now know ye, that I the said A M. for divers good causes and considerations me hereunto moving, have given, granted, assigned, and set over, and by these presents do fully and absolutely give, grant, assign, and set over, unto A S of ————, all such right, title, duty, term of years to come, service and demand whatsoever, which I the said A M have in or to the said A P or which I may or ought to have in him by force and virtue of the said indenture of apprenticeship And moreover, I the said A M do by these presents covenant, promise, and agree to and with the said A S, his executors and administrators, that notwithstanding any thing by me the said A M to be done to the contrary, the said A. P. shall, during the said term of ———— years, well and truly serve the said A S as his master, and his commandments lawful and honest shall do, and from his service shall not absent himself during the said term Provided, that the said A. S shall well entreat and use him the said A P. and him the said A. P in the craft, mystery, and occupation of a ———— which he the said A S now useth, after the best manner that he can or may, shall teach, instruct, and inform, or cause to be taught, instructed, and informed, as much as thereunto belongeth, or in any wise appertaineth, and shall also during the same term find and allow unto the said A P sufficient meat, drink, apparel, washing, lodging, and all other things needful or meet for an apprentice. In witness, &c

---

Approver.

AN approver (probator) is a person indicted of treason or felony, and in prison for the same, who upon his arraignment, before any plea pleaded, doth confess the indictment, and takes a corporal oath to reveal all treasons and felonies that he knoweth of, and therefore prays a coroner, before whom he is to enter his appeal or accusation, against those that are partners in the crime contained in the indictment. 3 Inst. 129.

This accufation of himfelf, and oath, makes his accufation of another perfon of the fame crime, to amount to an indictment , and if his partners are convicted, he fhall have his pardon of courfe. 3 *Inft* 129, 130

But juftices of the peace cannot take cognizance hereof, becaufe they have no authority by their commiffion to affign a coroner 3 *Inft* 130

And befides, as it is in the difcretion of the court, whether they will fuffer one to be an approver, this method of late hath been feldom practifed And in many cafes we have what feems to amount to the fame, by ftatute , where pardon is affured to offenders, on difcovering and convicting their accomplices.

Arbitration. See **Award**
Army. See **Soldiers and Militia.**
Arrack. See **Excife.**

Arraignment.

WHEN an offender comes into court, or is brought in by procefs, fometimes of *capias,* and fometimes of *habeas corpus* directed to the gaoler of another prifon , the firft thing that follows thereupon, is his arraignment 2 *H H* 216

Now arraignment is nothing elfe but the calling the offender to the bar of the court, to anfwer the matter charged upon him. 2 *H H* 216

And the word in Latin (lord *Hale* faith) is no other than *ad rationem ponere,* and in French *ad refon,* or abbreviated *a refn ,* for as the ancient word *difrain* or *derayn* imports in Latin *difp ationare,* to difprove or evince the contrary of any thing that is or may be affirmed, fo *arraigne* is *ad rationem ponere,* to call to account or anfwer. 2 *H H.* 216 And this perhaps may be fufficient to fhew the meaning of the word, altho' not to declare its derivation , for it feemeth to have flowed unto the French tongue, from its common origin with the Greek , of which we fhall have little doubt, when we confider the verbs αγορ ven, καληγορειν, and alfo διαγοριυιιν, as they are ufed in the claffical remains of that language, and compare them with the terms *arraigne, adraigne, difrayn, derayne*

The prifoner on his arraignment, tho' under an indictment of the higheft crime, muft be brought to the bar without irons and all manner of ſhackles or bonds, unleſs there be a danger of eſcape, and then he may be brought with irons. 2 *H H.* 219

Alſo there is no neceſſity that a priſoner, at the time of his arraignment, hold up his hand at the bar, or be commanded ſo to do, for is this only a ceremony for making known the perſon of the offender to the court, and if he anſwers that he is the ſame perſon, it is all one. 2 *Haw.* 308

Arreſt.

THIS is to be underſtood of arreſts in criminal caſes only, and not in civil caſes.

The word *arreſt* is the ſame, with very little variation, in the Engliſh, French, German, Belgic, and other languages of the weſtern empire, heretofore ſubject to the Roman power, and probably may have been derived unto us thro' the channels both of France and Saxony the French *arreſter* ſignifieth to ſtop or ſtay, and the Saxon *reſtan*, to reſt, and both perhaps have ſprung from the Italian *arreſto*, and that from the well known Latin verb *ſto*, to ſtand.

And, in law, an arreſt doth ſignify the reſtraint of a man's perſon, depriving him of his own will and liberty, and binding him to become obedient to the will of the law And it may be called the beginning of impriſonment, *Lamb* 93

Concerning which I will ſhew,

I. Who may or may not be arreſted.
II. For what cauſes of ſuſpicion an arreſt may be.
III. By whom the arreſt ſhall be made.
IV. The manner of an arreſt.
V. What is to be done after the arreſt.

I Who may or may not be arreſted.

Privilege of parliament. 1 Generally, a member of parliament ſhall have the privilege of parliament for himſelf and his ſervants to be freed from arreſts but for treaſon, felony, and breach of the peace there can be no privilege. 4 *Inſt.* 24, 25.

Peers and bodies corporate. 2 In caſes of peers and corporations, the proceſs is a diſtringas, for they cannot be arreſted 3 *Salk* 46

3 In

3. In the cafe of *K* and *Woodham*, *H.* 2 *G.* 2 upon a motion for an information againſt the defendant, who was a juſtice of the peace, it was held, that a perſon in execution in the king's bench may be there charged crimi‑ nally by a juſtice of the peace's warrant but that no ſuch juſtice can take a priſoner of this court out of the cuſtody of the court, and ſend him to the county gaol. *Str* 828 Perſons charged in execution

4 None ſhall arreſt prieſts or their clerks, or other per‑ ſons of holy church, whilſt they attend to divine ſervice, in churches, churchyards, or other places dedicated to God, on pain of impriſonment and ranſom at the king's will, and he ſhall alſo make gree to the parties arreſted 50 *Ed* 3 *c* 5   1 *R* 2 *c.* 15. In churchyards.

5 Alſo a warrant executed againſt any perſon whatſo‑ ever, on the Lord's day, is void, and the perſons ſerving the ſame ſhall ſuffer damages, as if they had done the ſame without warrant, except in caſes of treaſon, felony, and breach of the peace. 29 *C* 2. *c.* 7 *ſ.* 6 On Sundays

II *For what caufes of fufpicion an arreſt may be*

By the ſtatute of 34 *Ed* 3 *c* 1 Power is given to the juſtices of the peace, to arreſt all thoſe whom they find by indictment, or by *fufpicion*, and to put them in priſon Sufpicion

And the cauſes of ſuſpicion, which are generally agreed to juſtify the arreſt of an innocent perſon for felony, are theſe that follow Caufes of fufpi‑ cion.

(1) The common fame of the country, but it ſeems, that it ought to appear upon evidence, in an action brought for ſuch arreſt, that ſuch fame had ſome probable ground. 2 *Haw* 76 Common fame.

(2) The being found in ſuch circumſtances, as induce a ſtrong preſumption of guilt, as coming out of a houſe wherein murder hath been committed, with a bloody knife in one's hand, or being found in poſſeſſion of any part of goods ſtolen, without being able to give a probable account of coming honeſtly by them   2 *Haw* 76 Circumftances of guilt.

(3) The behaving one's ſelf in ſuch a manner as be‑ trays a conſciouſneſs of guilt, as where a man accuſed of felony, on hearing that a warrant is taken out againſt him, doth abſcond   2 *Haw* 76 Flight.

But the party who flies from an arreſt for a capital of‑ fence, is not thereby guilty of a capital offence, but only liable to forfeit his goods, when ſuch flight is found againſt him   2 *Haw.* 122.

(4) The being found in company with one known to be an offender, at the time of the offence, or generally at Evil company.

H 3   other

other times keeping company with perſons of ſcandalous reputation   2 *Haw.* 76   2 *Inſt* 52

Living idle
(5) The living an idle, vagrant, and diſorderly life, without having any viſible means to ſupport it   2 *Haw* 76

Hue and cry,
(6) The being purſued by hue and cry   2 *Haw* 76

For if a felony is done, and one is purſued upon hue and cry, that is not of ill fame, ſuſpicious, unknown, nor indicted, he may be attached and impriſoned by the law of the land   2 *Inſt* 52

Where no crime is committed
But generally, no ſuch cauſe of ſuſpicion, as any of the abovementioned, will juſtify an arreſt, where in truth no ſuch crime hath been committed, unleſs it be in the caſe of hue and cry   2 *Haw* 76

In the caſe of *Samuel* againſt *Payne* and others, *E* 20 *G* 3   The plaintiff *Samuel* brought an action of treſpaſs and falſe impriſonment againſt *Payne* a conſtable and two others.   The facts were theſe   *Hall*, one of the defendants, charged the plaintiff with having ſtolen ſome laces from him, which he ſaid were in the plaintiff's houſe   A ſearch warrant was granted by a juſtice upon this charge, but there was no warrant to apprehend him   On the ſearch, the goods were not found, however, *Payne*, *Hall*, and the other defendant an aſſiſtant of *Payne*, arreſted the plaintiff and carried him before a magiſtrate, who upon examination diſcharged him   The cauſe was tried before lord *Mansfield*, and a verdict found againſt all the three defendants   At the trial, his lordſhip, and the counſel on both ſides, looked upon the rule of law to be, that if a felony hath actually been committed, any man, upon reaſonable probable grounds of ſuſpicion, may juſtify apprehending the ſuſpected perſon to carry him before a magiſtrate, but that, if no felony has been committed, the apprehending of a perſon ſuſpected cannot be juſtified by any one   His lordſhip therefore left it to the jury to conſider, whether any felony had been committed.   The rule, however, was conſidered as inconvenient and narrow, becauſe if a man charges another with felony, and requires an officer to take him into cuſtody, and carry him before a magiſtrate, it would be moſt miſchievous that the officer ſhould be bound firſt to try, and at his peril exerciſe his judgment on the truth of the charge. He that makes the charge ſhould alone be anſwerable   The officer doth his duty in carrying the accuſed before a magiſtrate, who is authorized to examine, and commit or diſcharge.   On this ground, a motion was made for a new trial, and, after cauſe ſhewn, the court held, that the charge was a ſufficient juſtification to the conſtable and his assistant, and the rule for a new trial was made absolute. Which new trial came on before lord *Mansfield*, at the sittings after this term, when a verdict was found against *Hall*, and for the other two defendants. *Douglas.* 345

III. *By whom the arrest shall be made.*

1. In criminal cases, a person may be apprehended and restrained of his liberty, not only by process out of some court, or warrant from a magistrate, but frequently by a constable, watchman, or private person, without any warrant or precept.

Arrest without warrant.

2. Thus all persons, who are present when a felony is committed, or a dangerous wound given, are bound to apprehend the offender, on pain of being fined and imprisoned for their neglect. 2 *Haw.* 74.

By private persons.

Also, every private person is bound to assist an officer demanding his help, for the taking of a felon, or the suppressing of an affray. 2 *Haw.* 75.

Also by the vagrant act of 17 G. 2. Every private person may apprehend beggars and vagrants.

3. Also, a watchman may arrest a night walker, without any warrant from a magistrate. 2 *Inst.* 52.

By watchmen.

4. In like manner, a constable may *ex officio* arrest a breaker of the peace in his view, and keep him in his house, or in the stocks, till he can bring him before a justice. 1 *H. H.* 587.

By constables.

5. Or any person whatsoever, if an affray be made to the breach of the king's peace, may without any warrant from a magistrate, restrain any of the offenders, to the end the king's peace may be kept; but after the affray is ended, they cannot be arrested without an express warrant. 2 *Inst.* 52.

By others.

6. So much concerning an arrest without a warrant, next follows arresting with such warrant.

Arrest with warrant.

7. The warrant is ordinarily directed to the sheriff or constable, and they are indictable, and subject thereupon to a fine and imprisonment, if they neglect or refuse it. 1 *H. H.* 581.

By the sheriff or constable.

8. If it be directed to the sheriff, he may command his bailiff, under sheriff, or other sworn and known officer, to serve it, without writing any precept. But if he will command another man, that is no such officer, to serve it, he must give him a written precept, otherwise false imprisonment will lie. *Lamb.* 89.

Sheriff may depute.

9. But every other person to whom it is directed, must personally execute it; yet it seems, that any one may lawfully assist him. 2 *Haw.* 86.

Other cannot depute.

H 4

10 In

Where a constable may execute it out of his own district.

10. If a warrant be generally directed to all constables, no one can execute it out of his own precinct, for in such case it shall be taken respectively to each of them within their several districts, and not to one of them to execute it within the district of another, but if it be directed to a particular constable (Mr *Hawkins* says, to a particular constable *by name*), he may execute it any where within the jurisdiction of the justice, but is not compellable to execute it out of his own constablewick Lord *Raym* 546. 1 *H H* 581   2 *H H* 110   2 *Haw* 86

Any person may execute

11 The justice that issues the warrant, may direct it to a private person if he pleaseth, and it is good, but he is not compellable to execute it, unless he be a proper officer 1 *H H* 581

But not to be directed to the party

12 But by the justices oath of office, the warrant ought not to be directed to the party, but to some indifferent person, to execute it

Where directed to two jointly

13 If a warrant is directed to two or more jointly, yet any one of them alone may execute it. *Dalt c 169*

IV The manner of an arrest.

To be gone about immediately

1 The officer to whom a warrant is directed and delivered, ought with all speed and secrecy to find out the party, and then to execute the warrant *Dalt c 169*

Opposing the execution

2 It is certainly an offence of a very high nature, to oppose one who lawfully endeavours to arrest another for treason or felony and it seems, that a person who so opposes an arrest for treason, whereof he knows the party to have been guilty, is thereby guilty of the treason, and that he who so opposes an arrest for felony, is an accessary to the felony 2 *Haw*. 121

Arresting in the night

3. An arrest in the night is good, both at the suit of the king and of the subject, else the party may escape. 9 *Co* 66

Arresting in another county

4 By the 24 *G* 2. *c*. 55 Constables and others may, on having the warrant indorsed by a justice in another county, into which an offender shall have escaped, arrest an offender in such other county, and carry him before the justice who indorsed the warrant, or some other justice or justices of such other county, if the offence is bailable, to find bail, or else shall carry him back again before a justice in the county from whence the warrant did first issue,

Taking the power of the county

5 A private person cannot raise power to arrest or detain a felon 1 *H H* 601

But any justice, or the sheriff, may take of the county any number that he shall think meet, to pursue, arrest, and

and imprison traitors, murderers, robbers, and other felons, or such as do break, or go about to break, or disturb
the king's peace and every man being required, ought to
assist and aid them, on pain of fine and imprisonment.
Dalt c. 171

But it is not justifiable for a justice, sheriff, or other officer, to assemble the *posse comitatus*, or raise a power or
assembly of people, upon their own heads, without just
cause *Dalt c* 171

But where a justice, sheriff, or other officer, is enabled
to take the power of the county, it seemeth they may
command and ought to have the aid and attendance of all
knights, gentlemen, yeomen, husbandmen, labourers,
tradesmen, servants, and apprentices, and of all other
persons being above the age of fifteen years, and able to
travel *Dalt c.* 171 Because, by the statute of *Winchester*, all of that age are bound to have harness.

But women, ecclesiastical persons, and such as be de-
crepit, or diseased, shall not be compelled to attend them.
Dalt c 171.

And in such case it is referred to the discretion of the
justice, sheriff, or other officer, what number they will
have to attend on them, and how and after what manner
they shall be armed or otherwise furnished. *Dalt c* 171.

6 As to the case of breaking open doors, in order to
apprehend offenders, it is to be observed, that the law
doth never allow of such extremities, but in cases of necessity, and therefore, that no one can justify the breaking open another's door to make an arrest, unless he first
signify to those in the house the cause of his coming, and
request them to give him admittance. 2 *Haw* 86

But where a person authorized to arrest another, who
is sheltered in a house, is denied quietly to enter into it,
in order to take him, it seems generally to be agreed, that
he may justify breaking open the doors in the following
instances

(1) Upon a *capias* grounded on an indictment for any
crime whatsoever, or upon a *capias* from the chancery or
king's bench, to compel a man to find sureties for the peace
or good behaviour 2 *Haw* 86

(2) When one known to have committed a treason or
felony, or to have given another a dangerous wound, is
pursued either with or without a warrant, by a constable
or private person, but where one lies under a probable
suspicion only, and is not indicted, it seems the better
opinion at this day (Mr *Hawkins* says) that no one can
justify the breaking open doors in order to apprehend him·

Breaking open doors.

And

And this opinion he founds on *Coke's* 4 *Inſt* 177. and *Hale's pleas of the crown* 91 2 Haw 87

But Lord *Hale*, in his hiſtory of the pleas of the crown, ſays, that upon a warrant for probable cauſe of ſuſpicion of felony, the perſon to whom ſuch warrant is directed, may break open doors to take the perſon ſuſpected, if upon demand he will not ſurrender himſelf, as well as if there had been an expreſs and poſitive charge againſt him, and ſo (he ſays) hath the common practice obtained, notwithſtanding the contrary opinion of lord *Coke* for in ſuch caſe the proceſs is for the king, and therefore a *non omittas* is implied. 1 *H H* 580, 583 2 *H. H* 117

And as he may break open ſuch perſon's own houſe, ſo much more may he break open the houſe of another to take him , for ſo the ſheriff may do upon a civil proceſs But then he muſt at his peril ſee that the felon be there, for if the felon be not there, he is a treſpaſſer to the ſtranger whoſe houſe it is 2 *H. H* 117

But it ſeems that he that arreſts as a *private man* barely upon ſuſpicion of felony, cannot juſtify the breaking open of doors to arreſt the party ſuſpected, but he doth it at his peril, that is, if in truth he be a felon, then it is juſtifiable, but if he be innocent, but upon a reaſonable cauſe ſuſpected, it is not juſtifiable 1 *H H* 82

But a *conſtable* in ſuch caſe may juſtify, and the reaſon of the difference is this becauſe that in the former caſe it is but a thing permitted to private perſons to arreſt for ſuſpicion, and they are not puniſhable if they omit it , and therefore they cannot break open doors, but in caſe of a conſtable he is puniſhable if he omit it upon complaint. 2 *H. H* 92

(3) Upon a warrant from a juſtice of the peace, to find ſureties for the peace or good behaviour. 2 *Haw* 86. 1 *H H* 582 2 *H H.* 117.

And in general, Mr *Dalton* ſays, an officer upon any warrant from a juſtice, either for the peace or good behaviour, or in any caſe where the king is party, may by force break open a man's houſe, to arreſt the offender *Dc⁴ c* 169

(4) On a warrant to ſearch for ſtolen goods, the doors may be broke open if the goods are there , and if they are not there, the conſtable ſeems indemnified, but he that made the ſuggeſtion, is puniſhable 2 *H H* 151

(5) Where forcible entry or detainer is found by inquiſtion before juſtices of the peace, or appears on their view 2 *Haw* 86.

(6) On a *capias utlagatum*, or *capias pro fine* 2 Haw 86

(7) On the warrant of a juſtice of the peace for the levying of a forfeiture, in execution of a judgment, or conviction

viction for it, grounded on any ſtatute, which gives the whole or any part of ſuch forfeiture to the king *2 Haw.* 86

(8) Where an affray is made in a houſe, in the view or hearing of the conſtable, he may break open the doors to take them 1 *Haw* 137. 2 *Haw* 87

(9) If there be diſorderly drinking or noiſe in a houſe, at an unſeaſonable time of night, eſpecially in inns, taverns, or alehouſes, the conſtable or his watch, demanding entrance, and being refuſed, may break open the doors, to ſee and ſuppreſs the diſorder. 2 *H H* 95.

(10) Wherever a perſon is lawfully arreſted for any cauſe, and afterwards eſcapes, and ſhelters himſelf in an houſe 2 *Haw* 87.

(11) But upon a general warrant, without expreſſing any felony or treaſon, or ſurety of the peace, the officer cannot break open a door 1 *H H* 584

(12) Neither ought doors to be broke open to take a perſon, who is required to take certain oaths by virtue of a ſtatute, becauſe in ſuch caſe the warrant is not grounded on a precedent offence. 2 *Haw* 87 12 *Co* 131.

(13) In a civil ſuit, the officer cannot juſtify the breaking open an outward door or window in order to execute proceſs. If he doth, he is a treſpaſſer But if he findeth the outward door open, and entreth that way, or if the door be opened to him from within, and he entreth, he may break open inward doors if he findeth that neceſſary in order to execute his proceſs *Foſt* 319

For a man's houſe is his caſtle, for ſafety and repoſe to himſelf and family, but if a ſtranger, who is not of the family, upon a purſuit taketh refuge in the houſe of another, this rule doth not extend to *him*, it is not *his* caſtle, he cannot claim the benefit of ſanctuary therein. *Foſt* 320

And it is always to be remembred, that this rule muſt be confined to the caſe of arreſt upon proceſs in civil ſuits only For where a felony hath been committed, or a dangerous wound given, or even where a miniſter of juſtice cometh armed with proceſs founded on a breach of the peace, the party's own houſe is no ſanctuary for him in theſe caſes, the juſtice which is due to the publick muſt ſuperſede every pretence of private inconvenience *id*

(14) Finally, in all theſe caſes, if an officer, to ſerve any warrant, enters into a houſe, the doors being open, and then the doors are locked upon him, he may break them open in order to regain his liberty. 2 *Haw.* 87

7 If there be a warrant againſt a perſon, for a treſpaſs or breach of the peace, and he flies and will not yield to

Killing in the arreſt or purſuit.

the

the arrest, or being taken makes his escape, if the officer kills him it is murder. 2 *H. H.* 117.

But if such person, either upon the attempt to arrest, or after the arrest, assault the officer, to the intent to make his escape from him, and the officer standing upon his guard kills him, this is no felony, for he is not bound to go back to the wall as in common cases of *se defendendo*, for the law is his protection. 2 *H. H.* 118

But where a warrant issueth against a person for felony, and either before arrest, or after, he flies and defends himself with stones or weapons, so that the officer must give over his pursuit, or otherwise cannot take him without killing him, if he kill him it is no felony. And the same law is, for a constable that doth it by virtue of his office, or on hue and cry. 2 *H. H* 118

But then there must be these cautions. 1 He must be a lawful officer, or there must be a lawful warrant. 2 The party ought to have notice of the reason of the pursuit, namely, because a warrant is against him. 3 It must be a case of necessity, and that not such a necessity as in the former case, where an assault is made upon the officer, but this is the necessity, namely, that he cannot otherwise be taken. 2 *H H* 119

But tho' a private person may arrest a felon, and if he fly so as he cannot be taken without he be killed, it is excusable in this case for the necessity, yet it is at his peril, that the party be a felon, for if he be innocent of the felony, the killing (at least before the arrest) seems at least manslaughter, for an innocent person is not bound to take notice of a private person's suspicion. 2 *H H* 119.

Whether the constable need to shew his warrant 8 A person sworn and commonly known, and acting within his own precinct, need not shew his warrant, but he ought to acquaint the party with the substance of it. *2 Haw* 85

And an officer giveth sufficient notice what he is, when he saith to the party, I arrest you in the king's name, and in such case, the party at his peril ought to obey him, tho' he knoweth him not to be an officer, and if he have no lawful warrant, the party grieved may have his action of false imprisonment. *Dalt c* 169

But the learned editor of *Hale*'s history observes hereupon, that the books referred to intend the general warrant constituting such person an officer, as a bailiff, or the like, in a civil action, tho' it may be otherwise in case of felony, because in such case a private person may arrest a felon without any warrant at all. 2 *H. H.* 116

But

But if he acts out of his precinct, or is not ſworn and commonly known, he muſt ſhew his warrant if demanded. *2 Haw* 85, 86 Otherwiſe the party may make reſiſtance, and needs not to obey it. *Dalt. c.* 169.

But if the conſtable has no warrant, but doth it by virtue of his office, as a conſtable, it is ſufficient to notify that he is conſtable, or that he arreſts in the king's name. *1 H. H* 583

But in the caſe of a warrant of diſtreſs, iſſued by a juſtice of the peace, for the levying a pecuniary forfeiture or ſum of money, it is ſpecially provided by the ſtatute of the 27 *G* 2. *c.* 20 that the officer executing the ſame, ſhall, if required, ſhew his warrant to the perſon whoſe goods are diſtrained, and ſhall ſuffer a copy thereof to be taken.

9 If the conſtable come unto the party, and require *No arreſt by* him to go before the juſtice, this is no arreſt nor impri- *words only.* ſonment *Dalt c* 170.

For bare words will not make an arreſt without laying hold on the perſon or otherwiſe confining him. But if an officer comes into a room, and tells the party he arreſts him, and locks the door, this is an arreſt, for he is in cuſtody of the officer *1 Salk* 79   *2 Haw.* 129 *Caſes in the time of lord Hardwicke* 301

10. It hath been holden, that if a conſtable, after he *Retaking after* hath arreſted the party by force of a warrant, ſuffer him to *arreſt.* go at large, upon his promiſe to come again and find ſureties, he cannot afterwards arreſt him by force of the ſame warrant However if the party return, and put himſelf again under the cuſtody of the conſtable, it ſeems that it may be probably argued, that the conſtable may lawfully detain him, and bring him before the juſtice, in purſuance of ſuch warrant, but in this the law doth not ſeem to be clearly ſettled. *2 Haw* 81.

But if the party arreſted do eſcape, the officer upon freſh ſuit may take him again and again, ſo often as he eſcapeth, altho' he were out of view, or that he ſhall fly into another town or county *Dalt c* 169

V. *What is to be done after the arreſt.*

1 When a private perſon hath arreſted a felon, or one *By a private per-* ſuſpected of felony, he may detain him in cuſtody till he *ſon.* can reaſonably diſmiſs himſelf of him, but with as much ſpeed as conveniently he can, he may do any of theſe three things

(1) He may carry him to the common goal, but that is now rarely done. *1 H H.* 589. *2 H. H.* 77.

(2) He

(2) He may deliver him to the conſtable, who may either carry him to gaol, or to a juſtice of the peace. 1 *H. H* 589

(3) He may carry him immediately to a juſtice of the peace. 1 *H H* 589

By a watchman. 2. If the conſtable, or his watch, hath arreſted affray, ers, or perſons drinking in an alehouſe diſorderly at an unſeaſonable time of night, he may put the perſons in the ſtocks, or in a priſon if there be one in the vill, till the heat of their paſſion or intemperance is over, tho' he deliver them afterwards, or till he can bring them before a juſtice. 2 *H H* 95

By an officer by warrant. 3 If the arreſt is by virtue of a warrant, when the officer hath made the arreſt, he is forthwith to bring the party, according to the direction of the warrant If it be to bring the party before the juſtice who granted the warrant ſpecially, then the officer is bound to bring him before the ſame juſtice, but if the warrant be to bring him before any juſtice of the county, then it is in the election of the officer, to bring him before what juſtice he thinks fit, and not in the election of the priſoner. 1 *H. H* 582 2 *H H* 112

But if the time be unſeaſonable, as in or near the night, whereby he cannot attend the juſtice, or if there be danger of a preſent reſcue, or if the party be ſick, he may ſecure him in the ſtocks, or in an houſe, till the next day, or ſuch time as it may be reaſonable to bring him. 2 *H. H* 120

And when he hath brought him to the juſtice, yet he is in law ſtill in his cuſtody, till the juſtice diſcharge, or bail, or commit him. 2 *H H* 120

Returning the warrant. 4 But it is ſaid, the conſtable is not obliged to return the warrant itſelf, but may keep it for his own juſtification, in caſe he ſhould be queſtioned for what he had done, but only to return what he has done upon it. Lord *Raym* 1196

Conſtable indemnified. 5 And this ſeems to be implied in the ſtatute of the 24 *G* 2 *c* 44. which enacteth, that no action ſhall be brought againſt any conſtable or other officer, or perſon acting by his order, and in his aid, for any thing done in obedience to the warrant of a juſtice of the peace, until demand hath been made, or left at the uſual place of his abode, by the party, or by his attorney, in writing, ſigned by the party demanding the ſame, of the peruſal and copy of ſuch warrant, and the ſame hath been refuſed or neglected for ſix days after ſuch demand And if, after compliance therewith, any ſuch action ſhall be brought, without

out making the juſtice who ſigned the warrant defendant, on producing and proving ſuch warrant at the trial, the jury ſhall give their verdict for the defendant. *J* 6 And it is certain the conſtable cannot grant a peruſal or copy of the warrant, unleſs he hath it in his cuſtody

6. By an ancient ſtatute, 23 *H* 6 *c* 10 No ſheriff ſhall take for any arreſt, but 20 d, and the bailiff which maketh the arreſt 4 d, on pain of 40 l, half to the king, and half to him that will ſue in ſeſſions (or the courts above) and treble damages to the party injured

Fee for arreſt.

Upon which ſtatute perhaps may be founded the cuſtom in many places, of giving 4 d to the conſtable with the warrant, for his trouble in executing the ſame, which indeed at that time might be a reaſonable ſatisfaction, for 4 d then was worth more than ten times the value of 4 d now Which decreaſe in the value of money, in this and many other caſes depending upon ancient ſtatutes, may ſeem to require ſome conſideration

The rewards for arreſting or apprehending highwaymen and others, may be found under their reſpective titles

---

Aſſault and Battery.

I. *Aſſault, what*
II. *Battery, what.*
III *In what caſes they may be juſtified.*
IV. *How puniſhed.*

I. *Aſſault, what.*

ASSAULT, *aſſultus*, from the French *aſſailer*, is an attempt or offer, with force and violence, to do a corporal hurt to another, as by ſtriking at him with or without a weapon, or preſenting a gun at him, at ſuch a diſtance to which the gun will carry, or pointing a pitchfork at him, ſtanding within the reach of it, or by holding up one's fiſt at him, or by any other ſuch like act, done in an angry, threatning manner 1 *Haw* 133.

And from hence it clearly follows, that one charged with an aſſault and battery, may be found guilty of the aſſault, and yet acquitted of the battery But every battery includes an aſſault, therefore on an indictment of aſſault and battery, in which the aſſault is ill laid, if the

defendant

defendant be found guilty of the battery, it is sufficient.
1 *Haw.* 134

Notwithstanding the many ancient opinions to the contrary, it seems agreed at this day, that no words whatsoever can amount to an assault 1 *Haw* 134.

II. Battery, what.

Battery (from the Saxon *batte,* a club, or *beatan,* to beat, from whence cometh also the word *battle*) seemeth to be, when any injury whatsoever, be it never so small, is actually done to the person of a man, in an angry, or revengeful, or rude, or insolent manner, as by spitting in his face, or any way touching him in anger, or violently justling him out of the way, and the like 1 *Haw* 134

III In what cases they may be justified.

A man may justify an assault, in defence of his person, or of his wife, or master, or parent, or child within age, and even a *wounding* may be justified in defence of his person, but not of his possessions 3 *Salk* 46

Also if an officer having a lawful warrant lay hands on another, to arrest him, or if a parent in a reasonable manner chastise a child, a master his apprentice, a school master his scholar, in all these cases, and such like, it is justifiable 1 *Haw* 130

Likewise a person may justify an assault and battery of another, who doth menace or assault him, and attempt to beat him from his lawful watercourse or highway *Pult* 42

Likewise, if a person comes into my house, and will not go out, I may justify laying hold of him, and turning him out 3 *Black* 120

And where a man in his own defence beats another who first assaults him, he may take advantage thereof, both upon an indictment, and upon an action, but with this difference, that on an indictment he may give it in evidence upon the plea of not guilty, but on an action he must plead it specially 1 *Haw.* 134.

IV. How punished.

There is no doubt but that the wrong-doer is subject both to an action at the suit of the party, wherein he shall render damages, and also to an indictment at the suit of the king, wherein he shall be fined according to the heinousness of the offence 1 *Haw.* 134

But

But on an action of affault and battery, where the jury shall give lefs than 40 s damages, the plaintiff shall have no more cofts than damages, unlefs the judge shall certify on the back of the record, that an actual battery (and not an affault only) was proved upon the trial   43 *El. c* 6 22 & 23 *C* 2. *c* 9 *f* 136

By 6 *G c* 23 *f.* 11 Affaulting in the ftreet or high-way, with intent to fpoil people's cloaths, and fo fpoiling them, is felony and tranfportation.

By 7 *G* 2 *c* 21 Affaulting with intent to rob, is alfo made felony and tranfportation

And by 9 *Ann c* 16 Affaulting a privy counfellor in the execution of his office, is felony without benefit of clergy

A private affault is not inquirable in the leet, not being a common nufance, as all affrays are   1 *Haw.* 135

Warrant for an affault.

Weftmorland } To the conftable of ——

WHEREAS *complaint hath been made before me J P. efquire, one of his majefty's juftices of the peace in and for the faid county, upon the oath of* A I. *of* —— *in the faid county, taylor, that* A O. *of* —— *aforefaid, butcher, did on the* —— *day of* —— *violently affault and beat him the faid* A. I. *at* —— *aforefaid, in the county aforefaid · Thefe are therefore in his faid majefty's name, to command you forthwith to apprehend the faid* A O *and to bring him before me to anfwer unto the faid complaint, and to be further dealt withal according to law. Given under my hand and feal the* —— *day of, &c*

Indictment for an affault.

THE *jurors of our lord the king upon their oath prefent, that* A O *of* —— *in the faid county, butcher, on the* —— *day of* —— *in the* —— *year of the reign of* —— *at* —— *aforefaid, in the county aforefaid, in and upon* A I *taylor, then and there being in the peace of God and of our faid lord the king, with force and arms, an affault did make, and him the faid* A I *then and there did beat, wound, and evil intreat, and then and there to him other enormous things did, to the great damage and hurt of him the faid* A. I *to the evil example of all others offending in the like kind, and againft the peace of our faid lord the king, his crown and dignity*

Assizes.

1 ASSIZE (*affessio*) antiently signified in general, a court where the judges or assessors heard and determined causes, and more particularly upon writs of *assize* brought before them, by such as were wrongfully put out of their possession. Which writs heretofore were very frequent; but now mens possessions are more easily recovered by ejectments, and the like. Yet still the judges in their circuits have a commission of *assize*, directed to themselves and the clerk of assize, to take assizes, and to do right upon such writs.

2 To which commission of *assize*, four other commissions are now superadded, to wit,

(1) A commission of *general gaol delivery*, directed to the judges and the clerk of assize associate, which gives them power to try every prisoner in the gaol, committed for any offence whatsoever, but none but prisoners in the gaol.

(2) A commission of *oyer and terminer*, directed to the judges, and many other gentlemen of the county, by which they are impowered to *hear and determine* treasons, felonies, and other misdemeanors, by whomsoever committed, whether the persons to be tried be in gaol or not in gaol.

(3) A commission or writ of *nisi prius*, directed to the judges and clerk of assize, by which civil causes brought to issue in the courts above, are tried in the vacation by a jury of twelve men of the county where the cause of action arises, and on return of the verdict of the jury to the court above, the judges there give judgment.

(4) A commission of the *peace* in every county of their circuit.

3 By the precept for the general gaol delivery above mentioned, the sheriff is commanded to attend there in person, with his under-sheriff, and to give notice to all justices of the peace, mayors, coroners, escheators, stewards, and also to all chief constables and bailiffs of hundreds and liberties, that they be then and there in their own persons with their rolls, records, indictments, and other remembrances, to do those things which to their offices in that behalf appertain to be done.

By virtue whereof, all justices of the peace, mayors, and others abovementioned, of that county where the judges have their assizes, are bound to be present, and if they make default, without lawful impediment, the judges may

may fet a fine upon them for their negleҪ *Crown Circ.*
Comp 4

4 Alfo, by ancient cuftom (that is, by the common *Conſtables pre-*
law of the land) before the coming of the judges, the *ſentment*
high conftables iffue their warrants to the petty conftables,
to make prefentments of all crimes and offences cognizable at the affizes, to the intent (as it feemeth) that the
judges thereby may have a general information and knowledge, how the peace hath been kept which prefentments
being delivered to the high conftables, are by them delivered into court, and make up part of the rolls, and other
remembrances abovementioned

Which faid warrants of the high conftables perhaps
may be beft drawn upon the words of the commiffion of
over and terminer, which is the largeft of all the five commiffions abovementioned And then the form thereof may
be thus,

Weftmorland } To the conftable of —— in the faid
Eaft Ward } county

*THESE are to require you the faid conſtable, in his ma-
jeſty's name, to make out a preſentment in writing of all
treaſons, miſpriſons of treaſons, inſurrections, rebellions, counterfeiting, clippings, waſhings, falſe coinings, and other falſities of the money of* Great Britain, *and of other kingdoms and
dominions whatſoever, and of all the murders, felonies, manſlaughter, killings, burglaries, rapes of women, unlawful
meetings and conventicles, unlawful uttering of words, aſſem-
blies, miſpriſons, confederacies, falſe allegations, treſpaſſes,
riots, routs, retentions, eſcapes, contempts, falſities, negligences,
concealments, maintenance, oppreſſions, champerty, deceits, and all
other evil doings, offences and injuries whatſoever, and alſo the
acceſſaries of them, by whomſoever, and in what manner ſoever,
done, committed or perpetrated, within your conſtablewick Which
ſaid preſentment ſo made in writing as aforeſaid, and ſigned by
you, you are to deliver to me at —— in the ſaid county, on ——
the —— day of —— at the hour of —— in the fore-
noon of the ſame day, that I may have the ſaid preſentment ready
to be delivered to his ſaid majeſty's juſtices of oyer and terminer
and general gaol delivery at the next aſſizes to be holden for
the ſaid county Herein fail you not, as you will anſwer the
contrary at your peril Given under my hand, the —— day
of —— in the year of our Lord ——*

John Bownefs, *High Conſtable*

I 2   5 Whereas

In what caſes the judges may act, tho out of the proper county.

5 Whereas the courts of aſſiſe, niſi prius, oyer and terminer, and gaol delivery, for ſeveral counties at large, are often held in or near cities or towns that are counties of themſelves, and at the ſame time with the like courts for the ſaid cities or towns, and inconveniencies frequently ariſe in tranſacting the buſineſs of the ſeveral courts, for that the lodgings of the judges are ſituate either only in the county at large, or only in the county of ſuch city or town, it is therefore enacted, that whenever the ſaid courts for any county at large ſhall be held in or near any city or town which is alſo a county of it ſelf, with the like or any of the like courts for the ſaid city or town, the lodgings of the judges ſhall be conſtrued and taken to be ſituate both within the county at large, and alſo within the county of ſuch city or town, for tranſacting the buſineſs of the aſſizes for ſuch county at large, and for the county of ſuch city or town, during the time that ſuch judge or judges ſhall continue therein for the execution of their ſeveral commiſſions. 19 *G* 3 *c* 74 *ſ* 70.

Attachment.

THIS word, as a law term, we have immediately from the french *attacher*, to tye, or make faſt The Italian word is *attacare*, the Spaniſh *attacar*, and the Saxon *tæcan*, to take.

It ſignifieth the taking of a man's body by commandment of a writ or precept, and is properly grantable in caſes of contempts, againſt which for the moſt part all courts of record generally, but more eſpecially thoſe of *Weſtminſter-hall*, and above all the court of king's bench, may proceed in a ſummary manner, according to their diſcretion. 2 *Haw.* 141.

But in the caſe of *K.* and *Bartlett*, *H* 8 *G.* 2. it is ſaid that generally the ſeſſions have not a power to award an attachment, but the court ſaid, they would not determine how it would have been, if they had committed the perſon for contempt, but the ordinary and proper method is, by indictment *Seſſ. Ca. V* 2. 176

Attainder.

THE difference between a man attainted and convicted is, that a man is said to be convicted before he hath judgment, as if a man be convicted by verdict or confession, and when he hath his judgment upon the verdict or confession, then he is said to be attainted. 1 *Inst* 390.

That is to say, his blood is become *(attinctus) tainted,* stained, or corrupted insomuch that by the common law, in cases of treason or felony, his children or other kindred cannot inherit his estate, nor his wife claim her dower, and the same cannot be restored or saved, but by act of parliament, and therefore in divers instances, there is a special provision by act of parliament, that such or such an attainder shall not work corruption of blood, loss of dower, nor disherison of heirs.

Attaint.

ATTAINT is a writ that lieth, where a false verdict in a court of record, upon an issue joined by the parties, is given 1 *Inst* 294. Which is treated of under title **Jurors.**

Attorney.

1. AN *attorney* is one who is appointed to do any thing, in the *turn*, stead, or place of another. 1 *Inst* 51. — Who.

2 No attorney or solicitor shall be capable to continue or be a justice of the peace, during such time as he shall continue in the business and practice of an attorney or solicitor.—But this not to extend to any city or town being a county of it self, nor to any city, town, or liberty, having justices of their own. 5 *G.* 2 *c* 18 — Justice of the peace not to act as attorney

3 No under-sheriff, sheriff's clerk, receiver, nor sheriff's bailiff, shall be attorney in the king's courts, during the time that he is in office with any such sheriff. 1 *H* 5 *c* 4 — Under sheriff

4 No steward, bailiff, nor minister of lords of franchises, which have return of writs, shall be attorney in — Steward of a franchise.

I 3   any

any plea within the franchife or bailiwick, whereof he
fhall be officer 4 H 4 c 19

Recufant.

5 No recufant convict fhall practife as an attorney or
folicitor, on pain of 100 l. half to the king, and half to
him that fhall fue 3 J c 5 f 8

Perfons convict-
ed of perjury, &c.
or other crime

6 If any perfon, who hath been convicted of forgery,
perjury, or fubornation of perjury, or common barratry,
fhall practife as an attorney or folicitor, he fhall be tranfported for feven years 12 G c 29 f 4

To be bound 5
years.

7 No perfon fhall act as attorney or folicitor, unlefs
he fhall have been bound for five years 2 G 2 c 23
f 5, 6

Affidavit to be
made thereof

8 And every perfon bound to ferve as clerk to any
attorney or folicitor, fhall within three months caufe an
affidavit to be made of the actual execution of the contract, in which affidavit fhall be fpecified, the name of
the attorney and folicitor and of the perfon fo bound, their
places of abode, and the day of the date of fuch contract fuch affidavit to be filed within the faid time, in
the court where the attorney or folicitor is inrolled 22
G 2 c 46 f 3

But there is generally an indemnifying claufe in fome
act every two or three years for relief of perfons who
have omitted to caufe fuch affidavits to be made and filed,
provided they caufe the fame to be done within a time
therein limited.

And no perfon fo bound fhall be admitted or inrolled
an attorney or folicitor, before fuch affidavit fo filed fhall
be produced and openly read in court 22 G 2 c 46
f 4

Act 1
&c.
5 &c.

9 And fuch clerk fhall, during the whole time of fervice fpecified in the contract, continue and be actually
employed by fuch attorney or folicitor or his agent, in the
proper bufinefs of an attorney or folicitor. 22 G 2 c 46
f 6

Provided, that if the mafter fhall die or difcontinue
his practice, or if the contract fhall by confent be can-
celled, or fuch clerk be difcharged by order of court,
the clerk may be bound, during the refidue of the term
to another mafter fo as affidavit be made and filed as
aforefaid, of the execution of fuch fecond or other contract f 9

And fuch clerk, before he fhall be admitted attorney
or folicitor, fhall caufe an affidavit of himfelf, or of the
attorney or folicitor to whom he was bound, to be made
and filed as aforefaid, that he hath actually and really
ferved the faid term with fuch practifing attorney or
folicitor.

folicitor or his agent, during the faid whole term of five years. § 10

10 One of the judges in the courts of law, and the mafter of the rolls, or two mafters in chancery, and judge of the other courts of equity refpectively, fhall examine any perfon touching his fitnefs and capacity to be an attorney or folicitor and if approved of, he fhall be fworn in open court, and admitted and inrolled, without fee, except is for adminiftring the oath Which admiffion (on a treble 40 s ftamp) fhall be figned, and delivered to him 2 G 2 c. 23 § 4, 5, 6

And the attorney's oath fhall be this "I A B do "fwear, that I will truly and honeftly demean myfelf "in the practice of an attorney, according to the beft "of my knowledge and ability, fo help me God" § 13

The folicitor's oath, "I A B do fwear, that I will "truly and honeftly demean myfelf in the practice of a "folicitor, according to the beft of my knowledge and "ability, fo help me God" § 14

11 If any perfon fhall act as attorney or folicitor, for or in expectation of any gain or reward, without being admitted and inrolled as aforefaid, he fhall forfeit 50 l, and be incapable to act for the future The faid penalty to be recovered in any of the courts of record at Weftminfter, or in the counties palatine refpectively, or great feffions in Wales, or at the affizes or feffions, by any perfon who fhall fue for the fame within 12 months, together with treble cofts, and no proceedings thereupon fhall be removed before judgment, or ftayed by any certiorari or other writ 2 G 2 c 23 § 24, 25

And by the 7 & 8 W c 24 Any attorney or folicitor, acting as fuch, before he hath taken the oaths and fubfcribed the declaration, as other perfons qualifying for offices, fhall incur a præmunire

12 No attorney or folicitor fhall have more than two clerks at any one time 2 G 2 c 23 § 15

Except the prothonotaries in the common pleas, and the fecondary in the king's bench, and the feveral prothonotaries in the counties palatine, and great feffions in Wales, each of whom may have three, who fhall be bound and ferve for fuch time as aforefaid, and examined, admitted, and inrolled, as other perfons who have ferved to a fworn attorney § 16

13 A fworn attorney may, on examination as aforefaid, be admitted, fworn, and inrolled a folicitor, in any of the courts of equity, without fee or ftamp 2 G 2 c 23 § 20

14 In like manner, a fworn folicitor may be admitted, fworn, and inrolled an attorney, in the king's bench or common pleas. 23 G. 2. c 26 ſ 15

15 So alfo, a fworn folicitor in any of the courts of equity may, on examination as aforefaid, be admitted, fworn, and inrolled, in any other court of equity, without fee or ftamp. 2 G 2. c 23 ſ 21

16 And any attorney or folicitor in any of the courts refpectively, may, with the confent in writing of an attorney in any other court, in the name of fuch attorney, fue out any procefs, and carry on any fuit, in fuch court, notwithftanding he is not fworn and admitted to be an attorney of fuch court. 2 G. 2. c. 23. ſ. 10

17 And any perfon, who hath been admitted an attorney in any of his majefty's courts of record at Weftminfter, fhall be capable of being admitted to practife as an attorney in any inferior court of record, provided he be in all other refpects qualified according to the cuftom of fuch inferior court 6 G 2. c 27.

18 No perfon fhall act as attorney, folicitor, or agent, at any general or quarter feffions of the peace, without being duly inrolled; on pain of 50l, to him who fhall fue in 12 months, with treble cofts and if any attorney or folicitor fhall permit him to make ufe of his name in fuch feffions, he fhall forfeit 50 l in like manner 22 G 2. c 46 ſ 12

And no clerk of the peace or his deputy, or any underfheriff or his deputy, fhall act as folicitor, attorney, or agent, at any general or quarter feffions of the peace of the county or place where he fhall execute his faid office refpectively, on pain of 50l in like manner ſ 14

19 A perfon acting as attorney or folicitor in the county court, without having been legally admitted, fhall forfeit 20l with cofts, to him who fhall fue in 12 months in any of his majefty's courts of record 12 G 2. c. 13. ſ 7.

20 An attorney, in refpect of his attendance at the court, cannot be preffed for a foldier *Comyn's Dig* Attorney —But he is not privileged from ferving in the militia, or finding a fubftitute in his ftead *Blackſtone's Rep.* 1.23

An attorney fhall not be made conftable, though there be a cuftom that every inhabitant fhall be chofen in his turn. *id*

And, in general, it is faid, that he fhall not be elected into any other office, againft his will, as, to the office of overfeer of the poor, or churchwarden, or any office within a borough. *id.*

So he ſhall not be choſen collector of the lord's rent within a manor, where it is copyhold, though it be part of his tenure. *id.*

So he ſhall not be amerced for not doing his ſuit at the lord's court, when his attendance at Weſtminſter is required *id*

In the caſe of the corporation of *Norwich* v *Berry*, T 7 G 3 it was determined, that an attorney ought to have his privilege allowed from executing the office of ſheriff It was obſerved, that the conteſt was not between the city of *Norwich* and the attorney, but between the city of *Norwich* and the court of common pleas, that the privilege of the court was the matter in queſtion, which has exiſted as long as the court, and the crown could not, by a charter granted to a corporation, take it away *Burr. Manſf.* 2109.

If an attorney be denied his privilege, he may have a writ of privilege for his diſcharge 2 *Haw* 63.

21. If any attorney be notoriouſly found in any default, of record, or otherwiſe, he ſhall forſwear the court, and never after be received to make any ſuit in any court of the king. 4 H 4 c 18

And therefore, where an attorney ſued out a *capias*, without an original, he was ſtruck out of the roll, and ſworn, that he be not an attorney in any of the king's courts *Comyns' Dig* Attorney.

So an attorney, who gave names to the ſheriff to be returned upon a jury, was caſt over the bar *id.*

So if he takes money of his client, and afterwards wholly refuſes to intermeddle with his buſineſs, he ſhall be ſtruck out of the roll *id*

If he refuſe a re-delivery of writings intruſted to his peruſal, though ſome of them concern himſelf principally, the court, upon motion, will compel him to re-deliver them, on payment of all due to him in the cauſe for which they were delivered, for if the writings were delivered for a ſpecial purpoſe, he ſhall not detain them for another demand. *id*

And the court will award an attachment againſt him, for bad and fraudulent practice, and he ſhall pay coſts thereupon, or ſhall be committed But an attachment will not be granted before a day allowed to ſhew cauſe *id.*

22 No attorney or ſolicitor, being a priſoner, ſhall, in his own name, or in the name of any other attorney, during his confinement, ſue out any writ or proceſs, or commence any action, on pain that ſuch proceedings ſhall be void, and he ſhall be incapacitated to act as attorney

Miſbehaviour.

Acting when under confinement.

ney or folicitor for the future, and any attorney or fol citor permitting or impowering him to do fo in his name, fhall be in like manner incapacitated 12 G. 2 c. 13 ∫ 9

Provided, that fuch perfon fo confined may carry on or tranfact any fuit commenced before his confinement ∫ 10

Name to be in-fcribed on writs or other procefs.

23 Every writ or procefs for arrefting the body, and every writ of execution, or fome label annexed to fuch writ or procefs, and every warrant to be made out there-upon, fhall be fubfcribed or indorfed with the name of the attorney, clerk in court, or folicitor, and where fuch perfon fhall not be immediately employed by the plaintiff, then alfo with the name of the attorney or folicitor im medi itely employed And every copy of any writ to be ferved on the defendant fhall be fubfcribed or indorfed, with the name of the attorney or folicitor immediatly employed. 2 G 2 c 23 ∫. 22

But the not fubfcribing or indorfing the name of the attorney, clerk in court, or folicitor, on the warrant made out on the procefs, fhall not vitiate the fame, provided the writ be fubfcribed or indorfed but the fheriff making out fuch warrant, and not fubfcribing or indorfing the name of the attorney, clerk in court, or folicitor who fued out the fame, fhall forfeit 5 l, to be affeffed upon him as a fine, by the court out of which the procefs iffued, half to the king, and half to the party aggrieved by fuch omif fion 12 G 2 c 13 ∫ 4

Acting for a per-fon unqualified

24 If any fworn attorney or folicitor fhall knowingly act as agent for any perfon not qualified, he fhall, on proof thereof to the court in a fummary way, be ftruck off the roll and incapacitated, and fuch unqualified perfon fhall be committed to the prifon of the court, for any time not exceeding one year 22 G 2 c 46 ∫. 11

Suffering a per-fon unqualified to act in his name

25 If any fworn attorney fhall knowingly fuffer any perfon, not being a fworn attorney or folicitor, to act in his name, he fhall be incapable to act as an attorney 2 G. 2. c 23 ∫ 17

Suffering a fuit to delay.

26 If any attorney or folicitor fhall willingly delay his client s fuit, to work his own gain, the party grieved fhall have his action for the fame, and recover cofts and treble damages, and the faid attorney or folicitor fhall be difcharged from being an attorney or folicitor any more 3 ∫ c 7

In the cafe of *Ruffel* and *Stewart*, M 6 G 3 The de fendant being a prifoner, the plaintiff s attorney had ne-glected to charge him in cuftody within the time limited for his difcharge upon common bail, whereupon the plaintiff brought an action againft the attorney, and recovered againft him 1500 l damages *Bur Mansf* 1788.

27 All attornies and folicitors fhall give a true bill *To deliver a bill figned.* unto their clients fubfcribed with their own hands and names, before they fhall charge their clients with their fees or charges 3 *J. c* 7.

28 And if any attorney or folicitor fhall demand by his *Penalty for a wrong charge.* bill any other fum of money, or allowance upon his account of any money, which he hath not laid out, the party grieved fhall have his action for the fame, and recover cofts and treble damages, and fuch attorney or folicitor fhall be difcharged and incapacitated. 3 *J. c* 7.

29 No attorney or folicitor fhall fue for recovery of *Client to have a month to pay in.* his fees, until after one month from the time of delivering the bill figned 2 *G* 2 *c* 23 *f.* 23

30 And the client, on fubmiffion to pay the whole *Taxation.* fum that on taxation fhall appear due, may have the bill taxed by the proper officer And if the attorney or folicitor, or the party charged, having due notice, fhall not attend the taxation, the officer may proceed to tax the bill *ex parte* (And no fuit fhall be commenced for the faid fees during the taxation) And on taxation and fettlement of the bill, the party fhall forthwith pay to the faid attorney or folicitor, or to any perfon by whom authorized who fhall be prefent at the taxation, or otherwife as the court fhall direct, the whole fum that fhall be found due, and in default thereof, the party fhall be liable to an attachment, or to fuch proceedings at the election of the attorney or folicitor as the party fhall be otherwife liable to by law And if it appear on the taxation, that the attorney or folicitor hath been overpaid, he fhall forthwith refund, on pain of attachment, or fuch other proceedings as aforefaid If the bill taxed be lefs by a fixth part than the bill delivered, the attorney or folicitor fhall pay the cofts of taxation But if it fhall not be lefs, the court fhall charge the attorney or client according to their difcretion 2 *G* 2 *c* 23 *f* 23

Provided, that the faid act fhall not extend to any bill of fees due from any attorney or folicitor, to an other attorney or folicitor or clerk in court, but they may ufe fuch remedies for the recovery thereof, as they might have done before the making of the faid act 12 *G* 2 *c* 13 *f* 6

31 In fome cafes the attorney himfelf fhall be liable to *In what cafe the attorney fhall pay cofts* pay cofts As in the cafe of the King and ——— *G.* 2. On fhewing caufe why an information fhould

be granted against Mr *Fielding*, for a misdemeanour in his office of a justice of the peace, the complaint appeared to be frivolous and vexatious, so that the justice ought to have the costs he had been put to in defending himself against it. The only question was, who should pay them —The complaint was made on a joint affidavit made by the prosecutor (one *Taylor*), and his attorney (Mr *Callaghan.*) Which attorney (as was proved on oath) had also declared, that if it should cost him 100l he would lay *Fielding* by the heels —It was strongly urged on the behalf of Mr *Callaghan*, that it would be a very great discouragement to attornies, in the course of their practice, if they were to be made personally liable to costs, in case their clients motions should not succeed, which motions they had engaged in, at the application of their clients, and upon facts represented to them by their clients, as being true and candidly stated, and which they themselves could not know or suspect to be otherwise and that it would be still more hard upon them, to do this without hearing what they could urge in their own defence —But the court were clear and unanimous, that in this case, they might and ought to do it, because Mr *Callaghan* not only appeared as prosecutor, by joining in the original affidavit of complaint, but had also expressly declared, that if it should cost him 100l he would lay Fielding by the heels. Therefore they discharged the rule, with costs, to be paid by Mr *Taylor* and Mr *Callaghan*. Burrow, Mansfield 654

Auction, duty on. See **Excise,**

Award.

IT is judged not foreign to the office of a keeper of the peace, to have some knowledge of the law contained under this title. Concerning which we will shew,

I What things may be submitted to arbitration
II The several kinds of submission to arbitration
III. The award, and therein what shall be deemed a good award, and what not.

I What

I *What things may be submitted to arbitration.*

1 It is held clearly, that all matters of controversy, either of fact, or of a right in things and actions personal and uncertain, may be submitted to arbitration 9 *Co* 78.

2 Matters of freehold, or any right and title to a freehold, cannot be submitted to arbitrament, for a freehold is not transferrable from one to another, without livery and seifin Yet if there be a submission concerning the right, title, or possession of lands and tenements, and the parties enter into mutual bonds, to stand to the award made relating to them, they forfeit their bonds unless they obey it. 1 *Roll Abr* 242, 244 *Read* Arb *Wood*, b. 4 c 3

So if the condition of an obligation is, to stand to an award touching lands, and the arbitrator awards the land to one, and that the other shall release to him if he doth not release, the obligation is forfeited 1 *Bac Abr* Arbitrament.

But if the arbitrator awards the land to one, it seems the obligation is not forfeited, tho' the other do not convey to him to make him a good title, for the arbitrator hath not awarded any act to be done by the party, and the award itself cannot transfer the right, and so must be void, and then the condition of the obligation cannot be forfeited for the awarding the land to one, cannot be expounded, that the other shall infeoff him *id*

And altho' there be no bond, yet if the arbitrator do award that the one shall infeoff the other, it seems that an action on the case may be maintained for not doing it for the award in itself is as good as if there were a bond, and then there is the same reason an action should lie, as that the condition of the obligation should be forfeited, for if such an award were void, then the condition of the obligation to perform it could not be broken *id.*

In like manner, an *annuity* is not determinable by award, for it is reckoned in nature of a freehold, and therefore cannot pass without the deed of the party *id*

So a *partition* cannot be made by award, for a freehold cannot pass (as was said) without livery and seifin *id*

It hath been doubted, whether leases for years, being *chattels real*, could be transferred by award, therefore it seems safest, when the controversy relates to these, that the party be bound in mutual obligations to perform the award, and then, if the arbitrators award, that one shall assign or transfer the lease to the other, if he refuseth, he forfeits his obligation *id*

3 3 Debts

Matters of record.

3 Debts on arrearages of accounts before auditors, shall not be discharged by award, because it appears of record, and must be discharged by matters of as high a nature 1 *Bac Abr.* Arbitrament.

Debts due by specialty

4 Debts due by specialty cannot be discharged by a bare award, but if the submission was by bond, the award would be a good bar, for one specialty may be dissolved by another. 1 *Bac Abr* Arbitrament

A thing certain

5. A certain and fixed debt is not discharged by an award, for the end and design of an arbitration is, to reduce uncertain debts and duties to a certainty and to award a man a certain debt, is to give him no more, nor do any greater thing for him, than was done before, for now he can have but an action, and that he might have before, and to give him less than he had before, is to do him a manifest injustice, which the arbitrator cannot do. 1 *Bac Abr* Arbitrament

But if 20 l be due to a man, and he and another submit all personal things to arbitration, there, if the arbitrator award 10 l it is a good award because there were other uncertain things submitted, and the arbitrator had consideration of all, and set one against the other in making the award, so as perhaps the debt of 20 l was diminished, in consideration of some trespasses done by him to the other party *id*

Criminal offences.

6 Criminal matters, as treasons, murders, felonies, and other offences indictable at the suit of the king, cannot be submitted to arbitrament, for it is for the good of the commonwealth, that such offenders be made known and punished and the king in such cases is a party, for whom the other parties cannot undertake And altho' the submission be by bond, yet the obligation is void, and the parties may be punished for entring into such bonds 1 *Bac Abr* Arbitrament

But if the party injured proceeds by way of action, as he may in assaults and batteries, libels, and the like, the damages he sustained or expects to recover, may be submitted to arbitration for in such case the action is for himself, and not for the king *Compleat Arbitrator* 28

Matrimonial cause.

7 Also matrimonial causes, or any thing concerning the contract or dissolution of marriage, cannot be submitted to arbitrament 1 *Roll's Abr* 252

But the damages a person sustained by a promise of marriage, or any thing relating to a marriage portion, may be submitted 16 *Ed.* 4 2

II. The

II. *The several kinds of submission to arbitration.*

1 A submission by *words* is good, and the party in whose favour the award is made, hath a remedy to enforce a performance of it Yet it is not expedient that any submission should be by parol, because the party may revoke it at pleasure, at any time before the award made, and that by word likewise, and the judges will rarely enforce the performance of an award, when either the submission or the award is by parol, because it lays so great a foundation for perjury *Compl Arb* 21 *By parol.*

2 Submission may also be by *covenant*, but this method is seldom used for tho' it contains the same certainty with a bond, yet the method of suing on a covenant is different, and more difficult than in suing on a bond *Compl Arb.* 7, 46 *By covenant.*

3 Submission by *rule of court* (A) is made in pursuance of the statute 9 & 10 *W c.* 15. which enacteth as follows *By rule of court.*

It shall be lawful for all merchants and traders, and others desiring to end any controversy, suit, or quarrel (for which there is no other remedy but by personal action, or suit in equity) by arbitration, to agree that their submission to the award or umpirage be made a rule of any of his majesty's courts of record, which the parties shall choose, and to insert such agreement in their submission, or the condition of the bond or promise, whereby they submit themselves Which agreement being so made, and inserted in their submission or promise, or condition of their respective bonds, shall or may, on producing an affidavit thereof, made by the witnesses thereunto, or any one of them, in the court of which the same is agreed to be made a rule, and reading and filing the said affidavit in court, be entred of record in such court, and a rule shall thereupon be made by the said court, that the parties shall submit to, and finally be concluded by such arbitration or umpirage, and in case of disobedience to such arbitration or umpirage, the party neglecting or refusing to perform the same, or any part thereof, shall be subject to all the penalties of contemning a rule of court, and the court on motion shall issue process accordingly, which process shall not be stopped or delayed in its execution, by any order of any other court of law or equity, unless it shall be made appear on oath to such court, that the arbitrators or umpire misbehaved themselves, and that such award was procured by corruption, or other undue means

And

And this is allowed to be the most expeditious way; and the method is to get a counsel to move in any of the courts to have it made a rule, which in such case is never denied and then the party is liable to the same penalties that he would be for disobeying any other rule of court. *Compl Abr* 6, 47

By bond 4 Or lastly, the submission may be by bond (B) In which case each party must give to the other a bond; which bond, and condition, must contain exactly the same words, only changing the names of the parties And the penalty of the bond should at least be the value of the thing submitted, so that the party may rather abide by the award, than forfeit his obligation *Compl. Abr* 46

And undoubtedly a submission by bond in some respects, exceeds a submission by rule of court for an award made pursuant to bonds of submission, may bind the parties executors, but if the party who refuses to perform an award made pursuant to a rule of court, shall die, the act of parliament directing, that the prosecution shall be carried on by attachment, the remedy being lost, the award is lost likewise *Compl Abr* 34

Both by bond and rule of court 5. Sometimes the submission is both by bond and rule of court, by adding the parties consent at the bottom of the condition of the bond, and this is still the best way, for then the party may proceed which way he pleases and it is said, that he may proceed both ways, that is, to say, both on the bond, and have an attachment likewise for the contempt. 1 *Salk* 73

Restriction against filing a bill in equity. 6 It hath been usual also of late years, to insert in the submission a clause that no bill in equity shall be filed against the arbitrators which restriction will be a bar against such bill being brought As in the case of *Lingood* and *Croucher, Aug.* 6, 1742, One condition of the submission was, that the parties should be restrained from preferring a bill in equity against the arbitrators And on a bill being brought, the submission was pleaded in bar And by the lord chancellor *Hardwicke* the plea must be allowed And he mentioned a case of one Mr *Robins* in lord chancellor *King's* time, who being appointed arbitrator by the court, accepted of it with a proviso that the parties would enter into a rule not to bring a bill in equity, which was done accordingly notwithstanding which, the party against whom the award was made brought a bill against the arbitrator, and charged corruption and partiality. Upon which Mr. *Robins* moved, that he might be struck out from being a party to the cause His lordship granted the motion, and said it would be a very great hardship

hardſhip upon arbitrators if they ſhould be haraſſed with ſuits, and the allowing them to be liable to ſuch ſuits would effectually diſcourage perſons of worth from accepting the office of arbitrators And therefore he ſtruck him out from being a party 2 *Atkyns*, 395.

7 But in which way ſoever the ſubmiſſion is made, the ſame nevertheleſs may be revoked, tho' made irrevocable by the ſtrongeſt words, for a man cannot by his own act, make ſuch authority or power not countermandable, which by the law and in its own nature is countermandable 8 *Co.* 82 *Whether the ſubmiſſion may be countermanded.*

But if the ſubmiſſion be by bond, if the party revokes, he forfeits his obligation, for that he hath broken the words of the condition, which are, that he ſhall ſtand to and abide the award And if he revokes, he muſt likewiſe give notice of the revocation, and if the ſubmiſſion was by bond, the revocation muſt be in writing 8 *Co.* 82

And if the ſubmiſſion be made a rule of court, purſuant to the act of parliament, if either of the parties revokes, the court will grant an attachment *Compl Arb* 82.

But if the ſubmiſſion be by word, the party may revoke at pleaſure, and he forfeits nothing, but he muſt in this caſe likewiſe give notice of the revocation, tho' it need not be in writing and the notice muſt be to the arbitrators themſelves. 8 *Co.* 82.

III. *The award* (C), *and therein what ſhall be deemed a good award, and what not*

1. The arbitrators cannot injoin an oath to the witneſſes, there being no law which gives them any ſuch power *Arbitrators cannot adminiſter an oath*

2 It is highly convenient that the award be in writing, and ſo to be mentioned in the ſubmiſſion. *Compl Arb* 34 *Award beſt to be in writing.*

3 By the 23 G 3 c 58. Every award in writing ſhall be on a 5 s ſtamp *And upon ſtamp*

4. One thing eſſential to a good award is, that it be made with reſpect to perſons and things, according to the ſubmiſſion. *Wood.* b 4. c. 3. *Award to be according to the ſubmiſſion.*

Upon which ground, as the arbitrators are, with reſpect to the things ſubmitted, circumſcribed and tied down to the ſubmiſſion, ſo in ſeveral caſes it has been diſputed, whether their awarding releaſes to the time of the award, and not to the time of the ſubmiſſion, was good, it is therefore moſt adviſable to award releaſes to the time of

VOL I.   K   the

the fubmiffion, tho' it is now clearly held, that general releafes fhall extend only to the time of the fubmiffion, and that if there be releafes awarded to the time of the award, they fhall be good, unlefs it be fhewn on the other fide, that fome new matter hath arifen between the parties between the fubmiffion and award. 1 *Roll Abr.* 242. 6 *Mod* 34

That is to fay, an award of releafes to the time of making the award, includes all that is within the fubmiffion, and more, which fhall be good for fo much as is within the fubmiffion, and void for the refidue. 1 *Baz. Abr* Arbitrament

If the fubmiffion be of *all matters in difference*, the arbitrators, in difputes between two partners, may diffolve the *partnerfhip.* As in the cafe of *Green* and *Waring*, 1 4 G 3. It was moved to fet afide an award between two partners, becaufe the arbitrator, amongft other particulars, had directed the partnerfhip to be diffolved, which, it was argued, was exceeding his power. But by the court, when all matters in difference were referred, he had clearly a power to diffolve it. If a difference between a mafter and apprentice were referred, the arbitrators would have a power to order the indentures to be delivered up. And although it was fworn, that at the trial of this caufe, when the rule of reference was drawn up generally in the ufual form, referring *all matters in difference*, the plaintiff openly declared, that he would not have underftood that the arbitrator had a power to diffolve the partnerfhip, lord *Mansfield* obferved, that this is fufficient evidence, from the party's own mouth, that the diffolution of the partnerfhip was then a *matter in difference*. And the rule for fetting afide the award was difcharged. *Blackftone's Reports,* 475

If the fubmiffion be, *fo as the award be ready to be delivered to the parties or to fuch of them as fhall defire the fame,* the parties fo bound are themfelves obliged to take notice of the award at their peril, but if the words of the fubmiffion be, *fo that the award be delivered to each party by fuch a day,* then it muft be delivered to each party accordingly. *Read Arb Wood b* 4. *c* 3

But tho' the words of the fubmiffion may be fuch, as will oblige the parties to take notice of the award at their peril, yet if the arbitrators award that one of the parties fhall do an act, which depends upon another firft to be done of the other party, he muft have notice of it, at leaft the party who would take advantage of it, muft fhew that he hath done what was neceffary on his part. *Comp. Art* 12.

An award that one shall pay for the writings of the award, or the reckoning in the house where the award was made, is a void award, for such things are plainly out of the submission. 1 *Roll Abr* 254

5 Also, it is required, that the award be beneficial, and appoint something advantageous to either party, for an award of one side only, is not good : so if an award be that one of the parties shall go to *Rome*, when it appears that there is no advantage to the other party by his going, it is void. *Wood b* 4 *c.* 3

So if a man and woman submit themselves to an award, it is no good award that they shall *intermarry*, for this is not intended any advantage. 1 *Roll Abr* 252 And the bodies of the parties are not submitted to arbitration. 1 *Bac Abr.* Arbitrament.

Where an award was, that the defendant should pay to the plaintiff two sums at several times, and that several releases should be given presently, it was objected, that by giving such releases the bond and money would be discharged, and therefore the awarding the release was void against the plaintiff, and so there is nothing of his side to be done. And of this opinion was the court. But where the award was, that money should be paid at two several days, and releases given, so that it appears by the very method and order of the award, that the general releases were not to be given till after the money paid, the court were clear of opinion, that it was well enough, and so judgment was given for the plaintiff. 2 *Mod* 169

6 Also it is required in a good award, that it be possible and lawful. *Wood. b.* 4 *c* 3

Thus, if an award be, that one of the parties shall kill, steal, forge a deed, or the like, it is void. 1 *Inst* 206

In like manner, if it be awarded, that money shall be paid to an infant, and that he shall make a release, it is void, for the infant's release is not good in law.

Also it is held, that where a thing is awarded to be done, which afterwards becomes impossible by the act of God, the party is excused, as if an award be, to deliver a horse before such a day, and he dies before that day. 21 *Ed.* 4 70.

7 Also it is required, that the award be certain and final. *Wood. b.* 4 *c.* 3

Upon which ground it hath been resolved, that if the arbitrators award, that one of the parties beg the other's pardon before such a mayor, or such and such persons, it is good and certain enough, but if the award be, that he shall beg pardon in such manner and in such place as the

oth.r

other party shall appoint, it is not good. for the arbitra tors are to determine, and not to make such party his own judge in his own cause And tho' the time and place be but circumstances, yet in this sort of satisfaction they make the most considerable part. 1 *Salk* 71

Upon which ground also, the arbitrators cannot regu larly reserve any thing for their future judgment, when the time allowed them is expired, for then such their award is not certain and final. *Cro. Jac* 585

An award that the defendant shall *give security* to the plaintiff, for payment of a sum of money, is void for the uncertainty, not shewing what security he should give, whether by bond or otherwise. *Cro Jac* 314

In the case of *Winter* and *Garlick*, T 3 An. it was awarded, that the defendant should pay to the plaintiff 10l and all the *costs* of a suit then depending in an inferior court, and afterwards to give mutual releases By the court An award to pay such costs as the master shall tax is good, because it may be reduced to a certainty, but this is uncertain, and carries it farther than has hitherto been allowed And *Holt* chief justice said, that it hath been held a good award, to pay such costs as the protho notary shall tax, and that carries it far enough, but that surely the arbitrators should either ascertain it themselves, or refer it to a proper officer 1 *Salk* 75. 6 *Mod* 195

But in the case of *Dudley* and *Nettleford*, H. 13 C. where it was awarded, that the plaintiff should pay the costs, and nobody was appointed to tax them, the court supplied it by ordering the master to do it *Str* 737

And in the case of *Hawkins* v *Colclough*, E. 30 G 2 Lord *Mansfield* said, that awards are now considered with greater latitude and less strictness, than they were for merly, and it is right that they should be so, because they are made by judges of the parties own chusing And this was in the case of an award made by a cobler, upon a submission of all disputes, which award was in these words, "Whereas there has been a suit at law between the parties, that has run to a great expence on both sides, and it being left to me to make an end of it I de termine that they shall each of them pay their own charges at law, and that the defendant pay the plaintiff 5 s, for his making the first breach in the law" And the award was held to be sufficiently certain and final. *Bur ton*, Mansfield 274

And in the case of *Lucas* and *Wilson*, M 32 G 1 lord *Mansfield* said, the court will not enter at all into the merits

ments of the matter referred to arbitration, but only take into consideration such legal objections as appear upon the face of the award, and such objections as go to the misbehaviour of the arbitrators. *Burrow*, Mansfield 701

And in the case of *Tittenson* and *Peat*, in the chancery, *July* 20, 1747, lord *Hardwicke* said, the only ground to impeach an award is collusion, or gross misbehaviour in the arbitrators or other, it is final and binding upon all parties, or else no persons would ever undertake to be arbitrators. And a plea of an award is good, not only to the merits of the case, but also to a discovery, for a defendant to the bill is not obliged to set out the whole account between him and the plaintiff after an award in his favour, for that it is conclusive to all the parties, till an error is shewn in taking the account, or partiality and improper behaviour in the arbitrators ——— And in another case, *July* 30, 1748, a bill was brought to set aside an award, and the arbitrator was made a party, and the bill sought a discovery from him of the grounds on which he made his award, and to set it forth minutely in his answer. But by lord *Hardwicke*, unless there is corruption or partiality in an arbitrator, the party cannot set aside his award; and if it should be allowed to make arbitrators defendants, and give them all this trouble to set forth the particular reasons upon which they founded their award, it would introduce very great inconvenience, and be a discouragement to any person to undertake a reference. If there was a palpable mistake made by an arbitrator, or miscalculation in an account that had been laid before him, the party aggrieved might bring his bill against the party in whose favour the award was made, to have it rectified, and not against the arbitrator. And his lordship said, he did not know whether there was any established rule of the court with regard to arbitrators setting forth the reasons of their award, and how far they were obliged to discover, and how far not, but if there was none, he should not scruple to make one, because it would be unreasonable to put an arbitrator to so much trouble and expence, as such an answer must necessarily give him. 3 *Atk* 529, 644

8. It is settled that arbitrators cannot proceed on a reference, after they have once named an umpire, for then their authority ceaseth, tho' the time for making the award is not expired. *Rep of Pract in C B* 116 *Danes and Monsay. E 8 G 2*

Arbitrator may not proceed, after appointing an umpire.

But the appointment of an umpire, before their own time for making an award is expired, may be good. As

in the cafe of *Doyley* and *Pitfoe*, *T* 28 *G* 2. An action
of debt was brought upon a bond, conditioned that the
parties fhould fubmit to the award of two arbitrator,
provided they made their award on or before the 13th of
March next, and if they made no award, then that they
fhould appoint an umpire before the 17th of the faid
March. The defendant pleaded, that no award was made
on or before the faid 13th day of March, but that they
did, before the faid 17th of March, to wit, upon the 11th,
chufe and appoint an umpire, who had made an award.
By the court. There are no words, which by any conftruction can be intended to limit or circumfcribe the election of an umpire till after the 13th of March. The
plain fenfe of the fubmiffion is, that they fhould make
their award by a certain day, or in cafe they did not
make it, or could not agree, that then they fhould nominate an umpire. And they faid, the court has not
been nice in conftruing the time of the umpire's appointment, provided it was foon enough for him to make his
award. M S.

L 4 *G* 3 *Soulfby* and *Hodgfon*. An action of debt
was brought upon an arbitration bond. The arbitrators
were to chufe an umpire, in cafe they themfelves fhould
not agree within a limited time. They did not agree
within the limited time, but chofe an umpire. The
umpire accordingly made an umpirage. And they joined
in it. The only queftion was, whether the umpirage
was duly made according to the power given to the
umpire. Or whether it was vitiated and rendered void, by
the arbitrators joining in it. The court were unanimous
and clear, That this was the umpirage of the umpire only.
He was at liberty to take what advice, or opinion, or af-
fiftants he pleafed, and the joining of the arbitrators was
only furplufage. *Bur Manff* 1474. *Black Rep* 463.

Award to be
conftrued to
vourable, except
in cafe of par-
tiality or corrup-
tion.

9. Generally (as is aforefaid) the award fhall be expounded according to the intent of the arbitrators, and
not literally, and fhall not be unravelled in a court of
equity, unlefs there was corruption in the arbitrators.

But in the cafe of corruption, or other unfair practice,
it is enacted by the aforefaid ftatute of 9 & 10 *W* c. 15.
that any arbitration or umpirage procured by corruption
or undue means, fhall be deemed void, and accordingly
be fet afide by any court of law or equity, fo as complaint
thereof be made in the court where the rule is made, before the laft day of the next term after publifhing the arbitration. § 2.

But otherwife, as the arbitrators are perfons of the parties own chufing, and as the law prefumes that every man
will

will be fo wife as to pitch upon a perfon whofe underftanding and honefty he can rely on, it hath feldom happened, that an award was held void when there appeared
nothing elfe to vitiate it yet awards have been, and
are often fet afide in a court of equity, for corruption and
want of underftanding in the arbitrators. *Compl Arb* 73

Therefore it is the intereft of both parties, to chufe men
of honefty and underftanding to be their arbitrators, and
to acquaint them truly with the facts they are to go upon
for if they appear to be miftaken in a matter of fact, a
court of equity will fet afide the award 2 *Vern.* 705

So if the arbitrators, or any of them, appear to have
been deceived As where certain articles were fhewn
only to one of the arbitrators, and he to whom they
were not fhewn fwore that if he had feen them, he be-
lieved he fhould not have made fuch an award For in
fuch cafe, the award (according to the expreffion in the
ftatute) is procured by *undue means* 1 Atkyns, 64

If a fubmiffion is to three arbitrators, or any two of
them, and two of them by fraud or force will exclude
the other, that alone is fufficient to vitiate the award
or if they have private meetings, and admit one of the
parties, but give no notice to the other, but fuffer the attorney of the party whom they admitted, to draw up the
award, fuch award fhall be fet afide for partiality and un-
fairnefs 2 *Vern* 514

It is a general rule in equity, that when it appears that
any one of the arbitrators was any way *interefted* in the
matters in controverfy, the award is to be fet afide *Compl.
Arb.* 75.

And it is the ftrongeft argument of partiality, to fhew
that the arbitrators received from either of the parties any
confiderable fum of money, or any other prefent which
may be a temptation to act corruptly, but the fum or prefent muft be proved to be fo exorbitant, as to induce the
court to believe that it biaffed their judgments, otherwife
it will be of no effect *Compl Arb* 76

In the cafe of *Shepherd* and *Brand*, T 7 G 2 On a
rule to fhew caufe why an award fhould not be fet afide,
one exception was, that before making the award, the
arbitrators infifted upon three guineas apiece to be paid
to them by each of the parties for their trouble and expences, that the defendant refufed doing it on his part,
upon which the plaintiff paid the whole money By the
court, Where arbitrators, let their characters be otherwife
never fo unexceptionable, take money of one of the parties fingly, whether for charges or any thing elfe, before

making

making their award, as this is a matter of so tender a nature that even the appearance of evil is to be avoided, and this practice may be of dangerous example, it is sufficient cause to set aside the award, for if this should be suffered, it will be hard to distinguish what is corruption. 2 *Barnardist.* 463 *Cases in the time of lord Hardwicke,* 54

In the case of *Lingood* and *Croucher* above mentioned, lord *Hardwicke* said he remembered an instance in a famous case of *John Ward,* who being a party in a cause where one *John Warner* was an arbitrator, upon *Ward's* coming into the room he said, I *John Warner* will make you *John Ward* pay costs *Ward* complained to the court of this partial behaviour in the arbitrator, and the court inverted *Warner's* threats, for they made *Warner* pay costs to *John Ward* 2 Atk 396

Where the award appoints no time, the thing is to be done immediately.

10 If the arbitrators award a thing to be done, it may be proper for them to appoint a time and place for the doing of it, and the party who would take advantage of it, must shew that he has done what was requisite on his part. but if a thing is to be done generally, without mentioning time and place, it shall be done immediately, 2 *Brown* 311.

Demand to be before attachment

11 If the submission is by rule of court, it is necessary that there be a personal demand of the thing awarded, and the party must make affidavit of such demand, before he can have an attachment 1 *Salk* 83

On tender and refusal, the party refusing shall nevertheless sign a release

12. If a sum of money be awarded to one of the parties, and that upon the payment thereof they both shall give mutual releases, if he who is to receive the money, refuses it, yet upon a tender and refusal, he is as much obliged to sign a release as if he actually received it. 1 *Salk.* 75.

A Form of a submission by rule of court.

WHEREAS *divers disputes and controversies have arisen, and are now depending, between A. B of —— in the county of —— yeoman, of the one part, and C D of —— in the said county, yeoman, of the other part, Now for the ending and deciding thereof, it is hereby mutually agreed by and between the said parties, that all matters in difference between them shall be referred and submitted to the arbitrament, final end, and determination of A A of —— in the said county, gentleman, B A of —— in the said county, yeoman, and C A. of —— in the said county, yeoman, or any two of them, arbitrators indifferently elected by the said parties, so as the said arbitrators, or any two of them, do make and publish their award in writing ready to be delivered to the said parties, or such of them as shall desire the same, on or before the ——— day of ——— next ensuing the date hereof· And it is hereby mutally agreed by and between the said parties, that this submission shall be made a rule of his majesty's court of k ng's bench at* Westminster *In witness whereof the said parties to these presents have hereunto set their hands this ——— day of ——— in the ——— year,* &c

B. Arbitration bond.

KNOW *all men by these presents, that I A. B. of ——— in the county of ——— gentleman, am held and firmly* bound *to* C D *of ——— in the said county of ——— yeoman, in ——— pounds of good and lawful money of* Great Britain, *to be paid to the said* C. D *or to his certain attorney, his executors, administrators, or assigns To which payment well and truly to be made, I bind myself, my heirs, executors and administrators, firmly by these presents, sealed with my seal, and dated the ——— day of ——— in the ——— year of the reign of our sovereign lord* George *the third, of* Great Britain, France *and* Ireland, *king, defender of the faith, and so forth, and in the year of our Lord* ———.

Condition to stand to the award of two arbitrators, in common form·

THE *condition of the above obligation is such, that if the above bound* A B, *his heirs, executors, and administrators, and every of them, for and on his and their parts and behalfs, do and shall well and truly stand to, obey, abide, perform, observe and keep the award, order, arbitrament, final end and determination of* A A. *of ——— esquire, and* B A. *of ——— gentleman, arbitrators indifferently named, elected, and chosen, as well for and on the part and behalf of the above-bound* A B *as of the above named* C D *to arbitrate, award, order, adjudge and determine of and concerning all and all manner of action and actions, cause and causes of action and actions, suits, bills, bonds, specialties, judgments, executions, extents, accounts, debts, dues, sum and sums of money, quarrels, controversies, trespasses, damages and demands whatsoever, both in law and equity, or otherwise howsoever, which at any time or times heretofore have been had, made, moved, brought, commenced, sued, prosecuted, committed, omitted, done or suffered by or between the said parties, so as the said award be made in writing, and ready to be delivered to the said parties, on or before the ——— day of ——— now next ensuing , [and* *if the said A. B his heirs, executors, or administrators, or any of them, shall not prefer or cause to be preferred, any bill in equity against the said A. A. and B. A. or either of them, for or concerning their award in the premises ,*] *Then this obligation to be void, otherwise of force*

If the parties have a mind to make their submission a rule of court, then this may be added

And the abovebound A B doth agree and desire, that this his submission be made a rule of his majesty's court of king's bench at Westminster, *pursuant to the act of parliament in such case made and provided.*

Condition to stand to the award of three arbitrators, or any two of them, and an umpire appointed

THE *condition of this obligation is such, that if the above-bound A B his heirs, executors, and administrators, for and on his and their parts and behalfs, shall and do well and truly stand to, obey, abide, observe, perform, fulfil, and keep the award, order, arbitrament, final end and determination of* ———— *or any two of them, arbitrators indifferently elected and named, as well by and on the part and behalf of the said A B as by and on the part and behalf of the above named C D to arbitrate, award, order, judge and determine, of and concerning all and all manner of action and actions, cause and causes of action and actions, suits, bills, bonds, specialties, covenants, contracts, promises, accounts, reckonings, sums of money, judgments, executions, extents, quarrels, controversies, trespasses, damages and demands whatsoever, at any time heretofore had, made, moved, brought, commenced, sued, prosecuted, done, suffered, committed, or depending by or between the said parties, so as the award of the said arbitrators, or any two of them, be made and set down in writing, under their or any two of their hands and seals, ready to be delivered to the said parties in difference, on or before the* ———— *day of* ———— *now next ensuing, then this obligation to be void, otherwise of force*

And if the said arbitrators shall not make such their award of and concerning the premises, within the time limited as aforesaid, then if the said A. B. his heirs, executors, and administrators, for and on his and their part and behalf, do and shall well and truly stand to, observe, perform, fulfil and keep the award, determination, and umpirage [if the umpire be named] *of* ———— *being a person indifferently named and chosen between the said parties for umpire,* [if not named] *of such*

person

person as the said arbitrators shall indifferently chuse for umpire
in and concerning the premisses, so as the said umpire do make
and set down his award and umpirage in writing, under his
hand and seal, ready to be delivered to the said parties in difference, on or before the ———— day of ———— now next ensuing, and if the said A. B. his heirs, executors, or administrators,
or any of them, shall not prefer, or cause to be preferred, any
bill in equity, against them the said arbitrators and umpire, or
any of them, for or concerning the award of them the said arbitrators or umpire in the premisses Then this obligation to be
void, otherwise of force

[And the abovebound A. B. doth agree and desire, that this
his submission be made a rule of his majesty's court of king's
bench at Westminster, pursuant to the act of parliament in
such case made]

C Form of an award.

TO all to whom these presents shall come, we A B of
———— and C D of ———— do send greeting
Whereas there are several accounts depending, and divers
controversies have arisen, between ———— of ———— yeoman,
of the one part, and ———— of ———— yeoman, of the other
part, And whereas, for the putting an end to the said differences, they the said ———— and ———— by their several bonds
or obligations bearing date ———— last past, are reciprocally
become bound each to the other, in the penal sum of ———— to
stand to, abide, perform, and keep the award, order and final
determination of us the said ———— so as the said award be
made in writing and ready to be delivered to the parties in difference on or before ———— next ensuing, as by the said obligations and conditions thereof may appear Now know ye, that
we the said arbitrators, whose names are hereunto subscribed,
and seals affixed, taking upon us the burden of the said award,
and having fully examined and duly considered the proofs and
allegations of both the said parties, do make and publish this
our award between the said parties in manner following, that is
to say, First, we do award and order, that all actions, suits,
quarrels and controversies whatsoever, had, moved, arisen, and
depending between the said parties in law or equity, for any
manner of cause whatsoever touching the said premisses, to the
day of the date hereof, shall cease and be no further prosecuted,
and that each of the said parties shall pay and bear his own
costs and charges in any wise relating to, or concerning the
premisses And we do also award and order, that the said
———— shall deliver or cause to be delivered to the said ————
at ———— within the space of ———— &c. And further, we
do

do hereby award and order, that the said——shall on or before——pay or cause to be paid unto the said——the sum of——We do also award and order, &c And lastly, We do award and order, that the said——and——on payment of the said sum of——shall in due form of law, execute each to the other of them, or to the other's use, general releases, sufficient in the law for the releasing by each to the other of them, his heirs, executors and administrators, of all actions, suits, arrests, quarrels, controversies, and demands whatsoever, touching or concerning the premisses aforesaid, or any matter or thing thereunto relating, from the beginning of the world, until the——day of——last past (viz the day of the date of the arbitration bonds) In witness whereof we have hereunto set our hands and seals the—— day of——

Witnesses hereof,
A B.
C D.

Form of an umpirage.

(R'ECITE the arbitration bonds, as before) *Now know ye, that I——umpire indifferentl, chosen by ——having deliberately heard and understood the griefs, allegations, and proofs of both the said parties, and willing (as much as in me lieth) to set the said parties at unity and good accord, do by these presents arbitrate, award, order, decree, and judge as followeth, That is to say, &c.*

Backing a warrant. See **Warrant.**

Bail.

I. *What it is.*
II. *Difference between bail and mainprise.*
III *When a person may be discharged without bail.*
IV. *Who may or may not be bailed.*
V. *Who may bail, and the manner of it.*
VI. *Requiring excessive bail.*
VII. *Denying bail where it ought to be granted.*
VIII. *Granting bail where it ought to be denied.*
IX *Of bail by writ of* habeas corpus.
X. *Acknowledging bail in another man's name*
I. *What*

I. What it is.

BAIL (from the French *bailler*, to deliver) signifies the delivery of a man out of custody, upon the undertaking of one or more persons for him, that he shall appear at a day limited, to answer and be justified by the law. *Hale's Pl* 96

II. Difference between bail and mainprise.

The difference between bail and mainprise is, that mainpernors are only surety, but bail is a custody, and therefore the bail may retake the prisoner, if they doubt he will fly, and detain him, and bring him before a justice, and the justice ought to commit the prisoner in discharge of the bail, or put him to find new sureties. *Hale's Pl* 96.

III. Where a person may be discharged without bail.

If a person be brought before a justice, if it appears that no felony is committed, he may discharge him, but if a felony be committed, tho' it appears not that the party accused is guilty, yet he cannot discharge him, but must commit or bail him *Hale's Pl.* 98.

IV. Who may or may not be bailed.

At the common law, bail was allowed in all cases but homicide, but now the statute of the 3 *Ed* 1 *c.* 15 directeth what offenders shall be bailed, and what not. *Hale's Pl* 97

It is true the said statute only prescribeth who shall or shall not be let to bail by the *sheriff*, but by the 1 & 2 *P & M. c.* 13 it is enacted that no justice or justices of the peace shall let to bail or mainprise any person not replevisable by the said statute of 3 *Ed* 1. *c* 15.

Which statute is as follows *Forasmuch as sheriffs and others, which have taken and kept in prison persons detected of felony, and incontinent have let out by replevin such as were not replevisable, and have kept in prison such as were replevisable, because they would gain of the one party and grieve the other, and forasmuch as before this time it was not determined which persons were replevisable, and which not, but only those that were taken for the death of a man, or by commandment of the king, or his justices, or for the forest. It is provided, that*

such

such prisoners as before were outlawed, and they which have abjured the realm, provors, and such as be taken with the manner, and those which have broken the king's prison, thieves openly defamed and known, and such as be appealed by provors so long as the provors be living (if they be not of good name), and such as be taken for houseburning feloniously done, or for false money, or for counterfeiting the king's seal, or persons excommunicate taken at the request of the bishop, or for manifest offences, or for treason touching the king himself, shall be in no wise replevisable by the common writ, nor without writ. But such as be indicted of larceny by inquests taken before sheriffs or bailiffs by their office, or of light suspicion, or for petit larceny that amounteth not above the value of 12d if they were not guilty of some other larceny aforetime, or guilty of receipt of felons, or of commandment or force or of aid in felony done, or guilty of some other trespass for which one ought not to lose life nor member, and a man appealed by a provor after the death of the provor (if he be no common thief nor defamed), shall from henceforth be let out by sufficient surety, whereof the sheriff will be answerable, and that without giving ought of their goods

Sheriffs and others] That is to say, sheriffs and gaolers that have custody of gaols, so that this act extends not to any of the king's justices or judges of any superior courts of justice 2 *Inst* 185. But by a subsequent statute (as hath been said) it is extended to justices of the peace

But only those, &c] Here are first set down four sorts of persons which before this act were not bailable by the common writ *de homine replegiando*

1. *Those that were taken for the death of a man*] By the ancient law of the land, in all cases of felony, if the party accused could find sufficient sureties, he was not to be committed to prison, but afterwards it was provided by parliament, that in case of homicide the offender was not bailable. 2 *Inst* 186

And even if a person have dangerously wounded another, the justice ought to be very cautious how he takes bail, till the year and day be past, for if the party die, and the offender appear not, he is in danger of being severely fined 1 *Haw* 138

And this statute makes no distinction between such homicide as is malicious, and that which happens by misadventure or in self-defence and it seems agreed, that justices of the peace, who have power at this day to bail a man arrested for a *light suspicion* of homicide, cannot bail any

any such person for manslaughter, or even excusable homicide, if it manifestly appear that he was guilty of the fact, let it be ever so plain that it cannot amount to murder. 2 *Haw* 95, 105

2 *Or by commandment of the king*] That is, by matter of record in one of his courts, according to law, and not an *extrajudicial* commandment 2 *Inst* 186, 187. So also it is provided in the petition of rights 3 *Car.* that no person shall be detained in prison by the king's special command, without cause certified

And because some courts, as the king's bench, are before the king, and some before his justices, therefore the act saith, *by commandment of the king*, and the next words be, *or of his justices* 2 Inst 186

3 *Or of his justices*] That is, of any of the courts of *Westminster*, or justices of assize 2 *Haw* 96

4. *Or for the forest*] But as to imprisonment for offences in forests, the law hath been much mitigated by later statutes 2 *Haw* 98

All these four are excepted out of the common writ. *de homine replegiando*, that the sheriff in his county court, which is not a court of record, shall not replevy any of these four that are committed, altho' it should be by an unlawful commitment, but the superior courts at *Westminster*, upon an *habeas corpus*, shall do justice to the party in all these four cases. 2 *Inst* 187.

Next the act doth further provide, that these kinds of prisoners hereafter following (being 13 in number) shall not be replevisable.

1. *Such prisoners as before were outlawed*] Persons outlawed are *attainted* in law, and therefore are not bailable, for the intendment of the law is, that the person standeth indifferent whether he be guilty or no, and not if he be convicted or attained 2 *Inst* 188

2 *And they which have abjured the realm*] For these also are attainted upon their own confession, and therefore not bailable at all by law 2 *Inst* 188.

3 *Provors*] A provor, or *approver*, is a person that confesseth the felony with which he is charged, and undertakes to *prove* another guilty of the same crime, which if he does, he faves his own life, otherwise he shall be immediately executed And the reason why they are not bailable is, because they are guilty by their own confession, and therefore they do not stand indifferent. 2 *Inst.* 188

2

But

But this concerns not justices of the peace, because no man can become an approver before them, for that they cannot assign a coroner. *Hale's Pl.* 102.

4. *And such as be taken with the manner*] For in this case likewise, he standeth not indifferent whether he be guilty or no, being taken with the *mainer*, that is, with the thing stolen as it were in his *hand*, anciently called *hand-habbend*, and the like was anciently called *backberend*, as a bundle or fardle at his *back*, which was used to signifiy manifest theft   2 *Inst* 188

5. *And those which have broken the king's prison*] Here are two offences, first his breaking of the prison, for it is presumed that he who is innocent will never break prison and secondly, his flying, because he confesseth the fact who flies from judgment   2 *Inst.* 188.

6 *Thieves openly defamed and known*] Who, as it seems, ought not to be bailed for any fresh felony, whereof there is probable evidence against them   But this seems in a great measure to be left at the discretion of the person who has power to bail them, who on consideration of the circumstances of the whole matter, and the probabilities on both sides, if he finds it reasonable strongly to presume them to be guilty, ought not to bail but commit them. 2 *Haw.* 99.

7 *Such as be appealed by provors so long as the provors be living (if they be not of good name)*] The appeal of the approver is forcible against the appellee, because the approver confesseth himself guilty of the same felony, and therefore it serveth in nature of an indictment against the appellee, so long as the approver liveth, unless the appellee be of good fame   2 *Inst* 188.

8 *And such as be taken for housebuilding feloniously done*] This was felony by the common law   2 *Inst.* 188

9. *Or for false money*] This was treason by the common law. 2 *Inst* 188

10 *Or for counterfeiting the king's seal*] This was also treason by the common law   2 *Inst* 188.

11. *Or persons excommunicate taken at the request of the bishop*] That is, he that is certified into the chancery by the bishop to be excommunicated, and after is taken by force of the king's writ of *excommunicato capiendo*, is not bailable · For in ancient times men were excommunicated but for heresies, or other heinous causes of ecclesiastical cogni-

cognizance, and not for small or petty causes, and therefore in those cases the party was not bailable by the sheriff or gaoler without the king's writ but if the party offered sufficient caution *de parendo mandatis ecclesiæ in forma juris*, then should the party have the king's writ to the bishop to accept his caution, and to cause him to be delivered And if the bishop will not send to the sheriff to deliver him, then shall he have a writ out of the chancery to the sheriff for his delivery Or if he be excommunicated for a temporal cause, or for a matter whereof the ecclesiastical court hath no cognizance, he shall be delivered by the king's writ without any satisfaction. 2 *Inst* 189

12. *For manifest offences*] Which seems to be understood of inferior crimes of an enormous nature under the degree of felony, as dangerous riots, exorbitant rescoufes, misprifon of treafon, præmunire, and such like heinous offences Yet it seems to be in a great measure left to discretion, to judge in what cases their crime is so flagrant and enormous, that they ought not to have the benefit of it 2 *Haw* 99

13 *Or for treafon touching the king himself*] By the common law, a man accufed or indicted of high treafon, or of any felony whatsoever, was bailable upon good surety, until he were convicted, for at common law, the gaol was his pledge or surety, that could find none. 2 *Inst.* 189

Shall be in no wise replevifable by the common writ, nor without writ] That is, the sheriff shall not replevy them by the common writ *de homine replegiando*, nor without writ, that is, *ex officio* But all or any of these may be bailed in the king's bench 2 *Inst.* 189

Next the act setteth down feven kinds of offenders that may be bailed

1 *Such as be indicted of larceny by inquefts taken before sheriffs or bailiffs*] That is before sheriffs in their torns, or lords in their leets, or those that have *infangthief* and *outfangthief*; that is, who have the privilege to judge thieves taken *within* their fee, or thieves dwelling within their manor and taken for felony *out* of their fee. Yet this is expounded that they be of good fame 2 *Inst.* 190.

2 *Or of light fufpicion*] But if the prefumption be ftrong, or the defamation great, the justices may refufe to bail him *Hale's Pl* 102. And this is expounded also that they be of good fame. 2 *Inst* 190.

3. *Or for petit larceny that amounteth not above the value of 12d if they were not guilty of some other larceny aforetime]* This act divideth larceny into two kinds, grand larceny, when the thing stolen is above the value of 12d, and petit larceny when it is of the value of 12d or under   2 *Inst* 189

And it seems to be agreed, that there is no necessity that such persons be of good fame, yet upon the construction of the whole statute, if such persons be taken with the manner, or confess the fact, or their crime be otherwise open and manifest, it seems that they ought not to be bailed, but where there be any colour of probability for their innocence, it seems most agreeable to the intention of the statute to bail them   2 *Hawk* 101

4. *Or guilty of receipt of felons]* These are accessaries after the fact   2 *H H* 100

5. *Or of commandment or force or of aid in felony done]* These are accessaries before the fact   2 *H H* 100

But accessaries to felonies are not to be bailed, unless they be of good reputation   And it seems at this day to be settled, that where there are strong presumptions of guilt, such accessaries are not bailable by this statute   2 *Haw* 102

6. *Or guilty of some other trespass for which one ought not to lose life nor member,]* But it seems reasonable to qualify the generality of this expression, with this limitation, that such accusation ought to be either on a light suspicion, or else that the offence be inconsiderable, or that it be not excluded from bail by some special act of parliament   2 *Haw.* 99.   2 *H H* 135

7. *And a man appealed by a provor after the death of the provor if he be no common thief nor defamed]* And by parity of reason, he may be bailed, if the approver waive his appeal, or be vanquished   2 *Haw* 98

Be let out by sufficient surety] If a justice take insufficient surety, and the party appear not, he is finable by the judge of assize   *H P* 97   But if the prisoner appear thereupon, the justice is safe   2 *Haw* 89

And if a person who has power to take bail, be so far imposed upon, as to suffer a prisoner to be bailed by insufficient persons, it is said that either he, or any other person who hath power to bail him, may require the party to find better sureties, and to enter into a new recognizance with them, and may commit him on his refusal, for that insufficient sureties are no sureties   2 *Haw* 89

And

And the perſon who is to take the bail, may examine them on their oaths concerning their ſufficiency   *2 Haw.* 89 *2 H H.* 125.

It is to be obſerved, that the above ſtatute extends only to bail in criminal offices, and therefore gives no power at all to juſtices of the peace to bail any perſons on proceſs in civil actions, or for contempts to ſuperior courts *2 Haw* 106

There are furthermore many ſtatutes, which prohibit bail and mainpriſe in very many caſes, and allow the ſame in many others, which are interſperſed among the ſeveral titles which treat of thoſe matters

And where a ſtatute ordaineth, that an offender ſhall be impriſoned at the king's will or pleaſure, there the priſoner cannot be bailed, till he hath redeemed his liberty by ſuch fine or ranſom as ſhall be aſſeſſed by the king's juſtices in his courts   *Dalt. c* 167

Altho' a perſon be committed to be detained without bail or mainpriſe, yet if the offence be by law bailable, he that hath power of bailing may bail him. *2 H H* 135

V. Who may bail, and the manner of it.

By the common law, the ſheriff and every conſtable, being conſervators of the peace, might have bailed one ſuſpected of felony, but this authority is transferred from them to the juſtices of the peace by ſeveral ſtatutes. *Lamb.* 15

And it ſeems to be a good general rule, that ſo far as any perſons are judges of any crime, ſo far they have power of bailing a perſon indicted before them of ſuch crime And upon this ground it ſeems clear that any two juſtices (1 *Q*) may of common right bail perſons indicted at the ſeſſions, for that any two ſuch juſtices may hear and determine the indictment. Alſo it hath been holden, that any one juſtice hath the like power, and this ſeems to be implied by the ſtatute of 1 *R.* 3 *c* 3. which giving one juſtice power of bailing perſons arreſted for felony, *in like form as if ſuch perſon had been indicted at the ſeſſions,* clearly ſuppoſes, that if ſuch perſons had been indicted at the ſeſſions, they might have been bailed by any one juſtice   And if any one juſtice had ſuch power, before the ſtatute ſpecially relating to the power of juſtices in granting bail, it ſeems that he hath ſtill the ſame power in relation to perſons ſo indicted of any bailable crime under the degree of *felony,* becauſe the ſaid ſtatutes ſeem not to reſtrain him in any ſuch caſe, under the degree of

L 2

felony,

felony, from any power which he lawfully might claim before. 2 *Haw* 103

But it feems difficult to maintain the power of one juftice to bail a perfon, for any crime *before* indictment, unlefs by fome ftatute it be limited to the conufance of one juftice, or unlefs it be an offence directly tending to the breach of the peace, the bailing of perfons for which feems properly to come under their conufance as confervators of the peace 2 *Haw* 105

And Mr *Dalton* fays, if it is not in cafe of felony, it feemeth that any one juftice alone may bail a prifoner, except where it is otherwife ordered in particular inftances by fome fpecial ftatute *Dalt c* 12

And it feems to be agreed, that any one juftice might always in his difcretion either bail or imprifon one who has given another a dangerous wound, according as it fhall appear from the whole circumftances that the party is moft likely to live or die, for that every fuch juftice being a principal confervator of the peace, the offence at prefent being only an enormous breach thereof, and no felony, feems properly to come under his conufance 2 *Haw* 103.

But by 1 & 2 *P & M c* 13 *If a perfon be arrefted for manflaughter or felony, or fufpicion thereof, being bailable by law, he fhall not be let to bail or mainprife by any juftices, but in open feffions, except it be by two juftices at the leaft (1 Q) and the fame to be prefent together at the time of the faid bailment Which bail they fhall certify in writing fubfcribed or figned with their own hands, at the next general gaol delivery to be holden within the county where the perfon fhall be arrefted or fufpected*

And the faid juftices, or one of them, being of the quorum, when any fuch prifoner is brought before them, for any manflaughter or felony, before any bailment, fhall take the examination of the faid prifoner, and information of them that bring him, of the fact and circumftances thereof, and the fame or as much thereof as fhall be material to prove the felony, fhall put in writing before they make the bailment Which examination together with the bailment, the faid juftices fhall certify at the next general gaol delivery to be holden within the limits of their commiffion

And the faid juftices fhall have power to bind all fuch by recognizance as do declare any thing material to prove the offence, to appear at the next general gaol delivery to give evidence againft the party on his trial And fhall certify the fame in like manner

And any juftice offending contrary to this act, fhall on due proof by examination, be fined by the judges of affize.

But

But in London, Middlesex, *and in other cities and towns corporate, justices may let prisoners to bail, as they might before this act, but when they do bail, they are to take and certify the bail and examination as is here directed.*

VI. *Requiring excessive bail.*

By the declaration of rights 1 *W sess* 2 *c* 2. excessive bail ought not to be required

VII *Denying bail where it ought to be granted.*

To refuse bail where the party ought to be bailed (the party offering the same) is a misdemeanor punishable not only by the suit of the party, but also by indictment. 2 *Haw* 90. *H P.* 97

VIII. *Granting bail where it ought to be denied.*

Admitting bail where it ought not, is punishable by the judges of assize by fine, or punishable as a negligent escape at common law. *H P.* 97.

If the keeper of a prison bail any not bailable, he shall lose his fee and office, if another officer, he shall have three years imprisonment, and make fine at the king's pleasure. 3 *Ed.* 1 *c* 15

M 18 *G* 2 *K.* and *William Clarke,* esquire He as a justice of *Surry* committed a man on suspicion of stealing a mare, and bound over the owner to prosecute. Afterwards upon examining two other persons, he admitted the party to bail The prosecutor appeared at the assizes, and found a bill, but the party accused did not appear. And the court granted an information against the justice, declaring they should not have bailed the man themselves. *Str* 1216

IX. *Of bail by writ of* habeas corpus.

If bail cannot otherwise be obtained, the law hath provided a remedy in most cases by the *habeas corpus* act 31 *C* 2 *c* 2 The substance of which is briefly thus

If the commitment is for treason or felony plainly and specially expressed in the warrant of commitment, also if any person is committed and charged as accessary before the fact to any petty treason or felony, or upon suspicion thereof, or with suspicion of petty treason or felony, which petty treason or felony shall be plainly and specially expressed in the warrant of commitment in such cases the person shall not be bailed on a writ of habeas corpus, otherwise he may be bailed.

Also if a person is committed for treason or felony specially expressed, yet if he shall in open court the first week of the term, or first day of assize, petition to be tried, and shall not be indicted some time in the next term or assize after the commitment, he shall upon motion the last day of the term or assize, be bailed, unless it shall appear to the judge upon oath that the king's witnesses could not be produced within that time, and then if he is not tried in the second term or assize, he shall be discharged.

Previous to the aforesaid bailment, the prisoner or some person on his behalf, shall demand of the officer or keeper, a true copy of the warrant of commitment, which he shall deliver in six hours, on pain of 100l. to the party grieved for the first offence, and 200l. and forfeiture of his office for the second.

This application is to be made in writing, by the prisoner or any person for him, attested and subscribed by two witnesses who were present at the delivery thereof, to the court of chancery, king's bench, common pleas, or exchequer, or if out of term time, to the lord chancellor or one of the judges, and a copy of the warrant of commitment shall be produced before them, or oath made that such copy was denied.

But if any person hath wilfully neglected by the space of two terms to apply for his enlargement, he shall not have a habeas corpus granted in the vacation.

This being done, the lord chancellor, or judges respectively, shall award an habeas corpus under the seal of the court, a pain of 500l. to be marked in this manner, Per statutum tricesimo primo Caroli secundi regis, and signed by the person that awards the same; and shall be directed to the officer or keeper, returnable immediate.

And the charges of bringing the prisoner shall be ascertained by the judge or court that awarded the writ, and indorsed thereon, not exceeding 12 d. a mile.

Then the writ shall be served on the keeper, or left at the gaol with any of the under-officers, and the charges so indorsed, shall be paid or tendred to him, and the prisoner shall give bond to pay the charges of carrying him back if he shall be remanded, and that he will not make any escape by the way.

This done, the officer shall within three days after service (if it is within twenty miles) return the writ, and bring the body, and shall then likewise certify the true cause of the imprisonment, if above twenty miles and less than an hundred, then within ten days, if above an hundred, then within twenty days, on like pain as before.

But after the assizes are proclaimed for the county where the prisoner is detained, he shall not be removed.

Then

Then if it shall appear to the said lord chancellor or judges, that the prisoner is detained on a legal process, order, or warrant, out of some court that hath jurisdiction of criminal matters, or by warrant of a judge or justice of the peace for matters for which by law he is not bailable, in such case the prisoner shall not be discharged.

If he shall be discharged, he shall thereupon enter into recognizance to appear on his trial, and the writ, and return thereof, and recognizance shall be certified into the court where the trial must be.

But persons charged in debt, or other action, or with process in any civil cause, after their discharge for a criminal offence, shall be kept in custody for such other suit.

And persons so set at large, shall not be recommitted for the same offence, unless by order of court, on pain of 500 l, to the party grieved.

Two things I shall observe upon this statute.

1 That altho' the constable by his own authority, without any warrant of commitment, may carry offenders to gaol, and this was the method of securing prisoners, before there were any justices of the peace, yet since the institution of the office of justices of the peace, it is better that they be carried before a justice, to be sent by him to gaol by warrant of commitment, otherwise they have a right to be bailed upon this act, whatever the offence may be.

2 That the warrant of commitment ought to set forth the cause specially, that is to say not for treason, or felony in general, but treason *for counterfeiting the king's coin,* or felony *for stealing the goods of such a one to such a value,* and the like; that so the court may judge thereupon, whether or no the offence is such, for which a prisoner ought to be admitted to bail.

X *Acknowledging bail in another man's name.*

By the 21 J c 26 *If any person shall acknowledge, or procure to be acknowledged, any bail in the name of any other not privy to the same, he shall be guilty of felony, without benefit of clergy.*

In the name of any other] T 6 G Two people put in bail in feigned names, and because there were no such persons, they could not be prosecuted for personating bail on this statute. So the court ordered them and the attorney to be set in the pillory, which was done accordingly. *Str.* 384.

Bail taken before a judge is not within this statute, till it be filed of record 1 *H H* 696 But it is within the following statute of 4 *W c* 4 by which it is enacted, that *any who shall personate another before those who have authority to take bail, so as to make him liable to the payment of any sum of money in that suit or action, shall be guilty of felony* (but within clergy)

Form of bail.

Westmorland   BE it remembred, that on the —— day of —— in the —— year of the reign of —— A O of —— yeoman, A B of —— yeoman, and B B of —— yeoman, came before us John Moore, esquire, and Richard Burn, doctor of laws, two of his majesty's justices of the peace in and for the said county, one whereof is of the quorum, and severally acknowledged themselves to owe to our said lord the king, that is to say, the said A O, 20l, and the said A B and B B 10l each, to be respectively levied of their lands and tenements, goods and chattles, if the said A O shall make default in the performance of the condition indorsed, [or underwritten]
     John Moore,
     Richard Burn.

The condition of this recognizance is such, that if the within [above] bound A. O shall personally appear before the justices of our sovereign lord the king assigned to keep the peace within the said county, and likewise to hear and determine divers felonies, trespasses, and other misdemeanors in the said county committed, at the next general quarter sessions of the peace [or, before his majesty's justices of gaol delivery, at the next general gaol delivery] to be holden in and for the said county, then and there to answer to our said sovereign lord the king, for and concerning the felonious taking and stealing of —— the property of A M of —— yeoman, with the suspicion whereof the said A O stands charged before us the said justices, and to do and receive what shall by the court be then and there enjoined him, and shall not depart the court without licence, then the above [within] written recognizance shall be void

Or, if the party is in prison, and so absent, Lord *Hale* says, this is the true form from *Lambard.*

Westmorland   BE it remembred, that on the —— day of —— in the —— year of the reign of —— before us John Moore, esquire, and Richard Burn,
                                            doctor

doctor of laws, two of the justices of our said lord the king, assigned to keep the peace within the said county, and one of us of the quorum, at Grimeshill in the said county, did come A. B. and B. B of —— in the said county, yeoman, and took in bail until the next gaol delivery to be holden in the said county, one A O of —————— labourer, taken and detained in prison for suspicion of a certain felony in stealing —————— the property of —————— and took upon themselves each of the said A B. and B B under the penalty of 20l of good and lawful money of Great Britain, of the goods and chattles, lands and tenements, of them and each of them, to the use of our said lord the king, his heirs and successors, to be levied, if the said A O. shall not personally appear at the said next gaol delivery, before the justices of our said lord the king, assigned to deliver the said gaol, to stand to right concerning the felony aforesaid, according to the law and custom of England. Given under our seals, &c.

But the seal need not be, for they are judges of record; only it may be barely subscribed by them   or thus,

Taken and acknowledged the day and
  year abovewritten, before us the
  abovesaid
    John Moore,
    Ri Burn.

And hereupon a warrant issues for his deliverance, thus :

Westmorland. JOHN Moor, *esquire, and* Richard Burn, *doctor of laws, two of the justices of* ——— *and one of us of the quorum, To the keeper of his majesty's gaol at* —— *in the said county, greeting. Forasmuch as* A O. *of* —— *labourer, hath before us, found sufficient sureties to appear before the justices of gaol delivery at the next general gaol delivery to be holden in the said county, to answer to such things as shall be then on the behalf of our said sovereign lord objected against him, and namely, to the felonious taking of* —— *(for the suspicion whereof he was taken, and committed to your said gaol) We command you on the behalf of our said sovereign lord, that if the said* A. O. *do remain in your said gaol for the said cause, and for none other, then you forbear to detain him any longer, but that you deliver him thence, and suffer him to go at large, and that upon the pain that will thereon ensue Given under our seals at* Orton *in the said county, the* ——— *day of* —— *in the* —— *year* ——
                                                        Lord

Lord *Hale* says, the advantage of this latter kind of bail is this, that it is not only a recognizance in a sum certain, but also a real bail, and they are his keepers, and may be punished by fine beyond the sum mentioned in the recognizance, if there be cause, and may release him if they doubt his escape, and have him committed, and to be discharged of the recognizance.

Banks destroying.

Powake.

1 EVERY perverse and malicious person, cutting down and breaking up of any part of the dike called *New Powake* in *Marshland* in the county of *Norfolk*, and the broken dike called *Old field dike* by *Marshland* in the isle of *Ely*, or of any other bank being parcel of the rind and uppermost part of the said county of *Marshland*, made for the defence and salvation of the said county of *Marshland*, shall be adjudged felony And the sessions may determine the same 22 *H* 8 *c.* 11

Sea and river banks.

2. By the 6 *G* 2 *c* 37 If any person shall unlawfully and maliciously break down or cut down the bank of any river or any sea bank, whereby any lands shall be overflowed or damaged, he shall be guilty of felony without benefit of clergy *ʃ* 5

Piles for securing banks

3 And moreover, by the statute of 10 *G* 2 *c* 32 If any person shall unlawfully cut off, draw up, or remove and carry away any piles, chalk or other materials, driven into the ground, and used for the securing any marsh or sea walls, or banks, in order to prevent the lands lying within the same from being overflowed and damaged, on complaint or information thereof made upon oath to any justice residing near the place, such justice shall summon the party complained of, or shall issue his warrant to apprehend and bring such person before him, and upon his appearance, or neglect to appear, he shall proceed to examine the fact, and upon due proof thereof made either by confession, or oath of one witness, shall convict the offender, who shall thereupon forfeit 20 *l*, half to the informer, and half to the overseer for the use of the poor, to be levied by distress and sale for want of sufficient distress, to be committed to the house of correction, to be kept to hard labour for six months, *ʃ* 5.

Bankrupt.

1 LORD *Coke* says, that *banque* in *French* signifies the Derivation. same as *mensa* in *Latin*, and that *route* is a sign or mark, as we say a cart rout is the sign or mark where the cart hath gone, and that metaphorically a *bankrupt*, or *banqueroute*, is taken for him, that hath wasted his estate, and removed his banque so as there is left but a mention thereof 4 *Inst* 277

But as the first bankers came to us from *Italy*, it seemeth more probable that they brought their name along with them, and consequently that the word *bankrupt* or *banqueroute* cometh from the Italian *banco rotto*, the *bench* being *broken* The *banker* himself was so called from the *bench* or table which he used, with his name inscribed, and when he failed, his bench was broken Which word *rotto* is what remaineth in that country of the Latin *ruptus*; all which, both word and metaphor, we preserve in our language, when we say that a person is *bankrupt*, or that such a one is broken

2 The description of a bankrupt, within the several Description of a bankrupt statutes brought together into one view, seemeth to be as follows *Every person using the trade of merchandize, by way of bargaining, exchange, bartry, chevisance, or otherwise, in gross, or by retail, or seeking his trade of living by buying and selling, or that shall use the trade or profession of a scrivener receiving other mens monies or estates into his trust or custody, who shall (1) depart the realm, or (2) begin to keep his house, or otherwise to absent himself, or (3) take sanctuary, or (4) suffer himself willingly to be arrested for any debt or other thing not grown or due for money delivered, wares sold, or any other just or lawful cause or good consideration or purposes, or (5) shall suffer himself to be outlawed, or (6) yield himself to prison, or (7) willingly or fraudulently shall procure himself to be arrested, or his goods to be attached or sequestred, or (8) depart from his dwelling house, or (9) make any fraudulent grant or conveyance of his lands or goods, to the intent or whereby his creditors shall and may be defeated or delayed for the recovery of their just debts, or (10) shall obtain any protection, other than such person as shall be lawfully protected by privilege of parliament, or (11) shall prefer to any court any petition or bill against any of his creditors, thereby endeavouring to enforce them to accept less than their just debts, or to procure time, or longer days of payment than was given at the time of their original contract, or (12) being arrested for debt, shall lie in prison two months, or (13) being arrested for 100 l or more,*

I   *shall*

shall escape out of prison,—shall be adjudged a bankrupt, (and in the said cases of arrest, or lying in prison, from the time of his first arrest) 1 J. c 15. f 2. 21 J. c. 19 f 2, 1, 10 An c. 15 f 1.

Every person] An *Irishman*, who trades and hath contracted debts in England, and comes over here, may have a commission issued against him, at the petition of the creditors here, and the Irish creditors also upon the commission may come in and prove their debts And generally, if a person carries on a trade in any place belonging to the crown of Great Britain, and comes into England, a commission may be taken out by the creditors in England. And there have been several instances, where persons belonging to the plantations abroad, and which is their sole place of residence, yet happening to be in England, have had commissions of bankruptcy taken out against them here 1 *Atkyns*, 82.

A *clergyman*, if he trades, may be a bankrupt, for tho' by the 21 *H* 8. *c* 12 he is prohibited to trade, and his contracts in that kind are declared to be void, yet they are void with respect to himself only, and he shall not take advantage of the breach of one law, in order to avoid his being subject to another. 1 *Atk* 199.

An *infant*, tho' a trader, cannot be a bankrupt, for an infant can owe nothing but for necessaries, and the statutes of bankruptcy create no new debts, but only give a speedier and more effectual remedy for recovering such as were before due And no person can be made a bankrupt for debts, which he is not liable at law to pay 2 *Blackst.* 477

The daughter of a freeman of London, being a *married woman*, if she trades separately from her husband, may be a bankrupt 1 *Atk.* 206.

Using the trade of merchandize] As by exercising the calling of a merchant, a grocer, mercer, or in one general word a *chapman*, who is one that buys and sells any thing 2 *Blackst* 477.

But one single act of buying and selling will not make a man a trader, but there must be a repeated practice, and profit by it 2 *Blackst* 476

Of merchandize] But no person who shall adventure any money in the East India company, and shall receive his dividend in merchandize, and shall sell or exchange the same, shall be judged thereby a merchant or trader within any statute for bankrupts 13 & 14 C 2 c. 24 / 3, 4

And

And generally, buying and felling ftock in the public funds, or government fecurities, will not make a man a bankrupt, the fame not being goods, wares, or merchandize, within the intent of the ftatute, by which a profit may be fairly made. *2 Blackf.* 476

So alfo the members of the corporation of the Englifh *linen company* (for making cambricks and lawns), fhall not upon that account only be liable to bankruptcy *4 G.* 3. *c* 37.

Seeking his trade of living by buying and felling] He that buys only, or fells only, is not within this defcription, but it muft be botn buying and felling, and alfo getting a livelihood by it *2 Blackf* 476.

Alfo, by fpecial ftatute, 5 *G.* 2. *c* 30. No *farmer*, *grazier*, or *drover* of cattle, fhall be deemed a bankrupt. *f.* 40 ——But if fuch farmer or other fhall deal in wool, hops, or the like, he fhall be deemed a bankrupt, otherwife any perfon by taking a farm, might avoid the ftatutes And in the cafe of *Mayo* and *Archer*, *E* 8 *G.* a farmer who planted potatoes, but withal bought divers large quantities of potatoes, and fold the fame again, was adjudged a bankrupt. *Str.* 513.

Alfo, no *handicraft occupation*, where nothing is bought and fold, will make a man a bankrupt, as that of a hufbandman, a gardener, and the like, who are paid for their work and labour *2 Blackf.* 476

Alfo, an *innkeeper* or *victualler* cannot, as fuch, be a bankrupt, for his gain or livelihood doth not arife from buying and felling in the way of merchandize, but greatly from the ufe of his houfe, furniture, attendance, and the like · and tho' he may buy corn and victuals, to fell again at a profit, yet that no more makes him a trader, than a fchoolmafter or other perfon is, that keeps a boarding houfe and makes confiderable gains by buying and felling what he fpends in the houfe, and fuch an one is clearly not within the ftatute. *2 Blackf* 476 *Burr Marf* 2064.

But where perfons buy goods and make them up into faleable commodities, as *fhoemakers*, *fmiths*, *bakers*, and the like, here, tho' part of the gain is by bodily labour, and not by buying and felling, yet they are within the ftatutes of bankrupts for the labour is only in melioration of the commodity, and rendering it more fit for fale. *2 Blackf* 476

So alfo, for the like reafon, a *butcher* is within the ftatutes of bankruptcy *Bur Manf* 2148

But where a perfon bought a *coal mine*, and worked the mine, and fold the coals, he was adjudged not to be within the

the ftatutes for bankrupts But otherwife it would have been, if he had bought the coals and fold the fame again. 2 *Wilf* 169.

Or that fhall ufe th trade or profeffion of a fcrivener, receiving other mens monies or eftates into his truft or cuftody] Bankers, brokers, and factors are within this defcription 5 G 2 c 30 f 39

So alfo *pawnbrokers*, as it feemeth , being comprehended under the general word *brokers*, which includes the feveral fpecies of brokerage 1 *Atk* 206.

But no receiver-general of any taxes granted by act of parliament, fhall be deemed a bankrupt 5 G 2 c. 30 f. 40

Begin to keep his houfe, or otherwife to abfent himfelf] If a man keeps his houfe for a long time, this doth not immediately make him a bankrupt, but if he conceals himfelf within his houfe for a day or hour, to delay or defraud his creditors, he is a bankrupt. 1 *Bac Abr* 250.

Obtain any protection, other than fuch perfon as fhall be law fully protected by privilege of parliament] By the 4 G 3 c 33 in refpect to perfons having privilege of parliament, it is enacted, that the petitioners, on affidavit in any of his majefty's courts of record at Weftminfter, that the debt is juftly due, and that they verily believe that the debtor is a merchant, banker, broker, factor, fcrivener, or trader, within the ftatutes of bankruptcy, may fue out a fummons, or an original bill and fummons, againft fuch perfon, and ferve him with a copy thereof, and if he fhall not, within two months after perfonal fervice of fuch fummons, pay, fecure, or compound for fuch debt, or enter into bond in fuch fum and with two fuch fureties as any of the judges of that court out of which the fummons iffued fhall approve of, to pay fuch fum as fhall be recovered in fuch action, together with fuch cofts as fhall be given in the fame, he fhall be adjudged a bankrupt from the time of the fervice of fuch fummons, and the creditors may proceed againft him as againft other bankrupts Provided, that this fhall not extend to any debt contracted before March the 8th, 1764   And provided alfo, that nothing herein fhall fubject any perfon intitled to privilege of parliament to be arrefted or imprifoned during the time of fuch privilege, except in cafes made felony by any of the ftatutes of bankruptcy

For what debts a commiffion fhall be iffued, and what is to be done previous thereto

3 But notwithftanding that a perfon may have committed any of the abovefaid acts of bankruptcy, yet neverthelefs *no commiffion of bankrupt fhall be iffued on the petition of*

one

one or more creditors, unless the single debt of such creditor, or of two or more being partners, amount to 100 l, or of two such creditors petitioning amounts to 150 l, or of three or more to 200 l. 5 G 2 c 30 ſ 23

And the creditor or creditors petitioning, shall before the commission shall be granted, make affidavit before a master in chancery (to be filed with the proper officer) of the truth of the debt, and shall also give 200 l bond to the lord chancellor for proving the debt as well before the commissioners, as upon a trial at law, if the due iſſuing of the commission shall be contested, and also for proving the party a bankrupt, and further to proceed on such commission as hereafter is mentioned and if it shall appear, that the commission was taken out fraudulently, the lord chancellor may order satisfaction, and may assign such bond to the party injured *id*

4 But these circumstances abovementioned being ob- **Issuing the commission** served, then the lord chancellor may on such complaint in writing as aforesaid, by commission under the great seal, appoint such wise and honest discreet persons as to him shall seem good, to be commissioners 13 *El* c. 7 ſ 2.

5 Which commissioners before they act, shall admini- **Commissioners oath.** ster to each other the following oath, "I *A B*, do swear, "that I will faithfully, impartially, and honestly, ac- "cording to the best of my skill and knowledge, execute "the several powers and trusts reposed in me as a com- "missioner in a commission of bankrupt against —— and "that without favour or affection, prejudice or malice. "So help me God" 5 G 2 c 30 ſ 43

And they shall keep a memorial thereof signed by them, amongst the proceedings *id* ſ 44

6. Then the commissioners shall cause notice of the **Notice in the gazette of the commission being issued** commission being issued to be given in the gazette, and likewise notice in writing to be left at the bankrupt's usual place of abode, or personal notice to be given if he is in prison 5 G. 2 c 30 ſ 1.

7 In which notice also shall be appointed a time and **Bankrupt to surrender.** place of meeting of the commissioners, which meeting shall be at three several times within forty-two days, the last of which shall be on the forty-second day, within which time the bankrupt shall surrender himself, and dis- cover his estate and effects. 5 G 2 c 30 ſ 1, 2

But the lord chancellor may enlarge the time for such surrender and discovery, not exceeding fifty days from the end of the said forty-two days, so as such order be made by him, six days before the expiration of the forty-two. *id* ſ 3

8 A

Creditors to come in

8 A creditor may chuse whether he will come in under the commission or not But if he chuses to come in, he cannot proceed at law likewise for the same debt Therefore if a creditor has the bankrupt in execution, he must discharge him from the execution, before he can be admitted as a creditor under the commission. And a petitioning creditor, by the very petition, hath made his election. 1 *Atk* 83, 152.

Chusing assignees

9. The first meeting shall be for chusing an assignee or assignees of the bankrupt's estate and effects (which in *London* shall be at *Guildhall*) 5 G. 2 c. 30. f. 26.

The money with whom to be lodged.

10 But before assignees are chosen, the major part in value of the creditors may direct how and with whom the money to be received shall remain till divided, to which the assignees shall conform, as often as 100 l shall be got in 5 G 2. c 30. f. 32

Expences of the commission.

11. And the creditor or creditors who shall sue out the commission, shall prosecute the same at their own expence till assignees be chosen, and the commissioners shall at the meeting for chusing assignees ascertain such costs, and by writing under their hands order the assignees to reimbure the same, out of the first effects that shall be got in. 5 G. 2 c 30. f 25.

Who shall vote for assignees

12 At the said meeting for chusing assignees, the commissioners shall admit the proof of any creditor's debt, that lives remote from the place of meeting, by affidavit, and also permit any person duly authorized by letter of attorney from such creditors (oath being first made of the due execution thereof, either by affidavit sworn before a master in chancery, or before the commissioners *viva voce*, and in case of creditors residing in foreign parts, such affidavits to be made before a magistrate where the party shall be residing, and together with such creditors letters of attorney, to be attested by a notary publick) to vote in the choice of an assignee or assignees in the place of such creditor And every creditor shall be admitted to prove his debt, without paying any thing for the same And the commissioners shall assign the estate and effects unto such person or persons as the major part in value of the creditors, according to the debts then proved, shall chuse. 5 G. 2 c. 30 f 25, 26

But no creditor shall so vote, whose debt shall not amount to 10 l id f 27

Chusing new assignees.

13. And the commissioners may from time to time appoint new assignees, if the major part of the creditors, whose debts amount to 10 l, shall think fit, and the former assignees shall assign to them in ten days after notice of

such

such choice, and of the new assignees acceptance thereof, signified under their hands, on pain of 200 l, to the creditors, with full costs 5 G 2 c 30 f 30

And the lord chancellor, on petition of any creditors, may order former assignments to be vacated, and new assignments to be made of the effects not received, and the commissioners shall cause notice thereof to be given in the two next gazettes, and that the debtors do not pay to the assignees removed id f 31

And the new assignees, on filing a supplemental bill, shall be entitled to the benefit of the proceedings in a suit begun in the time of the first assignees, for there is no privity between the bankrupt and the assignees, or at most but an artificial one; and it would be hard, where there have been pleadings, examinations, and the like, in a former suit, that the new assignees should not have the benefit thereof, but should be obliged to begin again 1 Atk 88

14 On certificate under the hands and seals of the commissioners, that such commission is issued, and such person proved before them to become bankrupt, any judge or justice of the peace, shall on application to them for that purpose made, grant their warrant (A) for the taking and apprehending such person, and commit (B) him to the common gaol, there to remain until he be removed by order of the commissioners by their warrant And the gaoler shall forthwith give notice to one or more of the commissioners, of such person being in his custody, whereupon they shall send their warrant to him to deliver him to the person who shall be named in the warrant, who shall convey him to the commissioners to be examined And the commissioners by such or any other their warrant, may seize the goods and papers of such bankrupt which shall be in any prison (necessary wearing apparel of himself and wife, and children excepted). 5 G 2 c 30 f 14

Bankrupt not surrendring, to be apprehended

But if the person so apprehended shall, within the time allowed, submit to be examined, and in all things conform, he shall have the same benefit as if he had surrendred 5 G 2 c 30 f 15

By which last clause it seemeth, that the bankrupt shall not be apprehended and committed, until he shall have made default in not surrendring and making discovery, after due notice as aforesaid

15 The bankrupt, after assignees shall be appointed, shall deliver up to them on oath (to be administred by two of a master in chancery, or justice of the peace) all his books

Bankrupt to de-

of account, papers, and writings not feized by the mef-
fenger of the commiffion, and not before delivered up,
and th... in his power, and difcover fuch as are in the
power of others, and being not in cuftody, fhall at all
times attend the affignees, on reafonable notice given to
him in writing, or left for him at his place of abode, in
order to affift in making out the account of his eftate
5 G 2 c 30 § 4

16 And fuch bankrupt having furrendred, fhall at all
feafonable times, before the expiration of forty-two days,
or further term, be at liberty to infpect his papers, in
prefence of the affignees, or fome perfon appointed by
them, and to bring with him for his affiftance any perfons
not exceeding two at a time, and to make extracts from
thence, the better to enable him to difcover his effects
5 G 2 c 30 § 5

17 And in order thereto, he fhall be free from arreft
or imprifonment of his creditors, in coming to furrender,
and at his furrender, for the faid forty-two days or further term, provided he was not in cuftody at the time of
furrender And if he be arrefted for debt, or on an efcape
warrant, coming to furrender, or after furrender within
the faid term, then, on producing the notice under the
hands of the commiffioners or affignees, to the officer who
fhall arreft him, and making it appear to fuch officer that
fuch notice is figned by them, and giving the officer a copy
thereof he fhall be immediately difcharged And if any
officer fhall in fuch cafe detain him, he fhall forfeit to him
for his own ufe 5l a day, by action of debt, with full
cofts *id*

18 And if the bankrupt be in prifon or cuftody at the
time of iffuing the commiffion, and is willing to furrender
and be examined, and can be brought before the commiffioners and creditors, the expence thereof fhall be paid out
of his eftate but if he is in execution, or cannot be
brought before the commiffioners, then they fhall attend
him in prifon, and the affignees may appoint a perfon to
attend him in prifon, and to produce him his books and
papers, in order to prepare his laft difcovery and examination, a copy whereof the affignees fhall apply for, and
the bankrupt fhall deliver to them, ten days before fuch
laft examination 5 G 2 c 30 § 6

19 And the commiffioners may examine him (on oath,
21 J c 19 § 9) as well by word of mouth, as on interrogatories in writing, touching his trade, dealings, eftate, and
effects, and take down in writing his anfwer to verbal
interrogatories, which he fhall fign And if he fhall refufe

to anfwer, *or not anfwer fully* all lawful queftions, or refufe to fign the fame, the commiffioners may by warrant commit him to prifon without bail, *till he fhall fubmit to them, and full anfwer make*, and fign the fame, which warrant fhall fpecify fuch queftions   5 G 2 c 30. ſ 16, 17

As well by word of mouth, as on interrogatories in writing] M 4 G 2 K and *Solomon Nathan*   The defendant was committed by the commiffioners, who in their warrant recite, that he had been examined before them upon his oath, upon which examination he had notorioufly prevaricated, they therefore commit him without bail or mainprize, until he fhall make a full and true difclofure and difcovery of his eftate and effects, or be otherwife delivered by due courfe of law   Upon a *habeas corpus* it was moved, that the defendant might be difcharged   One reafon whereof was becaufe the ftatute requires, that there fhall be interrogatories exhibited for his examination, that ſ) he may have time to confider of his anfwer, and it can then appear to the court, whether he is bound to anfwer perhaps this prevarication might be in a matter they had no power to inquire into   And by the court, Interrogatories are a term known in law, and import that the queftions are put in writing   And they faid that *Holt* Ch J. held, that the bankrupt ought to have a copy, and time to confider of his anfwer   Str 880

Or not anfwer fully,] In the aforefaid cafe of *K* and *Solomon Nathan*, another objection againft the commitment was, that they commit him becaufe upon his examination he had *notorioufly prevaricated*, this being too loofe an expreffion, for he might prevaricate, and yet give a full anfwer at laft   And by the court, Where thefe fpecial authorities are given, the words of the act ought to be purfued   Str 880

The commiffioners may by warrant commit him] H 1 G 3 K and *Perrot*   The defendant being brought up by *habeas corpus*, appeared upon the return to have been committed, " until fuch time as he fhall fubmit himfelf " to the faid commiffioners or the major part of them, " and full anfwer make to their fatisfaction, to the que- " ftion fo put by them to him as aforefaid "   Which queftion was fpecified in the warrant to have been, that fince he did admit there was a deficiency of 13,513l, he fhould give a true and particular account what was become of it, and how he had difpofed thereof. His anfwer was, that on goods fold the laft year he had loft upwards of 2,000l; that by mournings he had loft upwards of 1000l, and that for 9 or ten years (he was forry to fay it) he had been extremely extravagant, and fpent large fums of money Which anfwer not being fatisfactory to the commiffioners, they committed him as aforefaid. And now the court, judging the anfwer to be very infufficient and unfatisfactory, ordered him to be remanded. Afterwards, he was brought up again, and it appeared that he had given a further anfwer, and particularized a woman upon whom he had fpent 5,000l, from December 1758 to December 1759, and particularized the times of fending and giving it to her, but that no other perfon was privy to this, and that the woman (whofe name was *Sarah Po—d*, otherwife *Taylor*,) is dead, as he has heard with feveral other improbable circumftances. It was urged, that now having given a full anfwer, he ought to be difcharged, that it is not material, in the prefent refpect, whether his anfwer be true or falfe, or whether his conduct was prudent or imprudent, and if he be not now difcharged, he muft be imprifoned for life. But the court ftill held the anfwer to be incompleat and unfatisfactory, and again ordered him to be remanded. [And this man was afterwards convicted and executed, for concealing his effects.] *Burrow, March'd* 1122, 1215

Till he fhall fubmit to them, and full anfwer make.] In the aforefaid cafe of *Solomon Nathan*, the commitment was, *until he fhall make a full and true difclofure and difcovery of his eftate and effects, or be otherwife deliver'd by due courfe of law.* And by the court, This commitment not purfuing the words of the ftatute, the prifoner muft be difcharged. *Sti 880*

M 8 W. Brice's cafe. A commitment *until he fhould conform himfelf to the authority*, was adjudged ill, becaufe too general, fince they have authority in other matters befides that; and it is beft in the like cafes, ftrictly to purfue the ftatute. *L Raym 100*

Another commitment *till difcharged by due courfe of law*, adjudged ill for the fame reafon. *id 851*

But if on an *habeas corpus* there appear infufficiency in the warrant of commitment, the judge neverthelefs fhall commit him to the fame prifon, to remain as aforefaid, unlefs it be made appear that he hath fully anfwered all lawful queftions, or unlefs it appear that he had fufficient reafon for not figning. *5 G 2 c 30 f 18*

And if the gaoler fhall fuffer him to efcape, or to go without the walls or doors of the prifon, he fhall, on

con

conviction by indictment or information, forfeit 500l to the creditors   *id*

Also, the gaoler shall, on request of any creditor who shall have proved his debt, and producing a certificate thereof under the hands of the commissioners, produce and shew him to such creditor, on pain of 100*l* to the creditors, by action of debt   *id / 19*

20 And by the said statute it is enacted, that if he shall not within the said time surrender himself to the commissioners, and sign such surrender, and also submit to be *Bankrupt not surrendring and conforming, felony.* examined from time to time on oath, and in all things conform to the statutes concerning bankrupts, and also on his examination fully discover all his estate, and how disposed of, except what hath been *bona fide* disposed of in the way of his trade and dealings, and except what hath been laid out in the ordinary expence of his family, and also deliver up to them all his effects (except the necessary wearing apparel of himself, and wife, and children), then in case of any default and wilful omission in not surrendring and submitting to be examined, or in case he shall remove, conceal, or embezzle any part of his estate to the value of 20l, or any books of account, or writings relating thereto, with intent to defraud his creditors, and be thereof convicted by indictment or information, he shall be guilty of felony without benefit of clergy, and his estate shall be divided among his creditors. 5 *G* 2 *c* 30 / 1

21 And every person who shall accept any trust, or *Other persons concealing the bankrupt's effects.* conceal any estate of the bankrupt, and shall not in forty-two days after issuing the commission, and notice thereof in the gazette, discover the same in writing to one or more commissioners or assignees, and submit himself to be examined, shall forfeit to the creditors 100*l* and double value of the estate concealed, by action of debt with full costs   5 *G* 2 *c* 30 / 21

22 Also the commissioners may examine on oath the *Bankrupt's wife may be examined.* bankrupt's wife, like as other persons   21 *J c* 19 /. 5, 6

23 As also they may examine in like manner every *And every other person.* other person duly summoned before, or present at their meeting, touching the person, trade, dealings, estate, and effects of the bankrupt, and any acts of bankruptcy by him committed, and may take down in writing the answers to verbal examinations, which the party shall sign. And if any of them shall refuse to answer, or not answer fully all lawful questions, or refuse to sign the same, the commissioners may by warrant commit him to prison

with-

without bail, till he shall submit to them, and full an-swer make, and sign the same, in like manner as is said before in section the 19th concerning the bankrupt him self 5 *G* 2 *c* 30 *f* 16, 17, 18, 19

24 The full commissioners shall have power by their discretions to take such order with the lands of such bank-rupt, as well copy or customary hold as freehold, which he had in his own right before he became a bankrupt, or which he purchased jointly with his wife or child to the only use of such bankrupt, or for such use or interest as he may lawfully part with, or with any person of trust to any secret use of such bankrupt, and also with all his money, goods, chattels, wares, merchandizes, and debts, and cause all the same to be searched and appraised to the best value they may, and the same to be sold by deed in-dented, and inrolled in a court of record, or otherwise ordered for payment of the creditors 13 *El. c* 7 *f* 2

25 And if any lands or goods shall descend or come to the bankrupt afterwards, before the debts be fully paid, the same shall be disposed of in like manner 13 *El. c* 7 *f* 11

26 But this shall not extend to lands assured by such person before he becomes bankrupt, provided the assur-ance be made *bona fide*, and not to his own use only, or of his heirs, and that the party to whose use they are as-sured, be not privy to the fraudulent purpose of the bank-rupt to deceive his creditors 13 *El. c* 7 *f* 12

27 Also the commissioners may by deed indented, and inrolled at *Westminster* in six months, sell the bankrupt's estate in tail, whereof no reversion or remainder is in the king or of the king's gift, which sale shall be good against all persons, whom the bankrupt by common recovery, or otherwise, might cut off 21 *f c* 19 *f* 12

28 Also, if the bankrupt hath conveyed any estate, on condition, or power of redemption, at a day to come by payment of money, or otherwise, the commissioners be-fore the time of the performance of such condition may appoint under their hands and seals any person to make such act or payment of money, or other performance, as fully as the bankrupt might have done, and may dispose of the estate redeemed for the use of the creditors, as fully as any other estate of the bankrupt 21 *J c* 19 *f* 13

29 Tenors purchasing copyhold or customary lands to pay a fine to the lord of the manor, who shall have the admission, 13 *El. c* 7 *f* 4

In order to save the expence of two fines, it was re-commended by the lord chancellor Hardwicke in case, to leave out the copyhold estate in the assignment, and then the commissioners, when they can meet with a purchaser, may convey to him in the first instance 1 *Alk.* 96

30. Effects which a bankrupt hath as executor only, shall not be applied to the use of the creditors, but shall go according to the direction of the testator 1 *Aƒ.* 101

31. Commissioners and others by warrant under their hands and seals, may break open the bankrupt's houses, doors, trunks, and chests, where he or any of his goods shall be reputed to be, and seize upon and order his body and goods as before is said 21 *J. c* 19 ƒ 8.

32. If the bankrupt shall convey to any of his children, or other person, any lands or goods, or transfer his debts in other mens names, except the same be conveyed or transferred on marriage of any of his children, or for some valuable consideration, the same may be disposed of in like manner 1 *J. c* 15 ƒ. 5

And if the bankrupt shall on his examination be found fraudulently to have conveyed his lands, goods, or estate, to the value of 20*l.* to defraud his creditors, and shall not discover the same, and (if it be in his power) deliver the same to the commissioners, or if he cannot make it appear to the commissioners, that he hath sustained some casual loss whereby he is disabled to pay what he owes, he shall, on conviction upon indictment at the assizes or sessions be set in the pillory in some public place for two hours, and have one of his ears nailed to the pillory, and cut off 21 *J. c* 19 ƒ 7

33. And if any bankrupt, after summons the commission, a bankrupt shall compound with the person suing out the same, for more than his proportion when released out to all others, such commission may be therefore, and the Lord Chancellor may award to any creditor petition such commission, and the person so compounding shall lose his whole debt, and deliver up to the new commissioners all he shall have so received for the use of the creditors 5 *G* 2 *c* 30 ƒ 24

34. If a debtor to a bankrupt pays him money, he must pay it over again, but he is not liable to it except by compulsion of law *Read 1 vol.*

35. But no real creditor of the bankrupt shall be liable to refund to the assignees, money paid, unless the same forth the commission sued out, and received by him of the bankrupt ten days before the person's becoming a bankrupt, or being indebted to *G* 2. *c* 19 ƒ 1

M 4

Purchafer not to be impeached after five years

36 And no purchaser for valuable confideration fhall be impeached, unlefs the commiffion be fued out in five years after the perfon fhall become bankrupt 21 J. c 19 f 14

Bankrupt con-veying their goods, in keep-ing poffeffion

37 If the bankrupt, at the time he fhall become bank-rupt, fhall by confent of the true owner, have in his pof-feffion and difpofition any goods whereof he fhall be re-puted owner, and take upon him the fale or difpofition thereof as owner the commiffioners may difpofe of the fame, as fully as any other part of the bankrupt's eftate 21 J. c 19 f 11

Debtor to the king

38 If any eftate of the bankrupt be extended after he is become a bankrupt, by any perfon under pretence of his being an accountant or indebted to the king, the com-miffioners may examine upon oath, whether the faid debt were due to fuch debtor or accountant, upon any contract originally made between fuch accountant and the bank-rupt, and if it was made with any other perfon than the faid accountant or for the ufe of any other perfon, the commiffioners proceedings fhall be available againft the faid extent 21 J. c 19 f 10

Otherwife, an extent of the crown is available againft a commiffion of bankruptcy, the crown not being with-in the ftatutes of bankrupts 1 Atk 262

Commiffioners or affignees to ftate ac-counts

39 The commiffioners or affignees may ftate accounts between the bankrupt and his debtors or creditors, and fet one debt againft another, and the balance only fhall be paid on either fide 5 G 2 c 30 f 28

May refer to arbitration, and compound

40 Alfo the affignees with confent of the major part in value of the creditors prefent at a meeting purfuant to notice to be given in the gazette, may fubmit difputes re-lating to the bankrupt's eftate to arbitration, and may compound for debts owing to the bankrupt 5 G 2 c 30 f 34, 35

Joint creditors

41 Creditors of a joint eftate, where there are no fe-parate creditors, may exhauft both the joint and feparate eftate, but where there are both joint and feparate credi-tors, the joint creditors (as they give credit to the joint eftate) fhall have firft their demand on the joint eftate, and the feparate creditors (as they give credit to the fe-parate eftate) fhall have firft their demand on the feparate eftate But if there be a furplus of the feparate eftate, the joint creditors are entitled to it, for a bankrupt has no right to any thing, till they are fully fatisfied But for the faving of expences, where there is a joint com-miffion depending, it feemeth beft for the feparate credi-tors not to take out a feparate commiffion, but to apply

to

to the court for an order to be admitted to come in and prove their debts under the joint commission   1 *Atk* 67, 138, 227.

42 Every person who shall, after the time of surrender, voluntarily make discovery to the commissioners or assignees, of any part of the bankrupt's estate, not before come to the knowledge of the assignees, shall have 5 *l per cent* and such farther reward as the assignees and the major part of the creditors in value, present at any meeting, shall think fit   5 G 2 c 30 ſ 20

Reward for discovering

43 Creditors having security by judgment, statute, recognizance, specialty with penalty or without, or other security, or having no security, or having made attachments in *London*, or elsewhere by any custom, of the goods of such bankrupt, whereof there is no execution or extent served and executed upon the lands, goods, or estate of such bankrupt before he shall become bankrupt, shall not be relieved for more than a rateable part with the other creditors, notwithstanding any penalty or greater sum contained in such security   21 J c 19 ſ 9

Persons having security, to have only their share.

44 Persons taking securities, payable at a future day, for goods delivered to persons who shall become bankrupts before the time of payment, shall be admitted to prove their securities, and receive their proportion, deducting interest from the time of payment to the time it would have become due   7 G c 31 ſ 1, 2.

Securities for money not become due.

But where the payment depends upon a future contingency, as if a security be made to pay to the wife so much in case she survives her husband, here she cannot come in amongst the creditors, because it is entirely uncertain whether she shall ever have any demand or not   And in case of the event happening afterwards, she can only come upon the bankrupt's future estate   1 *Barnard* 59

45 The obligee in any bottom-ree, or respondentia bond, and the assured in a policy of insurance, shall be admitted to claim, and after the loss or contingency, to prove the debt thereon, in like manner as if the same had happened before issuing the commission   19 G 2. c 32. ſ 2

Bottom rees insurance

46 The mortgagee may chuse whether he will come in as a creditor.   *Read* Bankr

Mortgagee.

47 A landlord may distrain for his rent upon a bankrupt's goods, either before or after the assignment, but if he neglects to do it, and suffers them to be removed, he can only come in upon an average with the rest of the creditors. But if the goods remain on the premises, he may distrain them, even after the messenger is in possession,

Landlord for his rent

fion, or after fale by the affignees And he is not re-
ftricted to one year only, as in the cafe of executions,
but may diftrain for his whole arrear   1 *Atk* 102, 3

Apprentice

48 An apprentice, for money to be refunded given with
him in his binding, fhall come in only amongft the reft of
the creditors   1 *Atk* 149

In cafe of notes, &c.

49 Where notes carry intereft, the fame fhall be continued down to &c. commiffion but note-
creditors have no right to prove intereft upon them, unlefs it is exprefled in the body of the notes Even at law,
where notes are for value received, and intereft is not exprefled, the jury do not give the plaintiff, in an action
upon the notes, intereft for them, but by way of damages
only and commiffioners of bankrupts cannot award damages 1 *Atk* 151, 259

Affignees not refponfible, &c.

50 Affignees fhall not be anfwerable for loffes occafioned by their own neceffary acts, but if an affignee
trufts a perfon with the payment of money, who fails, and
the money is loft, fuch affignee fhall be anfwerable over to
the creditors, unlefs he confulted the body of the creditors
in the appointment of fuch agent   1 *Atk* 87

An affignee cannot purchafe a debt, &c.

51 An affignee, who is an officer of the court, and an
officer of the commiffion, fhall not be allowed to ftop a
perfon's fhare in the dividend, on account of his own
private debt, which is owing to him from that perfon he
hath his remedy at law, and ought not to intermix his
own private affairs with the commiffion, to which he is
only a trustee   1 *Atk* 90

Swearing to a falfe debt

52 If any perfon fhall fwear that any fum is due to him
from the bankrupt, which is not due, or more than is due,
he fhall incur the offence of perjury, and moreover forfeit
double to the creditor   5 *G* 2 c 30 ſ 29

Affignees to keep books

53 The affignees fhall keep books of account of all
fums and effects received, which every creditor who hath
proved his debt may infpect at all feafonable times   5 *G*
2 c 30 ſ 2?

Final dividend

54 The affignees fhall, after four months, and within twelve months after iffuing the commiffion, caufe at
leaft twenty-one days notice to be given in the gazette,
of the time and place the commiffioners and affignees intend to meet to make a dividend, at which time, the creditors who have not before proved their debts may prove
them and the affignees fhall produce fair accounts, and
be fworn to them alfo to the commiffioners, if required by
the creditors, and thereafter deduct all neceffary
difburfements and expences and the commiffioners fhall make an order,
under their hands and feals, to juftify the creditors upon

tion ratelike, according to the quantity of his debts, 13
Eli c 7 ſ 2), which order ſhall contain the time and
place of making it, and the total of the debts proved, and
of the money in the hands of the aſſignees, and how much
in the pound ſhall be then diſtributed, one part of which
order ſhall be filed among the proceedings under the
commiſſion, and each of the aſſignees ſhall have a duplicate thereof. And the aſſignees ſhall take receipts for the
ſame, in a book to be kept for that purpoſe. 5 G 2
c 30 ſ 33.

Allowance to
the bankrupt.

55. The bankrupt ſurrendring and conforming, ſhall
be allowed 5l per cent. if after ſuch allowance, the neat
produce of his eſtate will pay 10s in the pound, ſo as the
ſaid 5l per cent amount not to above 200l.

And if the neat produce will pay 12s 6d in the pound
he ſhall be allowed 7l 10s per cent ſo as it amount not
to above 250l.

And if it will pay 15s in the pound, he ſhall be allowed
10l per cent. ſo as it exceed not above 300l.

If the neat produce will not pay 10s in the pound, the
bankrupt ſhall be allowed ſo much as the aſſignees and
commiſſioners ſhall think fit, not exceeding 3l per cent
5 G 2 c 30 ſ 7, 8.

But the ſame ſhall not be paid to the bankrupt, till a final
dividend ſhall be made, becauſe until that time, creditors
may ſtill come in to prove their debts. 1 Atk 228.

56. But no diſcovery on oath ſhall intitle the bankrupt
to the ſaid allowance, unleſs the commiſſioners ſhall, under their hands and ſeal, certify, to the lord chancellor,
that he hath made a full diſcovery of his eſtate, and in all
things conformed himſelf, and that there doth not appear
to them any reaſon to doubt of the truth of ſuch diſcovery,
or that the ſame is not a full diſcovery, and unleſs four
parts in five in number and value of the creditors, who
ſhall be creditors for not leſs than 20l, and who have
proved their debts or ſome perſon by them authoriſed
thereto, ſhall ſign the certificate, and teſtify their conſent
to ſuch allowance and certificate, and to the bankrupt's
diſcharge, to be alſo certified by the commiſſioners, but
the commiſſioners ſhall not certify the ſame, till they have
proof by affidavit of every creditor, or of the perſon by
them reſpectively authoriſed, ſigning the ſaid certificate,
and of the power by which any perſon is ſo authoriſed
(and brokers of attornies of perſons refuſing to fore ſwear
parts, as to be inconſiderable, ſhall be deemed evidence
in ſupport of ſaid power, 2 G 2 c 57 ſ 10) which
ſhall admit it, together with ſuch power to ſign, ſhall be
laid

laid before the lord chancellor with the certificate in order for allowing the fame,—and unless the bankrupt make oath, that the certificate and content of the creditors were obtained fairly and without fraud, and unless the certificate shall, after such oath, be allowed and confirmed by the lord chancellor, or two of the judges to whom he shall refer it and any of the creditors shall be allowed to be heard against making the certificate, and against the confirmation of it nor shall any commissioner sign the certificate, till after four parts in five in number and value of the creditors shall have signed it   5 G 2 c 30 ∫ 10

And every security given to the use of any creditor, to induce him to sign such allowance or certificate, shall be void   ia ∫ 11

Moreover, no bankrupt shall be intitled to such allowance, who hath upon marriage of any child given above 100 l, unless he prove by his books, or upon his oath, that he had remaining at the time sufficient to pay his debts, or who hath lost in one day the value of 5 l, or in the whole the value of 100 l, in 12 months next before his becoming bankrupt, at cards, dice, tables, tennis, bowl, billiards, shovelboard, cockfighting, horse-races, dog-matches, foot-races, or other pastime or game, or in bearing a part in the stakes, or by betting; or hath within one year before he became a bankrupt lost 100 l, by contracts for the stock of any company, or publick funds, where the contract was not to be performed within a week, or where the stock was not actually transferred   5 G 2 c 30 ∫ 12.

And moreover, by 24 G 2 c 57 When any person shall fraudulently swear, before the major part of the commissioners, or by affidavit exhibited to them, that a sum of money is due to him from the bankrupt, which shall in fact not be really owing, and shall, in respect of such fictitious debt, sign the certificate for such bankrupt's discharge, in such case, unless the bankrupt shall, before the major part of the commissioners have signed the certificate, by writing signed by him and delivered to one or more of the commissioners or assignees, disclose the fraud, and object to the reality of such debt, the certificate shall be void, and the bankrupt shall not be intitled to his discharge or allowance   ∫ 9

M 1766 A person became a bankrupt, and complied with all the directions of the act 5 G 2 c 30 so far that his certificate was signed by the creditors, but not allowed by the chancellor After signing the certificate, the assignees permitted the bankrupt to purchase his old stock

ftock in trade, for which they took collateral fecurity.
With this ftock the bankrupt carried on a new trade for about
four years, and then died poffeffed of about 3000l —By the
lord chancellor *Camden* Tho' the general pofition is true,
that a bankrupt is not cleared till his certificate is allowed
by the chancellor , yet in this cafe, from the circumftances
of the confent of the affignees, and the long acquiefcence
of the creditors, they fhall be barred from any claim on
this new acquired eftate And he compared it to the cafe
of a firft mortgagee who fees another mortgage executed
without giving notice

57 The bankrupt, after allowance of the certificate, *Bankrupt's duty after allowance.*
fhall attend on notice in writing from the affignees, to
fettle accounts, and fhall have 2 s 6 d a day allowed for
attendance , and if he fhall neglect or refufe, he fhall,
on oath made by the affignees before the commiffioner ,
be apprehended and committed to clofe gaol, by warrant
of the faid commiffioners, till he conform 5 G 2 c 30
f 36

58 To prevent expences, no money fhall be paid out *Commiffioners pay*
of the effects for eating or drinking of the commiffioners,
or of any other perfon, nor fhall the commiffioners have
above 20 s each for each meeting, nor any fchedule be
annexed to the deed of affignment Commiffioners acting
contrary hereto, fhall be difabled for ever to act as fuch.
5 G 2 c 30 f 42

59 If by the death of commiffioners, or otherwife, it *Half fees on renewing the commiffion*
be neceffary to renew the commiffion, half fees only fhall
be paid 5 G 2 c 30 f 45

60 All bills of fees or difburfements demanded by any *Attorney's bill*
folicitor, clerk, or attorney, fhall be fettled and certified
by a mafter in chancery, who fhall have for the fame 20 s.
5 G 2 c 30 f 46

61 Bankrupt dying before diftribution, fhall not hinder *Bankrupt dying.*
the diftribution 1 Jac c 15 f 17

And if the certificate be allowed in the life-time of the
bankrupt, it is good, tho' it be not confirmed by the lord
chancellor till after his death for the operative force of
it arifes from the confent of the creditors, and when
confirmed, it hath its effect from the beginning 1 Atk 77

And the allowance to the bankrupt, being a vefted intereft, fhall go to his executor 1 Atk 208

62 In 18 months after iffuing the commiffion, the af- *Second dividend.*
fignees fhall make a fecond dividend, and fhall caufe notice to be inferted in the gazette of the time and place the
commiffioners intend to meet to make a fecond diftribution, and for the creditors who have not proved their
debts

debts to come and prove them. And at such meeting, the assignees shall produce their account on oath, and what is in their hands shall by order of the commissioners be forthwith divided. Which second dividend shall be final, unless a suit in law or equity be depending, or part of the estate standing out that cannot have been disposed of, or that the major part of the creditors shall not have agreed to be sold, or unless some other or future estate of the bankrupt shall come to the assignees, which they shall, as soon as may be, convert into money, and in two months distribute the same in like manner. 5 G 2 c 30 ſ 37

But no suit in in equity, shall be commenced by the assignees, without consent of the major part in value of the creditors, who shall be present at a meeting of the creditors pursuant to notice in the gazette. id ſ 38

63. If the bankrupt shall be taken in execution, or detained in prison, for debt owing before his bankruptcy, by reason that judgment was obtained before the certificate was allowed and confirmed, any judge of the court, on producing the certificate, may order him to be discharged without fee. 5 G 2 c 30 ſ 13

And if the bankrupt's estate will pay 15 s in the pound, he shall be discharged from all the debts by him owing at the time he became bankrupt. And if he shall be arrested or prosecuted for any debt due before that time, he shall be discharged on common bail, and may plead in general, that the cause of action did accrue before he became bankrupt, and may give this act, and the special matter in evidence, and the certificate of his conforming, and allowance thereof, shall be sufficient evidence of the trading, bankruptcy, commission, and other proceedings precedent to the obtaining the certificate, and a verdict shall pass for the defendant, unless the plaintiff can prove that the certificate was obtained fraudulently, or can make appear a concealment by the bankrupt to the value of 10 l. And if the plaintiff is cast, the defendant shall have full costs. 5 G 2 c 30 ſ 7

But no commission of bankruptcy shall issue against any person who shall have been discharged by this act, or shall have compounded with his creditors, or delivered to them his estate, and been released by them, or been discharged by an act of insolvency, then the body only of such person conforming shall be free from arrest and imprisonment, but his future estate shall remain liable to his creditors (his tools of trade, necessary household goods and furniture, and necessary wearing apparel of himself and wife and children only excepted), unless the estate of such fuch perfon fhall produce clear of all charges 15 s in the pound *ra* § 9

64. But the bankrupt's difcharge, and allowance of his certificate, will not preclude the creditors from proceeding againft his fureties 1 *Atk* 83   *Sureties not difcharged*

65. The commiffioners fhall, on lawful requeft of the bankrupt, declare how they have beftowed his lands and goods, and pay to him the overplus, if any there be 13 *L* c 7 J 4   *Commiffioners to account and pay the overplus*

66. On petition to the lord chancellor, he may order the proceedings to be entred of record, to be at any time fearched and produced as evidence 5 G 2 c 30 J 41   *Proceedings to be entred of record*

67. Commiffioner fued for any thing done on the ftatute of 13 *El* and 1 *J* may plead the general iffue, and if he recovers, fhall have his cofts 1 *J* c 13 J 16 But there is no provifion for any thing done by them, or by the affignees, or any of the fubfequent ftatutes   *Remedy on commiffioner being fued*

68. The commiffion fhall not abate by the death of the king 5 G 2 c 30 J 45   *King's death not to abate the commiffion*

Note, the act of 5 C 2 c 30 fo often mentioned above, is but temporary, and by the laft continuance is of force till *Sept* 29, 1785, &c

A. Warrant to apprehend a bankrupt

Weftmoreland   {   To ————

WHEREAS a certificate under the hands and feals of ———— hath this day been produced before me ———— fetting forth that a commiffion of bankruptcy is iffued againft ———— and that the faid ———— is proved before them the faid ———— being the major part of the commiffioners authorized in the faid commiffion, to be a bankrupt And whereas application hath been made to me by ———— by order of the faid commiffioners, for the apprehending the faid ———— Thefe are therefore to require you, on fight hereof, to take and apprehend the faid ———— and bring him before me or fome other of his majefty's juftices of the peace for the faid county, to be proceeded againft according to law Given under my hand and feal this ———— day of, &c.

B Com-

B. Commitment thereon

Weftmorland $\left\{\begin{array}{l}\text{To the keeper of the common gaol}\\ \text{at ——— in the faid county, } \mathcal{J} \text{ P}\\ \text{efquire one of his majefty's juftices}\\ \text{of the peace for the faid county,}\\ \text{fendeth greeting}\end{array}\right.$

I Send to you herewith ——— being duly certified to be a bankrupt, requiring you to keep him in the faid gaol until he fhall be difcharged according to law Given ———

Baron Court.

THE *court baron* is a court which every lord of a manor (anciently called a *baron*) hath within the precinct of that manor The bufinefs thereof is, to inquire of matters concerning the lord and tenant in their *civil* capacity only, as of the death of tenants fince the laft court, of alienations, furrenders, incroachments, trefpaffes, efcheats, forfeitures, and fuch like. But with this court is frequently held, by grant or prefcription, a *court leet*, the jurifdiction whereof extendeth to all *criminal* matters within the precinct, for the prefervation of the king's peace For which fee the title *Leet*

Barratry.

I *What it is*
II *How punifhed*

I. *What it is.*

THIS word *barratry* we have received either from the *Danes*, or *Normans*, or both for *barratta* in the *Danifh*, and *baret* in the *Norman*, do equally fignify a quarrel or contention

And a *barrator*, in legal acceptation, doth fignify a common mover, exciter, or maintainer of fuits or quarrels, either in courts, or in the country, 1 Inft 368 1 Haw 243.

A

A common mover] It feems clear that no one can be a barrator in refpect of one act only , for every indictment for fuch crime muft charge the defendant with being a *common barrator*. 1 Haw. 243, 4.

Mover, exciter, or maintainer] Yet it feemeth, that an attorney is in no danger of being judged guilty of an act of barratry, in refpect of his maintaining another in a groundlefs action, to the commencing whereof he was no way privy. 1 *Haw* 243

Alfo it hath been holden, that a man fhall not be adjudged a barrator, in refpect of any number of falfe actions brought by him in his own right , for in fuch cafes he is liable to cofts. 1 *Haw* 243.

In courts] Either courts of record , or not of record, as in the county, hundred, or other inferior courts. 1 *Inft.* 368

Or in the country] In three manners 1 In difturbance of the peace. 2 In taking or keeping of poffeffion of lands in controverfy, not only by force, but alfo by fubtilty and deceit, and moft commonly in fuppreffion of truth and right 3 By falfe inventions, and fowing of calumniations, rumours, and reports, whereby difcord and difquiet may grow between neighbours 1 *Inft* 368

II. How punifhed.

By the ftatute of 34 *Ed* 3 c. 1 *The juftices of the peace fhall have power to reftrain all barratos, and to purfue, arreft, take and chaftife them, according to their trefpafs or offence*

And altho' this ftatute doth not create the offence, but fuppofes it at common law, and only appoints the punifhment, yet an indictment of barratry, concluding *againft the form of the ftatute*, is holden to be good, and agreeable to many precedents *Cro Eliz.* 148. 1 *Haw* 244.

But it hath been refolved, that fuch indictment is not good, without alfo concluding *againft the peace*, for this is an effential part of it, as being an offence by the common law. 1 *Haw* 244

And it hath been holden, that an indictment of this kind may be good, without alledging the offence at any certain *place* , becaufe, from the nature of the thing, confifting of the repetition of feveral acts, it muft be intended to have happened in feveral places, for which caufe it is faid, that a trial ought to be by a jury from the body of the county 1 *Haw* 244

Which cafe, and that of a common fcold, feem to be the only offences for which a general indictment will lie, without fhewing any of the particular facts in the indictment, for barratry is an offence of a complicated nature, confifting in the repetition of divers acts in difturbance of the peace, and it would be two prolix to enumerate them in the indictment, and therefore experience hath fettled it to be fufficient to charge a man generally as a common barrettor, and before the time to give the defendant a note of the particular matters which are intended to be proved againft him, for otherwife it will be impoffible to prepare a defence againft fo general and uncertain a charge, which may be proved by fuch a multiplicity of different inftances, and therefore the court generally will not fuffer the profecution to go on in the trial of the indictment, without fuch note being given to the defendant   1 *Haw* 244. 2 *Haw* 226, 7

As to the kind and manner of punifhment, it is faid, that if the offender be a common perfon, he fhall be fined and imprifoned, and bound to his good behaviour; and if he be of any profeffion relating to the law, he ought alfo to be farther punifhed, by being difabled to practife for the future   1 *Haw* 244

And by the 12 *G c* 29 If any perfon, who hath been convicted of forgery, perjury, fubornation of perjury, or common barratry, fhall practife as an attorney or folicitor, he fhall be tranfported for feven years   ſ 4

Baſtards.

Concerning the fettlement of baftard children, fee title **Poor.**

I *Who shall be deemed a bastard*

1. THE word *bastard* seemeth to have been brought unto us by the *Saxons*, and to be compounded of *base*, vile or ignoble, and *start*, or *steort* signifying a rise or original By the common people in the north (amongst whom is preserved much of the ancient *Saxon*) it is still pronounced *bystart*, denoting a person sprung from a vile or spurious origin, even as an *upstart* is a person suddenly risen from a mean extraction in general

Meaning of the word bastard.

2 Lord *Coke* says, We term all by the name of bastards that are born out of lawful marriage By the common law, if the husband be within the four seas, that is, within the jurisdiction of the king of *England*, if the wife hath issue, no proof is to be admitted to prove the child a bastard, unless the husband hath an apparent *impossibility* of procreation, as if the husband be but eight years old, or under the age of procreation, such issue is bastard, albeit he be born within marriage But if the issue be born within a month, or a day, after marriage, between parties of full lawful age, the child is legitimate. 1 *Inst.* 244

Bastard born in lawful marriage.

M 6 G 2 *Lomax* and *Holman* In ejectment the question on a trial at bar was, whether the lessor was son and heir of *Caleb Lomax*, esquire, deceased, which depended on the question of his mother's marriage. And that being fully proved, and evidence given of the husband's being frequently at *London*, where the mother lived, so that access must be presumed, the defendants were admitted to give evidence of his inability from a bad habit of body But their evidence not going to an *impossibility*, but an improbability only, that was not thought sufficient, and there was a verdict for the plaintiff. *Str.* 940

And it is said, that formerly if the husband was within the four seas, no proof of *non access* to his wife was admitted, but the child was deemed to be his, but as this notion was built on no rational foundation, it is now entirely departed from, and though the husband and wife are both in *England*, if there is sufficient proof that he had no access to her, the child will be a bastard And this was determined in the case of *Pendrell* and *Pendrell*, *M* 5 *G* 2 which was an issue out of chancery, to try whether the plaintiff was the heir at law of one *Thomas Pendrell* It was agreed, that the plaintiff's father and mother were married, and cohabited for some months, that they

they

they parted, ſhe ſtaying in *London*, and he going into *Staffordſhire*, that at the end of three years the plaintiff was born And there being ſome doubt upon the evidence, whether the huſband had not been in *London* within the laſt year, it was ſent to be tried And the plaintiff reſted at firſt upon the preſumption of law in favour of legitimacy, which was encountered by ſtrong evidence of no acceſs And it was agreed by court and counſel, on the trial at *Guildhall*, before Lord Ch J. *Raymond*, that the old doctrine of being within the four ſeas was not to take place, but the jury were at liberty to conſider of the point of acceſs, which they did, and found againſt the plaintiff. And the court of chancery acquieſced in the determination. *Str.* 925 *Andr.* 9.

T. 10 G. 2 *K* and the inhabitants of *Bedall* in *Yorkſhire*. An order was made upon one *Moor*, as the putative father of two baſtards, born of the body of *Elizabeth* the wife of *Richard Sharpleſs* in which it was ſtated, that for ſeven years before, the huſband had had no acceſs to her, ſhe having never ſeen or heard of him all that time, and not knowing whether he was alive or dead, which the juſtices adjudge to be true, and that *Moor* is the father of them, and order him to provide accordingly Upon appeal to the ſeſſions, the caſe is ſtated with ſome variation that in 1728, ſhe was married to *Sharpleſs*, then a ſoldier in *Mullin*'s troop, in a barn, by a perſon not in the habit of a clergyman, that there had been no acceſs for ſeven years but it appearing by a certificate from the commiſſary general's office, and from the evidence of *Simon Clarkſon*, that one *Richard Sharpleſs*, who he was told was formerly in *Mullin*'s troop, was muſtered as a private gentlemen in the third troop of horſe guards, from *June* 25, 1733, to *Feb* 23, 1736, though *Clarkſon* ſaid he could not take upon him to ſwear that it was the ſame *Richard Sharpleſs* pretended to be married as aforeſaid, upon this ſuppoſition of the huſband's being alive, the ſeſſions were of opinion, the children were not baſtards, and reverſed the order of the two juſtices And now upon debate, the order of ſeſſions was quaſhed, and the order of two juſtices confirmed for it being ſtated in both orders, that there was no acceſs according to the caſe of *Pendrell* and *Pendrell*, it was immaterial whether the huſband was alive or not *Str* 1076.

And, *M* 10 *W K* and *Abberton* The caſe was, a feme covert, during the abſence of her huſband at *Cadiz*, was brought to bed of a baſtard, and her huſband was not in *England* from the time of her conception, till ſhe was

brought

brought to bed. The queſtion was, whether this child was a baſtard, eſpecially within the words of the ſtatute of the 18 *Eliz.* (hereafter following) which ſaith, *children begotten and born out of lawful matrimony,* which cannot be ſaid of this caſe, the mother being married at the time of the birth of the child, and if ſuch a mother ſhould kill ſuch child, ſhe could not be guilty of murder within the ſtatute of the 21 *J. c.* 27   But by the court, He is a baſtard who is begotten and born of a feme covert, whilſt the huſband is beyond the four ſeas.   And in a real action if general baſtardy was pleaded, the biſhop ought to certify ſuch a one a baſtard   And where a man is a baſtard, he is ſuch to all purpoſes, and why not within the 18 *El* For though the ſtatute of 21 *J* is a penal law, yet the act of 18 *El.* is a remedial law. L *Raym* 395, 396

3 But this non-acceſs of the huſband ought to be prov- ed otherwiſe than upon the wife's oath , as in the follow- ing caſe, *M.* 8 *G* 2 *K* and *Reading*   The defendant *Reading* was adjudged by an order of baſtardy, to be the putative father of a baſtard child, begotten of the wife of one *Almort* of *Sherborn.*   The ſaid woman on the appeal, gave evidence, that the ſaid *Reading* had carnal knowledge of her body in or about *Auguſt* 1732, and ſeveral times ſince, and that her huſband had no acceſs to her from *May* 1731, to the time of her examination in that court, being the 3d of *October* 1733, and that the ſaid *Reading* was the father of the ſaid child   And the queſtion on removal of the ſame into the king's bench was, whether the wife in this caſe ſhould be admitted as an evidence for or againſt her huſband, and to baſtardize her own child   And the whole court were of opinion, that the wife could be a witneſs to no other fact but that of incontinence, and that this ſhe muſt be admitted to be witneſs to from the neceſſity of the thing; but not to the abſence of her huſband, which might properly be proved by other witneſſes, and likened it to the caſe of hue and cry, where the perſon robbed ſhall be admitted a witneſs of the fact of robbery, but not to prove any other matter relating thereto, as in what hundred the place was, and the like, becauſe that may be proved by others   2 *Seſſ Ca* 175.

How far the wife s oath ſhall be admitted in ſuch caſe.

And in the caſe of *K* and *Rooke, M.* 26 *G* 2.   The order of the two juſtices ſtates, it appears to us by exa- mination of *Dorothy* the wife of the reverend Mr. *Henry Bird,* that ſhe lived ſeparate from her huſband from *Mi- chaelmas* 1750, to *February* 1752, and that ſhe has not in all that time ſeen or been with him, he being a priſoner in *York* caſtle. That *John Rooke* had carnal knowledge of her

her

her body, on the 30th of *January* 1750, and got her with child of the baſtard Exception was taken, that the wife in this caſe was an incompetent witneſs By *Lee* Ch J and the court How far the evidence of the wife it is to be admitted upon orders of baſtardy, is now ſettled in the caſe of *K* and *Reading*, where the wife appeared upon the order to be the only witneſs to charge the putative father upon this, the order was quaſhed, and the reaſon given by the court was, that the wife might be admitted to prove the act of adultery *ex neceſſitate*, for of that there could be no other evidence, but not to prove other facts, of which there may be witneſſes The caſe being ſimilar, muſt be determined upon the authority of that caſe. The wife's examination alone does not make the order bad, but the facts to which ſhe is examined The neceſſity of the thing excepts her, as to the fact of adultery, out of the general rule, but not as to the fact of no acceſs, for that may be proved by particular circumſtances examinable by the juſtices below But upon this order ſhe appears to be the only evidence and her declarations are not admiſſible to baſtardize her iſſue And the order was quaſhed 1 *Wilſon*, 340

But in the caſe of *K* and *Bedall* abovementioned, The order reciting, that on the examination of the mother, and on other proof, it appeared that her huſband had no acceſs to her, was held to be good, for there the woman's oath is not ſet forth as the only evidence, but *other proof*, which muſt be intended legal proof *Andr* 8

Child born during a divorce

4 M 5 1 St George's and St *Margaret's Weſtminſter* Where a woman is ſeparated from her huſband by a divorce *a menſa & thoro*, the children ſhe has during the ſeparation are baſtards, for a due obedience to the ſentence ſhall be intended, unleſs the contrary be ſhewed but if a huſband and wife, without ſentence, do part and live ſeparate, the children ſhall be taken to be legitimate, and ſo deemed till the contrary be proved, for acceſs ſhall be intended But if a ſpecial verdict find the man had no acceſs, it is a baſtard, and ſo was the opinion of lord *Hale*, in the caſe of *Dickins and Collins* 1 Salk. 123.

Widow having a child after the huſband's death.

5 The law hath appointed no exact certain time, for the birth of legitimate iſſue, by the widow after the death of her huſband 1 *Danv* 726

M 7 J *Alſop* and *Bowtrell* The queſtion was, whether, the woman being delivered of a child forty weeks and nine days after the death of her huſband, ſuch child ſhould be deemed a baſtard. And it was proved, that her deceaſed

deceaſed huſband's father did much abuſe her, and cauſed her to lie in the ſtreets, and three phyſicians (two of them being doctors of phyſick) made oath, that the child came in time convenient to be the child of the party who died, and that the uſual time for a woman to go with child, is nine months and ten days, to wit, ſolar months, at thirty days to the month, and not lunar months, and that by reaſon of the want of ſtrength in the woman or the child, or by reaſon of ill uſage, ſhe might be a longer time, viz to the end of ten months or more. And the phyſicians further affirmed, that a perfect birth may be at ſeven months, according to the ſtrength of the mother or child, which is as long before the time of the proper birth. And by the ſame reaſon it may be as long deferred by accident, which is commonly occaſioned by infirmities of the body, or paſſions of the mind. And the child was adjudged to be legitimate. *Cro Jac* 541.

II. Securing the reputed father

By the 6 G 2 c 31. Whereas the laws now in being are not ſufficient to provide for the ſecuring and indemnifying pariſhes and other places, from the great charges frequently ariſing from children begotten and born out of lawful matrimony, it is enacted, *That if any ſingle woman ſhall be delivered of a baſtard child, which ſhall be chargeable, or likely to become chargeable to any pariſh or extraparochial place, or ſhall declare herſelf to be with child, and that ſuch child is likely to be born a baſtard, and to be chargeable to any pariſh or extraparochial place, and ſhall in either of ſuch caſes, in an examination (A) to be taken in writing, upon oath, before one juſtice of the county, city, or town corporate, where ſuch pariſh or place ſhall lie, charge any perſon with having gotten her with child, it ſhall be lawful for ſuch juſtice, upon application made to him by the overſeers of the poor of ſuch pariſh, or one of them, or by any ſubſtantial houſholder of ſuch extraparochial place, to iſſue out his warrant (B) for the immediate apprehending ſuch perſon ſo charged as aforeſaid, and for bringing him before ſuch juſtice, or before any other of his majeſty's juſtices of the peace of ſuch county, city, or town corporate. And the juſtice before whom ſuch perſon ſhall be brought ſhall commit (C) him to the common gaol or houſe of correction, unleſs he ſhall give ſecurity (D) to indemnify ſuch pariſh or place, or ſhall enter into a recognizance (E) with ſufficient ſurety, upon condition to appear at the next general quarter ſeſſions, or general ſeſſions, of the peace, to be holden for ſuch county or liberty, and to abide and perform ſuch order or orders as ſhall be made, in purſuance of an act paſſed in the 18th year of the reign of her late majeſty queen Eliſabeth, concerning baſtards begotten and born out of lawful matrimony.* § 1.

Iſſue out his warrant for immediate apprehending] If the conſtable, having a warrant to apprehend the reputed father, ſhall willingly or negligently ſuffer him to eſcape, he may be bound over to the ſeſſions, and there indicted, fined, and impriſoned, and under the influence thereof be compelled to make ſatisfaction to the proſecutors.

To appear at the next general quarter ſeſſions] It hath been uſual, to bind ſuch perſon to appear, not at the next ſeſſions generally, but at the next ſeſſions after the child ſhall be born, upon a principle of convenience, leſt, if the child ſhould not be born, or the mother not be able to go before the juſtices in order to filiate the child, before the next ſeſſions, the reputed father ſhould be gone, and the deſign of the act be fruſtrated   But the words of the act muſt be purſued, and therefore he muſt be bound *to appear at the next general quarter ſeſſions* [or, *general ſeſſions*] *of the peace to be holden for ſuch county or liberty, and to abide and perform ſuch order or orders as ſhall be made in purſuance of an act paſſed in the 18th year of the reign of her late majeſty queen Eliſabeth, concerning baſtards begotten and born out of lawful matrimony*

Eliſabeth} This ſtatute recites the name of queen *Eli-ſabeth* with the letter ſ, whereas the ſtatutes themſelves of that queen's reign do always exhibit her name with a z Which is noted here only, as not exactly agreeable to that preciſion which ordinarily is required in reciting acts of parliament in caſes penal

And if ſuch woman ſhall die, or be married, before ſhe ſhall be delivered, or miſcarry of ſuch child, or ſhall appear not to have been with child at the time of her examination, ſuch per-ſon ſhall be diſcharged from his recognizance at the next ſeſſions, or immediately releaſed out of cuſtody by warrant of one juſtice reſiding in or near the limits where ſuch pariſh or place ſhall be. § 2

And on application made by any ſuch perſon, who ſhall be committed to any gaol or houſe of correction, or by any perſon on his behalf, to any juſtice reſiding in or near the limits where ſuch pariſh or place ſhall be, ſuch juſtice ſhall ſummon the over-ſeers of the poor of ſuch pariſh, or one or more ſubſtantial houſ-holders of ſuch extraparochial place, to appear before him at a time and place to be mentioned in ſuch ſummons, to ſhew cauſe why ſuch perſon ſhould not be diſcharged And if no order ſhall appear to have been made, in purſuance of the 18th of

That

Ehf *within fix weeks after fuch woman fhall have been de-livered, fuch juftice may difcharge him from his imprifon-ment.* ſ 3

But *it fhall not be lawful for any juftice, to fend for any woman, before fhe fhall be delivered, and one month after, in order to her being examined concerning her pregnancy, or to compel any woman, before fhe fhall be delivered, to anfwer any queftions relating to her pregnancy* ſ 4

To compel any woman] M 11 G K and *Chandler.* In-dictment for fecreting a woman big with an illegitimate child, fo that fhe could not be had to give evidence about the father The defendant demurred. And by the court, Judgment muft be given for the defendant, for the child cannot be illegitimate before it is born, there being always a poffibility that it may be born in lawful wedlock And by this act the woman is not to be compelled. *Str* 612. L *Raym.* 1368

III. Bond to indemnify the parifh.

By the aforefaid ftatute of 6 *G.* 2 *c.* 31 The juftice before whom the party fhall be brought fhall commit him, unlefs he fhall give *fecurity to indemnify the parifh,* or enter into recognizance to appear at the feffions

In this cafe, whether a bond or other fecurity ought to be made to the churchwardens and overfeers and their fucceffors, or to their executors or adminiftrators, hath been queftioned , concerning which the author of the *Readings upon the Statutes* faith thus Thofe gentlemen who have taken upon them to direct the officers, to have fuch bonds or other fecurities made to them and their fucceffors, would do well to confider, whether the church-wardens and overfeers are fuch a corporation as can pur-chafe, fue and be fued And whether bonds, being things in action, it may not be difficult for the fucceffors of the churchwardens and overfeers, to whom they were made, to maintain an action on a bond made to their predecef-fors It is true, churchwardens may maintain an action for the goods of their church but they are not fuch a corporation, as can take or purchafe lands, or take fecu-rities for the ufe of their church, except in London. And it was never pretended, that the churchwardens and overfeers of the poor are a corporation in any refpect in relation to the poor, and confequently can neither fue nor be fued as fuch *Read Baft*

And indeed, upon the whole, the taking of a bond in any kind feemeth not fo convenient for the parifh, as an order made by the juftices , becaufe the fuing upon a bond is both tedious and expenſive, whereas the courſe of carrying an order into execution is very ſhort and eaſy

But then, on the other hand, a bond will bind a man's executors, but the order of the juſtices being obligatory only upon the man himſelf, when he dies, the order dieth with him

It ſometimes happens, by the mother's removing into another pariſh, that the child is not born in the pariſh indemnified, but this doth not abſolutely quit the bond becauſe there is a conſequential damage to the pariſh indemnified, which may affect the reputed father. For where the child goes with the mother for nurture, the pariſh where the child was born, and not the pariſh where it reſides with the mother, is bound to maintain it. As in the caſe of *Simpſon* and *Johnſon*, M 19 G 3 which was a caſe reſerved from the aſſizes for the opinion of the court, on an action of debt upon a bond. The defendant *Johnſon*, being apprehended by virtue of a warrant under the ſtatute of 6 G 2 gave bond in the uſual form to indemnify the pariſh of *Wickham St. Paul*, againſt all coſts, charges, and other demands, touching and concerning a child of which *Jemima Waaſs* was then pregnant, and likely to be born a baſtard. It happened, that before the birth of the child ſhe removed herſelf voluntarily from *Wickham St Paul* to the pariſh of *Gueſtingthorpe*, and was there delivered of the ſame baſtard child. After her delivery, ſhe returned to the pariſh of *Wickham St Paul*, where her legal ſettlement was, carrying her child with her, and received 1 s 6 d weekly from the plaintiff *Simpſon*, who was one of the overſeers of the poor there, for the maintenance of herſelf and her child. No order was made by any juſtice, directing the allowance of the ſaid 1 s 6 d or any other ſum to be made by the pariſh officers of *Wickham St Paul*. And no demand was made at any time on the defendant *Johnſon*, who lived in the adjoining pariſh of *Gueſtingthorpe*, but a demand was made on one of his ſureties, who refuſed to pay — The court were ſo clearly of opinion with the defendant, that they would not hear his counſel. Lord *Mansfield* ſaid, that the payment by the pariſh officers of *Wickham* was doubly voluntary, firſt, becauſe there had been no order upon them to pay, and ſecondly, becauſe they were not liable to maintain the child, but the pariſh where it was born, and they ſhould have applied to the officers of that pariſh *Douglas*, 7 — And this pariſh, by virtue of the bond, might have a remedy over againſt the reputed father

This queſtion, whether children under ſeven years of age, who are living with their mother for nurture at the

place

place of the mother's ſettlement, but whoſe own ſettlement is in another pariſh, are to be maintained by the pariſh where the mother lives and is ſettled, was determined in the caſe of *Darlington* and *Hemlington*, H 17 G 3 *Eleanor Gay* went with a certificate from the townſhip of *Hemlington* in the North Riding of the county of *York*, to the townſhip of *Darlington* in the county of *Durham*, and during her reſidence at *Darlington* bore two baſtard children there. Afterwards becoming chargeable, two juſtices removed the ſaid *Eleanor Gay* from the ſaid townſhip of *Darlington* to the ſaid townſhip of *Hemlington* which gave the certificate, but ſaid nothing in their order of removal concerning the two baſtard children, one of whom was then four years of age, and the other two years. The mother took them with her to *Hemlington* Whereupon *Hemlington* applied to ſome of the juſtices in the county of *Durham*, for an order upon the townſhip of *Darlington* to maintain the ſaid two baſtard children then reſiding at *Hemlington* with their mother as nurſe children And after ſummoning the overſeers of *Darlington* to ſhew cauſe, two juſtices of the county of *Durham* made an order upon the overſeers of *Darlington* to pay to the overſeers of *Hemlington* two ſhillings weekly, for the maintenance of the ſaid two baſtard children, whilſt nurſe children with their mother at *Hemlington*. The overſeers of *Darlington* appealed againſt this order of maintenance, but offered to receive and provide for the children in the townſhip of *Darlington* The ſingle queſtion before the ſeſſions was, " Whether the townſhip of *Darlington* was or " was not obliged to pay to the townſhip of *Hemlington* " any relief for the two baſtard children, whilſt they re- " mained with their mother as nurſe children at, and at " the expence of, the ſaid townſhip of *Hemlington*, ſhe re- " fuſing to part with them to the townſhip of *Darlington* " And the ſeſſions, being of opinion that they were not obliged, quaſhed the order of maintenance. The proceedings being removed into the court of king's bench, the court were of opinion, that the townſhip of *Darlington* was obliged to maintain the two children at *Hemlington*, whilſt reſiding there with their mother as nurſe children, and therefore quaſhed the order of ſeſſions, and affirmed the order of two juſtices *M S.*

And there is no difference as to this point between baſtards and legitimate children As in the caſe of *Shermandbury* and *Bolney (Carth 279)* A woman with three children, all under ſeven years of age, being ſettled in *Shermandbury*, married a man ſettled in *Bolney* After the marriage, the mother and three children were ſent to *Bolney*

The

The parish of *Shermandbury*, before the marriage, allowed 3 s a week for the three children, and the payment being diſcontinued after the marriage, two juſtices, on complaint of the parish of *Bolney*, made an order that *Shermandbury* ſhould continue to pay the 3 s The ſeſſions, and after wards the court of king's bench, confirmed the order of the juſtices. And the court ſaid, This caſe is within the equity of the ſtatute for relief of the poor, and there is no reaſon that *Shermandbury* ſhould be diſcharged of the chil dren by their mother's marriage *Douglas*, 10.

M 21 G 3 *Kirk* and *Strickland* It was moved for a rule to ſhew cauſe, why the defendant ſhould not be diſ charged upon filing common bail It was an action of debt upon a bond, conditioned for the indemnification of a pariſh againſt a baſtard child The penalty in the bond was 50 l, and the plaintiff, in his affidavit for holding the defendant to bail, had ſworn that he was juſtly in debted to him in that ſum. But the defendant, in the affidavit on which this motion was grounded, ſwore that only 3 l and ſome odd ſhillings were really due The court ſaid the conduct of the plaintiff was altogether un juſtifiable, and that he was liable to an action That in the caſe of a bond conditioned for the performance of a promiſe of marriage, and in ſome other inſtances, the penalty is the real debt, but, in other caſes, the bail could only be taken for the ſum to which the plaintiff would be intitled in damages for the breach of the con dition At firſt, however, they ſeemed to think they could not relieve the defendant upon this ſummary appli cation, it having been a uniform rule not to go into the merits, upon ſuch a motion, but to take the matter as it ſtood upon the affidavit to hold to bail, but at laſt they granted the rule, declaring that they were perſuaded the plaintiff would not venture to ſhew cauſe againſt it *Douglas*, 432

F 18 G , *Brangum* and *Perrot* It was moved for leave to pay 40 l (being the whole penalty of a bond to indemnify a pariſh againſt a baſtard child) into court, with coſts It was objected, that this was an action for a ſingle breach of the bond, on which the pariſh was in titled to recover, after which, the penalty ſhall ſtill re main in full force, to anſwer ſubſequent breaches, as they may ariſe, *in æquum tum* But not allowed by the court And the lord chief juſtice *De Grey* ſaid, This is ſo plain a caſe, that nothing that one can ſay can make it plainer The bond aſcertains the damage by conſent of parties If therefore the defendant pays the plaintiff the whole ſtated damages, what can he deſire more *Black Rep* 1190

If.

II. Order of filiation and maintenance by the juſtices.

If ſecurity hath not been given to indemnity the pariſh, the next thing in the courſe of proceeding is the order of filiation and maintenance to be made by the juſtices

By the 18 *El c 3 Concerning baſtards begotten and born out of lawful matrimony, the ſaid baſtards being now left to be kept at the charges of the pariſh where they were born, to the great burden of the ſame pariſh, and to the evil example and encouragement of lewd life, it is enacted, that two juſtices* (1 Q) *in or next unto the limits where the pariſh church is, within which pariſh ſuch baſtard ſhall be born, upon examination of the cauſe and circumſtances* (F), *ſhall and may by their diſcretion, take order* (G) *as well for the puniſhment of the mother and reputed father, as alſo for the better relief of ſuch pariſh, in part or in all, and ſhall and may, by like diſcretion, take order for the keeping of every ſuch baſtard child, by charging ſuch mother or reputed father, with the payment of money weekly, or other ſuſtentation, for the relief of ſuch child, in ſuch ways as they ſhall think meet and convenient And if after the ſame order by them ſubſcribed under their hands, the mother or reputed father, upon notice thereof, ſhall not for their part obſerve and perform the ſaid order, that then every ſuch party ſo making default in not performing the ſaid order, to be committed to ward in the common gaol, there to remain without bail or mainpriſe, except he or ſhe ſhall put in ſufficient ſurety* (H) *to perform the ſaid order, or elſe perſonally to appear at the next general ſeſſions of the peace, to be holden in that county where ſuch order ſhall be taken ; and alſo to abide ſuch order, as the ſaid juſtices, or the more part of them, then and there ſhall take in that behalf (if they then and there ſhall take any) , and if at the ſaid ſeſſions, the ſaid juſtices ſhall take no other order, then to abide and perform the order before made, as is aboveſaid*

And by the 3 *Cha c 4 All juſtices of the peace within their ſeveral limits and precincts, and in their ſeveral ſeſſions, may do and execute all things concerning that part of the ſaid ſtatute, that by juſtices of the peace in the ſeveral counties are by the ſaid ſtatute limited to be done.* Upon which ſtatute of the 3 *Cha* there hath been great diverſity of opinion, whether or no the ſeſſions hath power thereby to make an original order in the caſe of baſtardy, without the matter coming before them by way of appeal. As to thoſe who hold the negative, namely, that the ſeſſions cannot proceed originally upon the ſaid ſtatute of the 3 *Cha.* it is clearly obſervable, although their opinion may be true, that it riſeth upon a falſe foundation, namely, upon a ſuppoſition

S tion

tion that the said statute of 3 *Cha* is expired, which is no other than a palpable oversight committed by one author, and followed by others without examination (a thing not unusual in this kind of learning) For the said statute of 3 *Cha* c 4 was enacted to be in force until the end of the first session of the then next parliament Which next parliament was in the 16 *Cha* and by an act of that parliament, namely, by the 16 *Cha.* c 4 the said statute of 3 *Cha* c 4. together with many other statutes then near expiring, are enacted to be in force, until some other act of parliament shall be made touching their continuance or discontinuance Which other act was never made

Supposing therefore that the said act of 3 *Cha* c 4 is in force, the question is, Whether by virtue thereof the sessions have power to make an original order of bastardy Concerning which, in support of the negative opinion, the history and progress of the said statute of 3 *Cha.* seems considerable, which was thus The act of 18 *El* c 3 (as appears from *Rastal's* statutes) was supplementary to, and as it were incorporated with the act of 14 *El* c 5 which acts taken together made provision for the ordering and maintenance of the poor, and were in effect the groundwork of our present poor laws Which acts (among other particulars) enacted these four things 1 That the justices within the several counties, and also the justices within cities, boroughs, and towns corporate, within their respective limits, shall take order by a weekly taxation of all and every the inhabitants for relief of the poor 2 That with respect to bastard children in particular, two justices in or next unto the limits where the parish church is, within which parish such bastard shall be born, shall take order for the keeping such bastard child, by charging the mother or reputed father, with payment of money weekly, or other sustentation, for the relief of such child 3 That if any person is aggrieved with any such taxation, he may appeal to the next general sessions to be holden within the shire 4 With a proviso, that the county justices shall not intromit, or enter into any city, borough, or town corporate, having justices of its own, for the execution hereof, for any matter or cause arising within the precincts of such city, borough, or town corporate but the justices there shall proceed, as the justices elsewhere may do within the respective counties —Now both the said statutes were suffered to expire, except only so much as is contained in the second paragraph abovementioned, rendring the mother and reputed father of bastard children liable to maintain them, which was continued from time to time, and is yet in force, therefore the clause of appealing, and the power of justices in corporations, was gone. Upon which account, the said act of 3 *Cha c* 4 which revived or continued a great number of temporary acts that by the several intermissions of parliament in those days had expired or were near expiring, and at the same time explaining or amending divers of those acts as occasion might require, speaking of this act of 18 *El* says thus. *And so much of an act made in the eighteenth year of the reign of the late queen Elizabeth, intituled, An act for setting the poor on work and avoiding idleness, as concerneth bastards begotten out of lawful matrimony* [shall be continued] *With this, That all justices of the peace within their several limits and precincts, and in their several sessions, may do and execute all things concerning that part of the said statute, that by justices of the peace in the several counties are by the said statute limited to be done* —So that the power of proceeding originally in the sessions cannot (as it seemeth) hereby be supported, but the justices, whether of the counties at large, or of towns corporate or other franchises, out of their sessions, are to charge the mother and reputed father, and if any person is aggrieved, he may appeal to the sessions just in the same manner, as if the abovesaid four clauses were all still in force

The principal cases which have been adjudged in this matter are these following

H 9 *Cha Pridgeon's* case Pridgeon was brought to the bar upon an *habeas corpus*, and it appeared, upon the return thereof, that upon complaint to the two next justices he was by them ordered too keep a bastard child, he being according to the said order the reputed father. From this order he appealed to the next sessions, at which sessions the matter being examined, he was discharged, and the order of the two justices repealed. Afterwards, at another sessions, the matter being re-examined, it was ordered according to the first order of the two justices, that he should be accounted the reputed father of the bastard, and should keep it, and that if he did not perform it, he should be apprehended and committed. And thereupon being apprehended and committed, and all this matter returned, the court held, that he being discharged at the next sessions, to which he appealed according to the statute of 18 *El* the second sessions hath no power to alter it And because none were there to maintain this return, he was bailed, and day given, that if other matter were not shewed before such a time, he should be discharged. Afterwards, this matter being moved again, all the court delivered their opinions *seriatim*, that the order in the first

sessions

ſeſſions was concluſive, and the order in the laſt ſeſſions was merely void. For the ſtatute of 18 *El* appointing, that upon appeal to the ſeſſions from an order of two
juſtices, their order ſhall bind him who is adjudged to be
the reputed father, and in this caſe, having appealed to
the ſeſſions, and they making an order in court, that order
is final, and no other ſeſſions nor authority may meddle
therewith. And it was held, that the ſtatute of 3 *Cha.*
doth not aid this caſe, for the ſtatute there is, that *if the
two next juſtices make not proviſion for the baſtard, the juſtices
at their quarter ſeſſions ſhall ſettle an order for keeping of the
baſtard as the two next juſtices ought.* But it doth not give
more power or authority, nor gives authority to one ſeſſions to alter that which in a former ſeſſions was ordered.
Cro Car. 341, 350.

E 10 *Cha.* Slater's caſe. *William Slater* was by *Elizabeth Eton* charged with the getting of a baſtard child on
her body. The two next juſtices did not make any order
in it according to the ſtatute of 18 *El.* But the cauſe
came firſt to be heard at the ſeſſions, where the juſtices
ordered that *Slater* ſhould be diſcharged of the child, and
adjudged *Alexander Leigh* to be the reputed father. Afterwards, on complaint to the judges of aſſize, the judges
ordered, that two of the next juſtices to the pariſh where
the child was born (naming them) ſhould take conſideration thereof according to the ſtatute, and ſettle ſuch
courſe therein as to juſtice appertained. Whereupon
thoſe two juſtices declared the ſaid *William Slater* to be
the reputed father, and on his refuſing to pay the ſum
ordered by them for the maintenance of the child, they
committed him. Upon removal of the proceedings into
the court of king's bench, theſe two points were reſolved
by the whole court. 1 That before the ſtatute of 3 *Cha.*
the ſeſſions had no authority to meddle in the caſe of baſtardy, till the two next juſtices according to the ſtatute of
18 *El* had made an order therein, and that then, and not
before, on the party refuſing to perform the order, and
giving ſecurity to appear at the ſeſſions and abide ſuch
order as the juſtices then and there ſhould make, the juſtices at the ſeſſions might make a new order, otherwiſe
not. 2 That by the ſtatute of 3 *Cha* the juſtices in ſeſſions have power originally to make an order, and therefore that the firſt order made by the ſeſſions was in this
caſe good and legal, and the ſecond order made by the
two next juſtices void, and could not alter or revoke the
order which was firſt made by good authority. And for
proof thereof was cited *Pridgeon's* caſe. *Cro Car.* 470.

T 13

T 13 *Cha Wood*'s caſe   On complaint to the ſeſſions againſt a woman having a baſtard child, the matter was by them referred according to law to the two next juſtices to have the examination and ordering thereof   The ſaid two juſtices made an order againſt *John Wood* to be the reputed father, and ordered him to pay a weekly ſum towards the maintenance of the ſaid child   *Wood* appealed to the ſeſſions   And the juſtices there, on a re-examination of the matter, diſallowed of the order made by the two juſtices, and they there made a new order, by which they charged one *William Cole* to be the reputed father   On a reference of the matter to Sir *William Jones* judge of aſſize, and both the orders being read in court, that is, the order made by the two next juſtices, and the ſubſequent order made at the ſeſſions, he would not enter into the re-examination of this cauſe, but did, *in omnibus*, affirm the laſt order made by the ſeſſions upon appeal to them from the firſt order, which laſt order made at the ſeſſions was final, and no appeal to be admitted againſt it and this, he ſaid, had been adjudged divers times, and mentioned particularly *Pridgeon*'s caſe   2 *Bulſtr* 355

T 4 *An Q* and *Weſton Weſton*, being adjudged by the two next juſtices to be the reputed father, appealed to the ſeſſions, where the order was confirmed, and he committed for not paying the money ordered   It was objected, that the ſeſſions ſhould have proceeded againſt him upon his recognizance   By *Holt* chief juſtice   If they proceed on the 18 *El* the ſeſſions hath no power to commit, but to proceed upon his recognizance, but if on the 3 *Cha* the ſeſſions may commit as the two juſtices might have done, that is, unleſs the party put in ſecurity to perform the order, or to appear at the next ſeſſions. 1 *Salk* 122.

M 8 *G. K* and *Cleg.*   An order of baſtardy was made at the ſeſſions (which was admitted to have original juriſdiction), and it was objected, that it was not ſaid in the order that the defendant was ever ſummoned or appeared, and natural juſtice required that he ſhould at leaſt have an opportunity to defend himſelf ——— By *Pratt* chief juſtice   I believe theſe orders made originally at ſeſſions are very rare, the uſual way being to bring the matter before the ſeſſions by way of appeal from the order of two juſtices, Now if it ſhould be taken, that the order of two juſtices will be well enough, without their ſhewing a ſummons or appearance, yet I think this caſe will fall under a very different conſideration   For in the other caſe, the party has an opportunity to relieve himſelf by appeal, whereas upon an original order at ſeſſions he can have no opportunity to bring the matter to a farther examination, ſo that it is but a lewd woman's going behind his back and ſwearing a baſtard upon him, by which means the moſt innocent man in the world may be condemned —— But the matter went off upon the point, whether it was neceſſary that the ſummons ſhould appear upon the face of the order *Sti* 475

Finally, in the caſe of *K* and *Greaves*, *E* 21 *G* 3 An original order of baſtardy was made at ſeſſions, which being removed into the king's bench by certiorari, a rule was granted to ſhew cauſe why it ſhould not be quaſhed The principal objection was, that the ſeſſions have no original juriſdiction. In ſupport of the order it was ſaid, that there are four or five caſes which have decided that the ſtatute of 3 *Cha* gives to the ſeſſions an original juriſdiction And the order was confirmed *Douglas,* 610

So that whatever may be underſtood to have been the primary intention of the ſtatute, the point ſeems now to be ſettled upon the authority of theſe caſes, that the ſeſſions have power to make an original order in caſe of baſtardy But inſtances of this kind have been ſo exceeding rare, that no caſe hath occurred wherein it hath been determined, What or whether any remedy the reputed father is intitled to, if he is diſſatisfied with ſuch order In *Weſton's* caſe above-mentioned, *Holt* chief juſtice ſaid, that the ſeſſions may commit as the two juſtices might have done, unleſs the party put in ſurety to perform the order, or to appear at the next ſeſſions Which implies an appeal from the ſame court to the ſame court, a thing not uſual in other like caſes, an appeal importing the removal of a cauſe from an interior to a higher juriſdiction On the other hand, lord chief juſtice *Pratt,* in *Gleg's* caſe, ſaid, that upon an original order it ſeſſions, the party hath no opportunity to relieve himſelf by way of appeal, and from hence urges the extreme neceſſity of a ſtrict and regular ſummons of the reputed father, leſt he happen to be condemned unheard

The ſaid baſtards being now left to be kept at the charges of the pariſh where they be born] For at that time they could have no other ſettlement There were only two kinds of ſettlements then exiſting, the one was by birth, and the other where the perſon ſhould have reſided for the moſt part during the ſpace of three years So that till the child ſhould be three years of age, it could poſſibly have no other ſettlement And the place of birth continues to be
the

the settlement of bastard children still, unless in some few excepted cases

Two justices in or next unto the limits where the parish church is] By this measuring, as it were, from the parish church, it seemeth that no other justices can intermeddle And in this matter this statute of the 18 *El* is different from most other statutes for generally where power is given to two justices, the statutes express that two or more justices may do such a thing but here the statute saith only, that two justices, dwelling in or next unto the parish, shall have power to take order therein   And Mr *Dalton* makes a *query*, what shall be done, if the two next justices cannot agree in the order, or shall make no order And this case, tho' likely enough to happen, hath not yet been determined   If they will not proceed at all, there seemeth to be no doubt, but that they may be compelled by a *mandamus*   But if they cannot agree, whether one justice, not the next, may join with either of the other in making an order, doth not appear to have been determined   Or, in this case there seems to be a particular reason for applying to the sessions for an original order Or they may by consent make an order, and bring the matter to the sessions by way of appeal.

Shall and may by their discretion] Here is no *time* limited for their proceeding in this matter, so that the order may be made at any time after the birth of the child.

And in the cause of *K* and *Miles*, *M* 1 *G* On motion to quash an order of bastardy, it was resolved, that if the father run away, and return, tho' 14 years after, yet an order to fix the child on him is good, for there is no statute of limitation in these cases. 1 *Sess. C* 77.

But by the aforesaid statute of the 6 *G*. 2 if the reputed father is in prison, and no order shall be made in six weeks after the birth of the child, he may in such case be discharged from his imprisonment, but the order nevertheless made upon him afterwards, will be good

Take order] Herein they must proceed as in all other like cases, by giving the party accused an opportunity of being heard in his defence   In the case of *A* and *Cotton*, 16 & 7 *G* 2 An information was moved for against the defendant, who with another justice made an order of bastardy upon one *Fitzgerald*, without summoning him to appear before them to make his defence   Upon appeal to the sessions he was acquitted, and put to great expences, which it was insisted was contrary to natural justice By Mr Justice *Page*, No man in an office can be supposed to be fo ignorant, as not to know it is againft natural juftice, to convict a man without a fummons, the examination ought to be fo made, that the truth may appear, and this muft be by examining both fides, otherwife it is partial, the fcandal, the expence, and the diforder in Mr *Fitzgerald*'s family, are things that ought to be confidered, here was no taking by warrant, and therefore an action of falfe imprifonment would not lie, and this is the only method can be ufed to punifh the juftice. Mr J. *Probyn*, The principal objection about a fummons is right in law, and in reafon, poffibly an action on the cafe might be framed, there may poffibly have been only an error in judgment, and it is hard to grant an information. Mr J *Lee*, if this was ftrictly a conviction, againft which no appeal lies, an information ought to be granted; but he thought the matter was not fo very ftrong in the cafe of orders. And the rule was difcharged 1 *Seff. C.* 179

E 8 G 2. *K* v *Taylor* and *Neale*. Motion in the king's bench for an information againft the defendants, two juftices of *Devonfhire*, for making an order on one *Nicholas Mould*, adjudging him to be the putative father of a baftard child, without fummoning him, and alfo for refufing to hear his witneffes. On fhewing caufe, it appeared that he was fummoned by a third juftice, which the court held to be fufficient. And by Lord *Hardwicke* Ch J. If the party, being fummoned, will not attend himfelf, there is no reafon the juftices fhould hear any defence made for him, for if that were allowed, no offender of this fort would appear. Therefore the juftices in this cafe acted right. And it is but as this court does, when orders of baftardy are removed hither by certiorari for we never allow any exceptions to be taken to the order, unlefs the party attend in perfon, that the court may take care of him, and make him indemnify the parifh, if the order is good. 2 *Seff Caf.* 192. *Cafes in the time of Lord Hardwicke* 112.

By charging fuch mother] If the mother fhall *marry* before any order made, it hath been doubted whether the juftices can then charge her, as having no effects of her own, the fame by the marriage being vefted in the hufband. As in the cafe of *Ellen Bent*, E. 5 G. 3. She was delivered of a baftard child in the parifh of *Clifton*. After which, and before any order made, fhe married one *Abraham Taylor* of the parifh of *Middleton*. The overfeers of *Clifton* apply to the juftices, who made an order of filiation, charging her with 8 d a week towards the relief of
the

the pariſh. She pleaded her utter inability, and refuſed to pay Upon which the juſtices commit her to tne houſe of correction. She was brought up by *habeas corpus*, and her counſel moved for her diſcharge, inſiſting upon the illegality of her commitment, for that, being a married woman, ſhe was not an object of the juſtices juriſdiction, and the huſband was not ſummoned ——But by the court A feme covert is liable to be proſecuted for crimes committed by her. This woman has diſobeyed the order of the juſtices, and the ſtatute preſcribes the puniſhment here inflicted upon her There is no need to ſummon the huſband, in a criminal proſecution againſt the wife. *Burrow, Manſf* 1681.

With the payment of money weekly, or other ſuſtentation] That is, to the overſeers for the uſe of ſuch child But whether the overſeers ſhall have the ſole application of the money, and ordering of ſuch child, or the reputed father may take the child from the pariſh, and provide for it himſelf, hath been doubted, and ſeemeth not yet to have been fully ſettled by the unanimous reſolution of the court. And there are difficulties on both ſides If the reputed father indemnifies the pariſh, the intention of the act ſeemeth to be anſwered, and there may be ſuppoſed ſomething of natural affection (eſpecially if he acknowledges the child to be his) inclining him to be regardful of the child's welfare, at leaſt more than can be reaſonably expected from pariſh officers. But then, to be allowed to take the child from its mother, with whom the pariſh officers uſually and very properly leave it, whilſt very young, is unnatural and cruel, and it is very rare, that the reputed father ingenuouſly owns himſelf to be the real father. But if the child is of age and ability to be an apprentice or ſervant, and the reputed father can find a proper maſter, it is fit that he ſhould have power to put out the child accordingly, or that his contribution to the pariſh from that time ſhould ceaſe

In the caſe of *Richards* and *Samon* againſt *Hodges*, T. 2 *Cha* 2. this point came in queſtion, but the matter went off on an error in the proceedings, which was thus *Richards* and *Samon*, being churchwardens, brought an action againſt *Hodges*, on his bond in the uſual form to indemnify the pariſh in the caſe of a baſtard child. The defendant pleaded *Non damnificatus* generally The plaintiffs replied, that neither the defendant nor any other, for the ſpace of one month after the making of the bond, did provide any maintenance for the child, by reaſon

whereof

whereof, the pariſhioners, to prevent the ſud child's pe-
riſhing by hunger and cold, were forced for all the time
aforeſaid to pay, and have paid 4 s for the maintenance
and nouriſhment of the ſaid child   To which the defend
ant rejoined, that he would have nouriſhed the ſaid child
at his proper coſts and charges for all the time aforeſaid,
and offered ſo to do, as well to the plaintiffs as to other
the pariſhioners, but they refuſed to permit him, and of
their own wrong, and againſt the will of the defendant,
put the ſaid child to nurſe, and paid the ſaid 4 s   Upon
which rejoinder, the plaintiffs demurred in law   And
by the court, the rejoinder is not good, becauſe it is a
departure from the firſt plea in bar, for the defendant in
his plea ſays, that the pariſhioners were not damnified,
and when the plaintiffs by their replication ſhew how
they were damnified, there the defendant cannot rejoin
that this damnification was of their own wrong, as here
he hath done, but he ought to have pleaded that at firſt
in his plea in bar   And tho' it was urged for the defendant, that this was no damnification at all, becauſe it
was the voluntary act of the pariſh to put the child to
nurſe, when the defendant himſelf offered to maintain it,
and that they ought not to take advantage of their own
wrong, yet it was not allowed   For the court held clear
ly, that the rejoinder was a departure, and for that reaſon, it was adjudged for the plaintiffs   2 *Saunders*, 83

  M 21 *Cha* 2   *Birwell*'s caſe   Two juſtices order
the reputed father to pay ſo much a week to the pariſh,
until the child ſhou'd be 12 year of age   This was held
by the court to be wrong, and the reaſon given was, becauſe the father might take it away when he pleaſed, and
therefore the order ought to have been, that he ſhould pay
ſo long as the child ſhould be chargeable to the pariſh
1 *Vent* 48

  E 24 *Cha* 2   *Sherman*'s caſe   An order was made,
that the father ſhould pay ſo much a week, till the child
ſhould be able to get its living by working   It was laid
by *Twiſden* this order could not be good, for perhaps the
father would take it away and maintain it himſelf, which
he may do if he pleaſeth   1 *Ventr* 210

  E 11 *An* 2   *ard Smith*   Order to pay 1 s a week,
till the child is 8 years old   It was objected, that it
ſhould be ſo long as the child is chargeable, poſſibly he
may gain a ſettlement, or a perſon may give him an
eſtate, or the father may take him   By the court   This
is only a remote poſſibility   As to the father's taking
him, he ought to have done it at firſt, and by ſuffering

I

the

the order to be made, it ſhall be deemed a refuſal in law, beſides, he ſhall not then be ſuffered, he may ſell him, or make away with him, as too often happens *Caſ of S* 64.

T 27 *G* 2 *Newland* and *Oſman.* Debt upon a bond, with a condition to indemnify and ſave harmleſs the pariſh of *Eling* from a baſtard child Plea, that the defendant had maintained, ſupported, and nouriſhed the ſaid child to a certain day, that is to ſay, to the 27th of October laſt, and that then he offered to take the ſaid child to maintain, which they refuſed, and that if the churchwardens or any of them have been damnified, it is of their own wrong Replication, that for 3 weeks, from and after the ſaid 27th day of October, the defendant did not provide nouriſhment for the child, but failed, and by reaſon thereof the plaintiffs, after the three weeks, expended 3s for the maintenance of the child, and ſo were damnified Demurrer, and joinder in demurrer. The queſtion or law is, Whether a putative father may take a baſtard child into his own cuſtody to maintain it, or whether the pariſh ſhall have the care of it And the caſe in 2 *Saund* 83 was mentioned, wherein the court held this to be a good plea 1 *Vent* 48 that the father may maintain the child himſelf 1 *Ventr* 210 that the juſtices can only make an order to maintain, ſo long as the child ſhall be chargeable —By *Lee Ch J* The right way is, to make the order, ſo long as the child ſhall be chargeable It is not to be limited to any certain time And the reaſon given in all theſe caſes is, that the father or mother may take it before the time The intention of the ſtatute of Elizabeth was, to have a proviſion for the baſtard, and at the ſame time to indemnify pariſhes, And the law could never think of taking the care and education of children from their parents Nor could this enter into the mind of any judge Nouriſhing and maintaining certainly anſwers education It hath been objected, that the excuſe is collateral I do not think ſo, for all the inhabitants are parties, and the overſeers are but truſtees for them It ſeems a ſufficient excuſe, and there is no anſwer on the part of the plaintiff to it No objection has ever been thought of to pleas of this kind ——*Wright J* In the caſe in *Saunder*, it ſeems to have been admitted, that if this had been pleaded in the firſt inſtance, it would have been good I never did hear before, that the care of the child devolved upon the pariſh, where there was any other perſon to take care of it They are obliged to maintain the child, where it is in danger of ſtarving This court has conſtantly held, that the father has a right to take it away, by quaſhing the orders made in manner above mentioned This is not a collateral excuse, but such an one as will save the penalty And I cannot see that the parish has any sort of right or interest in the child ——*Dennison* J The material objection taken to this plea is, Whether or no the putative father of a bastard child can by the law of England take his bastard child from the parish I never did hear this doubted before. And I think that the notion that he cannot, is not to be countenanced nor encouraged The law does not suppose, that a man will not maintain his own child It is said, the next heir is not to be trusted with the guardianship I am sorry that was ever introduced into the law of England. It is an injurious notion of the people of England. I will rather suppose, that the parish officers will be cruel to the child, than the father All the cases admit tacitly that the father hath such a power And some of them say so expressly And I am very well satisfied that the law is so Inhabitants, churchwardens, overseers, are all the same, and every part of the condition is answered I have known this plea very often pleaded And that case in *Saunders* is the rule ——*Foster* J I am not so clear in these points. I think the care of educating bastard children, is not to be considered as a burden on the parish, but as a trust, and that it should not be so easy for fathers to take them out of their care and custody. The statute is express, that the justices shall order the father to contribute to the parish for the maintenance of the child Tho' it is not to be supposed that fathers will destroy their bastard children, yet they may look upon them as a burden and a shame, and therefore either neglect them, or put them into improper hands. The resolutions and orders of justices of the peace have been grounded upon this, not for requiring security till the child came to a certain age, but because the order intended the age too far. Therefore I am not so clear. The case in *Saunders* was only his own opinion ——Judgment for the defendant, unless desired to be argued again this term (This was at the desire of the plaintiff's counsel.) MS

Finally, in the case of *Hulland* against *Malken* and *Bristow*, T. 33 & 34 G. 2. In the common pleas. (Which was on a suit upon a bond for indemnifying the plaintiff from the charges of a bastard child, but it went off upon an error in the pleadings) The court said, we need not in this case say, whether the father or the mother hath a right to have the child while under 7 years of age And by the lord chief justice *Wilmot* I give no opinion, whether

whether the father has any power over the child, who is *vulgus filius* Grotius says truly, the mother is the only certain parent And an order of justices to remove the mother, always removes the child 2 *Wilson*, 126.

Upon the whole, there are two considerations, which seem to reduce the unlimited power in several of the aforesaid cases, of the reputed father taking the child when he pleases, into a very narrow compass One is, that nothing is more established, than that a child shall not be taken from its mother, without her consent, before it is seven years of age. The other is, That an order made by the justices, and confirmed at the sessions, or not appealed against, is binding upon the reputed father, and no other justices, in or out of sessions, have power to intermeddle And so it is laid down in one of the aforesaid cases, that "if the father take the child he must do it at first; " and by suffering the order to be made, it shall be deem-" ed a refusal in law, and he shall not then be suffered, " he may sell it or make away with it, as too often " happens." So that it should seem upon these premisses, that the time for the reputed father to insist upon taking the child cannot be until after it is seven years of age; nor even then, if an order has been made, and it is not to be supposed that the parish officers will forbear for seven years applying for an order, only to give the reputed father an opportunity to put in his claim.

After all Whatever exalted notions speculative and humane persons may entertain of the dignity of human nature and the tenderness of parents towards their children, it seemeth that large abatements ought to be made in respect of that kind of parents here spoken of In practice, it is seldom, if ever, known, that a reputed father, who applies to have the child taken off from the parish into his own management, even so much as pretends any advantage to the child thereby, but merely his own interest, to save charges: He does not want to have the child better provided for, but cheaper. If he should offer any thing for the good of the child, whereby he himself would not receive any benefit, much more if attended with some small additional expence to him, there is no doubt but the parish would be willing enough to accede to his proposal And it is well known in fact, that where the reputed father openly acknowledges the child, and is a man of some substance so as not to be likely to run away, the parish seldom gives him any disturbance, or if they be applied to in behalf of the child, they are for the most part ready to join with him in any reasonable accommodation.

S- ch

Such party ſo making default in not performing the ſaid order, to be committed] Until default ſhall be made, the juſtices have no power to commit, or to require ſureties for performance of the order, or for appearing at the ſeſſions L *Raym* 858   3 *Salk* 66   1 *Barnardiſt* 261.

And hereby a paſſage might be left open to avoid the future payments, by the reputed father complying at preſent, and afterwards running away. But the aforeſaid ſtatute of the 6 G 2. c 31 ſeemeth to have been intended to remedy this inconvenience, by which, one or more juſtices, either before or after the birth, may commit him to the gaol or houſe of correction, unleſs he ſhall give ſecurity to indemnify the pariſh, or otherwiſe enter into recognizance to abide ſuch order or orders as ſhall be made in purſuance of the act of the 18 El

To be committed to ward to the common gaol] In the aforeſaid caſe of *Ellen Bent*, the juſtices had committed her to the houſe of correction It was objected that the ſtatute gives no power to do this, but the commitment, if any, ought to have been to the common gaol But that was held by the court to be well enough For the ſtatute of the 7 J c 4 gives power to commit ſuch lewd women to the houſe of correction And by the 6 G c 19. a general power is given, for ſmall offences, or for want of ſureties, to commit either to the gaol or houſe of correction *Burn Manſf* 1681

Except he ſhall put in ſufficient ſurety to perform the ſaid order] That is, by recognizance, which, if the order is diſobeyed, ſhall be forfeited, and eſtreated into the exchequer But this makes nothing for the relief of the pariſh And therefore it were better if ſuch recognizance, or other ſecurity, upon default, might be made aſſignable to the pariſh officers, or elſe, that the perſon not paying, as well as not giving ſecurity, might be committed till payment ſhould be made Or if no ſecurity is given, it ſeemeth that the priſoner, diſobeying the order, may be indicted, fined, and impriſoned for the contempt ——If the orders are removed into the king's bench, and there confirmed, the court, on non-performance, will grant an attachment

It frequently happens, that the reputed father, by giving bond to indemnify the pariſh, eſcapes paying any thing towards the maintenance of the child, unleſs the mother, with her child, will throw herſelf upon the pariſh, which ſometimes perhaps her ability will not permit, or otherwiſe ſhe diſdains to do. In ſuch caſe it

hath

hath been advised fometimes, for the woman's father to bring an action againft the man for fpecial damage fuftained by the lofs of his daughter's fervice, and a jury according to circumftances, will give reasonable compenfation. —That is, if fhe be under the age of 21, and not emancipated from the father, or be, at the time, a part of her father's family and in his fervice   As in the two following cafes

E 6 G 3 *Poftlethwaite* and *Parkes*   This was an action of trefpafs with force and arms, for an affault upon the plaintiff's daughter, and getting her with child   And the declaration concluded, *whereby he loft her fervice*   It was tried at the affizes before Mr Juftice *Bathurft*, and a verdict given for the plaintiff, and 40s damages   A fpecial cafe was ftated, to this effect   The plaintiff's daughter, being 23 years of age, hired herfelf to one *Saul*, as a fervant, and went to live with *Saul* her mafter, and ferved him fome time   During her fervice, fhe was gotten with child, by the defendant, and becoming big with child, and unable thereby to perform her fervice as fhe was ufed and ought to do, fhe was difcharged by *Saul* her mafter, who paid her her wages in proportion to the fervice fhe had already done him, and the plaintiff her father received her, when no one elfe would, and lodged and boarded her in his houfe   She was there delivered of a baftard child, and the plaintiff, her father, maintained her in her lying-in, at his own expence   The queftion which arofe at the trial, and which was referved for the opinion of the court of king's bench was, " Whether the plaintiff can maintain this action "   In the argument of this caufe two points were made, 1. Whether the father and daughter can be confidered as mafter and fervant. 2 Whether her age makes any difference in the cafe, as fhe was upwards of 21, namely 23 years of age.—Mr *Davenport*, for the plaintiff, argued, That the action is maintainable by the father, upon the foot of being her mafter, as he has alledged, *whereby he loft her fervice*   He agreed, that no action would lie, but by reafon of the lofs of her fervice   Here, a daughter goes out to fervice, is gotten with child, difcharged, and returned upon her father, helplefs and unable, in that condition, to maintain her felf. He is obliged by law to maintain her, and did fo from the neceffity of the thing.   Therefore, from the confequential damage, an action is maintainable by her father, in whofe houfe fhe refided, and where fhe muft, in this cafe, be confidered as a fervant. And this cafe is not to be confidered upon

the

the foot of emancipation Her being 23 years of age makes no difference. This young woman's maſter could not bring an action againſt this defendant, he had ſuſtained no damage, having diſcharged her as ſoon as ſhe became unſerviceable to him No body but the father could ſue And the damage is the ſame to him, whether ſhe be over or under 21 ——Mr. *Wallace*, on the other ſide, argued for the defendant. The foundation of actions of this kind hath been, the *loſs of ſervice*. The father's intereſt in the child, whatever it might have been during infancy, ceaſes at the child's coming to the age of 21. Many injuries may be done to a child, which are not the ſubjects of actions by the father. Indeed an action will lie by a father, for taking away his ſon or his daughter, and there is a writ provided for him in the regiſter for that purpoſe But no action will lie for debauching his daughter If the father maintains the daughter in his own houſe, he is intitled to her ſervice, and may maintain an action for the loſs of her ſervice. But here, ſhe was hired out to ſervice in another man's houſe. If ſhe had been under age, and under her father's roof, I would agree that he had been intitled to an action as for the loſs of ſervice No inſtance can be produced, no precedent of ſuch an action as this is. And the principle will not hold, becauſe it depends upon the loſs of ſervice, which was not the preſent caſe ——Upon the whole it appeared that the parties were poor. The court therefore propoſed a compromiſe, which was accepted namely, that all proceedings be ſtayed, without coſts on either ſide. Lord *Mansfield* added, that it was not upon any doubt, in point of law, that he propoſed the compromiſe, meaning, as it ſeemeth, that he was clear that the action in this caſe would not lie. And upon that ſuppoſition, the reporter ſays he has ventured to report it, tho' it was not determined judicially and in form However, he ſays, there can be no doubt, but that the court were all of opinion, that the action could not be maintained And therefore, in compaſſion to the plaintiff, whoſe daughter had been injured by the defendant, they wiſhed to ſave him from the payment of coſts. *Bur Manſf* 1878

E. 9 G 3 *Tullidge* and *Wade* In the common pleas An action of treſpaſs was brought againſt the defendant, for that he with force and arms made an aſſault upon the daughter and ſervant of the plaintiff, and got her with child, whereby he loſt the benefit of her ſervice for a certain ſpace of time, and was put to great charge and expence

expence in her time of lying-in   The defendant pleaded
not guilty   The cauſe was tried at the aſſizes before
Mr. Juſtice *Gould*, when the jury found a verdict for the
plaintiff, and gave him 50l damages. It was moved for
a new trial, and the motion was grounded upon an affidavit tending to ſhew, that under the circumſtances of the
caſe appearing at the trial, the damages were exceſſive;
and alſo, that evidence was given at the trial, of a promiſe of marriage made by the defendant to the woman,
which ought not to have been permitted, becauſe ſhe may
have another ſort of action upon that promiſe   Whereupon Mr Juſtice *Gould* made his report to the court   And,
after ſtating the declaration as above, he ſaid, that this
daughter of the plaintiff was called as a witneſs at the
trial, and ſwore, that the plaintiff her father was a malt-
ſter, and kept a public houſe, that ſhe was his ſervant,
and was about 30 years of age, that the defendant was
an exciſeman, made his addreſſes to her as a lover, with
an intention (as ſhe then thought) to marry her, that he
was well received on that account by the plaintiff her father,
and very civilly treated by him and his family, and often
ſpent the evening with them   She alſo ſwore, that he pro-
miſed her marriage, and got her with child   Her brother
alſo was called, who depoſed, that the plaintiff was wholly
deprived of his ſaid daughter's ſervice and aſſiſtance in
his buſineſs, and paid ſome money on account of her
lying-in.   The counſel for the defendant, at the trial,
objected to the evidence given, as to the promiſe of marriage   Upon which, ſhe offered to give the defendant a re-
leaſe as to that promiſe, but the counſel for the defendant refuſed to accept thereof   Upon ſumming up the
evidence to the jury, the judge told them (as he was
pleaſed to ſay) over and over again, that in giving damages
in this action, they muſt not conſider the injury done to
the woman as to the promiſe of marriage, but muſt leave
that matter quite out of the queſtion, becauſe ſhe might
have her action for breach of that promiſe, that he
thought the plaintiff her father was by nature bound to
take care of her while ſhe laid-in, and that they ſhould
conſider his expences on that account, as well as his loſs
of his daughter's ſervice   Whereupon the jury gave 50l
damages, with which the judge ſaid he was not at all
diſſatisfied, and that he thought, if the jury had then
conſidered the promiſe of marriage, they would have given
ſix times as much damages —By the lord chief juſtice
Wilmot Actions of this ſort are brought for example's ſake.
And altho' the plaintiff's loſs in this caſe may not really
amount

amount to the value of twenty ſhillings, yet the jury have done right in giving liberal damages. And if the daughter brings another action againſt the defendant for the breach of promiſe of marriage, ſo much the better he ought to be puniſhed both ways Her being of the age of 30, is nothing to mitigate damages, or leſſen the defendant's fault And we will pay no regard to any affidavit read to us, the judge who tried the cauſe being ſatisfied with the verdict. If much greater damages had been given, we ſhould not have been diſſatisfied therewith, the plaintiff having received this inſult in his own houſe, where he had civilly received tne defendant, and permitted him to make his addreſſes to his daughter —And the motion for a new trial was rejected, and the plaintiff had judgment by the whole court. 3 *Wilſon*, 18.

THE uſual approved form of the order of filiation and maintenance is as follows :

Weſtmorland. THE *order of* J P *and* K. P *eſquires, two of his majeſty's juſtices of the peace in and for the ſaid county, one whereof is of the quorum, and both reſiding* [*in,* or] *next unto the limits of the pariſh church within the pariſh of* ——— *in the ſaid county, made the* ——— *da, of* ——— *in the* ——— *year* ——— *concerning a (male) baſtard child, lately born in the pariſh of* ——— *aforeſaid, of the body of* A M *ſingle woman*

Whereas it hath appeared unto us the ſaid juſtices, as well upon the complaint of the churchwardens and overſeers of the poor of the ſaid pariſh of ——— *as upon the oath of the ſaid* A M *that ſhe the ſaid* A. M. *on the* ——— *day of* ——— *now laſt paſt, was delivered of a (male) baſtard child at* ——— *in the pariſh of* ——— *in the ſaid county, and that the ſaid baſtard child is now chargeable to the ſaid pariſh of* ——— *and likely ſo to continue, and further, that* A F *of* ——— *in the ſaid county, yeoman, did beget the ſaid baſtard child on the body of her the ſaid* A M *And whereas the ſaid* A F *hath appeared before us, in purſuance of our ſummons for that purpoſe, but hath not ſhewed any ſufficient cauſe why he the ſaid* A F. *ſhall not be the reputed father of the ſaid baſtard child* [*Or, And whereas it hath been duly proved to us upon oath, that the ſaid* A F *hath been duly ſummoned to appear before us the ſaid juſtices, to the end we might examine into the cauſe and circumſtance of the premiſes, and whereas he the ſaid* A F. *hath neglected to appear before us, according to the ſaid ſummons*] *We therefore upon examination of the cauſe and circumſtance of the premiſſes, as well upon the oath of the*

ſaid

said A M. *as otherwise, do hereby adjudge him the said* A. F. *to be the reputed father of the said bastard child*

And thereupon we do order, as well for the better relief of the said parish of ——— as for the sustentation and relief of the said bastard child, that the said A F *shall and do forthwith, upon notice of this our order, pay or cause to be paid to the said churchwardens and overseers of the poor of the said parish of ——— or to some or one of them, the sum of ——— for and towards the lying-in of the said* A M *and the maintenance of the said bastard child, to the time of making this our order*

And we do also hereby further order, that the said A F *shall likewise pay or cause to be paid to the churchwardens and overseers of the poor of the said parish of ——— for the time being, or to some or one of them, the sum of ——— weekly and every week from this present time, for and towards the keeping, sustentation, and maintenance of the said bastard child, for and during so long time, as the said bastard child shall be chargeable to the said parish of ———.*

And we do further order, that the said A M *shall also pay or cause to be paid to the said churchwardens and overseers of the poor of the said parish of ——— for the time being, or to some or one of them, the sum of ——— weekly and every week, so long as the said bastard child shall be chargeable to the said parish of ——— in case she shall not nurse and take care of the said child herself.*

Given under our hands and seals the day and year first above written

One whereof is of the quorum] Many orders formerly have been quashed, for want of setting forth that one of the justices was of the *quorum*, but now by the statute of 26 *G* 2 *c* 27 no order shall be quashed for that defect only.

Whereas it hath appeared unto us] K and *Beard* The examination of the woman must be by two justices, as well as the ordering part, for the examination is a judicial act, and ought to be by both, and it is not enough that one should examine, and make report to the other, but if they are both present, and one only examine, it is well enough, for it is in fact the examination of both 2 *Salk* 478

So in the case of *Billings* against *Prin* and *D lobere* esquires, *T* 15 *G* 3 An action of trespass and false imprisonment was brought by the plaintiff, for committing her to prison for refusing to filiate a bastard child She

was

was examined ſeverally, at ſeparate times (but in the ſame day), and in ſeparate places, by the two juſtices the defendants, and they ſeparately ſigned the warrant of commitment. On trial at the aſſizes, a verdict was given for the plaintiff, with 5 l damages It was moved for a new trial, and argued, that it was ſufficient under the ſtatute, if the two juſtices joined in and conſented to the commitment, but that they might examine and adjudge the matter, and ſign the warrant, ſeparately. Unto which it was anſwered, that where two or more are required to do any act, they muſt meet together Elſe what they reſolve on is the mind of individuals, not of the whole body And this hath always been the doctrine with reſpect to juſtices of the peace By the court This caſe is ſo clear, that it cannot bear an argument There is no uſe in appointing two or more perſons to exerciſe judicial powers, unleſs they are to act together. Separate examinations by different magiſtrates may produce different facts On which then is the adjudication to proceed? It is exceeding clear, that in caſe of an action thus brought to try the validity of the commitment, it cannot be ſupported by law. *Black. Rep.* 1017

As well upon the complaint of the churchwardens and overſ rs] It hath been ſaid that an order made without the complaint of the pariſh officers, is not good *Blackerby,* 44

But in the caſe of *K.* and *Buckall,* M 3 G 2 where it was objected, that the order did not appear to be made up on complaint of the pariſh, it was anſwered, that the ſtatute does not require that the pariſh ſhould complain, but gives the juſtices power to make ſuch order on the complaint of any other And the order, as to that part, was confirmed. 1 *Barnardiſt.* 261.

As upon the oath of the ſaid A M] It ſeemeth, that the mother may be examined upon oath, concerning the reputed father, and of the time and other circumſtances, for that in this caſe, the matter, and the trial thereof, dependeth chiefly upon the examination and teſtimony of the mother *Dalt c.* 11

Was delivered of a (male) baſtard child] H. 8 G K and *England.* An order was quaſhed, becauſe the ſex of the baſtard, or the name of it were not mentioned, only, a certain baſtard child born of the body of ſuch a woman *Str* 503.

At ⸺ in the ſaid pariſh of ⸺] M 11 Ann 2 and *Caſh.* The order did not ſet forth that the child was born in the parish, and by the statute the justices cannot make an order to compel a man to contribute towards the maintenance of a bastard child, but in case of that parish where the child was born. And quashed for this reason. *Caf of S* 59.

T 7 *G K* and *Butcher*. Exception was taken to an order of bastardy, that it did not appear the child was born in the parish to which the relief is ordered, for it ran, *We two justices of the borough of* Lime Regis, *residing within the limits where the parish church is, within which parish the child was born* —— Which is only an averment, that the justices resided in that parish where the child was born, but that might not be the same parish ordered to be relieved. And for this fault the order was quashed. *Str* 437.

E 3 *G* 2. *K.* and *Childers*. On a rule to shew cause, why an order of two justices for relief of a bastard child, and an order of sessions confirming the same, should not be quashed, it was objected, that it was not directly adjudged that the child was born in the parish (of *Staplehurst*), and yet the order requires the defendant to pay the sum of 45 s to the churchwardens of that parish to reimburse them. It was answered, that it doth sufficiently appear in the order, that the child was born there, for it adjudges, that the defendant should pay this sum, for the charges the parish of *Staplehurst* were at upon account of the woman's lying in there. But the court said, that they do not allow of inferences to give the justices jurisdiction, and accordingly quashed both the orders. 1 *Barnardist* 326.

E 10 *G* 2 *K* and *Greaves*. The parish where the child is born, is only to be indemnified, and if the bastard has acquired a settlement elsewhere, the father is then discharged. *Niff.* Bast

Chargeable to the said parish] Order to provide for a bastard child. Exception was taken, that the order doth not set forth that he is chargeable to the parish, or likely to be so. And quashed by the court. *Comb* 39.

But in *K* and *Matthews*, H 8 W Exception was taken, that the order doth not set forth that the child is likely to become chargeable. But this exception was over-ruled, for that it is self-evident, that every bastard child's likely to become chargeable. 2 *Salk* 475, 6

And further, that A F of —— *in the said county, yeoman, did beget the said bastard child*] *T* 2 *G* 2 *K* and *Browne* Upon an order of bastardy it was stated, that the husband

had been abfent fix years, and that during his abfence
the defendant *had carnal knowledge* of the wife, and therefore they adjudge him to be the putative father. But by
the court, This order muft be quafhed, for his lying
with her is not a fufficient reafon to infer him the father
of this child and tho' the juftices need not fhew the
grounds they go upon, yet if they do, and it appears no
fufficient ground, their order will be bad   *Str* 811.

Do hereby adjudge] T 4 *Ann* Q and *Wefton* The great
objection which ftuck long with the court, was, that it
was faid in the order, we the faid juftices *doth* adjudge,
inftead of *do* adjudge, and after the cafe had depended
two terms, and been feveral times ftirred, the court for
that exception, the laft day of the term, quafhed the order   L *Raym* 1198

And afterwards, H 4 *Ann*   The fame juftices made
another order, with the very fame fault in it, *viz. doth*
adjudge, and upon a certiorari, that was quafhed L.
Raym 1198

Adjudge the faid A F. *to be the reputed father*] E 20 C
2 K. and *Perkaffe*   An order was quafhed, becaufe, there
was no adjudication, that the perfon againft whom the complaint was made, was the reputed father.   2 *Sid.* 363

H 9 G 2. K and *Jenkins*   Motion to quafh an order
of two juftices, whereby they adjudge, that fuch a perfon
is *not* the putative father of a baftard child, and therefore
they difcharge him, and the rather, becaufe in fuch a
cafe the parifh cannot appeal, becaufe an appeal is only,
when the party refufes to give fecurity to come to feffions
And by the whole court, the two juftices have no fuch
authority   for their whole power depends on the ftatute
of 18 *Eliz* and that is only to take order for punifhment
of the parties, and for relief of the parifh, and this order
is for neither the one nor the other.   2 *Seff. C.* 161 *Str.*
1050

The fum of ——— for and towards the lying-in] M. 12 *Ann*
Q and *Onam*   Order for maintenance of a baftard child,
was excepted to, becaufe the defendant is upon fight of
the order to pay 9 l in grofs, and after that, fo much
weekly   And by the court   By the ftatute the juftices
are to take order for relief of the parifh, and keeping of
the child, by payment of money weekly, or other fuf-
tentation, and this may be only indemnifying the parifh
for money laid out before the reputed father was found.
1 *Salk* 124

During

During so long time as the said bastard child shall be charge-able] E. 9 *W K* and *Barebaker* An order to pay so much money by the week, till the child shall be fourteen years of age, was adjudged to be bad for the justices have no power but to indemnify the parish, and that is only to oblige him to maintain the child, as long as it is or may be chargeable. 1 *Salk* 121 2 *Salk* 478

An order that the putative father should pay so much a week, until it should be able to get its living by work-ing, was quashed, it should have been for so long time, as the child shall be chargeable to the parish 1 *Vent* 210

But in the case of *K* and *Street*, *M* 1 *G* 2 An order of bastardy was made, to pay so much weekly, till the child was nine years old, if it should so long live And by the court, It is a good order, for we cannot intend it able to provide for itself sooner *Str* 788

So in the case of *K* and *Buckall*, *M* 1 *G* 2. Excep-tion was taken, that the order appointed the sum of 2s to be paid weekly, till the child should come to the age of twelve years, without saying, if the child shall be so long chargeable to the parish It was answered, that in-deed the old authorities lay it down in general, that orders of bastardy, as well as other orders relating to the poor, must be under the limitation mentioned, but the later au-thorities have been, that orders of bastardy need not and this, it was said, is founded upon good reason, for there cannot be any reasonable intendment, that bastards, who have no kindred, will have provision from any body, till such an age as is mentioned in the order And of that opi-nion was the court, and confirmed the order as to that point 1 *Barnardist* 261

But then the child may be bound an apprentice into another parish before that age, and having gained a set-tlement in such other parish, the effect of the order should then cease Therefore it is best in this and all such like cases to hold to the statute and the statute here only gives power to the justices *to take order for the relief of the parish where the child shall be born.*

In *Browne*'s case, *T* 9 *W* it was said, the justices can-not order a sum, for putting out the child an apprentice. *Comb* 448.

But in the aforesaid case of *K* and *Buckall*, *M* 3 *G* 2. Where it was objected, that the order was for the reput-ed father to pay 4 l to the overseers for binding the child out apprentice, when it should come to the age of 12 years, and did not say, if the child shall want it, so that tho' the child should be provided for in any other way, the sum must be still paid to the overseers The objection was over-ruled by the court, and the order, as to that, held good 1 *Barnardist* 261

But it seemeth not necessary to incumber the order therewith, for it may be the same thing if the parish bind him out, and pay the money, for until such sum shall be run off by the weekly payments, so long the child continues chargeable.

BUT after all, so far as these errors above rehearsed shall affect only the form of the order, and not the merits thereof, the same may be amended at the sessions, by the 5 *G* 2 *c* 19. before the appeal shall be proceeded upon, and then the court shall go upon the merits

V. *Appeal against the order.*

By the aforesaid statute of the 18 *El* *c* 3 the mother or reputed father refusing to perform the order of the two justices, shall be committed, unless they shall put in sufficient surety to perform the said order, or else *personally to appear at the next general sessions of the peace, to be holden in that county where such order shall be taken, and also to abide such order, as the said justices, or the more part of them, then and there shall take in that behalf (if they then and there shall take any), and that if at the said sessions, the said justices shall take no other order, then to abide and perform the order before made, as is abovesaid.*

Personally to appear] *H* 8 *W. K* and *Matthews*. It was moved to quash an order for maintaining a bastard child. It was answered, that no order relating to a bastard child can be quashed, unless the reputed father be present in court Unto which the court assented But it appearing to be a hard case, a rule was made to shew cause. On shewing cause, it was quashed, but the court would not quash it, till the reputed father came into court. 2 *Salk.* 475

H 3 *G* 2. *K* and *Gibson* It was moved to quash an order of bastardy, which, being indefensible, was accordingly done, the defendant entring into recognizance to abide the order of the sessions below which was the reason (the court said) why a personal appearance of the defendant was in these cases always required *Black Rep* 198.

At the next general sessions] That is to say, the next general sessions after notice of such order. 3 *Keb.* 551

General Sessions] *T.* 10 *W. K.* and *Shaw*. An order was made

made by two juſtices, adjudging *Shaw* to be the reputed father of a baſtard, whereupon he appealed to the next *quarter* ſeſſions after notice, where the order of the two juſtices was diſcharged   And now it was moved to quaſh the order of ſeſſions, becauſe by the ſtatute the appeal muſt be to the next *general* ſeſſions, and there might have been a general ſeſſions before the general quarter ſeſſions, as in *London* or *Middleſex*, where there are four general ſeſſions in the year, beſides the quarter ſeſſions. And quaſhed for this fault   2 *Salk* 482

To be holden in that county] It was moved to quaſh an order, for that it was at the ſeſſions of the peace in the county aforeſaid, and did not ſay *for* the county, but this was over-ruled, for that there is not ſo much ſtrict-neſs required in orders, as there is in indictments   1 *Ventr* 37

To which may be added alſo, that this is according to the words of the ſtatute

In that county where ſuch order ſhall be taken] T. 15 *Cha.* 2 *K* and *Coyſtan*   Reſolved, that this ſhall be intended of the next ſeſſions of that part of the county, where it was made, and not at the next ſeſſions in any county at large, for that would be miſchievous in many counties, where there are ſeveral ſeſſions in diſtinct parts of the county   1 *Sid* 149

To abide ſuch order as the ſaid juſtices, or the more part of them, ſhall then and there take] M 13 *G   K* and *Tenant.* The order of two juſtices being quaſhed upon the merits by the ſeſſions on an appeal, the defendant is thereby legally acquitted, and cannot be drawn in queſtion again for the ſame fact L. *Raym* 1423, 4   Str 716

But the order quaſhed for want of form, is as no order at all, and therefore the two juſtices may proceed *de novo.*

If the two next juſtices make an order, and the party appeals to the next ſeſſions, and they alter or diſcharge (upon the merits), or confirm that order, no other ſeſſions can order any thing contrary thereto, for the order upon the appeal is final *Cro Car* 350

T 1 *G* 2. *K.* and *Arunaʼl*   Two juſtices make an order, that the defendant ſhall pay a ſum in groſs, and alſo 2 s a week ſo long as the child ſhall be chargeable   The party appeals to the ſeſſions, who confirm the order   At a ſubſequent ſeſſions, the father of the baſtard deſired to have the keeping of it, and that the payment of the 2 s a week ſhould ceaſe, which the ſecond ſeſſions ordered Motion was made to quaſh this laſt order of ſeſſions, becauſe in this caſe they had no juriſdiction   And the court held, that the ſecond ſeſſions had no authority to order the ſubtraction of the 2 s a week, and the order was quaſhed, becauſe it was made out of time (being three years after the appeal, and therefore the juſtices had no juriſdiction   1 Seſſ. C 234

II. Puniſhment of the mother and reputed father.

By the 18 *El* c 3 *Concerning baſtards being left to be kept at the charges of the pariſh where born, to the great burden thereof, and to the evil example and encouragement of lewd life, it is enacted, that the two next juſtices ſhall take order therein, as well for the puniſhment of the mother and reputed father, as for the relief of the pariſh*

And by 7 *J* c 4   *Every lewd woman which ſhall have any baſtard which may be chargeable to the pariſh, the juſtices of the peace ſhall commit ſuch lewd woman to the houſe of correction, there to be puniſhed and ſet on work, during the term of one whole year, and if ſhe ſhall eftſoons offend again, then to be committed to the ſaid houſe of correction as aforeſaid, and there to remain until ſhe can put in good ſureties for her good behaviour, not to offend ſo again. ſ 7.*

Baſtard which may be chargeable] It ſeemeth by theſe words, that ſuch woman ſhall not be ſent to the houſe of correction, until after the child be born, and that it be living, for it muſt be ſuch a child as may be chargeable to the pariſh   *Dalt* c 11.

And if ſhe will diſcharge the pariſh of keeping the baſtard, ſhe cannot be puniſhed by this ſtatute of 7 *J*

But nevertheleſs ſhe may be puniſhed (Lord *Coke* ſays) by the ſtatute of 18 *El*   2 Inſt. 733.

Which opinion ſeems juſtly queſtionable   for the preamble of the ſaid act of 18 *El* (as hath been rehearſed) ſeemeth to reſtrain the juriſdiction of the juſtices to the parents of ſuch baſtard children only as are *left to be kept a the charges of the pariſh where born.*

The juſtices of the peace ſhall commit] It ſeemeth that ſuch commitment ought to be by two juſtices at the leaſt, and by comparing the two ſtatutes together, it ſeemeth fitteſt for the two next juſtices authorized by the 18 *El* Dalt. c 11.

Shall commit ſuch lewd woman] But ſuch puniſhment ſhall no. be until after the woman is delivered of her child, neither

neither are the juſtices to meddle with a woman, until the child be born, and ſhe ſtrong again. *Dal. c* 11

Alſo it ſeemeth, that ſuch baſtard child is not to be ſent with the mother to the houſe of correction, but rather that the child ſhould remain in the town where it was born (or ſettled with the mother) and there to be relieved by the work of the mother, or by relief from the reputed father, and yet the common opinion and practice is otherwiſe, *viz.* to ſend the child with the mother to the houſe of correction; and this may alſo ſeem reaſonable, where the child ſucketh on the mother *Dalt c* 11.

But it ſeemeth much the beſt, to commit the mother only, and not the child, but leave it to her choice whether ſhe will take it with her, and if ſhe will not, then to ſend it to its lawful place of ſettlement

Then to be committed to the ſaid houſe of correction as aforeſaid] Which words do imply that ſhe ſhall not be puniſhed as for a ſecond offence, unleſs ſhe hath been committed to and puniſhed in the houſe of correction for the firſt

VII. *Mother or reputed father running away.*

Whereas the putative fathers and lewd mothers of baſtard children run away out of the pariſh, and ſometimes out of the county, and leave the baſtard children upon the charge of the pariſh where they are born, altho' they have eſtates ſufficient to diſcharge the pariſh, it ſhall be lawful for the churchwardens and overſeers of the poor of ſuch pariſh where any baſtard child ſhall be born, to take and ſeize ſo much of the goods, and receive ſo much of the annual rents or profits of the lands of ſuch putative father or lewd mother, as ſhall be ordered by any two juſtices, towards the diſcharge of the pariſh, to be confirmed at the ſeſſions, for the bringing up and providing for ſuch baſtard child, and thereupon the ſeſſions may make an order for the churchwardens or overſeers of the poor of ſuch pariſh, to diſpoſe of the goods by ſale or otherwiſ, or ſo much of them for the purpoſes aforeſaid, as the court ſhall think fit, and to receive the rents and profits of the lands, or ſo much of them as ſhall be ſo ordered by the ſeſſions. 13 & 14 C. 2. c. 1 ſ. 19

E. 2 *Ann.* ℟ and *Chaffey* Order to the churchwardens and overſeers, to ſeize of the putative father's goods, what they ſhould judge proper for ſecuring of the pariſh, qualified, for that it ſhould be, what the juſtices think proper, and not what the churchwardens and overſeers think proper. L *Raym* 858

VIII Murdering a baſtard child.

1 By the 21 J c. 27. *If any woman be delivered of any iſſue of her body, male or female, which being born alive, ſhould by the laws of this realm be a baſtard, and ſhe endeavour privately, either by drowning, or ſecret burying thereof, or any other way, either by herſelf, or the procuring of others, ſo to conceal the death thereof, as that it may not come to light, whether it were born alive or not, but be concealed, ſhe ſhall ſuffer death as in caſe of murder, except ſhe can prove by one witneſs at leaſt, that the child was born dead*

And it hath been adjudged, that in order to convict a woman by force of this ſtatute, there is no need that the indictment be drawn ſpecially, or conclude againſt the form of the ſtatute, for the ſtatute doth not make a new offence, but only makes ſuch concealment an undeniable evidence of murder   2 *Haw* 438

Alſo, it hath been agreed, that where a woman appears to have endeavoured to conceal the death of ſuch child within the ſtatute, there is no need of any proof that the child was born alive, or that there were any ſigns of hurt upon the body, but it ſhall be undeniably taken that the child was born alive, and murdered by the mother. 2 *Haw* 438

But of late years, as this law ſeemeth to be ſomewhat ſevere, it hath been uſual, upon trials for this offence, to require ſome ſort of preſumptive evidence that the child was born alive, before the other conſtrained preſumption is admitted, that becauſe the death was concealed therefore it was killed by its parent.   4 *Blackſt* 198

Alſo, it hath been adjudged, that were a woman lay in a chamber by herſelf, and went to bed without pain, and waked in the night, and knocked for help, but could get none, and was delivered of a child, and put it in a trunk, and did not diſcover it till the following night, yet ſhe was not within the ſtatute, becauſe ſhe knocked for help 2 *Haw* 438

Alſo, it hath been agreed, that if a woman confeſs herſelf with child beforehand, and afterwards be ſurprized and delivered, no body being with her, ſhe is not within the ſtatute, becauſe there was no intent of concealment, and therefore in ſuch caſes it muſt appear by ſigns of hurt upon the body, or ſome other way, that the child was born alive   2 *Haw* 438

2 If a woman be with child, and any gives her a potion to deſtroy the child within her, and ſhe take it, and it works ſo ſtrongly that it kills her, this is murder, for

it was not given to cure her of a diſeaſe, but unlawfully to deſtroy her child within her, and therefore he that gives her a potion to this end, muſt take the hazard, and if it kills the mother, it is murder 1 *H H* 429, 30.

If a woman be quick or great with child, if ſhe take, or another give her any potion to make an abortion, or if a man ſtrike her, whereby the child within her is killed, tho' it be a great crime, yet it is not murder nor manſlaughter by the law of *England*, becauſe it is not yet in *rerum natura*, nor can it legally be known, whether it were killed or not 1 *H H.* 433

But if the child be born alive, and afterwards die of the poiſon or bruiſes it received in the womb, it is murder in ſuch as adminiſtred or gave them. 1 *Haw* 80 4 *Blackſt* 198

So if a man procure a woman with child to deſtroy her infant when born, and the child is born, and the woman in purſuance of that procurement kill the infant, this is murder in the mother, and the procurer is acceſſary 1 *H H* 433

IX. Capacity of a baſtard as to inheritance.

A baſtard can have no name of reputation as ſoon as he is born, but after he is born, and hath gained by time a name of reputation, he may purchaſe by his reputed name, to him and to his heirs, tho' he can have no heirs but of his body 1 *Inſt* 3 6 *Co* 65

A baſtard is *terminus a quo*, he is the firſt of his family, for he hath no relation of which the law takes any notice, but this muſt be underſtood as to civil purpoſes, for there is a relation as to moral purpoſes, therefore he cannot marry his own mother, or ſiſter, or the like 3 *Salk.* 66

Conſideration of natural affection will not raiſe an uſe to a baſtard, for though there is natural affection between them, yet the raiſing the uſe is a conſtitution of the law, and therefore the uſe ſhall never ariſe *Jenk* 47 *Dyer* 374.

If the iſſue of a man who is a baſtard purchaſe land, and dies without iſſue, tho' the land cannot deſcend to any heir on the part of the father, yet to the heir on the part of the mother (being no baſtard) it may, ſo if the baſtard was attained for the heirs of the part of the mother make not any conveyance by the baſtard *Noy,* 159

If a baſtard dies inteſtate, without wife or iſſue, the king is entitled to the *perſonalty*, and the ordinary of courſe grants adminiſtration to the patentee or grantee of the crown. 3 *P Will.* 33 2 *Black.* 505

A. Volun-

A. Voluntary examination of a woman with child of a baſtard. by 6 G. 2. c 31.

Weſtmorland. THE *voluntary examination of* A M *of* —— *in the ſaid county, ſinglewoman, taken on oath, before me* —— *one of his majeſty's juſtices of the peace in and for the ſaid county, this* —— *day of* ——

Who ſaith, that ſhe is now with child, and that the ſaid child is likely to be born a baſtard, and to be chargeable to the pariſh of —— *in the ſaid county, and that* A F *of* —— *in the ſaid county, weaver, is the father of the ſaid child.*

	The mark of
Taken and ſigned the day and year abovewritten, before me	† A M.
J P.	

Examination after the birth.

Weſtmorland. THE *examination of* A M *of* —— *in the ſaid county, ſinglewoman, taken upon oath before me* —— *one of his majeſty's juſtices of the peace in and for the ſaid county, this* —— *day of* ——.

Who ſaith, that on —— *the* —— *day of* —— *now laſt paſt, at* —— *in the pariſh of* —— *in the county aforeſaid, ſhe the ſaid* A M. *was delivered of a (male) baſtard child, and that the ſaid baſtard child is likely to become chargeable to the ſaid pariſh of* ——, *and that* A F. *of* —— *in the ſaid county, weaver, did get her with child of the ſaid baſtard child.*

	The mark of
Taken and ſigned the day and year abovewritten, before me	† A. M.
J P.	

B. Warrant for apprehending the reputed father before the birth, on 6 G. 2. c. 31.

Weſtmorland { To the conſtable of ——

WHEREAS A M *of* —— *in the ſaid county, ſinglewoman, hath by her voluntary examination taken in writing upon oath, before me* —— *one of his majeſty's juſtices of the peace in and for the ſaid county, this preſent day declared herſelf to be with child, and that the ſaid child is likely*

is be born a bastard, and to be chargeable to the parish of
—— *in the said county, and that A F. of* —— *in
the said county, weaver, is the father of the said child, And
whereas O P one of the overseers of the poor of the parish
of* —— *aforesaid, in order to indemnify the said parish in
the premisses, hath applied to me to issue out my warrant for
the apprehending of the said A. F. I do therefore hereby command you, immediately to apprehend the said A. F. and to
bring him before me or some other of his majesty's justices of
the peace for the said county, to find security to indemnify the
said parish of* —— *or else to find sufficient surety for his appearance at the next general quarter sessions, [or, next general
sessions] of the peace to be holden for the said county, and to
abide and perform such order or orders as shall be made, in pursuance of an act passed in the eighteenth year of the reign of her
late majesty queen Elisabeth, concerning bastards begotten and
born out of lawful matrimony Given under my hand and seal
the* —— *day of, &c*

The like after the birth.

Westmorland } To the constable of ——

WHEREAS A M of —— *in the said county,
singlewoman, hath by her examination taken in writing upon oath, before me* —— *one of his majesty's justices of
the peace in and for the said county, declared, that on the* ——
day of —— *now last past, at* —— *in the parish of* ——
*in the county aforesaid, she the said A M was delivered of a
(male) bastard child, and that the said bastard child is likely
to become chargeable to the said parish of* —— *and hath charged A F of* —— *in the said county, weaver, with having
gotten her with child of the said bastard child, And whereas
O. P. one of the overseers of the poor* [and so on, as in the
foregoing precedent to the end]

C. Commitment thereupon, by the 6 G. 2. c. 31.

Westmorland. { To the constable of —— in the said
county, and to the keeper of the house
of correction [or, common gaol] at
—— in the said county

WHEREAS A M of —— *singlewoman, in her
voluntary examination taken in writing upon oath,
the* —— *day of* —— *now last past, before me* ——

one of his majeſty's juſtices of the peace in and for the ſaid county, hath declared herſelf to be with child, and that the ſaid child is likely to be born a baſtard, and to be chargeable to the ſaid pariſh of ———— and hath charged A F of ———— gentleman, with having gotten her with child of the ſaid child, [Or, if it is after the birth, then ſay, _Whereas_ A M of ————— ſingle woman, in her examination taken in writing upon oath, before me ———— one of his majeſty's juſtices of the peace in and for the ſaid county, hath declared that on the ———— day of———— now laſt paſt, at ———— in the pariſh of ———— in the county aforeſaid, ſhe the ſaid A. M was delivered of a (male) baſtard child, and that the ſaid baſtard child is likely to become chargeable to the ſaid pariſh of ———— and hath charged A F of ———— weaver, with having gotten her with child of the ſaid baſtard child], _And whereas_ the ſaid A F being now perſonally preſent before me, being brought by my warrant, upon application for that purpoſe to me made, by O P one of the overſeers of the poor of the ſaid pariſh, hath refuſed to give ſecurity to indemnify the ſaid pariſh, and hath alſo refuſed to enter into a recognizance with ſufficient ſurety, upon condition to appear at the next general quarter ſeſſions [or, next general ſeſſions] of the peace to be holden for the ſaid county, and to abide and perform ſuch order or orders as ſhall be made in purſuance of an act paſſed in the eighteenth year of the reign of her late majeſty queen Eliſabeth, concerning baſtards begotten and born out of lawful matrimony _Theſe are therefore to command you_ the ſaid conſtable to take and convey the ſaid A F. to the houſe of correction at ———— in the ſaid county, and to deliver him to the keeper thereof, together with this warrant _And I do hereby command_ you the ſaid keeper of the ſaid houſe of correction, to receive the ſaid A F into your cuſtody in the ſaid houſe of correction, and him there ſafely to keep, until he ſhall give ſuch ſecurity, or enter into ſuch recognizance as aforeſaid, or be otherwiſe lawfully delivered from thence. Given under my hand and ſeal the ———— day of, &c.

D Bond to indemnify the pariſh.

KNOW all men by theſe preſents, that we A F of ———— in the county of ———— gentleman, and A, B. of ———— yeoman, are held and firmly bound unto ———— churchwardens, and ———— overſeers of the poor of the pariſh of ———— in the ſaid county (in truſt for the pariſhioners of the ſaid pariſh) in ———— pounds of good and lawful money of Great Britain, to be paid to the ſaid ———— or their certain attorney, their executors, adminiſtrators, or aſſigns To which

payment

payment well and truly to be made, we bind ourselves, and each of us, jointly and severally, and our and each and every of our heirs, executors, and administrators, firmly by these presents, Sealed with our seals, and dated the ——— day of ——— in the ———year of the reign of our sovereign lord George *the third, of* Great Britain, France, *and* Ireland, *king, defender of the faith, and so forth, and in the year of our Lord*———.

The condition of this obligation is such, that whereas A. M. *of ———singlewoman, hath in and by her voluntary examination, taken in writing and upon oath, before ——— one of his majesty's justices of the peace in and for the said county of ——— declared that she is with child, and that the said child is likely to be born a bastard, and to be chargeable to the said parish of ——— and that the abovebounden* A F *is the father of the said child,* [If it is after the birth, then say, *that whereas* A. M *of ———singlewoman, in her examination taken in writing upon oath, before ——— one of his majesty's justices of the peace in and for the said county, hath declared, that on the ——— day of ——— now last past, at ——— in the parish of ———in the county aforesaid, she the said* A. M. *was delivered of a (male) bastard child, and that the said bastard child is likely to become chargeable to the said parish of ——— and hath charged the abovebound* A F. *with having gotten her with child of the said bastard child,*] *If therefore the said* A F. *and* A S *or either of them, their or either of their heirs, executors, or administrators, do and shall from time to time, and at all times hereafter, fully and clearly indemnify and save harmless, as well the abovenamed churchwardens and overseers of the poor of the said parish of ———and their successors for the time being, as also all and singular the other parishioners and inhabitants of the said parish of ——— which now are, or hereafter shall be for the time being, of and from all manner of costs, taxes, rates, assessments, and charges whatsoever, for or by reason of the birth, education, and maintenance of the said child, and of and from all actions, suits, troubles and other charges and demands whatsoever, touching or concerning the same, then this present obligation to be void, otherwise of force.*

Signed, sealed, and delivered (having been first duly stamped) in the presence of   A F.
A S.

A. W.
B. W.

L. Re.

I

E. Recognizance for the reputed father to appear at the sessions, and to abide such order as shall be made, on 6 G. 2. *c.* 31.

Westmorland. BE it remembred, that on the ——— day of ——— in the ——— year of the reign of our lord George *the third*, of Great Britain, France, *and* Ireland, *king, defender of the faith, and so forth*, A F of ——— in the county aforesaid labourer, and A S of ——— in the county aforesaid yeoman, *personally came before me* J P. *esquire one of the justices of our said lord the king, assigned to keep the peace in the said county, and acknowledged themselves to owe to our said lord the king, that is to say, the said* A F *the sum of* ——— *and the said* A S. *the sum of* ——— *of good and lawful money of* Great Britain, *to be made and levied of their goods and chattels, lands and tenements respectively to the use of our said lord the king, his heirs and successors, if the said* A F. *shall make default in the condition under written.*

Whereas A M. *of* ——— *single woman, hath in and by her voluntary examination, taken in writing and upon oath, before* ——— *one of his majesty's justices of the peace in and for the said county of* ——— *declared that she is with child, and that the said child is likely to be born a bastard, and to be chargeable to the said parish of* ——— *and that the above bounden* A. F. *is the father of the said child;* [If it is after the birth, then say, *Whereas* A. M. *of* ——— *single woman, in and by her examination taken in writing upon oath, before me* ——— *one of his majesty's justices of the peace in and for the said county, hath declared that on the* ——— *day of* ——— *now last past, at* ——— *in the parish of* ——— *in the county aforesaid, she the said* A. M. *was delivered of a (male) bastard child, and that the said bastard child is likely to become chargeable to the said parish of* ——— *and hath charged the above-bound* A. F. *with having gotten her with child of the said bastard child*] *The condition of this recognizance is such, that if the abovebound* A F. *do and shall appear at the next general quarter sessions* [or, *the next general sessions*] *of the peace to be holden for the said county, and shall abide and perform such order or orders as shall be made in pursuance of an act passed in the eighteenth year of the reign of her late majesty queen* Elisabeth, *concerning bastards begotten and born out of lawful matrimony,* ——— *then this recognizance to be void, otherwise of force.*

Acknowledged before me

J. P.

F Warrant of the two next juſtices, for the mother, with a ſummons for the reputed father, to make the order of filiation and maintenance, on the 18 *El c* 3.

Weſtmorland. } To the conſtable of ——

WHEREAS *information hath been made unto us ——— two of his majeſty's juſtices of the peace in and for the ſaid county, one whereof is of the quorum, and both of us reſiding next unto the limits of the pariſh church within the pariſh of ——— in the ſaid county, as well upon the complaint of the churchwardens and overſeers of the poor of the ſaid pariſh, as on the oath of A M. of ———ſinglewoman, that on the ——— day of ——— laſt paſt, ſhe the ſaid A. M was delivered of a (male) baſtard child at ——— in the ſaid pariſh, and that A F of ——— in the ſaid county, taylor, is the father of the ſaid baſtard child, and that the ſaid baſtard child is now living, and chargeable [or, likely to become chargeable] to the ſaid pariſh of ——— Theſe are therefore to command you to bring the ſaid A M before us, at the houſe of ——— in ——— in the ſaid county, on ——— the ——— day of ——— at the hour of ——— in the afternoon of the ſame day, to be by us further examined, touching the premiſſes, and that you give notice thereof, unto the ſaid A F that he may likewiſe be at the time and place aforeſaid, to make his lawful defence To the end that upon the examination of the cauſe and circumſtance, we may take ſuch order therein, as to right doth appertain And what you ſhall do in the execution hereof, you are to make known unto us at the time and place aforeſaid Given under our hands and ſeals, the ——— day of, &c.*

G. The order of filiation and maintenance is inſerted before, in the body of the title.

H. Condition of a recognizance to appear at the next ſeſſions, after the order not performed, on the 18 *El. c.* 3.

WHEREAS *by an order under the hands and ſeals of us ——— two of his majeſty's juſtices of the peace for the ſaid county, one whereof is of the quorum, and both of us reſiding in [or, next unto] the limits of the pariſh church within the pariſh of ——— in the ſaid county A. F. of ——— in the*
ſaid

ſaid county, taylor, is adjudged to be the reputed father of a baſtard child lately born of the body of A M of ———— ſingle woman, at ———— in the ſaid pariſh of ———— [and then ſet forth what was ordered therein further] *And whereas the ſaid A F. hath not obſerved nor performed the ſaid order The condition therefore of this recognizance is ſuch, that if the abovebound A F ſhall obſerve and perform the ſaid order, or ſhall perſonally appear at the next general ſeſſions of the peace, to be holden in and for the ſaid county, and ſhall then and there abide ſuch order as ſhall be then made by the court, concerning the ſaid baſtard child, if any ſuch order ſhall be then made, and if no ſuch order ſhall be then made or taken by the ſaid court, if the ſaid A F. do and ſhall perform the order already by us made as aforeſaid, Then this recognizance to be void*

Battery. See **Aſſault.**

Bawdy houſes. See **Lewdneſs.**

Beer. See **Exciſe.**

Behaviour. See **Surety.**

Bent.

WHEREAS on the north-weſt coaſts of England, and eſpecially in the county of Lancaſter, the ſea is bounded, and the lands are prevented from being overflowed, by large hills, the ſand of which is ſo looſe, that in dry weather it is thrown by the winds on the adjacent lands, to the damage thereof, and the danger of the inhabitants, who are expoſed thereby to the inundation of the ſea, to prevent which, the land-owners are at great charges, annually to plant and maintain a ſort of ruſh or ſhrub called *ſtarr* or *bent*, but many diſorderly perſons pluck up and carry away the ſame, to make matts and bruſhes Therefore if any perſon without conſent of the owner, ſhall cut, pull up, or carry away any ſtarr or bent of the ſaid hills on the north-weſt coaſts of *England*, on complaint thereof on oath to one juſtice, the offender ſhall be ſummoned, and on default of appearing, the juſtice ſhall iſſue his warrant to apprehend and bring him before him, and being convicted on oath of one witneſs, or confeſſion, he ſhall forfeit 20 s, half to the informer and half to the owner of the bent, by diſtreſs, and for want of ſufficient diſtreſs, to be ſent to the houſe
of

of correction for three months, to be kept to hard labour; and for a second offence, to be committed to the house of correction for one year, to be whipt and kept to hard labour

And if any ftarr or bent fhall be found within five miles of the faid fand hills, the perfons convicted of having the fame in cuftody fhall forfeit 20 s in like manner, and for want of fufficient diftrefs fhall fuffer three months imprifonment, and hard labour in the houfe of correction

But this fhall not reftrain any perfons from the exercife of any ancient prefcriptive right, to cut ftarr or bent on the fea coafts in the county of *Cumberland.* 15 & 16 G. 2 c 33 f 6, 7, 8

𝕭𝖎𝖌𝖆𝖒𝖞.

AS *bigamy* in our law feems for the moft part to be ufed to fignify the having of two wives fucceffively one after the other, I fhall take the liberty to transfer the offence which is commonly treated of under this title unto the title 𝔓𝔬𝔩𝔶𝔤𝔞𝔪𝔶, which fignifies more properly the having two or more wives or hufbands at the fame time.

𝕭𝖑𝖆𝖈𝖐 𝖆𝖈𝖙.

IN order to avoid repeating the fame regulations fo many times over, as the offences hereunder mentioned are treated of under their refpective titles in the different parts of this book, it is thought proper, to infert here at large, the whole law relating to them all together, and to refer from thence to this title for the knowledge of the feveral particulars

By the 9 G c 22 (commonly called the *Waltham* black act, occafioned by the enormities committed in Epping foreft near Waltham in Effex, by perfons in difguife, or with their faces blacked) which act is required to be read at every feffions and leet, and by the 6 G 2 c 37 and the 10 G. 2 c 32 which by feveral continuances were in force till *Sept* 1, 1757, &c and finally by the 31 G 2 c 42 were made perpetual, and alfo by the 27 G 2. c. 15. it is enacted as followeth

If any perfon or perfons, being armed with fwords, fire-arms, or other offenfive weapons, and having his or their faces blacked, or being otherwife difguifed, fhall (1) appear in any foreft, chafe, park, paddock, or grounds inclofed with any wall, pale, or other fence, wherein any deer have been or fhall be ufually kept, or, (2) in any warren or place where hares or conies have been or fhall be ufually kept, or (3) in any high road, open heath, common, or down, or (4) fhall unlawfully and wilfully hunt, wound, kill, deftroy, or fteal any red or fallow deer, or (5) unlawfully rob any warren or place where conies or hares are ufually kept, or (6) fhall unlawfully fteal or take away any fifh out of any river or pond. Or if any perfon or perfons *(that is, whether armed and difguifed or not)* fhall (7) unlawfully and wilfully hunt, wound, kill, deftroy, or fteal any red or fallow deer, fed or kept in any places in any of the king's forefts or chafes, which are or fhall be inclofed with pales, rails, or other fences, or in any park, paddock, or grounds inclofed, where deer have been or fhall be ufually kept, or (8) fhall unlawfully and malicioufly break down the head or mound of any fifh pond, whereby the fifh fhall be loft or deftroyed, or (9) fhall unlawfully and malicioufly kill, maim, or wound any cattle, or (10) cut down or otherwife deftroy any trees planted in any avenue, or growing in any garden, orchard, or plantation, for ornament, fhelter or profit, or (11) fhall fet fire to any houfe, barn, or outhoufe, or to any hovel, cock, mow, or ftack of corn, ftraw, hay, or wood, or (12) fhall wilfully and malicioufly fhoot at any perfon in any dwelling houfe or other place, or (13) fhall knowingly fend any letter without any name fubfcribed thereto, or figned with a fictitious name, demanding money, venifon or other valuable thing, [or threatning to kill or murder any of his majefty's fubjects, or to burn their houfes, outhoufes, barns, ftacks of corn or grain, hay or ftraw, 27 G 2. c 15] or (14) fhall forcibly refcue any perfon being lawfully in cuftody of any officer or other perfon, for any the faid offences, or (15) fhall by gift or promife of money, or other reward, procure any of his majefty's fubjects to join him or them in any fuch unlawful act, or (16) fhall unlawfully and malicioufly break down, or cut down the bank of any river, or any fea bank, whereby any lands fhall be overflowed or damaged, or (17) fhall unlawfully and malicioufly cut any hop-binds growing on poles in any plantation of hops, or (18) fhall wilfully and malicioufly

fet

set on fire, or cause to be set on fire, any mine, pit, or delph of coal, or cannel coal

Every person so offending, being thereof lawfully convicted (in any county in *England)* shall be adjudged guilty of felony, and shall suffer death as in cases of felony, without benefit of clergy, but not to work corruption of blood, nor forfeiture of lands or goods

Note, I have added the words above *(whether armed and disguised or not)* to obviate an error which runs thro' most of the books, in a very material part of this statute. They do suppose that a person must be *armed and disguised* to commit any of the offences abovementioned, even the sending of a threatning letter, or persuading another to be an accomplice, whereas it seemeth somewhat clear, that to be armed and disguised is only necessary to constitute any of the six first offences, and that any person whatsoever may be guilty of any of the other following offences, whether armed and disguised or not

Shall appear in any high road] T 9 G 2 K against *Baylis* and *Reynolds*. The indictment was, that the defendants at *Ledford* in the county of *Hereford*, being armed with offensive weapons, and having their faces blacked, and being disguised, did feloniously appear in the high road there, against the form of the statute. The evidence was, that there was a great number of rioters assembled with intent to cut down some turnpikes set up in that county, and the prisoners were at the head of them, with their faces blacked so as it could not be known who they were, having on womens gowns, caps, and straw hats, and each an axe in his hand, and they advancing foremost were taken by the constables then assembled by the justices, and after they were taken and confined, the rest of the rioters did cut down the turnpikes. Lord *Hardwicke* Ch. J. directed the jury thus. The several facts mentioned in the act are not to be taken as being parts of the same offence, but are every of them several offences, and this is a direct separate crime from the rest. It is a single crime, and is for appearing in the high road with faces blacked, and being otherwise disguised. All the other matters proved are but as circumstances, but were properly enough given in evidence, in order to shew the nature of the fact. Therefore if upon the evidence you believe the prisoners did appear in the high road with their faces blacked, that is sufficient within the act, or that they were otherwise disguised, you are to find them guilty. The jury immediately, without going out of court, found them guilty, and they were ordered for execution. *Cases in the time of lord Hardwicke.* 291.

Kill, maim, or wound any cattle] M. 11 G 3 K. and
Paty At the affizes at *Abingdon*, before Mr juftice
Blackftone, the prifoner, a lad of 18 years of age, was capitally convicted, on an indictment for felonioufly, u
lawfully, knowingly, wilfully, and malicioufly fhooting
and killing one mare and one colt. It was moved in
arreft of judgment, that the mare and colt are not averred
in the indictment to be *cattle* within this ftatute, and that
the word *cattle* doth not by law neceffarily include ho.les,
mares, and colts That the ftatutes for regulating the
fale of cattle have t ought it neceffary to mention the
feveral fpecies of beafts to which the provifions of the faid
acts fhall extend That the book of rates diftinguifhes
between the fubfidy on *great cattle* imported, *viz* 50s,
and that on *horfes* and *mares*, *viz* 10l That the ftatute
of 22 C 2 c 13 diftinguifhes between the encouragement given for breeding *cattle of all forts*, and for breeding
horfes That when the ftatute of 14 G. 2. c 6. made it
felony without clergy to fteal *fheep* or *other cattle*, it was
found neceffary to fpecify, by 15 G 2 c 34 what cattle
were intended by the act Upon thefe objections, the
judge refpited fentence till the next affizes, and in the
mean time laid the cafe before all the judges, who unani
moufly agreed, that, as the ftatute of 22 & 23 C 2 c 7
had made the offence of killing horfes by night a fingle
felony, this ftatute was only to be confidered as an ex
tenfion of that ftatute And fome precedents were cited
of capital convictions (but none of executions) upon this
branch of the ftatute. Wherefore it was agreed, that
judgment of death fhould be given at the next affizes
[After which, he was reprieved for tranfportation, and
afterwards, upon ftrong applications from the country, received a free pardon] *Black Rep* 721

Being thereof lawfully convicted in any county in England.
In the fame manner and form, as if the fact had been com
mitted in fuch county And it is at the option of the
profecutor in what court he will profecute *Black Rep*
733

And for the more eafy and fpeedy bringing the offenders
to juftice, if any perfon fhall be charged with being guilty
of any the faid offences, before any two juftices where the
offence fhall be committed, by information of one or more
credible perfons on oath by them to be fubfcribed, the faid
juftices fhall forthwith certify under their hands and feals,
and return fuch information to one of the principal fecre
taries of ftate, who fhall lay the fame, as foon as conveniently

ently may be, before the king in his privy council
whereupon the king may make order in such his council,
requiring the offender to surrender himself in forty days, to
any of the justices of the king's bench, or to any justice
of the peace, to the end that he may be forthcoming to
answer the said offence according to due course of law,
which order shall be forthwith transmitted to the sheriff
of the county where the offence was committed, and shall
(in six days after receipt thereof) be proclaimed by him
or his officers, between ten and two of the clock, in the
market places, on the market days, of two market towns
in the county, near the place where the offence was committed, and a true copy of such order shall be affixed upon
some publick place in such market towns And if such
offender shall not surrender himself pursuant to such order,
he shall from the day appointed for his surrender, be
adjudged convicted and attainted of felony, and shall suffer pains of death, as in case of a person convicted and attainted by verdict and judgment of felony, without benefit of clergy And the court of king's bench, or judges
of assize, on producing to them such order in council,
under the seal of the said council, may award execution
accordingly.

And if any person, after the time appointed for surrender shall be expired, shall conceal, aid, abet, or suc-
cour such offender, knowing him to have been so charged,
and to have been required to surrender himself by such
order, and shall be lawfully convicted thereof, he shall be
guilty of felony without benefit of clergy

But this shall not hinder any judge, justice of the peace,
magistrate, officer, or minister of justice, from apprehending and securing such offender, by the ordinary course
of law And if be taken and secured before the time
of surrender, he shall have his trial by due course of
law

And the inhabitants of the hundred shall make satisfaction (not exceeding 200l) for the damages sustained
by the killing or maiming of cattle, cutting down or de-
stroying trees, setting fire to any house, barn, or outhouse, hovel, cock, mow, or stack of corn, straw, hay,
or wood, breaking or cutting down the bank of any river, or any sea bank, whereby any lands shall be overflowed or damaged, cutting hop-binds growing on poles
in any plantation of hops, setting on fire, or causing to
be set on fire, any mine, pit, or delph of coal or cannel
coal, the same to be rateably taxed and levied, as in cases
of robbery by the statute of 27 *El* c 13

Q 3 But

But no perfon fhall be enabled to recover damages, unlefs he fhall by himfelf or fervant, in two days after the damage done, give notice of the offence unto fome of the inhabitants of fome town, village, or hamlet near to the place where tne fact was committed, and fhall, in four days after fuch notice, give in his examination on oath, or the examination on oath of his fervant who had the care of the fame, before a juftice inhabiting in or near th. hundred, whether he knows the perfon or perfons tha committed the fact, or any of them, and if upon fuch examination it be confeffed, that the examinant knows the fud perfons or any of them, then fuch perfon con feffing fhall be bound by recognizance to profecute the offender by indictment or otherwife according to law

And if an offender be apprehended and lawfully con victed, in fix months after the offence committed, the hundred fhall not be liable

And the action fhall not be commenced but within one year after the offence committed

And if any perfon fhall apprehend, or caufe to be con victed, any fuch offender above mentioned, and fhall be killed, or wounded fo as to lofe an eye, or the ufe of any limb, in apprehending or fecuring, or endeavouring to apprehend or fecure any fuch offender, on proof thereof made it the feffions where the offence was committed, or the party killed or wounded, by the perfon fo apprehend ing or caufing the offender to be convicted, or the per fon fo wounded, or the executors or adminiftrators of the party killed, the juftices fhall give a certificate thereof to the perfon wounded, or the executors or adminiftrators of the perfon killed, by which they fhall be intitled to receive of the fheriff 50l, to be allowed in his accounts, which he fhall pay in thirty days from the time the certi ficate fhall be fhewed to him, on pain of forfeiting to the party 10l, for which, and for the penalty, the party may bring his action

Black lead.

IT having been found by experience, that wad, or black eauke, commonly called black lead, is neceffary for di vers ufeful purpofes, and more particularly in the cafting of bomb fhells, round fhot, and cannon balls, and that the fame hath been difcovered in one mountain or ridge of hills only in this realm, and great deftruction having been
ε   made

made thereof of late years by evil difposed perfons; therefore it is enacted, that every perfon who fhall unlawfully break, or by force enter into, any mine or wad hole of wad or black cawke, commonly called black lead, or into any pit, fhaft, or vein thereof, or fhall unlawfully take and carry away from thence any wad, black cawke, or black lead, or fhall aid, hire, or command any perfon to commit any the faid offences, fhall be guilty of felony, and the court or judge may order him to be committed to prifon, or the houfe of correction not exceeding one year, to be kept to hard labour, and to be publickly whipt by the common hangman, or by the mafter of fuch houfe of correction, at the times, and places, and in fuch manner as the court fhall think proper, or he may be tranfported for a term not exceeding feven years, and if he fhall voluntarily efcape, or break prifon, or return from tranfportation before the time, he fhall be guilty of felony without benefit of clergy   25 G 2 c 10 ʃ 1

And if any perfon fhall buy or receive any fuch wad, knowing the fame to be unlawfully taken and carried away as aforefaid, he fhall be guilty of felony, and be liable to all the penalties inflicted by the laws on perfons knowingly buying or receiving ftolen goods   ʃ 3.

Blafphemy and profanenefs.

1. ALL blafphemies againft God, as denying his being or providence, and all contumelious reproaches of Jefus Chrift, all profane fcoffing at the holy fcriptures, or expofing any part of them to contempt or ridicule, impoftures in religion, as falfely pretending to extraordinary commiffions from God, and terrifying or abufing the people with falfe denunciations of judgments, and all open lewdnefs grofsly fcandalous—are punifhable by fine and imprifonment, and alfo fuch corporal punifhment as to the court fhall feem meet, according to the heinoufnefs of the crime   1 Haw 6, 7   *Blafphemy*

2 Alfo feditious words, in derogation of the eftablifhed religion, are indictable, as tending to a breach of the peace   1 Haw 7   *Depraving the eftablifhed religion.*

3 No perfon fhall have any benefit of the toleration act, who fhall deny in his preaching or writing, the doctrine of the bleffed Trinity, as it is fet forth in the 39 articles   1 W feff. 1. c. 18 ʃ 17.   *Denying the Trinity*

Q 4   4 If

Representing the
Deity in stage
plays

4. If any person shall in any stage play, interlude, shew, may-game, or pageant, jestingly or profanely speak or use the holy name of God, or of Christ Jesus, or of the Holy Ghost, or of the Trinity, he shall forfeit 10l, half to the king, and half to him that shall sue   3 *J c* 21

Christians denying the christian religion

5. If any person having been educated in, or at any time having made profession of the christian religion in this realm, shall by writing, printing, teaching, or advised speaking, deny any one of the Persons in the holy Trinity to be God, or shall assert or maintain there are more gods than one, or shall deny the christian religion to be true, or the holy scriptures to be of divine authority, and shall be convicted thereof, in any of the courts at *Westminster*, or at the assizes, on the oaths of two witnesses, he shall for the first offence be incapable to have any office ecclesiastical, civil, or military, (unless he shall renounce such opinion in the court where he was convicted within four months after such conviction), and for the second offence he shall be disabled to be plaintiff, guardian, executor, or administrator, to take any gift or legacy, or to bear any office, and shall be imprisoned for three years   9 & 10 *W c* 32

But no person shall be prosecuted for any words spoken unless the information be given to a justice of the peace, within four days after the words spoken, and the prosecution of such offence be within three months after such information   *id.*

Case of Edmund
Curl

6. *M* 1 *G* 2 *K* and *Curl*   An information was exhibited by the attorney general, against *Edmund Curl*, for printing and publishing two obscene books, the one styled *The nun in her smock*, the other, *The art of flogging*, setting out the several lewd passages, and concluding against the peace   And of this the defendant was found guilty   It was moved in arrest of judgment, that however the defendant may be punishable for this in the spiritual court, as an offence against good manners, yet it cannot be a libel, for which he is punishable in the temporal courts   But after long debate and consideration, the court at last gave it as their unanimous opinion, that this was an offence properly within their jurisdiction, they said, that religion is a part of the common law, and therefore whatever is an offence against that, is evidently an offence against the common law   And the defendant was set in the pillory   *Str* 788   1 *Barnardist* 29

Case of Thomas
Woolston

7. *E* 2 *G* 2 *K* and *Woolston*   He was convicted on four informations, for his blasphemous discourses on the miracles of our Saviour   And attempting to move in arrest of judgment, the court declared they would not suffer

it

it to be debated, whether to write against christianity *in general* was not an offence punishable in the temporal courts at common law. They desired it might be taken notice of, that they laid their stress upon the word *general*, and did not intend to include disputes between learned men upon particular controverted points. The next term he was brought up, and fined 25 l for each of his four discourses, to suffer a year's imprisonment, and to enter into a recognizance for his good behaviour during his life, himself in 3000 l, and 2000 l by others. *Str.* 834

8. In the year 1656, *James Nayler* for personating our Saviour, and suffering his followers to worship him, and pay him divine honours, was sentenced to be set in the pillory, and to have his tong bored thro' with a red hot iron, and to be whipped, and stigmatized in the forehead with the letter B.

Case of James Nayler.

9. M 3 G 3 K and *Peter Annet*. The defendant was convicted on an information, for writing a most blasphemous libel in weekly papers, called the Free Inquirer; to which he pleaded Guilty. In consideration of which, and of his poverty, of his having confessed his errors in an affidavit, and of his being 70 years of age, and some symptoms of wildness that appeared on his inspection in court, the court declared, they had mitigated their intended sentence to the following, viz. To be imprisoned in Newgate for a month, to stand twice in the pillory, with a paper on his forehead, inscribed Blasphemy, to be sent to the house of correction, to hard labour, for a year, to pay a fine of 6 s 8 d, and to find security, himself in 100 l, and two sureties in 50 l each, for his good behaviour during life. *Blackst. Rep.* 395

Case of Peter Annet.

10. All persons in or belonging to his majesty's ships, or vessels of war, being guilty of profane oaths, cursings, execrations, drunkenness, uncleanness, or other scandalous actions, in derogation of God's honour, and corruption of good manners, shall incur such punishment as a court martial shall think fit to impose. 22 G 2. c 33 Art 2

Navy.

For profane cursing and swearing, see title **Swearing.**

Books.

IF any book shall be taken or otherwise lost out of any parochial library, any justice may grant his warrant to search for it, and if it shall be found, it shall by order

of

of such justice be restored to the library. 7 *Ann c* 14.
s. 10

Books popish. See **Popery.**
Brandy. See **Excise.**
Brass See **Pewter.**

Bread.

THE statute of the 31 *G* 2 *c* 29 repeals all the former laws relating to the assize of bread, and re-enacts the same, with additions and amendments Which, throughout the whole, is a very regular and judicious act, so that the author hath nothing more to do than to abridge the same in the order as it stands not being able, in point of method, to alter it for the better

Power to set the assize.
1 To the intent that a plain and constant rule and method may be duly observed, in making and assizing of the several sorts of bread which shall be made for sale, in any place where an assize shall be thought proper to be set, it is enacted, that it shall be lawful for the court, or for the person or persons herein authorized to set the assize of bread, to set or ascertain in any place within their jurisdiction, the assize and weight of all sorts of bread which shall be made for sale, or exposed to sale, and the price to be paid for the same, when and as often as they shall think proper 31 *G* 2 *c* 29 *s* 2

In proportion to the price of corn
2 And therein respect shall be had to the price, which the grain, meal, or flour shall bear, in the market or markets in or near to the places for which such assize shall be set *id*

Allowance to the baker.
3 And making reasonable allowance to the bakers for their charges, labour and profit, as they shall deem proper *id*

Penalty of disobeying the assize.
4 Where an assize shall be thought proper to be set, no person shall make for sale, or sell, or expose to or for sale, any sort of bread, except wheaten and houshold, (otherwise brown bread), and such other sorts of bread as shall be allowed in the assize but where it hath been usual to make, or the persons setting the assize shall allow the making of bread, with the meal or flour of rye, barley, oats, beans, or pease, or of any such different sorts of grain mixed together, the same may be there made and sold accordingly And if any person shall offend in the premisses, and be convicted thereof by confession or oath

of one witness, before any magiftrate or juftice within the limits of their jurifdiction, he fhall forfeit not exceeding 40 s, nor lefs than 20 s ∫ 3

5 And in every place where an affize fhall be thought Tables of affize. proper to be fet, the affize and weight of the feveral forts of bread which fhall be there made, fhall be fet according to the following tables.

TABLE

TABLE I

Of the assize and price of bread made of Wheat.

Price of the bushel of wheat and baking		Weight				Price											
		The penny loaf.				Quartern loaf				Halfpeck				Peck loaf			
		Wheaten		Houshold		Wheaten		Houshold		Wheaten		Houshold		Wheaten		Houshold	
s	d	oz	dr	oz	dr.	s	d	s	d	s	d	s	d	s	d	s	d
2	9	22	4	29	4	0	3¼	0	2¼	0	6¼	0	4¾	1	0½	0	9½
3	0	20	4	27	1	0	3½	0	2½	0	7	0	5¼	1	1¾	0	10¼
3	3	18	9	25	4	0	3¾	0	2¾	0	7½	0	5½	1	3	0	11
3	6	17	6	23	3	0	4	0	3	0	8	0	6	1	4	1	0
3	9	16	6	21	6	0	4¼	0	3¼	0	8½	0	6½	1	5	1	1
4	0	15	4	20	4	0	4½	0	3½	0	9	0	6¾	1	6½	1	1½
4	3	14	4	19	1	0	4¾	0	3¾	0	9½	0	7½	1	7½	1	2½
4	6	13	9	17	15	0	5	0	3¾	0	10¼	0	7¾	1	8½	1	3½
4	9	12	12	17	1	0	5½	0	4	0	10¼	0	8	1	9¾	1	4½
5	0	12	1	16	6	0	5¾	0	4¼	0	11½	0	8½	1	11	1	5
5	3	11	9	15	7	0	6	0	4½	1	0	0	9	2	0	1	6
5	6	11	2	14	10	0	6	0	4¾	1	0½	0	9½	2	1	1	7
5	9	10	8	14	4	0	6½	0	5	1	1½	0	9¾	2	2	1	7½
6	0	10	2	13	9	0	7	0	5¼	1	1¾	0	10¼	2	3½	1	8½
6	3	9	11	13	1	0	7¼	0	5½	1	2¾	0	10¾	2	4¾	1	9½
6	6	9	4	12	10	0	7	0	5½	1	3	0	11	2	6	1	10
6	9	9	0	12	1	0	7¾	0	5¾	1	3½	0	11½	2	7	1	11
7	0	8	11	11	9	0	8	0	6	1	4	1	0	2	8	2	0
7	3	8	7	11	2	0	8¼	0	6¼	1	4½	1	0½	2	9	2	1
7	6	8	3	10	11	0	8½	0	6½	1	5	1	1	2	10	2	2
7	9	7	14	10	6	0	8¾	0	6¾	1	5½	1	1½	2	11½	2	2¾
8	0	7	10	10	2	0	9¼	0	6¾	1	6¼	1	1¾	3	0½	2	3½
8	3	7	5	9	15	0	9½	0	7	1	7	1	2	3	2	2	4
8	6	7	2	9	9	0	9¾	0	7¼	1	7½	1	2½	3	3	2	5
8	9	6	15	9	4	0	10	0	7½	1	8	1	3	3	4	2	6
9	0	6	13	8	15	0	10¼	0	7¾	1	8½	1	3½	3	5	2	7
9	3	6	9	8	12	0	10½	0	8	1	9	1	3¾	3	6¼	2	7¾
9	6	6	7	8	8	0	10¾	0	8¼	1	9½	1	4¼	3	7¼	2	8¾
9	9	6	4	8	5	0	11	0	8½	1	10¼	1	4¾	3	8½	2	9½
10	0	6	1	8	2	0	11½	0	8½	1	11	1	5	3	10	2	10
10	3	5	15	7	15	0	11¾	0	8¾	1	11½	1	5½	3	11	2	11
10	6	5	13	7	12	1	0	0	9	2	0	1	6	4	0	3	0
10	9	5	11	7	9	1	0¼	0	9¼	2	0½	1	6	4	1	3	1

Price of the bushel of wheat and baking		Weight. The penny loaf Wheaten		The penny loaf Houshold		Price. Quartern loaf Wheaten		Quartern loaf Houshold		Half peck Wheaten		Half peck Houshold		Peck loaf Wheaten		Peck loaf Houshold	
s.	d	oz	dr	oz	dr	s	d	s	d	s	d	s	d	s	d	s	d.
11	0	5	9	7	5	1	0½	0	9½	2	1	1	7	4	2	3	2
11	3	5	6	7	3	1	0¾	0	9¾	2	1¾	1	7½	4	3¼	3	2¾
11	6	5	5	7	2	1	1	0	10	2	2¼	1	7¾	4	4½	3	3½
11	9	5	2	6	15	1	1½	0	10	2	3	1	8	4	5	3	4
12	0	5	1	6	13	1	1¾	0	10¼	2	3½	1	8½	4	7	3	5
12	3	4	15	6	10	1	2	0	10½	2	4	1	9	4	8	3	6
12	6	4	14	6	8	1	2¼	0	10¾	2	4½	1	9½	4	9	3	7
12	9	4	13	6	5	1	2½	0	11	2	5	1	10	4	10	3	8
13	0	4	11	6	4	1	3	0	11½	2	5¾	1	10¼	4	11½	3	8½
13	3	4	9	6	3	1	3¼	0	11¼	2	6½	1	10½	5	1	3	9
13	6	4	8	6	1	1	3½	0	11½	2	7	1	11	5	2	3	0
13	9	4	7	5	15	1	3¾	0	11¾	2	7¼	1	11½	5	3	3	11
14	0	4	5	5	13	1	4	1	0	2	8	2	0	5	4	4	0
14	3	4	4	5	11	1	4½	1	0¼	2	8½	2	0½	5	5	4	1
14	6	4	3	5	9	1	5	1	0½	2	9	2	1	5	6	4	2

In the first column is the price of the bushel of wheat *Winchester* measure, from 2 s 0 d, to 14 s 6 d a bushel, the allowance of the magistrates or justices to the baker for baking being included, and in the next two columns are the *weights* of the several loaves Then in the other columns are the *prices* So that, for example, if the price of wheat is 5 s a bushel, and the magistrates allowance 1 s 6 d to the baker for baking, then opposite to 6 s 6 d in the first column, will be found the weight and prices of the several loaves

And as the weight of the penny loaf is here only specified, the weight of larger loaves may be easily ascertained by addition, as for example, a twopenny loaf (when wheat is at the same rate) is twice as much as the penny loaf, the sixpenny loaf six times as much, and the eighteen penny loaf eighteen times as much

Note, the wheaten loaves are three fourths of the weight of the houshold loaves, and if the magistrates or justices shall think fit to allow any of the white loaves of the price of one penny or two pence, they are to weigh three fourths of the weight of the wheaten loaves of the same price

And

And note, that the prices of the houfhold loaves are always three fourths of the prices of the wheaten loaves, and where it fhall be thought proper to allow of half-quartern loaves, the prices of fuch loaves (if fold fingly) are to be half a farthing higher than is allowed by this table, when it fhall fo happen that the farthing is fplit.

And magiftrates and juftices being to fet the affize and fix the price of the feveral loaves of bread, having refpect to the price which the grain, meal, or flour, of which the fame are made, fhall bear in the market, but no provifion being made how they fhall know what price the refpective forts of meal and flour fhould be efteemed to bear, in proportion to the price of wheat, they are therefore to take notice, that the peck loaf of each fort of bread is to weigh when well baken, 17 lb 6 oz averdupois weight (which confifts of 16 drachms to the ounce, and 16 ounces to the pound), and the reft in proportion, and that every fack of meal or flour is to weigh 2 cwt and 2 qrs neat, and that from every fack of meal or flour there ought to be produced, on the average, 20 fuch peck loaves of bread, and, by obferving the faid rule, magiftrates and juftices may at all times know if the baker hath more or lefs than the allowance they intend to give him

T A B L E II.

Of the affize and price of bread made of the feveral grains here under mentioned

This table is divided into three columns. Column 1. contains the prices of the bufhel of grain, the allowance for baking included, which prices are adapted fo as to ferve either for the *Winchefter* bufhel of rye, barley, oats, beans, maflin (otherwife mifcellany, confifting of two thirds wheat and one third rye), the price of either of which bufhels in the market being known, the magiftrates are to add the intended allowance thereto, the amount of which being found in column 1 the weight which the loaves ought to be will be found under the column N° 2 and the price of the refpective peck loaves (which are to weigh 17 lb 6 oz. each) under N° 3.

Example When the price of the bufhel of barley in the market, with the allowance to the baker is 4 s, look for that fum in column 1, and under their refpective titles in the fame line will be found the weights which the feveral

veral

veral affize barley loaves fhould be of, and the price of the peck barley loaf, and fo of each of the other forts

Note, where bread is allowed at any time to be made for fale, of peafe only, the affize and price thereof are to be fet and fixed from the bean columns and where bread is ordered to be made for fale, of a coarfe fort of maflin or mifcellany grain, confifting of one third rye, one third barley, and one third either peafe or beans, the affize and price thereof are to be fet and fixed from the barley columns

Note alfo, that this table is framed for bread to be made of the whole produce of the faid feveral grains, except the bran or hull thereof only.

No I.

No. 1. Price of the bushel and baking		No. 2. Weight of the penny loaf.									
		Rye		Barley		Oats		Beans		Maslin	
s	d	oz	dr	oz	dr	oz	dr	oz	dr	oz	dr
1	0	62	8	67	8	21	4	83	12	70	0
1	3	50	0	54	0	25	0	67	0	56	0
1	6	41	10	45	0	25	14	55	12	46	10
1	9	35	11	38	9	17	14	47	14	40	0
2	0	31	4	33	12	15	10	41	14	35	0
2	3	27	13	30	0	13	14	37	4	31	2
2	6	25	0	27	0	12	8	33	6	28	0
2	9	22	11	24	9	11	6	30	7	25	6
3	0	20	13	22	8	10	7	27	14	23	5
3	3	19	4	20	12	9	10	25	12	21	8
3	6	17	13	19	4	8	15	23	15	20	0
3	9	16	11	18	0	8	5	22	5	18	10
4	0	15	10	16	14	7	13	20	15	17	8
4	3	14	12	15	14	7	6	19	11	16	8
4	6	13	14	15	0	6	15	18	10	15	9
4	9	13	2	14	4	6	9	17	11	14	12
5	0	12	8	13	8	6	4	16	12	14	0
5	3	11	14	12	14	5	15	15	12	13	5
5	6	11	5	12	4	5	11	15	3	12	14
5	9	10	13	11	12	5	7	14	9	12	2
6	0	10	6	11	4	5	3	13	15	11	10
6	3	10	0	10	13	5	0	13	6	11	3
6	6	9	10	10	6	4	13	12	14	10	12
6	9	9	4	10	0	4	10	12	6	10	6
7	0	8	15	9	10	4	7	11	15	10	0

No. 3. Price of the peck loaf									
Rye		Barley		Oats		Beans		Maslin	
s	d	s	d	s	d	s	d	s	d
0	4½	0	4¼	0	9	0	3¼	0	4
0	5½	0	5¼	0	11	0	4	0	5
0	6½	0	6¼	1	1¼	0	5	0	6
0	7¾	0	7¼	1	3¼	0	5¾	0	7
0	8¾	0	8¼	1	5¼	0	6¼	0	8
0	10	0	9¼	1	7¼	0	7½	0	9
0	11	0	10½	1	10	0	8¼	0	10
1	0	0	11½	2	1	0	9¼	0	11
1	1	1	0½	2	2½	0	10	1	0
1	2¼	1	1½	2	4¼	0	10¾	1	1
1	3¼	1	2¼	2	6½	0	11¾	1	2
1	4½	1	3¼	2	8¾	1	0¼	1	3
1	5¾	1	4½	2	11	1	1¼	1	4
1	6¼	1	5¼	3	0¾	1	2¼	1	5
1	8	1	7	3	2½	1	3	1	6
1	8¼	1	8	3	5¼	1	3¼	1	7
1	10	1	9	3	8	1	4¼	1	8
1	11	1	10	3	11	1	5¼	1	9
2	0¼	1	11	4	1	1	7¼	1	10
2	1¼	2	0	4	3	1	7¾	1	11
2	2¾	2	1	4	5½	1	8	2	0
2	3¼	2	2	4	7	1	8¾	2	1
2	5	2	3	4	9	1	9½	2	2
2	6	2	4	5	0	1	10½	2	3
2	7	2	5	5	[illegible]	1	11	2	4

6 Every affize which fhall be fet, in an, city, town corporate, hundred, divifion, liberty, rape, or wapentake, fhall be fet in averdupois weight, and not troy weight, and in the proportions directed by the fud tables, or as near as may be, and the faid tables fhall extend as well to fuch bread which fhall be made of the flour of wheat mixed with the flour of other grain, as alfo to bread which fhall be made with the flour of other grain than wheat, which fhall be publickly allowed in any place to be made into bread, and the affize of all fuch mixed bread fhall be fet as near as may be according to the faid tables *f* 5

Affize to be fet in averdupois weight

7 The prices which the feveral kinds of grain, meal, and flour, allowed to be made into bread, fhall *bona fide* fell for in the markets or places in *London*, where fuch grain, meal, and flour fhall be publickly fold during the whole market, and not at particular times thereof, or on particular contracts only, fhall from time to time be given in and certified on oath, on fome certain day in every week, as the court of mayor and aldermen fhall appoint, by the meal weighers of the faid city or fuch other perfons as the faid court fhall direct, and fhall alfo, on fome certain day in every week to be appointed by the faid court, be entred by fuch meal weighers or other perfons to be appointed as aforefaid, in writing under their hands, in fome book for that purpofe to be provided by the faid city, and kept at the town-clerk's office And the next day after every fuch price fhall be fo given in and certified, the affize and weight of all forts of bread to be fold or expofed to fale, and the price to be paid for the fame, fhall from time to time be fet by the faid court, if then fitting, if not, then by the mayor of the faid city And the affize fo fet fhall take place from fuch time as the faid court fhall order, and be in force for the faid city of *London* and the liberties thereof and the weekly bills of mortality (the city of *Westminster* and liberties thereof, the borough of *Southwark*, and weekly bills of mortality in the county of *Surry* excepted) until a new or other affize in *London* fhall be fet. And after the fetting of every fuch affize by the faid court, or by the mayor when the faid court fhall not fit, the affize fo fet fhall, with all convenient fpeed be made publick, in fuch manner as the faid court fhall direct But before any advance or reduction fhall in any week be made by the faid court or mayor, in the price of bread, the meal weighers or fuch other perfons as aforefaid appointed to make return of the prices of grain, meal, and flour, fhall leave in writing

Prices of grain &c. to be certified in London.

at the common hall of the company of bakers, a copy of every return fo made and entered by them as aforefaid, fome time of the fame day on which they fhall make the faid return and entry to the intent that the faid company may, in the morning of the next day after every fuch return and entry fhall be made, and before any time fhall be fet, have an opportunity to offer to the faid court or mayor refpectively, all fuch objections as they fhall think ht, againft any advance or reduction being that day made *f* 6

8 The court of mayor and aldermen of every other city where there fhall be any fuch court, and where fuch court fhall fit, and where there fhall be no fuch court, or being any fuch, when the fame fhall not fit, the mayor, bailiffs, or other chief magiftrate or magiftrates of every fuch other refpective city, and in towns corporate, or boroughs, the mayor, bailiffs, aldermen, or other chief magiftrate or magiftrates of every fuch town corporate or borough, or two juftices in fuch towns and places where there fhall be no fuch mayor, bailiffs, aldermen, or chief magiftrates, fhall and may from time to time as there fhall be occafion, caufe the refpective prices which the feveral forts of grain, meal, and flour (fit to make the different forts of bread allowed there) fhall *bona fide* fell for in the refpective publick markets in or near to fuch place, during the whole market, and not at particular times thereof, or on particular contracts only, to be given in to them and certified upon oath, in fuch manner, and by fuch perfons, and on fuch day in every week, as they fhall refpectively appoint And the price which fhall be fo certified, fhall be entered by the perfons who fhall certify the fame, in books to be provided and kept by them for that purpofe And within two days after every fuch price fhall be fo returned, the affize and weight of bread for fuch place, and the price to be paid for the fame, fhall be fet by fuch court or magiftrates refpectively as aforefaid And the affize fo fet fhall commence on fuch day in every week, and be in force for fuch time not exceeding feven days from the fetting of fuch affize, as fuch court or magiftrates refpectively fhall direct *f* 7

9 If two juftices of counties at large, ridings, or divifions, fhall at any time think fit to fet an affize of bread, for any place within the limits of their jurifdiction, in fuch cafe, it fhall be lawful for fuch two juftices, to caufe the price which grain, meal, and flour (fit to make the feveral forts of bread that fhall be made for fale in any fuch place) fhall *bona fide* fell for in the refpective

spective publick corn market or markets in or near any
such place, during the whole market, and not at any particular times thereon, or on special contracts only, to be
given and certified on oath to them at their respective
places of abode, on such day in every week as they shall
appoint, by the clerks of the market or markets in or
near such places, or such other person as they shall for
that purpose appoint. And the price so returned shall be
entred by the persons so returning the same in books to
be provided by them and kept for that purpose. And
within two days after such return, the assize may be by
them set for every such place, for any time not exceeding
14 days from the setting thereof. And the assize so set
from time to time, shall commence and be in force at
such time after every such setting thereof and be made publick in such places for which the same shall be so set, in
such manner as the justices who set the same shall direct.
ʃ 8

10. Any maker of bread for sale in any such other city,
town corporate, borough, or place, where the assize shall
at any time be thought proper to be set, shall have liberty
at all seasonable times, in the day-time, the next day after
such returns shall be made and entred as aforesaid, to see
the said entry, without paying any thing for the same,
to the intent every such maker of bread for sale may have
an opportunity on the said next day after such entry made
as aforesaid, to offer to any such court, mayor, bailiffs,
aldermen, or other chief magistrate or magistrates, or justices as aforesaid, who shall think fit to set such assize
within their respective jurisdiction, and before any such
assize shall be set, such objections as he can reasonably
make against any advance or reduction to be made in such
assize so to be set as aforesaid. *ʃ* 9

11. No baker of bread for sale shall be liable to pay
any fee, gratuity, or reward, to any person for or by
means of any assize to be set. *ʃ* 10

12. The form of the return or certificate shall be to
the effect following.

Bakers may in-spect the cer-tificate

Bakers to pay no fee for the assize

Form of the re-turn to be made

*The prices of grain, meal, and flour, as sold in the
corn market in ——— in the ——— of ——— the
——— day of ———.*

The best wheat at	———	———	by the bushel
The second at	———	———	by ditto
The third at	———	———	by the bushel
The best wheaten flour at	———		by the sack

Houshold

Houfhold flour at	———	by the fack
Rye at	——— ———	by the bufhel,
Rye meal or flour at	———	by ditto
Barley at	——— ———	by ditto.
Barley meal at	———	by ditto
Oats at	———	by ditto
Oatmeal at	——— ———	by ———
White peafe at	——— ———	by the bufhel
White pea flour or meal at	———	by ———
Beans at	——— ———	by the bufhel
Bean meal or flour at	———	by ———

To every of which returns the perfons appointed to make the fame fhall fign their names or marks § 11

Form of publication of the affize 13 When an affize fhall be fet, the fame fhall be made publick in the form or to the effect following

——— To u *, } The affize of bread fet the ——— day of ——— for ——— to take place on the ——— day of ——— now next enfuing, and to be in force ——— for the faid ——— of ——— ——

And in places where penny, two-penny, fix-penny, twelve-penny, and eighteen-penny loaves, fhall be made, as followeth

	lb	oz	dr
The penny loaf wheaten is to weigh			
Ditto houfhold is to weigh ———			
The two-penny loaf wheaten is to weigh ——— ——			
Ditto houfhold is to weigh ——			
The fix-penny loaf wheaten is to weigh ———			
Ditto houfhold is to weigh ——			
The twelve-penny loaf wheaten is to weigh ———			
Ditto houfhold is to weigh ——			
The eighteen-penny loaf wheaten is to weigh —— ——			
Ditto houfhold is to weigh ———			

And

And in places where quartern, half-peck, and peck loaves be made, then as follows

The peck loaf wheaten is to weigh	lb	oz	dr	and is to be sold for		s	d
Ditto houf-hold , to weigh				and is to be fold for			

And the half peck and quarter of a peck loaves of wheaten and houfhold bread are to weigh, in proportion to the weight a peck loaf of wheaten or houfhold bread ought to weigh , and to be fold accordingly in proportion And when any bread fhall be ordered to be made with the meal or flour of rye, barley, oats, peafe or beans, either alone, or mixed with the meal or flour of any other grain, the affize of fuch bread fhall be made publick, in fuch manner as the magiftrates or juftices, who fhall fet fuch affize, fhall from time to time direct ∫ 12

14 In places where any fix-penny, twelve-penny, and eighteen-penny loaves fhall be allowed to be made or fold, no peck, half peck, or quarter of a peck loaves fhall be allowed at the fame time to be made or fold , to the intent that one of thofe forts of loaves may not be fold, defignedly or otherwife, for the other fort thereof, to the injury of unwary people on pain that every one offending in the premiffes fhall forfeit not exceeding 40 s, nor lefs than 20 s, as the magiftrate or juftice before whom fuch offender fhall be convicted fhall think fit ∫ 13

Bread of different denominations not to be allowed at the fame time

15 If the juftices of any county, riding, or divifion, fhall in their feffions think fit to afcertain, that any hundred or other place within fuch divifion ought to be eftimated as of or in any one particular hundred, riding, or divifion of any fuch county, riding, or divifion, in order that the affize of bread which fhall be fet for fuch particular hundred or place may extend to or comprize fuch other hundred or place, in fuch cafe, it fhall be lawful for them fo to do but by fo doing thereof, no juftice of any fuch county, riding, or divifion fhall be excluded from acting as a juftice in any hundred, riding, or divifion of any fuch county, in which any fuch particular town, diftricts, or places fhall lie, or the affize fo then fhall be fet. ∫ 14

Hundreds may be divided for fetting the affize

R 3

Clerk of the market to keep book

16. An entry shall be made from time to time by the clerk of the market, or other person appointed to make return as aforesaid, in a book to be provided and kept by him, of every return by him made, and also of the rate at which the price, assize, and weight of bread shall be set within his jurisdiction, which book any inhabitant may, at all seasonable times in the day inspect without fee ʃ 15

Assize not to be altered till the price of wheat, &c. is varied

17. After the assize shall be set no alteration shall be made therein in any subsequent week, either to rise or sink the same, except when the price of wheat or other grain shall be returned as having risen or fallen 3d a bushel since the last return, no provision being made by the assize tables for altering any assize, when the variation in the price shall not have amounted to, and been returned 3d a bushel ʃ 16

Punishment of officers for default

18. If any meal weigher, clerk of the market, or other person appointed to make returns as aforesaid, shall neglect, omit, or refuse to do any thing by this act required to be done by him, or shall designedly or knowingly make any false return, or if any constable or other peace officer shall refuse or neglect to obey any warrant in writing delivered to him under the hand and seal of any magistrate or justice, or to do any other act requisite to be done by him for carrying this act into execution, he shall forfeit not exceeding 5l, nor less than 20s ʃ 17

Persons to declare the price of corn.

19. If a buyer or seller of or dealer in corn, grain, meal, or flour, on reasonable request to him made by the meal weighers of the city of *London*, or by the clerks of the market or other person respectively appointed to make returns as aforesaid, shall refuse to unclose and make known to them the true real prices which the several sorts of grain, meal and flour shall be *bona fide* bought at or sold by or for him, at any corn market, or other place where corn, grain, meal, or flour is usually openly or publickly sold, or shall knowingly give in any false or untrue price, or which hath been made by any deceitful means, he shall, on conviction thereof by confession, or oath of one witness, or affirmation of a quaker, forfeit not more than 10l, nor less than 40s ʃ 18

May be summoned before them

20. If any court, magistrate, or justices, who shall have ordered any return to be made as aforesaid, shall within three days after such return suspect, that the same was not truly and *bona fide* made, they may summon before them any person who shall have bought or sold, or agreed to buy or sell any grain, meal or flour within

their

I

their respective jurisdictions, or who shall be thought to
be likely to give any information concerning the premisses, and may examine them upon oath, touching the rates
and prices, which the several sorts of grain, meal and
flour, or any of them, were really and *bona fide* bought at
or sold for, or agreed so to be, by him, at any time within
seven days preceding such summons   And if any person
so summoned shall neglect or refuse to appear (proof of
such summons being made upon oath), or if any person
so summoned shall appear, and neglect or refuse to answer such lawful questions touching the premisses as shall
be proposed to him, without some just or reasonable excuse to be allowed by such court, magistrate, or justices,
he shall on conviction by oath of one witness, or by confession, forfeit not exceeding 10 l, nor less than 40 s.
And if any person so examined, shall wilfully forswear
himself, he shall suffer as in cases of perjury —Provided,
that the party summoned be not obliged to travel above
five miles from the place of his abode. § 19

21 Whenever any court, magistrate, or justices as
aforesaid, shall order any bread to be made with the flour
or meal of any other grain than wheat, or to be mixed
with the flour of wheat, or to be made with the flour or
meal of any other sorts of grain, either separate or mixed
together, all persons who shall make any bread for sale,
in any place where such order shall be made, shall make
bread with such mixed meal or flour, in such manner, and
of such weight and goodness, and shall sell the same at
such prices, as such court, magistrate, or justices respectively shall direct on pain of forfeiting not more than
5 l, nor less than 40 s § 20

Baker of bread made of other grain than wheat shall conform to the assize

22 The several sorts of bread which shall be made for
sale, or sold, or exposed to or for sale, shall always be
well made, and in their several and respective degrees, according to the goodness of the several sorts of meal or
flour whereof the same ought to be made, and no allum,
or preparation or mixture in which allum shall be an ingredient, or any other ingredient or mixture whatsoever
(except only the genuine meal or flour which ought to
be put therein, and common salt, pure water, eggs, milk,
yeast, and barm, or such leaven as shall be allowed to be
put therein by those who have set the assize, and where
no assize shall be set, then such leaven as any magistrate
or justice within his jurisdiction shall allow to be used in
making of bread) shall be put into, or in anywise used
in making dough, or any bread to be sold, or as or for
leaven to ferment any dough, or on any other account,

True making of bread.

R 4

in the trade or mystery of making bread, under any colour or pretence whatsoever, on pain that every person (other than a servant or journeyman) who shall knowingly offend in the premisses, and shall be convicted (A) thereof by confession, or oath of one witness, before any such magistrate or justice respectively, shall forfeit not more than 10 l, nor less than 40 s, or shall by warrant of such magistrate or justice be apprehended and committed to the house of correction, or some prison of the county, city, town corporate, borough, riding, division, or place, where the offence shall have been committed, or the offender shall be apprehended, there to remain and be kept to hard labour, for any time not exceeding one calendar month, nor less than ten days from the time of such commitment, as such magistrate or justice shall think fit And if any servant or journeyman baker shall knowingly offend in the premisses, and be convicted thereof as aforesaid, he shall forfeit not more than 5 l, nor less than 20 s, or shall in like manner be committed to the house of correction or prison as aforesaid And it shall be lawful for the magistrate or justice, before whom such offender shall be convicted, out of the money forfeited, when recovered, to cause the offender's name, place of abode, and offence, to be published in some news paper, which shall be printed or published in or near the county, city, or place, where any such offence shall have been committed. *f.* 21.

Adulterating meal

23. No person shall knowingly put into any corn, meal, or flour, which shall be ground, dressed, bolted, or manufactured for sale, either at the time of grinding, dressing, bolting, or in any wise manufacturing the same, or at any other time, any ingredient, mixture, or other thing whatsoever, or shall knowingly sell, offer, or expose to sale any meal or flour of any sort of grain, as or for the meal or flour of any other sort of grain, or any thing as or for or mixed with the meal or flour of any grain which shall not be the real and genuine meal or flour of the grain the same shall import to be and ought to be, on pain of forfeiting, not more than 5 l, nor less than 40 s *f* 22

Undue mixtures of meal

24. No person shall knowingly put into any bread which shall be made for sale, any mixture of meal or flour of any other sort of grain than of the grain the same shall import to be, and shall be allowed to be made of, in pursuance of this act, or shall put to any bread which shall be made for sale, any larger or other proportion of any other or different sort of grain, or the meal or flour thereof, than what shall be appointed or allowed to be put therein by

the

this act, or any mixture or thing as, for, or in lieu of flour, which shall not really be the genuine flour the same shall import to be and ought to be, on pain of forfeiting, not more than 5 l, nor less than 20 s *ſ.* 23

25 If any person who shall make any bread for sale, **Penalty for de-** or who shall send out, or sell, or expose to or for sale, **ficiency in** any bread which shall be deficient in weight, according **weight** to the assise which shall be set for the same, he shall for-feit (B) not exceeding 5 s, nor less than 4 s, for every ounce wanting in the weight every such loaf ought to be of, and for every loaf which shall be found wanting less than an ounce, shall forfeit not exceeding 2 s 6 d, nor less than 6 d, as such magistrate or justice before whom such bread shall be brought shall think fit so as such bread which shall be complained of for wanting weight, in any city, town corporate, borough, liberty, or fran-chise having jurisdiction thereof, or within the weekly bills of mortality, shall be brought before some magistrate, or justice having jurisdiction in the premisses, and weigh-ed before him, within 24 hours after the same shall have been baked, sold, or exposed to sale, and so as such bread which shall be complained of for wanting weight, in any hundred, riding, division, liberty, rape, wapen-take, or place, shall be brought before some justice with-in such jurisdiction, and weighed before him within three days after the same shall have been baked, sold, or exposed to sale, unless it be made out to the satisfac-tion of such magistrate or justice, on the behalf of the party complained of, that such deficiency in weight wholly arose from some unavoidable accident in baking, or otherwise, or was occasioned by some contrivance or confederacy *ſ* 24

26. Every person who shall make for sale, or sell, or **Mark.** expose, or send out to or for sale, any sort of bread what-soever, shall cause to be fairly marked on every loaf made, sold, carried out, or exposed to sale as wheaten bread, a large roman **W**, and upon every loaf made, sold, carried out, or exposed to sale as houshold or brown bread, a large roman **H**, on pain of forfeiting for every loaf not so marked, not more than 20 s, nor less than 5 s, (except as to such loaves which shall be rasped after the bespeaking or purchasing thereof, by the particular desire of any person who shall order the same to be rasped for his own use) *ſ* 25

27 No baker or other person shall ask or take, for any **Penalty for sell-** bread which he shall sell or expose to sale, any greater price **ing for a greater** than such bread shall be ascertained to be sold at by the as- **price than is set** sise **by the assise.**

size as aforesaid, and no baker, or other person who shall make any bread for sale, shall refuse or decline to sell any loaf or loaves of any of the sorts of bread which in pursuance of this act shall be allowed or ordered to be made, to any person who shall tender ready money in payment for the same, at the price set for the same by the assize, when such person shall have any loaf in his possession to be sold, more than shall be requisite for the immediate necessary use of his family or his customers, and which it shall be incumbent on such baker or other person complained of to prove before the magistrate or justice to whom such complaint shall be made, if thereunto required by the party complaining, on pain of forfeiting for every such offence, not more than 40 s, nor less than 10 s *f* 26

(And by the 2 & 3 *Ed* 6 *c* 15 If any baker shall conspire not to sell bread but at certain prices, every such person shall forfeit 10 l for the first offence, and if not paid in six days, he shall be imprisoned twenty days, and have only bread and water for his sustenance, for the second offence 20 l, or the pillory, and for the third offence 40 l, or the pillory, and loss of an ear, and to become infamous And the sessions or leet may hear and determine the same)

Bread inferior to wheaten shall not be sold for a higher price than houshold

28 No person shall sell or offer to sale any bread of an inferior quality to wheaten bread, at a higher price than houshold bread shall be set at by the assize, on pain of forfeiting (being convicted thereof by confession, or oath of one witness, before one magistrate or justice) the sum of 20 s. *f* 27.

Houses may be entred to search for bread

29 It shall be lawful for any magistrate or justice, or for any peace officer authorized by warrant of such magistrate or justice, at seasonable times in the day-time, to enter into any house, shop, stall, bakehouse, warehouse or outhouse, of or belonging to any baker or seller of bread, to search for, view, weigh, and try all or any the bread, which shall be there found And if any bread, on any such search, shall be found to be wanting either in the goodness of the stuff whereof it shall be made, or to be deficient in the due baking or working thereof, or shall be wanting in the due weight, or not truly marked, or shall be of any other sort of bread than shall be allowed to be made by virtue of this act, any such magistrate, justice, or peace officer may seize the same, and such magistrate, or justice may dispose thereof, as he in his discretion shall think fit for the better carrying of this act into execution *f* 28. 32 *G* 2. *c* 18 *f*. 2.

30 If information fhall be given on oath, to any magiftrate or juftice, that there is reafonable caufe to fufpect, that any miller who grinds any grain for toll or reward, or any perfon who doth drefs, bolt, or in anywife
manufacture any meal or flour for fale, or any maker of
bread for fale, doth mix up with, or put into any meal or
flour ground or manufactured for fale, any mixture, ingredient, or thing whatfoever, not the genuine produce
of the grain fuch meal or flour fhall import and ought to
be, or whereby the purity of any meal or flour in the
poffeffion of any fuch miller, mealman, or baker fhall be
in anywife adulterated, it fhall be lawful for any fuch
magiftrate or juftice, and alfo for any peace officer authorized by the warrant of fuch magiftrate or juftice, at all
feafonable times in the day-time, to enter into any houfe,
mill, fhop, bakehoufe, ftall, bolting-houfe, paftry, warehoufe, or outhoufe, of or belonging to any fuch miller,
mealman, or baker, and to fearch and examine whether
any mixture, ingredient, or thing, not the genuine produce of the grain fuch meal or flour fhall import or ought
to be, fhall have been mixed up with or put into any
meal or flour in the poffeffion of any fuch miller, mealman or baker, either in the grinding of any grain at the
mill, or in the dreffing, bolting, or manufacturing thereof,
or whereby the purity of any meal or flour fhall be in any
wife adulterated And if on fuch fearch it fhall appear,
that any offence hath been committed in any place allowed to be fearched as aforefaid, it fhall be lawful for
any magiftrate, juftice, or officer, authorized as aforefaid, to feize any meal or flour which fhall be deemed on
fuch fearch to have been adulterated, and all mixtures
and ingredients which fhall be found and deemed to have
been ufed or intended to be ufed for fuch adulteration,
and fuch thereof as fhall be feized by fuch peace officer
fhall, with all convenient fpeed, be carried to fome magiftrate or juftice And if any magiftrate or juftice, who
fhall make any feizure in purfuance of this act, or to
whom any thing feized fhall be brought, fhall adjudge
that any mixture or ingredients, not the genuine produce of the grain any fuch meal or flour which fhall
have been fo feized fhall import and ought to be, fhall
have been put into any fuch meal or flour, or that the
purity of any fuch meal or flour fo feized was adulterated
by any mixture or ingredient put therein, in fuch cafe,
every fuch magiftrate or juftice is hereby required to difpofe of the fame, as he in his difcretion fhall think proper.
31 G 2 c 29 f 29.

Mills and other
places may be
en red to fearch
for adulterated
meal.

31.

31 Every miller, mealman, baker, or feller of bread as aforefaid, in whofe houfe, mill, fhop, bakehoufe, ftall, bolting houfe, paftry, warehoufe, outhoufe, or poffeffion, any mixture or ingredient fhall be found, which fhall re adjudged by any magiftrate or juftice to have been lodged there with an intent to have adulterated the purity of meal, flour, or bread, fhall on conviction by confeffion, or oath of one witnefs before any fuch magiftrate or juftice, forfeit not exceeding 10l, nor lefs than 40s, unlefs the party charged with fuch offence fhall make it appear to the fatisfaction of fuch magiftrate or juftice, that fuch mixture or ingredient was not brought or lodged where the fame was feized, with defign to have been put into any meal or flour, or to have adulterated the purity thereof, but that the fame was there for fome other lawful purpofe. And it fhall be lawful for fuch magiftrate or juftice, out of the forfeiture when recovered, to caufe the offender's name, place of abode, and offence, to be publifhed in fome news-paper printed or publifhed in or near the county, city, or place, where fuch offence fhall have been committed. ƒ 30

32. If any perfon fhall obftruct or hinder fuch fearch, or the feizure of any bread or ingredients as aforefaid, he fhall forfeit not exceeding 5l, nor lefs than 20s ƒ 31

33 No perfon who fhall follow or be concerned in the bufinefs of a miller, mealman, or baker, fhall act as a magiftrate or juftice in the execution of this act, on pain of 50l, to him who will inform and fue for the fame in any court of record at *Weftminfter.* ƒ 32

34. If any perfon who fhall follow the trade of a baker, fhall make complaint to any magiftrate or juftice, and make appear to him by the oath of any credible witnefs, that any offence which he hath been charged with, and for which he fhall have paid any penalty by this act, fhall have been occafioned by the wilful neglect or default of any journeyman or other fervant employed by him, fuch magiftrate or juftice fhall iffue his warrant to bring fuch journeyman or fervant before himfelf or any magiftrate or juftice of the place where the offender can be found, and on his being apprehended and brought before fuch magiftrate or juftice, the faid magiftrate or juftice fhall examine into the matter of fuch complaint, and on proof thereof upon oath fhall under his hand adjudge and order what reafonable fum fhall be paid by fuch journeyman or fervant to his mafter, by way of recompence for the money he fhall have paid by reafon of the wilful neglect or default of fuch journeyman or fervant. And if he

fhall

shall neglect or refuse, on conviction, to pay immediately; such magistrate or justice shall commit him to the house of correction, or some other prison, of the place where he shall be apprehended or convicted, to be kept to hard labour not exceeding one calendar month, unless payment thereof shall be made after such commitment, and before the expiration of the said term of one calendar month.

l 33

35 It shall be lawful for the mayor of *London*, or any alderman thereof, within the said city or liberties, and for one justice within the several counties, ridings, divisions, cities, towns corporate, boroughs, liberties, or jurisdictions, to hear and determine, in a summary way, all offences against this act, and for that purpose to summon before him the party accused, and if he shall not appear, or offer some reasonable excuse for his default, then on oath made of the offence by one witness, such magistrate or justice shall issue his warrant for apprehending the offender And on appearance of the party accused, or if he shall not appear, on notice being given to or left for him at his usual place of abode, or if he cannot be apprehended on a warrant granted against him, as aforesaid, such magistrate or justice shall proceed to inquire of the offence, and to examine any witness or witnesses who shall be offered on either side upon oath; and shall convict or acquit the party accused And if the penalty, on such conviction, shall not be paid within 24 hours after such conviction, such magistrate or justice shall issue his warrant directed to any peace officer to make distress, and if any offender shall convey away his goods out of the jurisdiction of such magistrate or justice, or so much thereof that the penalty cannot be levied, then some magistrate or justice within whose jurisdiction the offender shall have removed his goods shall back the said warrant, and thereupon the penalty shall be levied by distress, and if within five days the forfeiture shall not be paid, the distress shall be appraised and sold, rendring the overplus after deducting the forfeiture and the costs and charges of the prosecution, distress, and sale, which charges shall be ascertained by the magistrate or justice before whom the offender was convicted, or who backed the warrant, if either of them shall continue alive, and if not, then by some other magistrate or justice where the offender was convicted, and for want of such distress, every such magistrate or justice within whose jurisdiction such offender shall reside or be, shall on application of the prosecutor, and proof made of the conviction and non-

payment

Manner of conviction, offenders.

payment of the penalty and charges, commit such offender to the common gaol or house of correction of the division or place where the offender shall be found, there to remain for one calendar month from the time of such commitment, unless payment shall be sooner made ∫ 34.

And if it shall be made out on oath, to the satisfaction of any magistrate or justice, that any one is likely to give material evidence on behalf of the prosecutor or of the person accused, and will not voluntarily appear to be examined, such magistrate or justice shall issue his summons to convene such witness before him, at such reasonable time as in such summons shall be fixed. And if any persons so summoned shall neglect or refuse to appear, and no just excuse shall be offered for such neglect or refusal, then (after proof upon oath of such summons) such magistrate or justice shall issue his warrant to bring such witness before him, and if on his appearance, or on being brought before such magistrate or justice, he shall refuse to be examined on oath, without offering any just excuse for such refusal, such magistrate or justice may commit him to the publick prison of the county, city, or other division, in which the person so refusing to be examined shall be, there to remain not exceeding 14 days, nor less than three, as such magistrate or justice shall direct ∫ 35

Form of the conviction.

36. And the conviction shall be in the form or to the effect following

———To wit BE it remembred, that on this ——— day of ——— in the ——— year of the reign of ——— A. O is convicted before me one of his majesty's justices of the peace for the said county of ——— for ——— and I do adjudge him to pay and forfeit for the same the sum of ———

Given under my hand and seal the day and year aforesaid. s. 35.

Appropriation of the forfeitures.

37 By a general clause in this same act, ∫ 34 All penalties and forfeitures, when recovered, shall be paid to the informer

But by the 32 G 2 c 18 Such of the penalties by the aforesaid act, as thereby are not *particularly* disposed of, shall be one moiety thereof, where any offender shall be convicted by confession, or oath of one witness, to him who shall inform and prosecute, and the other moiety thereof, and also all penalties and forfeitures incurred on the weighing, trying, or seizure of any bread by any magistrate or justice, shall be applied for the better carrying

the

the faid act into execution, as fuch magiftrate or juftice fhall think fit ſ 2

38. No certiorari fhall be granted, to remove any con- Certiorari. viction, or other proceeding had thereupon. 31 G 2 c 29 ſ 37

39 If any perfon convicted fhall think himfelf ag- Appeal. grieved, he may appeal to the next feffions, and the execution fhall in fuch cafe be fufpended, fuch perfon convicted entering into recognizance, at the time of the conviction, with two fufficient fureties, in double the fum which he fhall have been adjudged to forfeit, upon condition to profecute fuch appeal with effect, and to be forthcoming to abide the judgment and determination of the juftices at the faid feffions, who fhall finally determine the matter of the faid appeal, and award fuch cofts as to them fhall appear juft and reafonable, to be paid by either party and if the conviction fhall be affirmed, the appellant fhall immediately pay down the fum adjudged, together with fuch cofts as the juftices in their faid feffions fhall award, and in default of payment thereof, any two fuch juftices, or any one magiftrate or juftice having jurifdiction in the place to which fuch appellant fhall efcape or where he fhall refide fhall commit him to the common gaol of the county, city, divifion, or place, where he fhall be apprehended, until he fhall make payment of fuch penalty and of the cofts and charges which fhall be adjudged on the conviction, to the informer But if the appellant fhall be difcharged, reafonable cofts fhall be awarded to him againft the informer, who would in cafe of fuch conviction have been intitled to a fhare of the penalty, and which cofts fhall and may be recovered by the appellant againft fuch informer, in like manner as cofts given at the feffions are recoverable ſ 38

Provided, that if the conviction fhall be within fix days before the feffions, the party on entring into fuch recognizance as aforefaid, fhall be at liberty to appeal, either to the then next, or to the next following feffions ſ 39

40 Every action which fhall be brought againft any Indemnity of magiftrate, juftice, or peace officer, for any thing done perfons profunder this act, fhall be commenced within fix months, cuted for any and laid in the proper county, and the act of the 24 G 2, thing done un-c 44 fhall extend to fuch magiftrate or juftice acting under this act And no action fhall be commenced againft fuch peace officer, till feven days after notice in writing fhall have been given to or left for him at his ufual place of abode by the profecutor's attorney, which notice fhall contain the name and place of abode of the perfon intending

tending to bring fuch action, and alfo of his attorney, and likewife the caufe of action and fuch peace officer may within the faid feven days tender fatisfaction, and if the fame is not accepted, the defendant may plead fuch tender in bar of the action, together with the general iffue or any other plea with leave of the court, and if the jury fhall find the amends tendred to have been fuffi- cient, or if the plaintiff fhall be nonfuit, or difcontinue, or judgment be given for the defendant upon demurrer, or if the action be brought after the time limited, or not within the proper county, the jury fhall find for the de- fendant, and he fhall be intitled to his cofts, but if the jury fhall find, that no fuch tender was made, or not fuf ficient, or fhall find againft the defendant on any plea pleaded, they fhall give a verdict for the plaintiff, and fuch damages as they fhall think proper, and the plaintiff fhall thereupon recover his cofts againft fuch defendant / 40

And other perfons fued for any thing done on this act, may plead the general iffue, and if they recover fhall have treble cofts. ſ 41

Limitation of actions

41 Provided always, that no perfon fhall be convicted for any of the aforefaid offences, unlefs the profecution be commenced within three days after the offence committed. ſ 42

Saving of the right of others.

42. Provided alfo, that nothing herein fhall extend to prejudice any right or cuftom of the city of *London*, or of the lord of any leet, or clerk of the market, or the dean of *Weftminster*, or high fteward of *Weftminster* or his de- puty, or of the univerfities ſ 43, 44, 45

Note, the reafon why the indemnifying ftatute of the 24 G. 2 c 44 is here particularly mentioned, feems to be upon the account of fuch magiftrates or chief officers who are empowered to act in fetting the affize, and other- wife carrying this act into execution, that are not juftices of the peace, as for inftance, the court of mayor and al- dermen, in moft of the boroughs and towns corporate, confifteth of perfons fome of whom are not juftices, and in others, efpecially the more ancient, not one of them is a juftice of the peace, (the corporation having been efta- blifhed before there were any juftices of the peace in the kingdom) but yet they are enabled fpecially to proceed in this and in many other inftances by act of parliament Which obfervation is applicable alfo to the power herein given to them, to iffue precepts, to examine upon oath, and the like, which power is implied in the general of- fice of a juftice of the peace, but is not applicable to thofe others, without fpecial words granting the fame.

So

So alſo it was neceſſary for the act to be particular, with regard to the indemnification of conſtables and others acting under ſuch warrants, as alſo of the meal weighers, clerks of the market, and others appointed to make returns of the price of grain, flour, and the like, who are not under the general protection of the law for their proceedings in theſe matters, and therefore require an expreſs declaration in the act itſelf, of their authority and privilege in this reſpect.

43. All that hath been ſaid above, as to the price and weight of bread, and the like, proceeds upon the ſuppoſition of an aſſize being ſet. By the 3 G 3 c 11. regulations are made altho' no aſſize is ſet, and further proviſions are enacted as followeth *Proceedings where the aſſize hath not been ſet.*

No loaf or loaves of bread, called or deemed aſſize loaf or loaves in the table of the aſſize and price of bread in the act of the 31 G. 2. and the weight of which varies according to the variation in the price of grain, ſhall be made for or expoſed to ſale, in any place where loaves called prized loaves in the ſaid tables ſhall be allowed to be ſold at the ſame time, that is to ſay, no aſſize loaves of the price of three pence and prized loaves called half quartern loaves, nor aſſize loaves of the price of ſix pence and prized loaves called quartern loaves, nor aſſize loaves of the price of twelve pence and prized loaves called half peck loaves, nor aſſize loaves of the price of eighteen pence and prized loaves called peck loaves, ſhall at the ſame time in any place be made for or expoſed to ſale, to the end that unwary perſons may not be impoſed on by buying aſſize loaves for prized loaves, or prized loaves for aſſize loaves, on pain that every perſon offending ſhall forfeit not exceeding 40 s, nor leſs than 10 s   *ſ* 1

And the juſtices in their general, quarter, or petty ſeſſions, may from time to time appoint, which of the ſorts of aſſize or prized loaves, and what other ſorts of bread, and what ſorts of grain, ſhall be allowed to be made and ſold within their juriſdiction or any part thereof, their order to be entred in a book, which may be inſpected by the makers of bread for ſale at all ſeaſonable times of the day without fee, and they ſhall cauſe a copy thereof to be put up in ſome market or other public town of the place, or elſe be inſerted in ſome public news-paper circulated there ——— Provided, that the juſtices ſhall not at any time allow the making for ſale or ſelling any ſorts of aſſize bread made of the flour of wheat, other than wheaten and houſhold bread, and loaves of white bread of the price of two pence or under   *ſ* 2, 3

And every maker of bread for fale fhall obferve the fame proportion as to weight, as where the affize is fet, that is to fay every white loaf of the price of 2 d or under, fhall weigh three parts in four of the weight of the wheaten loaf of the like price, and every wheaten affize loaf, of whatever price the fame fhall be, fhall weigh three parts in four of the weight of every houfhold affize loaf of the like price, and every houfhold affize loaf, fhall weigh one third part more than a wheaten affize loaf of the like price, on pain of forfeiting not exceeding 40 s ʃ 4

And every peck, half peck, quarter of a peck, and half quarter of a peck loaf, made for fale of the flour of wheat, and called *Wheaten Bread*, fhall be fold in proportion to each other, as to price, and the like, as to loaves of *Houfhold Bread*, which fhall be fold proportionably to each other, and for one fourth lefs than *Wheaten Bread* of the fame denomination on pain of forfeiting for every loaf, not exceeding 40 s, nor lefs than 10 s ʃ 5

And the weight of every fort of bread made for fale fhall be in averdupois weight as follows Every peck loaf, feventeen pounds fix ounces, half peck loaf, eight pounds eleven ounces, quarter of a peck loaf, four pounds five ounces and a half, half quarter of a peck loaf, two pounds two ounces and three quarters, on pain of forfeiting for every ounce wanting not exceeding 5 s, nor lefs than 1 s, and for lefs than an ounce not exceeding 2 s 6 d, nor lefs than 6 d, fo as the fame in any city, town corporate, or within the bills of mortality, be brought before a juftice and weighed before him within 24 hours after the fame fhall have been baked or found in any perfon's cuftody for fale, and elfewhere within three days, — unlefs it be made out to the fatisfaction of fuch juftice, that the deficiency in weight wholly arofe from fome unavoidable accident, or was occafioned by fome contrivance or confederacy ʃ 6

And no perfon fhall fell or offer to fale any bread of an inferior quality to wheat bread, at an higher price than houfhold bread, on pain of forfeiting not exceeding 20 s ʃ 7

Every wheaten loaf fhall be marked with a large Roman W, houfhold with a large Roman H and if any perfon fhall fell or offer to fale any fuch loaf unmarked (except as to fuch loaves which fhall be ftamped by the defire of the purchafor for his own ufe), he fhall forfeit for every fuch loaf, not exceeding 40 s, nor lefs than 10 s, unlefs it fhall appear to the fatisfaction of the juftice to whom complaint fhall

shall be made, that the not marking arose from some unavoidable accident, or was occasioned by some contrivance
or confederacy ∫ 8

And bread made of any other grain than wheat shall be
marked with some letter or letters not more than two, as
the justices in their general, quarter, or special sessions
shall order, which order shall be entred in a book, unto
which the bakers may resort in the day time without fee,
and the justices shall cause a copy thereof to be put up in
some market or other publick town or place within the
division, or otherwise to be inserted in some publick news-
paper usually circulated there And if the justices shall
neglect to make such order, then the baker shall mark
every such loaf with any two distinct capital letters as he
shall think fit And every person who shall make or
have in his custody for sale any such loaf made of other
grain than wheat, which shall not be so marked, so as
the same may on view thereof be ascertained under what
denomination it was made (except such loaves as shall be
rasped by the desire of the purchasor for his own use);
shall forfeit not exceeding 40 s, nor less than 5 s, for every
loaf not so marked ∫ 9

And it shall be lawful for any justice, or peace officer
authorized by warrant of such justice, to enter into any
house, shop, stall, bakehouse, wharehouse, outhouse, or
other place, of or belonging to any baker or seller of
bread, and to search, view, weigh, and try all or any bread
which shall be there found And if any bread shall, on
any search or trial by any justice, or on proof made before
him by the oath of one witness, be found to be deficient
in weight, or not truly marked, or deficient in the due
baking or working thereof, or wanting in the goodness
of the stuff, or made with any mixture of meal or flour
of any other grain than the same shall import to be made
with, or with any larger or other proportion of any other
grain than what ought to be put therein, or with any
mixture or ingredient which by the aforesaid act ought not
to be put therein, or with any thing in lieu of flour
which shall not be the genuine flour the same shall
import to be, or made with any leaven not allowed by the
said former act, such justice or peace officer may seize the
same, and dispose thereof to poor persons as to such justice
shall seem fit, and the maker or seller, whose bread shall
be found wanting in the goodness of the stuff, or made
with such undue mixture as aforesaid, or undue proportion, or made with any thing in lieu of flour which shall
not be the genuine flour the same shall import to be, or

with

with any leaven not allowed by the said act, shall forfeit not exceeding 5 l, nor less than 20 s, unless the default shall appear to have wholly arisen from some unavoidable accident, or some contrivance or confederacy ∫ 10

And if any person, shall obstruct or oppose any such search, or seizure of such bread, he shall forfeit not exceeding 40 s, nor less than 20 s ∫ 11

And no person, who shall follow or be concerned in the business of a miller, mealman, or baker, shall be capable of acting as a justice in the execution of this act, and if he shall presume so to do, he shall forfeit 50 l, to him who shall inform or sue for the same ∫ 12

Provided, that if such baker shall make it appear to any such justice, that any offence for which he shall have paid the penalty, was occasioned by the neglect or default of his journeyman or servant, the said justice shall issue his warrant for bringing such offender before him or some other justice, and, on conviction, such justice shall order what reasonable sum shall be paid by the said offender by way of recompence, and if he do not immediately pay the same, the said justice shall commit him to the house of correction or other prison of the place where he shall be apprehended, there to be kept to hard labour for any time not exceeding one calendar month, unless payment be sooner made ∫ 13

And one justice may hear and determine offences in like manner as by the said former act ∫ 14, 15.

And no certiorari shall be granted, to remove any conviction or other proceedings had thereupon ∫ 17

With like liberty of appeal as by the said former act ∫ 18, 19

And persons convicted on this act, shall not be prosecuted for the same offence under any other law ∫ 23.

And all penalties and forfeitures on this act shall go, half to the informer, and half as the justice shall order for carrying this act into execution ∫. 24.

Finally, it is provided, that nothing herein shall extend to the universities ∫ 25

Concerning standard wheaten bread   44 By the 13 G 3 c 62 Whereas by the 31 G 2 c 29 and 3 G 3 c 11. only two sorts of bread made of wheat are allowed to be made for sale, that is to say, Wheaten and Houshold, and whereas according to the ancient order and custom of the realm there hath been from time immemorial a STANDARD WHEATEN BREAD, being the whole produce of the wheat whereof it was made it is therefore enacted, that from henceforth a bread made of the flour of wheat, which flour, without
any

any mixture or divifion, fhall be the whole produce of the grain, the bran or hull thereof only excepted, and which fhall weigh three fourth parts of the weight of the wheat whereof it fhall be made, may be made and fold, and fhall be called and underftood to be a *ftandard wheaten bread* ſ 1

And the maker fhall mark every loaf thereof with the capital letters S W, and the fame may be made and fold, altho no affize be fet, of the weight and in the proportions following, viz That every ftandard wheaten peck loaf fhall weigh 17 lb 6 oz averdupois, every half peck loaf 8lb 11oz, and every quartern loaf 4lb 5½oz And every peck loaf, half peck loaf, and quartern loaf fhall always be fold as to price in proportion to each other refpectively And that when wheaten and houfhold bread, made as the law directs, fhall be fold at the fame time, together with this ftandard wheaten bread, they be fold in refpect of and in proportion to each other as followeth; namely, That the fame weight of wheaten bread, which cofts 8 d, the fame weight of this ftandard wheaten bread fhall coft 7 d, and the fame weight of houfhold bread fh ll coft 6d, or 7 ftandard wheaten affized loaves fhall weigh equal to 8 wheaten affized loaves, or to 6 houfhold affized loaves of the fame price, as near as may be ſ 2.

Provided, that the faid ftandard wheaten bread fhall not be made into or expofed to fale as prized loaves, at one and the fame time, together with affized loaves of the fame ftandard wheaten bread ſ 3.

And the magiftrates may, whenever they think proper, fix the affize of this ftandard wheaten bread, according to the following tables.

S 3   T A B L E

TABLE I

Or the ASSIZE table of standard wheaten bread

The first column contains the price of the bushel of wheat, Winchester measure, from 2 s 9 d to 14 s 6 d the bushel, the allowance of the magistrates to the baker included. The other columns contain the *weight* of the several loaves.

Price of the bushel of wheat and baking	Small Bread		Large Assize Bread.		
	Penny	Twopence	Six pence	Twelve Pence	Eighteen Pence
s d.	oz. dr	lb oz dr	lb oz dr	lb oz dr	lb oz, d.
2 9	25 4	3 2 9	9 7 11	18 15 5	28 7 0
3 0	23 3	2 14 5	8 11 0	17 6 1	26 1 1
3 3	21 6	2 10 12	8 0 5	16 0 11	24 1 0
3 6	19 14	2 7 12	7 7 3	14 14 5	22 5 8
3 9	18 9	2 5 1	6 15 4	13 14 7	20 13 11
4 0	17 6	2 2 12	6 8 4	13 0 9	19 8 13
4 3	16 6	2 0 11	6 2 2	12 4 4	18 6 7
4 6	15 7	1 14 4	5 12 11	11 9 6	17 6 1
4 9	14 10	1 13 4	5 7 13	10 15 10	16 7 7
5 0	13 14	1 11 13	5 3 7	10 6 13	15 10 4
5 3	13 4	1 10 8	4 15 7	9 14 14	14 14 5
5 6	12 10	1 9 4	4 11 13	9 7 11	14 3 8
5 9	12 1	1 8 3	4 8 9	9 1 1	13 9 10
6 0	11 9	1 7 3	4 5 8	8 11 1	13 0 9
6 3	11 2	1 6 4	4 2 12	8 5 8	12 8 5
6 6	10 11	1 5 6	4 0 3	8 0 5	12 0 8
6 9	10 5	1 4 10	3 13 13	7 11 9	11 9 6
7 0	9 15	1 3 14	3 11 9	7 7 3	11 2 12
7 3	9 9	1 3 3	3 9 8	7 3 1	0 12 9
7 6	9 4	1 2 9	3 7 10	6 15 4	10 6 13
7 9	9 0	1 1 15	3 5 13	6 11 0	10 1 7
8 0	8 11	1 1 6	3 4 2	6 8 4	9 12 7
8 3	8 7	1 0 14	3 2 9	6 5 2	9 7 11
8 6	8 3	1 0 6	3 1 1	6 2 2	9 3 3

Price of the bushel of wheat and baking	Small Bread.		Large Assize Bread		
	Penny.	TwoPence	Six Pence	Twelve Pence	Eighteen Pence
s d	oz. dr	lb oz dr	lb. oz dr	lb oz dr	lb oz dr
8 9	7 15	0 15 14	2 15 11	5 15 5	8 15 0
9 0	7 12	0 15 7	2 14 5	5 12 11	8 11 0
9 3	7 8	0 15 0	2 13 1	5 10 3	8 7 4
9 6	7 5	0 14 10	2 11 14	5 7 13	8 3 11
9 9	7 2	0 14 4	2 10 12	5 5 9	8 0 15
10 0	6 15	0 13 14	2 9 11	5 3 7	7 13 2
10 3	6 13	0 13 9	2 8 11	5 1 6	7 10 1
10 6	6 10	0 13 4	2 7 12	4 15 7	7 7 3
10 9	6 7	0 12 15	2 6 13	4 13 10	7 4 6
11 0	6 5	0 12 10	2 5 15	4 11 13	7 1 12
11 3	6 3	0 12 0	2 5 1	4 10 2	6 15 4
11 6	6 1	0 12 1	2 4 4	4 8 9	6 12 13
11 9	5 15	0 11 13	2 3 8	4 7 0	6 10 8
12 0	5 13	0 11 9	2 2 12	4 5 8	6 8 4
12 3	5 11	0 11 6	2 2 1	4 4 2	6 6 2
12 6	5 9	0 11 2	2 1 6	4 2 12	6 4 2
12 9	5 7	0 10 14	2 0 11	4 1 7	6 2 2
13 0	5 6	0 10 11	2 0 1	4 0 3	6 0 4
13 3	5 4	0 10 8	1 15 8	3 14 15	5 14 7
13 6	5 2	0 10 5	1 14 14	3 13 13	5 12 1
13 9	5 1	0 10 2	1 14 5	3 12 11	5 11 0
14 0	4 15	0 9 15	1 13 13	3 11 9	5 9 6
14 3	4 14	0 9 12	1 13 4	3 10 9	5 7 13
14 6	4 13	0 9 9	1 12 12	3 9 8	5 6 5

S 4 TABLE

TABLE II.

Or the PRICE table of standard wheaten bread

The first column contains the price of the bushel of wheat, allowance to the baker included The other columns contain the *prices* of the several loaves

Price of the bushel of wheat and baking		Quartern Loaf		Half Peck Loaf		Peck Loaf		Price of the bushel of wheat and baking		Quartern Loaf		Half Peck Loaf		Peck Loaf	
s	d	s	d	s	d	s	d	s	d	s	d.	s	d	s	d
2	9	0	2¾	0	5½	0	11	8	9	0	8¾	1	5½	2	11
3	0	0	3	0	6	1	0	9	0	0	9	1	6	3	0
3	3	0	3	0	6½	1	1	9	3	0	9¼	1	6½	3	1
3	6	0	3½	0	7	1	2	9	6	0	9½	1	7	3	2
3	9	0	3¾	0	7½	1	3	9	9	0	9¾	1	7½	3	3
4	0	0	4	0	8	1	4	10	0	0	10	1	8	3	4
4	3	0	4¼	0	8½	1	5	10	3	0	10¼	1	8½	3	5
4	6	0	4½	0	9	1	6	10	6	0	10½	1	9	3	6
4	9	0	4¾	0	9½	1	7	10	9	0	10¾	1	9½	3	7
5	0	0	5	0	10	1	8	11	0	0	11	1	10	3	8
5	3	0	5¼	0	10½	1	9	11	3	0	11¼	1	10½	3	9
5	6	0	5	0	11	1	10	11	6	0	11½	1	11	3	10
5	9	0	5¾	0	11½	1	11	11	9	0	11¾	1	11½	3	11
6	0	0	6	1	0	2	0	12	0	1	0	2	0	4	0
6	3	0	6¼	1	0½	2	1	12	3	1	0¼	2	0½	4	1
6	6	0	6½	1	1	2	2	12	6	1	0	2	1	4	2
6	9	0	6¾	1	1½	2	3	12	9	1	0¾	2	1½	4	3
7	0	0	7	1	2	2	4	13	0	1	1	2	2	4	4
7	3	0	7¼	1	2½	2	5	13	3	1	1¼	2	2½	4	5
7	6	0	7½	1	3	2	6	13	6	1	1½	2	3	4	6
7	9	0	7¾	1	3½	2	7	13	9	1	1¾	2	3½	4	7
8	0	0	8	1	4	2	8	14	0	1	2	2	4	4	8
8	3	0	8	1	4½	2	9	14	3	1	2¼	2	4½	4	9
8	6	0	8	1	5	2	10	14	6	1	2½	2	5	4	10

And

And the bakers and fellers of the faid ftandard wheaten bread fhall be liable to all the penalties of the former acts, Provided, that if any information be laid againft a baker, for making, marking, or expofing to fale any bread purporting to be the ftandard wheaten bread aforefaid, made of flour, not being the whole produce of the wheat, the bran or hull thereof only excepted, and weighing three fourth parts of the weight of the wheat whereof it was made and fhall prove that he bought the faid flour, as and for fuch flour, of the miller or mealman, naming his name and place of abode, in fuch cafe, the baker fhall be acquitted, and the miller or mealman fhall forfeit as in the cafe of adulterating corn, meal, or flour, by the faid act of 31 G 2 ʃ 5, 6

And when the magiftrates have fet the affize of the faid ftandard wheaten bread, they may, if they think proper, omit fetting the affize of any other fort of bread. ʃ 7

And the juftices at any general or quarter feffions may prohibit for three months (unlefs they fhall fee caufe fooner to revoke the prohibition, which they may do at any adjourned quarter feffions or any fpecial feffions) the makers of bread for fale, from making or expofing to fale any other one or more forts of bread, purporting to be of a fuperior quality, and fold at a higher price, than the ftandard wheaten bread aforefad. Provided, that no fuch order of prohibition fhall take place, until one kalendar month at leaft after the date of the making thereof. And fuch order fhall be entred by the faid juftices in a book, to be infpected by the bakers at all feafonable times in the day time without fee. And the juftices fhall caufe a copy of fuch order to be put up in fome market or other publick town within the diftrict, or fhall caufe the fame to be inferted in fome publick news paper publifhed within fuch diftrict. And provided, that the bakers may have an opportunity, whilft the faid prohibition is under confideration, of offering to the juftices their objections againft it. ʃ 8, 9

Provided alfo, that nothing herein fhall extend to prevent the magiftrates or others who have power to fet the affize of bread, from allowing (even during the time of fuch prohibition as aforefaid), if they think fit, any white loaves or wheaten loaves of the price of one penny or two pence to be made and fold, fo that they be made, marked, and fold, according to the regulations of the affize table of the 31 G 2 ʃ 10.

And whereas in many places, the inferior claffes of people are ufed to be fupplied with bread made of wheat,

I

of

of a coarse and cheaper sort than the standard wheaten
bread aforesaid, therefore it shall be lawful for the baker,
to make and sell such inferior and coarser bread, provided
he sells the same at a price under that of houshold bread,
as directed by the said act of 31 G 2 (altho' nothing in
this act extends to setting any assize thereon) But if he
sells such inferior or coarser bread by weights and prices
whereat the houshold bread aforesaid is at that time assized,
he shall be liable to the same penalties as bakers for any
misdemeanor in making and selling any other sort of bread
ſ 11, 12

Provided always, that nothing herein shall extend to
prejudice any right or custom of the city of London, or
the dean of the collegiate church of Westminster, or the
high steward of the city of Westminster, or either of the
two universities ſ 14, 17

A Information of an undue mixture used in making of bread, on the 31 G. 2. c 29 ſ 21.

Westmorland   BE *it remembred, that* this ——— *day of*
——— *in the* ———*year of the reign*
of ——— *at* ——— *in the said county,* A I *yeoman, in his*
proper person, exhibiteth to me J P *esquire, one of his ma-*
jesty's justices of the peace for the said county, a complaint and
information, and thereby informeth me, that A O *late of* ———
in the county aforesaid, baker, on the ——— *day of* ———
[Here specify the time of the offence, that the prosecution
may appear to be commenced within three days after the
offence committed, according to the 42d section of the
aforesaid statute] *did put into and use, in the making of bread*
to be sold, a preparation or mixture in which allum was an in-
gredient, contrary to the form of the statute in such case made
and provided, whereby the said A O *hath forfeited a sum of*
money, not exceeding 10 l, *nor less than* 40 s, *and thereupon the*
said A I *prayeth the judgment of me the said justice in that*
behalf, and that he the said A I *may have one moiety of the*
said forfeiture, according to the form of the statute in such case
made, and that the said A O *may be summoned to answer the*
premises before me the said justice

Summons thereupon

Westmorland ⎰ To the constable of ———

WHEREAS *complaint and information hath been*
exhibited before me J P *esquire, one of his majesty's*
justices

justices of the peace for the said county, by A I yeoman, that A O late of ——— in the county aforesaid, baker, on the ——— day of ——— in the ——— year of the reign of ——— did put into and use, in the making of bread to be sold, a preparation or mixture in which alum was an ingredient, contrary to the form of th statute in such case made and provided These are therefore to require you forthwith to summon the said A O. to appear before me at ——— on the ——— day of ——— at the hour of ——— in the forenoon of the same day, then and there to answer to the said information And be you then there, to certify what you shall have done in the premisses Herein fail you not. Given under my hand and seal, the ——— day of ——— in the year aforesaid

If the party shall not appear on such summons, or offer some reasonable excuse for his default, then on oath made of the offence by one witness such justice shall issue his warrant (mutatis mutandis) to apprehend the offender, and bring him before the said justice, to answer the said information.

On the party's appearance, or if he do not appear, then on proof of the summons being given to him or left at his usual place of abode, or if he cannot be apprehended by warrant as aforesaid, the justice may proceed to hear and determine the offence

The form of the conviction, by the words of the statute, shall be as follows.

Westmorland, to wit. BE it remembred, that on this ——— day of ——— in the ——— year of the reign of ——— A O is convicted before me J P esquire, one of his majesty's justices of the peace for the said county, for putting into and using in the making of bread to be sold, a preparation or mixture in which alum was an ingredient And I do adjudge him to pay and forfeit for the same, the sum of five pounds Given under my hand and seal the day and year aforesaid

Warrant of distress, on non payment of the penalty within 24 hours after his conviction.

Westmorland { To the constable of ———

FOrasmuch as A O late of ——— in the county aforesaid, baker, was on the ——— day of ——— duly convicted, before me J P esquire, one of his majesty's justices of the peace for

*for the faid county, by the oath of A. W a credible witnefs,
for that he faid A O on the —— day of —— did
put into and ufe, in the making of bread to be fold, a prepa
ration or mixture in which allum was an ingredient, againft
the form of the ftatute in fuch cafe made and provided, by reafon whereof, I did adjudge and have adjudged him to pay and
forfeit for the faid offence the fum of 5 l, to be diftributed as is
herein after mentioned And whereas it appears to me, that
the faid fum, or any part thereof, is not yet paid I do therefore hereby authorize and require you forthwith to make diftrefs
of the goods and chattels of him the faid A O and if within
the fpace of five days next after fuch diftrefs by you taken, the
faid fum of 5 l fhall not be paid, that then you do caufe the
faid goods by you feized to be appraifed and fold, rendring the
overplus to him the faid A. O. after deducting the faid fum of
5 l, and alfo the cofts and charges of the profecution for the faid
offence, and of the faid diftrefs and fale, which cofts and
charges I do hereby afcertain at the fum of 30 s And out of
the faid fum of 5 l fo forfeited as aforefaid, you are to pay one
moiety to A. I yeoman, who informed me of the faid offence,
and profecuted to conviction him the faid A O before me for
the fame, and the other moiety you are to apply for the better
carrying the act of parliament for the due making of bread and
for the other purpofes therein mentioned into execution, according
as I fhall hereafter give you directions And if fufficient diftrefs
cannot be had or found whereupon to levy the faid fum of 5 l as
aforefaid, you are hereby required to certify the fame to me together with the return of this precept Herein fail you not.
Given under my hand and feal, the —— day of —— in the
—— year of the reign of ——.*

Return of the want of diftrefs, indorfed upon the warrant

Weftmorland   *I A C conftable of —— in the faid county,
do hereby certify J P efquire, one of his
majefty's juftices of the peace for the faid county, that by virtue of this warrant, I have made diligent fearch for the goods
and chattels of the within mentioned A O and that I can find
no fufficient goods and chattels of him the faid A O whereon
to levy the within mentioned fum of 5 l Witnefs my hand,
the —— day of —— in the year ——*

A. C.

Sworn before me the faid juftice,
   the day and year aforefaid

J. P.

Commitment for want of diftrefs.

Weftmorland. { To the conftable of ——— in the faid county, and to the keeper of the common gaol at ——— in the faid county.

FOrefmuch as A O late of ——— in the county aforefaid, baker, was on the ——— day of ——— duly convicted before me J P efquire, one of his majefty's juftices of the peace for the faid county, by the oath of A W. a credible witnefs, for that he the faid A O on the ——— day of ——— did put into and ufe in the making of bread to be fold, a preparation or mixture in which allum was an ingredient, againft the form of the ftatute in that cafe made and provided, by reafon whereof I did adjudge him to pay and forfeit for the faid offence the fum of 5 l And whereas on the ——— day of ——— in the year aforefaid, I did iffue my warrant to the conftable of ——— to levy the faid fum of 5 l by diftrefs of the goods and chattels of him the faid A O And whereas it appears to me, as well upon the oath of the faid conftable of ——— as otherwife, that he the faid conftable of ——— hath ufed his beft endeavours to levy the faid fum on the goods and chattels of the faid A O as aforefaid, but that no fufficient diftrefs can be found whereon to levy the fame Therefore I do hereby command you the faid conftable of ——— him the faid A O to apprehend and fafely convey to the faid common gaol, and him to deliver to the keeper thereof aforefaid, together with this precept And I do hereby command you the faid keeper of the gaol aforefaid, to receive into your cuftody in the faid gaol him the faid A O and him there fafely to keep for the fpace of one calendar month from the time of this commitment, unlefs the faid fum of 5 l, and the cofts and charges of the profecution which I have afcertained at the fum of ———ſhall be fooner paid Given under my hand and feal, the———day of——— in the year aforefaid

B. The like procefs as above may be for bread deficient in weight, beginning the information, which is the ground work of the whole, thus

THAT A O late of ——— in the county aforefaid, baker, on the ——— day of ——— in the ——— year of the reign of ——— did expofe to fale one loaf of houfhold bread importing to be a two penny loaf, deficient in weight one
ounce,

ounce, according to the affize then and there fet for the faid bread

And fo in other like cafes

Breaking gaol See $\mathfrak{Prifon\ breaking}$.
Breaking open doors. See $\mathfrak{Arreft}$
Brewers See $\mathfrak{Excife}$.

$\mathfrak{Bribery}$.

BRIBERY in a ftrict fenfe is taken for a great mif prifion of one in a judicial place, taking any thing whatfoever, except meat and drink of fmall value, of any one who has to do before him any way, for doing his office, or by colour of his office, but of the king only, and is punifhable at the common law by fine and impri fonment 1 *Haw* c 67

$\mathfrak{Bricks\ and\ Tiles}$.

True making of tiles

1 **B**Y the 17 *Ed* 4 *c* 4 Every perfon, ufing the occupation of making of tile called Plain tile (otherwife called Thik tile), roof tile or cres tile, corner tile, and gutter tile, fhall make it good, feafonable, and fufficient, and well whited and annealed

And the earth, whereof any fuch tiles fhall be made, fhall be digged and caft up before Nov 1, next before they fhall be made, and ftirred and turned before Feb 1, next following, and not wrought before Mar 1, next af ter and the fame earth, before it be put to making of tile, fhall be truly wrought and tried from ftones

And the veins called malin or marle, and chalk, lying commonly in the ground near to the land convenient to make tile, after the digging of the faid earth whereof any fuch tile fhall be made, fhall be well fevered from the earth of which the tile fhall be made

And every fuch plain tile fo to be made fhall be 10' inches long, 6' inches broad, and half an inch and half a quarter thick —Roof tile or cres tile, 13 inches long, half an inch and half a quarter thick, with convenient deep-

deepnefs.—Gutter tile and cover tile 10½ inches long, with convenient thicknefs, breadth, and deepnefs.

And if any perfon fhall fet to fale any fuch tile otherwife made, he fhall forfeit to the buyer double value of the tile, and make fine and ranfom at the king's will.—To be recovered by action of debt, with cofts.—And alfo the juftices of the peace and every of them may hear and determine offences againft this act, who fhall affefs upon the offender no lefs fine than for every 1000 plain tiles 5 s, for every 100 roof tile 6 s 8 d, and for every 100 corner or gutter tile 2 s.

And the faid juftices fhall have power to call before them or any of them perfons having experience or knowledge in making tile, to fearch and examine the digging, cafting, turning, parting, making, whiting, and annealing aforefaid, and no perfon fhall put any fuch tile to fale before it be fearched, on pain of forfeiture. And if the fearcher fhall find any perfons offending againft this act, they fhall prefent the defaulters at the next feffions, which fhall be equal to a prefentment of 12 men. And the fearcher fhall have of the tile maker for his labour for every 1000 plain tile fearched 1 d, for every 100 roof tile an halfpenny, and for every hundred corner and gutter tile a farthing. Searcher neglecting his duty fhall forfeit 10 s, and the juftices may hear and determine the defaults of the fearchers, in like manner as of the tile makers.

2. By the 17 G 3 c 42. All bricks made for fale, fhall, when burned, be not lefs than eight inches and an half long, two inches and an half thick, and four inches wide, and all pantiles, not lefs than thirteen inches and an half long, nine inches and an half wide, and half an inch thick on pain that the maker fhall forfeit 20 s for every 1000 bricks, and 10 s for every 1000 pantiles § 1, 2. [Note, the reafon why no provifion was made concerning *pantiles*, among the other forts of tiles, by the above mentioned act of the 17 Ed 4 1, becaufe *pantiles* are a modern invention, long after the date of that act.]

And the fize of the fieve or fcreens for fifting or fcreening fea coal afhes, to be mixed with brick earth in making of bricks, fhall not exceed one fourth part of an inch between the mafhes § 3.

3. All combinations for inhancing the price of bricks or tiles fhall be void, and every brick maker or tile maker offending therein fhall forfeit 20 l, and every clerk, agent, or fervant, 10 l, half to the poor, and half to him who fhall fue in fix calendar months in one of the courts at Weftminfter § 4.

Penalties. 4. All other penalties and forfeitures, not herein otherwise directed, fhall be recovered before one juftice, on proof by confeffion or oath of one witnefs; to be levied by diftrefs, and diftributed half to the informer, and half to the poor of the parifh where the offender dwells and if fufficient diftrefs fhall not be found, or fuch penalties and forfeitures fhall not be forthwith paid, the juftice fhall commit the offender to the common gaol or houfe of correction for the place where the matter fhall arife, for any time not exceeding two calendar months, unlefs fuch penalties and forfeitures, and all reafonable charges, fhall be fooner paid. *ſ* 5.

The conviction to be in this form, or to the like effect

BE it remembred, that on the ——— day of ——— in the year of our Lord ——— A B is convicted before me C D one of his majefty's juftices of the peace for the ——— of——— (fpecifying the offence, and the time and place when and where the fame was committed, as the cafe fhall be) Given under my hand and feal, the day and year aforefaid. ſ 6

But no penalty, in refpect of the dimenfions of bricks or tiles, fhall be recovered, unlefs the information fhall be laid within one calendar month after fale or delivery of the bricks or tiles *ſ* 7.

Appeal 5 Perfons aggrieved may, within four calendar months after the caufe of complaint fhall have arifen, appeal to the general quarter feffions, giving 21 days notice at the leaft, in writing, to the perfon or perfons whofe acts are complained againft, and within eight days after fuch notice entring into recognizance before a juftice with two fureties, conditioned to try fuch appeal at, and abide the order of, and pay fuch cofts as fhall be awarded by the court. And the juftices at fuch feffions, on proof of fuch notice and recognizance, fhall hear and determine the appeal in a fummary way, and award fuch cofts to the party appealing or appealed againft, as they fhall think reafonable And their determination fhall be conclufive, and no order or other proceedings in the premifes fhall be quafhed for want of form, or removed by *certiorari* or other procefs into any of his majefty's courts of record at *Weftminfter, ſ.* 8.

Bridges.

Bridges.

NOTE, This title treateth only of county bridges · Those which are under the cognizance of the surveyor of the highways, as being repaired by the several parishes or districts, are treated of under the title **Highways**

I. *Who shall repair.*

1 By the great charter, 9 H 3 c 15· *No town nor freeman shall be distrained to make bridges nor banks, but such as of old time and of right have been accustomed*

And none can be compelled to make new bridges, where never any were before, but by act of parliament 2 *Inst* 701

2 By the common law, some persons (spiritual or temporal, corporate or not corporate) are bound to repair bridges by reason of the *tenure* of their lands or tenements, and some by reason of *prescription* only

By *tenure*, by reason that they and those whose estate they have in the lands or tenements, are bound in respect thereof to repair the same   2 *Inst* 700

By reason of *prescription only*, but herein there is a diversity between bodies politick or corporate, spiritual or temporal, and natural persons   for the bodies politick or corporate, spiritual or temporal, may be bound by usage and prescription only, because they are local and have a succession perpetual, but a natural person cannot be bound by act of his ancestor, without a lien, or binding, and assets   2 *Inst* 700

3 If a man make a bridge for the common good of all the subjects, he is not bound to repair it, for no par-

ticular man is bound to reparation of bridges by the common law, but by tenure or prescription 2 *Inst* 701.

And if none are bounden by tenure or prescription at common law, then the whole county or franchise shall repair it 2 *Inst* 701.

E 10 G 3 K and the Inhabitants of the *West Riding* of the county of *York* The case was, There was an ancient foot bridge over *Glusburne* beck in the said West Riding, and a ford for horses, and another for carriages, being in the king's common highway, leading from *Ot*, to *Clu* in the county of *Lancaster* The inhabitants of *Glusburn* had always repaired the said foot bridge. In the year 1743, the inhabitants of *Glusburne* aforesaid, being desirous of having a bridge for carts and carriages over the said stream, applied for assistance to the sessions for the said West Riding, and thereupon the justices ordered the sum of 10l to be issued for that purpose, with a proviso, that the same should not be construed to extend to charge the inhabitants of the said Riding, in time to come, with the reparation of the said bridge or any part thereof In pursuance whereof, the inhabitants of *Glusburn* aforesaid pulled down the ancient foot bridge, and sold the materials thereof, and received the money for the same, and built a bridge, about sixty yards higher up the stream, in the same highway, for foot passengers, horses, carts, and carriages Which bridge so built was of public utility, and used constantly afterwards by all persons passing that road, till the year 1767, when the same was carried away by a flood And the question was, Whether the inhabitants of the said West Riding were obliged to rebuild the said bridge And, in behalf of the said Riding, a case was cited from 1 *Roll's Abr* 368. which is as follows " If a man erects a mill for his own profit, and makes a " new cut for the water to come to it, and makes a new " bridge over it, and the subjects use to go over this as " over a common bridge, this bridge ought to be repaired " by him who has the mill, and not by the county, because " he erected it for his own benefit " But the court were clear and unanimous, that the riding was obliged to repair this new bridge. The inhabitants of the county are of common right bound to repair all publick bridges, because they are for the benefit of the county By *Magna Charta*, none shall be distrained to *make* bridges, but such as of old time have been accustomed The inhabitants of *Glusburn* were not bound to *make* or build this new bridge for carts or carriages Nor are they obliged to *repair* more than they were before bound to repair And they never

were

rere bound to repair a bridge for horfes, carts, and carriages. What they were bound by prefcription to repair,
was only a foot bridge. They have built a quite different
bridge, in a different place. The cafe in *Roll's Abr* about
a mill erected for a perfon's own benefit is different. There
the private emolument continued to the perfon who erected
it. And it was not reafonable for him to make the county contribute to it, whilft the private benefit continued to
himfelf. But this bridge for horfes, carts, and carriages
was for the common publick utility of the county, and
therefore is within the rule, that "if a man builds a bridge,
" and it becomes ufeful to the county in general the coun-
" ty fhall repair it." The common law therefore attached upon this bridge, and the county ought to repair
it. *Barrow* Mansf 2594. *Black Rep* 685.

4. By the 22 *H* 8 *c* 5 *Whereas in many places, it cannot be certainly proved, what hundred, town, p..., perfon,
or body politick ought to repair bridges b... in the highways, in every fuch cafe, the faid bridge... if they be without a
... or town corporate, fha'l be ma... by the whole fhires of the
..., if within a city or town corporate, then by the inhabitants of fuch city or town corporate, if part be in one fhire, city,
or town corporate, and part in another, or part within the
limits of a city or town corporal, and part without, the inhabitants of the fhire, cities, or towns corporat, fhall repair
fuch part as lies within their limit.* i 3

Bridges broken in the highways] This extendeth only to
common bridges in the king's highways, and not to private bridges to mills, or the like, the remedy in which
cafe is not by indictment but by action. 2 *Inft* 701

Within a city or town corporate] It hath been queftioned,
whether a borough which hath no bridge within it's own
limits, be not liable to contribute to the repairs of a county
bridge. 1 *Haw* 225

By the inhabitants] The perfons to be charged by this
act are comprehended under the word *inhabitants*, which
word, being the largeft word of the kind, is needful to be
explained.

Firft, altho' a man be dwelling in an houfe, in a foreign
county, city, or town corporate, yet if he hath lands in
his own poffeffion and manurance in the county, city, or
town corporate, where the decayed bridge is, he is an inhabitant, both where his perfon dwelleth, and where he
hath lands in his own poffeffion.

Secondly,

Secondly, If a man dwelleth in a foreign fhire, city, or town corporate, and keepeth a houfe and fervants in another fhire, city, or town corporate, he is an inhabitant in each fhire, city, or town corporate within this ftatute.

Thirdly, *Ex vi termini*, every perfon that dwelleth in any fhire, city, or town corporate, tho' he hath but a perfonal refidence, yet he is faid in law to be an inhabitant, or a dweller there, as fervants, or the like, but this ftatute extendeth not to them, but to fuch houfholders who may be diftrained for non-payment And it would be infinite and impoffible, to tax every inhabitant being no houfholder

Fourthly, Every corporation and body politic, refiding in any county, city, or town corporate, or having lands or tenements in any county, city, or town corporate, which they keep in their own hands and occupation, are faid to be inhabitants there, within the purview of this ftatute

Fifthly, An infant, that hath houfe or lands by defcent or purchafe, is liable to this public charge, and fo is the hufband of a feme covert 2 *Inft* 702.

5 A tenant at will of an houfe, which adjoins to a common bridge, is bound to repair the houfe, fo that the publick be not prejudiced by the want of repair, although he be not bound to repair as to his landlord. L *Raym.* 856

6 The freehold of bridges is in him that hath the freehold of the foil, but the free paffage is for all the king's liege people 2 *Inft.* 705

II Power of the leet to inquire thereof.

Decays of bridges are prefentable in the leet, or torn 2 *Inft* 701

III. Power of the juftices in feffions

The juftices, or four of them at the leaft (1 Q) fhall have power to inquire, hear and determine in the general feffions, of all manner of annoyances of bridges broken in the highways, to the damage of the king's liege people, and to make fuch procefs and pains upon every prefentment againft fuch as ought to be charged to make or amend them, as the king's bench ufually doth, or as it fhall feem by their difcretions to be neceffary and convenient, for the fpeedy amendment of fuch bridges 22 H 8 c. 5 1 1.

Fourt

Four of them at the leaſt] If the bridge be within a franchiſe, which hath not four juſtices, and a ſeſſions of its
own, the juſtices of the county ſhall inquire but if the
franchiſe be a county of itſelf, and hath not four juſtices
(1 *Q*) it is not within this ſtatute, but is left to the remedy
which it had at common law 2 *Inſt* 702

And to make proceſs] Where the bridge is in one ſhire,
and the perſons or lands which ought to be charged are
in another ſhire, or where the bridge is within a city or
town corporate, and the perſons or lands that ought to be
charged are out of the ſaid city, the juſtices of ſuch ſhire,
city, or town corporate, ſhall have power to hear and determine ſuch annoyances, being within the limits of their
commiſſion and if the annoyance be preſented, then to
make proceſs into every ſhire of the realm, againſt ſuch
as ought to repair the ſame, and to do further in every
behalf as they might do, if the perſons or lands chargeable
were in the ſame ſhire, city, or town corporate where the
annoyance is 22 *H* 8 *c* 5 ſ 5

As the king's bench uſually doth] The preſentment at
common law, might be before the king's bench, or at the
aſſizes 2 *Inſt* 701

IV Concerning the 300 foot at the ends of bridges

Such part and portion of the highways, as well within
franchiſes as without, as lie next adjoining to any ends of
any bridges, diſtant from any of the ſaid ends by the ſpace
of 300 foot, ſhall be made, repaired, and amended as
often as need ſhall require, and the juſtices, or four of
them, (1 *Q*) ſhall have power to inquire, hear and determine, in the general ſeſſions, all manner of annoyances
of and in ſuch highways, ſo being and lying next adjoining to any ends of bridges, diſtant from any one of the
ends of ſuch bridges 300 foot, and to do in every thing
concerning the making, repairing, and amending of ſuch
highways, in as ample manner as they may do for the
making, repairing, and amending of bridges. 22 *H* 8.
c 5 ſ 9.

V Indictment of bridges.

1 *No money ſhall be applied to the repair of bridges, until
preſentment be made by the grand jury at the aſſizes or ſeſſions,
of their inſufficiency, inconveniency, or want of reparation.*
12 *G* 2. c. 29. ſ. 13.

2, An indictment for not repairing a bridge, ought to shew what fort of a bridge it is, whether for carts and carriages, or for horses, or for footmen only. L *Raym* 1175

3 If a man be indicted for that by reason of the tenure of certain lands he is bound to repair a bridge, it must be alledged where those lands lie. 2 *H H* 18.

4 Any particular inhabitant of a county, or tenant of land charged to the repairs of a bridge, may be made defendant to an indictment for not repairing it, and be liable to pay the whole fine affessed by the court, for the default of repairs, and shall be put to his remedy at law for a contribution from those, who are bound to bear a proportionable share in the charge; for the neceffity of the case requires the greateft expedition in cafes of this nature for bridges being of abfolute neceffity, are not to lie un repaired till fuits are determined. 1 *Haw* 221

5 If a manor be held by the fervice or tenure of repairing a common bridge or highway, and that manor afterwards comes to be divided into feveral hands, every one of their fuccceffes being tenants of any parcel, either of the demefnes or fervices, fhall be liable to the whole charge, and are contributory among themfelves. And tho' the lord of the manor might, upon the feveral alienations, agree to difcharge thofe that purchafed of him, of fuch repairs, yet that fhall not alter the remedy for the publick, but only bind the lord and thofe that claim under him. As the whole manor, and every part of it, in the poffeffion of one tenant, was once chargeable with the reparation, fo it fhall remain, notwithftanding any act of the proprietor. It fhall not be in his power to apportion the charge whereby the remedy for publick benefit fhould be made more difficult, or by alienations to perfons unable, to render it, in refpect of the parts which fhould come into fuch hands, quite fruftrate. 1 *Salk.* 358

6 It hath been refolved, that it is not fufficient for the defendants to an indictment for not repairing a bridge, to excufe themfelves, by fhewing either that they are not bound to repair the whole, or any part of the bridge, without fhewing what other perfon is bound to repair the fame, and it is faid, that in fuch cafe the whole charge fhall be laid upon fuch defendants, by reafon of their ill plea. 1 *H H.* 221

7 It feemeth, that no inhabitant of a county ought to be a juror, for the trial of an iffue, whether the county be bound to fuch repairs or not, and therefore the jury muft come from fome adjacent county. 1 *Haw* 222.

And

And it seemeth that the same objection may lie as to the *justices*, where they are (as it may probably happen) all interested. In which case it seemeth that the trial shall be in the next county For where an impartial trial cannot be had in the proper county, it shall be tried as near to the same as may be As in the case of the king and the inhabitants of the county of the city of *Norwich*, concerning a county bridge, the trial was in *Suffolk* Burrow *Mansfield* 859, 860.

But by a special statute, an inhabitant of the county, in such case, may be a *witness* 1 An ft 1 c 18

8 *No fine, issue, penalty, or forfeiture, upon any presentment, or indictment for not repairing bridges, or the highways at the ends of bridges, shall be returned into the exchequer, but shall be paid to the treasurer, to be applied towards the said repairs, and not otherwise* 1 Ann ft 1 c 18 f. 4

9 *And no presentment or indictment for not repairing bridges, or highways at the ends of bridges, shall be removed by certiorari out of the county into another court* 1 Ann ft 1 c 18 f 5

But a *certiorari* lies to remove an order made by the justices, concerning the repair of a bridge, pursuant to a private act of parliament, and the justices ought to return the private act upon which their order is founded *Dalt* 504.

E 4 *G* 2 *K* and the inhabitants of *Handsworth* Upon motion to quash a *certiorari* to remove an indictment against the defendants at sessions, for not repairing a bridge, it was insisted, that by the 1 *An c* 18 the *certiorari* is taken away To which it was answered, and resolved by the court, that this act extendeth only to bridges where the county is charged to repair, and that where a private person or parish is charged, and the right will come in question, the act of the 5 & 6 *IV c* 11 hath allowed the granting a *certiorari* And therefore they refused to quash. *Str.* 900.

VI Charges of repairing.

By the 12 *G* 2. *c.* 29 The charges of repairing and amending bridges, and highways at the ends of bridges, shall be paid out of the general county rate f. 1.

VII. Surveyors of the work.

The four justices in sessions as aforesaid may appoint two surveyors, with salaries, to see the bridges amended 22 *H* 8. *c* 5 f 4

And

And this bufinefs of furveying the bridges, for the more convenience, is ufually annexed by the juftices to the office of the high conftables, for which they have by this clause power to allow them falaries.

VIII. *Manner of repairing.*

1 It feemeth to be clear, that thofe who are bound to repair bridges, muft make them of fuch height and ftrength, as fhall be anfwerable to the courfe of the water, whether it continue in the old channel, or make a new one.　1 *Haw* 221

2 And perfons are not trefpaffers, for entring on any adjoining lands for repairing bridges, or laying thereon the requifite materials　1 *Haw* 221

IX *Purchafing lands adjoining*

The juftices at their feffions may purchafe any parcel of land, adjoining or near to any county bridge, for the more commodious enlarging, or convenient rebuilding the fame, not exceeding one acre, to be paid for by the treafurer out of the county rates, by order under the hands and feals of the faid juftices in their faid feffions, which lands fo purchafed, fhall be conveyed to fuch perfon or perfons as the juftices in the faid feffions fhall appoint, in truft, for enlarging or rebuilding the faid bridges　14 *G* 2 *c* 33

X. *Contracting for a term of years*

By the 12 *G* 2 *c* 29 ʃ 14　When any publick bridges, ramparts, banks, or cops, are to be repaired at the expence of the county, the juftices at their general or quarter feffions, after prefentment made by the grand jury of their want of reparation, may contract with any perfon for rebuilding, repairing, and amending the fame, for any term not exceeding feven years, at a certain annual fum

In order to which they fhall give publick notice of their intention of contracting with any perfon, for rebuilding, repairing, and amending the fame.

And fuch contracts fhall be made at the moft reafonable price which fhall be propofed by the contractors, who fhall give fufficient fecurity for the due performance thereof, to the clerk of the peace.

　　　　　　　　　　　And

And all contracts when agreed to, and all orders relating thereto, shall be entred in a book to be kept by the
clerk of the peace for that purpose, who shall keep the
same amongst the records of the county, to be inspected by
any of the justices at all seasonable times, and by any person employed by any parish or place, contributing to the
same without fee

Indictment for a bridge out of repair.

Westmorland. } BY the oaths of ———— good and lawful men of the county aforesaid, then
and there sworn and charged to inquire for our said lord the
king, and the body of the county aforesaid, it is presented, that
a certain common bridge, over the river ———— commonly called ———— bridge, lying and being in the parish of ———— in
the county aforesaid, in the king's common highway there, leading
from the market town of ———— to the market town of ————
in the said county, altogether and from the time whereof the
memory of man is not to the contrary, being a common king's
highway for all the lieges and subjects of our said lord the king
and of his ancestors, with their horses, carts, and carriages to
go, pass, ride, and travel at their pleasure, on the ————
day of ———— in the ———— year of the reign of ———— was,
and yet is in great decay, broken, and ruinous, so that the lieges
and subjects of our said lord the king, upon and over the said
bridge with their horses, carts, and carriages could not and cannot go, pass, ride, and travel, without great danger, to the
grievous damage and nusance of all the lieges and subjects of our
said lord the king, upon and over the same bridge going, passing,
riding, and travelling, and against the peace of our said lord the
king, his crown and dignity

And that the inhabitants of the county aforesaid, the common bridge aforesaid (so as aforesaid being in decay) ought to
repair and amend, when, and so often as it shall be necessary.

[Or, And that A. O. late of ———— in the said county,
gentleman, by reason of his tenure of certain lands lying in the
parish of ———— aforesaid, and elsewhere in the said county,
ought to make, repair, and amend the said common bridge, as
often as and when it shall be necessary]

Buggery.

What it is. 1 BUGGERY (from the *Italian bugarone*, a buggerer, this vice being said to have been brought into *England* out of *Italy* by the *Lombards*) is a detestable and abominable sin, amongst christians not to be named, committed by carnal knowledge, against the ordinance of the Creator, and order of nature, by mankind with mankind, or with brute beast, or by womankind with brute beast *3 Inst 58*

The punishment. 2 And by the statute of 25 *H* 8 *c* 6. Buggery committed with mankind or beast is made felony without benefit of clergy. And the justices of the peace may hear and determine the same, as in cases of other felonies.

Principal and accessary. 3. Which said statute making it felony generally, there may be accessaries both before and after But those that are present, aiding and abetting, are all principals And altho' none of the principals are admitted to their clergy, yet accessaries before and after are not excluded from clergy *1 H H 670*

Infants. 4 If the party buggered be within the age of discretion (which is generally reckoned the age of 14) it is no felony in him, but in the agent only But if buggery be committed upon a man of the age of discretion, it is felony in them both *3 Inst 59. 1 H. H 670*

Navy. 5 By the articles of the navy (22 *G.* 2 *c* 33) if any person in the fleet shall commit the unnatural and detestable sin of buggery or sodomy, with man or beast, he shall be punished with death by the sentence of a court martial.

Burglary.

Offences againſt the houſe of another, which fall
ſhort of burglary, belong to title **Larceny**, under the head **Larceny from the houſe**.

I *What is burglary.*
II *Puniſhment thereof.*
III. *Reward for convicting a burglar.*

I. *What is burglary.*

1 THE word *burglar* ſeemeth to have been brought
unto us out of *Germany* by the *Saxons*, and to be
derived of the German *burg*, a houſe, and *larron* a thief,
probably from the Latin, *latro, latronis* | Derivation of burglary.

2 Burglary *is a felony at common law, in breaking and
entring the manſion houſe of another, in the night, with intent
to commit ſome felony within the ſame, whether the felonious
intent be executed or not.* Hale's Pl 79 | Definition of burglary.

—*Breaking*] Every entrance into the houſe by a treſpaſſer, is not a breaking in this caſe, but there muſt be an
actual breaking   As if the door of a manſion houſe ſtand
open, and the thief enter, this is not breaking.   So it is
if the window of the houſe be open, and a thief with a
hook or other engine draweth out ſome of the goods of
the owner, this is no burglary, becauſe there is no actual
breaking of the houſe   But if the thief breaketh the
glaſs of the window, and with a hook or other engine
draweth out ſome of the goods of the owner, this is burglary, for there was an actual breaking of the houſe.
3 *Inſt* 64

And Lord *Hale* ſays, theſe acts amount to an actual
breaking, opening the caſement or breaking the glaſs
window, picking open the lock of a door, or putting back
the lock, or the leaf of a window, or unlatching the door
that is only latched   1 H H 552.

At a meeting of the judges upon a ſpecial verdict, in
January 1690, they were divided upon the queſtion, whether breaking open the door of a *cupboard* let into the
wall of the houſe was burglary or no   Concerning which,
Sir *Michael Foſter* ſays, with regard to cupboards, preſſes,
lockers, and other fixtures of the like kind, it ſeemeth,
that, in favour of life, a diſtinction ought to be made
between caſes relating to mere property and ſuch wherein

life

life is concerned   In queſtions between the heir or de
viſee and the executor, whoſe fixtures may with propriety
enough be conſidered as annexed to, and parts of the
freehold.   The law will preſume, that it was the inten
tion of the owner, under whoſe bounty the executor
claimeth, that they ſhould be ſo conſidered, to the end
that the houſe might remain to thoſe, who by operation
of law, or by his bequeſt, ſhould become intitled to it,
in the ſame plight he put it or ſhould leave it, intire and
undefaced.   But in capital caſes, it ſeemeth, that ſuch
fixtures, which merely ſupply the place of cheſts and
other ordinary utenſils of houſhold, ſhould be conſidered
in no other light than as mere moveables, partaking of
the nature of thoſe utenſils, and adapted to the ſame uſe.
Poſt 108, 9.

M 8 *G K* and *Gray*   One of the *ſervants* in the houſe,
opened his lady's chamber door (which was faſtened with
a braſs bolt) with deſign to commit a rape, and it was
ruled to be burglary, and the defendant was convicted and
tranſported   *Str* 481

By the ſtatute of the 12 *An c* 7   If any perſon ſhall
enter into the manſion houſe of another, by day or night,
without breaking the ſame, with an intent to commit
felony, or being in ſuch houſe ſhall commit any felony,
and ſhall in the night time break the ſaid houſe to get out,
he ſhall be guilty of burglary, and ouſted of the benefit
of clergy, in the ſame manner as if he had broken and
entred the houſe in the night time, with intent to commit
felony

M 4 *G* 2 *Joſhua Cornwall's* caſe   He was indicted
with another perſon for burglary   And upon the evidence
it appeared, that he was a ſervant in the houſe, where the
robbery was committed, and in the night time opened the
ſtreet door, and let in the other priſoner, and ſhewed him
the ſide-board, from whence the other priſoner took the
plate   then the defendant opened the door and let him
out, but the defendant did not go out with him, but
went to bed   Upon the trial it was doubted, whether
this was burglary in the ſervant, he not *going out* with the
other   But afterwards at a meeting of all the judges at
Serjeants Inn, they were all of opinion that it was burglary
in both, and not to be diſtinguiſhed from the caſe where
one watches at the ſtreet end, whilſt another goes in and
commits the burglary, which hath often been ruled to be
burglary in both   and upon report of this opinion the defendant was executed.   *Str* 881.

And entring] It is deemed an entry, when the thief breaketh the houſe, and his body, or any part thereof, as his foot, or his arm, is within any part of the houſe, or when he putteth a gun into a window which he hath broken, or into a hole of the houſe which he hath made of intent to murder or kill, this is an entry and breaking of the houſe but if he doth barely break the houſe, without any ſuch entry at all, this is no burglary   3 *Inſt* 64

In the caſe of *George Gibbons*, at the *Old Bailey* in *June* 1752, *Gibbons* was indicted for burglary in the dwelling houſe of *John Allen*   It appeared in evidence, that the priſoner in the night time cut a hole in the window ſhutters of the proſecutor's ſhop, which was part of his dwelling houſe, and putting his hand thro' the hole, took out watches and other things, which hung in the ſhop within his reach   but no entry was proved, otherwiſe than by putting his hand thro' the hole   This was held to be burglary, and the priſoner was convicted. *Foſt* 107, 8

If divers come in the night to do a burglary, and one of them break and enter, the reſt of them ſtanding to watch, at a diſtance, this is burglary in all   3 *Inſt.* 64.

The manſion houſe] This includes alſo churches, and the walls and gates of a walled town   1 *Haw* 103

Mr *Hawkins* ſays, all out-buildings, as barns, ſtables, dairy houſes, adjoining to a houſe, are looked upon as part thereof, and conſequently burglary may be committed in them   but if they be removed at any diſtance from the houſe, it ſeems that it hath not been uſual of late to proceed againſt offences therein as burglaries   1 *Haw* 104

And lord *Hale* ſays more explicitly, the manſion houſe doth not only include the dwelling houſe, but alſo the outhouſes that are parcel thereof, as barn, ſtable, cowhouſe, dairy-houſe, if they are parcel of the meſſuage, tho' they are not under the ſame roof, or joining contiguous to it, and ſo, he ſays it was agreed by all the judges   but if they be no parcel of the meſſuage, as if a man take a leaſe of a dwelling houſe from one, and of a barn from another, or if it be far remote from the dwelling houſe, and not ſo near to it as to be reaſonably eſteemed parcel thereof, as if it ſtand a bow-ſhot off from the houſe, and not within or near the curtilage of the chief houſe, then the breaking is not burglary, for it is not a manſion houſe, nor any part thereof   1 *H. H* 558, 9

To break and enter a *ſhop*, not parcel of the manſion houſe, in which the ſhopkeeper never lodges, but only

works

works or trades there in the day time, is not burglary, but only larceny, but if he, or his servant usually, or often lodge in the shop at night, it is then a mansion house, in which burglary may be committed. 1 *H. H* 557, 8.

It is not necessary to make it burglary, that any person be actually in the house, at the very time of the offence committed. 1 *Haw* 103

At *Newgate* sessions, in *January* 1750, *John Nutbrown*, and *Miles Nutbrown* were indicted for burglary in the dwelling house of one Mr *Fakney* at *Hackney*, and stealing divers goods. It appeared by Mr *Fakney*'s evidence, that he held this house for a term of years not yet expired, and made use of it as a country house in the summer, his chief residence being in *London* That about the latter end of the last summer, he removed with his whole family to his house in the city, and brought away a considerable part of his goods That in *November* last, his house was broke open, and in part rifled, upon which he removed the remainder of his houshold furniture, except a clock, and a few old bedsteads, and some lumber of very little value, leaving no bed, or kitchin furniture, or any thing else for the accommodation of a family Mr *Fakney*, being asked, whether at the time he so disfurnished his house, he had any intention of returning to reside there, declared that he had not come to any settled resolution whether to return or not, but was rather inclined totally to quit the house, and to let it for the remainder of his term The fact the prisoners were charged with was sufficiently proved, and was committed about midnight the first of *January* last. The court was of opinion, that the prosecutor having left his house, and disfurnished it in the manner before mentioned, without any settled resolution of returning, but rather inclining to the contrary, it could not, under these circumstances, be deemed his dwelling house, at the time the fact was committed, and accordingly directed the jury to acquit the prisoners of the burglary, which they did, but found them guilty of felony in stealing the clock and some other small matters And they were ordered for transportation —————— And the distinction is this Where the owner quitteth the house, *animo revertendi*, it may still be considered as his mansion house, tho' no person be left in it, many citizens, and some lawyers, do so from a principle of good husbandry, in the summer, or for a long vacation But there must be an intention of returning, otherwise it will be no burglary *Foft* 76, 77

In the night] Lord *Coke* says, as long as the day continues, whereby a man's countenance may be discerned, it is called day, and when darkneſs comes, and day light is paſt, ſo as by the light of day you cannot diſcern the countenance of a man, then it is called night And this doth aggravate the offence, ſince the night is the time wherein man is at reſt, and wherein beaſts run about ſeeking their prey Hence in ancient records, the twylight was ſignified, when it was ſaid, *inter canem & lupum*, (between the dog and the wolf,) for when the night begins, the dog ſleeps, and the wolf ſeeketh his prey   3 *Inſt* 63

At the *Lancaſter* Lent aſſizes 1771, K and *Waddington*. There was an indictment for burglary, alledging the fact to be committed in the night, but not expreſſing about what hour it was done. Mr juſtice *Gould* held the indictment inſufficient as for a burglary, and directed the priſoner to be found guilty of a ſimple felony only He ſaid, that according to the old doctrine, a burglary might be committed at any time between ſun ſetting and ſun riſing, but that the rule now eſtabliſhed is, that it cannot be committed during the *crepuſculum*, that therefore it is neceſſary to ſpecify the *hour*, in order that the fact may appear upon the face of the indictment to be done between the twylight of the evening and that of the morning

Accordingly, Sir *William Blackſtone* ſays, the better opinion ſeems to be, that if there be daylight enough, begun or left, to diſcern a man's face withal, it is no burglary. But this doth not extend to moonlight, for then many midnight burglaries would go unpuniſhed and beſides, the malignity of the offence doth not ſo properly ariſe from its being done in the dark, as at the dead of night, when all the creation, except beaſts of prey, are at reſt, when ſleep has diſarmed the owner, and rendered his caſtle as it were defenceleſs.   4 *Black*. 224.

With intent to commit felony] There can be no burglary, but where the indictment both expreſly alledges, and the verdict alſo finds, an intention to commit ſome felony; for if it appear, that the offender meant only to commit a treſpaſs, as to beat the party, or the like, he is not guilty of burglary   1 *Haw* 105

However it ſeems the much better opinion, that an intention to commit a rape or other ſuch crime, which is made felony by ſtatute, and was a treſpaſs only at common law, will make a man guilty of burglary, as much as if ſuch offence was a felony at common law, becauſe wherever a ſtatute makes any offence felony, it incidentally gives it all the properties of a felony at common law. 1 *Haw* 105

Whether

Whether the felonious intent be executed or not] Thus they are burglars, who break any houfe, or church in the night, although they take nothing away And herein this offence differs from robbery, which requires that fomething be taken, tho' it is not material of what value

Where a man commits burglary and at the fame time fteals goods out of the houfe, it is alfo larceny, and if he be acquitted of the burglary, he may notwithftanding be indicted of the larceny, for they are feveral offences, tho' committed at the fame time And burglary may be, where there is no larceny, and larceny may be, where there is no burglary. 2 *H. H* 246

II *Punifhment thereof.*

By the 18 *El c* 7 and 3 *W c* 9 Benefit of clergy is taken away in cafes of burglary, both from the principal, and the acceffary before, but in all cafes of burglary, acceffaries after muft have their clergy 2 *H H* 364 1 *Haw* 357, 358

But by the 10 *G* 3 *c* 48. Every perfon who fhall buy or receive any ftolen jewel or jewels, or any ftolen gold or filver plate, watch or watches, knowing the fame to have been ftolen, fhall in all cafes where fuch jewel or jewels, or gold or filver plate fhall have been feloniously ftolen, accompanied with a burglary actually committed in ftealing the fame, be triable as well before conviction of the principal felon whether he be in or out of cuftody, as after his conviction and if fuch perfon fo buying or receiving fhall be convicted thereof, he fhall be guilty of felony, and tranfported for 14 years.

III *Reward for convicting a burglar.*

Indemnity for killing him

1 It may be obferved, in the firft place, that it is provided by the 24 *H.* 8. *c* 36 That there fhall be no forfeiture of lands or goods, for killing any perfon that attempts to commit burglary.

But befides this indulgence to a perfon killing fuch an offender in defence of his houfe, there are fpecial advantages and rewards for apprehending and convicting him in due courfe of law, which are as follows

Charges of convicting him to be reimburfed.

2 By the 25 *G* 2 *c* 36 The charges of profecuting and convicting a burglar, fhall be paid by the treafurer of the county where the burglary was committed, on producing to him the order of the court for that purpofe, which

which the clerk of affize, or of the peace, fhall make out, for the fee of 1 s   / 11

And alfo the charges of poor witneffes appearing on their recognizance, by the 27 G 2 c 3 on paying 6 d for the order   except in *Middlefex*, where the faid charges fhall be paid by the overfeers of the poor where the perfon was apprehended

And by the 18 G 3 c 19 The court, before whom any perfon hath been tried and convicted, or tried and acquitted, in cafe it fhall appear to the faid court that there was a reafonable ground of profecution, and that the profecutor had *bona fide* profecuted, may order the treafurer to pay to fuch profecutor fuch fum as they fhall think reafonable, not exceeding the expences he was *bona fide* put unto, making alfo, if he fhall appear to be in poor circumftances, a reafonable allowance for his trouble and lofs of time ——— And the juftices in feffions may lay down or alter from time to time fuch rules and regulations, as to fuch cofts or charges thereafter to be allowed to any perfon, as to them fhall feem juft   which rules and regulations, having received the approbation and fignature of one or more of the judges of affize, fhall be binding, and not otherwife, on all perfons whatfoever.

/ 7 9

3 Every perfon who fhall apprehend any one guilty of burglary and profecute him to conviction, fhall have a certificate without fee, under the hand of the judge, certifying fuch conviction, and within what parifh or place the burglary was committed, and alfo that fuch burglar was difcovered and taken, or difcovered or taken, by the perfon fo difcovering or apprehending , and if any difpute arife between feveral perfons fo difcovering or apprehending, the judge fhall appoint the certificate into fo many fhares to be divided among the perfons concerned, as to him fhall feem juft and reafonable

Exemption from parifh offices for taking and convicting him.

And if any perfon fhall happen to be flain by fuch burglar, in endeavouring to apprehend him, the executors or adminiftrators of fuch perfon flain fhall have the like certificate

Which certificate fhall be inrolled by the clerk of the peace of the county in which it fhall be granted, for which he fhall have 1 s and no more

And the faid certificate fhall be once affigned over , and the original proprietor, or the affignee of the fame, fhall by virtue thereof be difcharged from all manner of parifh and ward offices, within the parifh and ward where the felony was committed   10 & 11 *W*. c. 23

In the cafe of the *King* and *Derbyfhire*, *T* 1 *G* 3. The defendant *John Derbyfhire* was indicted at the feffions for refufing to take upon him the office of *conftable* for the manor of *Birmingham* The indictment being removed by certiorari, the caufe was tried at *Warwick* affizes, and the jury found fpecially, that the defendant was a fit perfon in all refpects to be nominated and elected to the office, unlefs difcharged or exempt therefrom by reafon of a certificate he had under this act It appeared that the ufage at *Birmingham* had been, annually at the court leet there, for the jury to elect two conftables for the manor of *Birmingham* generally, and one conftable for the hamlet of *Deritend* (a diftinct vill within the faid manor) particularly that the manor of *Birmingham* extends into and comprehends the whole town and parifh of *Birmingham*, and alfo the faid hamlet of *Deritend* that the conftables fo elected for the faid manor of *Birmingham* generally, have jurifdiction and authority, as conftables, not only throughout the faid town and parifh of *Birmingham*, but alfo within and throughout the faid hamlet of *Deritend* that the conftable of *Deritend* is elected out of the inhabitants of *Deritend* only, and the conftable fo elected for *Deritend* particularly, and the faid conftables fo elected for the faid manor of *Birmingham*, have feverally equal and concurrent jurifdiction within the faid hamlet of *Deritend*. The queftion referved for the opinion of the court was, whether the faid *John Derbyfhire*, notwithftanding the certificate, is liable to ferve the faid office Againft him, it was urged, that the difcharge by the act is, from all parifh and ward offices, within the parifh or ward wherein the felony was committed But the limits of this man's office extend beyond the parifh of *Birmingham*, therefore this is not a parifh office And there is no fuch divifion in this place as a ward, therefore no ward office But a conftable is not a parifh officer at all It was a common law office, before parifhes exifted, and is as ancient as towns or leets and a parifh is not a common law divifion, but an ecclefiaftical one On the other hand, it was anfwered, that he is at leaft a parifh officer (whatever more he may be), becaufe his office extends throughout the whole parifh of *Birmingham* And he is an inhabitant of the parifh of *Birmingham*. Therefore, though he be alfo conftable of the manor, which includes the parifh, yet he is certainly a parifh officer, notwithftanding that greater extent of his jurifdiction or power By the court The only queftion is, whether the conftable of the manor of *Birmingham* is a parifh officer of the parifh of *Birmingham*

This

This term *parish officer* doth not include every office exer⹂
cised in the parish; if it did, it might even take in the
office of high sheriff of the county. A parish officer is
relative to the parish, and confined to the parish only A
constable of a *parish*, may be called a parish officer, but
this man hath a much larger jurisdiction than the parish
only, for he hath the jurisdiction over the whole manor,
which extends much beyond the parish, and the parish is
only a part of that district, over which it is to be exer⹂
cised And the act doth not intend the certificate to be a
discharge from an office, whereof the functions are to be
exercised out of the limits of the parish This man can⹂
not be esteemed a parish officer, either from the origin of
his office, or from the nature, or from the exercise of it.
Burrow Mansfield 1182

4 And moreover, as a further reward, every person
who shall apprehend any person guilty of burglary, and
prosecute him to conviction, shall have a certificate under
the hand of the judge, without fee, to be made out and
delivered before the end of the assizes, certifying the con⹂
viction, and in what parish the burglary was committed,
and also that the burglar was taken by the person claiming
the reward, and if any dispute shall happen to arise be⹂
tween the persons claiming, the judge shall by the said
certificate appoint the same to be paid amongst the parties
claiming the same, in such share and proportion as to him
shall seem just and reasonable

And on tender of such certificate to the sheriff, and
demand made, he shall pay to the person so intitled, the
sum of 40 l, without fee or deduction, within one month
after such tender and demand, on pain of forfeiting
double, with treble costs. 5 *Ann.* c 31 6 G c. 23.
f 10.

40l for taking and convicting.

5 And if any watchman, or any other person, be killed,
in endeavouring to apprehend any such burglar, his exe⹂
cutors or administrators shall have a certificate delivered
under the hand and seal of the judge, or of the two next
justices of the peace, of such person being so killed,
which certificate they shall, on sufficient proof before them
made, give without fee, whereupon, such executor or
administrator shall be intitled to receive the like sum of
40l in like manner 5 *Ann.* c 31 f 2

40l to the executor of a person killed

6 And moreover, if any person, being out of prison,
shall commit any burglary, and afterwards discover two
or more the like offenders, so as two or more be convic⹂
ted, he shall have the like reward and allowance of 40 l,
and also all other advantages which are given to persons

40l and a pardon, for convicting two accomplices

who

who shall apprehend and convict any the like offenders; and shall also have the king's pardon for all burglaries, robberies, and felonies (except murder and treason) by him committed before such discovery made, which pardon shall be likewise a good bar to an appeal *5 Ann. c. 31 f. 4.*

Sher if how to be repaid

7 And the sheriff on producing the certificates, and receipts for the said rewards, may deduct the same on his accounts, and if he have not money in his hands, he shall be repaid out of the treasury, on certificate from the clerk of the pipe *5 Ann c 31 f 3*

Or instead of charging the same in his accounts, he may immediately apply to the commissioners of the treasury, who shall forthwith repay the same without fee *3 G. c. 15 f 4.*

Warrant to apprehend a burglar

Westmorland. } To the constable of ———

FORASMUCH as A I. of ——— in the county of ——— yeoman, hath this day made information and complaint upon oath, before me J P. esquire, one of his majesty's justices of the peace for the said county, that yesterday in the night the dwelling house of him the said A I at ——— aforesaid in the county aforesaid, was feloniously and burglariously broken open, and one silver tankard of the value of 5l, of the goods and chattels of him the said A I feloniously and burglariously stolen, taken and carried away from thence, and that he hath just cause to suspect, and doth suspect, that A. O. late of ——— in the county of ——— labourer, the said felony and burglary did commit These are therefore, in his said majesty's name to command you, that immediately upon sight hereof you do apprehend the said A O. and bring him before me to answer the premisses, and to be further dealt withal according to law. Herein fail you not Given under my hand and seal the ——— day of ——— in the year ———.

Indictment for proper burglary.

Westmorland THE jurors for our lord the king upon their oath present, That A O late of ——— in the county of ——— labourer, on the ——— day of ——— in the ——— year of the reign of ——— at the hour of one in the night of the same day, with force and arms, at ——— in the county of ——— the dwelling house of A I.

feloniously

feloniously and burglariously did break and enter, with intent ... in the said A. I of his goods in the same dwelling house then being, feloniously and burglariously to spoil and rob, and the same goods feloniously and burglariously to steal, take, and carry away, against the peace of our said lord the king, his crown and dignity.

Indictment for burglary and larceny.

Westmorland THE jurors for our lord the king upon their oath present, That A O late of ———— in the county of ———— labourer, on the ———— day of ———— in the ———— year of the reign of ———— betwixt the hours of ten and eleven in the night of the same day, with force and arms, at ———— in the county of ———— the dwelling house of A I feloniously and burglariously did break and enter, and one silver tankard of the value of 5 l, of the goods and chattels of him the said A I in the same dwelling house then and there feloniously and burglariously did steal, take, and carry away, against the peace of our said lord the king, his crown and dignity.

𝔅𝔲𝔯𝔫𝔦𝔫𝔤.

1 MAliciously and voluntarily burning the house of another, by night or by day, is felony at the common law 1 Haw 105.

Houseburning at the common law

Maliciously and voluntarily] For if it be done by mischance or negligence, it is no felony   3 *Inst.* 67

Yet if a man maliciously intending only to burn one person's house, happens thereby to burn the house of another, it is certain that he may be indicted as having maliciously burned the house of that other, for where a felonious design against one man misseth its aim, and takes effect upon another, it shall have the like construction as if it had been levelled against him who suffers by it. 1 *Haw.* 106.

Burning] Neither a bare intention to burn a house, nor even an actual attempt to do it by putting fire to a part of a house, will amount to felony, if no part of it be burned, but if any part of the house be burnt, the offender is guilty of felony, notwithstanding the fire afterwards be put out, or go out of itself   1 *Haw.* 106

The houſe] Not only a manſion-houſe, and the princi-pal parts thereof, but alſo any other houſe, and the out buildings, as barns and ſtables adjoining thereto, and alſo barns full of corn, whether they be adjoining to any houſe or not, are ſo far ſecured by law, that the mali-cious burning of them is felony at common law. 1 *Haw.* 105

Of another] Mr *Hawkins* ſays, A perſon ſeiſed in fee, or but poſſeſſed for years, of a houſe ſtanding by itſelf at a diſtance from all others, cannot commit felony in burn-ing the ſame Alſo, that it ſeems the much ſtronger opi-nion, that a man ſo ſeiſed or poſſeſſed of a houſe in a town, who burns his own with an intent to burn his neighbour's, but in the event burns his own only, is not guilty of fe-lony, but however it is certainly an offence highly pu-niſhable, in regard of the malice thereof, and the great danger to the publick which attends it, and the offender may be ſeverely fined, and impriſoned during the king's pleaſure, and ſet on the pillory, and bound to his good behaviour 1 *Haw* 106.

And ſo it was in *Holmes*'s caſe, *M* 10 *Cha Holmes* was indicted at *Newgate* ſeſſions, and convicted, for that he, being poſſeſſed of a houſe in *London* for ſix years, remainder to another for three years, reverſion to the cor-poration of *Haberdaſhers* in fee, did burn the ſaid houſe And the indictment being removed into the king's bench by certiorari, it was held by three juſtices, againſt the opinion of *Croke* juſtice, that it was not felony to burn a houſe whereof he was in poſſeſſion by virtue of a leaſe for years. For they ſaid, the burning of a houſe is not fe-lony, unleſs it be the houſe of *another*. Wherefore he was diſcharged of the felony But becauſe it was an exorbi-tant offence, they ordered, that he ſhould be fined 500l to the king, and impriſoned during the king's pleaſure, and ſhould ſtand upon the pillory, with a paper on his head ſignifying the offence, at *Weſtminſter* and at *Cheap-ſide*, upon the market day, and in the place where he committed the offence, and ſhould be bound to his good behaviour during life. *Cro. Car.* 376.

In the caſe of *Elizabeth Harris*, at *Ayleſbury*, Lent aſ ſizes 1753, before Mr Juſtice *Deniſon*, *Elizabeth Harris*, a girl of 14 years of age, and of ſufficient underſtanding for her years, was indicted for maliciouſly ſetting fire to, and burning a dwelling houſe in the poſſeſſion of *Ed-ward Stokes* and *Anne*, the wife of *William Courſe*, was indicted as an acceſſary to the felony before the fact.

The

The prisoner *Elizabeth Harris* was the daughter of the prisoner *Anne* by a former husband, *John Harris* It appeared in evidence at the trial, that *John Harris* died seised of the equity of redemption of this house and of another adjoining to it, subject to a mortgage term for 20 *l*. And that the equity descended to his eldest son, a child left with other children under the care of their mother the prisoner *Ann*, who was intitled to dower out of these houses, but no dower was ever assigned That *Anne* having the care of her son and his estate, let these houses to *Edward Stokes* at the rent of 5 *l* a year, and received the rent for some time, but having a large family of children, she was obliged to ask relief of the parish where she lived That she was denied such relief, on account of these houses, the parishioners insisting, that the overseers of of the poor should be let into the receipt of the rent, before she should be intitled to any parochial relief That thereupon she frequently declared, she would set the housing on fire, if the parish did not relieve her, that she had young children, whom the parish could not punish, tho' they might punish her, and she would order the least child she had who could carry a coal of fire, to burn the housing down And many other declarations of the like kind she made, which discovered an obstinate resolution in her to burn the houses, rather than submit to the terms the parishioners insisted on It appeared further, that the prisoner *Elizabeth* set the house on fire by the direction of her mother the prisoner *Anne*, who went from home on purpose to be absent at the time the fact was committed, and that no other house was burnt ——The jury found both the prisoners guilt, But a doubt arising by reason of the interest the prisoner *Anne* had in the house, Mr justice *Denison* thought proper to respite judgment, in order to take the opinion of the judges, on the case ——*July* 2d, 1753, at a meeting of the judges, it was unanimously agreed, that both the prisoners were guilty of felony The only doubt was, with regard to the interest the prisoner *Anne* had in the house, and it was grounded on the reasoning in *Holmes*'s case for had she had such estate in the house as would have cleared her of the charge of the felony, the prisoner *Elizabeth*, who acted by her directions, could not have been guilty of felony —— But all the judges agreed, that the prisoner *Anne*'s title to dower was not such an interest as could bring her within the rule in *Holmes*'s case *Holmes* had the possession by legal title, and during the continuance of his lease could maintain his possession against all mankind, and

there-

therefore the houfe m ght in a limited fenfe be called his own But in the prefent cafe, the poffeffion was in *Edward Stokes*, under a demife from *Anne* in behalf of her fon, and fubject to a yearly rent which fhe received And her title to dower, had *Edward Stokes's* intereft been out of the cafe, did not fo much as give her a right of entry, it being a bare right of action Mr juftice *Denifon* faid, that he had no doubt upon him from the beginning But it being a new cafe, and fome of the bar being doubtful, he thought it advifeable to take the opinion of the judges ——— At the next affizes, judgment of death was pronounced upon both the prifoners, and *Anne* the mother was executed But *Elizabeth* being young, and acting under her mother s direction, was reprieved, and recommended to mercy on condition of tranfportation ——— It was faid in the debate of this cafe by fome of the judges, and not denied by any, that had *Anne* been feifed of the freehold and inheritance of the houfe, and *Stokes* in poffeffion under a leafe, it would have been felony in *Anne* to have burnt it otherwife all tenants and their concerns would be very much at the mercy of their land lords And the principle the three judges went upon in *Holmes's* cafe, doth feem to warrant this opinion. They confidered the houfe then under confideration as the property of *Holmes*, as *his own houfe*, by reafon of the eftate he had in it under his leafe *Croke* (who differed from them) did not difpute the principle, but argued againft the conclufion the other judges drew from it. And if this be fo, Mr juftice *Fofter* fays, he does not fee why it **may** not with ftrict legal propriety be faid of a reverfioner, who fhould malicioufly fet fire to houfes in the poffeffion of his tenants under leafes from himfelf or his anceftors, that he burned the *houfes of another* The judgment in *Holmes's* cafe, to fay no more of it, was a very merciful judgment The houfe might with ftrict legal propriety have been confidered as the houfe of the landlord Both landlord and tenant have a property, one temporary and limited, the other abfolute and perpetual, like the perfon to whom goods are delivered, and the abfolute owner thereof, in the cafe of larceny.——— Note, it was ftated in this cafe, that the daughter, who committed the fact at the inftigation of the mother, was *of the age of 14, and of fufficient difcretion* But if the mother had employed, as fhe threatened fhe would, the eldeft of her children, then *fhe* muft have been indicted as principal, fince the child not being of years of difcretion was innocent *Fof.* 113, 349

2. By the statutes of 23 *H* 8 *c* 1 and 25 *H* 8 *c* 3.
No person who shall be found guilty for wilful burning
of any dwelling house, or barn wherein any corn shall
be, nor persons abetting, procuring, helping, maintaining, or counselling the same shall be admitted to the benefit of clergy

There hath been much learned debate, how far these
statutes, which are repealed by 1 *Ed* 6 *c* 12, are revived by 5 & 6 *Ed* *c* 10. But as the same is enacted
in effect by other subsequent statutes, it is now not very
material

By the 4 & 5 *P* & *M* *c* 4. Every person who shall
maliciously command, hire, or counsel any person, wilfully to burn any dwelling house, or any part thereof, or
any barn then having corn or grain in the same, shall not
have the benefit of his clergy

But accessaries after shall have their clergy. 1 *H* *H.*
573

3. Whoever shall wilfully and of malice burn, or cause
to be burned, or aid, procure, or consent to the burning
of any barn, or stack of corn or grain, within any of the
counties of *Cumberland*, *Northumberland*, *Westmorland*, and
Durefme, shall be guilty of felony without benefit of clergy
And justices of the peace in sessions may hear and determine the same. 43 *El* *c* 13.

4. If any person shall in the night time, maliciously,
unlawfully, and willingly burn, or cause to be burned
or destroyed, any ricks or stacks of corn, hay, or grain,
barns, or other houses or buildings, or kilns, he shall be
guilty of felony, but without corruption of blood, or dif-
inheritance of heirs

And the judges of assize, or three justices of the peace
(1 *2*) may determine the same, so that the prosecution
be within six months

And the said justices, on request of the party injured,
shall issue their warrant for apprehending all such persons as shall be suspected thereof, and take their examination.

And shall cause all others who to them shall seem likely
to make discovery, to appear before them, and give information on oath, yet so, as no person to be examined shall
be proceeded against for any offence, concerning which he
shall be examined as a witness and shall upon his examination make a true discovery

And if such witness, being duly summoned shall refuse to appear, or to be examined, they may commit him
to the common gaol, till he submit to be examined upon
oath

And they shall sue warrants for summoning jurors

And if any person, being found guilty (in order to avoid judgment of death, or execution thereupon) shall make his election to be transported, the court shall cause judgment to be entred that he be transported to some of the plantations (to be mentioned in the judgment) for seven years and if he shall return before the expiration of the term, he shall suffer death as a felon, and as if no such election to be transported had been made by him 22 & 23 C 2 c 7

Burning by the Black Act

5 By the 9 G c 22 commonly called the Black Act, (which is inserted more at length under the title Black Act,) If any person shall set fire to any house, barn, or outhouse, or to any hovel, cock, mow, or stick of corn, straw, hay, or wood, [And by the 10 G 2 c 32 f 6 If any person shall wilfully and maliciously set on fire any mine, pit, or delph of coal or cannel coal, which offence, by f 4 of this act, is incorporated with the offences in the Black Act] he shall be guilty of felony without benefit of clergy

And the hundred shall be chargeable, as in cases of robbery, for the damages sustained (not exceeding 200l)

And if any person shall apprehend, or cause to be convicted, any offender, and shall be killed, or wounded so as to lose an eye or the use of a limb in endeavouring to apprehend him, on proof thereof made at the sessions, and on certificate thereof from thence, he shall be entitled to the sum of 50l, to be paid by the sheriff in thirty days, the same to be repaid to him out of the treasury.

House burning not bailable

6 Such as be taken for houseburning feloniously done, are not bailable by justices of the peace. 3 Ed 1 c 15 2 Inst. 189

Burning a ship.

7 If any ship officer or mariner shall wilfully burn the ship to which he belongeth, or procure the same to be done, to the prejudice of the owner of the ship or goods, he shall be guilty of felony without benefit of clergy. 1 Ann st 2 c 9

And by the articles of the navy, 22 G 2 c 33 Every person who shall unlawfully burn or set fire to any magazine, or store of powder, or ship, boat, ketch, hoy, or vessel, or tackle or furniture thereunto belonging, not appertaining to an enemy or rebel, shall be punished with death, by the sentence of a court martial. Art 25

Burning mills, or engine belonging to mine.

8 If any person shall burn or set fire to any wind saw mill, or other wind or water mill, or any of the works belonging thereto, he shall be guilty of felony without benefit of clergy And if any person shall burn or set fire

3

to any machine or engine belonging to any mine, he shall be guilty of felony, and transported for seven years 9 G 3 c 29

9 If any person shall, by day or by night, in a riotous, **Burning wood growing.** open, tumultuous, or in a secret and clandestine manner, forcibly, or wrongfully and maliciously, burn any wood, or springs of wood, or coppice wood, he shall be guilty of felony 1 G. st 2. c 48   6 G c 16

And any two justices, or the justices in sessions, may cause the offender to be apprehended, and hear, and determine and adjudge the offence 6 G c 16.

But if the offender is not known, then the person injured shall have satisfaction from the inhabitants of the parishes, towns, or places joining thereon, in the same manner as for dikes and hedges overthrown in the night, by the statute of 13 Ed 1. c 46 (which enacts, that if it cannot be known by the verdict of assize or jury who did the fact, the towns near adjoining shall be distrained to levy the hedge at their own cost, and to yield damages) unless the offender be by such parish, town, or place, convicted in six months. 6 G. c. 16

10 No person shall on any mountains, hills, heaths, **Burning ling,** moors, forests, chases, or other wastes, burn between **gofs, furze or fern.** Feb 2, and June 24, any grig, ling, heath, furze, gofs or fern, on pain of being committed to the house of correction for any time not exceeding one month, nor less than ten days, there to be whipt, and kept to hard labour 4 & 5 W. c 23 ∫ 11

11 If any person shall set fire to, burn, or destroy any **Burning gofs,** gofs, furze, or fern, in any forest or chase without consent **furze, or fern in** of the owner or person chiefly entrusted with the custody **for sts.** of such forest or chase, or some part thereof, or shall be aiding therein, and being brought before a justice, shall be thereof convicted by confession, or oath of one witness, or on view of the justice, he shall forfeit not exceeding 5 l, nor less than 40 s, half to the informer, and half to the poor, if not forthwith paid, to be levied by distress, and if no sufficient distress can be found, the justice shall commit him to the common gaol for any time not exceeding three months, nor less than one month 28 G. 2 c 19 ∫ 3

12 If any person shall maliciously, willingly, and un- **Burning a laden** lawfully, burn or cause to be burnt, any wain or cart, **cart, or fire** laden with coals, or with any goods or merchandizes, **wood.** or any heap of wood prepared, cut, or felled for making coals, or billets, or talwood, he shall forfeit treble damages to the party grieved, to be recovered by action of

trespass

trefpafs and alfo 10l, as a fine to the king. 37 H. 8.
c 6 f 4

Punifhment of a fervan carelefly firing a houf.

13 If any fervant, through negligence or carelefnefs, fhall fire or caufe to be fired any dwelling houfe, or outhoufe or houfes, and be thereof convicted on the oath of one witnefs before two juftices, he fhall forfeit 100l, to the churchwardens of the parifh where the fire fhall happen, to be diftributed by them to the fufferers, in fuch proportions as to them fhall feem juft, and if he do not pay the fame immediately on demand to the churchwardens, the faid juftices fhall commit him to fome workhoufe or houfe of correction for eighteen months, there to be kept to hard labour. 6 An c 31

Threatning to burn a houfe

14 By the commiffion of the peace, any juftice may caufe to come before him, all thofe who to any of the people concerning the firing of their houfes have ufed threats, to find fufficient fecurity for the peace or their good behaviour towards the king and his people, and if they fhall refufe to find fuch fecurity, may caufe them to be fafely kept in the king's prifons, until they fhall find fuch fecurity

And by the 9 G. c. 22. If any perfon fhall fend any letter, without any name fubfcribed thereto, or figned with a fictitious name, threatning to burn any houfe, outhoufe, barn, ftack of corn or grain, hay or ftraw, he fhall be guilty of felony without benefit of clergy

Burying in Woollen. See **Woollen Manufacture.**

Butcher.

Confpiring to raife the price of victuals.

1 IF any butchers fhall confpire not to fell their victuals but at certain prices, every fuch perfon fhall forfeit for the firft offence 10l to the king, and if not paid in fix days, he fhall fuffer twenty days imprifonment, and fhall only have bread and water for his fuftenance, for the fecond offence 20l in like manner, or the pillory, and for the third offence 40l or pillory, and the lofs of an ear, and to be taken as a man infamous, and not to be credited in any matter of judgment.   And the feffions or leet may determine the fame. 2 & 3 Ed 6, 15.

Not to kill in a walled town

2 No butcher fhall flay any beaft within any walled town, except *Carlifle* and *Berwick*, on pain of forfeiting for every ox 12 d, every cow and other beaft 8 d, half to the king, and half to him that will fue 4 H 7 c 3

3. A butcher that felleth fwines flefh meazled, or flefh dead of the murrain, fhall for the firft time be grievoufly amerced, the fecond time fuffer judgment of the pillory, the third time be imprifoned and make fine, and the fourth time forfwear the town Ordinance for bakers *Hauk Stat* V 1 p. 181 — *Selling unwholfome flefh.*

4 If any butcher fhall kill or fell any victual on the Lord's day, he fhall forfeit 6 s 8 d, one third to the inform-r, and two thirds to the poor, on conviction before one juftice, on his own view, or confeffion, or on h of two witneffes, to be levied by the conftable or churchwarden 3 C ι 1 — *Not to kill or fell on the Lord's day.*

5 No butcher fhall water any hide, except in *June*, *July*, and *Auguft*, on pain of 3 s 4 d for each offence, one third to the king, one third to the informer, and one third to the town or lord of the liberty 1 J c 22 ſ 2, 50 — *Not to water hides.*

And the feffions or leet may hear and determine the fame ſ 50

Or, any two juftices, near the place, may (in three months after the offence committed) fummon the party accufed, and the witneffes, and upon the party's appearance, or contempt in not appearing, on proof of notice given, may examine the witneffes on oath, and give judgment, and iffue warrants under their hands to levy the penalty by diftrefs, and, if not redeemed in fix days, the fame to be fold. They may alfo mitigate the penalties, fo as they reduce them not to lefs than a fourth part, over and above the cofts and charges. And any perfon aggrieved may appeal to the next feffions, who may finally determine the fame, and in cafe of conviction, iffue warrants for levying the penalties 9 *An* c 11 ſ 36, 37

6 No butcher fhall put to fale any hide putrified or rotten, on pain of 3 s 4 d for each offence, in like manner. 1 J c 22 ſ 2. — *Selling rotten hides*

7. No butcher fhall be a tanner or currier, on pain of 6 s 8 d a day, to be recovered and levied in like manner 1 J c 22 ſ 2, 25 — *Exercifing the trade of a tanner.*

8 If any raw hide fhall wilfully or negligently be gafhed, in the flaying thereof, or being gafhed, be offered to fale by any butcher or other, the offender fhall forfeit 2 s 6 d for fuch hide, and 1 s for a calf fkin, half to the poor, and half to the informer To be levied by two juftices in like manner 9 *An. c.* 11. ſ. 11. — *Gafhing hides.*

Butter and cheese.

I *Concerning the packing, weight, and goodness of butter.*

II *Concerning the shipping of butter and cheese for* London

I. *Concerning the packing, weight, and goodness of butter.*

Weight of the cask to be marked.

1 EVERY farmer and other person packing up butter for sale, shall set upon every firkin and cask, when the same is fully seasoned in water, a continuing visible mark of the just weight of the empty cask, on pain of forfeiting for every offence the sum of ten shillings for every hundred weight of butter otherwise packed, and so proportionably for a greater or lesser quantity, half to the churchwardens and overseers for the use of the poor, and half with double costs to him who shall sue for the same in sessions, by action of debt, indictment, information, or presentment 13 & 14 C 2 c 26 ∫ 5, 6

Weight of a pot to be marked

2 Also every potter shall set upon every pot which he shall sell for packing up butter, the just weight of the pot when it is burnt, together with the first letter of his christian name, and his surname at length, on pain of 1 s And no person shall expose to sale any butter packed up in any pot not so marked, on pain of 2 s for every such pot To be recovered and applied in like manner 13 & 14 C 2 t. 26 ∫ 6

Weight and goodness

3 Every kilderkin of butter shall contain 112 pounds, and every firkin 56 pounds neat, or above every pound containing 16 ounces, besides the tare of the cask, of good and merchantable butter, and every pot of butter shall contain 14 pounds neat, or above, besides the weight of the pot,

And no butter which is old or corrupt shall be mixed or packed up with any butter which is new and found,

Nor any whey butter shall be packed or mixed with any butter made of cream,

And every cask or pot of butter shall be of one sort and goodness,

And no butter shall be salted with any great salt, but shall be salted and saved with small salt, nor more salt shall be intermixed with it than shall be needful for its preservation

O n

On pain that every owner, farmer, or packer of butter, not putting up in each kilderkin, firkin, and pot, to be fold or expofed to fale, fuch quantities as aforefaid, or offending in falfe packing as aforefaid, for every offence fhall forfeit the value of all the butter fo falfe packed, and for every offence where any kilderkin, firkin, or pot fhall be found to contain a leffer quantity of butter than as above, fix times the value of every pound of butter that fhall be wanting in fuch cafk or pot, to be recovered and applied as aforefaid   13 & 14 C 2 c. 26 ſ 2

4 And when the farmer or other perfon hath filled the cafk with butter, he fhall, befides the former mark of the weight of the cafk, fet alfo on the cafk the firft letter of his chriftian name, and his furname at length with an iron brand, on pain of forfeiting for every offence the fum of 10s, for every hundred weight of butter otherwife packed, and for more or lefs proportionably, to be recovered and applied in like manner   13 & 14 C 2 c 26 ſ 5

Owner to fet his name on the cafk.

5 And every cheefemonger and other who fhall fell any kilderkin, firkin, pot, or other cafk of butter, fhall deliver therein the full quantity and due quality, or fhall be liable to make fatisfaction, according to the price thereof   13 & 14 C 2 c 26 ſ 3

Cheefemonger to deliver due quantity and quality.

6 And no cheefemonger or other perfon fhall repack for fale, any butter, in any kilderkin, firkin, or other cafk, or pot, on pain of forfeiting double value thereof, to be recovered and applied in like manner   13 & 14 C 2 c 26 ſ 4.

Cheefemonger fhall not repack butter.

7 The profecution for the offences above, fhall be commenced in four months after the fale of the butter   13 & 14 C 2 c 26 ſ 7

In what time the profecution fhall be

8 But provided neverthelefs, that no feller of butter fhall be charged with any of the faid penalties, after the buyer hath bought the butter and approved it.   4 W c 7 ſ 2

Profecution not to be, if the buyer hath approved it

9 And for preventing any fraud in the feller, after the factor or buyer hath bought the butter, the faid factor or buyer fhall fet his feal, or mark, or name upon it, or upon the cafk, and if it fhall be afterwards exchanged or opened, and the cafk changed, or any bad butter mixed or packed up with good butter, or any other fraud be committed by the feller, and he be convicted thereof, before one juftice, by oath of one witnefs, or confeffion, he fhall forfeit 20s for every firkin and offence, to be levied by the conftable, by diftrefs, and to be diftributed by the juftice, half to the churchwardens and overfeers for the ufe of the poor, and half to the informer   4 W c 7 ſ 3.

Fraud after fale, by the feller.

But

But any perfon aggrieved may appeal to the next fef. fions, giving 20 l bond to the party, to pay cofts (in a month after) if he is not relieved on his appeal *id f 10*

II *Concerning the fhipping of butter and cheefe for* London

No undue pre-ference.

1 Every warehoufekeeper, weigher, fearcher, or fhip-per of butter and cheefe, fhall receive all butter and cheefe that fhall be brought to him, for the *London* cheefemongers, and fhip the fame without undue preference , and fhall have for his pains 2 s 6 d for every load and if he fhall make default, he fhall, on conviction before one juftice, on oath of one witnefs, or confeffion, forfeit for every firkin of butter 10 s, and for every weigh of cheefe 5 s, half to the churchwardens and overfeers for the ufe of the poor, and half to the informer, to be levied by the conftable by diftrefs and fale. *4 W. c. 7 f 4*

Book of entry.

2 And he fhall keep a book of entry of receiving and fhipping the goods, on pain of 2 s 6 d for every firkin of butter, and weigh of cheefe, to be levied and applied in like manner, and for want of diftrefs, to be committed till paid *4 W c 7 f 5*

Mafter of a fhip refufing to take in.

3 A mafter of a fhip refufing to take in butter or cheefe, before he is full laden (except it be a cheefe monger's own fhip fent for his own goods), fhall forfeit for every firkin of butter refufed 5 s, and for every weigh of cheefe 2 s 6 d, to be levied and applied in like manner *4 W c 7 f 6*

Appeal.

4 Perfon aggrieved by the determination of the juftice, may appeal to the next feffions, giving 20 l bond with one or more fureties, to the party, to pay cofts (within a month after) if he is not relieved on his appeal. *4 W c. 7. f. 10*

Exception.

5 But this act fhall not extend to any warehoufe in *Chefhire* or *Lancafhire* *4 W c 7. f 9*.

Note, There are fpecial directions in the act of *8 G c 27* concerning the felling of butter in the city of *York*, and the act of the *17 G 2 c 8.* concerning the fame in *New Malton*, which are not general enough to be here in ferted.

Buttons.

1. NO perſon ſhall ſell or offer to ſale, or import, any foreign bone lace, cut-work, embroidery, fringe, band ſtrings, buttons, or needle-work, made of thread and ſilk, or either of them, or any foreign buttons whatſoever on pain that he who ſhall offer them to ſale ſhall forfeit the ſame and 50 l, and the importer ſhall forfeit the ſame and 100 l, half to the king, and half to him that ſhall ſue 13 & 14 C 2. c 13 ſ 2   4 W. c 10. ſ 2.

And on complaint and information given to a juſtice of the peace, at times reaſonable, he ſhall iſſue his warrant to the conſtable, to enter and ſearch for ſuch manufactures in the ſhops being open, or warehouſes, and dwelling houſes of ſuch perſons as ſhall be ſuſpected, and to ſeize the ſame   13 & 14 C. 2   c 13 ſ. 3   4 W. c 10. ſ 3

And foreign lace and needle-work condemned, ſhall not be ſold or delivered out of the warehouſe wherein the ſame ſhall be ſecured, otherwiſe than on condition of exportation 7 G 3 c 47. ſ 9

And Engliſh bone-lace, needle work, point, or cut-work, may be exported cuſtom free   11 & 12 W c 3 ſ 15.

2. No perſon ſhall make, ſell, or ſet on any buttons made of wood only, and turned in imitation of other buttons, on pain of 40 s a dozen, half to the king, and half to him that ſhall ſue in any court of record   10 W c 2

Made of wood only] H 13 W King and *Roberts* An information was exhibited againſt the defendant, for having made wooden buttons, contrary to the ſtatute Upon trial, the jury found a ſpecial verdict, that all the button was of wood, but there was in it a ſhank of wire And after argument, judgment was given for the king, namely, that this was a button of wood, notwithſtanding the ſhank, which is no eſſential part of buttons, for buttons of ſilk and hair have no ſhanks Lord *Raym* 712

3 By the ſaid act of the 10 W c. 2 No perſon ſhall make, ſell, or ſet on, any buttons made of cloth, ſerge, drugget, frize, camlet, or other ſtuffs of which clothes are uſually made, on pain of 40 s a dozen, half to the king, and half to him that ſhall ſue in any court of record

And by the 8 An c 6 No taylor or other perſon ſhall make, ſell, ſet on, uſe, or bind on any clothes, any buttons or button-holes, made of or ufed, or bound with ferge, drugget, frize, camlet, or other ftuffs of which clothes are ufually made, on pain of 5l a dozen, half to the king, and half to him that fhall fue in any court of record, or on complaint to two juftices, they may fummon witneffes, and levy the penalty, and return the overplus if any be, and if any perfon is aggrieved, he may appeal to the next feffions.

But by this act no power is given to make diftrefs The next that occurs, is the ftatute of 4 G c 7 which in the ftatutes at large is a loofe, injudicious, and ungrammatical act, and by its garb may well enough feem to have been drawn up by the taylors or button-makers, whereby it is enacted as follows

No taylor or other perfon fhall make, fell, fet on, or bind on any clothes, any buttons, or button-holes made of, or ufed, or bound with cloth, ferge, drugget, frize, camlet, or any ftufts that clothes are ufually made of (velvet excepted), on pain of 40 s a dozen To be determined by one juftice where the offence fhall be difcovered, or the offender fhall inhabit, on oath of one witnefs, in three months after the offence committed, and to be diftributed (charges of conviction firft deducted) half to the informer, and half to the poor of the parifh or place where the offence fhall be difcovered if not paid (being lawfully demanded) in 14 days after conviction, the juftice fhall iffue his warrant to the conftable where the offender dwells, or can be found, to levy it by diftrefs and fale, and where no fufficient diftrefs can be found, he fhall be committed to the common gaol of the county or place where he fhall be found, to be kept to hard labour for three calendar months. Perfons aggrieved may appeal to the feffions, giving fufficient notice, and the feffions may allow cofts to the party aggrieved

And taylors caufing their apprentices or fervants to make fuch clothes, fhall themfelves be fubject to the penalties

And all fuch clothes, made with fuch buttons and button-holes, expofed to fale, fhall be forfeited and feized, and recovered and difpofed of as the other penalties

And by the ftatute of the 7 G ft 1 c 12 No perfon fhall ufe or wear on any clothes (velvet excepted) any fuch buttons or button-holes, on pain of 40 s a dozen, on conviction by confeffion, or oath of one witnefs, and any juftice of the peace, where the offence fhall be committed, or the offender fhall inhabit, fhall on complaint or information on oath, of any credible perfon, in one month

after

after the offence, fummon the party, and on his appearance or contempt, examine the matter, and on due proof by confeffion, or oath of one witnefs, convict the offender, and caufe the forfeiture by his warrant to be levied by diftrefs and fale, the faid penalties to be half to him on whofe oath the party fhall be convicted, and half to the poor of the parifh where the offence fhall be committed And perfons aggrieved may appeal to the next quarter feffions giving 8 days notice

To him on whofe oath the party fhall be convicted] This is almoft the only inftance where a fhare of the penalty is given in exprefs words, in a popular action, to tne party on whofe oath any perfon is convicted, and the contrary doctrine feems generally to prevail, that the defendant fhall not be condemned upon the fole teftimony of the plaintiff fwearing for his own intereft And it is certainly againft the common law, that fuch a perfon fhould be a witnefs at all, and therefore his right to give evidence in his own caufe, and the power to convict the defendant upon that fole evidence, muft depend on the exprefs words of fome ftatute —Not to mention, that here is no difpofal of one moiety of the penalty, if the party is convicted by his own *confeffion*.

Buying of titles.

I By the common law
II. By ftatute.

I By the common law.

IT feemeth to be an high offence at common law, to buy or fell any doubtful title to lands known to be difputed, to the intent that the buyer may carry on the fuit, which the feller doth not think it worth his while to do, and on that confideration fells his pretenfions at an under rate, and it feemeth not to be material whether the title fo fold be a good or bad one, or whether the feller were in poffeffion or not, unlefs his poffeffion were lawful and unconteefted, for all practices of this kind are by all means to be difcountenanced, as manifeftly tending to oppreffion, by giving opportunities to great men to purchafe the difputed titles of others, to the great grievance of the adverfe parties, who may often be unable or difcouraged to defend their

titles

titles againſt ſuch powerful perſons, which perhaps they might ſafely enough maintain againſt their proper adverſary 1 *Haw* 261

II　*By ſtatute.*

1　By the ſtatute of 13 *Ed* 1 *c* 49. *No perſon of the king's houſe ſhall buy any title whilſt the thing is in diſpute, on pain of both the buyer and ſeller being puniſhed at the king's pleaſure*

2　And by 32 *H.* 8 *c* 9　*None ſhall buy any pretenced right in any land, unleſs the ſeller hath been in poſſeſſion of the ſame, or of the reverſion or remainder thereof, or taken the rents and profits thereof, for one year next before, on pain that the ſeller ſhall forfeit the land, and the buyer the value, half to the king, and half to him that ſhall ſue within one year.* ſ 2, 6.

Pretended title} But he who is in lawful poſſeſſion may purchaſe the pretended title of any others　32 *H* 8 *c.* 9. ſ. 4

One year before] But no conveyance made by one who hath the uncorteſted poſſeſſion, and undiſputed abſolute propriety of lands, is any way within the meaning of this ſtatute 1 *Hau* 265

3　*And the offence of buying of titles may be laid in any county, at the pleaſure of the informer* 31 El. c. 5 ſ 4.

Cabbages, Stealing　The ſame penalty as for ſtealing turnips.　For which, ſee the Title **Turnips**

Callico　See **Exciſe.**
Cambricks.　See **Linen**
Candles.　See **Exciſe**
Capias　See **Proceſs.**

Cards and Dice.

Importation prohibited.　1　BY the 10 *Ann* c. 19　No playing cards or dice ſhall be imported.

2　Bv

2 By the 9 *An. c* 23 Shall be paid, for every pack of cards made in Great Britain, a duty of 6 d   By 29 *G* 2. *c* 13 a further duty of 6 d   And by 16 *G* 3 *c* 34. a further duty of 6 d Duty on cards and dice.

And by 9 *An. c* 23 for every pair of dice 5 s   By 29 *G* 2 *c* 13 a further duty of 5 s   And by 16 *G* 2. *c* 34 a further duty of 2 s 6 d

The same to be under the management of the commissioners of the stamp duties

3 All makers of cards or dice, before they begin to make them, shall give notice in writing of the house or place where they intend to make them, to the commissioners or their officer next adjacent, on pain of 50 l. 9 *An. c* 23 *s.* 41. And also all the cards, dice, materials, and utensils shall be forfeited.   10 *An c.* 19 *s* 166 Places of making to be entred.

4 And every maker of cards shall send to the commissioners a sufficient quantity of paper, in order to have as many aces of spades impressed thereon as such maker shall desire, and every pack of cards shall have one such ace so impressed   And the commissioners shall cause a stamp to be prepared, with such device as they shall think proper, to denote the said ace of spades, as well in every pack made for use in Great Britain, as in every pack made for exportation, so as in such device there be some distinguishing mark, between cards for home, and cards for foreign consumption   5 *G* 3 *c* 46 *s* 9 Providing materials.

And the maker shall also send to the commissioners or their officers, jews or wrappers made for inclosing cards for use in Great Britain, with his name and any other particular word or thing printed thereon, as the commissioners shall direct, in order that the same may be stamped and delivered again, from time to time, to such maker, as occasion shall require   And the commissioners shall denote one of the six-penny duties charged on cards in Great Britain, on such jew or wrapper.   5 *G* 3 *c* 46. *s* 10.

5. And the officers may enter any house or place where cards or dice are made, sold, or exposed to sale, or suspected to be privately made, or into any publick gaming house, room, or place, and there search and see what quantity of cards or dice shall be making, and whether they be stamped, and if the owner or occupier shall refuse entrance or liberty of search, he shall forfeit 10 l.   10 *An c* 19. *s* 169 Officers may enter and search.

And if the commissioners be informed, or have cause to suspect, that any person makes cards or dice in a place not entred, on affidavit thereof by the informer before a justice

of

of the peace declaring the grounds of his fufpicion, the officer may in the day time, and in the prefence of a conftable, by warrant of fuch juftice break open the door, or any part of fuch private place, and enter, and feize all fuch cards, dice, tools, or materials, and if not replevied in five days, they fhall be forfeited and fold   6 G 2. c 21 ∫ 59

Materials not to be removed till finifhed.
6 And no materials begun to be wrought for cards or dice, fhall be removed until they be compleatly made, or the duties paid, on pain of double duty   10 An c 19, ∫ 166

And no maker of cards or dice fhall remove the fame from the place of making, until fuch mark upon the dice, and fuch feal upon the paper and thread inclofing every pack of cards fhall be put thereon, as the commiffioners fhall appoint, on pain of forfeiting the fame and treble value   9 A. c 23 ∫ 41

Entry and payment of the duties.
7 The makers of cards and dice fhall once in every 28 days make entry upon oath with the proper officer, of all the cards and dice by them made within the faid time, on pain of 20l   9 An c 23 ∫ 42

And fhall once in every fix weeks clear off the duties, on pain of double duty   id

Selling or ufing without ftamp.
8 And no cards or dice fhall be expofed to fale, or ufed in play in any publick gaming houfe, unlefs the paper and thread inclofing the fame fhall have been refpectively fealed and ftamped, and unlefs one of the cards of each pack fhall be alfo ftamped on the fpotted fide, on pain that every perfon who fhall expofe to fale any fuch cards or dice not ftamped, fhall forfeit for every fuch pack, and for every one of fuch dice, 5l, with full cofts   10 An c 19 ∫ 162

Ufing ftamped.
9 If any maker fhall ufe in the making up of any pack of cards, any ace of fpades, jew, or wrapper, that has been ufed before, he fhall forfeit 20l   5 G 3 c 46 ∫ 13

And if any perfon fhall fell or buy any fuch ace of fpades, jew, or wrapper, in order to be made ufe of for the inclofing any pack or parcel of cards, he fhall forfeit 20l And if either the buyer or feller fhall inform againft the other, his evidence fhall be admitted, and he fhall be indemnified   ∫ 14, 15

And if any perfon fhall take off the ftamp of any playing cards, or outfide paper of any parcel or pack of cards, with intent to ufe the fame again, he fhall be guilty of felony, and tranfported for any time not exceeding feven years   12 G 3 c 48

Selling wafte or remnant cards.
10 If any perfon fhall fell any cards called wafte cards, unlefs before fale he mark the back or plain fide of every fuch card,

card, so as to render it unfit to be used in playing, he shall forfeit 20 l   29 G 2 c 13 ſ 10

And if any person shall sell any cards, by way of second hand cards, in packs or parcels, after the wrapper or cover shall have been broke open, unless before sale he mark the backside of every card so as to render it unfit for play, he shall forfeit 5 l for each pack.   16 G. 3 c 34

11. If any person shall counterfeit the stamps on cards or dice, or on any jew, wrapper, or thread inclosing the same, or knowingly sell the same with a counterfeit stamp, or fraudulently use any of the stamps provided by the commissioners, he shall be guilty of felony without benefit of clergy   10 An. c 19 ſ 163   29 G 2 c 13 ſ 5   5 G 3 c 46 ſ 10

Counterfeiting the stamp

12 In the case of exportation, it shall be lawful to remove cards or dice from the place where they are made, without stamping or paying duty, provided that within a month after they are made, and before they be removed, bond of double duty be given, that they shall be exported and not relanded   10 An c 19 ſ 170   5 G c. 19 ſ. 48.

Exportation

But cards intended for exportation shall before packing for exportation be inclosed in paper and thread, in packs or parcels, and be marked on the spotted side, in such manner as the commissioners shall direct, and if any person shall sell or expose to sale to be used in Great Britain, or shall use or permit to be used in any publick gaming house, any cards so marked as for exportation, he shall forfeit 20 l for every such pack   29 G 2 c 13 ſ 6

And if any person shall reland, or procure to be relanded, any parcel of cards, after having been entred and shipped for exportation, he shall forfeit 50 l.   And if any person concerned shall inform against an accomplice, he shall be admitted to give evidence, and himself be indemnified   5 G. 3 c 46 ſ 16, 17

Carriers.

1. ALL persons carrying goods for hire, as masters and owners of ships, lightermen, stage-coachmen, and the like, come under the denomination of common carriers, and are chargeable on the general custom of the realm, for their faults or miscarriages   1 Bac Abr 343

Carrier, who.

2 By the 3 W. c 12   The justices in Easter sessions yearly, shall rate prices of all land carriage of goods

Rates for carriage

X 4

to

to be brought *into* any place within their jurisdiction, by any common waggoner or carrier, and shall certify the rates so made to the mayors and other chief officers of the several market towns within their jurisdiction, to be hung up in some publick place to which all persons may resort And no such common waggoner or carrier shall take for carriage above the rates so set, on pain of 5l, by distress, by warrant of two justices where such waggoner o carrier shall reside, to the use of the party grieved ʃ 24

And by 21 G 2 c 28 If any common waggoner or carrier shall demand and take any greater price for bringing goods *to* London, or to any place within the bills of mortality, than is allowed and settled by the justices for the place from whence the same are brought for the carrying of goods *from* London to the said place, he shall forfeit 5l to the party grieved, to be recovered as by the said act of the 3 W or by distress and sale of his goods, by warrant from two justices of *Middlesex, Surry, London,* or *Westminster* ʃ 3

And the clerk of the peace in the country shall, immediately after *Easter* sessions yearly, certify to the lord mayor of *London*, and to the respective clerks of the peace for *Middlesex, Surry,* and *Westminster*, the rates made for the carriage of goods in their respective counties and places, which certificate, or an attested copy thereof, signed by the officer to whom the same shall be transmitted, shall be sufficient evidence of the prices so set ʃ 3

And every common waggoner or carrier shall have his christian and surname and place of abode, in large or capital letters, placed upon some conspicuous part of his carriage, before he shall drive the same, on pain of 20s, to be levied and recovered as aforesaid. ʃ 4

[Note, This act of the 21 G 2 c. 28 stands repealed, by the 7 G 3 c 40 & 13 G 3 c 84 by mistake, as it seemeth, for the repeal was intended, most probably, only for so much of the said act as relates to turnpike roads, and not for what relates to the price for carriage of goods]

A carrier shall not evade the law, by refusing to carry goods at the prices limited For if a common carrier, who is offered his hire, and who hath convenience, refuses to carry goods, he is liable to an action in the same manner as an innkeeper who refuses to entertain a guest, or a smith who refuses to shoe a horse. 1 Ba. Abr. 344

So

So an action will lie againſt a common ferryman, who refuſeth to carry paſſengers. *id*

But if the porter puts up the box of a paſſenger behind a ſtage coach, and the maſter as ſoon as he knows of it ſays, he is already full, and refuſes to take the charge of it, the maſter ſhall not be liable. For this is the ſame with an hoſt who refuſeth his gueſt, his houſe being full, and yet the party ſays he will ſhift, or the like, if he be robbed, the hoſt is diſcharged. *id*

So a carrier may refuſe to admit goods into his warehouſe at an unſeaſonable time, or before he is ready to take his journey, but he cannot refuſe to do the duty incumbent upon him by virtue of his publick employment. *L. Raym.* 652

3 No carrier with any horſe or horſes, nor waggon-man, carman, or wain-man, with their reſpective carriages, ſhall by themſelves, or any other, travel on the Lord's day, on pain of 20 s, on conviction in ſix months, before one juſtice (or mayor), on view, or confeſſion, or oath of two witneſſes, to be levied by the conſtable or churchwardens by diſtreſs, to the uſe of the poor, except that the juſtice may reward the informer with any ſum not exceeding a third part. *3 G c 1* — *Carrier travelling on Sundays*

4 It hath been holden, that a carrier imbezilling goods which he has received to carry to a certain place, is not guilty of felony, becauſe there was not a felonious *taking*, but is liable only to a civil action. *1 Haw.* 89, 90 — *Carrier imbezilling goods*

5 But it hath been reſolved, that if a carrier open a pack, and take out part of the goods, with intent to ſteal it, he may be guilty of felony, in which caſe it may be ſaid, not only that ſuch poſſeſſion of a part diſtinct from the whole, was gained by wrong, and not delivered by the owner, but alſo that it was obtained baſely, fraudulently, and clandeſtinely, in hopes to prevent its being diſcovered at all, or fixed upon any one when diſcovered. *1 Haw.* 90 — *Carrier opening a pack*

6 Alſo it ſeems clear, that if a carrier, after he has brought the goods to the place appointed, take them away again ſecretly, with intent to ſteal them, he is guilty of felony, becauſe the poſſeſſion, which he received from the owner, being determined, his ſecond taking is in all reſpects the ſame, as if he were a mere ſtranger. *1 Haw.* 90 — *Carrier ſtealing goods after brought to the place*

7 Alſo it hath been reſolved, if goods be delivered to a carrier, to be carried to a certain place, and he carries them to another place, and diſpoſeth of them to his own uſe, — *Carrying to another place.*

ufe, that this is felony, becaufe this declareth that his
intention originally was not to take the goods, upon the
agreement and contract of the party, but only with a defign of ftealing them *Kelynge* 82

Carrier robbed. 8 Where goods are delivered to a carrier, and he is
robbed of them, he fhall be charged, and anfwer for
them, by reafon of the heir And this was at the common law, before the hundred was anfwerable over to him,
becaufe fuch robbery might be, by confent and combina-
tion, carried on in fuch a manner, that no proof could be
had of it 1 *Salk* 143

And altho' it may be thought a hard cafe, that a poor
carrier who is robbed on the road, without any manner
of default in him, fhould be anfwerable for all the goods
he takes, yet the inconvenience would be far more into-
lerable, if he were not fo, for it would be in his power
to combine with robbers, or to pretend a robbery, or fome
other accident, without a poffibility of remedy to the party, and the law will not expofe him to fo great a temptation, but he muft be honeft at his peril 12 *Mod*
482

One delivering or carrying goods. 9. And generally, if a man delivers goods to a common carrier, to carry to a certain place, if he lofes or
damages them, an action upon the cafe lies againft him
for by the cuftom of the realm, he ought to carry them
fafely 1 *Bac* 343

And if he be a common carrier, tho' there be no agreement, or rate fettled, or promife of payment, yet he fhall
recover his hire on a *quantum meruit*, and therefore fhall
be liable for lofs and damages *id*

Alfo if a perfon, who is no common carrier, takes upon
himfelf to carry my goods, tho' I promife him no reward,
yet if my goods are loft or damaged by his default, I fhall
have an action againft him *id.*

For the very taking of the goods is a general confideration, tho' he be not a common carrier and the acceptance of the goods makes him liable *Stra* 104

Who fhall have the action for the goods loft. 10 M 11 G 3 *Davis & James* On an action againft
a common carrier, the queftion was, In whofe name the
action ought to have been brought The declaration
charged, that the plaintiff being poffeffed of cloth, as of
his own proper goods, delivered the fame to the defendant
to be carried to London and delivered to a certain perfon there The goods were loft, and the plaintiff obtained a verdict againft the carrier It was moved for
a new trial, on the objection, that the action ought to
have been brought in the name of the perfon to whom
the

the goods were confign<mark>ed</mark>, and not in the name of the confignor For the confignor parted with his property upon his delivering the goods to the carrier, and no property remained in him after the delivery Unto this it was anfwered, that the queftion doth not turn upon the ftrict property The carrier has nothing to do with the vefting of the property It does not lie in his mouth to fay, that the confignor is not the owner He is the owner with refpect to the carrier, who undertook to him, and was to be paid by him.——Lord *Manffeld* faid there was neither law nor confcience in the objection The vefting of the property may differ according to the circumftances of cafes But it does not enter into the prefent queftion. This is an action upon the agreement between the plaintiff and the carrier The plaintiff was to pay him Therefore the action is properly brought by the plaintiff, who agreed with him, and was to pay him *Bur Manf* 2680

11 A delivery to the carrier's fervant, is a delivery to the carrier, and if goods are delivered to a carrier's porter, and loft, an action will lie againft the carrier *Read Car.*

Goods delivered to the carrier's fervan

At Bury affizes, 1732, in the cafe of *Harvey* againft *Syhard* and his wife, the plaintiff brought his action againft *Syhard* and his wife, for a box with 80l in it, which was delivered to her as book-keeper for her brother, who was a carrier, in order to be fent by the waggon to London, which 80l was afterwards loft It was adjudged, that the action would not lie againft her, but it ought to have been brought againft the brother himfelf. And the plaintiff was nonfuited 2 *Barnard* 234

12. If a box is delivered generally to a carrier, and he accepts it, he is anfwerable, tho' the party did not tell him there is money in it But if the carrier afks, and the other fays no, or if he accepts it conditionally, provided there is no money in it, in either of thefe cafes the carrier is not liable *Sti* 145

How far it is neceffary that the carrier fhould know what the goods are

If a man delivers a box to a carrier to carry, and he afks what is in it, and the man tells him, a book and tobacco (as the cafe was) and in truth there is 100l befides, yet if the carrier is robbed, he fhall anfwer for the money, for the other was not bound to tell him all the particulars in the box, and it was the bufinefs of the carrier to have made a fpecial acceptance 1 *Bac Abr* 345.

But if a perfon, being a common carrier, receives by his book-keeper from another man's fervant, two bags of money fealed up, containing as was told him 200l, and the

the book-keeper gives a receipt for his master to this effect, Received of such a one two bags of money sealed
up, said to contain 200 l, which I promise to deliver on
such a day at such a place unto such a person, he to pay
10 s *per cent* for carriage and risque, tho' the bags contain 400 l, and the carrier is robbed, he shall be answerable only for 200 l, for this is a particular undertaking,
and as it is by reason of the reward that the carrier is
liable, when the plaintiff endeavours to defraud him of
it, it is but reasonable he should be barred of the remedy, which is only founded on the reward   1 *Bac. Abr*
346

A man took a place in a stage coach, and in the journey the defendant by negligence lost the plaintiff's
trunk, upon not guilty pleaded, the evidence was, that
the plaintiff gave the trunk to the man that drove the
coach, who promised to take care of it, but lost it   *Holt*
chief justice held, that the master was not chargeable,
and that a stage coachman is not within the custom as
a carrier is, unless the master makes a distinct price for
the carriage of the goods as well as of the persons   1 *Salk*
282

But by the custom and usage of stage coaches, every
passenger uses to pay for the carriage of goods above such
a weight, and in such case the coachman shall be charged
for the loss of goods beyond such weight   *Comyn* 25

In the case of *Gibbon* and *Paynton*, E 9 G 3   An
action was brought against the *Birmingham* stage coachman, for 100 l in money, sent from *Birmingham* to *London* by his coach, and lost   It was hid in hay, in an old
nail-bag   The bag and the hay arrived safe, but the
money was gone   The coachman had inserted an advertisement in a *Birmingham* news paper, with a *nota bene*,
that the coachman would not be answerable for money
or jewels or other valuable goods, unless he had notice
that it was money or jewels or valuable goods that was
delivered to him to be carried   He had also distributed
hand bills, of the same import   It was notorious in that
country, that the price of carrying money from *Birmingham* to *London* was three pence in the pound   The
plaintiff was a dealer at *Birmingham*, and had frequently
sent goods from thence   It was proved that he had
been used, for a year and an half, to read the news
paper in which this advertisement was published, though
it could not be proved that he had ever actually read or
seen the individual paper wherein it was inserted   A
letter of the plaintiff's was also produced, from whence

it

it appeared that he knew the course of this trade, and that money was not carried from that place to London at the common and ordinary price of the carriage of other goods. And the jury found a verdict for the defendant. On behalf of the plaintiff, it was moved for a new trial, and a rule was obtained to shew cause. On shewing cause, the court were of opinion that the verdict was right. By the general custom of the realm, a common carrier insures the goods, at all events. And it is right and reasonable that he should do so. But he may make a special contract, or he may refuse to contract, in extraordinary cases, but upon extraordinary terms. And certainly, the party undertaking ought to be apprized what it is that he undertakes, and then he will, or at least may, take proper care. But he ought not to be answerable where he is deceived. Here he was deceived. The money was hid in an old nail-bag, and it was concealed from him, that it was money. The true principle of a carrier's being answerable, is the reward. And a higher price ought in conscience to be paid him for the insurance of money and other valuable things, than for insuring common goods of small value ——And the rule was discharged. *Burrow Mansf* 2298

13. Where goods are stolen from the carrier, he may prefer an indictment against the felon, as for his own goods, for tho' he has not the absolute property, yet he has such a possessory property, that he may maintain an action of trespass against any one who takes them from him, and so may indict a thief for taking them, and the indictment were good also, if it had been brought by the real owner. *Kelynge* 39

Carrier may indict for goods stolen, as his own property.

14. And there is a special case, wherein it is said, that a man may commit larceny by stealing his own goods delivered to the carrier, with intent to make him answer for them, for the carrier had a special kind of property in the goods, in respect whereof, if a stranger had stolen them, he might have been indicted generally as having stolen the said carrier's goods, and the injury is altogether as great, and the fraud as base, where they are taken away by the very owner. 1 *Haw* 94

Persons stealing his own goods from the carrier.

15. E 1 An. *Skinner* and *Upshaw*. The plaintiff brought an action of trover against the defendant who was a common carrier, for goods delivered to him to carry. On not guilty pleaded, the defendant gave in evidence, that he offered to deliver the goods to the plaintiff, if he would pay him his hire, but that the plaintiff refused, and therefore he retained them. And it was ruled by *Holt* chief

Carrier may retain goods for his hire.

ch ef juftice at *Guildhall* (before whom the caufe was tried) that a carrier may retain the goods for his hire And on d rection, the defendant had a verdict given for him *L Raym* 752

And even if the goods be ftolen goods, yet the right owner fhall not have them without paying for the carriage For the carrier being obliged to receive and carry the goods, the law will not deprive him of the remedy for the reward due for the carriage *Ibid* 166.

Carrots.

The penalty for ftealing *carrots* is the fame as that for ftealing *turnips, potatoes, cabbages, parfnips,* and *peafe* which are treated of together under the title **Turnips.**

Cafual death. See **Deodand.**

Cattle.

I Concerning the bringing of cattle into England.
II Buying and felling of cattle
III Stealing, killing, or maiming of cattle.
IV. Prohibiting the importation of hides, fkins, or other parts of cattle, to prevent infection

I Concerning the bringing of cattle into England.

Cattle of the
ifle of Man.

1 **BY** the 5 *G* 3 *c* 43 Beftials may be freely im-ported from the ifle of *Man*

Scotch cattle

2 By the fixth article of the union, no *Scotch* cattle, carried into *England*, fhall be liable to any other duties, than thofe to which cattle of *England* are liable. 5 *An. c* 8

Irifh cattle

3 By the 5 *G* 3 *c* 10 which was of temporary con-tinuance, but by the 16 *G* 3 *c* 8 made perpetual, all forts of cattle may be imported from *Ireland* duty free

II. Buyers

II. *Buying and selling of cattle.*

No person shall buy any ox, steer, runt, cow, heifer, or calf, and sell the same again alive in the same market or fair, on pain of forfeiting double value, half to the king, and half to him who shall sue   3 & 4 Ed 6 c 19 *s. 4 f* 7, 8 And the said act of 3 & 4 Ed 6 c 19 is not repealed by the 12 G 3 c 71 which repeals the general forestalling, ingrossing, and regrating act of 5 & 6 Ed 6 c 14 and other subsequent acts inforcing the same; but hath no reference to any preceding act.

None shall buy and sell in the same market.

III *Stealing, killing, or maiming of cattle.*

1 By the 22 & 23 C 2 c. 7. If any person shall in the night time maliciously, unlawfully, and willingly *kill or destroy* any horses, sheep, or other cattle, he shall be guilty of felony, but without corruption of blood, or loss of dower But to avoid judgment of death, or execution thereupon, he may chuse to be transported to some of the plantations, to be mentioned in the judgment, for seven years

Killing or wounding in the night.

And if any person shall in the night time maliciously, unlawfully, and willingly *maim, wound, or otherwise hurt* any horses, sheep, or other cattle, whereby the same shall not be killed or utterly destroyed, he shall forfeit treble damages, by action of trespass, or upon the case

And three justices (1 Q) may inquire by a jury and witnesses, and may issue warrants for summoning jurors, and for apprehending persons suspected, and take their examinations, and cause witnesses to come before them to give information on oath, so as no person to be examined shall be proceeded against, for any offence concerning which he is examined as a witness, and shall make a true discovery and if such witness, being summoned, refuse to appear, they may commit him till he submit to be examined on oath

2 And by the 14 G 2 c 6 and 15 G 2 c. 34 If any person shall feloniously drive away, or in any other manner feloniously steal any ox, bull, cow, calf, steer, bullock, heifer, sheep, or lamb, or shall wilfully kill any ox, bull, cow, calf, steer, bullock, heifer, sheep, or lamb, with a felonious intent to steal the whole carcass, or any part thereof, or shall assist or aid in committing any such offence, he shall be guilty of felony without benefit of clergy

Stealing, or killing with intent to steal, 10l reward

And

And every perfon who fhall apprehend and profecute to conviction any offender, fhall have 10 l reward. In order to which, he fhall have a certificate figned by the judge, before the end of the affizes, certifying the conviction, and where the offence was committed, and that fuch offender was apprehended and profecuted by the perfon claiming the reward, and if there are feveral claimants, the judge fhall in the faid certificate direct what fhare fhall be paid to each claimant. Which certificate being tendred to the fheriff, he fhall within a month pay the fame without deduction, on pain of forfeiting double, with treble cofts. The fame to be allowed in his accounts, or to be paid to him out of the treafury.

Killing or wounding by the Black Act. 3. And by the 9 G c 22. commonly called the Black Act, which is inferted at large under the title of that name, If any perfon fhall unlawfully and malicioufly kill, maim, or wound any cattle, he fhall be guilty of felony without benefit of clergy, but without corruption of blood.

And the hundred fhall be anfwerable for the damages, not exceeding 200 l.

And if any perfon fhall apprehend, or caufe to be convicted, any offender, and fhall be killed, or wounded, fo as to lofe an eye or the ufe of any limb, in endeavouring to apprehend or fecure him, on proof thereof at the feffions, and on certificate thereof from thence, the fheriff fhall within thirty days pay to the perfon intitled the fum of 50 l, to be repaid to him out of the treafury.

IV. Prohibiting the importation of hides, fkins, or other parts of cattle, to prevent infection

It fhall be lawful for the king, his heirs or fucceffors, as often as he or they fhall find it neceffary, by proclamation with the advice of his privy council, or by his order in council, to be publifhed in the *London Gazette*, to prohibit generally, or from any particular country or countries, the importation of any hides or fkins, horns or hoofs, or any other part of any cattle or beaft, into *Great Britain* or *Ireland*, for fuch time, and under fuch rules, orders, and regulations, as he or they by the advice aforefaid fhall judge moft expedient and effectual to prevent any contagious diftemper from being brought into thefe kingdoms. 9 G 3 c 39.

Certiorari.

Certiorari.

A Certiorari is an original writ, issuing out of the court Certiorari, what. of chancery or the king's bench, directed in the king's name to the judges or officers of inferior courts, commanding them to *certify* or to return the records of a cause depending before them, to the end the party may have the more sure and speedy justice, before the king or such justices as he shall assign to determine the cause   1 *Bac. Abr.* Certior A

Also, the justices of the peace may deliver or send into the king's bench, indictments found before them, or recognizances of the peace taken before them, or force recorded by them, without any certiorari. *Dalt c* 195 What things may be certified without a writ of certiorari

Concerning which writ of certiorari, it is here shewn,

I *In what cases it is grantable.*
II *How to be granted and allowed.*
III *The effect of it.*
IV *The return of it.*

I. *In what cases it is grantable.*

1 A certiorari lies in all judicial proceedings, in which a writ of error does not lie, and it is a consequence of all inferior jurisdictions erected by act of parliament to have their proceedings returnable in the king's bench L *Raym* 469, 580 In cases where a writ of error lies not

2 And therefore a certiorari lies to justices of the peace, even in such cases which they are empowered by statute finally to hear and determine, and the superintendency of the court of king's bench is not taken away without express words   2 *Haw* 286 Where not specially prohibited by statute

3. But it seems agreed, that a certiorari shall never be granted to remove an indictment after a conviction, unless for some special cause, as where the judge below is doubtful what judgment to give   2 *Haw* 288. After conviction

And, *E* 18 *G* 2 *K.* and *Nicholls* An indictment was removed into the court of king's bench by certiorari, after conviction, and before judgment Upon which a doubt arose, what the court could do, the certiorari being brought before judgment, and this court not being apprized of the circumstances of the offence, could not tell what judgment to give And in *Carth* 6 it is said, they cannot give judgment A rule therefore was made to shew cause why the certiorari should not be quashed, so as to remit it back to the sessions, which was afterwards made absolute *Str* 1227

And in the case of the *King* against *Gwynne* and others, *H* 32 *G*. 2. The court (on a defended motion) granted a *Procedendo*, at the instance of the defendants, upon an indictment for an assault at the quarter sessions at *Brecon*, removed into the king's bench by certiorari, because the certiorari had not issued till after the defendants had confessed the assault below, tho' the conviction was not after a trial, and tho' several of the justices were sworn to be near relations of Mr *Gwynne* one of the defendants, namely, his father, two brothers, and an uncle. *Burrow.* Mansfield 749.

After issue joined

4 Also, it seems a good objection against the granting a certiorari, that issue is joined in the court below, and a *venire* awarded for the trial of it 2 *Haw* 288.

Where the court is bound of right to grant it

5 It hath been adjudged, that wherever a certiorari is by law grantable for an indictment, the court is bound of right to award it at the instance of the prosecutor, because every indictment is the suit of the king, and he has a prerogative of suing in what court he pleases. But it seems to be agreed, that it is left to the discretion of the court, either to grant or deny it at the prayer of the defendant 2 *Haw* 287. *Burr. Mansf* 2456.

Not for heinous crimes

6 And it seems that the court will not ordinarily, at the prayer of the defendant, grant a certiorari for the removal of an indictment of perjury, or forgery, or other heinous misdemeanor, for such crimes deserve all possible discountenance, and the certiorari might delay, if not wholly discourage the prosecution 2 *Haw*. 287

But in extraordinary circumstances the court will sometimes dispense with this rule As in the case of *K & Fawle, M* 13 *G* The court granted a certiorari to remove an indictment for felony found at the quarter-sessions, upon affidavits that the defendant could not have a fair trial there. *L Raym.* 1452

II. How to be granted and allowed.

How to be granted on indictment or presentment.

1. On *indictment or presentment* By the 5 *W* c. 11. and 8 & 9 *W* c 33 *it is enacted, that in term time, no writ of certiorari, at the prosecution of any party indicted, shall be granted out of the king's bench, to remove any indictment or presentment of trespass or misdemeanor, before trial had, from before the justices in sessions, unless such certiorari shall be awarded upon motion of counsel, and by rule of court made for the granting thereof.*

But

But in the vacation, writs of certiorari *may be granted by any justice of the king's bench, whose name shall be indorsed on the writ, and also the name of the person at whose instance it is granted*

And all the parties indicted, prosecuting such certiorari *shall, before the allowance thereof, find two sufficient manucaptors, who shall enter into a recognizance before a justice of the king's bench (who shall endorse the same on the writ), or before a justice of the peace of the county or place, in the sum of 20 l, with condition, at the return of the writ, to appear and plead to the said indictment or presentment, in the said court of king's bench, and at his own costs and charges to cause and procure the issue that shall be joined thereupon, or any plea relating thereunto, to be tried at the next assizes for the county wherein the indictment or presentment was found, after such* certiorari *shall be returned, or the next term if in* London, Westminster, *or* Middlesex, *unless the court shall appoint another time, and if so, then at such other time, and to give due notice of such trial, to the prosecutor or his clerk in court, and also that the party prosecuting the writ of* certiorari, *shall appear from day to day, in the said court of king's bench, and not depart until he shall be discharged by the court*

And the said recognizance shall be certified into the king's bench, with the certiorari *and indictment, and there filed, and the name of the prosecutor (if he shall be the party grieved), or some publick officer, shall be indorsed on the indictment.*

And if the defendant prosecuting the writ of certiorari, *be convicted of the offence for which he was indicted, then the court of king's bench shall give reasonable costs to the prosecutor, if he be the party grieved or injured, or be a justice, constable, or other civil officer, who prosecutes on account of any thing that concerned him as officer, to be taxed according to the course of the said court, who shall, for the recovery thereof, within ten days after demand, and refusal of payment, on oath, have an attachment awarded, and the recognisance not to be discharged till the costs are paid*

But if the person procuring the certiorari, *being the defendant, shall not, before allowance thereof, procure such manucaptors to be bound as aforesaid, the justices may proceed to the trial of the indictment in sessions, notwithstanding the writ of* certiorari *delivered.*

At the prosecution of any party indicted] This extends only to certiorari's procured by persons indicted, from whence it follows, that those which are procured by the prosecutor of an indictment, remain as they were at common law. 2 Haw 292.

Y 2

To be tried at the next affizes] But the recognizance fhall not be forfeited, unlefs the profecutor give rules according to the courfe of the court   2 *Haw* 293

Reafonable cofts] The mafter of the crown office, in taxing the cofts, ought only to confider thofe which are fubfequent to the certiorari   2 *Haw.* 292

To the profecutor, if he be the party grieved or injured] M 20 G 2 K and *Ingleton*   The defendant was indicted for attempting to fet fire to the houfe of one *Efton* in *York*, and the indictment alfo charged that the defendant folicited *Mafon*, one of the profecutors, to help to fet fire to the houfe   *Mafon* and one *Glenton* informed the mayor of *York* of this, who bound *Mafon* and *Glenton* over to profecute the defendant   The faid defendant removed the indictment by certiorari into the court of king's bench, and was thereupon convicted and fined   On payment of the fine, it was moved that the recognizance fhould be difcharged.   Unto which it was objected, that the defendant was obliged, before the difcharge thereof, to pay the cofts of the profecutors   But by the court, this cafe is not within the act, for the act extends only to officers and perfons really injured, which neither *Glenton* nor *Mafon* are, for there was no damage done to the houfe, but only intended to be done, nor are either of them officers   And the recognizance was difcharged   1 *Wilfon* 139

In a like cafe, M 30 G 2 K and *Smith*   It was moved, that before the recognizance fhould be difcharged, the profecutor fhould have his cofts   The objection was, that no name of any perfon, as being either the party grieved or injured, or a public civil officer, was indorfed upon the indictment   It was anfwered, That this is not neceffary in order to giving cofts, that to this purpofe it is fufficient, if the profecutor actually be a civil officer, and of that in the prefent cafe there was an affidavit and the act does not fay, that the profecutor fhall not have his cofts, unlefs his name be indorfed   By the court, It is enough, if it be proved that the profecutor was fuch officer, and here it is proved by affidavit   And it was ruled, that the profecutor fhould have his cofts, before the recognizance fhould be difcharged. *Burrow, Mansfield.* 54

May proceed to the trial] Neverthelefs they muft make a return to the certiorari, otherwife they will be in contempt to the court, for all writs muft be obeyed, unlefs good caufe be fhewn to the contrary, and the proper way of fhewing it, is to return it.   2 *Haw* 292

2 On

2 On a *conviction or order*. By the 13 G 2. *c* 18 it is enacted, that *no certiorari shall be granted, to remove any conviction, judgment, order, or other proceedings, before any justice of the peace, or the general or quarter sessions, unless it be applied for in six calendar months after such proceedings had or made, and unless it be duly proved upon oath, that the party suing forth the same, hath given six days notice thereof in writing, to the justice or justices, or two of them (if so many there be), before whom such proceeding have been, to the end that such justices, or the parties therein concerned, may shew cause if they so think fit, against issuing the* certiorari

And by 5 G 2 *c* 19 *No such* certiorari *shall be allowed, to remove any such judgment or order, unless the party prosecuting the* certiorari, *before the allowance thereof, enter into a recognizance with sufficient sureties, before a justice of the county or place, or before the justices at sessions where such judgment or order shall have been given or made, or before a justice of the king's bench, in* 50*l, with condition to prosecute the same, at his own costs and charges with effect, without wilful delay, and to pay the party in whose favour the judgment or order was made, within a month after the same shall be confirmed, his full costs to be taxed according to the course of the court where such confirmation shall be. And if he shall not enter into such recognizance, or shall not perform the conditions, the justices may proceed and make such further order for the benefit of the party for whom the judgment shall be given, in such manner as if no* certiorari *had been granted*

The said recognizance to be certified into the king's bench, and there filed, with the certiorari *and order or judgment removed thereby.*

And if the order or judgment shall be confirmed by the court, the person intitled to the costs, for the recovery thereof, within ten days after demand made, upon oath of such demand and refusal of payment, shall have an attachment granted for the contempt, and the recognizance not to be discharged till the costs are paid and the order complied with

E 1 *An.* A rule was made in the court of king's bench, that no certiorari should be granted to remove orders of justices, from which the law has given an appeal to the sessions, before the matter be determined on the appeal, because it hinders the privilege of appealing, and that if any order be removed before appeal, it should be sent down again. But if the time of appeal be expired, that case is not within the rule By *Holt* Ch J —But afterwards, *M.* 4 *Ann* in the case of *Shellington,* it was held, that advantage must be taken of this rule upon the motion to file the order, for that after it is filed it is too late. 1 *Salk.* 147

But in the cafe of the borough of *Warwick,* M 8 G 2. There was an appeal from a poor rate, and the feffion made an order that the churchwardens fhould produce the books at an adjourned day, before which, a certiorari was brought to remove that order. And it was held to lie, though the appeal was depending, elfe the order muft be obeyed before the validity of it can be determined. It was alfo held, that an appointment of overfeers may be removed before an appeal to the feffions, for the rule laid down in 1 *Salk.* 147 extends only to the cafe where there is a limited time for appealing, as to the next quarter feffions, but the ftatute of the 43 *El* c 2 is not fo reftrained and confequently it can never be faid, that the time for appealing is out. And if the appeal from an appointment is lodged, there can be no certiorari, till the feffions hath made a determination, and a certiorari brought, pending fuch appeal, fhall be fuperfeded. *Str.* 991.

III The effect of it.

Subfequent proceedings void.	1 After a certiorari is allowed by the inferior court, it makes all the fubfequent proceedings on the record that is removed by it erroneous 2 *Haw* 293
Except where the jury is fworn.	2 But it hath been adjudged, that if a certiorari for the removal of an indictment before juftices of the peace be not delivered, before the jury be fworn for the trial of it, the juftices may proceed 2 *Haw* 294
And after judgment	3 And the juftices may fet a fine to compleat their judgment, after a certiorari delivered, L *Raym* 1515.
Removes all after the tefte of it	4 A certiorari removes all things done between the tefte and return. L *Raym* 835, 1305
Removes the record itfelf.	5 A certiorari removes the record itfelf out of the inferior court, and therefore if it remove the record againft a principal, the acceffary cannot there be tried 2 *Haw* 325
In what cafe the perfon of the defendant fhall be removed	6 And if the defendant be convicted of a capital offence, the perfon of the defendant muft be removed by habeas corpus, in order to be prefent in court, if he will move in arreft of judgment And herein the cafe of a conviction differs from that of a fpecial verdict, where the prefumption of innocence may be fuppofed to continue, and therefore the perfonal prefence of the defendant in that cafe is not neceffary at the argument of it. *Buriet* Mansfield 930 K and *pragg* M 33 G 2

7 It

7. It hath been holden, that a certiorari for the removal of a recognizance for the good behaviour, or an appearance at feffions, will fuperfede the obligation of it but this would be highly inconvenient, and the contrary feems to be fupported by the better authority. *2 Haw* 292 {.sidenote}How far it fuperfedes the obligation of a recognizance

8 If a *fuperfedeas* come out of a fuperior court, to the juftic s, they ought to furceafe, altho' the *fuperfedeas* be awarded againft law, for they are not to difpute the command of a fuperior court, which is a warrant to them *Crom.* 129. {.sidenote}Cafe where it is awarded againft law.

IV. *The return of it*

1 Every return of a certiorari ought to be under feal. *2 Hav* 294 {.sidenote}Return of the certiorari

2 And altho' the *cuftos rotulorum* keep the records, yet muft the juftices, to whom it is directed, return the certiorari, and therefore if it is directed to the juftices of the peace, and the clerk of the peace only return it, nothing is thereby removed. *2 Haw* 294

3. The certiorari may be fometimes to remove and fend up the record itfelf, and fometimes but only the tenor of the record (as the words therein be), and it muft be obeyed accordingly *Dalt. c.* 195 *2 Haw* 295.

4 A return was in paper, (and not upon parchment), and for that reafon was held by the court not good. 1 *Barnardift.* 113 H. 2 G 2 K and the inhabitants of Darlington.

5 Upon a certiorari to remove an indictment of a riot, or forcible entry, or the like, the return muft have thefe words, *as alfo to hear and determine divers felonies,* &c according to the commiffion, for if the return mentions only that they are juftices of the peace, without fuch words, the return is infufficient. *Dalt c.* 195

6 If the perfon to whom a certiorari is directed, do make a falfe return, yet the court will not ftay filing it on affidavit of its being falfe, except in publick cafes, as in cafes of commiffioners of fewers, or for not repairing highways, or for fome fuch fpecial caufes, becaufe the remedy for a falfe return is either an action on the cafe at the fuit of the party grieved, or an information at the fuit of the king *Dalt. c* 195

7 If the perfon to whom the certiorari is directed, do not make a return, then an *alias,* that is, a fecond writ; then a *pluries,* that is, a third writ, or *caufam nobis fignifices,*

fices, fhall be awarded, and then an attachment. *Crom.* 116.

Befides thefe general rules, in common to all certiora-ri's, there are many times fpecial directions about granting and allowing or not allowing them, in particular cafes, which are treated of under their refpective titles, fuch as highways, game, tithes, fwearing, and many others

The return of a certiorari may be thus
Firft, on the backfide of the writ indorfe thefe or the like words.

The execution of this writ appears in a fchedule to the fame writ annexed.

And that fchedule may be thus, on a piece of parchment by itfelf, and filed to the writ.

Weftmorland　I *Sir Philip Mufgrave, baronet, one of the keepers of the peace and juftices of our lord the king, affigned to keep the peace within the faid county, and alfo to hear and determine divers felonies, trefpaffes, and other mifdemeanors in the fame county committed, by virtue of this writ to me delivered, do under my feal certify unto his majefty in his court of king's bench, the indictment of which mention is made in the fame writ, together with all matters touching the fame indictment. In witnefs whereof I the faid Sir P M. have to thefe prefents fet my feal Given at ——— in the faid county, the ————— day of ——— in the ——— year of the reign of ———.*

Then take the record of the indictment, and clofe it with-in the fchedule, and feal and fend them up both together with the certiorari

Challenge.　See **Jurors**.
Champerty　See **Maintenance**.
Chance medley.　See **Homicide**.

Cheat.

OF cheats punifhable by publick profeccution, there are two kinds,

I. *By the common law.*

II. *By ftatute.*

I *By the common law.*

1 Cheats which are punifhable by the common law, may in general be defcribed to be deceitful practices, in defrauding or endeavouring to defraud another of his known right, by means of fome artful device, contrary to the plain rules of common honefty, as by playing with falfe dice, or by caufing an illiterate perfon to execute a deed to his prejudice, by reading it over to him in words different from thofe in which it was written, or by perfuading a woman to execute writings to another, as her truftee, upon an intended marriage, which in truth contained no fuch thing, but only a warrant of attorney to confefs a judgment, or by fuppreffing a will, and fuch like. 1 *Haw* 188.

2. It feemeth to be the better opinion, that the deceitful receiving of money from one man, to another's ufe, upon a falfe pretence of having a meffage and order to that purpofe, is not punifhable by a criminal profecution, becaufe it is accompanied with no manner of artful contrivance, but wholly depends on a bare naked lie, and it is faid to be needlefs to provide fevere laws for fuch mifchiefs, againft which common prudence and caution may be a fufficient fecurity 1 *Haw.* 188.

3 A perfon for a counterfeit pafs, was adjudged to the pillory, and fined. *Dalt. c* 32.

4. On an indictment againft the defendant, a miller, for changing corn delivered to him to be ground, and giving bad corn inftead of it, it was moved to quafh the fame, becaufe it is only a private cheat, and not of a publick nature It was anfwered, that being a cheat in the way of trade, it concerned the publick, and therefore was indictable And the court unanimoufly agreed not to quafh it *T.* 16 *G.* 2 *K* and *Wood.* 1 Seff C 217.

5 A perfon falfely pretending that he had power to difcharge foldiers, took money of a foldier to difcharge him; and

and being indicted for the same, the court held the indictment to be good. *T* 3 *C.* Serlested's case. 1 *Lord,* 202.

6. As there are frauds which may be relieved civilly, and not punished criminally (with the complaints whereof the courts of equity do generally abound), so there are other frauds, which in a special case may not be helped civilly, and yet shall be punished criminally. Thus if a minor goes about the town, and pretending to be of age, defrauds many persons by taking credit for considerable quantities of goods, and then insists on his non-age, the persons injured cannot recover the value of their goods, but they may indict and punish him for a common cheat. *Barl* 100.

7. Finally, the distinction which, as it seemeth, will solve almost all cases of this kind, was taken in the case of *K.* and *Wheatly,* *H* 1 *G* 3. The defendant was indicted and convicted for selling beer short of the due and just measure, to wit, 16 gallons as and for 18. It was moved in arrest of judgment. And by the court, This is only an inconvenience and injury to a private person, arising from that private person's own negligence and carelessness in not measuring the liquor, upon receiving it, to see whether it held out the just measure or not. Offences that are indictable must be such as affect the publick. As if a man uses false weights and measures, and sells by them to all or to many of his customers, or uses them in the general course of his dealing, so if there is a conspiracy to cheat. For these are deceptions that common care and prudence are not sufficient to guard against. These are much more than private injuries, they are publick offences. But in the present case, it is a mere private imposition or deception. No false weights or measures are used, no conspiracy. Only an imposition upon the person he was dealing with, in delivering him a less quantity instead of a greater, which the other carelessly accepted. It is only a non-performance of his contract, for which non-performance he may bring his action. So, the selling an unsound horse for a sound one, is not indictable. The buyer should be more upon his guard. And the distinction which was laid down, as proper to be attended to in all cases of this kind, is this. That in such impositions or deceits where common prudence may guard persons against their suffering from them, the offence is not indictable, but the party is left to his civil remedy for the redress of the injury that has been done to him, but where false weights and measures are used, or false tokens produced, or such methods taken to cheat and deceive, as people cannot by

any ordinary care or prudence be guarded againſt, there it
is an offence indictable *Burrow* Mansfield 1125 *Black J.
Rep* 273.

II *By ſtatute*

1 By the 33 H 8 c 1 If any perſon ſhall falſely and
deceitfully obtain, or *get into his lands or poſſeſſion* any
money goods, chattels, jewels, or other things, of any
other perſon, by colour and means of any *falſe privy token*,
or counterfeit letter made in another man's name, and
ſhall be convicted thereof, by examination of witneſſes, or
confeſſion, at the aſſizes or ſeſſions, or by action in any
court of record, he ſhall have ſuch puniſhment by impriſonment, pillory, or other *corporal pain* (except death),
as the court ſhall appoint Saving to the party grieved
ſuch remedy by action or otherwiſe, for the goods ſo obtained, as he might have had by the common law

And two juſtices (1 Q) may call and convent by proceſs or otherwiſe (A), to the aſſizes or ſeſſions, any perſon
ſuſpected, and commit or bail him to the next aſſizes or
ſeſſions

Get into his hands or poſſeſſion] A perſon endeavouring by
a counterfeit letter to defraud another of goods, and being
apprehended on ſuſpicion of ſuch fraud, before he hath got
the goods into his poſſeſſion, ſeems not to be within this
ſtatute E 3 G 2. K. and *Brian* Seſſ C. V 2 27.

Falſe privy token] On motion to quaſh an indictment,
which was, that the defendant came pretending that ſuch
a perſon had ſent him to receive 20l, and received it,
whereas ſuch perſon did not ſend him By the court, It is
not indictable, unleſs he came with *falſe tokens*, for we are
not to indict one man for making a fool of another.
Blackerby. 79.

H 13 G 2 K. and *Munoz.* It was adjudged, that an
indictment averring the offence to be by falſe tokens, without ſhewing what thoſe falſe tokens are, is not ſufficient,
and that the fraudulently procuring a note from a perſon,
by falſely affirming that there was one in the next room
that would pay the money due upon it, whereas in fact
there was no ſuch perſon in the next room, is not a *falſe
token*, but a falſe affirmation only 1 *Seſſ* C 201. *Str.*
1127

Note, the ſtatute ſays a falſe *privy* token

Corporal pain] Lord *Coke* obſerves hereupon, that for
this offence the offender cannot be fined, but corporal pain
only inflicted. 3 *Inſt.* 133.

But Mr *Hawkins* obſerves, that there is a precedent in
Cro Car 564 by which it appears, that one convicted on

such a profecution hath been adjudged not only to ftand on the pillory, but alfo to pay a fine of 500 l, and to be bound with good fureties to the good behaviour 1 *Haw* 188

Commit or bail him] In this cafe the juftices fhall do well to take examination of the offence, and to certify the fame to the feffions or gaol delivery, and withal to bind over the informers and witneffes to give evidence therein *Dall c* 32

2 By the 30 G. 2 *c* 24 All perfons who knowingly and defignedly, by falfe pretence or pretences, fhall obtain from any perfon, money, goods, wares, or merchandizes, with intent to cheat or defraud any perfon of the fame, fhall be deemed offenders againft law and the publick peace, and the court before whom any fuch offender fhall be tried, fhall on conviction order him to be fined and imprifoned, or to be put in the pillory, or publickly whipped, or to be tranfported as foon as conveniently may be for feven years *f* 1

And any juftice, before whom any perfon charged on oath with having committed any of the offences aforefaid, fhall examine by oath and fuch other lawful means as to him fhall feem meet touching the matters complained of, and deal with the offender according to law and if the party charged as being the offender fhall be committed to prifon, or admitted to bail, to anfwer the matters complained of at the next feffions or affizes, the faid juftice fhall bind over the profecutor to appear and profecute fuch offender with effect, and if fuch goods fo fraudulently obtained appear to fuch juftice to exceed the value of 20 l, the recognizance fhall be in not lefs than double the value of the goods *f* 2

A Warrant of two juftices to apprehend an offender, on 33 *H*. 8. *c*. 1.

Weftmorland } To the conftable of——

WHEREAS *complaint hath been made unto us whofe names and feals are hereunto fet, two of his majefty's juftices of the peace for the faid county, and one of us of the quorum, upon the oaths of* A. I *of——yeoman, and* B I *of——yeoman, that on the——day of—— A O of——yeoman, did by a falfe privy taken [or, counterfeit letter] that is to fay, by [here particularize the offence] falfely and deceitfully obtain and get into his hands and poffeffion [here mention the things] from* C I *of—— contrary to the ftatute in that cafe made Thefe are therefore to* command

command you, upon sight hereof, forthwith to bring the said
A O before us at ———— on the ———— day of ———— to
answer to the said complaint, and further to be dealt withal ac-
cording to law Given under our hands and seals the ———— day
of ——— .

Cheese. See **Butter.**
Chocolate. See **Excise.**

Church and Church yard.

1 THE ancient Saxon word is *cyrce*, the Danish **Original of the word church** *kircke*, the Belgick *kercke*, the Cimbrick *kirkia* or *kurk*, probably from the Greek word κυριακὸς, belonging to the Lord, or κυρίου οῖκος, the Lord's house so that we have lost the ancient pronunciation of the word (except in the northern parts of *England* and in *Scotland*) by softening the letters *c* or *ch*, as we have done in many cases, which letters the ancient *Greeks* and *Romans* always pronounced hard, as the letter *k*.

2 *In cities and towns corporate, the bishop (with the con-* **Uniting of churches.** *sent of the mayor, aldermen, and justices of the peace, and of the patron) may unite two churches or chapels, and make order with the like consent, that the patrons present by turns, having regard to the value of the livings united and the incumbents thereof shall be graduates* 17 Car 2 c 3

3 Clauses are commonly inserted in the several acts of **New churches.** parliament for making provision for the rectors of new churches, which clauses give certain powers to justices of the peace, in relation to the assessments to be made for that purpose And in the case of borrowing money for rebuilding clergymens houses, by the 17 G 3 c 53 the estimates are to be sworn to before a justice of the peace or master in chancery

4 *No fairs nor markets shall be kept in church yards* 13 **Markets in the church yard.** Ed 1 st 2 c 6

5 *Clergymen shall not be arrested, and drawn out of any* **Arrest in the church or church** *church or church yard, whilst they attend to divine service, on* **yard** *pain of imprisonment of the offender, and ransom at the king's will, and satisfaction to the party arrested* 50 Ed. 3 c 5 1 R 2 c 15

Also it is said, that arrests in civil cases ought not to be of persons going to or coming from church, but that a warrant from a justice of the peace for the king may be executed

cuted in such cases *Cro Car* 602 *Cro Jac.* 321. 2 *Bulst* 2

But altho' the officer may be punished for the same either in the spiritual or temporal courts, yet the arrest (if not on a Sunday) is good in law. *Watson, c* 34 *p* 344

brawling in the church or church yard

6. *If any person shall, by words only, quarrel, chide, or brawl, in any church or church yard, the ordinary (on proof of two witnesses) may suspend every layman, being an offender, ab ingressu ecclesiae, and every clergyman from the ministration of his office, so long as he shall think meet* 5 & 6 Ed 6 c 4 f 1

Striking in the church or church yard.

7 *If any shall smite, or lay any violent hands on another in any church or church yard, he shall be deemed ipso facto excommunicate, and be excluded from the fellowship and company of Christ's congregation* 5 & 6 Ed 6 c 4 f 2

Lay violent hands] But churchwardens, or perhaps private persons, who whip boys for playing in the church, or pull off the hats of those who obstinately refuse to take them off themselves, or gently lay their hands on those who disturb the performance of any part of divine service, and turn them out of the church, are not within the meaning of this statute. 1 *Haw* 139.

Shall be deemed ipso facto excommunicate] And he shall not excuse himself by shewing that the other assaulted him. 1 *Haw* 139.

Ipso facto] Nevertheless, in this and other like cases, there ought either to be a precedent conviction at law, which must be transmitted to the bishop, or else the excommunication must be declared in the spiritual court upon a proper proof of the offence there, for it is implied in every penal law, that no one shall incur the penalty thereof, till he be found guilty upon a lawful trial. 1 *Haw.* 139.

Striking with a weapon in the church or church yard.

8 *If any shall maliciously strike another with any weapon, in any church or church yard, or shall there draw any weapon with intent to strike, and shall be convicted thereof by verdict of 12 men, or confession, or by two witnesses, before the judges of assize, or justices of the peace in their sessions, he shall be adjudged to have one of his ears cut off, and if he have no ears, he shall be burned in the cheek with a hot iron having the letter* F, *whereby he may be known and taken for a fray maker and fighter, and he shall also stand ipso facto excommunicate.* 5 & 6 Ed 6. c 4 f 3

Sacrilege.

9 He who steals goods belonging to a parish church, may be indicted for stealing the goods of the parishioners. 1 *Haw* 94.

For other matters, see title **Churchwardens.**

Churchwardens.

I. *Who are exempted from being churchwardens.*

1. **A** Counsellor or attorney ought not to be chosen churchwarden and if he is, he may have a prohibition, by reason of his attendance on the courts at *Westminster* 2 Roll's Abr 272 — *Attorneys.*

2 Apothecaries, who have served 7 years, shall be exempted from the office of churchwarden. 6 *W c* 4 — *Apothecaries and surgeons*

And by the 18 *G* 2. *c* 15 Freemen of the corporation of surgeons in *London* are exempted from being churchwardens

3 Dissenting teachers or preachers, in holy orders, or pretended holy orders, being duly qualified, are exempted from the office of churchwarden 1 *W sess* 1 *c* 18 — *Dissenting ministers*

4. Other dissenters, scrupling to take upon them the office, may execute the same by a sufficient deputy, to be approved of in like manner as other churchwardens 1 *W. sess* 1. *c* 18 — *Other dissenters.*

5 All persons who have prosecuted a felon to conviction, and the first assignee of the certificate thereof, are exempted from the office of churchwarden, in the parish where the offence was committed 10 & 11 *W c* 23 *s* 2. — *Persons having convicted a felon*

6. No private man, personally serving for himself in the militia, during the time of such service, shall be liable to serve as churchwarden 2 *G* 3 *c* 20 — *Persons serving in the militia*

II. Chusing and swearing churchwardens, with their duty thereupon

When to be chosen and by whom

1 Churchwardens shall be chosen yearly in *Easter* week, by the joint consent of the minister and parishioners, if it may be, but if they cannot agree, the minister shall chuse one, and the parishioners another   *Canons of* 1603 89.

But where there is a custom for the parishioners to chuse both, that custom shall continue   *Gibs Codex,* 242

Refusing to take the office.

2 A person chosen churchwarden, refusing to take his office and oath, may be excommunicated for the refusal, and no prohibition will lie   *Gibs* 243

Refusing to swear them

3 And the ecclesiastical judge, refusing to swear him, may be compelled by a mandamus   *Gibs* 243

Churchwarden's oath.

4 The churchwarden's oath, as said to have been agreed on, upon mutual consultation between the civilians and common lawyers, is as follows

" You shall swear truly and faithfully to execute the " office of a churchwarden within your parish, and ac " cording to the best of your skill and knowledge present " such things and persons as to your knowledge are pre " sentable by the laws ecclesiastical of this realm   so help you God and the contents of this book." *Gibs* 243

Churchwardens a body corporate.

5 Churchwardens being thus sworn, are so far incorporated by law, as to sue for the goods of the church, and to bring an action of trespass for them, and also to purchase goods for the use of the parish, but they are not a corporation in such sort as to purchase lands, or take by grant, except in *London* by custom   *Gibs* 241

How long they shall continue

6 Churchwardens shall continue in office, till the new churchwardens be sworn.   *Can* 118.

III. Their duty in levying rates, and therein of vestries and select vestries.

Summoning a vestry

1 The rates must be made with the consent of the major part of the parishioners, housekeepers, or occupiers of land   In order to which, publick notice of a vestry (a place so called from the vestments of the minister kept there) ought to be given the *Sunday* before, either in the church after divine service is ended, or else at the church door as the parishioners come out, both of the calling of the said meeting, and also of the time and place of the assembling of it   And it will be fairest then also to declare for what business the said meeting is to be held, that no one may be surprized, but that all may have full time before,

3

before, to confider what is to be propofed at the faid meeting. And it is ufual that for half an hour before it begins, one of the church bells be tolled to give the parifhioners notice when they are met. 5 Co 67 *Shaw Par. Law* 54

2 At the common law, every parifhioner who paid to the church rates, and no other, had a right to vote *Shaw* 55. And thofe that pay no church rates fhall have no vote in affairs relating to it, except it be the rector or vicar *Wood, b.* 1 c 7

Who fhall have a vote in the veftry

3 All perfons who have a vote in the veftry have an equal right, and neither the minifter nor churchwardens, without a fpecial cuftom, can adjourn the veftry, but this can only be done by a majority of the whole affembly. *Str* 1047

Who may adjourn the veftry.

4 When the churchwardens and parifhioners are there met, they are to confider what fum of money it will be neceffary to raife for fuch repairs as fhall then be needful, and after they have agreed what fum is fit, they are to make an equal levy *Degge* 171

Laying the rates.

5 And the major part of them that appear, fhall bind the parifh; or if none appear, the churchwardens alone may make the rate, becaufe they, and not the parifhioners, are to be cited and punifhed, in defect of repairs *Gibf* 220

Majority to bind the parifh

6. It is moft convenient, that every parifh act there be entred in the parifh book of accounts, and every man's hand confenting to it be fet thereto, for then it will be a certain rule for the churchwardens to go by. *Shaw* 55

Entring in a book.

7 By cuftom there may be felect veftries, of a certain number of perfons elected yearly, to make rates, and manage the concerns of the parifh for that year: and fuch cuftom is a good cuftom *Read* Ch Service *Gibf* 246. *Str* 428

Select veftry.

8 It is holden, that a rate for the reparation of the fabrick of a church is real, charging the land, and not the perfon, but a rate for ornaments is perfonal, upon the goods, and not upon the land. *Gibf* 220.

Two rates, one for the fabrick another for ornaments.

And in *Jeffery's* cafe, 5 Co 67 it was folemnly adjudged, that the rates for the repair of the church fhall be laid upon every occupier of lands in the parifh, altho' fuch occupier live in another parifh; and fuch perfon may come to the veftries of the parifhioners, and vote in the making a rate: but he fhall not be charged towards the ornaments of the church, as for bells, repair of feats, bread and wine, clerk's wages, vifitation charges, and the like, by reafon of fuch lands, for that the perfonal eftates of the inhabitants are chargeable with every thing that doth not relate to the fabrick of the church, or repairs of the fences of the church yard, or such other things as concern the freehold

And therefore some have been of opinion, that church-wardens should make two rates, one upon lands and house, which may concern the freehold of the church, and another upon personal estates and stock, to defray other expences. But as this method creates confusion, so it is seldom practised

And Sir *Simon Degge* says, that he conceives the law to be clear otherwise, and that a foreigner who holds lands in the parish is as much obliged to pay towards the bells, seats, and ornaments, as to the repair of the church, otherwise there would be great confusion in making several levies, which he never observed to be practised within his knowledge But he leaves it a query, among a diversity of opinions p 173

And Mr *Shaw*, in his parish law, having cited the authors who hold these different opinions, says, that the practice generally now goes according to the opinion last mentioned, namely, that foreigners occupying lands within the parish shall be charged to both, and that the ecclesiastical judges, as well as the temporal, for the case and convenience which accrues from the making of one levy for all do give countenance thereto, and begin to treat the contrary opinion as obsolete and out of doors p 92

Equal pound rate. 9 A taxation by the pound rate is the most equitable way, and not according to the quantity of the land *Wood*, b 1. c 7

Tenant to be charged, and not the landlord 10 Where lands are in farm, not the lessor, but the tenant shall be rated and pay *Gibs* 221

Impropriator how far chargeable 11 An impropriator, tho' bound to repair the chancel, is also bound to contribute to the reparations of the church, if he hath lands in the parish, which are not parcel of the parsonage *Gibs* 221, 223

Appeal against the rate 12 If any person find himself aggrieved at the inequality of the assessment, his appeal must be to the ecclesiastical judge *Degge* 172

And in such case, if he will be relieved, he must shew, that he is illegally or unequally taxed in respect of the quantity of his land, as being rated for more than he has, or that the land which he hath is over-rated, or that the rate was needless, or that some lands in the parish are omitted in the rate *Wood*, b 1 c 7

Rates how to be recovered. 13. If any refuse to pay the rates, being demanded by the churchwardens, they are to be sued for in the ecclesiastical

fiaftical courts and not elfewhere *Gibf* 219 *Degge.*
171
Alfo a quaker, refufing to pay church rates, may be
fued, as other parifhioners, in the ecclefiaftical court, or
he may be profecuted before the juftices of the peace, in
the fame manner as for his tithes

IV Their duty as to repairs, and therein concerning
church feats

1 Of common right, the foil and freehold of the church
is the parfon's, the ufe of the body of the church,
and the repair of it, common to the parifhioners, and
the difpofing of the feats therein, the right of the ordinary
Gibf 221

Who fhall repair.

2 The fpiritual court may compel the parifhioners to
repair the body of the church, and may excommunicate
every one of them till it be repaired, but thofe that are
willing to contribute fhall be abfolved, till the greater
part agree to a tax *Read Ch Service*

Who may compel the repairs to be made

3 If the churchwardens erect or add any thing new,
either to the fabrick of the church, utenfils, or churchyard,
they muft have the confent of the parifhioners, and if fuch
additions are in the church, the bifhop's licence is alfo
neceffary. But where neceffary repairs are wanting, the
greater part of the parifh will bind the lefs. and if the major
part will not confent, where repairs are neceffary, the
churchwardens may repair without their confent, if upon
notice given they refufe to meet, or when they are
met, refufe to make a rate But if a church fall down,
the parifhioners are not bound to rebuild it *Read Ch*
Service 1 *Vent* 367

Difference between adding fomething new, and repairing the old.

4 But if a church be fo much out of repair, that it is
neceffary to pull it down, or fo little, that it needs to be
enlarged, the major part of the parifhioners may make a
rate for new building, or enlarging, as there fhall be
occafion This was declared in the 29 *C* 2. by all the
three courts fucceffively, notwithftanding the caufe was
laboured by a great number of quakers, who oppofed the
rate *Gibf* 221

When they may rebuild.

5 The parfon, that is, the fpiritual rector, as alfo the
lay impropriator, are bound by common right to repair
the chancel, and is thereupon intitled to the chief feat
therein, unlefs another hath it by prefcription, yet he
hath not the difpofal of the feats therein, but the bifhop.
Gibf 223, 224

Repairing the chancel

6 An ifle in a church, which hath time out of mind
belonged to a particular houfe, and been maintained and

Repairing an ifle

repaired by the owner of that houſe, is part of his frank tenement, and the ordinary cannot diſpoſe of it, or inter-meddle in it *Gibſ* 221

Seat inſeparable from the houſe

7 A ſeat, or priority in a ſeat, in the body of the church, may be preſcribed for as belonging to a houſe, if it hath been uſed, and alſo repaired, time out of mind, by the inhabitants of ſuch houſe. *Gibſ.* 221

And no one can claim a ſeat in a church by preſcrip-tion as appendant or belonging to land, but it muſt be laid as belonging to a houſe, in reſpect to the inhabitancy thereof. *Wood, b* 1 *c.* 7.

And therefore a ſeat may not be granted to a perſon and his heirs abſolutely, for the ſeat doth not belong to the perſon, but to the inhabitant. *Gibſ* 221.

V. Their duty as to ſundry other matters.

Overſeer.

1. Every churchwarden is an overſeer of the poor, al-tho' every overſeer of the poor is not a churchwarden. 43 *El c* 2 ſ 1.

And in *M* 15 *C* 2. A churchwarden was committed by the two next juſtices, as churchwarden, for refuſing to account for the money received and diſburſed by him, but on an *habeas corpus* he was diſcharged becauſe by the warrant of commitment it ought to appear that he was overſeer of the poor, for by the ſtatute of 43 *El* that is annexed to his office of churchwarden, and the juſtices have no juriſdiction over him as churchwarden, but as overſeer. *Dalt.* 186.

Church way.

2. They are to ſee that the church ways be well kept and repaired And the right to a church way may be claimed and maintained by a libel in the ſpiritual court. 2 *Roll's Abr* 287

Vacancy.

3 Churchwardens have the care of a benefice during its vacancy Having firſt taken out a ſequeſtration from the ſpiritual court, they are to manage all the profits and expences of the benefice for him that ſhall next ſucceed, plough and ſow his glebe; take in the crop, collect tithes, thraſh out and ſell corn, repair houſes and fences, and the like And they ſhall take care that during the vacancy the church ſhall be duly ſerved by a curate approved by the biſhop, whom they are to pay out of the profits of the benefice And if the ſucceſſor thinks himſelf aggrieved by them, he may appeal to the eccleſiaſtical judge. *Par. L* 99 *Com Par. Off* 90.

Worldly calling on the Lord's day

4 They (or the conſtable) ſhall levy the penalties for perſons exerciſing their worldly calling on the Lord's day 29 *C* 2 *c* 7

5. They shall suffer no plays, feasts, banquets, suppers, church ales, drinkings, temporal courts or leets, lay juries, musters, or any profane usage to be kept in the church or church yard *Can* 88 *Profanation of the church*

6 They shall see that the parishioners resort to church, and continue there orderly, during divine service, and shall present the defaulters *Can* 90 *Attending divine service*

7 They shall not suffer any idle persons to abide either in the church yard, or church porch, during the time of divine service or preaching, but shall cause them to come in, or to depart *Can* 19 *Loitering in the church yard*

8 They shall levy the forfeiture of 12d a Sunday, on the goods of persons not coming to church. 1 *El c* 2 *Levying 12 d Sunday for not coming to church*

9 They (or the constable) shall levy the penalty of 3s 4d, for using unlawful pastimes on the Lord's day. 1 *C c* 1 *Sports on the Lord's day*

10. They (or the constables or overseers) shall levy the penalties for being present at unlawful conventicles. 22 *C 2 c.* 1 *Conventicle*

11 They shall, on pain off 20l, present at the sessions once a year, the monthly absence from church of all recusants, and the names and ages of their children above nine years old, and the names of their servants And if the party presented shall be indicted and convicted, the churchwardens shall have a reward of 40s, to be levied of the recusants goods, by warrant of the justices in sessions. 3 *J c* 4 *Recusant.*

12 They shall keep excommunicated persons out of the church *Can* 85 *Excommunicate persons*

13 They shall take care to have in the church a large bible, book of common prayer, book of homilies, a font of stone, a decent communion table, with proper coverings, the ten commandments set up at the east end, and other chosen sentences upon the walls, a reading desk, and pulpit, and chest for alms, all at the charge of the parish. *Can* 80, 81, 82, 83, 84. *Ornaments of the church*

14 They ought to keep the keys of the belfrey, and to take care that the bells be not rung without good cause, to be allowed by the minister and themselves *Can* 88 *Bells.*

15 They shall have a box, wherein to keep the register, with three locks and keys, two keys to be kept by them, and one by the minister, and every Sunday they shall see that the minister enter therein all christenings, weddings, and burials that have been the week before, and at the bottom of every page, they shall (with the minister) subscribe their names. And they shall, within a month after *March* 25, yearly, transmit to the bishop a copy thereof for the year before, subscribed as above *Register.*

And

And such register, being carefully preserved, is good evidence, and the falsifying of it is punishable at the common law. *Gibf* 229

Communion

16 They shall, at the charge of the parish, with the advice and direction of the minister, provide bread and wine against the communion. *Can* 20

Incumbent.

17 They (or the overseers) shall levy the penalty of 5l. for an incumbent not reading the common prayer once a month. 13 & 14 C 2 c 4

Charity briefs.

18 They shall collect money on charity briefs, on pain of 20l. 4 *An.* c 14

Strange preachers

19 They shall not suffer any strangers to preach, but such as shall appear qualified on shewing their licence, and they shall see that such preachers register or subscribe their names in a book to be kept for that purpose, with the day when they preached, and the bishop's name who granted the licence. *Can* 50, 52

Burying in woollen

20 They shall, on certificate from the minister, apply to the magistrates for conviction of offenders in not burying in woollen. 30 C 2 c 3,

Persons denied christian burial.

21 Persons who murder themselves, or die excommunicated, are denied christian burial, and therefore the churchwardens are not to suffer them to be buried in the church or church yard, without special licence from the bishop. *Degge* 183

Eating flesh on fish days

22. They shall levy the penalties for eating flesh on fish days. 5 *El.* c 5

Gaming

23 They shall receive the penalties for servants, labourers, apprentices, or journeymen gaming in publick houses. 30 G 2. c 24.

Drunkenness

24 They shall receive the penalties for tipling and drunkenness. 4 G c 5 21 G 2 c. 7

Suffering tipling

25 They (or the constable) shall levy the penalty for suffering tipling. 1 J c 9.

Spirituous liquors

26 They shall receive the penalties for hawking spirituous liquors. 9 G 2 c 23

Corn.

27 They (or the overseers) shall levy the penalty for selling corn by a wrong measure. 22 C 2 c 8

Butter and cheese

28 They (or the overseers) shall receive the penalties relating to butter and cheese. 13 & 14 C. 2. c 26

Weights and measures

29 They (or the overseers) shall levy the penalties relating to weights and measures. 16 C. c. 19. 22 C 2 c 8

Hawkers and pedlars,

30 They shall carry hawkers and pedlars trading without licence, before a justice of the peace. 9 & 10 W. c 27.

31 They

31 They shall provide chests wherein to lock up the arms, clothes, and accoutrements of the militia. 2 G 3. c 20 — *Militia.*

32 They, together with the minister, are to sign certificates for the out-pensioners of *Greenwich* hospital, residing within their parish, with respect to the identity of their persons, in order to the receiving of their pensions 3 G 3 c. 16. — *Greenwich hospital.*

33. They (or the overseers) shall pay to the high constables the general county rate, out of their money collected for the poor. 12 G 2 c 29. — *County rate.*

34 They shall receive the penalty for servants carelesly firing houses 6 An c 31 — *Servants firing houses*

35 They shall receive the penalties for tracing hares in the snow (and other game penalties) 1 J c 27 — *Tracing hares.*

36 They shall join with the constable and surveyor of the highways in chusing and returning new surveyors. 13 G 3. c 78 — *Surveyors of the highways*

VI. Of presentments, and therein concerning sidesmen or assistants.

1. Churchwardens by their oath are to present or certify to the bishop, or his officer, all things presentable by the ecclesiastical laws, which relate to the church, minister, and parishioners — *Oath to present.*

2 The articles delivered to them for their direction, are for the most part founded on the book of canons made in the year 1603, and the rubricks of the common prayer — *Book of articles.*

3 There are also several things which they are bound to present by act of parliament, as tipling or drunkenness, by the statute of 4 J c 5 recusants by 3 J c 4 — *Statute presentments*

4 They may present as often as they please, but shall not be obliged above once a year where it hath so been used, and not above twice any where, except it be at the bishop's visitation *Can* 116, 117 — *When to present*

5 For the presentments of any church or chapel for one year, the register shall have only 4d *Can.* 116. — *Fee for taking in presentments.*

6 The minister may present where the churchwardens neglect *Can* 113 But such presentment ought to be upon oath 2 *Vent* 42 — *Minister may present.*

7 In larger parishes, there are officers called sidesmen (antiently synodsmen, otherwise called questmen) to assist the churchwardens in their inquiries and presentment of offenders They shall be chosen yearly in *Easter* week by the minister and parishioners, if they can agree, if not, by the bishop *Can.* 90. — *Sidesmen.*

Z 4

8. The

Sidesman's oath

8 The sidesman's oath, said to have been agreed on by the civilians and common lawyers, is this

" You shall swear, that you will be assistant to the
" churchwardens in the execution of their office, so far
" as by law you are bound. So help you God." *Gibs.*
242

VII. Their accounting.

When to account.

1 At the end of the year, or within a month after at most, they shall before the minister and parishioners (at a vestry) give up a just account of such money as they have received, and also what they have particularly bestowed in reparations, and otherwise, for the use of the church, and shall deliver up to the parishioners the money and parish goods in their hands, to be delivered over by them to the next churchwardens by bill indented. *Can.* 89

How compelled to account.

2 And if they refuse, they may be presented at the next visitation by the new churchwardens, or any of the parish that are interested may by process call them to account before the ordinary, or the succeeding churchwardens may have a writ of account at common law. And if they have disbursed more than they have received, the succeeding churchwardens shall pay what is due to them, and account it among their disbursements. 1 *Roll's Abr.* 121

Accounting to a select vestry.

3. If the custom of the parish is, for a certain number of persons to have the government thereof, and the account is given up to them, the custom is a good custom, and the account given to them a good account. *Gibs.* 242

Vouchers.

4 Mr *Barlow* says, that for disbursements of any sum not above 40 s, their own oath is held sufficient proof, but for all sums above, receipts must be produced. *Barl.* 105 But it may be more satisfactory if receipts be produced for all.

Allowance of the account.

5 The allowance of the account may be by entring it in the church book of accounts, and having it signed by those in the vestry who allow the accounts. *Barl.* 105

Account allowed, final.

6. When they have faithfully accounted, and their account is allowed by the minister and major part of the parishioners present, it shall not afterwards be in the power of any to make them account again, unless some fraud in their accounts is afterwards discovered. *Wood, b* 1. *c* 7

E 7 G. 2 *Wainwright* and *Bagshaw.* The churchwardens were cited into the court of *Litchfield* to account. They pleaded, that they had accounted at the vestry according to law. Which plea was rejected, and thereupon a prohibition was granted: for the ordinary is not

to

to take the account, he can only give a judgment that they do account, and to what purpose should they be sent back, to those who have taken their accounts already. *Str.* 974, 1133.

VIII. *Their punishment on misbehaviour.*

1 If the churchwardens waste the goods of the church, the new churchwardens may call them to an account before the bishop, or bring their action at common law *Read Ch Service* — Churchwardens committing waste

2. And whereas many churchwardens and overseers, and other persons intrusted to receive collections for the poor, and other publick monies relating to the churches and parishes whereunto they belong, do often misspend the same, to the prejudice of such parishes, and of the poor and other inhabitants thereof, and the parishioners, who are the only persons sometimes who can make proof thereof, have not been allowed to be witnesses against them: is enacted, that in all actions to be brought in any court at *Westminster*, or at the assizes, for the recovery thereof, the evidence of the parishioners, other than such as receive alms, shall be taken and admitted. 3 *W. c.* 11. ſ 12. — Parishioners may be evidence against them.

3 But churchwardens are not answerable for indiscretion, but for deceit only, if they lay out more money than is needful. *Wood, b* 1. *c* 7 — Not answerable for indiscretion.

XI *Their indemnity on doing their duty.*

If any action be brought against any churchwardens, or persons called sworn men, executing the office of churchwarden, for any thing done by virtue of their office, they may plead the general issue, and give the special matter in evidence and if a verdict is given for them, or the plaintiff shall be nonsuit, or discontinue, they shall have double costs. 7 *J c.* 5. 21 *J c* 12. — Double costs.

In *Kerchival's* case, *M.* 8 *Car* An action was brought against the churchwardens for a presentment upon common fame of incontinency Upon not guilty, it was found for the churchwardens, and moved, that they might have double costs But it was resolved, that this being merely ecclesiastical, is not within this statute, for that the statute was never intended, but where they shall be vexed concerning temporal matters, which they shall do by virtue of their office, and not for presentments concerning matters of fame. *Cro Car* 285, 286

Clergy.

I Clergymen.
II Benefit of clergy,

I. Clergymen

Liable to the poor

1 BY the 43 *El c* 2 Clergymen are liable to the poor rates, for their glebe and tithe

And to the highways.

2 And Mr. *Hawkins* says, clergymen are within the purview of the statutes relating to the repair of highways, in respect of their spiritual possessions, as much as any other persons whatsoever in respect of any other possessions, for the words are general, and there is no kind of intimation therein that any particular persons shall be exempted more than others 1 *Haw* 204

And to other publick charges

3 And it seems to be now generally settled, that clergymen are liable to all publick charges imposed by act of parliament, where they are not specially excepted

Shall not farm.

4 No clergyman shall take to farm any lands (except he have not sufficient glebe for the expences of his houshold), on pain of 10 l a month, half to the king, and half to him that shall sue 21 *H* 8 *c* 13

Shall not buy to sell again.

5 No clergyman shall buy to sell again any cattle, corn, fish, wool, wood, victual, or any manner of merchandize, on pain of treble value, half to the king, and half to him that shall sue and the contract shall be void 21 *H* 8 *c* 13

Shall not keep a tanhouse or brewhouse

6 No clergyman shall keep any tanhouse, or any brewhouse but for his own house, on pain of 10 l a month, half to the king, and half to him that shall sue 21 *H* 8 *c* 13

May be imprisoned for incontinency

7 The ordinary may punish clergymen for incontinency, by committing them to ward or prison by his discretion 1 *H* 7 *c* 4

Privilege against an assault

8 A person laying violent hands on a clergyman, may be punished in the ecclesiastical court 13 *Ed* 1 *st* 4 2 *Inst* 492.

May have the benefit of clergy more than once

9 Clergymen in holy orders may have the benefit of clergy a second, or third time, or oftener 2 *H H* 374, 375

Shall not be burn in the hand

10 A clerk in holy orders shall not be burned in the hand, but shall have the same privilege as if he had been burned in the hand, and therefore shall not be drawn in question in the ecclesiastical court, to deprive him, or inflict any ecclesiastical censure upon him 2 *H. H.* 389

11. Io

11 To the intent that clergymen may the better dif- *Shall not ferve in temporal offices.*
charge their duty in celebration of divine fervice, and not
be intangled with temporal bufinefs, if any of them be
chofen to any temporal office, he may have his writ to be
difcharged 1 *Inft* 96

12 Ecclefiaftical perfons have this privilege, that they *Shall not ferve in war*
ought not in perfon to ferve in war 2 *Inft* 4

13 Ecclefiaftical perfons are not bound to appear at *Need not appear at the torn.*
the torn, or view of frankpledge 52 *H* 3 *c* 10. 9 *Ed* 2
c 3 2 *Inft* 4

14 No clergyman fhall be arrefted in any church or *Shall not be arrefted in the church.*
church yard, whilft he attends to divine fervice, on pain
of imprifonment of the offender, and ranfom at the king's
will, and gree to the party arrefted. 50 *Ed* 3. *c* 5.
1 *R* 2 *c* 15

\ But the arreft notwithftanding (if not on a Sunday) is
good in law. *Watfon, c* 34 *p* 344

15 The body of a clergyman may not be taken by *Shall not be taken on a ftatute ftaple*
force of any procefs upon a ftatute ftaple, or ftatute mer-
chant 2 *Inft* 4

16 If an action of trefpafs, debt, account, or other *Nor on a cap as.*
action wherein procefs of *capias* lies, be brought againft a
clerk in holy orders, and the fheriff return that he is a
clergyman beneficed, having no lay fee in which he may
be fummoned, in this cafe the plaintiff cannot have a *capias*
to arreft his body, but a writ to the bifhop to compel him
to appear. 2 *Inft* 4 *Degge* 157

17 If a perfon be bound in a recognizance in the chan- *Sheriff fhall not levy on his ecclefiaftical goods.*
cery, or in any other court, and he pay not the fum at the
day, by the common law, if the perfon had nothing but
ecclefiaftical goods, the recognizee could not have a *levari
facias* to the fheriff to levy the fame of thefe goods, but the
writ ought to be directed to the bifhop to levy the fame
of his ecclefiaftical goods 2 *Inft* 4

18 A clergyman fhall be amerced only according to his *Shall not be amerced of his fpiritual goods*
lay tenement, and not after the quantity of his fpiritual
benefice. *Mag Chart. c* 14 *Gibf* 15

19 Diftreffes fhall not be taken by fheriffs, or other of *Diftrefs not to be made on his fpiritual inheritance*
the king's minifters, in the inheritance of the church
wherewith it was anciently endowed, but otherwife it is of
late purchafe 9 *Ed* 2 *c* 9 2 *Inft* 4 *Gibf* 18

20 A clergyman is not bound to pay tolls or other like *Shall not pay toll of his fpiritual goods*
cuftoms, for his ecclefiaftical goods, and if he be mo-
lefted therefore, he may have a writ for his difcharge.
2 *Inft* 4 *Gibf* 21

And this not only for all the goods and merchandizes
of clergymen gotten upon their church livings, but alfo

for all goods and merchandizes by them bought, to be spent upon their rectories and church livings. *Degge* 153

21. Lord *Coke*, in his readings on the *Magna Charta*, says thus, " True it is, that ecclesiastical persons have " more and greater liberties than other of the king's sub " jects, wherein to set down all would take up a whole " volume of itself, and to set down no example agreeth " not with the office of an expositor, therefore some few " examples shall be expressed, and the studious reader " left to observe the rest as he shall read them in our " books, and other authorities of law." And the in stances he gives, are chiefly those which are mentioned above, nevertheless I do not find any author since his time, who hath said what are those other many and great privileges of the clergy, but the authors do generally ad here to these particular instances, probably as being sup ported by so great an authority. Other privileges have been abolished, since his time, by acts of parliament, and the adjudications of the temporal courts, and others per haps lost by disuse, and possibly some of the instances abovementioned would have been gone likewise, or not looked upon as of so much authority, if they had not been vouched by lord *Coke*.

II. Benefit of clergy.

I. Original of the benefit of clergy
II. By what persons it may be demanded.
III. In what cases it may be demanded.
IV. At what time it must be demanded.
V. Effect of clergy allowed.

I. Original of the benefit of clergy.

ANciently princes and states, converted to Christia- nity, in favour of the clergy, and for their encou- ragement in their offices and employments, and that they might not be so much intangled in suits, did grant to the clergy very bountiful privileges and exemptions, and par- ticularly, an exemption of their persons from criminal pro- ceedings, in some capital cases before secular judges, which was the true original of the benefit of clergy.

The clergy increasing in wealth, power, honour, num- ber, and interest, afterwards set up for themselves, and that which they obtained by the favour of princes and states at first, they now began to claim as their right, and a right of the highest nature, namely, by the law of God; and

and by their canons and conftitutions endeavoured, and in fome places obtained, vaft extenfions of thefe exemptions both with regard to the perfons concerned, to wit, not only to perfons in holy orders, but alfo to all that had any kind of fubordinate miniftration relative to the church, and likewife in refpect of the caufes, exempting as far as they could all caufes of clergymen, as well civil as criminal, from the jurifdiction of the fecular power, and wholly fubordinating them immediately and only to the ecclefiaftical jurifdiction, which they fuppofed to be lodged firft in the pope by divine right and inveftiture from Chrift, and from the pope fhed abroad into all fubordinate and eccle-fiaftical jurifdiction.

And by this means they endeavoured, and in fome kingdoms and for fome ages obtained, that there was a double fupreme power in every kingdom the one ecclefiaftical, abfolute, and independent upon any but the pope, over ecclefiaftical men and caufes, and the other fecular, of the king, or civil magiftrate

But this claim of exemption, altho' it obtained much in this kingdom, yet grew fo burdenfome, that it was from time to time qualified and abridged by the civil power, fometimes by acts of parliament t king it away in fome cafes, fometimes by the interpretation and conftruction of the judges, and fometimes by the contrary ufage of the kingdom for ecclefiaftical canons never bound in *England* farther than they were received, and fo had not their authority from their own ftrength and obligation, but from the ufages and cuftoms of the kingdom that admitted them, and only fo far forth as they were fo admitted.

And therefore if they were indicted in cafes criminal, but not capital, nor wherein they were to lofe life or limb, there the privilege of clergy was not allowed, and therefore not in indictments of trefpafs or petit larceny.

Alfo it was not allowed them in high treafon

But, at the common law, in all cafes of felony or petit treafon, clergy was allowable, excepting two, lying in wait, and burning of houfes, (which were looked upon as hoftile acts, and the authors of them therefore not intitled to the common privileges of fubjects) 2 *H. H* 323 -330

II. *By what perfons it may be demanded.*

1 By a favourable interpretation of the ftatutes relating to the benefit of clergy, not only thofe actually admitted into fome inferior order of the clergy, but alfo thofe who were

Who may demand it

Others befides clergymen.

were never qualified to be admitted into orders (which was formerly tried by putting them to read a verfe) have been taken to have a right to this privilege, as much as perfons in holy orders   2 *Haw* 338.

Women.

2 But by the common law, a woman could not have the benefit of clergy   but now by the ftatute of 3 *W c* 9 a woman convicted or outlawed for any felony, for which a man might have his clergy, fhall upon praying the benefit of that ftatute, be fubject only to fuch punifhment as a man would be in the like cafe.

Hereticks, Jews, Turks, perfons excommunicate

3 Lord *Hale* fays, A perfon convicted of herefy, a Jew, or a Turk, fhall not have their clergy, but a perfon excommunicate fhall have his clergy   2 *H H* 373.

But by the 5 *An c* 6 which abolifhed the ceremony of reading, the wall of partition (as Sir *Michael Fofler* expreffes it) between fubject and fubject under one and the fame degree of guilt, is taken away, which meafure intitled to the indulgence of the law, in common with the reft of their fellow fubjects, all thofe who before were fuppofed to be under a legal incapacity for orders as Jews, and fome others were, and likewife thofe who in prefumption of law were not qualified in point of learning, of which reading a fcrap of Latin (viz. *miferere mei Deus*) which they called the *neck verfe*, was commonly made the teft. And from this period, the meafure of punifhment hath been governed by the degrees of real guilt, and not by the function or abilities of the offender   *Fofl* 305, 6.

Perfons having had clergy once

4 By the 4 *H.* 7 *c.* 13   Every perfon (not being within orders) who hath once been admitted to his clergy, fhall not be admitted to the fame a fecond time

Burning in the hand

5 And if he is convicted of murder, he fhall be marked (unlefs he is a peer, 2 *H. H* 376) with an M, on the brawn of the left thumb, and if for any other felony, with a T. 4 *H* 7 *c* 13.

Burning not a conclufive proof of the conviction.

6 But he fhall not be oufted of his clergy, by the bare mark in his hand, or by a parol averment, without the record teftifying it, or a tranfcript thereof (according to the following ftatutes). 2 *H H* 373

And therefore the burning in the hand feemeth now to be of little ufe, and (as Sir *Michael Fofler* obferves) can fcarcely be called even fo much as a flight punifhment, but rather a piece of abfurd pageantry, tending neither to the reformation of the offender, nor for example to others, to wit, burning the offender in the hand with an iron fcarcely heated   *Fofl* 372

Conviction how to be certified

7. By 34 & 35 *H* 8 *c* 14   The clerk of the crown, or of the peace, or of affize, fhall certify a tranfcript briefly

briefly of the tenor of the indictment, outlawry, or conviction, and attainder, into the king's bench in 40 days And the clerk of the crown, when the judges of affize or justices of the peace write to him for the names of such persons, shall certify the same with the causes of the conviction or attainder

8 Another method is given by the 3 *W c* 9 which enacts, that the clerk of the crown, clerk of the peace, or clerk of affize, where a person admitted to clergy shall be convicted, shall at the request of the prosecutor, or any other on the king's behalf, certify a transcript briefly and in few words, containing the effect and tenor of the indictment and conviction, of his having the benefit of clergy, and the addition of the party, and the certainty of the felony and conviction, to the judges where such person shall be indicted for any subsequent offence *ſ* 7

9 Also it seems, that if the party deny that he is the same person, ſsue must be joined upon it, and it must be found upon trial that he is the same person, before he can be ousted of clergy 2 *H H* 373

How it may be otherwise certified.

How tried whether he is the same person

III In what cases it may be demanded.

1 By the 25 *Ed* 3 *ſ* 3 *c* 4 All manner of clerks, who shall be convicted before the secular judges, for any treasons or felonies, touching other persons than the king himself, shall have the privilege of the holy church

2 Clergy was never allowed in this nation in cases of high treason, nor is it allowed on indictments of petit larceny or trespass, but by the above recited act, clergy was allowed in all treasons and felonies, except treason against the king So that after this statute the benefit of clergy might be pleaded and allowed in all other treasons and felonies *Hale's Pl* 230   2 *H H* 326

3 Consequently, wherever clergy is not allowable in any other cases, it is taken away by some subsequent act of parliament *Hale's Pl* 230

4 Consequently, where a new felony is made by an act of parliament, clergy is to be allowed, unless expressly taken away by such statute *Hale's Pl* 230

And if it maketh a new felony, and takes away clergy not generally, but in such or such cases, regularly in other cases, clergy is allowable 2 *H H* 335

But if the statute enacts generally, that it shall be felony without benefit of clergy, or that he shall suffer as in case of felony without benefit of clergy, this excludes in all circumstances, and to all intents. 2 *H H* 335

Formerly allowed in all felonies.

But not in treason or petit larceny

Clergy taken away by statutes.

Allowed in new felonies, unless expressly taken away

5 It

Therefore where clergy is excluded, the indictment must bring the offence within the statute

5 It follows further from what hath been said, that in all cases where an act of parliament ousteth clergy, in case of any felony, the indictment must precisely bring the party within the case of the statute, otherwise, altho' possibly the fact itself be within the statute, and it may so appear upon the evidence, yet if it be not so alledged in the indictment, the party, tho' convict, shall have his clergy. 2 *H H.* 336

But altho' the case be so laid in the indictment, that it comes within the statute, to exempt the prisoner from clergy, yet if upon the evidence it fall out, that tho' it be a felony, yet it is not so qualified as laid in the indictment, the jury ought to find him guilty of the felony simply, but not as to the matter laid in the indictment, and thereupon the prisoner shall be admitted to his clergy, and this is commonly done. 2 *H H* 366.

Indictment on a statute which ousteth of clergy an offence which was felony at common law.

6 But if the offence was capital at the common law, and a statute only excludes it from clergy, the indictment, in such case need not conclude *against the form of the statute*, because the statute doth not alter the nature of the offence, but leaves it to its proper judgment, and only takes away a personal privilege of exemption from such judgment 2 *Haw* 342

Accessary.

7 Furthermore, from what hath been observed above, it follows, that where an act taketh away clergy from the principal, and saith nothing of the accessary, the accessaries, as well before as after, shall have their clergy, 11 *Co* 37. *Fost.* 355.

IV. At what time it must be demanded.

To be demanded after conviction

1 By the ancient common law, the benefit of clergy was demanded as soon as the prisoner was brought to the bar, before any indictment or other proceeding against him, but this was found a great inconvenience to the prisoner, because possibly he might have been acquitted of the felony, or if not, yet in case of an inquest of office, he lost his challenges to such inquest, and yet upon such inquest found, he forfeited his goods, and the profits of his lands, and therefore *Prisot* Ch. J with the advice of the other judges, in the reign of *H*. 6 for the safety of the innocent, would not allow the prisoner the benefit of clergy before he had pleaded to the felony, and (having the benefit of his challenges and other advantages) had been convicted thereof which course hath been generally observed ever since. 2 *Inst* 164 2 *H H* 378

May be allowed tho' not demanded

2 And this benefit of clergy may be allowed by the court in discretion, tho' the party challenge it not *Hal's Pl* 230.

V. *Effect of clergy allowed.*

1 Perfons admitted to their clergy, may be continued in prifon as a further punifhment, not exceeding one year 18 *El c* 7. Perfons having their clergy may be continued in gaol.

2 And by 4 *G c.* 11. Perfons convicted of offences within benefit of clergy (except receivers and buyers of ftolen goods) may, inftead of being whipped and burnt in the hand, be tranfported for feven years May be tranf-ported.

3 And by the 19 *G* 3. *c* 74 When any perfon fhall be convicted of any felony within the benefit of clergy, for which he fhall be liable to be burned in the hand, the court may, if they think fit, inftead thereof, impofe upon the offender a moderate pecuniary fine, or otherwife, inftead of fuch burning, in any of the cafes aforefaid, except manflaughter, may order the offender to be once or oftener, but not more than thrice, either publickly or privately whipped, fuch private whipping to be in the prefence of not lefs than two perfons, befides the offender and the officer who inflicts the fame, and in cafe of female offenders, in the prefence of females only *ſ* 3. May be fined or whipped.

Provided, that this fhall not extend to deprive the court of the power now vefted in them, of detaining fuch offender in prifon for any time not exceeding one year, or of committing him to the houfe of correction or other public workhoufe, to be kept to hard labour for any time not lefs than fix months, nor exceeding two years but fuch perfon, after fuch burning, or after fuch whipping or fine, may be fo detained or committed, and with fuch accumulated punifhment, in cafe of efcape from fuch houfe of correction or workhoufe, as if this act had not been made *ſ* 4

4 A perfon admitted to his clergy, forfeits all his goods that he hath at the time of the conviction 2 *H H* 388 Shall forfeit their goods.

5 But prefently upon his burning in the hand, he ought to be reftored to the poffeffion of his lands, and from thenceforth to enjoy the profits thereof 2 *H H* 388 But not lands.

6 Alfo, it reftores him to his credit, and confequently enables him to be a good witnefs 2 *Haw* 364 Credit reftored.

7. And it is holden that after a man is admitted to his clergy, it is actionable to call him felon, becaufe his offence being pardoned by the ftatute, all the infamy and other confequences of it are difcharged 2 *Haw* 365. Actionable to call him felon.

Clerk of the peace.

1 THE *custos rotulorum* shall appoint an able and sufficient person, residing in the county or division, to execute the office of clerk of the peace, by himself or his sufficient deputy (to be allowed of by the said *custos rotulorum*, 37 *H* 8 *c* 1), and to take and receive the fees, profits, and perquisites thereof, for so long time only as such clerk of the peace shall well demean himself in his said office 1 *W* c. 21. *f*. 5

Office not to be sold
2 But the *custos rotulorum* shall not sell the place of clerk of the peace, or take any bond or other assurance to receive any reward, fee, or profit, directly or indirectly, to him or to any other person for such appointment, on pain that such *custos rotulorum* selling, and such clerk of the peace buying, shall be disabled to hold their respective places, and shall each forfeit double value of the thing given, to him who shall sue. 1 *W* c. 21 *f* 8.

3 And every clerk of the peace, before he enters upon the execution of his office, shall in open sessions take the oath following

" I *A* B do swear, that I have not, nor will pay any
" sum or sums of money, or other reward whatsoever, nor
" given any bond or other assurance to pay any money,
" fee, or profit, directly or indirectly, to any person or
" persons whomsoever, for such nomination and appoint-
" ment So help me God." 1 *W*. c. 21 *f* 9

4 He shall moreover take the oaths of allegiance, supremacy, and abjuration, and perform the other requisites, as other persons who qualify for offices

Not to act as solicitor.
5 No clerk of the peace, or his deputy, shall act as solicitor, attorney, or agent, or sue out any process at any general or quarter sessions, where he shall execute the office of clerk of the peace or deputy, on pain of 50 *l*, to him who shall sue in twelve months, with treble costs. 22 *G* 2 *c* 46 *f* 14

Shall certify outlawries.
6 The clerk of the peace shall certify into the king's bench, the names of such as be outlawed, attainted, or convicted of felony 34 & 35 *H* 8. *c* 14

Shall deliver estreats to the sheriff.
7 He shall deliver to the sheriff, within twenty days after *Sept* 29, yearly, a perfect estreat or schedule of all fines, and other forfeitures in sessions 22 & 23 *C* 2. *c* 22 *f* 7

8 And

8 And shall also yearly, on or before the second *Mon-* Shall deliver estreats into the exchequer.
day after the morrow of All Souls, deliver into the court of
exchequer a perfect duplicate, certificate, and estreat of
all such estreats and schedules delivered to the sheriffs, on
pain of 50l, half to the king, and half to him that shall
sue 22 & 23 C 2 c. 22 ∫ 8 And moreover he may
be amerced for the same, by the barons of the exchequer
3 G c 15.

9 And he shall, upon delivery of the said estreats into Upon oath
the court of exchequer, take the following oath, to be
administred by one of the barons,

" You shall swear, that these estreats, now by you de-
" livered, are truly and carefully made up and examined,
" and that all fines, issues, amerciaments, recognizances,
" and forfeitures, which were set, lost, imposed, or for-
" feited, and in right and due course of law ought to be
" estreated in the court of exchequer, are, to the best of
" your knowledge and understanding, therein contained,
" and that in the same estreats are also contained and ex-
" pressed, all such fines as have been paid into the court,
" from which the said estreats are made, without any
" wilful or fraudulent discharge, omission, misnomer, or
' defect whatsoever " 4 & 5 W c 24 ∫ 5

10 And if he shall spare, take off, discharge, or con- Penalty of concealing fines.
ceal any such fine or forfeiture, unless it be by rule of
court, he shall forfeit treble value, half to the king, and
half to him that shall sue, and shall also forfeit his office,
and be incapable to be employed in any office where the
revenue is concerned 22 & 23 C 2 c 22 ∫ 9

11 The clerk of the peace is not bound to enter judg- Fees
ment, or the like, at the suit of any, without having the
fee due for the same, but if the court order any thing
without suit of another, to wit, *ex officio*, there he ought
to enter the same without having any fee for the entring
thereof *Crom* 159

Also Mr *Crompton* says, he shall have for every recognizance of the peace taken in court 2 s, and for every release of the peace there 2 s, and for process awarded
against any to find surety of the peace 2 s *Crom* 160

And by 10 & 11 W c 23 he shall have only 2 s for
drawing an indictment of felony ; and if it is defective he
shall draw a new one *gratis*, on pain of 5 l with full costs
to him that shall sue ∫. 7, 8

His fees also in divers other cases are specially limited by
act of parliament and it seemeth to be one of the *desiderata*

in

in the juſtices law, that the clerk of the peace's fees are not aſcertained in all inſtances, even as thoſe of the other clerks to juſtices of the peace by the ſtatute of the 26 G 2 c 14 And withal it might be requiſite to inſert in the table to be agreed on for that purpoſe, by whom the ſame ſhall be paid in the ſeveral inſtances reſpectively, and what ſhall be the courſe of recovering the ſame on non-payment

12 If any clerk of the peace ſhall miſdemean himſelf in the execution of his office, and thereupon a complaint and charge in writing of ſuch miſdemeanor ſhall be exhibited againſt him, to the juſtices in ſeſſions, the ſaid juſtices may, on examination and due proof thereof openly in the ſaid ſeſſions, ſuſpend or diſcharge him from the ſaid office, and in ſuch caſe, the *cuſtos rotulorum* ſhall appoint another able and ſufficient perſon, reſiding in the ſaid county or diviſion, to be clerk of the peace And in caſe of refuſal or neglect to make ſuch appointment, before the next general quarter ſeſſions, the juſtices in ſeſſions may appoint one. 1 *W* c 21 ſ 6

His duty in other matters is interſperſed where it falls in amongſt the other titles of this book

Appointment of a clerk of the peace, on the 37 *H* 8 c 1 and 1 *W* c. 21

FOraſmuch as the office of clerk of the peace for the county of —— is now void, by the death of —— gentleman, late clerk of the peace for the ſaid county, Know all men by theſe preſents, that I —— cuſtos rotulorum of the county aforeſaid, do hereby nominate, elect, appoint and aſſign C P gentleman, an able and ſufficient perſon, inſtructed and learned in the laws of England, and reſiding in the ſaid county, to be clerk of the peace for the ſaid county, to hold, execute, and enjoy the office of clerk of the peace for the county aforeſaid by himſelf or his ſufficient deputy, and to take and receive the fees, profits and perquiſites thereof, ſo long as he ſhall well, juſtly, and honeſtly demean himſelf in his ſaid office. In witneſs whereof I the ſaid —— have hereunto ſet my hand and ſeal, the —— day of —— in the —— year ——.

Clipping money See **Coin**
Clockmaking See **Servants.**
Cloth and Clothier See **Woollen Manufacture.**
Coaches and Chairs See **Excise** and **Hackney coaches.**

Coals

Coals.

BY the 30 C 2 ſ 1 c 8 and 6 & 7 W c 10 and 11 G 2. c 15. for the admeaſurement of keels, boats, waggons, wains, carts, and other carriages, uſed for the carrying of coals in the ports of *Newcaſtle*, *Sunderland*, and the other members of the port of *Newcaſtle*, and by the 15 G. 3 c 27 for extending the like regulations to the other ports of this kingdom If, after the admeaſurement thereof by the commiſſioners appointed for that purpoſe, the marks ſhall be removed or altered, every perſon who had a hand in or was privy to the doing thereof, ſhall, on conviction upon the oath of one witneſs before one juſtice, forfeit 10 l by diſtreſs, half to the king and half to the diſcoverer, and for want of diſtreſs, ſhall be committed to the common gaol for three months

Concerning the weights, meaſures, and prices of coals, eſpecially in and about *London*, and alſo concerning the duties thereupon, there are regulations made by above forty different acts of parliament, which, not being of general concern, are here omitted

For the deſtroying of coal works   See Mines
Cocoa nuts   See Exciſe.
Coffee   See Exciſe.

Coin.

For matters common to this with other treaſons, ſee title Treaſon.

COIN, in French, ſignifieth a corner, and from thence hath its name (according to Lord *Coke*) Le- *Original of he word* cauſe in antient times money was ſquare, with corners, as it is in ſome countries to this day   1 Inſt 207

Others derive this word, which in the old *French* is written *coign*, as alſo the Italian *cuno*, and the Spaniſh *cuno*, from the Greek word κοινω, *communis*, becauſe money is the common mean or inſtrument of traffick

But theſe derivations ſeem too artificial   The word doth properly ſignify a wedge, as the Latin *cuneus*, and hath a verb belonging to it in the ſeveral languages   and is tranſlated to lawful money, either from the form of a wedge, ingot, or lingot (*linguetta*) in which bullion was tranſported from all antiquity, or elſe from the inſtrument, a

A a 3   wedge

weage or chisfel, with which, in trade, thefe lingots were occafionally cut to the weight required, as they are at this day in the *Eaſt Inues*, with sheers

Weights for coin. 2 No other weight, than fuch as fhall be ftamped or marked by the officer appointed by his majefty for that purpofe, fhall be fufficient in law for determining the weight of the gold and filver coin And if any perfon fhall counterfeit fuch ftamp or mark, or krowingly fell any weight with the impreffion of fuch counterfeit ftamp thereon, or fhall wilfully increafe or diminifh any fuch weight after it has been fo ftamped or marked, or ufe any fuch weight in weighing the gold and filver coin of this realm, knowing the fame to be fo increafed or diminifhed he fhall, on conviction before two juftices, forfeit any fum not exceeding 50 l, half to the king, and half to him that fhall inform or fue, and in default of payment, he fhall be committed to the common gaol or houfe of correction for any time not exceeding three months 14 G. 3 c. 92

Determining the value of coin. 3. The legitimation of money, and the giving it its denominated value, is one fpecial part of the king's pre rogative 1 H H 188

But in order to fix the value, the weight and finenefs of the metal are to be taken into confideration When a given weight of gold and filver is of a given finenefs, it is then of the true ftandard, and called Sterling metal, and of this fterling metal all the coin of the kingdom muft be made by the ftatute of the 25 *Ed.* 3 ſt 5 c. 13. So that the king's prerogative feemeth not to extend to the de- bafing or enhancing the value of the coin below or above the fterling value 1 *Blackſt* 278

Legitimating foreign coin 4 And the king may by his proclamation legitimate foreign coin, and make it current money of this kingdom, according to the value impofed by fuch proclamation 1 H. H 192.

And therefore both *Engliſh* money, coined by the king's authority, and foreign coin made current by proclamation, are within the denomination of lawful money of *England* 1 Inſt 207

But of this latter fort there is none at prefent in *England*, *Portugal* money being only taken by confent, as approach- ing neareft to our ftandard, and falling in tolerably well with our divifions of money into pounds and fhillings, but no perfon is obliged to take it 4 *Blackſt* 89

Copper coin 5 And only gold or filver coin, and not brafs or cop- per, are within this denomination 1 *Haw* 42

And no perfon can be inforced to take in payment any money but of lawful metal, that is of filver or gold 2 *Inſt* 577 Except for fums under fixpence. 1 H H 195

4

6 By

6 By the ftatute of 25 *Ed* 3 *ft* 5 *c* 2 it is made trea- Counterfeiting the coin of this realm.
ion to counterfeit the coin of this realm   That is to fay, whether the perfon utter it or not 3 *Inft* 16   1 *Haw* 42

7 And if any perfon fhall falfely forge and counterfeit Counterfeiting foreign current coin
any fuch kind of coin of gold or filver, as is not the pro-per coin of this realm, and fhall be current therein by the king's confent   he, his counfellors, procurers, aiders and abettors fhall be guilty of high treafon. 1 *Mar.* *feff* 2 *c.* 6

8 By the 5 *El* *c* 11   Clipping, wafhing, rounding, Clipping, wafh-ing, filing.
or filing, for lucre or gain, any the proper coin of this realm, or the dominions thereof, or of any other realm current within this realm by proclamation, fhall be ad-judged treafon in the offenders, their counfellors, con-fenters and aiders

9. And by the 18 *El. c.* 1   If any perfon fh ll, for Impairing, diminifhing, falfifying
lucre or gain, by any art, ways, or means, impair, di-minifh, falfify, fcale, or lighten the proper coin of this realm, or any the dominions thereof, or the coin of this realm allowed to be current (at the time of the offence committed) by the king's proclamation, he, his counfel-lors, confenters, and aiders fhall be guilty of treafon.

10 And if any perfon (not employed in the mint) Edging
fhall mark on the edges any the current coin of this king-dom, or, if any perfon whatfoever fhall mark on the edges any of the diminifhed coin of this kingdom, or any coun-terfeit coin refembling the coin of this kingdom, with let-ters or grainings, or other marks or figures like unto thofe on the edges of money coined in the mint, he, his coun-fellers, procurers, aiders, and abettors fhall be guilty of high treafon 8 & 9 *W. c.* 26. *f* 3   Profecution to be in fix months   1 *An. ft* 1 *c* 9

11. Alfo, if any perfon fhall colour, gild, or cafe over Colouring
with gold or filver, or with any wafh or materials pro-ducing the colour of gold or filver, any coin refembling any the current coin of this kingdom, or any round blanks of bafe metal, or of coarfe gold or coarfe filver, of a fit fize and figure to be coined into counterfeit milled money, refembling any the gold or filver coin of this kingdom, or if any perfon fhall gild over any filver blanks of a fit fize and figure to be coined into pieces refembling the current gold coin of this kingdom, he, his counfellors, procurers, aiders, and abettors fhall be guilty of high treafon 8 & 9 *W. c.* 26 *f* 4   Profecution to be in three months *f.* 9

And by the 15 & 16 *G* 2 *c* 28. If any perfon fhall wafh, gild, or colour any lawful or counterfeit filver coin called a fhilling or fixpence, or add to or alter the impreffion, or any part thereof, on either fide, with intent to make fuch fhilling or fixpence refemble a guinea or half guinea, or fhall any way alter or colour halfpennies or farthings, with intent to make them refemble a fhilling or fixpence he, his counfellors, aiders, and abettors fhall be guilty of high treafon Profecution to be in fix months

Counterfeiting halfpence and farthings.

12 Lord *Hale*, fpeaking of copper halfpence and farthings, makes it a quæry, whether the counterfeiting of them be not treafon within the ftatute of 25 *Ed* 3 but inclines to the negative. 1*H. H* 195, 211, 212

And with this agrees the fenfe of the legiflature, in the ftatute of 15 & 16 *G* 2 *c* 28 which reciting that whereas the counterfeiting of the copper coin of this kingdom is only a mifdemeanor, and the punifhment often very fmall, therefore enacteth, that if any perfon fhall coin or counterfeit brafs or copper halfpence or farthings, he, his counfellors, aiders, and abettors, fhall fuffer two years imprifonment, and find fureties for their good behaviour for two years more   *s* 6

And further, by the 11 *G* 3 *c* 40 If any perfon fhall make, coin, or counterfeit any of the copper monies of this realm, commonly called an halfpenny or farthing, or fhall buy, fell, take, receive, pay, or put off any counterfeit copper money, not melted down or cut in pieces, at or for a lower rate or value than by its denomination it doth import or was counterfeited for, he fhall be guilty of felony [but within clergy] And one juftice, on complaint upon oath that there is juft caufe to fufpect, that any perfon hath been concerned in counterfeiting the copper monies of this realm, may by his warrant caufe the dwelling houfe, room, workfhop, out-houfe, yard, garden, or other place, belonging to fuch fufpected perfon, to be fearched for tools and implements for coining fuch copper monies And if any fuch tools or implements fhall at any time be found hid or concealed in any place fo fearched, or be found in the cuftody of any perfon whatfoever not employed in his majefty's mint, nor having the fame by fome lawful authority, it fhall be lawful for any perfon whatfoever difcovering the fame, to feize fuch tools or implements, and carry the fame forthwith to a juftice, who fhall caufe the fame to be fecured and produced in evidence againft any perfon who fhall be profecuted for any the offences aforefaid in fome court proper for the determination thereof, and after they fhall have been produced in evidence, as well the fame fo produced, as the other fo feized and not produced in evidence, fhall forthwith by order of the court, or by order of a juftice if there fhall

be

be no trial, be defaced and destroyed, or otherwise disposed of as such court or justice shall direct

Counterfeiting coin no current,

13 If any person shall falsely forge or counterfeit any such kind of coin of gold or silver, as is not the proper coin of this realm, nor permitted to be current within this realm, he, his procurers, aiders, and abettors shall be guilty of misprision of high treason 14 El c. 3

Bringing in false money,

14 If any person shall bring false money into the realm, counterfeit to the money of *England*, knowing the same to be false, to merchandise or make payment, in deceit of the king and his people, he shall be guilty of high treason. 25 Ed 3 st 5 c 2.

Also, if any person shall bring from the parts beyond the sea, any forged and counterfeit money like to the gold or silver coin of foreign realms, current in payment within the king's realm by the king's sufferance and consent, knowing the same to be false and counterfeit, to the intent to utter or make payment of the same within this realm, by merchandizing or otherwise, he, his counsellors, procurers, aiders, and abettors shall be guilty of high treason. 1 & 2 P & M c 11 s 2

Note, This must be brought from a foreign nation, and not from *Ireland*, or other place subject to the crown of *England*, because the counterfeiting there, is punishable by the laws of our king, is much as in *England* 1 Haw 43

Sir *Michael Foster* observing upon these offences (and of the offence above mentioned, of counterfeiting foreign current coin) says, prosecutions for importing money counterfeit to the similitude of *English* coin have been very rare, and for the offences of counterfeiting foreign coin legitimated by proclamation, and of importing such coin, there can be none, as things stand at present, till the crown shall be advised to legitimate some species of foreign coin I know of none (says he) now current among us that is legitimated, and most probably none will For if the offences of counterfeiting and diminishing foreign coin, and of importing such counterfeit and diminished coin, which are great evils and daily growing, were made more penal than they are at present, he says he knows of no good end that could be answered by legitimating any species of it, on the other hand, there seem to be great inconveniences that would attend it Fost 227

Bringing in light money.

15 By the 14 G 3 c 42 (which by the 16 G 3 c 45 hath continuance to *May* 1, 1783, &c) all silver coin of this realm, or purporting so to be, which is not of the established standard of the mint in weight and fineness,

nefs, tnat is, of 62 fhillings to a pound troy, and 11 ounce, and 2 penny weights of fine filver, and 18 penny weights of alloy in the pound troy, fhall be prohibited to be imported, and if any quantity thereof exceeding 5 *l* fhall be found by any officer of the cuftoms, the fame fhall be forfeited, and profecuted in any court of record at *Weft-minfter*, or if it do not amount in value to 20*l*, the fame may be profecuted in a fummary way before two juftices where the feizure fhall be made, at the election of the commiffioners of the cuftoms And after condemnation, the fame fhall be melted down or otherwife defaced, and fhall be half to the king and half to the officer who fhall profecute

And no tender in the payment of money in filver coin of any fum above 25 *l*, at any one time, fhall be allowed to be legal, for more than according to its value by weight, after the rate of 5 s 2 d an ounce

Coining prefs and tools. 16. If any prefs for coinage, fhall be found in the cuftody of any perfon (other than the officers of the mint), it fhall be feized for the king's ufe, and every perfon in whofe cuftody fuch prefs fhall be found, fhall forfeit 500 *l*, half to the king, and half to the informer. 7 & 8 *W*. *c* 19 *f* 4

And by 8 & 9 *W c* 26 No perfon, unlefs employed in the mint, fhall knowingly make or mend, or begin or proceed to make or mend, or affift in the making or mending of any puncheon, counter-puncheon, matrix, ftamp, dye, pattern or mould, of fteel, iron, filver, or other metal, or of fpaud, or fine founders earth, or fand, or of any other materials whatfoever, in or upon which there fhall be, or be made or impreffed, or which will make or imprefs the figure, ftamp, or refemblance of both or either of the fides or flats of any gold or filver coin, current within this kingdom, nor fhall knowingly make or mend, or begin or proceed to make or mend, or affift in the making or mending of any edger or edging tool, inftrument, or engine, not of common ufe in any trade, but contrived for making of money round the edges with letters, grainings, or other marks or figures refembling thofe on the edges of money coined in the mint, nor any prefs for coinage, nor any cutting engine for cutting round blanks by force of a fhrew, out of flatted bars of gold, filver, or other metal, nor fhall knowingly buy or fell, hide or conceal, or without lawful authority or fufficient excufe for that purpofe, knowingly have in his houfe, cuftody, or poffeffion, any fuch puncheon, counter-puncheon, matrix, ftamp, dye, edger, cutting engine, or other tool or inftrument before mentioned, on pain that fuch perfon, his counfellors, procurers, aiders, and abettors, fhall be guilty of high treafon ∫ 1   Profecution to be in three months ∫ 9   But by the 1 *An fl* 1 c 9 ∫ 2   The profecution for offences by making or mending, or beginning or proceeding to make or mend any coining tool or inftrument in the abovefaid act prohibited, or by marking of money round the edges with letters or grainings, may be commenced at any time within fix months

And if any perfon fhall, without lawful authority, knowingly convey, or affift in conveying out of the mint, any puncheon, counter-puncheon, matrix, dye, ftamp, edger, prefs or other tool, engine, or inftrument ufed for or about the coining of monies there, or any ufeful part of fuch tool or inftrument, he, his counfellors, procurers, aiders, or abettors, fhall be guilty of high treafon 8 & 9 *W.* c 26 ∫ 2   Profecution to be in three months   ∫ 9

And if any puncheon, dye, ftamp, edger, cutting engine, prefs, flafk, or other tool, inftrument, or engine, ufed or defigned for coining or counterfeiting gold or filver monies, or any part of fuch tool or engine, fhall be hid or concealed in any place, or found in the houfe, cuftody, or poffeffion of any perfon not employed in the mint, nor having the fame by fome lawful authority, any perfon whatfoever difcovering the fame, may and fhall feize the fame, and carry them forthwith to fome juftice of the peace to be by him fecured, to be produced in evidence, againft any perfon who fhall be profecuted for any fuch offence   And after they have been produced in evidence, they fhall forthwith by order of the court (or by order and in the prefence of a juftice of the peace, if there hath been no trial) be totally defaced and deftroyed   8 & 9 *W.* c. 26 ∫ 5

17. For the better preventing the clipping, diminifhing, Selling of clippings. or impairing the current coin, if any perfon fhall buy or fell, and knowingly have in his cuftody or poffeffion, any clippings or filings of the current coin of this kingdom, he fhall forfeit the fame, and alfo 500 l, half to the king, and half to the informer, and fhall be branded in the right cheek with the letter R, and be imprifoned till the payment of the 500 l.   6 & 7 *IV.* c 17. ∫ 4

18 And if any fhall caft ingots or bars of filver, in Bullion. imitation of *Spanifh* bars or ingots, or ftamp them in likenefs of the *Spanifh* ftamp, he fhall forfeit the fame, and alfo 500 l, half to the king, and half to the informer 6 & 7 *IV.* c 17 ∫ 3

And if any broker, not being a trading goldfmith or refiner of filver, fhall buy or fell any bullion or molten filver, he fhall be imprifoned fix months   ∫ 7

And

And the warden of the company of goldsmiths, with two of the court of assistants within the bills, and two justices elsewhere, may enter into the house, room, or workshop of any person suspected, and with the help of a constable may break open any door, box, trunk, chest, cupboard, or cabinet, to search for bullion suspected to be concealed, and if found, they shall seize the same, and the person in whose possession it shall be found. And the said wardens, assistants, and constables, within the bills, shall carry him before the next justice, which justice, and the said two justices elsewhere, may examine him, and if he shall not prove by the oath of himself, or of a credible witness, that it is lawful silver, and was not current coin, nor clippings thereof, he shall be committed, and if on his trial he shall not prove the same by one witness, he shall be imprisoned six months *f* 8

And no person shall ship any molten silver or bullion, without certificate from the court of the lord mayor and aldermen of *London*, and oath made before them by the owner and two witnesses, that it is foreign bullion, and that no part of it was the coin of this realm, or clippings thereof, nor plate wrought within this kingdom, on pain that the same shall be forfeited, half to the king, and half to the officer or other person who shall seize the same. And the owner shall forfeit double the value thereof, half to the king, and half (with costs) to him that shall sue. And the captain or master of a ship (if it belong to a subject) permitting the same, shall forfeit 200 l, to him who shall sue, and if it is a king's ship, he shall moreover forfeit his employment. And if any officer of the customs shall grant a cocquet for exporting the same, before such certificate and entry thereof made, he shall forfeit 200 l and his office. And in case of seizure of such bullion, or action brought for the forfeitures, the proof shall lie upon the owner, and for want of proof it shall be forfeited *f* 8 *W. c* 19 *f* 6, 7, 8, 9.

And if any bullion is entered to be exported, other than in the name of the true owner or importer, the exporter shall forfeit the same, or the value thereof, half to the king, and half to him who shall seize or discover the same 6 *& 7 W. c* 17 *f* 14.

Blanched copper and other base metal

19 And whereas several mixtures of metals have been invented in imitation of gold and silver, and blanched copper is principally made use of in imitation of silver, and seldom, if ever, for any honest or good purpose, it is enacted, that if any person shall blanch copper for sale, or mix blanched copper with silver, or knowingly buy, or sell or

offer to fale blanched copper alone, or mixed with filver; or fhall knowingly and fraudulently buy or fell or offer to fale any malleable compofition or mixture of metals or minerals, which fhall be heavier than filver, and look, and touch, and wear like ftandard gold, but be manifeftly worfe than ftandard, he fhall be guilty of felony, and fhall fuffer death as in cafe of felony. Profecution to be in three months. 8 & 9 *W* c 26 f 6, 9

20 If any perfon fhall take, receive, pay, or put off **Paying coin under value.** any counterfeit milled money, or any milled money whatfoever unlawfully diminifhed, and not cut in pieces, at or for a lower rate or value than the fame by its denomination doth or fhall import, or was coined or counterfeited for, he fhall be guilty of felony, and fuffer death as in cafe of felony. Profecution to be in three months. 8 & 9 *W* c 26 f 6, 9

21 If one perfon counterfeits, and by agreement before **Uttering falfe money** the counterfeiting, another perfon is to take off and vent the counterfeit money, fuch other is an aider and abettor, and confequently a principal traitor (for in high treafon there are no acceffaries). 1 *H H* 214

If one perfon counterfeits, and another (knowing that he did fo) puts it off, but without any fuch previous agreement, fuch other perfon feems to be all one with a receiver of him, becaufe he maintains him. 1 *H H* 214.

If one perfon counterfeits, and another perfon knows that he did fo, and doth neither receive, maintain, or abet him, but conceals his knowledge, this is mifprifion of treafon. 1 *H. H.* 214.

But, formerly, where it did appear, that the utterer of counterfeit money knew who counterfeited it, but barely uttered it for his own benefit, although he knew it was counterfeit, yet it was only a cheat and mifdemeanor, punifhable by fine and imprifonment (contrary to the opinion in *Stanford* and *Dalton*), but now by the ftatute of 15 G. 2. c. 28 it is enacted, that whereas the uttering falfe money is a crime frequently committed all over the kingdom, and the offenders are not deterred, becaufe it is only a mifdemeanour, and the punifhment generally fmall, tho' there is reafon to believe that the utterers are often the coiners, or in confederacy with them, therefore, if any perfon fhall tender in payment any counterfeit coin, knowing it to be fo, he fhall for the firft offence fuffer fix months imprifonment, and find fureties for his good behaviour for fix months longer, for the fecond offence, fhall fuffer two years imprifonment, and find fureties for two years more, and for the third offence, fhall be guilty of felony without benefit of clergy. f 2

And

And if any perfon fhall tender in payment an, coun terfeit money (knowing it to be fo), and fhall either the fame day, or within ten days after, knowingly tender other falfe money in payment, or at the time of fuch tendring have more in his cuftody, he fhall for the firft offence fuffer a year's imprifonment, and find fureties for his good behaviour for two years more, and for the fecond offence, fhall be guilty of felony without benefit of clergy ∫ 3

Perfons guilty of the faid crimes fhall be tried and con victed in fuch manner as is ufed againft offenders for coun terfeiting the coin and the clerk of affize, or clerk of the peace, where the firft conviction was had, fhall certify the fame by a tranfcript in few words, containing the tenor of fuch conviction (for which he fhall have 2 s 6 d), and fuch certificate being produced in court, fhall be fufficient proof of the former conviction. Profecution to be in fix months ∫. 5, 9

Note, By this it fhould feem, that the juftices of the peace in feffions have power to try fuch offenders, other-wife this direction to the clerk of the peace to certify the conviction is incongruous, for he is not the proper perfon to certify what is done in another court, where he is not neceffarily fuppofed to be prefent albeit no power is given to the feffions by any exprefs words in this ftatute to hear and determine fuch offences

By the ftatute 9 G 3. c 37. If any churchwarden or overfeer of the poor, (or perfon authorized by him, fhall make any payments to the poor in any bafe or counterfeit money, one juftice, on complaint, may fummon the of fender, and on his non-appearance, or confeffion, or proof of the offence by the oath of one witnefs, may adjudge him to forfeit not lefs than 10 s, nor more than 20 s, to be le-vied by diftrefs, and to be applied to the ufe of any poor perfon or perfons of the parifh or place refpectively as the juftice fhall appoint. ∫. 7.

Having falfe money in poffef-fion

22 If falfe or clipt money be found in a man's hands, if he be fufpicious, he may be arrefted till he have found his warrant. 3 *Inft* 18. *Hale's Pl.* 21. 1 *Haw* 43

Falfe money what to be done with.

23. Any perfon to whom any *filver* money fhall be ten dred, any piece whereof fhall be diminifhed, otherwife than by reafonable wearing, or that by the ftamp, impref-fion, colour, or weight thereof, he fhall fufpect to be coun terfeit, may cut, break, or deface fuch piece and if any piece fo cut, broken, or defaced fhall appear to be a coun-terfeit, the perfon tendring the fame fhall bear the lofs thereof, but if the fame fhall be of due weight, and ap pear to be lawful money, the perfon that cut, broke, or

defaced

defaced the fame, fhall receive the fame at the rate it was coined for And if any queftion arife, whether the piece fo cut be counterfeit, it fhall be determined by the next juftice of the peace, or chief magiftrate in a corporation 9 & 10 *W* c 21 f 1

And if any perfon to whom any *gold* money fhall be tendred, any piece or pieces whereof fhall be diminifhed otherwife than by reafonable wearing, or that by the ftamp, impreffion, colour, or weight thereof, he fhall fufpect to be counterfeit, may cut, break, or deface fuch piece or pieces And if any piece fo cut, broken, or defaced fhall appear to be diminifhed otherwife than by reafonable wearing, or counterfeit, the perfon tendring the fame fhall bear the lofs thereof But if the fame fhall be of due weight, and appear to be lawful money, the perfon that cut, broke, or defaced the fame, fhall receive the fame at the rate it was coined for And if any queftion fhall arife, whether the piece fo cut be counterfeit or diminifhed in manner aforefaid, it fhall be determined by the mayor or other head officer in a corporation, and elfewhere by one juftice inhabiting near where the tender was made. 13 *G* 3 c 71

And if any counterfeit or unlawfully diminifhed money fhall be produced in any court of juftice, either in evidence or otherwife, the judge fhall caufe it to be cut in pieces in open court, or in the prefence of a juftice of the peace, and then to be delivered to or for the perfon to whom it belongs 8 & 9 *W* c 26 f 5.

24 By the 3 *Ed* 1. c 15 Perfons taken for falfe money are not bailable by juftices of the peace **Bail.**

But they muft take the examinations and informations, and bind over the witneffes to the proper court, and commit the perfons accufed. 1 *H H.* 372

25 It is not neceffary there fhould be two witneffes in **Evidence.** cafes of counterfeiting the coin, as it is in other high treafons; but perfons may be convicted according to the courfe of the common law, by one witnefs only 1 *H H* 318, 328

26 The judgment for high treafon, relating to the **Judgment.** coin, is, to be drawn to the place of execution, and there hanged by the neck till he be dead 2 *Haw* 444.

But it is generally provided by the feveral ftatutes, that this fhall work no corruption of blood, nor lofs of dower.

27 Every perfon who fhall apprehend any perfon who **Reward for convicting an offender.** hath counterfeited any of the current [gold or filver] coin of this realm, or that for lucre or gain hath clipped, wafhed, filed, or any way diminifhed the fame, or hath altered

fhillings

shillings and sixpences to make them resemble guineas and half guineas, or halfpennies and farthings to make them look like shillings and sixpences, or shall bring or cause to be brought into this kingdom, any clipt, false, or counterfeit coin, and prosecute such person to conviction every such person shall have a reward of 40 l In order to which, the judge shall give him under his hand, a certificate certifying the conviction, and the county in which it was made, and that the offender was taken and prosecuted by such person, and if any dispute shall arise between several persons apprehending and prosecuting, the judge shall in the certificate appoint the reward to be paid amongst them, in such proportion as he shall think reasonable The said certificate to be tendred to the sheriff, who shall thereupon pay the same without fee, within one month after such tender and demand, on pain of forfeiting to the party double the sum, with treble costs The sheriff to be repaid out of the treasury. 6 & 7 W. c 17. ſ 9, 10, 11 15 & 16 G 2 c 28. ſ. 7.

In like manner a reward of 10 l shall be paid, for apprehending and convicting a counterfeiter of the copper money 15 & 16 G 2 c 28. ſ 7

Pardon to accomplices informing.

28 If any person being out of prison, shall be guilty of clipping, coining, counterfeiting, washing, filing, or otherwise diminishing the [gold or silver] coin of this realm, and afterwards discover two or more persons who have committed any of the said crimes, so as two or more be convicted, he shall have the king's pardon, and if he is an apprentice, he shall be made a freeman 6 & 7 W c 17 ſ 12

In this clause at large in the statute, is an instance of that multiplicity of words, which is sometimes ridiculed in our laws, where it is said, *two or more person or persons,* and again, *two or more of the person or persons*

Further, if any person being out of prison, shall be guilty of altering sixpences or shillings, to make them look like half guineas or guineas, or altering farthings or halfpennies, to make them look like sixpences or shillings, or of counterfeiting birts or copper halfpennies or farthings, or of uttering false money, —— and afterwards discover two or more persons who have committed any of the said crimes, so as two be convicted, he shall have the king's pardon 15 & 16 G 2 c 28 ſ 8

Charges of prosecuting.

29 The commissioners of the treasury may issue a sum not exceeding 600 l yearly, for the charges and expences of the officers and others employed in the prosecution of offences in counterfeiting, diminishing, or otherwise concurring

concurring

cerning the current coin of this realm 7 *Ann. c* 24.
f 4 15 & 16 G 2. *c.* 28. f 10

Commitment.

ANciently there were more felons committed to gaol without mittimus in writing, than were with it such were all the commitments by constables, watchmen, and private persons arresting for felony, and bringing to the common gaol, long before there were any justices of the peace, and yet mittimus's are not of so ancient date even as they 1 *H H* 610

But now, since the *habeas corp is* act, a commitment in writing seems more necessary than it was in former times, otherwise the prisoner may be admitted to bail upon that act, whatsoever his offence may have been

When a statute appoints imprisonment, but limits no time when, it is to be understood that he shall be imprisoned presently *Dalt c* 170

Concerning which I will set forth,

I *Who may be committed.*
II *To what place.*
III *The form of the commitment.*
Iv *Charges of the commitment.*
V *That the goaler shall receive the prisoner.*
VI *Shall certify the commitment.*
VII *Commitment discharged*

I *Who may be committed.*

1 There is no doubt but that persons apprehended for offences which are not bailable, and also all persons who neglect to offer bail for offences which are bailable, must be committed 2 *Haw* 116

2 And it is said, that wheresoever a justice is impowered by any statute to bind a person over, or to cause him to do a certain thing, and such person being in his presence shall refuse to be bound, or to do such thing, the justice may commit him to the gaol, to remain there till he shall comply 2 *Haw* 116

3 If a prisoner be brought before a justice, expressly charged with felony upon oath, the justice cannot discharge him, but must bail or commit him 2 *H H* 121

Persons charg'd on suspicion

4 But if he be charged with suspicion only of felony, yet if there be no felony at all proved to be committed, or if the fact charged as a felony be in truth no felony in point of law, the justice may discharge him, as if a man be charged with felony for stealing a parcel of the freehold, or for carrying away what was delivered to him, and such like, for which tho' there may be cause to bind him over as for a trespass, the justice may discharge him as to felony, because it is not felony. But if a man be killed by another, tho' it be by misadventure, or self defence, (which is not properly felony), or in making an assault upon a minister of justice in execution of his office (which is not at all felony), yet the justice ought not to discharge him, for he must undergo his trial for it, and therefore he must be committed, or at least bailed 2 *H. H* 121

Persons not paying their fine

5 But commitment by the justices of the peace almost in all cases (except for the peace, good behaviour, felony, or higher offences) is but to retain the party till he hath made fine to the king, and therefore if he offer to pay it, or find sureties by recognizance to pay it, he ought not to be committed, but to be delivered presently *Dalt c* 170

II To what place

To the gaol

1 By the 5 *H* 4 *c* 10 All felons shall be committed to the common gaol, and not elsewhere

House of correction

2 But by the 6 *G c* 19 Vagrants and other criminals, offenders, and persons charged with small offences, may for such offences, or for want of sureties, be committed either to the common gaol, or house of correction, as the justices in their judgment shall think proper.

Stocks

3 And they may commit other offenders to the stocks, or other custody, by particular statutes

Different county

4 Generally, if a man commit felony in one county, and be arrested for the same in another county, he shall be committed to gaol in that county where he is taken *Dalt c* 170

Yet if he escapes, and is taken on fresh suit, in another county, he may be carried back to the county where he was first taken *Dalt c.* 170

Also by the 24 *G* 2 *c* 55 If a person is apprehended, upon a warrant indorsed, in another county, for an offence not bailable, or if he shall not there find bail, he shall be carried back into the first county, and be committed (or if bailable, bailed) by the justices in such first county.

III Form

III. Form of the commitment.

1 It muſt be in writing, either in the name of the In whoſe name,
king, and only teſted by the perſon who makes it, or it
may be made by ſuch perſon in his own name, expreſſing
his office, or authority, and muſt be directed to the gaoler,
or keeper of the priſon. 2 *Haw* 119

Yet the mention of the name and authority of the juſtice (lord *Hal.* ſays) in the beginning of the mittimus, is
not always neceſſary, for the ſeal and ſubſcription of the
juſtice to the mittimus, is ſufficient warrant to the gaoler,
for it may be ſupplied by averment, that it was done by
the juſtice 2 *H H* 122

2 It ſhould contain the name and ſurname of the party The party's
committed, if known, if not known, then it may be name.
ſufficient to deſcribe the perſon by his age, ſtature, com-
plexion, colour of his hair, and the like, and to add that
he refuſeth to tell his name 1 *H H* 577

3 It is ſafe, but not neceſſary, to ſet forth, that the Oath
party is charged upon oath 2 *Haw* 120

4 It ought to contain the cauſe, as for treaſon, or fe- Cauſe.
lony, or ſuſpicion thereof, otherwiſe if it contain no cauſe
at all, if the priſoner eſcape it is no offence at all, whereas
I the mittimus contained the cauſe, the eſcape were treaſon
or felony, tho' he were not guilty of the offence, and
therefore for the king's benefit, and that the priſoner may
be the more ſafely kept, the mittimus ought to contain the
cauſe 2 *Inſt* 52

And hereupon it appeareth, that a warrant or mittimus
to anſwer to ſuch things as ſhall be objected againſt him,
is utterly againſt law 2 *Inſt* 591

Alſo, it ought to contain the certainty of the cauſe, and
therefore if it be for felony, it ought not to be generally for
felony, but it muſt contain the ſpecial nature of the felony, briefly, as for felony *for the death of ſuch an one*, or
for burglary *in breaking the houſe of ſuch an one*, and the
reaſon is, becauſe it may appear to the judges of the king's
bench, upon an *habeas corpus*, whether it be felony or no
2 *H H* 122

But the want hereof ſeems not to make the commitment abſolutely void, ſo as to ſubject the gaoler to a falſe
impriſonment, but it lies in averment to excuſe the gaoler
or officer, that the matter was for felony 1 *H H* 584

5 It muſt have an apt concluſion, as if it is for felony, Concluſion,
to detain him till he be thence delivered by law, or by
order of law, or by due courſe of law 2 *H* 120 2 *H
H* 123

But

But if the conclusion be irregular, it doth not seem to make the warrant void, but the law will reject that which is surplusage, and the rest shall stand, so that if the matter appear to be such, for which he is to remain in custody, or be bailed, he shall be bailed or committed as the case requires, and not discharged, but the wrong conclusion shall be rejected. 1 *H H* 584

It is also to be observed, that a commitment grounded on an act of parliament, ought to be conformable to the method prescribed by it. As where the overseers were committed for refusing to account, and the warrant concluded in the common form, until they be duly discharged according to law, upon the return of an *habeas corpus* the court held the commitment void, because the warrant ought to have concluded, there to remain until he shall account, as the 43 *El c* 2 doth appoint. And a difference is, where a man is committed as a criminal, and where only for contumacy, in the first case, the commitment must be, until discharged according to law, but in the latter, until he comply. 2 *Haw Not* 33

Where a statute appoints imprisonment, but limits no time how long, in such case the prisoner must remain at the discretion of the court. *Dalt c* 170

Seal 6 It must be under seal, and without this, the commitment is unlawful, the gaoler is liable to false imprisonment, and the wilful escape by the gaoler, or breach of prison by the felon, makes no felony. 1 *H H* 583

But this must not be intended of a commitment by the sessions, or other court of record, for there the record itself, or the memorial thereof, which may at any time be entred of record, are a sufficient warrant, without any warrant under seal. 1 *H H* 584

Place 7 It should also set forth the place at which it is made (that it may appear to be within the jurisdiction of the justice) 2 *Haw* 119

Time 8 It must also have a certain date, of the year and day 2 *H H* 123

IV. *Charges of the commitment*

By the 3 *J c.* 10 Every person who shall be committed to the common or usual gaol, within any county or liberty, by any justice of the peace, for any offence or misdemeanor, the said person so to be committed, having means or ability thereunto, shall bear his own reasonable charges for so conveying or sending him to the said gaol, and the charges also of such as shall be appointed to guard him

him to such gaol, and shall so guard him thither. And if any such person so to be committed, shall refuse at the time of his commitment and sending to the said gaol, to defray the said charges, or shall not then pay or bear the same, then such justice shall, by writing under his hand and seal, give warrant to the constable of the hundred, or constable of the township where such person shall be dwelling and inhabit, or from whence he shall be committed, or where he shall have any goods within the county or liberty, to sell such and so much of the goods and chattels of the said person so to be committed, as by the discretion of the said justice shall satisfy and pay the charges of such his conveying and sending to the said gaol, the appraisement to be made by four of the honest inhabitants of the parish where such goods shall be, the overplus to be delivered to the party.

And by the statute of the 27 G 2 c 3 When any person, not having goods or money in the county where he is taken, sufficient to bear the charges of himself and of those who convey him, is committed to gaol, or to the house of correction, by warrant from a justice, then on application by the constable or other officer who conveyed him, to any justice for such county or place, [such justice] shall upon oath examine into and ascertain the reasonable expences, and shall without fee by his warrant order the treasurer to pay the same. But in *Middlesex*, the same shall be paid by the overseers of the poor of the parish where the person was apprehended

Note, By the *habeas corpus act*, the charges of conveying an offender is limited not to exceed 12d a mile, which may be an argument for allowing as much in this case, especially as security is to be given before a man is removed on that act by *habeas corpus*, that he shall not escape by the way, which renders guards in that case not so necessary

V. Gaoler shall receive the prisoner

If the gaoler shall refuse to receive a felon, or take any thing for receiving him, he shall be punished for the same, by the justices of gaol delivery. 4 Ed 3 c. 10 *Dalt.* 170

But if a man be committed for felony, and the gaoler will not receive him, the constable must bring him back to the town where he was taken, and that town shall be charged with the keeping of him, until the next gaol delivery or the person that arrested him, may in such case

keep

keep the prifoner in his own houfe, as it feemeth *Dalt c 170*

But in other cafes it feems, that regularly no one can juftify the detaining a prifoner in cuftody out of the common gaol, unlefs there be fome particular reafon for fo doing, as if the party be fo dangeroufly fick, that it would apparently hazard his life to fend him to the gaol, or there be evident danger of a *refcous* from rebels, or the like. *1 Haw. 118.*

VI. The gaoler fhall certify the commitment.

By the 3 *H* 7 *c* 3 The fheriff or gaoler fhall certify the commitment to the next gaol delivery.

VII. Commitment difcharged.

It feems that a perfon legally committed for a crime, certainly appearing to have been done by fome one or other, cannot be lawfully difcharged by any one but the king, till he be acquitted on his trial, or have an *ignoramus* found by the grand jury, or none to profecute him on a proclamation for that purpofe by the juftices of gaol delivery. But if a perfon be committed on a bare fufpicion, without an indictment, for a fuppofed crime, where afterwards it appears that there was none, as for the murder of a perfon thought to be dead, who afterwards is found to be alive, it hath been holden, that he may be fafely difmiffed without any farther proceeding, for that he who fuffers him to efcape is properly punifhble only as an acceffary to his fuppofed offence, and it is impoffible that there fhould be an acceffary, where there can be no principal, and it would be hard to punifh one for a contempt, in difregarding a commitment founded on a fufpicion, appearing in fo uncontefted a manner to be groundlefs. *2 Haw. 121.*

Mittimus for felony.

Weftmoreland. J. P. *efquire, &c. one of the juftices of our lord the king, affigned to keep the peace in the faid county, and alfo to hear and determine divers felonies, trefpaffes, and other mifdemeanors in the faid county, committed, To the keeper of the gaol of our faid lord the king at —— in the faid county, or to his deputy there, and to each of them, greeting. Whereas A. O. late of —— in the faid county, labourer, hath been arrefted by the conftable of*

—— in the said county, for suspicion of a felony by him as it is said, committed, in stealing a black mare, of the value of 40 s. the property of A P of —— in the said county, yeoman Therefore on the behalf of our said lord the king, I command you and each of you, that you or one of you receive the said A O into your custody in the said gaol, there to remain till he be delivered from your custody by the law and custom of England Given under my hand and seal at —— in the said county, the —— day of —— in the —— year of the reign of our said lord ——.

Another.

Westmorland. J. P esquire, &c To the keeper of the common gaol at —— in the said county, or to his deputy there These are in his majesty's name to charge and command you, that you receive into your said gaol, the body of A O late of —— in the said county, yeoman, taken by A C constable of —— in the said county, and by him brought before me for suspicion of felony, that is to say, for stealing —— And that you safely keep the said A O in your said gaol, until the next general gaol delivery for the said county [if he be not bailable, or if bailable, then thus] until he shall thence be delivered by due course of law. And herein fail you not, &c.

Another.

Westmorland J. P esquire, &c To the keeper of —— I send you herewithal the body of A O. late of —— in the said county, labourer, brought before me this present day, and charged with the felonious taking and carrying away forty sheep, the property of —— which also he hath confessed upon his examination before me [by which he is not bailable] Therefore these are on the behalf of our said lord the king to command you, that immediately you receive the said A O and him safely keep in your said gaol, until he be thence delivered by the due order of law Hereof fail you not, as you will answer for your contempt at your peril Given under my hand and seal at —— &c

Or thus, in the king's name

Westmorland GEORGE the third by the grace of God, of Great Britain, France, and Ireland, king, defender of the faith, and so forth To the keeper

B b 4 of

of our gaol at ———— in our *said county of* W *or to his
deputy, greeting Whereas* A. O *late of* ———— *in our said
county, yeoman, is arrested for suspicion of felony, by him, as
it is said, committed, in feloniously taking and carrying away
———— of the value of* ———— *the property of* ———— *We
therefore command you, and each of you, that you receive him
the said* A O *into your custody in our said gaol, or that one of
you do receive him, there to remain till he be delivered from
your custody, according to the law of our kingdom of* England
Witness J P *esquire, one of the justices assigned to keep the
peace in our said county, and also to hear and determine divers
felonies, trespasses, and other misdemeanors in our said county
committed, at* ———— *in the said county, the* ———— *day of
in the* ———— *year of our reign*

Form of a warrant of commitment in general.

Weſtmorland. **J.** P *esquire, one of the justices of our lord
the king, assigned to keep the peace within
the said count, To the constable of* ———— *in the said county,
and to the keeper of* ———— *at* ———— *in the said county*

    *These are to command you the said constable, in his majesty's
name, forthwith to convey and deliver into the custody of the
said keeper of the said* ———— *the body of* A O *charged before me with* [here specify the offence] *And you the said
keeper are hereby required to receive the said* A O *into your
custody in the said* ———— *and him there safely to keep, &c
Given under my hand and seal, the* ———— *day of* ———— *in
the* ———— *year of the reign of his said majesty king* George
the third

Common prayer.

Impugners of
the book of
common prayer

1   IMpugners of the form of worship in the church of
England, established by law, and contained in the
book of common prayer, of the 39 articles, of the rites
and ceremonies of the church, and of episcopal government, shall be excommunicated *ipſo faĉto*, and not restored
but by the biſhop or archbiſhop on their repentance   *Can.*
5, 6, 7

Miniſters dero-
gating from the
book of common
prayer

2   If any parſon, vicar, or other miniſter, that ought to
uſe the common prayer, or to miniſter the ſacraments,
ſhall refuſe to do the ſame, or (wilfully ſtanding in the ſame)
ſhall uſe any other form, or ſhall ſpeak any thing in derogation of the ſame book or of any thing therein contained, he
ſhall, on conviction, for the firſt offence forfeit to the king
one

one year's profit of all his fpiritual promotions, and be imprifoned for fix months, for the fecond offence, fhall be deprived of all his fpiritual promotions, and be imprifoned for a year, and for the third offence, fhall be deprived of all his fpiritual promotions, and be imprifoned during life. And if he has no fpiritual promotion, he fhall for the firft offence be imprifoned for a year, and for the fecond offence, during life. 1 *El* c 2 ſ 4 —— 8

But this fhall not reftrain the fpiritual court, from proceeding againft thefe offenders, and they may be deprived by the faid court, according to the courfe of the fpiritual law, for the firft offence *id* ſ 16, 23 1 *Haw* o

Any perfon depraving the book of common prayer.

3 It any perfon whatfoever fhall in plays, fongs, or by other open words, fpeak any thing in derogation of the nine book, or any thing therein contained, or fhall by open fact caufe or procure any minifter in any place to fay common prayer openly, or to minifter any facrament, in other form, or fhall interrupt or let any minifter to fay the faid common prayer, he fhall (being indicted for the fame at the next affizes) forfeit to the king for the firft offence 100 marks, and for the fecond 400 marks, (which if not paid in 6 weeks after conviction, he fhall fuffer 6 months imprifonment for the firft offence, and 12 months for the fecond,) and for the third offence fhall forfeit all his goods and chattels, and be imprifoned during life. 1 *El.* c. 2 ſ. 9, 10, 11, 12, 13, 20.

Refident incumbent to read the common prayer once a month

4 Where an incumbent refides upon his living, and keeps a curate, the incumbent himfelf (not having lawful impediment to be allowed by the bifhop) fhall at leaft once a month openly and publickly read the common prayer, and (if there be occafion) adminifter the facraments, and other rites of the church, on pain of 5l to the poor, on conviction by confeffion, or oath of two witneffes, before two juftices, and in default of payment in ten days, the fame to be levied by the churchwardens or overfeers by diftrefs and fale, by warrant of fuch juftices. 13 & 14 C 2. c 4 ſ 7

Confeffion.

CONFESSION is twofold, either *expreffed* or *implied*

An *exprefs* confeffion is, where a perfon directly confeffes the crime with which he is charged, which is the higheft conviction that can be. 2 *Haw.* 333

But

But it is usual for the court, especially if it be out of clergy, to advise the party to plead and put himself upon his trial, and not presently to record his confession, but to admit him to plead 2 *H H* 225

An *implied* confession is, where a defendant in a case not capital, doth not directly own himself guilty, but in a manner admits it by yielding to the king's mercy, and defiring to submit to a small fine, which submission the court may accept of if they think fit, without putting him to a direct confession 2 *Haw* 333

It seems that the confession of the defendant taken upon an examination before justices of the peace, or in discourse with private persons, may be given in evidence against the party confessing, but not against others 2 *Haw* 429

All those who on their examination own themselves guilty of a felony alledged against them, and are charged in their *mittimus* with the felony so confessed, seem to be excluded from bail, for bail is only proper where it stands indifferent whether the party be guilty or innocent 2 *Haw.* 97.

Conies. See **Game.**
Conjuration. See **Witchcraft.**

Conspiracy.

I. *What it is*
II. *How punishable.*

I. *What it is.*

B the common law
¹⁴ ¹⁴

1. **B**Y the common law there can be no doubt, but that all confederates whatsoever, wrongfully to prejudice a third person, are highly criminal, as where divers persons confederate together by indirect means to impoverish a third person, or falsly and maliciously to charge a man with being the reputed father of a bastard child, or to maintain one another in any matter whether it be true or false. 1 *Haw.* 190

B, statute.

2 And conspiracy by statute is as follows *Conspirators are they, that do confederate or bind themselves by oath, covenant, or other alliance, that every of them shall aid and bear the either falsly and maliciously to indict, or cause to indict, or*

fals.

falsly to move or maintain pleas, and such as retain men in the country, with liveries or fees to maintain their malicious enterprises, and this extendeth as well to the takers, as to the givers. And stewards and bailiffs of great lords, who by their office or power, undertake to bear or maintain quarrels, pleas, or debates, that concern other parties than such as touch the estate of their lords or themselves. 33 Ed 1 ft 2

From this definition of conspirators, it seems clearly to follow, contrary to the opinion of Lord *Coke*, that not only those who actually cause an innocent man to be indicted, and also to be tried upon the indictment, whereupon he is lawfully acquitted, are properly conspirators, but that those also are guilty of this offence, who barely conspire to indict a man falsly and maliciously, whether they do any act in prosecution of such conspiracy or not. 1 *Haw* 189. L *Raym* 1169

But an *action* will not lie for the conspiracy, unless it be put in execution, for in such case, the *damage* is the ground of the action. L *Raym* 378

Also it plainly appears from the words of the statute, that one person alone cannot be guilty of conspiracy, within the purport of it, from whence it follows, that if all the defendants who are prosecuted for such a conspiracy be acquitted but one, the acquittal of the rest is the acquittal of that one also. And upon the same ground it hath been holden, that no such prosecution is maintainable against a husband and wife only, because they are esteemed but as one person in law. But it is certain, that an action on the case, in the nature of a conspiracy, may be brought against one only. Also, it hath been resolved, that if such an action be brought against several persons, and all but one be acquitted, yet judgment may be given against that one only. 1 *Haw* 192

In the case of *K* against *Cope* and others, H 5 G. The husband, and wife, and servants were indicted for a conspiracy to ruin the trade of the prosecutor, who was the king's card-maker. The evidence against them was, that they had at several times given money to the prosecutor's apprentices, to put grease into the paste, which had spoiled the cards. But there was no account given, that ever more than one at a time was present, tho' it was proved they had all given money in their turns. It was objected, that this could not be a conspiracy, for several persons might do the same thing, without having any previous communication with each other. But it was ruled, that the defendants being all of a family, and concerned in making of cards, it would amount to evidence of a conspiracy. *Str.* 144.

In

In the cafe of *K* againft *Kimnerfley* and *Moore*, *T.* 5 G An information was brought, fetting forth that the defendants being evil difpofed perfons, in order to extort money from my lord *Sunderland*, did confpire together to charge my lord with endeavouring to commit fodomy with the faid *Moore* The defendant *Kinnerfley* only appears, and pleads to iffue, and is found guilty And now exception was taken in arreft of judgment, that to every confpiracy there muft be two perfons at leaft, whereas here is only one brought in and found guilty, and the other poffibly may be acquitted But it was anfwered, that this is arguing from what has not happened, and probably never will, for tho' *Moore* may have an opportunity to acquit himfelf, and is not concluded by the verdict as *Kinnerfley* is, yet as the matter now ftands, *Moore* himfelf is found guilty, for the confpiracy is found as it is laid, and therefore judgment may be given againft one, before the trial of the other And a cafe was quoted, where feveral were indicted for a riot, *with many others*, and two only were found guilty, and it was objected, that there muft be three to make a riot, but upon the words, *with many others*, judgment was given againft the defendants And the court over-ruled the exception And the defendant had fentence And in the *Eafter* term following, *Moore* alfo was convicted, and had judgment. *Stra* 193

And, *E* 18 G 2 *K* againft *Eliz Nicols* She was indicted for confpiring with *Tho Bygrave*, unjuftly to charge *William Frankland* with a robbery, and for that purpofe going before a juftice, where *Bygrave* fwore it upon him *Nicols* only came in, and pleaded not guilty And the jury found that fhe was guilty, but that *Bygrave* died before the indictment was preferred Exception was taken, that one alone cannot be guilty of a confpiracy, and here is but one convicted But the court over-ruled this, on the authority of *Kinnerfley's* cafe, in which cafe there was a poffibility of contradictory verdicts, which here cannot be *Stra* 1227

II How punifhed

On action   1 It is clear, that thofe who are convicted of confpiracy at the fuit of the party, fhall have judgment of fine and imprifonment, and to render the plaintiff his damages 1 *Haw* 193

On indictment or information.   2 Alfo it is certain, that he who is convicted at the fuit of the king, of a confpiracy to accufe another of a matter

ter

ter which may touch his life, shall have judgment that he shall lose the freedom and franchise of the law (whereby he is disabled from being put upon any jury, or to be sworn as a witness, or even to appear in person in any of the king's courts), and also that his houses, lands and goods shall be seized into the king's hands, and his houses and lands stripped and wasted, his trees rooted up, and his body imprisoned   And this is commonly called *villa nous* judgment, and is given by the common law, and not by any statute, and is said generally in some books to be the proper judgment upon every conviction of conspiracy at the suit of the king, without any restriction to such as endangered the life of the party, but this point doth not seem to be any where settled. 1 *Haw* 193.

But this judgment hath been but seldom given, there being no instance of it since the reign of *Edward* the third. *Burro v.* Mansfield 996, 1027

In the case of *Kinnersley* and *Moore* above mentioned, *Kinnersley* was sentenced to be fined 500l, to suffer a year's imprisonment, and to find sureties for his good behaviour for seven years *Moore* was sentenced to stand in the pillory, suffer a year's imprisonment, and to find sureties in the like manner for seven years *Str* 196

T 2 *G* 3 *K* and *Rispal* An indictment was found at the sessions, against the defendant and two others, for a conspiracy The indictment set forth, that the defendants, wickedly and maliciously devising and intending unjustly to vex and aggrieve one *John Chilton*, and to deprive him of his good name, fame, credit, and reputation, wickedly and unlawfully did among themselves conspire, combine, confederate, and agree, falsly and without any reasonable or probable cause, to charge and accuse the said *John Chilton*, that he the said *John Chilton* had then lately taken out of a bag a quantity of human hair, of the goods and chattels of the said *Rispal* That the two other offenders, in pursuance of the said conspiracy, said to *Chilton*, that he was a man of credit, and had better make it up than have his credit blasted And that *Rispal*, in further pursuance of the said conspiracy, unlawfully and wickedly did extort from the said *Chilton* 30l, and a promissory note of 33l, as a composition for the said offence, and to desist from prosecution On the indictment being removed by certiorari, motion was made in arrest of judgment, upon two objections First, that the justices at their sessions have no jurisdiction over conspiracies, any more than over perjury, usury, and forgery, it being not

specified

specified in their commission, nor given them by any special statute. Secondly, the indictment doth not charge them to have conspired to fix any crime on the defendant, but only taking hair out of a bag, which might be a lawful act. To the first objection it was answered, That the justices in sessions, under the general words of the commission, have cognizance of all crimes that tend, either directly or consequentially, to a breach of the peace. That conspiracies have this tendency, in the same manner as libels, which are indictable at the sessions, without being specified in the commission, so is extortion also, and this is a conspiracy to extort. To the second objection it was answered, That the charge is, a conspiracy to extort money, by what means is not material. That *Rispal* did actually extort it, which is a direct and positive charge against him. So that either way there is ground sufficient for the court to give judgment against *Rispal*— By lord *Mansfield* chief justice. The case lies in a narrow compass. The first question is, Whether the justices in sessions have a jurisdiction over conspiracies. No authority has been cited to shew, that they have not, nor that they have. It must therefore be determined upon general principles. The cases of perjury, forgery, and usury stand upon their own special grounds, and it has been determined, that the justices have no jurisdiction there. This offence of a conspiracy is a trespass, and trespasses are indictable at sessions, tho' not committed with force and arms. They tend to the breach of the peace, as much as cheats or libels, which are established to be within the jurisdiction of the sessions. As therefore there is no authority to the contrary, I think that the justices had a jurisdiction here. The second question is, Whether a sufficient crime be laid in the indictment, to enable the court to give judgment. The crime is laid as an unlawful conspiracy. This, whether it be to charge a man with criminal acts, or such only as may affect his reputation, is fully sufficient. The several facts in the indictment are not to be considered as distinct and separate charges, but as one and the same united and continued offence pursued thro' its different stages. And then it is clear, that the whole will amount to an indictable offence, namely, the getting money from a man, by conspiring to charge him with a false fact. *Bur Mansf* 1320. *Black Rep* 368.

Constable.

Constable.

THE office of a constable, in executing of warrants, is treated of under the titles **Arreſt**, and **War=** **rant**, and in like manner the other particulars of his duty may be found under the reſpective titles throughout the book, this title treating only of the office of a con-ſtable in general.

I Of the antiquity and original of conſtables.

II Who ſhall be a conſtable.

III How choſen and ſworn.

IV. His power as a conſervator of the peace.

V. His duty as a ſuboı dinate officer to juſtices of the peace

VI His indemnity and protection in his office.

VII Concerning the expences of his office.

VIII. Concerning his account and removal from his office.

I Of the antiquity and original of conſtables.

1 The ſundry names of high conſtables, or conſtables of lathes, rapes, wapentakes, hundreds, and franchiſes, and the divers names alſo of petty conſtables, tythingmen, borſholders, boroheads, headborows, chief pledges, and ſuch other (if there be any) that bear office in towns, pariſhes, hamlets, tythings, or borows, are all in effect but two, that is to ſay, *conſtables* and *boꞃſholdeꞃs* Lamb Conſt

This word *conſtable* hath afforded matter of much diſqui-ſition to the learned It is evidently a compound, but from what two original words it hath ſprung, hath been varıouſly conjectured Hiſtory traceth it from its arrival in *England*, backwards through *France*, and *Germany*, and *Greece*, to the imperial ſeat at *Conſtantınople* in the days of *Conſtantıne* the Great From whence we aſcend farther ſtill towards the eaſt, where we find the word *cône* or *cûne* in *Paleſtine*, which ſignified in the times of the old teſtament a ſtability, ſtrength, or ſtay Of which word there ſeem to be ſome traces in the mongrel name of *Laocoon* at *Troy*, and more eſpecially of this ſame *Conſtantıne*, who was him-ſelf of oriental extraction, having ſprung from *Dardanıa*, a country of the upper *Moeſia*, and was ſaid by his flat-

terers

Antiquity of conſtables in general.

terers to have been defcended from *Dardanus* and the *Trojans* And perhaps this appellation of the emperor might give occafion to the adopting of the word into the *Roman* language at that time For it was then that the word *count* (the genuine offspring of *cône* or *cûne*) firft became a name of dignity, and from thence travelled weftwards (with a little variation according to the genius of each language) throughout the provinces Amongft the *Saxons*, the word was *koning* or *kyninge*, from whence un doubtedly we receive our *Englifh* word *king* Again, the word *ftole*, *ftalle*, *ftafle*, *ftable*, by an eafy tranfmutation of thofe letters frequent in almoft all languages (and which feemeth the other conftituent of the word *conftable*) is likewife common to thofe languages of the middle ages, and fignifieth a ftanding place, divifion, or department, called by the Romans *ftatio*, and all of them probably from the fame origin with the Latin *fto*, and the ancient *Greek* word *ςαω*. So that, according to this etymology, the word *conftable* will properly fignify the ftability or ftay of the place, or the ftrong man of the divifion The *German* word is *conneftafle*, the French *conneftable*, the Italian *coneftabile*, the Spanifh *condeftable*, from the word *coi de* which they ufe for *count* All which feem to be comprehended in the imperial denominations of the *Conftantine* family, fuch as *Conftans, Conftantius, Conftantinus, Conftantia, Conftantina, Conftantianus, Conftantinacius*, and the like.

As touching *borfholders* (which is the other general name, and doth contain within it the meaning of tything-men, borowheads, headborows, thirdborows, and chief pledges) that is made up of the Saxon *borg*, *borrow* or *borhoe*, a pledge, and *ealder*, the elder, chief, or head, and *borfhealder* in one word doth mean the chief or head of the fureties or pledges For the underftanding whereof, it is to be remembered, that by the ancient laws of this realm (before the coming in of king *William* the conqueror) it was ordained for the more fure keeping of the peace, and for the better repreffing of thieves and robbers, that all free-born men fhould caft themfelves into feveral companies, by ten in each company, and that every of thofe ten men of the company fhould be furety and pledge for the forthcoming of his fellows fo that if any harm were done by any of thefe ten, againft the peace, then the reft of the ten fhould be amerced, if he of their company that did the harm fhould fly, and were not forthcoming to anfwer to that wherewith he fhould be charged And for this caufe, the companies are yet in fome places of *England* called *boroes*, of the faid word *borge*, *borrow*, or

borhoe,

borboe, signifying a pledge or furety, and in other places they are called *tythings*, becaufe they contain (as hath been faid) the number of ten men with their families And even as ten times ten do make an hundred, fo becaufe it was then alfo appointed that ten of thefe companies fhould at certain times meet together for their matters of greater weight, therefore that general affembly, or court, was and yet is called a *hundred* Furthermore, it was then alfo ordained, that if any man were of fo evil credit, that he could not get himfelf to be received into one of thefe tythings or boroes, then he fhould be fhut up in prifon, as a man unworthy to live at liberty amongft men abroad Now whereas every of thefe tythings or boroes did ufe to make choice of one man amongft themfelves, to fpeak and to do, in the name of them all, he was therefore in fome places called the tythingman, in other places the boroes elder, (whom we now call borfholder), in other places the borohead, or headborow, and in fome other places the chief pledge, which laft name doth plainly expound the other three that are next before it, for head or elder of the boroes, and chief of the pledges are all one, and in fome fhires, where ever, third borough hath a conftable, there the officers of the other two are called *wardborows* And in thefe tythings, or boroes, fundry good orders were obferved, and amongft others, firft, that every man of the age of 12 years fhould be fworn to the king Then, that no man fhall be fuffered to dwell in any town or place, unlefs he were alfo received into fome fuch furetifhip and pledge as is aforefaid Thirdly, that if any of thefe pledges were imprifoned for his offence, then he ought not to be delivered without the affent of the reft of his pledges Again, that no man might remove out of one tything or boroe, to dwell in another, without lawful warrant in that behalf Laftly, that every of thefe pledges fhould yearly be prefented and brought forth by their chief pledge, at a general affembly for that purpofe, which we yet in remembrance thereof do call the *view of frankpledge*, or the leet court *Lamb.* Conft

Some fmall fhadow of which antiquity we feem ftill to retain in a common phrafe in drinking, when a man fays to another that he will *pledge* him, which is faid to have begun when the *Danes* tyrannized in this land, and the meaning was, to encourage the perfon to drink freely, for that the other would be furety to him that no one fhould do him any bodily harm whilft he was drinking

Alfo we do ftill retain the word *forrow* as a verb in our language, fignifying to take money upon a pledge or furety

In ſome places, at this day, there is both a tithingman and conſtable, where the tithingman is as it were a deputy to execute the office in the conſtable's abſence but there are ſome things which a conſtable hath power to do, that tithingmen cannot intermeddle with, for the conſtable may do whatever the tithingman may do, but not on the contrary, the tithingman not having an equal power with the conſtable. But in places where there is no conſtable, the office and authority of tithingman ſeems to be all one under a different name. 1 *Black* 357

Antiquity of High conſtables

2 By the ſtatute of *Wincheſter*, *In every hundred and franchiſe two conſtables ſhall be choſen to make the view of armour, and they ſhall preſent defaults of armour, and of ſuits of towns, and of highways, and ſuch as lodge ſtrangers in uplandiſh towns, for whom they will not anſwer.* 13 Ed 1 ſt 2 c 6

And from hence lord *Coke*, and others, will have it, that high conſtables are no ancienter than this ſtatute. But Mr *Hawkins*, (agreeably with *Lambard*, *Dalton*, and other authorities) ſays, that it ſeems to be the better opinion, that both conſtables of hundreds, which are commonly called high conſtables, and alſo conſtables of tythings, which are at this day commonly called petty conſtables, or tithingmen, were by the common law, and not firſt ordained by the ſaid ſtatute of *Wincheſter*, for that ſtatute doth not ſay, that there ſhall be ſuch officers conſtituted, but clearly ſeems to ſuppoſe that there were ſuch before the making of it. 2 *Haw* 61

In ſhort, the truth of the matter ſeems to be this. The far greateſt part of the buſineſs of high conſtables, at this day, is not at all appropriated to them, as high conſtables, but only as officers to execute the precepts of the juſtices of the peace, which any other perſon may do as well as they. The original and proper authority of an high conſtable, as ſuch, ſeems to be the very ſame and no other, within his hundred, as that of the petty conſtable within his vill; and therein, moſt probably, he is coeval with the petty conſtable. The other uſual branches of his office, ſuch as the ſurveying of bridges, the iſſuing precepts concerning the appointing of overſeers of the poor, ſurveyors of the highways, aſſeſſors and collectors of the land tax and window duties, and in like manner the viewing of armour by the above mentioned ſtatute, are in him, not of neceſſity, but as matter of convenience, and it is diſcretionary in the juſtices whom they will appoint to be their officers in theſe caſes; others have been ſuperadded to the office, for the like reaſon of convenience, by ſundry

Acts of parliament, such as the issuing precepts for the licensing of alehouses, for levying county rates, and for returning lists of jurors, for that one person can do all the same much easier and cheaper than so many different persons

II *Who shall be a constable.*

1 It hath been said, that a custom in a town, that the Women. inhabitants shall serve the office of constable by turns, according to the situation of their several houses, is not good, for that, by such a course, it may come to a woman's turn to be a constable, as inhabitant of one of those houses, yet we find such customs allowed to be good in later books, and it seems, that the consequence of the reasoning above mentioned may well be denied, since a woman in such case may procure another to serve for her   2 *Haw* 63

2 Also it seems, that a practising physician, being Physicians. chosen constable in pursuance of such custom, has no remedy for his discharge, for that there are no precedents of this kind, and his calling is private   2 *Haw* 63

But by the 32 *H* 8 *c* 40   The president, commons, and fellows of the faculty of physick in *London*, shall not be chosen constables

3 And by the 5 *H* 8 *c* 6 and 18 *G* 2 *c* 15 Sur- Surgeons geons in *London* shall be freed and exempted from the office of constable

In the case of *K* and *Pond*, *M* 5 *G* On an indictment against *Pond*, a surgeon, for refusing to be constable, it was moved to the attorney general that a *noli prosequi* might be granted, for that by the 5 *H* 8 *c* 6 (and by the 32 *H* 8 *c* 40 for the incorporating of barbers and surgeons, which incorporation was dissolved by the above act of 18 *G* 2) all persons of the corporation of surgeons within *London* are exempt, and tho' it hath been held that physicians are not exempt, yet by the equity of those statutes, and by the custom of the realm, *all* surgeons have been allowed the same privilege and therefore a *noli prosequi* was allowed, unless cause shewn   And no cause was shewed, the reporter says, that ever he heard of   *Comyns* 312

4. By the 6 & 7 *W* *c.* 4 Apothecaries in *London*, and Apothecaries. within seven miles thereof, being free of the company of apothecaries, and also those in the country who have served seven years apprenticeship, shall be exempted from the office of constable

5 Also

Attornies

5 Alſo it ſeems certain, that if a ſworn attorney, or other officer, of the courts at *Weſtminſter*, be choſen into this office, he may have a writ of privilege for his diſcharge, by reaſon of his neceſſary attendance in thoſe courts and it hath been reſolved, that ſuch officers ſhall have this privilege, not only where there is no ſpecial cuſtom concerning the election of conſtables, but alſo where they are choſen by a particular cuſtom, in reſpect of their eſtates, or otherwiſe, for that no ſuch cuſtom ſhall be intended to be more ancient than the uſages of thoſe courts, and therefore ſhall give way to them 2 *Haw.* 63.

Barriſters at law, ſervants to members of parliament

6. And upon the like reaſons, it is taken for granted, that practiſing barriſters at law, and the ſervants of members of parliament, have the ſame privilege, but there ſeem to have been no reſolutions to this purpoſe 2 *Haw* 63

Aldermen of London.

7 Alſo it hath been reſolved, that an alderman of *London*, for the like reaſons, is not compellable to be a conſtable 2 *Haw* 63

Captain of the guards

8 But it hath been holden, that a captain of the king's guards, being preſented to ſerve as conſtable, in purſuance of a cuſtom in reſpect of his lands in a town, cannot claim this privilege, for that notwithſtanding he is bound by his office to perſonal attendance on the king's perſon, yet ſuch office being of late inſtitution, ſhall not prevail againſt an ancient cuſtom 2 *Haw* 63.

Militia man.

9 But a perſon ſerving for himſelf as a private man in the militia, ſhall during the time of ſuch ſervice be exempted from the office of conſtable. 2 *G* 3 *c* 20 ſ 76

Where there are others ſufficient.

10. Yet if ſuch an officer as before mentioned, or a gentleman of quality who hath no ſuch office, or a practiſing phyſician, be choſen conſtable of a town, which hath ſufficient perſons beſides to execute this office, and no ſpecial cuſtom concerning it, perhaps he may be relieved by the king's bench, but it ſeems that even a cuſtom cannot exempt fitting perſons from ſerving the office of conſtable, where there are not ſufficient beſides them to execute it But theſe points ſeem not to be ſettled 2 *Haw* 63

Diſſenting teachers

11 By the 1 *W c* 18 ſ 11 Every teacher or preacher in holy orders, or pretended holy orders, in a congregation tolerated by law, ſhall from the time of his ſubſcription and taking the oaths, be exempted from the office of conſtable.

Proſecutors of felons

12 And by 10 & 11 *W c* 23 ſ 2, 3 The proſecutor of a felon to conviction, or perſon to whom he ſhall aſſign

affign the certificate thereof, ſhall be diſcharged from the office of conſtable

13 Inaſmuch as the office of a conſtable is wholly mi- *Whether he* niſterial, and no way judicial, it ſeems that he may ap- *may appoint a* point a deputy to execute a warrant directed to him, *deputy.* when by reaſon of ſickneſs, abſence, or otherwiſe, he cannot do it himſelf, yet it doth not ſeem to be ſettled, that a conſtable can make a deputy, without ſome ſpecial cauſe *2 Haw. 62.*

In the caſe of *Medhurſt* and *Waite*, M 2 G 3 The high conſtable appointed a deputy to billet ſoldiers under the mutiny act This appointment was by parol only, and the deputy was not ſworn. By lord *Mansfield* and the court The high conſtable hath power by the act to billet ſoldiers, and he may appoint a deputy to this particular miniſterial act This is a miniſterial (not a judicial) act And a conſtable may appoint a deputy to do miniſterial acts *Burr. Mansf.* 1259

And the ſuperior muſt be anſwerable for his deputy, upon any miſcarriage, unleſs the deputy is duly allowed and ſworn, for then he is conſtable *Wood. b. 1. c. 7.*

14. And by 1 *W. c.* 18. ſ. 7 If any perſon diſſenting *Diſſenters ap* from the church of *England*, ſhall be choſen conſtable, *pointing a de* and ſhall ſcruple to take upon him the office, in regard *puty.* of the oaths, or any other matter required to be done in reſpect of ſuch office, he may execute it by a ſufficient deputy by him to be provided, to be allowed by ſuch perſons, and in ſuch manner, as ſuch officer ſhould have been allowed.

III. *How choſen and ſworn.*

1 It ſeemeth, regularly, that the petty conſtable ought *By whom to be* to be choſen in the leet, and the high conſtable (properly *choſen.* ſo called) in the torn, which is the general leet of the whole hundred · and if there be no leet, then that the petty conſtable ought to be choſen alſo in the torn.

But whether they are to be choſen and appointed by the ſuitors in the reſpective courts, or by the lord or his ſteward in the leet, and the ſheriff in his torn, ſeemeth not clearly determined *2 Haw. 62.*

2 But by which of them ſoever they ſhall be choſen *By whom to be* and appointed, it ſeemeth clear, that they are to be ſworn *ſworn.* and placed in their office, by the lord or his ſteward, or by the ſheriff reſpectively, as being judge of the court. *2 Haw. 62.*

3 Alſo

Custom of chusing

3 Also it seems certain, that a custom for chusing a constable either way is good, and it seems to have been the opinion of the makers of the act of 13 & 14 C 2 hereafter following, that the lords of the courts leet have this power of common right, and consequently the sheriff in his torn, where there is no court leet   2 *Haw* 93

Anciently the practice was, that in every hundred where there was a feudal lord, the constables were sworn in and admitted by the lord or his steward in his leet, but where there was no such feudal lord, the sheriff in his torn had the swearing and placing of them in also if there was no feudal lord of the hundred, an annual officer was chosen, who was to preside over the whole hundred, who was called the high constable, but if the hundred was feudal, as it often anciently was, then such lord of the hundred administered the office himself   1 *Bac Abr* Const A

Chusing high constables

4 But now the usual manner is, that the high constables of hundreds be chosen either at the sessions, or by the greater number of the justices of the division, and likewise that they be sworn at sessions, or by warrant from the sessions, which course hath been often allowed and commended by the justices of assize   *Dalt c* 28

And the reason thereof may be this, as hath been intimated above, namely, that their office at present doth not so much consist in executing the office of high constable as such, as in executing the justices precepts, which they may do for the most part, whether they be indeed high constables or not

Petty constables appointed by justices of the peace

5 And moreover, every petty constable, being a principal peace officer, and it being necessary for the preservation of the peace, that every vill should be furnished with one, the justices of the peace have ever since the institution of their office, taken upon them as conservators of the peace, not only to swear the petty constables, which have been chosen at a torn or leet, but also to nominate and swear those who have not been chosen at any such court, on the neglect of the sheriffs or lords to hold their courts, or to take care that such officers are appointed in them.   And this power of justices of the peace having been confirmed by the uninterrupted usage of many ages, shall not now be disputed, but shall be presumed to have been grounded on sufficient authority   And some have carried this point so far, as to allow the justices at their sessions, to swear one who was chosen at the leet, and unduly rejected by the steward, who had sworn another in his place.   2 *Haw* 65.

And

And in the caſe of *K* and *Dr Franchard*, *H* 14 *G* 2. Dr Franchard was choſen conſtable of *Milborne Port* at the leet, which immediately adjourned, and he was afterwards ſworn in by a ſingle juſtice of the peace And upon motion for an information as not being duly ſworn, the court held this to be a good ſwearing *Str* 1149

6. *M* 21 *C* 2 The juſtices of the county of *North-* *ampton*, at their general ſeſſions choſe a conſtable for *Holm-* *by*, and for not coming in to take the oath, proceeded againſt him Which proceedings being removed by certiorari into the king's bench, it was moved on affidavits that there had not been a conſtable there for 50 years before, that he might be diſcharged, alledging likewiſe, that *Holmby* was a privileged place, and that all the inhabitants were the duke of *York's* tenants But the court held, that they could not diſcharge him on motion, and ſaid, that they muſt determine the matter by action of falſe impriſonment, or ſome other way, and inclined ſtrongly that he could not any way be diſcharged For, by the court, tho' originally conſtables were choſen in leets, yet the conſtable being an officer whoſe duty it is to keep the peace, the juſtices may chuſe him in caſes of neceſſity, as in the hamlets about the tower, the juſtices, by reaſon of the increaſe of buildings, where there was formerly but one conſtable, did chuſe five, and it was ruled they might do ſo, and they ſeemed to incline, that tho' formerly there had been none, yet they might chuſe one if they ſhould think it convenient 1 *Bac Abr* Conſt A

(marginal note) Where no conſtable hath been before

7 However, it is certain, that juſtices of the peace had power to nominate and ſwear conſtables, on the default of the torn or leet, before the ſtatute of 13 & 14 *C* 2 *c* 12. and therefore, that they have ſuch authority in ſome caſes not mentioned in that ſtatute, which enacts, that if a conſtable ſhall die, or go out of the pariſh, any two juſtices may make and ſwear a new one, until the lord ſhall hold a leet, or till the next quarter ſeſſions, who ſhall approve of the officer ſo made and ſworn, or appoint another and if any officer ſhall continue above a year in his office, the juſtices in their quarter ſeſſions may diſcharge him, and put in another till the lord ſhall hold a court as aforeſaid 2 *Haw.* 65 13 & 14 *C* 2 *c* 12 ſ 15

(marginal note) Where the leet ſhall make default

8 And it ſeems to be clear in this day, that the king's bench hath power by mandamus to compel the court or judge to ſwear a conſtable duly choſen 2 *Haw* 65

(marginal note) Mandamus to compel the lord to ſwear a conſtable

9. Conſtables lawfully choſen, if they ſhall refuſe to be ſworn, a juſtice of the peace may bind them over to the aſſizes or ſeſſions (there to be indicted) *Dalt* c. 26

(marginal note) Conſtable refuſing to be ſworn,

10 But

How puniſhed.

10 But it ſeemeth that the ſheriff, or ſteward of the leet, cannot lawfully commit them for ſuch refuſal, without more, but it is ſaid, that if the party be preſent in the court, he may be fined, and that if he be abſent, and have a certain time and place appointed him by the ſheriff or ſtew..d, for the taking of the oath before a juſtice of the peace, and have alſo expreſs notice of ſuch appointment, and be preſented at the next court, for having refuſed to take it accordingly, he may be amerced alſo it ſeems, that in either caſe he may be indicted (A) either at the aſſizes or ſeſſions. And it is adviſeable in all pleadings, in any action concerning ſuch a fine or amerciament, and in all indictments for ſuch refuſal, ſpecially and expreſsly to ſet forth the manner of every ſuch election, appointment, notice, and refuſal, and before whom the court was holden and it hath been adjudged, that it is inſufficient to ſay in general, that the party was duly elected, or lawfully elected. or that he had notice, without ſetting forth the ſpecial circumſtances thereof Alſo it is ſaid to have been adjudged, that an indictment for not finding a ſufficient perſon to ſerve the office of conſtable, without ſhewing that the party refuſed to ſerve it himſelf, is inſufficient 2 Haw 64.

Conſtable's oath.

11 There is a long form of a conſtable's oath, in Dalton, which is adopted by Mr. Bailow, expreſſing his duty in many inſtances, but as that form nevertheleſs doth not contain the hundreth part of the conſtable's duty, nor indeed the moſt material inſtances of it, it may be more elegible (as no particular form is directed by any ſtatute) to ſweat him (B) to the due execution of his office in general, than to deſcend to thoſe particulars; leſt by mentioning ſome parts of his duty, and not others, he may be induced to think, that thoſe others are not ſo neceſſary,

Oaths of allegiance and ſupremacy

12. By the 1 G ſt 2 c 13 High conſtables are to take the oaths of allegiance, ſupremacy, and abjuration, as other perſons who qualify for offices, but they are not within the ſtatute of the 25 C 2. c. 2 as to receiving the ſacrament, and ſubſcribing the declaration againſt tranſubſtantiation, and petty conſtables are exempted both from the one and from the other

IV His power as a conſervator of the peace.

Conſtable a conſervator of the peace

1 Every high and petty conſtable are by the common law conſervators of the peace 2 Haw 33 Crom 6. Dalt c 1

May commit for an affray in his preſence,

2 And therefore if any man ſhall make an affray or aſſault upon another in the preſence of the conſtable, or
ſhall

ſhall threaten to kill, beat, or hurt another, or ſhall be in
a fury ready to break the peace, the conſtable may com‐
mit him to the ſtocks, or other ſafe cuſtody for the preſent,
and after may carry him before a juſtice, or to gaol, until
he ſhall find ſurety for the peace, which ſurety the con‐
ſtable himſelf may alſo take by obligation, to be ſealed and
delivered to the king's uſe, and if the party will not find
ſurety to the conſtable, he may impriſon the party until he
ſhall do it. *Dalt. c* 1.

3 But he may not require ſurety of the peace, unleſs **But not when he**
the offence be upon his own view, and not if it be com‐ **is abſent**
mitted out of his ſight, for he cannot take any man's
oath that he is afraid of death, becauſe he is not a judge
of record, which is the reaſon that an obligation taken by
him ſhall be in his own name, and not in the king's name;
and the ſame ſhall be certified in the ſeſſions of the peace.
Cro. Eliz 375, 376

V. *his duty as a ſubordinate officer to juſtices of the*
peace.

It hath always been holden, that the conſtable is the **Subordinate to**
proper officer to a juſtice of the peace, and bound to exe‐ **the juſtices of**
cute his warrants, and therefore it hath been reſolved, **the peace.**
that where a ſtatute authorizes a juſtice of the peace to
convict a man of a crime, and to levy the penalty by war‐
rant of diſtreſs, without ſaying to whom ſuch warrant
ſhall be directed, or by whom it ſhall be executed, the
conſtable is the proper officer to ſerve ſuch warrant, and
indictable for diſobeying it. 2 *Haw* 262

VI. *His indemnity and protection in his office.*

1. If an action is brought againſt a conſtable for any **Double coſts.**
thing done by virtue of his office, he, and alſo all others
which in his aid, or by his command, ſhall do a thing
concerning his office, may plead the general iſſue, and give
the ſpecial matter in evidence, and if he recovers, he ſhall
have double coſts 7 *J. c* 5

2 And ſuch action ſhall be laid in the county where the **Proper county.**
fact was committed, and not elſewhere. 21 *J c* 12

3 Formerly the conſtable was bound to take notice of **No action if he**
the juriſdiction of the juſtice inſomuch that if the juſtice **delivers a copy**
iſſued a warrant in any matter wherein he had no juriſ‐ **of the warrant,**
diction, the conſtable was puniſhable for the execution
of it but now, by the ſtatute of 24 G. 2 *c* 44 it is
enacted,

That

That no action ſhall be brought againſt any conſtable, or other perſon acting by his order, and in his aid, for any thing done in obedience to the warrant of a juſtice of the peace, until demand hath been made, or left at the uſual place of his abode, by the party, or by his attorney, in writing, ſigned by the party demanding the ſame, of the peruſal and copy of ſuch warrant, and the ſame hath been refuſed or neglected for ſix days after ſuch demand and if after compliance therewith, any ſuch action ſhall be brought, without making the juſtice who ſigned ſuch warrant defendant, on producing and proving ſuch warrant at the trial, the jury ſhall give their verdict for the defendant, notwithſtanding any defect of juriſdiction in the juſtice And if ſuch action be brought jointly againſt the juſtice and conſtable, on proof of ſuch warrant, the jury ſhall find for the conſtable, notwithſtanding ſuch defect of juriſdiction as aforeſaid, and if the verdict be given againſt the juſtice, the plaintiff ſhall recover his coſts againſt him, to be taxed in ſuch manner by the proper officer, as to include ſuch coſts as the plaintiff is liable to pay to ſuch defendant, for whom ſuch verdict ſhall be found as aforeſaid ſ 6

Note, By this it ſeemeth, that the conſtable ought not to return the warrant to the juſtice, but to keep it for his own juſtification, for he cannot grant to the party the peruſal of the warrant, unleſs he hath it but he muſt certify to the juſtice what he hath done in the execution thereof.

4 And no action ſhall be brought againſt any conſtable, but within ſix months after the act committed. 24 G 2 c 44 ſ 8

5 And if the conſtable is aſſaulted in the execution of his office, he need not go back to the wall, as private perſons ought to do and if in the ſtriving together, the conſtable kills the aſſailant, it is no felony, but if the conſtable is killed, it ſhall be conſtrued premeditated murder. *Hale's Pl* 37 1 H H 457

VII. Concerning the expences of his office.

1 By the 27 G. 2. c. 20. The conſtable executing a juſtice's warrant, for levying a penalty, or other ſum of money directed by an act of parliament, by diſtreſs, may deduct his own reaſonable charges of taking, keeping, and ſelling the goods diſtrained, returning the overplus on demand, after ſuch penalty or ſum of money and charges deducted.

2 A

2 A perſon committed to gaol, for any miſdemeanor, Charges of conveying an offender to gaol ſhall bear his own charges (if able) for conveying or ſending him to the ſaid gaol, and the charges of thoſe that guard him thither, and if he ſhall refuſe at the time of commitment to defray the ſame, or ſhall not then pay the ſame, the juſtice committing him, ſhall by warrant to the high or petty conſtable where the perſon ſhall inhabit, or from whence he ſhall be committed, or where he ſhall have any goods within the county, order ſo much to be ſold thereof, as by his diſcretion ſhall ſatisfy the ſame, the appraiſement to be made by four honeſt inhabitants 3 J.
, 10 J I

And if he have not money nor goods within the county, ſufficient to bear the charges of himſelf and of thoſe who convey him to the gaol, or houſe of correction, the conſtable may make application to a juſtice, who may upon oath examine into and aſcertain the reaſonable expences, and ſhall by his warrant (without fee) order the treaſurer to pay the ſame, except in *Middleſex*, where the ſame ſhall be paid by the overſeers of the pariſh where the perſon was apprehended 27 G 2. c 3.

3 And by the 18 G 3 c 19 Whereas conſtables, Charges in the buſineſs of the pariſh head-boroughs, and tithingmen, are or may be at great charge in doing the buſineſs of their pariſh, townſhip, or place, and in many caſes are not ſufficiently indemnified by law, it is therefore enacted, that every conſtable or other ſuch officer ſhall every three months, and within 14 days after he ſhall go out of his office, deliver to the overſeers a juſt account in writing, fairly entred in a book to be kept for that purpoſe, and ſigned by him, of all ſums ſo by him expended on account of the ſaid pariſh, townſhip, or place, in all caſes not hitherto provided for by law, and alſo of all ſums received by him on the account of the ſaid pariſh, townſhip, or place, and the overſeers ſhall, within the next 14 days after the account ſhall be ſo delivered, lay the ſame before the inhabitants, and if approved by the majority of tnem, the overſeers ſhall pay out of the poor rate ſuch ſum as ſhall appear to be due on the ſaid account But if the account, or any part thereof, ſhall be diſallowed, the overſeers ſhall deliver back to the conſtable or other officer ſuch book of accounts, who may then produce the ſaid book to a juſtice, giving reaſonable notice thereof to the overſeer, which juſtice ſhall examine the ſame, and hear and determine any objection that ſhall be made to the account, and ſettle the ſum which ſhall appear to him to be due, and enter the ſame in the account, and ſign his name thereto, and the overſeers ſhall pay the ſame accordingly J 4

2

Pro-

Provided, that if the overſeer ſhall find that the pariſh, townſhip, or place is aggrieved by any thing done or omitted by the ſaid conſtable or other officer, or by the juſtice, or ſhall have any material objection to the account, or to ſuch determination as aforeſaid, he may, giving reaſonable notice to the ſaid juſtice, conſtable, or other officer, appeal to the next general or quarter ſeſſions for the county or liberty where ſuch pariſh, townſhip, or place lies, who ſhall hear and finally determine the ſame But if it ſhall appear to the juſtices that reaſonable notice was not given, they ſhall adjourn the appeal to the next quarter ſeſſions And the juſtices may order to the party for whom the appeal ſhall be determined reaſonable coſts, in like manner as concerning ſettlements by the 8 & 9 *W* *c* 30 ——Provided, that in corporations which have not four juſtices, the overſeer may appeal, if he thinks fit, to the ſeſſions of the county. *ſ* 5, 6.

And the juſtices in ſeſſions may from time to time lay down or alter ſuch rules and regulations as to any coſts or charges to be allowed to any perſon by virtue of this act, as to them ſhall ſeem juſt which rules and regulations, having received the approbation and ſignature of one or more of the judges of aſſize, ſhall be binding, and not otherwiſe, on all perſons whatſoever. *ſ.* 9

VIII *Concerning his account and removal from his office.*

Account 1 The high conſtables ſhall at the general or quarter ſeſſions, if thereunto required, account for the general county rate by them received, on pain of being committed to gaol until they ſhall account, and ſhall pay over the money in their hands, according to the order of the ſaid court, on the like pain And all their accounts and vouchers ſhall, after having been paſſed at the ſaid ſeſſions, be depoſited with the clerk of the peace, to be kept amongſt the records, and inſpected by any juſtice without fee. 12 G 2 *c* 29 *ſ* 8

Removal, 2. And in ſuch manner as conſtables are to be choſen, in the ſame manner, and by the like authority are they to be removed, ſo as if there ſhall be cauſe to remove and put an high conſtable from his place, it hath not been thought fit, that any one or two juſtices ſhould do it upon their diſcretion, but that it ſhould be done by the greater part of the juſtices of that diviſion, and that for ſome juſt cauſe, or elſe that it be done at the ſeſſions *Dalt. c.* 28.

And

And it ſeems clear, that the ſheriff or ſteward of the leet, having power to place a conſtable in his office, have by conſequence a power of removing him   2 *Haw.* 63

And alſo the juſtices of the peace have alſo uſed, for good cauſe, to diſplace all ſuch conſtables, as have been choſen and ſworn by them.   2 *Haw.* 65

And by the 13 & 14 C. 2 c 12. If a conſtable ſhall continue above a year in his office, the ſeſſions may diſcharge him, and put another in his place, till the lord ſhall hold a leet   ſ. 15.

And if the court, or other judge, ſhall refuſe to diſcharge a conſtable, the king's bench may compel them by *mandamus.*   2 Haw 65.

A. Indictment for not taking the office.

THE *jurors for our lord the king upon their oath preſent, that A O late of ——— in the townſhip of ——— in the ſaid county, yeoman, on the ——— day of ——— in the ——— year of the reign of ——— and long before, and always after until the day of the preferring of this indictment, was and is an inhabitant and reſiding within the townſhip of ——— aforeſaid, in the county aforeſaid, and an able perſon to ſerve the office of conſtable for the ſaid townſhip, and he the ſaid A O on the ſaid ——— day of ——— in the year aforeſaid, in the townſhip aforeſaid, at the court leet of A L. lord of the manor of ——— aforeſaid, holden before A S gentleman, ſteward of the ſaid court, by the ſuitors of the ſaid court, was elected and choſen, according to the ancient cuſtom of chuſing conſtables for the ſaid townſhip, for one year from thence next following, to do and execute all and ſingular thoſe things which belong to the office of conſtable, [or otherwiſe as the cuſtom ſhall be for chuſing conſtables] and that the ſaid A. O afterwards, to wit, on the ——— day of ——— in the year aforeſaid, at the townſhip of ——— aforeſaid, had due notice given to him by A B bailiff of the aforeſaid manor, of his being ſo elected and choſen conſtable as aforeſaid, and then and there was by him the ſaid A B required to appear before J P. eſquire, then and yet one of his majeſty's juſtices aſſigned to keep the peace within the ſaid county, and alſo to hear and determine divers felonies, treſpaſſes, and other miſdemeanors in the ſaid county committed, on the ſaid ——— day of ——— in the year aforeſaid, to take his oath for the due executing the ſaid office of conſtable for the ſame townſhip, according to the duty of that office, nevertheleſs the ſaid A O his duty in that behalf not regarding, but continuing and intending wholly to neglect to ſerve the ſaid office of conſtable, after he the ſaid A. O was ſo elected and choſen into*
the

the ſaid office as aforeſaid, to wit, on the ſaid——day of
——in the year aforeſaid, and contin ually afterwards until
the day of taking this inquiſition, at the townſhip aforeſaid, in
the county aforeſaid, unlawfully and contemptuouſly did refuſe,
and ſtill doth refuſe, to take his ſaid oath for the due executing
the ſaid office of conſtable, and in any wiſe to execute the
ſame office, to the great hindrance of juſtice, in contempt of
our ſaid lord the king, and to the evil example of all others in the
like caſe offending, and againſt the peace of our ſaid lord the king.

B Conſtable's oath.

YOU *ſhall well and truly ſerve our ſovereign lord the*
king, [*and the lord of this leet, if ſworn in a court*
leet] *in the office of conſtable, for the townſhip of——for*
the year enſuing, according to the beſt of your ſkill and know-
ledge. So help you God.

Convicſion.

THE power of a juſtice of the peace is in reſtraint of
the common law, and in abundance of inſtances
is a tacit repeal of that famous clauſe in the great charter, that a man ſhall be tried by his equals, which alſo
was the common law of the land long before the great
charter, even for time immemorial, beyond the date of
hiſtories and records. Therefore generally nothing ſhall
be preſumed in favour of the office of a juſtice of the
peace, but the intendment will be againſt it. Therefore
where a ſpecial power is given to a juſtice of the peace by
act of parliament to convict an offender in a ſummary
manner, without a trial by jury, it muſt appear that he
hath ſtrictly purſued that power, otherwiſe the common
law will break in upon him, and level all his proceedings.
Therefore where a trial by jury is diſpenſed withal, yet he
muſt proceed nevertheleſs according to the courſe of the
common law in trials by juries, and conſider himſelf only
as conſtituted in the place both of judge and jury. Therefore there muſt be an information or charge againſt a perſon, then he muſt be ſummoned or have notice of ſuch
charge, and have an opportunity to make his defence,
and the evidence againſt him muſt be ſuch as the common law approves of, unleſs the ſtatute ſpecially directeth
otherwiſe, then, if the perſon is found guilty, there muſt
be a conviction, judgment, and execution, all according

to the courfe of the common law, directed and influenced by the fpecial authority given by ftatute, and in the conclufion, there muft be a *record* of the whole proceedings, wherein the juftice muft fet forth the particular manner and circumftances, fo as if he fhall be called to account for the fame by a fuperior court, it may appear that he hath conformed to the law, and not exceeded the bounds prefcribed to his jurifdiction

The difficulty of drawing up a conviction in due form, hath induced the legiflature to inftitute a more apt and compendious method in divers inftances, and it were to be wifhed, in eafe of the juftices, that this provifion might be made more general. Thefe fummary forms of convictions, which are fpecially directed by act of parliament, are interfperfed throughout this book under the titles to which they do refpectively belong

Other forms of convictions, which are left at large according to the courfe of the common law (having no prefcriptive form of words directed by any act of parliament) are likewife drawn forth at length under divers titles, particularly, concerning fuch matters as have been often controverted in the courts above, occafioned either by the largenefs of the penalties, or fometimes by the greatnefs of the offenders, as in cafes of riots, forcible entries, game deftroying, and fuch like

It remaineth, under this title, to infert one general precedent or form of conviction for the whole, which may be to the effect following

General form of conviction.

Weftmorland ⟩ BE it remembred, that on the ——— day of ——— in the ——— year of the reign of ——— by the grace of God, of Great Britain, France, and Ireland, king, *defender of the faith, and fo forth,* at ——— in the county of ——— aforefaid, A I of ——— cometh before me I P efquire, one of the juftices of our faid lord the king, affigned to keep the peace of our faid lord the king in the faid county, and alfo to hear and determine divers felonies, trefpaffes, and other mifdemeanors in the faid county committed, [refiding near to the place where the offence herein after mentioned was committed, or as the ftatute requires] and giveth me the faid juftice to underftand and be informed, that one A O of ——— in the faid county, yeoman, on the ——— day of ——— now laft paft, at ——— in the faid county, did [here fet forth the fact, in the words of the ftatute as near as may be] againft the form of the ftatute in fuch cafe made and provided. and afterwards,

terwards, upon the aforesaid —— day of —— in the year
aforesaid, at —————— aforesaid, in the county aforesaid, he the
said A. O. after being duly summoned in this behalf before me
the justice aforesaid appeareth and is present, in order to make
his defence against the said charge contained in the said information, and having heard the same, he the said A. O. is asked by
me the said justice, if he can say any thing for himself, why he
the said A. O. should not be convicted of the premisses above
charged upon him in form aforesaid, who pleadeth that he is not
guilty of the said offence Nevertheless on the —————— day
of —————— aforesaid, in the year aforesaid, at —————— aforesaid,
in the county aforesaid, one credible witness, to wit, A. W.
of —————— yeoman, cometh before me the justice aforesaid, and before me the same justice upon his oath on the holy gospel to him
then and there by me the justice aforesaid administred, deposeth,
sweareth, and on his oath aforesaid affirmeth and saith, that
the aforesaid A. O. on the —— day of —— aforesaid, in the
year aforesaid, at —————— aforesaid, in the county aforesaid,
did [here again set forth the fact, or so much thereof as is
sufficient to convict the offender] And thereupon the aforesaid A. O. the —————— day of —— aforesaid, in the year aforesaid, before me the justice aforesaid, by the oath of one credible
witness aforesaid, according to the form of the statute aforesaid
is convicted, and for his offence aforesaid hath forfeited the
sum of —— of lawful money of Great Britain, to be distributed
as the statute aforesaid doth direct. In witness whereof, I the
said justice to this present record of the conviction as aforesaid,
have set my hand and seal at —————— aforesaid, in the county
aforesaid, the day and year first above-written.

If he confesses the fact then say, —————— And because the said
A. O. hath nothing to say, nor can say any thing in his own defence touching and concerning the premisses aforesaid, but doth
of his own accord freely and voluntarily acknowledge and confess
all and singular the said premisses to be true, in manner and form
as the same are charged upon him in the said information and
because all and singular the premisses being heard and fully understood by me the said justice, it manifestly appears to me ——————
Or, if the party hath been summoned, and doth not appear, then say, —————— Whereupon, on the said —————— day
of —————— in the year aforesaid, at —————— aforesaid, in the
county aforesaid, he the said A. O. was duly summoned in this
behalf, to appear before me, in order to make his defence against
the said charge contained in the said information, but the said
A. O. doth neglect to appear before me, and doth not appear,
nor make any defence against the said charge as aforesaid Therefore I the said justice, on the said —————— day of —————— in the
year aforesaid, at —————— aforesaid, in the county aforesaid, do

pro-

ffeeed to examine into the truth of the said complaint , And A W. of ——— a credible witness, cometh before me the justice aforesaid, and before me the same justice upon his oath, &c

Cometh before me] A conviction ought to be in the present tense, and not in the time past. L *Raym* 1376 *Str* 608. *Roberts*'s case.

And giveth me to understand and be informed] A conviction ought to be on an information or complaint precedent M 11 *W K* and *Fuller*. L Raym. 510

That one A O. *of* ——— *in the said county, yeoman*, &c] All acts which subject men to new and other trials, than those by which they ought to be tried by the common law, ought to be taken strictly ; and the court of king's bench will require, that it do appear upon the face of such proceedings, that the fact was an offence within the act, and that the justices have proceeded accordingly M 1 *An. K.* and *Chandler* 1 Salk. 578 L. Raym. 581.

Therefore the particular manner of the offence ought to be set forth. Thus in the case of swearing, before the legislature by the act of the 19 *G* 2 had directed a summary form of words, for the conviction, it was required not only to set forth that the person had cursed or sworn in general, but the particular oaths and curses were to be set forth, that the court might judge thereupon, whether they were indeed oaths and curses or not. H. 8 *G. K* and *Sparling*. Str 497.

And in the case of *K* and *Roberts*, M 11 *G* which was a conviction for swearing 150 oaths in these words *by God*, and cursing 150 curses in these words *God damn you*, this matter was carried so far, that it was insisted this was not sufficient, but that the oaths and curses ought to have been set forth 150 times each. But the oaths and curses being all only in the same words over again, the court held the conviction good *Str*. 608 L *Raym* 1376

And it seemeth, that a conviction on a penal statute ought expressly to shew, that the defendant is not within any of its provisoes , for since no plea can be admitted to such a conviction; and the defendant can have no remedy against it, but from an exception to some defect appearing in the face of it, and all the proceedings are in a summary manner, it is but reasonable that such a conviction should have the highest certainty, and satisfy the court, that the defendant had no such matter in his favour, as the statute itself allows him to plead 2 *Haw.* 250

But in the cafe of *K* and *Ford*, *T* 9 *G* There was a conviction on the 3 *C c* 3. for keeping an alehoufe without licence, and it was objected, that in the act there was a provifo to exempt perfons who had been punifhed by the former law of the 5 & 6 *Ed* 6 *c* 25 and therefore it fhould have been faid, he had not been proceeded againft upon that act But by the court, That coming in by way of provifo, he fhould have infifted on it in his defence, it appears he was afked what he had to fay, and therefore we may reafonably prefume he had no fuch defence to make And the conviction was confirmed *Str* 555

And in the cafe of *K* and *Bryan*, *M* 12 *G* 2 The defendant was convicted on the gin act, and an exception was taken, that there was no averment, that it was not fold to be ufed in medicine and the cafes on the game act were mentioned, where in convictions it is neceffary to exclude all the qualifications for killing game On the other hand, it was infifted, that the reafon of that was, becaufe thofe were in the enacting claufe, whereas this about medicine comes in by way of provifo, and is by way of defence to be fhewn on the defendant's part And for that purpofe was cited, *M* 11 *G. K* and *Theed*, where in a conviction for obftructing an excife officer on the 8 *An c* 9 it was objected, that it not being averred to be in the day, it fhould have been fhewn that there was a conftable prefent, which is made neceffary in the night, but was held to be well, and its being in the night fhould have been fhewn on the defendant's part. And by the court, This is brought within the general enacting claufe and the true diftinction is, where the extenuation comes in by way of provifo or exception And the conviction was confirmed. *Str* 1101

Being duly fummoned] *T* 11 *G K* and *Venables* The court were unanimoufly of opinion, that the party ought to be heard, and for that purpofe ought to be fummoned in fact, and that if the juftices proceeded againft a perfon without fummoning him, it would be a mifdemeanor in them, for which an information would lie. *L Raym* 1406.

And in the cafe of *K* and *Allington*, *H* 12 *G* On affidavit that no fummons was had, the court granted an information againft the juftice who made the conviction *Str* 678

H 6 *G K* and *Johnfon* The defendant was convicted for keeping a gun And exception was taken, that there was not a *reafonable* fummons, for it was made to appear

the

3

the same day, which might be impossible upon account of the distance, or the summons being served late, and his witnesses might not be got together on so short a warning then it was to appear *at the parish aforesaid*, whereas there were two parishes mentioned before, so the man might have gone to one, whilst they were convicting him at the other. It was answered, that the defendant appeared at the time, and made defence, so that cures all defects in the summons. And by the court, The answer is right. *Sh* 261.

H 3 *G. K.* and *Simpson.* The defendant was convicted for deer-stealing, and the conviction set forth, that he had been summoned to appear before the justices, but it did not appear he ever was before them. Exception was taken to this, that as no appeal lies in this case, the justices should have not proceeded in the absence of the party, especially where it may end in a corporal punishment as it may do here for want of a distress. And at another day, on consideration, *Parker* C. J. delivered the resolution of the court. We are all of opinion, the offender may be convicted, without appearing. The statute is silent as to the method of proceeding, and the law of *England*, it is true, in point of natural justice, always requires the party charged with any offence, to be heard before he be condemned in judgment; but that rule must have this exception, unless it is through his own default, were it otherwise, every criminal might avoid conviction. *Str* 44.

But, generally, it is not necessary to *set forth the summons in the conviction*, for although no summons is set forth, yet the court will intend one; but where a summons is set forth, and that summons appears to be irregular, the court will quash the conviction, there being then no room to intend any other summons. 11 *G. K.* and *Venables,* 1 Sess. C 210. L. Raym. 1405.

One credible witness, to wit, A W *of —— yeoman*] It is requisite to name the witness, that it may appear he is not the same person who was the informer, for an informer who hath a share of the penalty, is never allowed to be a witness, unless in case where a statute shall specially so direct it.

On his oath aforesaid affirmeth and saith] In all convictions, being in the nature of judgments, the whole evidence ought to be set forth, or at least so much thereof as is sufficient to warrant the conviction, that the court of king's bench may judge of the sufficiency thereof; but

other-

otherwise it is in orders which are authoritative And
so it was laid down in the case of *K* and *Floyd*, *M* 8 *G* 2
which was thus, A motion was made to quash an order of
seſſions, made under the ſtatute of the 1 *W. c.* 21 *ſ.* 6
whereby the defendant was adjudged guilty *upon full proof*
of the charge againſt him, and that he be diſcharged from
his office of clerk of the peace, upon the objection that
the evidence is not ſet out But it was adjudged after conſideration, that this was an order, and therefore the evidence
need not be ſhewn but that it would be otherwiſe if it
was a conviction *Andr* 82 *Str* 996

M 5 *G* 2 *K* and *Theed* A conviction on the candle
act was quaſhed, becauſe the evidence was not ſet out, it being only alledged, that the offence was *fully and duly proved*
Str 919 2 *Barnard* 16, 73

T 6 *G* *K* and *Bates* A conviction for taking pil-
chards, againſt the form of the ſtatute, quaſhed, becauſe
the witneſs ſwears generally that the defendant *is guilty of*
the premiſſes, and that is taking upon himſelf to ſwear the
law *Str* 316

E 1 *G* 3 *K* againſt *Vipont* and others The conviction was, that the defendants, *having heard the charge,*
(of conſpiring to advance their wages in the woollen manufacture), and being called upon by the juſtices to ſhew
cauſe why they ſhould not be convicted, and having nothing to ſay whereby to defend themſelves, are therefore convicted And quaſhed by the court, becauſe the evidence
ought to be particularly ſet forth, that the court may
judge thereof, and it muſt be given in preſence of the defendant, that he may have an opportunity of croſs-exa-
mination *Burrow, Mansfield* 1163

L 7 *G* 3 *K* and *Killett* The defendant, being a clergyman, was convicted for neglecting to read the act
againſt profane curling and ſwearing. The conviction
fully ſet forth the offence as charged in the information,
and then goes on, ſetting forth that the defendant was
ſummoned, and having neglected to appear, the juſtice proceeded to examine into the truth of the charge, *and the*
ſame, as ſet forth, being duly proved before him, he adjudges
the defendant guilty By the court It is now fully ſettled, that upon a conviction the evidence ought to be ſet
out, that the court may judge whether the juſtices have
done right, but upon an order it is not neceſſary *Burr*
Mansfield 2063

And for his offence aforeſaid hath forfeited] *H* 3 *G* 2 *K*
and *Hawkes*, A conviction for killing a deer was quaſhed
be

because it was only ———— *he is convicted* without any judgment of forfeiture. *Str.* 858.

And in the aforesaid case of the *King* against *Lupint* and
others, the conviction *not adjudging the forfeiture*, was for
that reason, as well as the other above mentioned, determined to be ill, especially as the statute, upon which the
conviction was made, leaves the judgment discretionary
concerning the duration of the punishment, the offender
being to be imprisoned by the justices for any time not exceeding three months. *Burrow, Mansfield* 1163.

To be distributed as the statute aforesaid doth direct] *M.
9 An. K.* and *Barret.* A conviction for deer stealing did
set forth, that———— *he is convicted, and shall forfeit* 30 l *according to the form of the statute,* without making a distri-
bution, which ought to be 10 l to the informer, 10 l to
the party grieved, and 10 l to the poor. But by the court.
This is well enough, for by the statute he is only to forfeit in case ne has goods, which is conditional, and not
absolute. 1 *Salk.* 383.

After all, these convictions, being tedious and trouble-
some, are never drawn up in form, till occasion calls them
forth, as if they be to be recorded at the sessions, or removed into a higher court by certiorari.

Note, On a suggestion that the defendant hath a title
to the thing in question, a prohibition will be granted by
the king's bench, before or after conviction, to stay the
justice from proceeding, for without doubt if the defendant have but a colour of title, the justices have no jurisdiction in the cause, as where the defendant was convicted
for cutting trees, where he had a right of common. L,
Raym 901.

Corn.

I *The measure of corn*

Buying corn in the sheaf without measuring

1. TO buy or sell corn in the sheaf, before it is threshed and measured, is against the common law of *England*, and the reason thereof seemeth to be, for that by such sale the market is in effect forestalled 3 *Inst* 197

Penalty of selling otherwise than by Winchester measure

2 If any person shall sell corn otherwise than by *Winchester* measure, sealed and stricken by the brim, he shall forfeit 40 s, on conviction before one justice, on the oath of one witness, to be levied by the churchwardens and overseers, or some of them, to the use of the poor, by distress and sale In default of distress, imprisonment till paid 22 *C* 2 *c* 8. *f* 2.

And if any mayor, or other head officer, shall knowingly permit the same, he shall, upon conviction thereof at the county sessions, forfeit 5 l, half to the prosecutor, and half to the poor, by distress and sale ; for want of distress, to be imprisoned by warrant of the justices, till payment be made *f* 3

Further penalty

3 And moreover, every person who shall sell or buy corn, without measuring, being thereunto required, or in any other manner than is by the 22 *C* 2 *c* 8 directed, and that without shaking of the measure by the buyer, he shall, beside the penalty of that act, forfeit all the corn so bought or sold, or the value thereof, to the party complaining 22 & 23 *C* 2 *c* 12 *f* 2

And on complaint made to a justice of the peace, that corn hath been bought, sold, or delivered contrary to this act, the proof shall lie upon the defendant, to make it appear by the oath of one witness, that he sold or bought the same lawfully wherein if he shall fail, he shall forfeit as is said before, to be levied by distress and sale, which shall by the justice be distributed, half to the poor, and half to the informer 22 & 23 *C* 2 *c* 12 *f* 3

Difference of measures

4 But notwithstanding all the statutes that have been made, for the uniformity of measures throughout the realm, yet

yet the meaſure of corn differs in many places, the buſhel being greater in one place than in another. And altho' regularly, a cuſtom or preſcription againſt a ſtatute is void, except it be confirmed by the ſtatute, or ſaved by another ſtatute; yet it is ſaid, that in the meaſure of corn, the cuſtom of the place is to be obſerved, if it be a cuſtom beyond all memory, and uſed without any viſible interruption. *Bacl* 578.

II *Cutting corn growing, or burning ſtacks of corn.*

1. Every perſon who ſhall unlawfully cut or take away any corn or grain growing, being convicted thereof by confeſſion, or oath of one witneſs, before one juſtice, ſhall for the firſt offence pay ſuch damages as the juſtice ſhall appoint; and if the juſtice ſhall think him not able or ſufficient, or if he do not pay ſuch damages, he ſhall commit him to the conſtable where the offence is committed, or where the party is apprehended, there to be whipped; and for every other offence he ſhall in like manner be whipped. The conſtable refuſing, ſhall be committed by the juſtice, till he conform. 43 *El. c.* 7 *Cutting corn growing*

but if he cut it at one time, and then come again at another time and take it away, it is felony. 1 *Haw.* 93.

2. If any perſon ſhall in the night time, maliciouſly and wilfully burn or cauſe to be burnt, any rick or ſtack of corn, he ſhall be guilty of felony; but to avoid judgment of death, he may make his election to be tranſported for ſeven years. And three juſtices (1 2) may determine the ſame. 22 & 23 C. 2 c. 7 *Burning corn in the night.*

3. But by the 9 G. c. 22. commonly called the Black Act, which is inſerted more at large in the title of that name, If any perſon ſhall ſet fire to any mow or ſtack of corn, he ſhall be guilty of felony without benefit of clergy. ſ 1. *Burning by night or day.*

And the hundred ſhall anſwer the damages, not exceeding 200l. ſ 7, 8, 9, 10.

And if any perſon ſhall apprehend, or cauſe to be convicted, ſuch offender, and ſhall be killed, or wounded ſo as to loſe an eye, or the uſe of any limb, in apprehending or endeavouring to apprehend ſuch offender, on proof thereof at the ſeſſions, and certificate thereof from thence, the ſheriff ſhall pay to the perſon intitled the ſum of 50l. in 30 days, to be repaid to him out of the treaſury. ſ 12.

III *Afcertaining the prices of corn*

1 By the 10 G 3 c 39 (which is in force for seven years, &c and by 17 G. 3. c 44 for seven years further) The justices, at *Michaelmas* sessions yearly, shall order returns to be made weekly of the prices of wheat, rye, barley, oats, and beans, (and in *Scotland* also of beer or big), from such market towns as they shall think proper, not less than two nor more than six within any county, riding, or division, and shall appoint a proper person, being an inhabitant of such market town, to make such returns from every such market town, to the persons appointed to receive the same (as hereafter mentioned) And if such person appointed shall die, neglect his duty, or become incapable of performing it, two justices may appoint another till the next sessions, and the justices there may confirm their choice, or appoint another till the next *Michaelmas* sessions And if the justices shall neglect to appoint proper persons to make returns, the commissioners of the treasury shall appoint them until the *Michaelmas* sessions next following ſ 1, 3

In *London*, the meal weighers shall take an account the prices of wheat, rye, barley, oats, and beans, at the markets within the said city, and return the average price weekly to the person to be appointed as aforesaid to receive the same ſ 2

2 And the justices shall cause a standard *Winchester* bushel of eight gallons to be provided and kept at each market town from whence the return shall be made ſ 4

3 And such returns shall be the average prices of wheat, rye, barley, oats, and beans, by the customary measure of each respective market, and the average prices by the said standard or *Winchester* bushel id

4 And every person making such returns (except from *London*) shall be paid such sums as the said justices shall direct, not exceeding 2s for each return, to be paid quarterly by the treasurer out of the publick stock, on receiving a certificate from the person appointed to receive the returns, that the said returns have been made according to the directions of this act, and upon receipt of duplicates of such returns, which duplicates, the persons making the same shall transmit to the clerk of the peace or his deputy, four times in every year, to be laid before the justices at their next general or quarter sessions ſ 5

5 The commissioners of the treasury shall appoint a fit person to receive the returns at the treasury, which person shall enter the returns in a book to be kept for that purpose

purpofe, and fhall once in every week caufe the fame or an abſtract thereof to be publifhed in the *London* gazette, and fhall alſo four times in every year tranſmit a certificate to the clerk of ne peace for each county or diviſion, and to the court of the mayor and aldermen of *London*, of the returns which have been made by the ſeveral perſons appointed to make the ſame within ſuch county or diviſion, and alſo whether the ſame were regularly made ſ 6

And he fhall receive and ſend all his letters and packets free from the duty of poſtage ſ 7

IV. *Importation of corn*

1 When corn doth not exceed the following prices, the cuſtom and poundage for corn imported ſhall be as follows: wheat not above 53s 4d a quarter, fhall pay 16s, if above 53s 4d, and not above 4l, it ſhall pay 8s, rye, not above 40s a quarter, fhall pay 16s, barley and malt, not above 32s a quarter, fhall pay 16s, buck wheat, not above 32s a quarter, fhall pay 16s, oats not above 16s a quarter, fhall pay 5s 4d, peaſe or beans, not above 40s a quarter, fhall pay 16s. 22 C 2 c 13 ſ 1 *Duty on importation*

But when the prices exceed theſe rates, then the duties payable before this act, fhall only be paid id ſ 2 That is to ſay, for every quarter of wheat imported 5s 4d, or rye 4s, barley or malt 2s 8d, buck wheat 2s, oats 1s 4d, peaſe or beans 4s 15 C 2 c 7 ſ 3

2 And that it may be known what price corn bears where ſuch foreign corn is imported, the juſtices of the peace for the counties where foreign corn is imported, fhall at every their quarter ſeſſions give in charge to the grand jury to make inquiry and preſentment upon their oaths, of the common market prices of the ſeveral ſorts of middling *Engliſh* corn, as the ſame is uſually commonly bought and ſold in the county, which preſentment ſhall be certified by the juſtices to the chief officer and collector of the cuſtoms at the port where the corn is imported, to be hung up in ſome publick place in the cuſtom houſe And the ſame ſhall be done in the city of *London* in *October* and *April* (and in *January* and *July*, 9 G 3 c 17,) yearly, by the mayor, aldermen and juſtices there, by the oaths of two perſons, neither of whom ſhall be corn chandler, meal man, factor, merchant, or other perſon, intereſted in ſuch corn to be imported, but by ſubſtantial houſholders in *Middleſex* or *Surry*, and each of them having a freehold eſtate of 20l a year, or leaſehold of 50l a year, *Price of corn how to be aſcertained for that purpoſe*

a year, above reprizes, and being skilful in the prices of corn 5 G 2 c 12 1 J. 2 c 19

But during the continuance of the 10 G 3 c 39 aforesaid, the prices shall be ascertained by persons specially appointed to make returns from the several counties as is above expressed, and the commissioners of the treasury shall order an account of the quantities of all corn and grain exported and imported from and into *Great Britain*, together with an account of all bounties and duties paid and received thereon, to be transmitted annually by the commissioners of the customs in *England* and *Scotland*, and be registred in proper books to be kept for that purpose, by the person appointed to receive the returns from the several counties as by the said act is directed 10 G 3 c. 39 ∫ 8 And by the act of 21 G 3 c 50 So much of the former acts as concerns the ascertaining of the prices, either for exportation or importation, is repealed with respect to the city of *London* and the counties of *Kent* and *Essex*, and many new regulations established, which act being of considerable length and minuteness, and affecting only a small part of the kingdom in comparison, it is judged necessary for the particulars to refer to the act itself

The said duties on importation, in what cases to cease.

3 Whenever the price of middling *British* wheat, at the ports and places where wheat shall be imported, shall be at or above 48 s a quarter, rye, pease, or beans, 32s, barley, beer, or bigg, 24s, oats, 16s, all customs and duties payable on importation thereof shall cease, and in lieu thereof, shall be paid on importation a duty of only 6d a quarter for wheat, 2d an hundred weight for wheat flour, 3d a quarter for rye, pease, and beans, and 2d a quarter for barley, beer, bigg, and oats And the same may be carried coastwise, under the same regulations as corn, flour, or grain of the growth of this kingdom 13 G 3 c 4, ∫ 1

Corn liable to the former duties on importation to be warehoused.

4 In case any wheat, or wheat flour, rye, pease, beans, barley, beer, bigg, or oats shall be imported into any of the ports of *Bristol, Berwick, Beaumaris, Dover, Exeter, Falmouth, Harwich, Hull, London, Lynn Regis, Lancaster, Liverpool, Milford, Newcastle, Newhaven, Poole, Southampton, Stockton, Whitehaven, Yarmouth, Ayr, Leith, Port Glasgow, Aberdeen, Kirkwall,* (*Preston,* 16 G 3 c 39 *Portsmouth, Sandwich, Chichester, Chester,* 18 G 3 c 25 and *Cowes,* 19 G 3 c 29) at any time when the duties not repealed by this act shall be payable for such species of corn, grain, or flour, the same, upon due entry thereof, may be forthwith landed, in presence of
2p

an officer, without payment of the duties, provided that
an account be taken of the quantity, and entred in a
book to be kept by the proper officer, and that the same
be secured under the joint locks of the king and the importer in a warehouse to be provided at the expence of the
importer or proprietor, with the approbation of the commissioners of the customs or three of them, or the collector and comptroller of the customs where the same
shall be imported, with liberty for the proprietor to screen,
turn, and take such other care of the same as necessity
shall require, in the presence of an officer. And such
corn, grain, or flour, shall not be delivered out but on
the following conditions, viz If the same shall be for
home consumption, the person taking out the same shall
pay such duties as shall at the time of taking out be payable for the like sort imported, and the same shall be
measured out, and shall pay the duties, by the stricken
bushel, and not by the heaped bushel And if the same
shall be delivered out for exportation, the owner or exporter, with one surety, shall enter into bond that the
same shall not be relanded in *Great Britain, Ireland,
Guernsey, Jersey, Alderney, Sark*, or *Man*, or the islands of
Faro —Provided, that this shall not extend to prohibit
corn, grain, or flour, imported from *Ireland* and warehoused here, to be carried back to *Ireland*, subject to the
like securities and restrictions as upon exportation of any
other foreign corn, grain, or flour   13 G 3 c 43
§ 2, 3

And all such corn, grain, or flour so delivered as aforesaid for exportation, shall be exported directly from the
port where the same was so delivered, and not removed or
carried to any other port or place in this kingdom, on
pain (besides the forfeiture of the bond) that all such
corn, grain, or flour shall be forfeited, together with the
boats, vessels, horses, carts, or carriages, and also the
ship from whence the same was unloaded, and may be
seized by any officer of the customs And all persons
assisting therein shall forfeit treble value of such corn,
grain, or flour The said penalties and forfeitures to be
recovered and applied, as in case of uncustomed goods.
§ 4

And in all cases, where any corn, grain, or flour, for
which the duties have been paid, shall be again exported
within six calendar months from the importation thereof;
the duty shall be *drawn back* and repaid to the person exporting the same to any place where a drawback is allowed on the exportation of any foreign goods. §. 13

V Ex-

V. Exportation of corn

1 Whenever the price of middling *British* wheat, at any port or place from whence the same shall be intended to be exported, shall be at or above 44s a quarter, no person shall export, or cause to be laid on board for exportation, any wheat, wheat meal or flour, malt, bread, biscuit, or starch, made of wheat When the price of rye, pease, or beans shall be at or above 28s a quarter, no person shall export, or cause to be laid on board for exportation, any rye, pease, or beans, ground or unground, or any bread or biscuit made of rye, pease, or beans When the price of barley, beer, or bigg, shall be at or above 22s a quarter, no person shall export, or cause to be laid on board for exportation, any barley, beer, or bigg, or malt, bread, or biscuit, made of barley, beer or bigg And when the price of oats shall be at or above 14s a quarter, no person shall export, or cause to be laid on board for exportation, any oats or oatmeal, or malt, bread, or biscuit, made of oats The said prices to be ascertained in manner aforesaid (save that the prices of corn and grain and of oatmeal exported shall be governed by the average prices at which the same shall be sold in the publick market at or nearest to the port of exportation on the last market day preceding, 14 G 3 c. 64) And if any person shall offend in the premises, the said commodities so exported or shipped for exportation shall be forfeited, and every offender therein shall forfeit 20s for every bushel of wheat, wheat meal or flour, rye, pease, beans, barley, beer or bigg, oats, oatmeal, and malt made of any of the grains aforesaid, ground or unground, and also the ship or vessel and furniture shall be forfeited, and may be seized by any officer of the customs, half to the king, and half to him that shall sue in the courts at *Westminster* or at the assizes And where the value of the penalties or forfeitures shall not exceed 50l, the same may be recovered by information before the justices in sessions. And the master or mariners knowingly assisting therein, shall on conviction in any such courts respectively, be imprisoned three months 13 G 3 c 43 f 5

Provided, that this shall not extend to prohibit the exportation or carrying out of so much of any of the said articles as shall be necessary for any ships in their voyage or for his majesty's ships of war, forces, forts, or garrisons. f. 6.

No

Nor to prohibit carrying the same coastwise, with the usual coquets *ſ. 7.*

Provided also, that nothing herein shall extend to prohibit the exporting yearly from the port of *London* to *Gibraltar*, any quantity of wheat, meal, flour, rye, barley, or malt, not exceeding 2500 quarters in the whole, to *Minorca*, 3500, to *St Helena*, (or any of the settlements of the *East India* company, 1000, 16 G 3 c 37. From the port of *Southampton* to *Guernsey*, *Jersey*, and *Alderney*, any quantity of wheat, meal, flour, rye, barley, malt, bread, biscuit, or pease, not exceeding 500 quarters in the whole, 14 G 3 c. 5 *ſ. 4*) From the ports of *Whitehaven* and *Liverpoole* to the Isle of *Man*, any quantity of wheat, barley, oats, meal, or flour, not exceeding 2500 quarters in the whole, half thereof from *Whitehaven*, and half from *Liverpoole* *ſ* 8

Provided also, that this shall not extend to prohibit the exportation of beans to the *British* forts or factories in *Africa*, or for the use of the ships trading on that coast which have been usually supplied from *Great Britain*, or to prohibit the *African* company from exporting annually any quantity of wheat flour not exceeding 200 quarters, or any quantity of bread or biscuit, or of bread and biscuit together, not exceeding 15 tons, to the said forts or factories *ſ* 9.

Nor to prohibit corn, grain, or flour, from being exported to *Ireland*, during such time as any general prohibition or embargo on the exportation of corn, grain, or flour shall be in force in that kingdom *ſ* 10

Nor to prohibit the exporting yearly, from the port of *London* only, any wheat, meal, flour, bread, and starch, made of wheat, not exceeding 2000 quarters in the whole, nor, from the port of *London* or any other port, any other sort of corn and grain, pease and beans, ground or unground, malt and oatmeal,—to any of his majesty's sugar colonies in *America* 14 G. 3 c 5 *ſ* 1. (And for the purposes of carrying this act into execution, four hundred weight avoirdupois of meal, and three hundred weight avoirdupois of flour, bread, biscuit, and starch, made of wheat, shall be deemed equal to one quarter of wheat *ſ* 6)

Provided also, that it shall be lawful to export yearly from the port of *Bristol* biscuit and pease not exceeding in the whole 150 tons of biscuit and 300 quarters of pease, from the port of *Poole* not exceeding 250 tons of biscuit and 700 quarters of pease, from the port of *Dartmouth* not exceeding 150 tons of biscuit and 300 quarters of pease,

from

from the ports of *Topsham* and *Tingmouth* within the port of *Exeter* not exceeding 150 tons of biscuit and 300 quarters of pease, to the island of *Newfoundland*, for the benefit of the fishery there. 14 G. 3 c 11.

And provided, that it shall be lawful to export yearly, from the port of *London* only, wheat meal or flour not exceeding in the whole 200 quarters, and oats, oatmeal, grotts, barley, pease, beans, malt, and biscuit, not exceeding together in the whole 250 quarters, to *Hudson's Bay*, for the benefit of the company there. 14 G 3 c 26.

And by the 18 G 3 c 16 for the use of the *British* fisheries at the island of *Newfoundland*, *Nova Scotia*, *Bay Chaleur*, and *Labrador*, further quantities of wheat flour, biscuit, and pease, are permitted to be exported from the ports of *London*, *Bristol*, *Poole*, *Dartmouth*, *Topsham*, *Tingmouth*, *Barnstaple*, *Liverpoole*, *Weymouth*, and *Chester*.

Bounty on exportation.

2 By the aforesaid act of the 13 G 3 c 43, the former bounties on exportation shall cease, and instead thereof there shall be allowed on the exportation of corn or grain, either ground or unground, being the growth of this kingdom, and put on board in *British* shipping, the master and at least two thirds of the mariners being his majesty's subjects, the several bounties following That is to say, when the price of middling *British* wheat shall be under 44s a quarter (to be ascertained as aforesaid), there shall be allowed a bounty of 5s for every quarter of wheat, and 5s for every quarter of malt made of wheat When rye shall be under 28s a quarter, there shall be allowed a bounty of 3s for every quarter of rye When barley, beer, or bigg shall be under 22s a quarter, there shall be allowed a bounty of 2s 6d for every quarter of barley, beer, or bigg, and 2s 6d for every quarter of malt made of barley, beer, or bigg And when oats shall be under 14s a quarter, there shall be allowed a bounty of 2s for every quarter of oats, and 2s 6d for every quarter of oatmeal, computed at the rate of 276 lb avoirdupois to a quarter. ∫ 11

Provided, that if any person shall have entered outwards any of the said articles, and begun to ship or lay the same on board, during the time that the prices of middling *British* corn shall be under the rates aforesaid, he shall not be prohibited from exporting the same, or so much thereof as shall be so shipped, within 20 days from the entry thereof at the custom house, nor from receiving the bounty, altho' the prices may have arisen above the rates herein before specified, after the said shipping, and before the exportation ∫ 12.

3. It

3 If any perfon fhall wilfully and malicioufly beat, wound, or ufe any other violence to any perfon, with intent to hinder him from buying corn in any market or other place, or fhall unlawfully ftop or feize upon any waggon, cart, or other carriage, or horfe, loaden with wheat, flour, meal, malt, or other grain, in or on the way to or from any city, market town, or fea port, and wilfully and malicioufly break, cut, feparate, or deftroy the fame or any part thereof, or the harnefs of the horfes drawing the fame, or fhall unlawfully take off, drive away, kill, or wound any fuch horfes, or unlawfully beat or wound the driver, or fhall, by cutting of the facks or otherwife, fcatter or throw abroad fuch wheat, flour, meal, malt, or other grain, or fhall take and carry away, fpoil or damage the fame, or any part thereof he fhall, on conviction before two juftices or the feffions, be fent to the gaol or houfe of correction, for any time not exceeding three months, nor lefs than one month, and be once publickly and openly whipped by the mafter of fuch gaol or houfe of correction, in fuch city, market town, or fea port, in or near which the offence fhall be committed, on the firft convenient market day, at the market crofs or market place there, between the hours of eleven and two 11 G 2 c 22 f 1

And if any fuch perfon, fo convicted, fhall commit any of the offences aforefaid a fecond time, or if any perfon fhall wilfully or malicioufly pull down, throw down, or otherwife deftroy any ftorehoufe, or granary, or other place where corn fhall be then kept in order to be exported; or fhall unlawfully enter any fuch ftorehoufe, granary, or other place, and take and carry away any corn, flour, meal, or grain therefrom, or fhall throw abroad or fpoil the fame or any part thereof, or fhall unlawfully enter on board any fhip or veffel, and fhall wilfully and malicioufly take and carry away, caft out therefrom, or otherwife fpoil or damage any meal, flour, wheat, or grain therein, intended for exportation he fhall be guilty of felony, and tranfported for feven years f 2, 3

And the hundred fhall anfwer damages (not exceeding 100l) as in cafes of robbery, the perfon injured giving notice of the offence in two days, by himfelf or fervant, to a conftable of the hundred, or the conftable of the place in or near which the fact fhall be committed, and within ten days after fuch notice, giving in the examination on oath of himfelf or of his fervant prefent at the time of the fact, or having the care of fuch his property, before a juftice of the peace, whether he knows the perfons that committed

mitted the fact, or any of them, and if he does, then entring into recognizance to prosecute ∫ 5, 6.

But if an offender is convicted in 12 months the hundred shall not be liable, and therefore the action must not be brought till after one year nor shall it be commenced but within 2 years. ∫ 7, 8

Coroner.

CORONERS are ancient officers by the common law, so called because they deal principally with the pleas of the crown, and were of old time the principal conservators of the peace. 2 *Haw* 42

Concerning whom I shall shew,

I *Who may be a coroner.*
II *How chosen*
III *His power and duty in taking an inquisition of death*
IV *His power and duty in other matters.*
V *His fees*
VI. *Punishment for not doing his duty.*

I *Who may be a coroner.*

Dignit

1 Of ancient time this office was of great estimation, for none could have it under the degree of a knight. 3 *Ed* 1 *c* 10   4 *Inst* 271

Estate.

2 And by the 14 *Ed* 3 *st* 1 *c*. 8. No coroner shall be chosen unless he have land in fee, sufficient in the same county, whereof he may answer to all manner of people.

II *How chosen*

To be chosen in the county court

1. The coroner (as of ancient time the sheriffs and conservators of the peace) shall be chosen in full county, that is, in the county court, by the commons of the same county. 28 *Ed* 3 *c.* 6

And this must be in pursuance of the king's writ for that purpose, issuing out of, and returnable into the chancery, and none but freeholders have a voice at such
2   election

election, for they only are fuitors to the county court.
2 *Haw.* 43, 44

2 And being elected by the county, if he be infuffi- Count to ancient, and not able to anfwer fuch fines and other duties fwer for him
in refpect of his office, as he ought, the county, as his
fuperior, fhall anfwer for him   2 *Inft* 175

3. And being chofen by the county, his office continues, Office not void
notwithftanding the demife of the king   4 *Inft* 271   by the king s
death

4. And after he is chofen, he fhall be fworn by the To be fworn
fheriff, for the due execution of his office   2 *Hale's
H* 55

5 But in the ftatute of 28 *Ed* 3 which enacts that O he s not cho-
they fhall be chofen by the county, there is a faving to the fen by the coun-
king and other lords, who ought to make coroners, their ty
franchifes

6 The lord chief juftice of the king's bench, by vir- Chiefjuftice.
tue of his office, is the chief coroner of *England*   2 H
H 53

III *His power and duty in taking an inquifition of death.*

1 When it happens that any perfon comes to an un- Notice.
natural death, the townfhip fhall give notice thereof to the
coroner. Otherwife if the body be interred before he
come, the townfhip fhall be amerced   *Hale's Pl* 170.

2 And by *Holt* Ch. J   It is a matter indictable to Burying without
bury a man that dies a violent death, before the coroner's notice.
inqueft have fat upon him.   2 *Haw Not.* 8.

3 And if the townfhip fhall fuffer the body to lie till Lying unburied
putrefaction, without fending for him, they fhall be amerced   *Hale's Pl* 270   2 *Haw* 48

4 When notice is given to the coroner, he is to iffue Precept to fum-
a precept to the conftables of the four, five, or fix next mon a jury
townfhips, to return a competent number of good and
lawful men of their townfhips, to appear before him in
fuch a place, to make an inquifition touching that matter   4 *Ed* 1 *ft.* 2   2 *H H* 59   Or he may fend his
precept to the conftable of the hundred. *Wool,* b 4 c. 1

But the aforefaid ftatute being wholly directory, and in
affirmance of the common law, doth neither reftrain the
coroner from any branch of his power, nor excufe him
from the execution of any part of his duty not mentioned
in it, which was incident to his office before   Upon which
ground, it hath been holden, that there is no neceffity that
it appear in a coroner's inqueft, that it was taken by the
oaths of perfons of the next adjacent towns, but that it

is sufficient to say, that it was taken by the oaths of lawful persons of the county, inasmuch as such inquisitions, being good before the statute, which is wholly declaratory, must needs be so still But it seems that it ought to appear in every such inquisition, at what place, and by what jurors by name it was taken, and that such jurors were sworn 2 *Haw* 47

Jur.

5 These are to be at least 12, and it is said, that all persons of the neighbouring towns, above the age of twelve years, are bound to attend at the taking the inquisition, unless they have a reasonable excuse to the contrary 2 *Inst* 148 2 *Haw* 54

Default in not appearing.

6 If the constables make not a return, or the jurors returned appear not, their defaults are to be returned to the coroner and the constables or jurors in default shall be amerced before the judges of assize 2 *H H.* 59

Swearing and charge

7. The jury appearing is to be sworn and charged by the coroner to enquire, upon the view of the body, how the party came by his death 2 *H H* 60.

View of the body.

8 For he can take inquisition of death, only upon view of the body, and not otherwise, therefore if the body be interred before he come, he must dig it up And this he may do lawfully within any convenient time, as in 14 days *Hale's Pl* 170. 2 *Haw.* 48

Where the body cannot be viewed

9 If the body cannot be viewed, the coroner can do nothing, but the justices of the peace shall enquire thereof *Hale's Pl* 170 2 *Haw* 48

Form of the charge where a person is slain

10 The jury being sworn, and the body upon view, he shall enquire upon the oaths of them, in this manner, by the statute of 4 *Ed* 1 *st* 2 called the statute *de officio coronatoris*, viz

If they know where the person was slain; whether it were in any house, field, bed, tavern, or company

Who are culpable, either of the act, or of the force, and who were present, either men or women, and of what age soever they be, if they can speak, or have any discretion

And how many soever be found culpable, they shall be taken and delivered to the sheriff, and shall be committed to the goal

And such as be found, and be not culpable, shall be attached until the coming of the judges of assize

Where a person slain is found in the field or woods.

11 And, by the same statute, if it fortune any such man be slain, which is found in the fields, or in the woods, first it is to be enquired, whether he were slain in the same place or not

And

And if he were brought and laid there, they should do so much as they can to follow their steps that brought the body thither, whether he were brought upon a horse, or in a cart

It shall also be enquired, if the dead person were known, or else a stranger, and where he lay the night before

12 Also, by the same statute, all wounds ought to be viewed, the length, breadth, and deepness, and with what weapons, and in what part of the body the wound or hurt is, and how many be culpable, and how many wounds there be, and who gave the wound. **Wounds,**

13 And they must hear evidence on all hands, if it be offered to them, and that upon oath, because it is not so much an accusation or an indictment, as an inquisition or inquest of office 2 H. H 157 **Defendant's evidence,**

14 And by the aforesaid statute, if any be found culpable of the murder, the coroner shall immediately go to his house, and shall enquire what goods he hath, and what corn he hath in his graunge, and if he be a freeman, they shall enquire how much land he hath, and what it is worth yearly, and further, what corn he hath upon the ground : and likewise of his freehold, how much it is worth yearly, over and above the service due to the lord of the fee, and the lands shall remain in the king's hands, until the lords of the fee have made fine for it **To enquire of the murderer's lands and goods,**

And when they have thus enquired upon every thing, they shall cause all the land, corn, and goods to be valued, in like manner as if they should be sold immediately ; and, thereupon they shall be delivered to the whole township, which shall be answerable before the judges for all.

15 In like manner, by the said statute, it is to be enquired of them that be drowned, or suddenly dead, whether they were so drowned, or slain, or strangled by the sign of a cord tied streight about their necks, or about any of their members, or upon any other hurt found upon their bodies And if they were not slain, then ought the coroner to attach the finders, and all other in the company **Persons drowned or suddenly dead,**

16. He shall also enquire, whether the persons so found guilty, fled, for which flight they forfeit goods and chattels 2 Haw 48, 53 **Flight.**

And it hath been formerly held, that if a person were slain, and upon the coroner's inquest on view of the body, it were found that such a person fled, tho' the said person were afterwards acquitted both of the felony and flight, yet he forfeited his goods, for the coroner's inquest is so solemn, that it is not traversable, also when the goods are once lawfully vested in the king, by that inquest, the property of them cannot be devested　But this opinion seemeth harsh and unreasonable, that a man shall be liable to forfeit all his goods, which may perhaps be all that he is worth, by an inquest taken in his absence, without either hearing him, or giving him an opportunity of defending himself　1 *Bac Abr* Coron D　2 *Haw* 54

Also it is strongly holden in some books, that an inquest of self murder, found before a coroner, cannot be traversed　but the contrary opinion being also holden by books of as great authority, and seeming also to be more agreeable to the general tenor of the law in other cases, it seems to be the better opinion, that such inquest by being removed into the king's bench by certiorari, may be there traversed by the executor or administrator of the person deceased, or in case the coroner's inquest find him to have been a lunatick, by the king or the lord of the manor. 1 *Bac Abr* Coron D　2 *Haw* 54

Township amerced for an escape

17. And if any person be slain or murdered in the day time, and the murderer escape untaken, the township shall be amerced　3 *H* 7 *c* 1

Deodands.

18 Concerning horses, boats, carts, and the like, whereby any are slain, which properly are called deodands, they also shall be valued, and delivered unto the towns as before　4 *Ed* 1 *st* 2.

Coroner's rolls.

19 All which things must be inrolled in the rolls of the coroner　4 *Ed* 1 *st* 2

Sheriff's rolls

20 And the sheriffs shall have counter rolls with the coroner, of things belonging to their office　3 *Ed* 1 *c* 10

Adjourning after view

21 But it is not necessary that the inquisition be taken in the very same place where the body was viewed, but they may adjourn to a place more convenient 2 *Haw* 48

Burial

22 Immediately upon these things being enquired, the bodies of such persons being dead, or slain, shall be buried 4 *Ed* 1 *st* 2

Certifying to the assizes

23 By the 1 & 2 *P & M c* 13 *s* 5　Every coroner, upon any inquisition before him found, whereby any person shall be indicted for murder or manslaughter or as accessary before the offence committed, shall put in writing the effect of the evidence given to the jury before him, being material , and shall bind over the witnesses to the next general gaol delivery to give evidence , and shall certify the evidence, the recognizance, and the inquisition or indictment before him taken and found, at or before the trial, on pain of being fined by the court

B*f*

By the exprefs words of which ftatute, he may enquire of *acceffaries befoie the fact*, but he cannot enquire of acceffaries *after* the fact 2 *Haw* 48

24 He ought alfo to enquire of the death of all perfons who die in prifon, that it may be known, whether they died by violence, or any unreafonable hardfhips for if a prifoner by the durefs of the gaoler, comes to an untimely death, it is murder in the gaoler, and the law implies malice in refpect of the cruelty 3 *Inft* 52, 91 Perfons dying in gaol

And this inqueft upon prifoners ought to confift of a party jury, that is, fix of the prifoners (if fo many there be), and fix of the next vill or parifh, not prifoners *Umfreville's Coron* 212

25 If the inquifition fha'l be quafhed in the court of king's bench, the coroner by leave of the court may take up the body again, and take a new inquifition *E* 5 *G K.* and *Saunders* Str 167. *M* 9 *G.* Cafe of the coroner of *Wenlock.* Str. 533 Inquifition quafhed

And if a coroner appear to have been corrupt in taking an inqueft, it feems that a *melius inquirendum* fhall go to fpecial commiffioners, who fhall proceed not on view, but upon teftimony, and the coroner fhall have nothing to do with fuch inqueft But where the inqueft is quafhed for want of form only, he fhall take a new one in like manner, as if he had taken none before. 1 *Bac. Abr.* Coron D

IV His power and duty in other matters

1 He ought to inquire of treafure that is found, who were the finders, and likewife who is fufpected thereof, and that may well be perceived, where one liveth riotoufly, haunting taverns, and hath done fo of long time hereupon he may be attached for this fufpicion, by four, or fix, or more pledges, if he may be found. 4 *Ed* 1 *ft* 2 Treafure trove.

2 Befides his judicial place, he hath alfo an authority minifterial as a fheriff, namely when there is juft exception taken to the fheriff, judicial procefs fhall be awarded to the coroner, for the execution of the king's writs and in fome fpecial cafes, the king's original writ fhall be immediately directed to him 4 *Inft.* 271 Executing procefs

3 He is bound to be prefent in the county court, to pronounce judgment of outlawry upon the exigent, after *quinto exactus*, at the fifth court, if the defendant doth not appear *Wood, b* 4 *c* 1. Outlawry.

4. He

4 He had anciently alſo a power in certain appeals, as of rape, and maim, and alſo in caſes of abjuration for felony or other offences, which are now out of uſe.

V His fees.

Fee of 13 s 4 d.

1 By the ſtatute of 3 H 7 c 1 The coroner ſhall have for his fee, upon every inquiſition taken upon the view of the body ſlain, 13 s 4 d of the goods and chattels of him that is the ſlaver and murderer, if he have any goods, and if not, he ſhall have for his ſaid fee, of ſuch amercia ments as ſhall fortune any townſhip to be amerced for eſcape of ſuch murderer

Fee of 20 s and alſo 9 d a mile

2 Moreover, by the 25 G 2 c 29 For every inqui ſition (not taken upon view of a body dying in gaol) he ſhall have 20s, and alſo 9d for every mile he ſhall be com pelled to travel from his uſual place of abode to take ſuch inquiſition, to be paid by order of the juſtices in ſeſſions, out of the county rates, for which order no fee ſhall be paid ſ 1

And for every inquiſition taken on view of a body dying in priſon, he ſhall be paid ſo much, not exceeding 20 s, as the juſtices in ſeſſions ſhall allow to be paid in like manner ſ 2

But no coroner of the king's houſhold, and of the verge of the king's palaces, nor any coroner of the admiralty, nor of the county palatine of *Durham*, nor of the city of *London* and borough of *Southwark*, nor any franchiſes be longing to the ſaid city, nor of any city, town, or fran chiſe, not contributing to the county rates, or within which ſuch rates have not been uſually aſſeſſed, ſhall be intitled to any benefit by this act, but they ſhall have ſuch fees and ſalaries as they were allowed before this act, or as ſhall be allowed by the perſons by whom they have been appointed ſ 5

VI His puniſhment for not doing his duty

His puniſhment for neglect of duty.

1 Coroners concealing felonies, or not doing their duty thro' favour to the miſdoers, ſhall be impriſoned a year, and fined at the king's pleaſure 3 Ed 1 c 9

2 And by the 3 H 7 c. 1 If any coroner be remiſs, and make not inquiſitions upon the view of the body dead, and certify the ſame to the gaol delivery, he ſhall forfeit to the king an hundred ſhillings.

3 And by the 25 G 2 c 29 If any coroner, not ap pointed by an annual election or nomination, or whoſe office is not annexed to any other office, ſhall be convicted of

of extortion for taking more than his lawful fees, or of wilful neglect of his duty, or misdemeanor in his office, the court before whom he shall be convicted may adjudge him to be removed from his office, and thereupon, if he shall have been elected by the freeholders, a writ shall issue for the amoving him, and the electing another in his stead; and if he hath been appointed by the lord of any liberty or franchise, or in any other manner than by the free-holders, the person intitled to nomination, shall on notice of such judgment of amoval, nominate another person in his stead $\int$ 6.

4 And he ought to execute his office in person, and not by deputy, for he is a judicial officer *Wood, b* 4 *c* 1 Otherwise it seemeth that he shall incur the aforesaid penalties, for remissness or neglect of duty.

The coroner's precept to summon a jury.

Westmorland $\}$ To the constable of ———— in the said county.

THESE are in the name of our sovereign lord the king, to require you, immediately upon sight hereof to summon and warn 24 good and lawful men of the four next townships to ———— in the said county, to be and appear before me A C. gentleman, one of the coroners of the county aforesaid, at ———— aforesaid, in the said county, on the ———— day of ———— then and there to enquire of, do, and execute all such things as on his majesty's behalf shall be lawfully given them in charge, touching the death of A D And be you then there to certify what you shall have done in the premisses, and further to do and execute what in behalf of our said lord the king shall be then and there enjoined you Given under my hand and seal the ———— day of ————.

The juror's oath on the coroner's inquest.

YOU shall diligently enquire, and true presentment make, on the behalf of our sovereign lord the king, how and in what manner A D (or, a person unknown, as the case is) here lying dead, came to his death, and of such other matters relating to the same as shall be lawfully required of you, according to your evidence. So help you God.

After the foreman is sworn, the rest may be sworn, three or four together, as follows

Such oath as A. T. the foreman of this inquest hath for his

*part taken, you and every of you shall well and truly observe and
keep on your parts respectively So help you God*

Witnesses oath

THE evidence which you shall give to this inquest, on the
behalf of our sovereign lord the king, touching the death
of A D. shall be the truth, the whole truth, and nothing but
the truth So help you God.

Inquisition of murder.

Westmorland AN inquisition indented, taken at ———
in the county of —— aforesaid, the ——
day of ———— in the —— year of the reign of —— before me A C gentleman, one of the coroners of our lord the
king, for the county aforesaid, upon the view of the body of
A D then and there lying dead, upon the oaths of A B.
C D E. I &c good and lawful men of ———— aforesaid,
and of twelve other of the next towns, to wit, K L and M.
in the said county, who being sworn and charged to enquire on
the part of our said lord the king, when, where, how, and
after what manner, the said A D came to his death, do say,
upon their oath, that one A M late of ———— aforesaid,
gentleman, not having God before his eyes, but being moved and
seduced by the instigation of the devil, on the —— day of ——
in the ———— year of ———— aforesaid, at the first hour in
the night of the same day, with force and arms, at ———— in
the county aforesaid, in and upon the aforesaid A D then and
there being in the peace of God, and of the said lord the king,
feloniously, voluntarily, and of his malice forethought, made
an assault And that the aforesaid A M. then and there with
a certain sword made of iron and steel, of the value of 5s,
which he the said A. M then and there held in his right hand,
the aforesaid A. D in and upon the left part of the belly of the
said A D a little above the navel of the said A D. then
and there violently, feloniously, voluntarily, and of his malice
forethought, struck and pierced, and gave to the said A D
then and there with the sword aforesaid, in and upon the aforesaid left part of the belly of the said A D a little above the
navel of the said A. D. one mortal wound of the breadth of
half an inch, and of the depth of three inches, of which said
mortal wound the aforesaid A D then and there instantly
died, and so the said A M then and there feloniously killed
and murdered the said A. D against the peace of our said lord
the king, his crown and dignity,

And

And the said jurors further say, upon their oath aforesaid, that A A of ———— yeoman, and B A of ———— yeoman, were feloniously present with drawn swords, at the time of the felony and murder aforesaid in form aforesaid committed, that is to say, on the said ———— day of ———— in the ———— year aforesaid, at ———— aforesaid, in the county aforesaid, at the first hour in the night of the same day, then and there comforting, abetting, and aiding the said A M to do and commit the felony and murder aforesaid in manner aforesaid, against the peace of our said lord the king, his crown and dignity.

And moreover, the jurors aforesaid, upon their oath aforesaid, do say, that the said A M A. A. and B A had not, nor any of them had, nor as yet have or hath any goods or chattels, lands or tenements, within the county aforesaid, or elsewhere, to the knowledge of the said jurors. [Or, And the jurors aforesaid, upon their oath aforesaid, do say, that the said A B at the time of the doing and committing of the felony and murder aforesaid, had goods and chattels, contained in the inventory to this inquisition annexed, which remain in the custody of B C.]

In witness whereof, as well the aforesaid coroner, as the jurors aforesaid, have to this inquisition put their seals, on the day and year, and at the place first above mentioned.

A C. *coroner.*

A. B.
C D
E F *&c. jurors*

An inquisition where one hangs himself.

———— As above to ———— not having God before his eyes, but being seduced and moved by the instigation of the devil, at ———— aforesaid, in a certain wood at ———— aforesaid, standing and being, the said A D being then and there alone, with a certain hempen cord of the value of 3 d, which he then and there had and held in his hands, and one end thereof then and there put about his neck, and the other end thereof tied about a bough of a certain oak tree, himself then and there, with the cord aforesaid, voluntarily and feloniously, and of his malice forethought, hanged and suffocated, and so the jurors aforesaid, upon their oath aforesaid say, that the said A D then and there in manner and form aforesaid, as a felon of himself, feloniously, voluntarily, and of his malice forethought, himself killed, strangled, and murdered, against the peace, &c.

An

An inquisition where one drowns himself.

———— at ———— aforesaid, in the county aforesaid, then and there being alone, in a common river there, called ———— himself voluntarily and feloniously drowned And so the jurors aforesaid, upon their oath aforesaid say, that the aforesaid A D. in manner and form aforesaid, then and there himself voluntarily and feloniously as a felon of himself killed and murdered, against the peace ————

An inquisition on one drowned by accident.

———— that the said A D on the ———— day of ———— in the year aforesaid, at the parish and in the county aforesaid, going into the river ———— there to bathe himself, it so happened, that accidentally, casually, and by misfortune, he the said A D was in the water of the said river then and there suffocated and drowned, of which said suffocation and drowning he the said A D then and there instantly died And so the jurors aforesaid do say, that the said A D in manner, and by the means aforesaid, accidentally, casually, and by misfortune, came to his death, and not otherwise. In witness, &c

An inquisition where one dies a natural death

———— that the said A D on the ———— day of ———— in the year aforesaid, at the parish and in the county aforesaid, to wit, in a certain place called ———— was found dead, that he had no marks of violence appearing on his body, and died by the visitation of God, in a natural way, and not otherwise. In witness, &c.

An inquisition upon one who dies in gaol

———— who say upon their oath, that the aforesaid A D on the day of the taking of this inquisition, being a prisoner in the gaol at ———— in the county aforesaid, then and there died of the visitation of God, and then and there in manner and form aforesaid came to his death, and not otherwise. In witness, &c.

An inquisition on one *non compos mentis*

———— who say upon their oath, that the aforesaid A D on the day and year aforesaid, and at the time of his death, to wit,

wit, from the ———— day of ———— to the time of his death, and at the time of his death aforesaid, was a lunatick, and a person of insane mind, and that the said A D being a luna-tick and a person of insane mind as aforesaid, did on the ———— day of ———— come alone to a certain river, called ———— in the said county, and did then and there cast himself into the said river, and drowned himself in the water of the said river. And so the jurors aforesaid, upon their oath aforesaid say, that the aforesaid A D from the cause aforesaid, in man-ner and form aforesaid, came to his death, and not otherwise. In witness, &c.

An inquisition on one for cutting his throat

———— by the instigation of the devil, at ———— aforesaid, in the county aforesaid, in and upon himself, then and there being in the peace of God and of the said lord the king, felo-niously, voluntarily, and of his malice forethought, made an assault. And that the aforesaid A D then and there with a certain knife, of the value of one penny, which he the said A D then and there held in his right hand, himself upon his throat then and there feloniously, voluntarily, and of his malice fore-thought did strike, and gave to himself then and there with the knife aforesaid, upon his throat aforesaid one mortal wound of the breadth of four inches, and the depth of one inch, of which said mortal wound the said A D at ———— aforesaid in the county aforesaid, languished, and languishing lived, from the said ———— day of ———— in the ———— year aforesaid, to the ———— day of ———— and that the said A D on the ————day of ———— aforesaid, in the ———— year aforesaid, at ———— aforesaid, in the county aforesaid, of that mortal wound died. And so the jurors aforesaid, &c

For killing another in his own defence

———— upon their oaths say, that A K late of ———— gentleman, at ———— aforesaid in the said county, on the ———— day of ———— in the ———— year of ———— in the peace of God and of our said lord the king then being, A M late of ———— in the county of ———— at the hour of ———— in the afternoon of the same day, did come, and upon him the said A K then and there of his malice forethought did make an assault, and him the said A K had then and there endeavour to beat and kill, by continu-ing the assault aforesaid, from the house of one W H in ———— aforesaid to a certain place called ———— in the county afore-said, and the said A K seeing that the said A M was so maliciously disposed to a certain wall in the said place, called ———— did flee, and from thence for fear of death could not escape,

escape, and so the said A K himself, in preservation of his life, against the said A M. continued to defend, and in his own defence him the said A K upon the right part of the breast of him the said A M with a certain sword of the price of one shilling, which the said A K then and there held in his right hand, did strike, then and there giving to the said A. M one mortal wound, of the breadth of one inch, and of the depth of three inches, of which said mortal wound the said A M at ——— aforesaid in the county aforesaid languished, and languishing lived from the said ——— day of ——— to the ——— day of ——— from thence next ensuing, and that the said A M on the said ——— day of ——— in the ——— year aforesaid, at ——— aforesaid in the said county, of that mortal wound died, And so the said A K did then and there kill him the said A M in his own defence

An inquisition where the murderer is unknown.

——— The same as before, only say, ——— *that a certain person unknown, &c and add ——— And the said jurors upon their oath aforesaid further say, that the said person unknown, after he had committed the said felony and murder in manner aforesaid, did fly away. Against the peace, &c*

Costs.

BY the 18 G 2 c 19 Whereas by the laws now in being, justices of the peace are not sufficiently authorised, on complaints that come before them out of sessions, to award costs against either the person complaining, or the person against whom the complaint is made, it is therefore enacted, that where any complaint shall be made before any justice or justices, and a warrant or summons shall issue in consequence thereof, it shall be lawful for such justice, who shall have heard and determined the matter of the complaint, to award (A) such costs to be paid by either party, and in manner and form as to him shall seem meet, to the party injured And if the person so ordered by the justice shall not forthwith pay, or give security for the same to the satisfaction of the justice, the same shall be levied by distress (B) And if goods and chattels of such person cannot be found (C), the justice shall commit him (D) to the house of correction for the place where such person shall reside, to be kept to hard labour not exceeding one month, nor less than ten days, or until ſuch ſum, together with the expences attending the commitment, be firſt paid ſ 1

Provided, that upon the conviction of any perſon upon a penal ſtatute, where the penalty ſhall amount to or exceed the ſum of 5 l, the ſaid coſts ſhall be deducted by the juſtice, according to his diſcretion, out of the penalty, ſo that the ſaid deduction ſhall not exceed one fifth part of the penalty, and the remainder of the penalty ſhall be paid to or divided among the perſon or perſons who would have been intitled to the whole of the penalty, if this act had not been made ſ. 2

And the juſtices in ſeſſions from time to time may lay down or alter ſuch rules and regulations concerning coſts or charges to be allowed to any perſon by virtue of this act, as to them ſhall ſeem juſt which rules and regulations, having received the approbation and ſignature of one or more of the judges of aſſize, ſhall be binding, and not otherwiſe, on all perſons whatſoever ſ 9

The following forms are inſerted in the act itſelf.

A. Form of awarding coſts.

County or borough of ——— to wit } *I A J one of his majeſty's juſtices of the peace in and for the ——— aforeſaid, in purſuance of an act made in the eighteenth year of his majeſty king George the third, intituled,* An act for the payment of coſts to parties, on complaints determined before juſtices of the peace out of ſeſſions, for the payment of the charges of conſtables in certain caſes, and for the more effectual payment of charges to witneſſes and proſecutors of any larceny or other felony, *on the complaint of ——— ——— [here ſtate the names of the parties and the offence generally, and the date] againſt ——— for ——— which ſaid complaint was heard and determined by me on the ——— day of ——— Do award the following coſts to be paid by ——— videlicet [here ſtate the coſts] Given under my hand and ſeal this ——— day of ——— in the year of our Lord ———*

B. Form of warrant of diſtreſs and ſale.

——— to wit. } To the conſtable of ——— ——— and to all other his majeſty's conſtables in and for ——— in ——— ·——— aforeſaid

Whereas I J P eſquire, one of his majeſty's juſtices of the peace in and for the ——— aforeſaid, in purſuance of an act made

in the eighteenth year of his majefty king George *the third, intituled,* An act for the payment of cofts to parties, on complaints determined before juftices of the peace out of feffions,
for the payment of the charges of conftables in certain
cafes, and for the more effectual payment of charges to
witneffes and profecutors of any larceny or other felony,
*have awarded, on the ——— day of ——— now laft paft, on the
complaint of ——— againft ——— for ——— the following cofts to
be paid by ——— videlicet* [here ftate the fum] *And whereas
the faid ——— being ordered by me the faid juftice to pay fuch
fum as aforefaid, hath not paid down or given fecurity for the
fame to the fatisfaction of me the faid juftice, Thefe are therefore to command you, and each and every of you, to levy the
faid fum of ———ly diftrefs and fale of the goods and chattels of the faid ——— and I do hereby order and direct the
goods and chattels fo to be diftrained to be fold and difpofed of
within ——— days, unlefs the faid fum of ——— for which
fuch diftrefs fhall be made, together with the reafonable charges
of taking and keeping fuch diftrefs, fhall be fooner paid, and you
are hereby alfo commanded to certify unto me what you fhall have
done by virtue of this my warrant. Given under my hand and
feal at ——— the ——— day of ——— in the year of our
Lord ———.*

C. Conftables return thereon, for want of diftrefs.

——— } *I ——— conftable of ——— do hereby certify
to wit. } to ——— juftice of the peace of ——— that I have
made diligent fearch for, but do not know, nor can
find any goods and chattels of ——— by diftrefs and fale whereof I may levy the fum of ——— purfuant to his warrant for
that purpofe dated the ——— day of ———. Given under my
hand, this ——— day of ——— in ———.*

D Commitment thereupon to the houfe of cor-
rection.

——— } To the conftable of ——— and alfo to the
to wit } keeper of the houfe of correction at ———
*Whereas, in purfuance of an act made in the eighteenth year
of his majefty king* George *the third, intituled,* An act for the
payment of cofts to parties, on complaints determined
before juftices of the peace out of feffions, for the payment of the charges of conftables in certain cafes, and
for the more effectual payment of charges to witneffes and
profecutors of any larceny or other felony, *I J P efquire,
one of his majefty's juftices of the peace in and for the faid* ———

did

did issue my warrant of distress and sale, directed to —— of —— constable of the said —— of —— ordering the said constable to levy the sum of —— of the goods and chattels of the said —— in manner and form as therein is mentioned And whereas it appears to me by the return of —— constable of —— dated the —— day of —— that he hath made diligent search, but doth not know of nor can find any goods and chattels of the said —— by distress and sale whereof the said sum of —— may be levied pursuant to the said warrant. These are therefore to command you the said constable of —— to apprehend the said —— and convey the said —— to the said house of correction at —— and to deliver the said —— there to the said keeper of the said house of correction And these are also to command you the said keeper of the said house of correction, to receive the said —— into the said house of correction and there to keep to hard labour for the space of —— from the date hereof, or until such sum of —— together with the expences attending the commitment of the said —— to the said house of correction, be first paid, or until the said —— be discharged by due course of law Given under my hand and seal at —— the —— day of ——

The costs and charges of prosecutors and witnesses in cases of felony are treated of under the title **Felony.**

Cottages.

COTTAGE (Sax. *Cote*) is a little house for habitation, without any land belonging to it. By the 31 El c 7 cottages were prohibited to be erected without laying at least four acres of land to the same, and divers other restrictions were thereby injoined, but the same was repealed by the 15 G 3 c 32 setting forth, that the said statute of 31 El. had laid the industrious poor under great difficulties to procure habitations, and tended very much to lessen population, and in divers other respects was inconvenient to the labouring part of the nation in general

County court.

County.

1 ANCIENTLY, the *comites, counts,* or *earls,* had the government of the counties, and afterwards the *vicecomites* or *sheriff.* And the *county* seemeth to be nothing else, but the district of the *comes* or *count.* Shire is a *Saxon* word, from *scyran,* to share or divide, for that the shires and counties are divided by certain metes and bounds from each other. And the *sheriff,* in Saxon *scyregerefa,* is the *reve, grave,* or governor of the *shire,* wherein he hath great power, being therein the chief officer under the king.

County court.

2 The sheriff holdeth in his county two courts, the *torn* and the *county court.* The *torn* is the king's court of record, for criminal causes, and for redressing of common grievances within the county, the *county court* is not a court of record, but only a court baron, for civil causes, and this is the court'of the sheriff himself

When to be holden.

3 By the 2 & 3 *Ed* 6 *c* 25 No county court shall be longer deferred than one month from court to court, so that the county court shall be kept every month, and not otherwise.

And this is to be accounted 28 days to the month, and not according to the month of the calendar. 2 *Inst.* 71

Where to be kept

4 It may be kept at any place within the county, unless restrained by statute. *Wood,* b 4. *c.* 1

How far the sheriff is judge

5 The suitors, that is, the freeholders, are the judges in this court, except that in re-disseisin, by the statute of *Merton,* the sheriff is judge. And by the statutes concerning parliamentary elections, he is judge at the election of knights, for he must make a true return at his peril. *Barl* County Court

Of what sum this court hath cognizance

6 This court shall hold pleas betwixt party and party, where the debt or damage is under 40 s. 4 *Inst* 266

But in a *replevin,* the sum may be above 40 s. 4 *Inst.* 266.

Of what offences this court hath cognizance

7 Also it hath not cognizance of trespass *vi et armis,* because a fine is thereby due to the king, which it cannot impose. 4 *Inst* 266

One plaint for one trespass or contract.

8 And by the 11 *H* 7 *c* 15 No plaint shall be entered in the county court, but where the plaintiff, or his attorney is present, and the plaintiff shall find pledges to pursue his plaint, and he shall have but one plaint for one trespass or contract, on pain of 40 s, half to the king, and half to the prosecutor. And one justice may examine the

the sheriff or other officer, making default, and shall, within a quarter of a year, certify the examination into the exchequer

But as to the pledges above mentioned, they are now disused in this court; and were formerly used only in cases where the plaintiff lived out of the county   *Greenw.* 11 *Read* County C

9 But by virtue of a writ of *justicies*, the court may hold plea of trespass *vi & armis*, and of any sum, or of all actions personal above 40s   For this writ is in the nature of a commission to the sheriff, for the sake of dispatch, to do the same *justice* in his county court, as might otherwise be had in the courts at *Westminster*   4 *Inst* 266   **Writ of justicies**

10 By the 12 *G* 2 *c* 13 *f* 7   If any person shall commence or defend any action, or sue out any writ, process, or summons, or carry on any proceedings in the county court, who shall not be admitted attorney or solicitor according to the act of 2 *G* 2 *c* 23 he shall forfeit 20l with costs, to him who shall sue in any court of record   **Who shall act as attorney in this court**

11 The plaintiff in this court first takes out a summons returnable at the next county court, and if the defendant do not appear, an attachment or *distringas* is to be made out   but if the defendant appear, the plaintiff is to file his declaration, shewing his cause of action, or matter of complaint, in what manner the action accrued, at what time and place the wrong was done, and the damage he hath sustained   *Greenw* 11   *Read* County C   **Summons.**

12 If the defendant doth appear, and the next court after gives a rule to declare, and the plaintiff doth not file his declaration within the time, he may be nonsuited   *id*   **Declaration.**

13 When the plaintiff hath declared, he must continue his suit from court day to court day, otherwise the defendant may take advantage of it, and this is called a continuance, being an adjourning of the suit from time to time, to keep it on foot   *id*   **Continuance.**

14 The rule, or *dies datus*, is when farther day is given to the plaintiff to declare, or to the defendant to plead, and the time given is usually to the next court day, but upon occasion may be enlarged   *id*   **Dies datus**

15 The next court after filing the declaration, and imparlance given, the defendant is to put in his answer or plea, and if the plaintiff join issue, they may proceed to trial the next court day, if they proceed not farther by replication, rejoinder, surrejoinder, and the like   *id*   **Answer.**

16 But if freehold is pleaded by the defendant, this court can proceed no further, for freehold shall never be   **Plea of freehold.**

tried without writ, therefore the cause must be removed, as when a defendant avoweth for damage feasant, and the plaintiff justifieth by reason of common of pasture *Wood.* b 4 c 1

Judgment and diftrifs

17 Where a verdict is given for the plaintiff, and judgment entred thereupon, a *fieri facias* may be awarded against the defendant's goods, which may be taken by virtue thereof, and appraised and sold, to satisfy the plaintiff, but if the defendant hath no goods whereupon to levy, the plaintiff remains without remedy in this court, for it being no court of record, no *capias* lies there, but an action may be brought at common law upon the judgment entred *Greenw* 22 *Read* County C.

Removal by recordare

18 Causes are removed out of this court, by a writ of *recordare*, which issues out of the chancery, directed to the sheriff, commanding him to send the plaint that is before him in his county court (without writ of *justicies*) into the court of king's bench, or common pleas, to the end the cause may be there determined And the sheriff is hereupon to summon the other party to be in that court, (into which the plaint is to be sent) at a day certain And of all this he is to make certificate under his own seal, and the seals of four suitors of the same court *Read* County C

Removal by pone

19 Causes are also removed by *pone*, which differs in nothing from a *recordare*, but that it removes such suits as are before the sheriff by writ of *justicies*, and a *recordare* is to remove the suit that is by plaint only, without writ *id*

Removal after discontinuance

20 And altho' the plea be discontinued in the county, yet the plaintiff or defendant may remove the plaint into the common pleas or king's bench, and it shall be good, and he shall declare upon the same *id*

Of outlawry pronounced

21 In this court, after the *quinto exactus*, the coroner gives judgment of outlawry 4 *Inst* 266

Hundred court.

22 Out of the county court is derived the hundred court, for the ease of the subject, and it hath like jurisdiction as the county court, and may be held every three weeks 2 *Inst* 71

County hall. See **Shire hall.**

County rate.

THE feveral rates hereafter following, in order to avoid the inconveniencies of feparate collections, fhall for the future be levied and raifed by one general county rate

That is to fay,

(1) For repairing county bridges, and highways thereto adjoining, and falaries for the furveyors of bridges, as directed by the 22 H 8 c 5 and 1 An ft. 1 c 18.

(2) For building and repairing county gaols, by 11 & 12 W c 19

(3) For repairing fhire halls, by the 9 G. 3 c 20

(4) For the mafter of the houfe of correction his falary, and relieving the weak and fick in his cuftody, by the 7 J c 4

(5) For relief of the prifoners in the king's bench and marfhalfea prifons, and of poor hofpitals in the county, and of thofe that fhall fuftain loffes by fire, water, the fea, or other cafualties, and other charitable purpofes for relief of the poor, as the juftices in feffions fhall think fit; b. tne 43 El c 2 f 15

(6) For relief of prifoners in the county gaol, by the 14 El c 5

(7) For the prefervation of the health of prifoners, by the 14 G 3. c 59

(8) For the chaplain's falary of the county gaol, by the 13 G 3 c 58

(9) For fetting prifoners on work, by the 19 C 2. c 4

(10) The treafurer's falary, by the 12 G 2 c 29.

(11) Salary of perfons making returns of the prices of corn, by the 10 G 3 c 39

(12) Charges attending the removal of any of the faid general county rates by certiorari, by the 12 G. 2 c 29.

(13) Money for purchafing lands at the ends of county bridges, by the 14 G 2. c 33

(14) Charges of building or repairing houfes of correction, and for fitting up and furnifhing the fame, and employing the perfons fent thither, by the 17 G 2 c 5 f 33.

(15) Charges of apprehending, conveying, and maintaining rogues and vagabonds, by the 17 G 2 c 5

(16) Charges of the foldiers carriages, over and above the officers pay for the fame, by the feveral yearly acts

F f 2   againft

against mutiny and defertion, and by the militia act of the 2 G 3 c 20

(17) The coroners fee of 9d a mile for travelling to take an inquisition, and 20s for taking it, by the 25 G 2 c 29

(18) Charges of carrying persons to the gaol, or house of correction, by the 27 G 2 c 3

(19) The gaoler's fees for persons acquitted of felony, or discharged by proclamation, by the 14 G 3 c 20

(20) Charges of prosecuting and convicting felons, by the 25 G 2 c 36. 27 G. 2. c. 3. 14 G 3 c. 20 and 18 G 3 c 19

(21) Charges of prosecuting and convicting persons plundering shipwrecked goods, by the 26 G. 2 c 19

(22) Charges of maintaining the militia men's family, by the several militia acts

(23) Charges of bringing insolvent debtors to the assizes, in order to their discharge, if themselves are not able to pay, by the 32 G 2 c 28

(24) The charges of transporting felons, or conveying them to the places of labour and confinement, by the 6 G c 23 & 19 G 3 c 74.

(25) Charges of carrying parish apprentices, bound to the sea-service, to the port to which the master belongeth, by the 2 & 3 An c 6.

Sessions to lay the rate

2 And that the same may be collected with as much ease, and as little expence as possible, the justices at their general or quarter sessions, or the greater part of them, shall have power to make one general rate to answer all the purposes aforesaid 12 G 2 c 29 ſ 1

Which rate shall be assessed in such proportions in every parish or place, *as any of the rates by the said several former acts have been usually assessed* id

By which last words reference being made to the former acts, as to the manner of proportioning the rate, it is proper to insert here, how the case stands upon the said former act, as to such laying of the assessments, and it is thus

(1) By the above mentioned act of the 22 H 8 (in regard to *bridges*) the justices were to rate every inhabitant within their jurisdiction, in such reasonable sum, as they should think convenient   And by the 1 *An* ſt 1 c. 18 Every town, parish, or place was to be assessed as they usually had been assessed towards the repair of bridges

(2) By the 14 *El* c 5 (for *relief of prisoners*) the justices were to rate every parish at such reasonable sums as they should think convenient

(3) By the 44 *El* c 2 (for *hospitals and the marshalsea*) the same was to be rateably assessed upon every parish

(4) By

(4) By the 7 *J c* 4 (for *the master of the house of correction his salary*) the same was to be rated, as for hospitals and the marshalsea, by the 43 *El c* 2

(5) By the 19 *G* 2 *c* 4 (for *setting prisoners on work*) to be raised as other county charges

(6) By the 11 *G* 12 *W c* 19 (for *repairing gaols*) to be assessed by the justices in equal proportions, on every hundred, ward, or other division

(7) And for *vagrants* (by the 12 *An* now repealed) the money was to be raised as for bridges and gaols

So that upon the whole here seems to be intended an equal, proportionable rate, upon every division

3 And where any person, liberty, division, or place hath usually contributed, or is liable to pay, only to one or more of, and not to all the rates hereby intended to be raised and thrown into one general rate, the justices at their general or quarter sessions may order and ascertain, what proportion thereof shall be assessed on, and paid by such person, liberty, division, or place 12 *G* 2 *c* 29 *f* 5

As for instance, where by the statute of 22 *H* 8 *c* 5 towns corporate are charged for the repairing of bridges within their respective liberties, and the counties, for the bridges out of such liberties, in such case, a town corporate ought not to be charged towards the bridges in the county at large, and consequently ought to have an abatement in the rate charged upon them, in such proportion as the expence of bridges is to the whole expence of the several articles charged upon the said general county rate, as if the expence of bridges be a tenth part of the whole expence chargeable upon the county rate, then such town corporate shall have an abatement of one shilling for every ten, which it would otherwise be charged with in such rate

4 And by the 13 *G* 2 *c* 18. *f* 7 Where any liberties or franchises have commissions within themselves, and are not subject to the county justices, and do not, nor did before the 12 *G* 2 contribute to the county rates, the justices within such liberties may exercise the same powers within their liberties, as justices in their counties

5. Which said rates the high constable shall, at such times as the said justices by their order in sessions shall direct, demand of the churchwardens and overseers; which demand shall be made in writing (A) and given to them, or any of them, or left at their dwelling houses, or affixed on the church doors by the said high constables 12 *G*. 2 *c* 29 *f* 2

6 Whereupon the said churchwardens and overseers shall in 30 days after such demand made, of the mo-

F f 3   ney

ney collected for relief of the poor, pay the fums fo affeffed on each parifh or place 12 *G* 2 *c* 29 *f* 2

7 And if the churchwardens or overfeers, or any of them, fhall neglect or refufe fo to pay, the high conftable fhall levy the fame by diftrefs and fale of the goods of fuch churchwardens or overfeers fo refufing or neglecting, by warrant of two or more juftices refiding in or near fuch parifh or place 12 *G* 2 *c* 29 *f* 2

8 And the receipt of fuch high conftable fhall be a full difcharge to the churchwardens and overfeers, or other perfon paying the fame 12 *G* 2 *c* 29 *f* 2

9 Where there is no poor rate, the juftices, in their general or quarter feffions, fhall by their order direct the fum affefled on fuch parifh, townfhip, or place, to be rated and levied by the petty conftable, or other peace officer, *as money, for relief of the poor is by law to be rated or levied* Which fum fo rated and levied fhall be paid by him to the high conftable, and fhall be demanded of, paid by, or levied on fuch petty conftable, in the fame manner as before of the churchwardens and overfeers And if any petty conftable fhall pay fuch fum before he hath collected it, he may afterwards rate and levy the fame, or may be allowed and reimburfed the fame, out of any conftable's or other rate, which the juftices in their feffions fhall order and direct 12 *G* 2 *c* 29 *f* 3

As money for relief of the poor is to be rated or levied] That is to fay, by taxation of every inhabitant, parfon, vicar, and other, and of every occupier of lands, houfes, tithes, coal mines, or faleable underwoods 43 *El c* 2 *f* 1

10 And whereas it will be inconvenient to many towns, parifhes, and places, in the counties of *York, Derby, Durham, Lancafter, Chefter, Weftmorland, Cumberland*, and *Northumberland*, that the faid rates fhould be paid out of the poor rate, the juftices at their general or quarter feffions, *if they fhall think convenient*, may order the fum affefled on any fuch town, parifh, or place, to be paid by and levied on the petty conftable [B] in fuch manner as is above directed, in cafes where no rate is made for the poor. 12 *G* 2. *c* 29 *f* 4

If they fhall think convenient] By which words, the juftices in thofe counties may order the rate to be paid by either of the two methods before mentioned, according to their difcretions, that is to fay, either by the churchwardens and overfeers out of the poor rate, or by the petty

conftables

constables by an assessment after the manner of the poor rate And the reason of this clause seems to be, because some parishes in the northern counties being very large, and for that reason subdivided into several townships with regard to the poor, it may happen that some townships in the same parish may be high rated, and others low rated, towards the relief of their poor, therefore if a general sum for the county rate upon the whole parish were to be charged upon all the inhabitants, in proportion to their poor rate, it would lay the burden very unequally To remedy which, the justices by this clause may charge separately such sum as they shall think reasonable upon each subdivision or constablewick, in order to lay the same equally throughout the parish and if any township shall be aggrieved thereby, they may appeal as hereafter is directed, or remove it by *certiorari*

11. The said high constables, at or before the next sessions respectively after they have received the money, shall pay the same to the treasurer, and the money so paid, shall be deemed the publick stock 12 G 2 c 29 f 6

High constable to pay to the treasurer

12 And the treasurer's receipt shall be a sufficient discharge to the high constable 12 G 2 c 29 f 9

Treasurer's receipt

13 And the said high constables shall deliver in a true account on oath (if required) of the money by them received, before the said justices at their general or quarter sessions and if any such high constable shall neglect or refuse to demand or levy as aforesaid, or to account, the said justices at their general or quarter sessions may commit him to the common gaol, until he shall have caused such rates to be demanded and levied, and shall have rendered a true account And if it shall appear by such account, that any sum is remaining in his hands, and he shall not pay over the same to the treasurer, they may commit him till he pay the same 12 G 2 c 29 f. 8.

High constable to account.

14 And the justices, at their general or quarter sessions, may oblige by their order, the petty constables or any other person empowered to levy, collect, or receive any sum for the purposes aforesaid, and who have any sum in their hands, to account and pay over the same, in like manner as the high constables 12 G 2 c 29 f 17

Petty constables and others to account

15 And the treasurer shall pay so much of the money in his hands, to such persons, as the justices in sessions shall by their order from time to time appoint, for the uses and purposes of the said above mentioned acts, and for any other uses and purposes to which the public stock of any county, city, division or liberty, is or shall be applicable 12 G 2. c 29 f 6.

Treasurer disbursements

Ff4

16 And

16 And the treafurer fhall keep a book of entries, of the fums by him received and paid, and fhall deliver in a true account, on oath if required, of his receipts and difburfements, to the juftices at every general or quarter feffions, and alfo the proper vouchers for the fame, to be kept amongft the records of the feffions. 12 G 2 c. 29 f. 7, 8

17 And the difcharge of the faid juftices, by their order at their general or quarter feffions, fhall be a fufficient difcharge to the treafurer 12 G 2 c 29. f 9

18 And no new rate fhall be made, until it appear by the treafurer's accounts, or otherwife, that three fourths of the money collected have been expended for the purpofes aforefaid 12 G 2 c 29 f 10

19 If the churchwardens and overfeers of any parifh or place, fhall think fuch parifh or place is over-rated, they may appeal to the next general or quarter feffions, againft fuch part of the rate only as may affect fuch parifhes or places but fuch rate, upon the appeal, fhall not be quafhed in regard to any other parifhes or places 12 G 2 c 29. f 12.

20 No *certiorari* to remove any rates, or any orders or other proceedings of the feffions touching fuch rates, fhall be granted but upon motion the firft week of the next term after the time for appealing from fuch rates or orders is expired, and on making it appear to the court by affidavit or otherwife, that the merits of the queftion on fuch appeal or orders, will by fuch removal come properly in judgment And no fuch *certiorari* fhall be allowed, until fufficient fecurity be given to the treafurer, in the fum of 100l, to profecute the *certiorari* with effect, and to pay the cofts if the rates or orders fhall be confirmed Nor fhall any fuch rates, orders, or proceedings be quafhed for want of form only 12 G 2 c 29 f 21

And no action fhall be commenced againft any perfon who fhall have collected or received any money on any rate which fhall be quafhed on a *certiorari* or otherwife, for any money collected or received on fuch rate before the *certiorari* was brought, but the perfons who have paid on fuch rate more than they ought to have paid, fhall be repaid, or have the fame allowed in the next rate 12 G 2 c 29 f 18

A High conſtable's warrant to levy the rate.

Weſtmorland. } To the churchwardens and overſeers of
Kendal Ward. } the poor of the townſhip [or pariſh] of
—— in the ſaid county

BY virtue of an order of his majeſty's juſtices of the peace in and for the ſaid county, in their general quarter ſeſſions aſſembled, you are hereby required in thirty days time from your receipt of this precept, or otherwiſe having had due notice thereof, to pay to me, out of the money by you collected or to be collected for the relief of the poor, the ſum of —— being the proportion of your ſaid townſhip [or pariſh] for and towards the general county rate, for the repairing of bridges, repairing of the goal, and for the reſt of priſoners therein, and for the relief of the priſoners in the king's bench and marſhalſea priſons, repairing the ſhire hall, repairing and furniſhing the houſe of correction, with the ſalary of the keeper thereof, the treaſurer's ſalary, the coroner's fees, the charges concerning vagrants, priſoners carriages, conveying and tranſporting felons, and other county charges. And herein you are not to fail, on the peril that ſhall enſue thereof. Given under my hand the —— day of —— .

John Bracken, *High conſtable.*

B Or, in the northern counties above mentioned, the juſtices, if they think proper, inſtead of ordering the money to be paid by the churchwardens and overſeers, may order it to be paid by the petty conſtables, and then the high conſtable's precept to the petty conſtables may be thus,

Weſtmorland } To the conſtable of —————— in the ſaid
Kendal Ward } county

BY virtue of an order from his majeſty's juſtices of the peace in and for the ſaid county, in their general quarter ſeſſions aſſembled, you are hereby required to raiſe the ſum of —— within your conſtablewick, for which you are to make an equal rate within your ſaid conſtablewick, and to levy the ſame, in ſuch manner as money for the relief of the poor is to law to be rated or levied which ſaid ſum you are to pay into me, in thirty days time from your receipt of this precept, or otherwiſe having had due notice thereof, the ſame being the proportion of your ſaid
conſ

conſtablewick, for and towards the general county rate, for the repairing of bridges ——

And ſo repeat the ſeveral particulars as in the laſt precedent, and that for this reaſon, that the people may know what it is they pay their money for

---

Cuſtoms.

THE laws relating to the cuſtoms, ſo far as juſtices of the peace, conſtables, and other ſuch officers, are concerned therein, being conſiderably connected with the laws of exciſe, it is thought proper to refer this ſubject to the title **Exciſe,** where the whole will be more clearly comprehended under one view

---

Cuſtos rotulorum

BY the 37 *H.*8 *c* 1 (which was altered by the 3 *&* 4 *Ed.* 6 *c.* 1 but reſtored by 1 *W c* 21) No perſon ſhall be appointed to the office of *cuſtos rotulorum,* but ſuch as ſhall have a bill ſigned with the king's hand for the ſame , which bill ſigned ſhall be a ſufficient warrant to the lord chancellor to make a commiſſion, aſſigning and authorizing thereby the ſame perſon to be *cuſtos rotulorum,* until the king hath by another bill with his own hand appointed one other perſon to have the ſame office, by himſelf, or his ſufficient deputy, learned in the laws, and meet and able to ſupply the ſaid office

In purſuance whereof, the laſt clauſe in the commiſſion of the peace is generally to this effect " Laſtly, we have " aſſigned you the aforeſaid —— —— keeper of the rolls " of our peace in our ſaid county, and therefore you ſhall " cauſe to be brought before you and your ſaid fellows, " at the days and places aforeſaid, the writs, precepts, " proceſſes, and indictments aforeſaid, that they may " be inſpected, and by a due courſe determined, as is afore- " ſaid "

Cyder See **Exciſe.**

Debtors.

Debtors.

HOW prisoners for debt shall be demeaned   See title Ga

Insolvent debtors brought to the assizes, in order to be discharged, shall pay for their bringing thither, not exceeding 12 d a mile, and if they are not able to pay, then the same shall be paid by the treasurer, out of the county stock   32 G. 2 c 28 s 15

Deer.   See **Game**.
Defamation   See **Slander.**

Demurrer.

A Demurrer (from *demorari*) signifies an abiding in point of law, upon which the defendant joins issue, allowing the fact to be true as laid in the indictment. *Wood* b 4 c 5

In criminal cases not capital, if the defendant demur to an indictment, the court will not give judgment against him to answer over, but final judgment.   2 *Haw* 334

But regularly in all cases of felony, where a man pleads a special matter, tho he conclude his plea with not guilty to the felony, or do not conclude it so, yet if his plea be tried, or found, or ruled against him, he shall be put to his plea of not guilty, and be tried for the felony, for tho' a man shall lose his land in some cases, for mispleading, yet he shall not lose his life for mispleading.   2 *H.* H 257

Deodand.

1. DEODAND is, when any moveable thing inanimate, or beast animate, doth move to or cause the untimely death of any reasonable creature, by mischance, without the will or fault of himself, or of any person 3 *Inst* 57

2. This, altho' it be not properly homicide, nor punishable as a crime, yet is taken notice of by the law, as far as the nature of the thing will bear, in order to raise the

greater

greater abhorrence of murder, and the unhappy instru-
ment or occasion of such death is called a deodand *(deo-
dandum)*, and forfeited to the king, and was anciently paid
into the hands of the king's almoner, to be applied to pious
uses for the soul of the deceased. Also all such weapons,
whereby one man kills another, are forfeited   3 *Inst.* 57
1 *Haw.* 66   *Post* 265

3 This forfeiture is still part of the casual revenue of
the crown, unless where lords of franchises are intitled to
it by grant. For no man can *prescribe* to t, or to the
goods of self-murderers or other felons, or of out-laws,
happening within his royalty   *Post* 265

4 It seems clearly settled, contrary to the former opinions, that a horse, or the like, killing an *infant* within
the age of discretion, is as much forfeited as if he were of
age. 1 *Haw.* 66.

5 Also, it was anciently holden, that things *fixed to
the freehold*, as the wheel of a mill, or a bell hanging in the
steeple, may be deodands, but by the later resolutions they
cannot, unless they were severed before the accident happened 1 *Haw* 66

6 It is agreed by all, that a *ship* in salt water, from
which a man falls and is drowned, is not forfeited, because
persons at sea are continually exposed to so many perils,
that the law imputes not such misfortunes to the ship.
Also it seems clear, that when a man riding on a horse
over a river, is drowned thro' the violence of the stream,
the horse is not forfeited, because not that, but the water
caused his death. But it is said, that a ship, by a fall
from which a man is drowned in the fresh water, shall be
forfeited, but not the merchandize therein, because they
no way contribute to his death. And by the same reason
it seems that if a man riding on the shafts of a waggon,
fall to the ground and break his neck, the horses and waggon only are forfeited, and not the loading, because it no
way contributed to his death, for which reason, where a
thing not in mot on causes a man's death, that part thereof
only, which is the immediate cause, is forfeited. As where
one climbing upon the wheel of a cart, while it stands
still, falls from it, and dies of the fall, the wheel only is
forfeited. But if he had been killed by a bruise from one
of the wheels being in motion, the loading also would have
been forfeited, because the weight thereof made the hurt
the greater. and it is a general rule, that wherever the
thing which is the occasion of a man's death is in motion
at the time, not only that part thereof which immediately
wounds him, but all things which move together with it.

2

and help to make the wound more dangerous, are forfeited also 1 *Haw* 66.

7 Thus a cart met a waggon loaded upon the road, and the cart endeavouring to pass by the waggon, was driven upon an high bank and overturned, and threw a person that was in the cart, just before the wheels of the waggon, and the waggon ran over him and killed him, it was resolved in this case, that the cart, waggon, loading, and all the horses were deodands, because they all moved to the death. 1 *Salk* 220

8 If a weight of earth fall upon a worker in a mine, and kill him, the weight of the earth is forfeit, and not the whole mine 1 *H H* 420

9 In all these cases, if the party wounded die not of his wound, within a year and a day after he received it, there shall be nothing forfeited, for the law doth not look on such a wound as the cause of a man's death, after which he lives so long But if the party die within that time, the forfeiture shall have relation to the wound given, and cannot be saved by any alienation or other act whatsoever in the mean time 1 *Haw* 67

10 However nothing can be forfeited as a deodand, nor seized as such, till it be found by the coroner's inquest to have caused a man's death, but after such inquisition, the sheriff is answerable for the value of it, and may levy the same on the town where it fell, and therefore the inquest ought to find the value of it 1 *Haw* 67

11 And if the coroner omits his duty in this case, the inquisition may be made by the commissioners of gaol delivery, oyer and terminer, or of the peace. 1 *H H* 419.

12 After all, as this forfeiture seemeth to have been originally founded, rather in the superstition of an age of ignorance, than in the principles of sound reason and policy, it hath not of late years met with great countenance in *Westminster-hall* And when juries have taken upon them to use a judgment of discretion, not strictly within their province, for reducing the quantum of the forfeiture, the court of king's bench have refused to interpose in favour of the crown or lord of the franchise In the case of *K* and *Rolfe*, coroner of *Kent*, *H* 5 *G* 2 the coroner's inquest found, that a man sitting on his waggon accidentally fell to the ground, and that the horses drawing the waggon forward, one of the fore wheels crushed his head, of which he instantly died, and then concluded that only the wheel, on which they set a small value, moved to his death A motion was made, in behalf of Mr *Mompesson*, lord of the franchise, for quashing this inquisition, upon

affidavits

affidavits tending to fhew, that the cart and horfes were equally inftrumental, which indeed the finding of the jury did fufficiently imply But the court was very clear, that neither this court nor the coroner can oblige the jury to conclude otherwife than they have done, and would not fuffer the affidavits for quafhing the inquifition to be read A like cafe came on, M 29 G 2 A nd *Drew*, coroner of *Middlfex* The coroner's jury, upon view of the body of a perfon killed by the like accident, found that only one wheel of the waggon moved to the death The court, on motion in behalf of the lord of the franchife, granted a rule for fhewing caufe why the inquifition fhould not be quafhed for this mifbehaviour of the jury On the day for fhewing caufe, Mr *Hume Campbell*, counfel for the lord of the franchife, informed the court, that upon looking into precedents, he was fatisfied he could not fupport the rule and thereupon it was difcharged The cafe of the *King* and *Rolfe* was mentioned on this occafion, and greatly relied on. *Taft* 266.

Dice See **Stamps.**

Diffenters.

I Of proteftant diffenters in general.
II. Diffenting minifters
III. Diffenting fchoolmafters.

I. Of proteftant diffenters in general.

(1) BY the 1 *El c* 2 f 14 Every perfon not having reafonable excufe, fhall refort to their parifh church or chapel, or upon reafonable let thereof, to fome ufual place where common prayer fhall be ufed, on every funday and holiday, on pain of punifhment by the cenfures of the church, or of forfeiting for every offence 12 d.

(2) By the 23 *El. c* 1 Every perfon above the age of 16, who fhall not repair to fome church, or chapel, or ufual place of common prayer, fhall forfeit for every month 20 l. And if he fhall forbear for 12 months he fhall be bound to the good behaviour till he conform

(3) By the 29 *El c* 6 Every offender in not repairing to church, having been once convicted, fhall without any other indictment or conviction, pay half yearly
into

into the exchequer 20 l for every month afterwards, until he conform, which if he shall omit to do, the king may seize all his goods, and two parts of his lands

(4) And by 3 J. c 4 The king may refuse the 20 l a month, and take two parts of the land, at his option

(5) And by the 3 J c 5 No recusant in not repairing to church, being convicted thereof, shall enjoy any publick office, or shall practise law or physick, or be executor, administrator, or guardian

(6) And by the 35 El c 1 If any person refusing to repair to church, shall be present at any assembly, meeting, or conventicle, under pretence of any exercise of religion, he shall be imprisoned till he conform, and if he shall not conform in three months, he shall abjure the realm, which if he shall refuse to do, or after abjuration shall not go, or shall return without licence, he shall be guilty of felony without benefit of clergy. And whether he shall abjure or not, he shall forfeit his goods, and shall forfeit his lands during life

(7) And by the 22 C 2 c 1 If any person, being sixteen years of age, shall be present at any conventicle or meeting, under pretence of any exercise of religion, in other manner than according to the liturgy and practice of the church of *England*, at which there shall be five persons or more assembled, besides those of the houshold, if it be in an house where there is a family, or if it be in a house, field, or place, where there is no family, then where any five persons or more are so assembled, — every justice of the peace before whom information shall be made, shall (on pain of 100 l, half to the informer) on proof by confession, or oath of two witnesses, or the notorious evidence of the fact, make a record thereof (which shall be afterwards certified to the sessions), which record shall be a full conviction Whereupon he shall impose upon every offender a fine of 5 s for the first offence, and for every other offence 10 s, to be levied by distress and sale of the goods of the offender, or in case of the poverty of such offender, upon the goods of any other person then convicted of the like offence, so as the sum to be levied on any one person in case of the poverty of other offenders amount not in the whole to above 10 l on occasion of any one meeting, one third to the king, one third to the poor, and one third to the informer and to such persons as the justice shall appoint, having regard to their diligence in discovering, dispersing, and punishing of the said conventicles

And every person who shall suffer any such meeting in his house, outhouse, barn, or backside, shall forfeit 20 l in

like

like manner, and in case of his inability, it shall be levied on the goods of such persons who shall be convicted of being present.

If the penalty exceeds 10 l, an appeal lies to the sessions And if the party is there found guilty by a jury, he shall pay treble costs and no other court whatsoever shall intermeddle, but the quarter sessions only.

And justices and constables may with what force they think fit, upon refusal to open, break open doors where they shall be informed such conventicle is, and take the offenders into custody And on certificate from any justice of peace of his particular information or knowledge of such unlawful meeting, and that he is not able, with such assistance as he can get, to suppress the same, any commissioned officer of the militia, or other his majesty's forces, with such troops or companies of horse and foot, and also the sheriff, and, other ministers of justice, with such other assistance, as they shall think meet, or can get in readiness with the soonest, shall repair to the place, and by the best means they can, shall dissolve, dissipate, and prevent such meeting, and take the offenders into custody

Thus stood the laws at the revolution.

Now by the 1 _W_ _c_ 18 commonly called the act of toleration, which by the 19 _G_ 3 _c_ 44 is declared to be a publick act, it is enacted, that neither the statutes aforesaid, nor any other made against papists and popish recusants (except the 25 _C_ 2 _c_ 2 concerning the qualifying for offices, and _C_ 30 2 _st_ 2 _c_ 1 containing the declaration against popery,) shall extend to any person dissenting from the church of _England_, who shall at the general sessions of the peace to be held for the county or place where such person shall live, take the oaths of allegiance and supremacy, and subscribe the said declaration against popery, of which the court shall keep a register and no officer shall take any fee above 6 d for registering the same and 6 d for a certificate thereof signed by such officer

Provided, that the place of meeting be certified to the bishop of the diocese, or to the archdeacon of the archdeaconry, or to the justices of the peace at the general or quarter sessions And the register or clerk of the peace shall register or record the time, and give certificate thereof to any who shall demand the same, for which no greater fee shall be taken than 6 d And provided, that during the time of meeting the doors shall not be locked, barred, or bolted.

And if any perfon diffenting from the church of *England* as aforefaid fhall be appointed to the office of high conftable, petty conftable, churchwarden, overfeer of the poor, or any other parochial or ward office, and fhall fcruple to take upon him the office, in regard of the oaths or otherwife, he may execute the fame by a fufficient deputy, that fhall comply with the laws on this behalf Provided that the deputy be allowed and approved, by fuch perfon, and in fuch manner, as fuch officer fhould by law have been allowed and approved

II *Diffenting minifters.*

(1) By the 17 *C* 2 *c* 2 No perfon, who fhall take upon him to teach or preach in any meeting or conventicle, under pretence of any exercife of religion, fhall, unlefs only in paffing upon the road, or unlefs required by legal procefs, come within five miles of a city, town corporate, or borough, without taking an oath of allegiance therein mentioned, on pain of 40 l, one third to the king, one third to the poor, and one third to him who fhall fue in the courts at *Weftminfter*, affizes, or feffions And two juftices, on oath of the offence, may commit him for fix months.

(2) And by the 22 *C* 2 *c*. 1. If any perfon fhall take upon him to preach or teach in any meeting or conventicle, in other manner than according to the practice of the church of *England*, he fhall forfeit for the firft offence 20 l, and for every other offence 40 l. And if he be a ftranger, or in the judgment of the juftice of the peace before whom he is convicted, unable to pay, it may be levied on the goods of any perfon prefent

(3) And by the 13 & 14 *C* 2 *c* 4 ſ 14 No perfon fhall prefume to confecrate and adminifter the facrament before he be ordained prieft, according to the form and manner of the church of *England*, on pain of 100 l.

Now by the aforefaid act of toleration, and by the 19 *G* 3. *c* 44. No perfon diffenting from the church of *England*, in holy orders, or pretended holy orders, or pretending to holy orders, nor any preacher or teacher of any congregation of diffenting proteftants, fhall be liable to any of the aforefaid penalties, who fhall at the feffions as aforefaid of the place where he fhall live, take the faid oaths of allegiance and fupremacy, and fubfcribe the faid declaration againft popery, and alfo make and fubfcribe a declaration in the words following viz *I A B do ſolemnly declare, in the preſence of almighty God, that I am a chriſtian and a proteſtant, and as ſuch, that I believe that the ſcriptures of the old and new teſtament, as commonly received among proteſtant churches, do contain the revealed will of God, and that I do receive the ſame as the rule of my doctrine and practice* For the regiſtring of which he ſhall pay 6 d to the officer of the court and no more, and 6 d for a certificate thereof ſigned by ſuch officer.

And any preacher or teacher, duly qualified, ſhall be allowed to officiate in any congregation, although the ſame be not in the county where he was ſo qualified, provided that the place of meeting hath been duly certified and regiſtred, and ſuch teacher or preacher ſhall, if required, produce a certificate of his having ſo qualified himſelf, under the hand of the clerk of the peace where he was qualified, and ſhall alſo before any juſtice of ſuch county where he ſhall ſo officiate, make and ſubſcribe ſuch declaration and take ſuch oaths as aforeſaid, if required (10 *An.* c. 2 ſ. 9)

And every ſuch teacher and preacher, having taken the oaths and ſubſcribed as aforeſaid, ſhall from thenceforth be exempted from ſerving in the militia of this kingdom, and from ſerving on any jury, or of being appointed to bear the office of churchwarden, overſeer of the poor, or any other parochial or ward office, or other office in any hundred, city, town, pariſh, diviſion, or wapentake.

III. Diſſenting ſchoolmaſters.

(1) By the 23 *El* c 1 If any perſon ſhall keep a ſchoolmaſter, who ſhall not repair to church, or be allowed by the biſhop, he ſhall forfeit 10 l a month, and the ſchoolmaſter ſhall be impriſoned for a year

(2) By the 17 *C* 2. c 2 No perſon ſhall be ſchoolmaſter, or take any boarders or tablers to be inſtructed by himſelf or any other, without taking an oath of allegiance therein mentioned, on pain of 40 l.

(3) By the 13 & 14 *C* 2 c. 4. Every ſchoolmaſter keeping any publick or private ſchool, and every perſon inſtructing or teaching any youth in any houſe or private family as a tutor or ſchoolmaſter, ſhall before his admiſſion ſubſcribe before the ordinary the declaration of conformity to the liturgy of the church of *England*, on pain of being diſabled to hold the ſaid ſchool. And if any ſchoolmaſter, or other perſon, inſtructing or teaching youth in any private houſe or family as tutor or ſchoolmaſter, ſhall teach any youth as tutor or ſchoolmaſter, before

licence

licence obtained from the bifhop or ordinary of the diocefe, and before fuch fubfcription as aforefaid, he fhall for the firft offence be imprifoned three months, for the fecond and every other offence be imprifoned three months, and forfeit 5 l.

But by the 19 G 3 c 44 No diffenting minifter, nor any other proteftant diffenting from the church of *England*, who fhall take the aforefaid oaths, and make and fubfcribe the abovementioned declaration againft popery, and the declaration herein before mentioned, fhall be profecuted in any court whatfoever, for teaching and inftructing youth as a tutor or fchoolmafter.

Provided, that this fhall not extend to the enabling any perfon diffenting from the church of *England* to hold the mafterfhip of any college or fchool of royal foundation, or of any other endowed college or fchool for the education of youth, unlefs the fame fhall have been founded fince the firft year of king *William* and queen *Mary*, for the immediate ufe and benefit of proteftant diffenters

Note, The forms of the faid oaths and declaration are inferted in the title **Oaths**

Diftrefs.

A Diftrefs is the taking of a perfonal chattel out of the poffeffion of the wrong doer, into the cuftody of the party injured, to procure a fatisfaction for the wrong committed and is of two kinds, either for cattle trefpaffing and doing damage, or for non-payment of rent or other duties

The remedy for recovering rent by way of diftrefs feems firft to have come over to us from the civil law. For anciently in the feudal law, the not paying attendance at the lord's courts, or not doing the feudal fervice, was a forfeiture of the eftate But thefe feudal forfeitures were afterwards turned into diftreffes, according to the pignorary method of the civil law, that is, the land that is let out to the tenant is hypothecated, as a pledge in his hands, to anfwer the rent agreed to be paid to the landlord, and the whole profits arifing from the land are liable to the lord's feifure for the payment and fatisfaction thereof.

Concerning which we will fhew,

I. *For what caufes a diftrefs fhall be.*

II.

I *For what cauſes a diſtreſs ſhall be.*

Rent in arrear. 1. Diſtreſs for rent muſt be, for rent in arrear, therefore it may not be made on the ſame day on which the rent becomes due, for if the rent is paid in any part of that day, whilſt a man can ſee to count money, the payment is good.

Tender of payment. 2 It muſt not be after tender of payment, for if the landlord come to diſtrain the goods of his tenant for rent behind, before the diſtreſs the tenant may upon the land tender the arrearages, and if after that a diſtreſs be taken it is wrongful and if the landlord have diſtrained, if the tenant, before the impounding thereof, tender the arrearages, the landlord ought to deliver the diſtreſs, and if he doth not, the detainer is unlawful Even ſo it is, in caſe of a diſtreſs for damage feaſant (or damage done by cattle treſpaſſing), the tender of amends before the diſtreſs, maketh the diſtreſs unlawful, and after the diſtreſs, and before the impounding, the detainer unlawful 2 *Inſt.* 107

But in this caſe, altho' the owner tender ſufficient amends, yet he cannot take his beaſts out of the pound, if the amends be refuſed, but he muſt replevy and if it be found at the trial that the amends was not ſufficient, the perſon on whom they treſpaſſed ſhall have damages, if the amends tendred were ſufficient, then the owner of the beaſts ſhall have damages *Di. & St.* 112.

2

3. The

3 The like remedy may be had by diſtreſs, impound- See rents and chief rent
ing and ſale, in caſes of rent-ſeck, rents of aſſize, and
chief rents, as in caſe of rents reſerved upon leaſe 4 G 2
c 28 ſ 5

Note, there are three kinds of rents, rent *ſervice*, rent
charge, and rent *ſeck*.

Rent *ſervice* is, where the tenant holdeth his land of his
lord by fealty and certain rent, or by homage, fealty, and
certain rent, or by other ſervice, and certain rent And
it is called a rent ſervice, becauſe it hath ſome corporal
ſervice incident to it, which at the leaſt is fealty 1 *Inſt*
141, 2

Rent *charge* is ſo called, becauſe the land for payment
thereof is charged with a diſtreſs, but before this act ſuch
diſtreſs could not be ſold, but only detained till the rent
ſhould be paid

If the rent be reſerved, without any clauſe put in the
deed of diſtreſs for the ſame, then it is called a rent *ſeck*,
redditus ſiccus, or dry rent and the difference between a
rent charge and a rent ſeck is, that there is a clauſe of
diſtreſs annexed to one, and no ſuch clauſe to the other,
and therefore the one is a charge upon the land, but for
the other the grantee had formerly no remedy but to
charge the perſon of the grantor in a writ of annuity
1 *Inſt* 143

Rents of *aſſize* are the certain rents of freeholders and
ancient copyholders, ſo called becauſe they are aſſized and
certain, and thereby diſtinguiſhed from *redditus mobiles*,
farm rents for life, years, or at will, which are variable
and uncertain 2 *Inſt* 19

4 On a parol demiſe, or verbal leaſe, where the quan- Agreement no by deed
tum of the rent agreed upon can appear in certain, the
landlord may diſtrain But whereas there are often difficulties when the agreement is not by deed, the landlord in
ſuch caſe may recover a reaſonable ſatisfaction in an action
on the caſe, for the uſe and occupation of the lands
And if in evidence on the trial, any parol demiſe, or any
agreement (not being by deed) whereon a certain rent
was reſerved, ſhall appear, the plaintiff ſhall not therefore be nonſuited, but may make uſe thereof as an evidence of the quantum of the damages to be recovered
11 G 2 c 19 ſ 14

5 So an action of debt may be brought againſt a tenant Rent reſerved on a leaſe for life
for life, in purſuance of the ſtatute of the 8 Ar c 14
which enacteth, that whereas before the ſaid ſtatute no
action of debt did lie againſt a tenant for life or lives, for
any arrears of rent during the continuance of ſuch eſtate

for

for life or lives, it ſhall be lawful, for any perſon having any rent in arrear or due upon any leaſe or demiſe for life or lives, to bring an action of debt for ſuch arrears, in like manner as he might have done in caſe ſuch rent were reſerved upon a leaſe for years *ſ* 4

Leaſe deter-mined

6 Perſons having rent in arrear, upon any leaſe determined, may diſtrain for ſuch arrears after the determination of the leaſe in the ſame manner as if it had not been determined; provided that ſuch diſtreſs be made in ſix kalendar months after the determination of ſuch leaſe, and during the continuance of ſuch landlord's title or intereſt, and during the poſſeſſion of the tenant from whom ſuch arrear became due 8 *An c* 14 *ſ* 6, 7

Leaſe renewed

7 Whereas many perſons hold conſiderable eſtates by leaſes for lives or years, and leaſe out the ſame in parcels to ſeveral under tenants, and where as many of thoſe leaſes cannot be renewed without a ſurrender of all the under leaſes derived out of the ſame, whereby it is in the power of any ſuch under tenants to prevent or delay the renewing of the principal leaſe, it is enacted, that in ſuch caſe, the chief leaſes may be renewed, without ſurrendring all the under leaſes, and the like diſtreſs or entry may be had, as if the former chief leaſe had been ſtill kept on foot and continued, or the under leaſes had been renewed under ſuch new principal leaſe 4 *G* 2 *c* 28 *ſ* 6

Two diſtreſſes for one rent

8 Before the ſtatute of the 17 *C* 2 *c* 7 in caſe a diſtreſs was too little, where ſufficient diſtreſs was to be had, a man could not diſtrain again, be the demand never ſo great, for it was his folly that at firſt he diſtrained no more *Mo* 7 *Comb* 546

But now, by the ſaid ſtatute, in all caſes where the value of the cattle diſtrained ſhall not be found to be to the full value of the arrears diſtrained for, the party to whom ſuch arrears were due, his executors or adminiſtrators, may diſtrain again for the reſidue of the ſaid arrears. *ſ* 4

So in like manner, where the diſtreſs is made by virtue of the warrant of a juſtice of the peace, in nature of an execution. And the diſtinction ſeemeth to be this where a perſon hath an entire duty, he ſhall not ſplit the entire ſum, and diſtrain for part of it at one time, and for part of it at another time, and ſo *totus quoties,* for ſeveral times, for that is great oppreſſion. But if a man ſeiſeth for the whole ſum that is due to him, and only miſtakes the value of the goods ſeiſed (which may be of very uncertain, or even imaginary value, as pictures, jewels, race horſes, and the like), there is no reaſon why he ſhould

not

not afterwards complete his execution by making a further seizure *Burrow* Mansfield 589

9 If any distress and sale shall be made, for rent in arrear and due, when none is in truth due, the owner shall recover double value with full costs. 2 *W. Sess* 1. *c* 5 *f* 5

And if the distress be taken of goods without cause, the owner may make *rescous*, but if they be distrained without cause, and impounded, the owner cannot break the pound and take them out, because they are in the custody of the law 1 *Inst.* 47

Distraining where no rent is due.

II. *What goods may be distrained, and what not.*

1 Distress for rent must be of a thing, whereof a valuable property is in somebody, and therefore dogs, bucks, does, conies, and the like, that are *feræ naturæ*, cannot be distrained 1 *Inst* 47

Valuable property.

2 Altho' it be of valuable property, as a horse, yet when a man or woman is riding on him, or an axe in a man's hand cutting of wood, and the like, they are for that time privileged, and cannot be distrained 1 *Inst* 47

Separate from the person

But it is said, that if one be riding upon a horse damage feasant, the horse may be led to the pound with the rider upon him 1 *Sid* 440, 442

And it hath been held, that horses joined to a cart, with a man upon it, cannot be distrained for rent (altho' they may for damage feasant), but both cart and horses may, if the man be not upon the cart. 1 *Vent* 36.

3 Valuable things shall not be distrained for rent, for benefit and maintenance of trades, which by consequent are for the commonwealth, and are there by authority of law as a horse in a smith's shop shall not be distrained for the rent issuing out of the shop, nor an horse in an hostry, nor the materials in a weaver's shop for making of cloth, nor cloth or garments in a taylor's shop, nor sacks of corn or meal in a mill, nor any thing distrained for damage feasant, for it is in custody of the law, and the like. 1 *Inst* 47

For maintenance of trades.

In the case of *Francis* and *Wyatt*, *T* 4 *G.* 3 Mr. *Wyatt* the landlord distrained for rent a chariot of Mr *Francis*, who thereupon brought a replevy, setting forth, that the coach house in which his chariot was taken, was part of certain other coach houses and stables known by the appellation of the *Talbot livery stables*, whereof one *Matthew Wilkinson* was the tenant and occupier under a demise from the said Mr *Wyatt* for a term of years, at the annual rent

of 60l That *Matthew Wilkinſon*, during ſuch his occupation of the premiſſes, uſed and followed the trade and
buſineſs of a common public livery ſtable keeper, for
keeping gentlemen's horſes and ſetting up their coaches
and carriages That the plaintiff Mr *Francis* ſet up his
chariot there, at livery, with the ſaid *Matthew Wilkinſon*
as at a common public livery ſtable keeper's, and that the
landlord Mr *Wyatt* took his chariot, ſo ſtanding in the
ſaid coach houſe, as a diſtreſs for rent due to him from
the ſaid *Matthew Wilkinſon*, to the wrong and injury of
the ſaid Mr *Francis* The queſtion was, Whether a
gentleman's chariot, which ſtood in a coach houſe belonging to a common livery ſtable keeper, was diſtrainable
for rent due to the landlord from the livery ſtable keeper —
For the plaintiff Mr *Francis* it was argued, that the livery
ſtable is exactly upon the foot of a common inn, and intitled to the ſame privileges and exemptions, and is
equally to be protected, upon the principles of neceſſity,
utility, and convenience to the community, and if horſes
and carriages are not privileged therein, it will put an end
to that branch of commerce And the common caſes
were cited, of goods carried to a fair or market and the
horſe carrying the ſame, of corn ſent to a mill, cloth to
a taylor, wool ſent to be ſpun, ſtuffs ſent to a dyer, goods
ſent by a carrier or left at a common wharf, all which
are privileged from diſtreſs.—For the landlord, it was argued, that theſe coach houſes are not in the nature of
common inns, for the maſter of them is not bound to take
in horſes and carriages as an innkeeper is, any more than
the maſter of a public boarding ſchool is bound to receive
all boarders, or a common brewer to ſerve all cuſtomers
That the right of putting up horſes and carriages in the
one ariſes from private contract, in the other, from authority of law, which is the ground of the protection extended to theſe houſes by law If indeed the plaintiff's
carriage had been ſent to a coachmaker's to be repaired,
it might for the time have been privileged, but here is no
ſuch neceſſity By hiring the coach houſe (whether by
the week, the quarter, or the year) he becomes an under-
tenant, and muſt be liable to the landlord's diſtreſs, as
much as a man who hires an unfurniſhed room in a
lodging houſe —By lord *Mansfield* chief juſtice Whatever may be the law of this caſe, it is worth the landlord's
while, to conſider the conſequences of taking ſuch a
diſtreſs, which will ruin his eſtate. For if it ſhould be
determined, that carriages and horſes ſtanding at livery
are liable to be diſtrained by the landlord for rent, the

livery ſtables will be all deſerted and undone, for no prudent man will make himſelf liable to ſuch an hazard
Therefore let this caſe ſtand over for farther argument,
and let the landlord in the mean time ſeriouſly conſider,
how far in prudence he ought to preſs the queſtion.——
But Mr *Francis* perceiving the opinion of the court to be
againſt him, did not think proper to bring the matter to a
further argument   And afterwards, in the Eaſter term
following the landlord moved for judgment, and judgment
was given for him, upon the ground of its being part of
the profits of the premiſes, which diſtinguiſhes it from
the caſe of goods ſent to be manufactured, and the like.
Bur Manſf 1498   *Black Rep* 483

4 Beaſts belonging to the plough ſhall not be diſtrained   **Tools of a man s**
(which is the ancient common law of *England*, for no man   **profeſſion.**
ſhall be diſtrained by the utenſils or inſtruments of his
trade or profeſſion, as the axe of the ca penter, or the book
of a ſcholar) while goods or other beaſts may be diſtrained
1 *Inſt* 47.

But this rule holds only in diſtreſſes for rent arrear,
amerciaments, and the like, but doth not extend to caſes,
where a diſtreſs is given, in the nature of an execution, by
any particular ſtatute, as for poor rates, and the like
3 *Salk* 136

So in the caſe of *Hutchins* and *Chambers*, E 31 G 2.
On a ſpecial verdict   Several geldings were diſtrained for
the poor rate, which were ſtated to be beaſts of the plough
and cart, when there were other goods more than ſufficient to anſwer the value of the demand.   It was objected, that by the ſtatute of 51 *H* 3 ſt 4. (which was
alſo in affirmance of the common law) *no e ſhall be diſtrained by his beaſts that gigne his land*   In the argument
of this cauſe, it was obſerved, that this duty on the ſtatute of the 43 *Eliz* is not a tax upon the land, nor payable out of it, but a charge upon the perſon   and it is a
tax throughout the kingdom, and for publick benefit
That it is not to be conſidered upon the foot of a common law diſtreſs   That the nature, deſign, and end of this
publick duty, required the moſt effectual and ſpeedy remedy that could be deviſed   That the reaſon why beaſts
of the plough could not be diſtrained at common law, will
not hold in the preſent caſe.   This is ſimilar to an execution, and eſſentially different from a diſtreſs at common
law   By the common law the diſtreſs could not be ſold
It was only taken *nomine pœnæ*, not as a ſatisfaction
(which this is) for the duty   The reaſons for the privilege do not now hold.   Agriculture then wanted and required

quired encouragement, and muſt have been impeded by a common law diſtreſs. Now it doth not. Then, the thing diſtrained could not be ſold, and remained uſeleſs. Now, it may be ſold. This diſtreſs is not taken as a pledge, or a mean to compel, but for a ſatisfaction for the duty itſelf, a perſonal duty, and of a publick nature —And by lord *Mansfield* Ch. J. This ſeiſing is but partly analagous to the common law diſtreſs, but is much more analagous to the common law execution. In the old common law diſtreſſes, which were in nature of a *nomine pœnæ* to compel payment, it would have been abſurd to have ſuffered the implements by which a man gained his livelihood to be holden as a pledge, becauſe that would have been taking from the man the only means he had of being able to pay the debt. But this reaſon doth not hold, where the things diſtrained may immediately be ſold by way of ſatisfaction, which, tho' called a diſtreſs, yet really is, in this reſpect, an execution. And in caſes of execution, beaſts of the plough may be diſtrained, altho' there be other ſufficient diſtreſs. And the court were unanimouſly of opinion, that beaſts of the plough are diſtrainable under the ſtatute of the 43 *Eliz.* and ſuch like acts of parliament. *Burrow.* Mansfield 579

Things fixed to the freehold

5. Furnaces, cauldrons, or other things fixed to the freehold, or the doors or windows of a houſe, or the like, cannot be diſtrained. 1 *Inſt.* 47.

Things for which a replevin will not lie

6. Things for which a replevin will not lie, ſo as to be known again, as money out of a bag, cannot be diſtrained. 2 *Bac. Abr.* 109.

Corn or hay cut.

But money in a bag ſealed may be diſtrained, for that the bag ſealed may be known again.

7. By the 2 *W. ſeſſ.* 1 *c.* 5. Perſons having rent arrear on any demiſe, leaſe, or contract, may ſeize and ſecure any ſheaves or cocks of corn, or corn looſe or in the ſtraw or hay being in any barn or granary, or upon any hovel, ſtack, or rick, or otherwiſe upon any part of the land charged with rent, and may lock up or detain the ſame in the place where found, in the nature of a diſtreſs, ſo as the ſame be not removed to the damage of the owner, out of the place where found and ſeized, but be kept there (as impounded) till replevied or ſold *ſ* 3.

Corn or hay growing.

8. Alſo by the 11 *G.* 2. *c.* 19. The landlord may take and ſeize corn, graſs, hops, roots, fruits, pulſe, or other product growing, as a diſtreſs, and the ſame may cut, gather, make, cure, carry and lay up, when ripe, in the barns or other proper place on the premiſſes, and if there ſhall be no barn or proper place on the premiſſes, then in any

any other barn or proper place which he ſhall procure, ſo
near as may be to the premiſſes, the appraiſement whereof
ſhall be tiken when cut, gathered, cured, and made, and
not before *ſ* 8

And notice of the place where the goods ſo diſtrained
ſhall be lodged, ſhall in one week after the lodging thereof
be given to the tenant, or left at the laſt place of his abode.
ſ 9

9 Generally, whatever goods and chattels the landlord **Cattle de-**
finds upon the premiſes, whether they in fact belong to the **paſtured**
tenant or a ſtranger, are diſtrainable by him for rent, for
otherwiſe a door would be opened to infinite frauds upon
the landlord, and the ſtranger hath his remedy over by
act on on the caſe againſt the tenant, if by the tenants default the goods are diſtrained, ſo that he cannot render them
when called upon 3 *Blackſt.* 8

But on particular circumſtances perhaps a court of equity
may relieve As in the caſe of *Fowkes* and *Joyce, T. 1 W.*
in the common pleas, a perſon driving ſheep to *London* to
ſell, by agreement with a maſter of an inn, put them into
the ground at ſo much a ſcore for a night. The landlord
ſeeing them, aſked whoſe they were, but conſented to their
ſtaying there, and afterwards diſtrained them for rent due
to him from the maſter of the inn. And it was adjudged
for the landlord. 3 *Lev* 260 2 *Ventr.* 50.——— But
in the ſame caſe, upon a bill for relief in equity, the lords
commiſſioners ſeemed to think, that the grounds lying to the
inn, and uſed therewith, ought to have the ſame privilege
as the inn hath, and that paſſenger's cattle ought not to
be diſtrainable there 2 *Vern* 129 ———And it appeared
in this caſe, that on the landlord's coming and ſeeing the
ſheep, he pretended to be angry Upon which the owner
offered to take out the ſheep, at which time they were not
diſtrainable for the rent, having not been levant and
couchant (that is, having not ſo long remained upon the
ground, as to have laid down and riſen up again to feed).
So that the court looked on the conſent as a fraud, to get
them to be left all night, by which they became liable to the
diſtreſs And it was decreed, that the landlord ſhould anſwer for the value of the ſheep, and pay coſts both in law
and equity *Prec Chan.* 7

10 Where a ſtranger's beaſts eſcape into the land, **Cattle eſcaped**
they may be diſtrained for rent, tho' they have not been **on the premiſ-**
levant and couchant, provided they are treſpaſſers But if **ſes.**
the tenant of the land is in default, in not repairing his
fences, whereby the beaſts came into the land, the landlord

lord cannot diſtrain ſuch beaſts, tho' they have been levant and couchant, unleſs he nave cauſed notice to be given to the owner, and the owner ſuffers them to remain there afterwards *Lutw* 364

But in caſe of an ancient ſeigniory, the lord may diſtrain cattle for ſervices, which came in by eſcape, tho' they were not levant and couchant, altho' it be in default of the fences, which the tenant of the land ought to maintain, becauſe the lord hath nothing to do with the repairing of the fences, and he hath no remedy but by diſtreſs But the owner may prevent the diſtreſs, by making freſh purſuit, for then the cattle remain as it were in his own poſſeſſion. L *Raym.* 168, 9. H 8 W Kemp and Crews

But in caſe of rent reſerved upon a leaſe for years, the landlord cannot diſtrain ſuch cattle, until they be levant and couchant, for if the landlord had had the lands in his own hands, he ought to have repaired the fences, and when he puts in a leſſee, he ought by covenant to oblige him to repair and therefore in that caſe, if the law would allow the landlord to diſtrain the cattle of a ſtranger which come in by eſcape, before that they be levant and couchant, it would be in effect to allow a man to take advantage of his own wrong. Therefore if the cattle come in by default of the owner of the cattle, then they may be diſtrained before they be levant and couchant, and if in default of the tenant of the land, there they cannot be diſtrained until they have been levant and couchant, that is to ſay, for rent upon leaſes for years And in ſuch caſe the landlord ſhall not take the cattle before that he has given notice to the owner, that they are upon the land liable to his diſtreſs, and if he doth not come to take them away, then they become diſtrainable, And by *Treby* chief juſtice, where the cattle eſcape accidentally, there they are not diſtrainable, until they have been levant and couchant, but if they eſcape by default of their owner, they are diſtrainable the firſt minute *id.*

In the caſe of *Brodon* and *Pierce* H 1690, where a rent charge was arrear for 20 years, and cattle eſcaped out of the next ground, and were diſtrained, lord *Nottingham* (in equity) relieved againſt it. 2 *Vern.* 231

Cattle damage feaſant. 11 If ten head of cattle were doing damage, a man cannot take one of them and keep it till he be ſatisfied for the whole damage, but he may bring an action of treſpaſs for the reſt. 12 *Mod* 660 H. 13 W Vaſper and Edwards,

If a man hath common for ten cattle, and he puts in more, the ſurpluſage above ten may be taken damage feaſant. 1 *Roll's Abr* 665

If a man come to diſtrain, and ſee the beaſts in his ground, and the owner chaſe them out, of purpoſe before the diſtreſs taken, yet the owner of the ſoil cannot diſtrain them, and if he doth, the owner of the cattle may reſcue them, for the beaſts muſt be damage feaſant at the time of the diſtreſs. 1 *Inſt* 161

For diſtreſs damage feaſant is the ſtricteſt diſtreſs that is, and the thing diſtrained muſt be taken in the very act, for if the goods are once off, tho' on freſh purſuit, the owner of the ground cannot take them. 12 *Mod* 661

III At what time the diſtreſs ſhall be taken

For a rent or ſervice the lord cannot diſtrain in the night, but in the day time, and ſo it is of a rent charge, but for damage feaſant, one may diſtrain in the night, otherwiſe, it may be, the beaſts may be gone before he can take them. 1 *Inſt* 142

For before ſun riſing, or after ſun ſet, no man may diſtrain but for damage feaſant. *Mirrour* c 2 ſ 26

IV Where the diſtreſs ſhall be made.

1 The king's officers, as ſheriffs and others, ſhall not take diſtreſses in the fees wherewith churches in times paſt have been endowed, but diſtreſſes may be taken in poſſeſſions of the church newly purchaſed. 9 *Ed* 2 *c* 9 — Church lands.

2 A man may diſtrain in places or lands within the fee, liable to diſtreſs, and not elſewhere. 52 *H* 3 *c*. 51. 2 *Inſt* 131 *Mir* c 2 ſ 26 — On the premiſſes.

3. And by the 11 *G* 2 *c* 19 The landlord may diſtrain any cattle or ſtock of the tenant, depaſturing on any common appendant or appurtenant, or any ways belonging to the premiſſes demiſed. ſ 8 — On the common.

4 No perſon (except the king's officers) ſhall take diſtreſſes in the king's highway. 52 *H* 3 *c* 15 — In the highway.

And the reaſon is, becauſe the king's ſubjects ought to have free paſſage, as well to fairs and markets, as about their other affairs. But yet this ſhall not be taken, to make the diſtreſs utterly unlawful, ſo as to take advantage thereof in bar to an avowry, but to this purpoſe, that if the lord diſtrain in the highway, the tenant may have an action againſt him upon this ſtatute. 2 *Inſt* 131, 132

5 But by the 11 G. 2 c 19. If any tenant for life, years, at will, ſufferance, or otherwiſe, ſhall fraudulently or clandeſtinely convey off the premiſſes his goods or chattels, to prevent the landlord from diſtraining, ſuch landlord, or any perſon by him lawfully impowered, may in 30 days next after ſuch conveying away, ſeize the ſame wherever they ſhall be found, and diſpoſe of them in ſuch manner, as if they had been diſtrained on the premiſſes. ſ 1

But no landlord ſhall diſtrain any goods ſold *bona fide*, and for a valuable conſideration, before ſuch ſeizure made, to any perſon not privy to ſuch fraud ſ 2

And if any tenant ſhall ſo fraudulently remove and convey away his goods or chattels, and if any perſon or perſons ſhall wilfully and knowingly aid or aſſiſt him in ſuch fraudulent conveying away or carrying off of any part of his goods or chattels, or in concealing the ſame, every perſon ſo offending ſhall forfeit to the landlord double the value of ſuch goods, to be recovered in any court of record at *Weſtminſter* ſ. 3

But if the goods and chattels ſo fraudulently carried off or concealed ſhall not exceed the value of 50 l, the landlord or his agent may exhibit a complaint in writing (A) before two juſtices of the peace of the ſame county or diviſion, reſiding near the place where ſuch goods and chattels were removed, or near the place where the ſame were found, not being intereſted in the lands or tenements whence ſuch goods were removed, who may ſummon (B) the parties concerned, examine the fact and all proper witneſſes upon oath, (or if it is a quaker, upon affirmation required by law,) and in a ſummary way determine whether ſuch perſon or perſons be guilty of the offence, with which he or they are charged, and to enquire in like manner of the value of ſuch goods and chattels, and upon full proof of the offence, by order (C) under their hands and ſeals the ſaid juſtices ſhall adjudge the offender or offenders to pay double the value of the ſaid goods and chattels, to ſuch landlord, his bailiff, ſervant, or agent, at ſuch time as the ſaid juſtices ſhall appoint and if the offender or offenders, having notice of ſuch order, ſhall refuſe or neglect ſo to do, they ſhall by their warrant (D) levy the ſame by diſtreſs and for want of ſuch diſtreſs (E) may commit the offender or offenders to the houſe of correction (F) there to be kept to hard labour, without bail or mainprize, for the ſpace of ſix months, unleſs the money ſo ordered to be paid as aforeſaid ſhall be ſooner ſatisfied. ſ 4

Perfons aggrieved by order of fuch juftices, may appeal to the next general or quarter feffions, who may give cofts to either party   *J* 5

And where the party appealing fhall enter into recognizance, with one or two fureties, in double the fum fo ordered to be paid, with condition to appear at fuch feffions, the order of the juftices fhall not be executed againft him in the mean time   *J* 6

T 29 & 30 *G* 2 *K* and *Biffex.*   Order made by two juftices, reciting that a complaint had been made to them in writing, by *A Clavey* againft *J Biffex*, that he the faid *Clavey* demifed his eftate in the parifh of *Shelley* in the county of *Somerfet*, to *William Thatcher*, at the yearly rent of 44 l, and that there was due and in arrear from *Thatcher* to him for rent of the faid eftate, on the fifth day of *April* laft, 24 l 15 s 8½ d, and that he the faid *Clavey* would have diftrained the goods and chattels of the faid *W. Thatcher* upon the faid eftate, in order to obtain fatisfaction of the faid rent, but to prevent him from fo doing, the faid *Biffex*, on or about the 27th, 28th, and 29th days of *Auguft* laft, did knowingly and wilfully aid and affift the faid *Thatcher*, in fraudulently conveying and carrying off from the faid eftate his the faid *Thatcher*'s good and chattels, and alfo in concealing the fame, being under the value of 50 l, that is to fay two cows, one heifer, and ten hundred weight of cheefe, of the value of 20 l, whereby the faid *Clavey* was prevented from diftraining the fame, in order to obtain fatisfaction for the faid rent, and contrary to the ftatute 11 *G* 2, and therefore praying us to grant him our warrant of fummons, requiring you the faid *J Biffex* to appear before us, and that we would examine the fact, and thereupon make fuch order therein for his relief, as the faid ftatute directs and requires, and as fhould be agreeable to juftice. Whereupon we the faid juftices, refiding near the faid eftate from whence the faid goods and cattle were removed, and neither of us any way interefted in the faid eftate, did iffue our warrant of fummons, requiring you the faid *J Biffex* to attend us thereon to anfwer the faid complaint, and you having attended accordingly, and we in your prefence having examined the witneffes produced by the faid *A Clavey* upon oath, and heard what was alledged by you in your defence, do adjudge that the faid complaint is true, and that the faid goods and cattle of the faid *W Thatcher*, which you fo aided and affifted in conveying and carrying off from the faid eftate, and alfo in concealing the fame, were of the value of 20 l, and that you have thereby forfeited double of the value of the

faid

ſaid goods and cattle, being the ſum of 40l, to the ſaid complainant *A Clare*, by virtue of the ſaid ſtatute We therefore in purſuance of the ſaid ſtatute, do adjudge, order, and require you the ſaid *J Biſſex*, within the ſpace of three days from the date hereof, to pay to the ſaid *A Cavy* the ſum of 40l, which if you ſhall neglect to do, ſuch further proceedings will be then had againſt you to inforce the payment thereof, as the ſaid ſtatute directs and requires Given under our hands and ſeals, this fifth day of *January* 1756 — This order was affirmed by the ſeſſions upon appeal Both the orders were removed by *cert nar*. into the king's bench It was moved to quaſh the ſame. Objections taken 1 The complaint is ſaid to be taken in writing, but not upon oath 2 It is only ſaid, that he demiſed to *W Thatcher*, but not ſaid for what eſtate or term. 3 It is ſtated, ſo much was due for rent, but not ſaid for what term, it might be due 20 years ago it is not ſtated to be due, when *Thatcher* removed his goods. 4 The words of the order are, goods and *cattle*, of the ſtatute, goods and *chattels* 5 No certain time is alledged when the defendant aided and aſſiſted, only ſaid, on or about the 26th, 27th, or 28th of *Auguſt* 6 Not ſtated that *Thatcher* did carry off his goods only that *Biſſex* did aid and aſſiſt him in carrying them off 7 They adjudge the complaint true, but do not ſtate the evidence and this is a conviction, not an order and for any thing that appears, it might be upon *Clare*'s evidence alone. 8 It is not ſtated that the goods were under the value of 50l, which is the ground of the juſtices juriſdiction 9 The words of the ſtatute are, if any perſon ſhall be a tenant of any lands, tenements, or hereditaments the word uſed in the order is *eſtate*, which may be a thing incorporeal, or may mean the intereſt in the land, and ſo not within the ſtatute 10 It ſhould appear, whether the landlord has a right to diſtrain by the 8 *An c.* 14 the landlord may diſtrain at any time within ſix months after the expiration of the term it doth not appear theſe ſix months were not expired, and if they were, this is no offence ———After conſideration, Mr juſtice *Deniſon* delivered the reſolution of the court I think the moſt material objection is, whether this is an order or a conviction If a conviction, the evidence ought to have been ſet out And there has been no doubt (notwithſtanding the caſe of *K* and *Pulteine.* 1 *Salk* 369) that in a conviction the evidence muſt be ſet out, that the court may judge upon it So it was held by lord *Hardwicke* in the caſe of *K* and *Lloyd, St* 906 and in that caſe it was objected, that as it ſubjected the party to a penalty, tho' in the ſtatute it was called an order, yet it ſhould be conſtrued as a conviction but the court ſaid, every act of the juſtices, which ſubjects the party to a penalty, ſhall not be conſtrued as a conviction *K.* and *Venables,* Str 630 2 *L Raym* 1406 upon the ſtatute for licenſing alehouſes, conſidered as an order. *K* and *Blackwell,* *M* 4 *Geo.* which the court ſaid was a ſtrong caſe, and muſt be conſidered as an order I underſtood from my lord *Hardwick,* in the caſe of *K* and *Lloyd,* that his ground of the difference was founded upon the expreſſions of the ſtatute, and not upon the penalty, as where the words of the ſtatute are, " of which he ſhall be con-" victed," it is to be conſtrued as a conviction Here it is extremely ſtrong, the ſtatute calls it an order and in the nature of it, it is an examination upon a complaint. If the party was never ſummoned, this court upon affidavit will grant an information againſt the juſtices but the ſummons need not be ſet out, and the court will intend the juſtices have done right, in caſe the contrary does not appear upon the face of the order. As to the 1ſt objection this is not an information, but a complaint when the party is ſummoned, the witneſſes are to be examined upon oath, but the complaint need not be upon oath In anſwer to the 2d objection as the order has followed the words of the ſtatute, we will not intend it a caſe wherein the juſtices had not a juriſdiction The court will not, in caſe of an order, intend that the juſtices have done wrong. As to the third objection it is ſufficiently alledged, in an order, his aſſiſting the tenant to carry away the goods, as it is here alledged, is ſufficient to ſhew the rent continued then to be in arrear, and the rather, as the defendant might have availed himſelf of the rent paid, by proving it before the juſtices I much doubt, whether in a declaration it would not be ſufficient to ſay, the rent was in arrear at ſuch a day, and I think it would lie upon the defendant to prove that the rent does not remain in arrear. As to its not being ſaid, for what time the rent was due, this is mere matter of form As to the 5th objection. *about,* in common parlance, means in this caſe three days or near it They might be three days in carrying the goods away The days are not material, even in legal proceedings. 1 L. *Raym.* 581 And in the caſe of *K* and *Simpſon,* *H.* 3 *Geo* 2 *Str.* 46 the day and hour in a conviction are not material. By this ſtatute no time is limited, when the complaint ſhall be made it may be made at any time Suppoſe that the defendant had paid the penalty on a different complaint made, he might eaſily have ſhewn it.

As to the 6th the anſwer is obvious, If *Thatcher* had not carried his goods away, the defendant could not have aided in carrying them. The ſtatute makes two offences, one, carrying the goods away, the other, aiding in carrying them away It is only neceſſary here to ſtate the offence which the defendant had been guilty of, which this order does in the words of the ſtatute In the caſe of *K* and *Monk*, M 13 *Geo* 2 there was a conviction for aiding and aſſiſting in killing a buck. It was objected, that it was not charged the buck was killed. But the court held, that as the conviction was in the words of the ſtatute, it was ſufficient And the court held they were all principals, as well thoſe that killed the buck, as thoſe that aſſiſted And this was the caſe of a conviction ——— All the other objections may have this general anſwer, that in the caſe of orders, where the juſtices have juriſdiction, we will intend they have acted right, and if they have done wrong, they may be puniſhed by an information ——— Let the orders be confirmed *MS*

So in the caſe of *K* and *Middlehurſt*, T 30 & 31 G 2 Two juſtices make an order againſt one *Thomas Middlehurſt*, for wilfully and knowingly aiding or aſſiſting *John Cheſterton*, the tenant of Sir *Thomas Fleetwood*, in fraudulently removing and conveying away five cows and other goods, *or* in concealing the ſame Which order, on appeal to the ſeſſions, was confirmed It was mov'd to quaſh theſe orders, upon two objections 1. The whole adjudication refers to the complaint of one *Thomas Weſton*, wherein there is no charge upon *Cheſterton* the tenant at all neither is it ſtated, that *Cheſterton* the tenant did remove the goods 2. The act creates two offences, *viz* aſſiſting in *removing*, and aſſiſting in *concealing* the goods Now, it is not ſpecifically charged upon the defendant *Middlehurſt*, that he wilfully and knowingly did either of theſe two things It is only alledged that he wilfully and knowingly did one or the other In 1 *Salk.* 371 *Rex* v. *Stocker*, an indictment for forging, *or* cauſing to be forged, was holden ill, becauſe the charge was in the diſjunctive So, 2 *Haw.* 225 An indictment charging a man diſjunctively, is void For the offences are diſtinct, and it appears not, of which of them the defendant is accuſed So here, it doth not appear, of which of the two offences the juſtices have convicted him.——— On a rule to ſhew cauſe, To the 1ſt objection, that it is not deſcribed ſufficiently what the offence is, it was anſwered, that this is an order, and the court will not intend it to be ill To the 2d objection, as to the charge being in the diſjunctive,

that

that he aſſiſted the tenant in removing or concealing the
goods, it was anſwered, that the crime and the puniſhment
are the ſame upon both, and the defendant was heard —
By lord *Mansfield* Ch. J. Upon indictments, it hath been
determined, that an alternative charge is not good (as,
forged *or* cauſed to be forged), tho' one only need be
proved, if laid conjunctively (as, forged *and* cauſed to be
forged) but I do not ſee the reaſon of it the ſubſtance
is exactly the ſame, the defendant muſt come prepared
againſt both and it makes no difference to him in any
reſpect. But this is an order and being good in ſubſtance,
needs not be literally ſo ſtrict —And by the court, the
rule to ſhew cauſe was diſcharged, and conſequently both
orders affirmed. *Burrow*, Manſield 399

THE following form of a conviction, drawn by the late
Mr ſerjeant *Poole*, ſeeming to be very accurate and judicious, may be uſeful as a precedent in this and other like
caſes ——" *Lancaſhire*, to wit, Be it remembred, that
on the 25th day of September in the twelfth year of the
reign of our lord the preſent king, at *Liverpoole* in the
county of *Lancaſter*, *Samuel Brown* of *Liverpoole* aforeſaid
cometh before us *John Goodwin* and *Richard Gildart* eſquires,
juſtices of the lord the preſent king aſſigned to keep the
peace in and for the county aforeſaid, and alſo to hear and
determine divers felonies, treſpaſſes and other offences
committed in the ſaid county, and reſiding near to the
cloſe from whence the mare herein after mentioned was
conveyed away, we or either of us not being intereſted in
that cloſe, and then and there exhibiteth before us a certain complaint in writing againſt *John Elliſon* of *Liverpoole*
aforeſaid labourer, by which he giveth us to underſtand
and be informed, that he the ſaid *Samuel Brown*, on the
ſecond day of February in the year of our Lord 1738, at
Liverpoole aforeſaid, had demiſed to one *Thomas Elliſon* a
certain cloſe of paſture called —— containing by eſtima-
tion —— acres, with the appurtenances, of the ſaid
Samuel, ſituate, lying, and being in *Liverpoole* aforeſaid,
near to a certain place there called The Loggerheads, to
hold the ſame to the ſaid *Thomas Elliſon* from thenceforth
for one whole year from thence next enſuing and fully to
be compleat and ended, at and under the yearly rent of ſix
pounds ſeventeen ſhillings and ſixpence, to be paid by the
ſaid *Thomas Elliſon* to the ſaid *Samuel* at two payments in
the year, to wit, upon the firſt day of Auguſt and upon
the ſecond day of February called Candlemaſs-day by equal
portions, the firſt payment whereof was to begin and be
made on the firſt day of Auguſt then next following, and

that

that by virtue of that demiſe the ſaid *Thomas Elliſon* entred into the ſaid cloſe and was poſſeſſed thereof, and that on the firſt day of Auguſt now laſt paſt, the ſum of three pounds eight ſhillings and nine pence of the rent aforeſaid was and became due and in arrear to the ſaid *Samuel Brown* from the ſaid *Thomas Elliſon* for half a year ended at that day in the year aforeſaid and yet is unpaid, and that after the ſaid ſum of three pounds eight ſhillings and nine pence of the rent aforeſaid ſo became due and in arrear to the ſaid *Samuel Brown*, and whilſt the ſame was due to him and unpaid, to wit, on the ———— day of Auguſt now laſt paſt, one bay mare of the ſaid *Thomas Elliſon*, under the value of 50 l, that is to ſay, of the value or price of four pounds and four ſhillings, was depaſturing and feeding upon the ſaid demiſed premiſſes, and was then ſubject and liable to be taken as a diſtreſs for the ſaid arrear of rent ſo due and payable; and that the ſaid *Thomas Elliſon*, to prevent the ſaid *Samuel Brown* from diſtraining the ſaid mare for the ſaid arrear of rent ſo reſerved due and payable as aforeſaid, afterwards, that is to ſay, on the ſame day and year laſt mentioned, fraudulently and clandeſtinely conveyed away the ſaid mare off and from the ſaid demiſed premiſſes, and hath ever ſince that time concealed the ſame, and that one *John Elliſon* of *Liverpoole* aforeſaid labourer, well knowing the premiſſes, did wilfully aid and aſſiſt the ſaid *Thomas Elliſon*, in the fraudulent conveying away the ſaid mare off and from the ſaid demiſed premiſſes, and in concealing the ſame, and thereupon, afterwards, that is to ſay, on the ſixth day of October in the ſame year, at *Liverpoole* aforeſaid, the ſaid *John Elliſon* and the ſaid *Samuel Brown*, being in that behalf in due manner ſummoned, come before us the ſaid juſtices in their proper perſons on occaſion of the ſaid complaint, And one *Richard Bradley* and one *Chriſtopher Clitherall*, being credible witneſſes in that behalf, likewiſe then and there come before us, and then and there take their corporal oaths, and each of them then and there taketh his corporal oath, upon the holy goſpel of God, to ſpeak the truth of and upon the premiſſes in the ſaid complaint ſpecified, before us the ſaid juſtices then having ſufficient power and authority to adminiſter the ſaid oaths to them the ſaid *Richard Bradley* and *Chriſtopher Clitherall* in that behalf, and the ſaid *Richard Bradley* and *Chriſtopher Clitherall* then and there are examined before us upon their ſaid oaths, and each of them is examined before us upon his oath of and upon the premiſſes in the ſaid complaint ſpecified, and the ſaid *John Elliſon* being then and there preſent before us the ſaid juſtices

tices in his proper perſon on occaſion of the ſaid complaint, and the complaint aforeſaid and the examination of the ſaid *Richard Bradley* and *Chriſtopher Clitherall* of and upon the premiſſes, and the evidence of the ſaid *Richard Bradley* and *Chriſtopher Clitherall* thereupon then and there given upon their ſaid oaths, being heard and fully underſtood by the ſaid *John Ellſon*, he the ſaid *John Ellſon* by us the ſaid juſtices is then and there required if he hath or knoweth any thing to ſay for himſelf, why he the ſaid *John Ellſon* ought not to be convicted of the premiſſes aforeſaid above laid to his charge; and becauſe upon hearing and fully underſtanding the ſaid complaint and the evidence of the ſaid *Richard Bradley* and *Chriſtopher Clitherall* of and upon the premiſſes given before us upon their ſaid oaths, and alſo upon hearing and fully underſtanding all and ſingular the matters and things by the ſaid *John Ellſon* alledged in his defence of and upon the premiſſes, it appears manifeſtly to us, that the ſaid *John Ellſon* is guilty of the premiſſes above laid to his charge in manner and form as by the ſaid complaint is above alledged, and becauſe upon enquiry made by us the ſaid two juſtices on the oath of the ſaid *Chriſtopher Clitherall* in that behalf likewiſe in due manner taken before us the ſaid juſtices then having power and authority to adminiſter that oath to him the ſaid *Chriſtopher* in that behalf, it manifeſtly appears to us the ſaid juſtices, that the ſaid mare in the ſaid complaint mentioned, at the time of conveying the ſame away as in the ſaid complaint is mentioned was of the value of four pounds and four ſhillings of lawful money of this realm Therefore it is conſidered by us the ſaid juſtices, and we the ſaid juſtices do order and adjudge, that the ſaid *John Ellſon* be convicted of the premiſſes by the complaint aforeſaid ſo as aforeſaid laid to his charge, and that he pay to the ſaid *Samuel Brown* the ſum of eight pounds and eight ſhillings of lawful money of Great Britain on the —— day of —— now next enſuing, being double the value of the ſaid mare in the ſaid complaint mentioned, according to the form of the ſtatute in that behalf made and provided In witneſs whereof we the ſaid juſtices have hereunto put our hands and ſeals this ſixth day of October in the thirteent year of the reign of our lord George the ſecond king of Great Britain, France, and Ireland, defender of the faith, and ſo forth, and in the year of our Lord one thouſand ſeven hundred and thirty nine."

V. That reaſonable diſtreſs ſhall be taken.

Diſtreſs to be reaſonable

Diſtreſſes ſhall be reaſonable, and not too great, and he that taketh great and unreaſonable diſtreſſes, ſhall be grievouſly amerced   52 *H.* 3 *c* 4

For example, if the lord diſtrain two or three oxen for 12 d, or the like ſmall ſum, and the owner bring a replevy of the oxen, and the lord avow the taking of them for the 12 d, of his own ſhewing, he ſhall make fine   or the party may have his action upon this ſtatute, 2 *Inſt.* 107

If the lord diſtrain an ox, or horſe, for a penny, if there were no other diſtreſs upon the land holden, the diſtreſs is not exceſſive but if there were a ſheep, or a ſwine, or the like, then the taking of the ox or horſe is exceſſive, becauſe he might have taken a beaſt of leſs value, 2 *Inſt.* 107,

VI. Manner of taking diſtreſs.

Breaking gates.

1 Gates or incloſures may not be broken open, nor thrown down, to make a diſtreſs 1 *Inſt* 161.

Opening doors

2 Nor may the leſſor enter into the tenant's houſe, unleſs the doors are open   *Read* Diſtr 2 *Bac. Abr.* 111.

Upon a queſtion about taking a diſtreſs, it was held by the lord chief juſtice *Hardwicke*, at the ſummer aſſizes at *Exeter*, 1735, that a padlock put on a barn door could not be opened by force, to take the corn by way of diſtreſs. 9 *Viner* 128

But if the outer door of an houſe is open, one may break an inner door to take a diſtreſs   *Caſes in the time of lord Hardwicke* 168

Aid of the conſtables and juſtices

3. Where any goods or chattels fraudulently or clandeſtinely conveyed or carried away, ſhall be put, placed, or kept in any houſe, barn, ſtable, outhouſe, yard, cloſe, or place, locked up, faſtened, or otherwiſe ſecured, ſo as to prevent ſuch goods or chattels from being taken and ſeized as a diſtreſs for arrears of rent, it ſhall be lawful for the landlord, or his ſteward, bailiff, receiver, or other perſon or perſons impowered, to take and ſeize, as a diſtreſs for rent, ſuch goods and chattels (firſt calling to his aſſiſtance the conſtable, headborough, borſholder or other peace officer of the hundred, diſtrict or place, where the ſame ſhall be ſuſpected to be concealed, and in caſe of a dwelling houſe, oath being alſo firſt made (G) before a juſtice of the peace, of a reaſonable ground to ſuſpect that ſuch goods or chattels are therein) in the day time to break open (H) and enter into ſuch houſe, barn, ſtable, outhouſe,

houfe, yard, clofe, and place, and to take and feize fuch goods and chattels for the faid arrears of rent, as he might have done if they had been in any open place. 11 G 2 c. 19 ſ 7

But except it be in this cafe where the goods are clandeſtinely conveyed, it may feem from what hath been faid, that the landlord hath no mean to come at the goods in order to make diſtrefs, if the tenant fhall think fit to lock up his gates, and fhut the doors And the like may be obferved in cafes of diſtrefs for the levying a penalty, by warrant of juſtices of the peace (unlefs fuch penalty, or part thereof, be given to the king) Which matter may feem to require fome confideration

4 If a landlord comes into a houfe, and feizes upon fome goods as a diſtrefs, in the name of all the goods of the houfe, that will be a good feizure of all 6 *Mod* 215

Part in the name of the whole

VII. Diftrefs how to be demeaned.

1 By the 52 H 3 c 4. *None fhall caufe any diſtrefs that he hath taken, to be driven out of the county where it was taken and if one neighbour do fo to another of his own authority (as for damage feafant, or rent charge, 2 Inſt 106) he fhall make fine as for a thing done againſt the peace, and if the lord fo prefume to do againſt the tenant, he fhall be grievoufly punifhed by amerciament*

Impounding off the premiffes.

Before this act, at the common law, a man might have driven the diſtrefs to what county he pleafed which was mifchievous, for two caufes, 1 Becaufe the tenant was bound to give the beafts being impounded in an open pound fuftenance, and being carried into another county, by common intendment he could have no knowledge where they were 2 He could not know where to have a replevy, but the party was, before this ftatute, driven to his action upon his cafe 2 *Inſt* 106

And albeit this ftatute be in the negative, yet if the tenancy be in one county, and the manor in another county, the lord may drive the diſtrefs which he taketh in the tenancy to his manor in the other county, for that the tenant is out of both the faid mifchiefs for the tenant by doing of fuit and fervice to the manor, by common intendment may know what is done there, and therefore may give his beaft fuftenance And to know where to have his replevy, the bailiff of the manor ufually drives the cattle diſtrained to the pound of the manor And hereby it is to be noted, that a cafe out of the mifchief, is out of

the

the meaning of the law, tho' it be within the letter 2 *Inſt* 106.

And by the 1 & 2 *P & M c* 12 It is further enacted, that *no diſtreſs of cattle ſhall be driven out of the hundred, rape, wapentake, or lathe, where ſuch diſtreſs ſhall be taken, except it be to a pound overt within the ſame ſhire, not above three miles diſtant from the place where the ſaid diſtreſs was taken, and no cattle or other goods diſtrained for any cauſe of one time, ſhall be impounded in ſeveral places, whereby the owner may be conſtrained to ſue ſeveral replevies, on pain of* 100 s *to the party grieved, and treble damages* ſ 1

T 21 *G* 2 *Gimbar* and *Pelah* The defendant juſti-fied impounding cattle damage feaſant And on evidence it appeared, he put them into the next pound, though it happened to be in another county And *Lee* Ch J held, it did not make him a trefpaſſer, though it ſubjected him to the penalty of the ſtatute of the 1 & 2 *P & M* Str 1272

Note, a pound is either *overt* or open, as in a pinfold made for ſuch purpoſes, or in his own cloſe, or in the cloſe of another by his conſent, and it is therefore called open, becauſe the owner may give his cattle meat and drink, without trefpaſs to any other, and then the cattle muſt be ſuſtained at the peril of the owner Or it is a pound *covert* or cloſe, as to impound the cattle in ſome part of his houſe, and then the cattle muſt be ſuſtained with meat and drink at the peril of him that diſtraineth, and he ſhall not have any ſatisfaction therefore. 1 *Inſt* 47

But if the diſtreſs be of utenſils of houſhold, or ſuch like dead goods, which may take harm by wet or weather, or be ſtolen away, there he muſt impound them in a houſe, or other pound *covert*, within three miles in the ſame coun-ty, for if he impound them in a pound *overt*, he muſt an-ſwer for them 1 *Inſt* 47.

Impounding on the premiſſes

2 By 11 *G*. 2. *c*, 19. Any perſon diſtraining, may im-pound or otherwiſe ſecure the diſtreſs, of what kind ſo-ever it be, in ſuch place, or on ſuch part of the premiſſes, as ſhall be moſt convenient; and may appraiſe, and ſell the ſame, as any perſon before might have done off the premiſſes ſ. 10.

Uſing the good diſtrained.

3 Cattle diſtrained may not be worked or uſed, unleſs for the owner's benefit, as a cow milked, or the like, much leſs may they be abuſed or hurt *Cro Jac.* 148.

And it hath been ſaid in this caſe, that even a cow may not be milked, for tho' the cow be better for this, yet he who took the diſtreſs ought not to do good to the owner with-

without his confent, and perhaps the owner would have come before any damage came by this to the cow, and if it perifh by this, yet he who took the diftrefs may diftrain again 2 *Bac Abr* 112

4 So if the diftrefs be loft by the act of God as if the diftrefs dies in the pound, without any default in the diftrainer, in fuch cafe, he who made the diftrefs may diftrain again 1 *Salk* 248.

Diftrefs dying.

5 It is the diftrainer's own fault, if he puts the diftrefs in a pound which will not hold it, but he cannot juftify the tying of cattle in the pound, and if he ties a beaft, and it is ftrangled, he muft pay damages 1 *Salk* 248.

Killed.

VIII. *Of refcous and pound breach.*

1. By the common law, if a man break the pound, or the lock of it, or part of it, he greatly offendeth againft the peace, and doth trefpafs to the king, and to the lord of the fee, and to the fheriffs, and hundredors, in breach of the peace, and to the party, and to the delaying of juftice, and therefore hue and cry is to be levied againft him, as againft thofe who break the peace *Mn c* 2. *f* 26 And the party who diftrained may take the goods again, wherefoever he fhall find them, and impound them again 1 *Inft* 47

Refcous and pound breach.

2 And by ftatute, on any pound breach or refcous, of goods diftrained for rent, the perfon grieved thereby, fhall in a fpecial action upon the cafe, recover treble damages and cofts againft the offender, or againft the owner of the goods, if they be afterwards found to have come to his ufe or poffeffion. 2 *W c* 5. *f* 4.

Treble damages and cofts] In the cafe of Sir *Wilfred Lawfon* v. *Storcy*, M 6 *W* It was adjudged, that the cofts fhall be trebled as well as damages L *Raym* 20.

3 When a man hath taken diftrefs, and the cattle diftrained, as he is driving them to the pound, go into the houfe of the owner, if he that took the diftrefs demand them of the owner, and he deliver them not, this is refcous in law. 1 *Inft* 161.

IX *Replevying the diftrefs.*

1 It is worthy of obfervation, how provident the law is, that mens beafts, cattle, or other goods be not unjuftly or exceffively diftrained, and if they be, that deliverance be fpeedily made of them by replevy (or taking back

Replevy.

the

the pledge) otherwise the husbandry of the realm, and mens other trades, might be overthrown or hindred 2 *Inst* 137

2 To which purpose, it is enacted by the 1 & 2 P & M c 12 that the sheriff of every county shall, at his first county day, or in two months after he hath received his patent of office, appoint and proclaim in the shire town four deputies at the least, dwelling not above 12 miles one distant from another, to make replevies, on pain of 5l for every month that he shall lack such deputy or deputies, half to the king, and half to him that shall sue in any court of record. *f* 3

3 And the *sheriff, or other officer* having authority to grant replevins, shall in every replevin of a distress for rent, take in his own name, from the plaintiff and two sureties, a bond in double the value of the goods distrained, to be ascertained on the oath of one witness, and conditioned for prosecuting the suit with effect, and without delay, and for duly returning the goods distrained, in case a return shall be awarded, before any deliverance be made of the distress, and the sheriff shall assign such bond *to the avowant, or person making conusance.* 11 G 2 c 19 f 23

Sheriff or other officer] T 18 G. 3. *Richards* and *Acton* A rule was made on *Joseph Garmeson* the replevin clerk, *Robert Jeffreys* the under sheriff, and *Edward Pembury* the clerk of the county court, to discover the names of the pledges taken upon granting the replevin in this cause, and to shew cause why they should not pay the defendant 57l 15s, being the damages and costs recovered by him in this cause, together with the costs of the application. The distress was for rent, and on replevin brought, the defendant had a verdict with the damages and costs abovementioned. On application to *Garmeson* for the names of the pledges, he from time to time evaded and delayed so doing, having it was supposed taken none, or at least insufficient sureties, and being (as it was sworn) attorney for the plaintiff in this action. On shewing cause, *Garmeson* made an affidavit of his illness and inability to do any business. The under-sheriff and county court clerk shewed for cause, that they were intirely ignorant of this matter, having nothing to do with the replevin clerk who was appointed by the high sheriff in pursuance of the statute. The court inlarged the rule to a further day, and ordered the high sheriff to be added, when it was held, that as well the high sheriff and under-sheriff as the replevin clerk (who is their deputy) are answerable to the defendant in replevin for the sufficiency of the pledges. They therefore discharged the rule against the county court clerk, but with re-

regard to the high and under-sheriff, and the replevin clerk, they made the rule absolute. *Black. Rep.* 1220.

To the avowant or person making conusance] Avowry is, where one takes a distress, and the person distrained sues a replevin, then he that took the distress must *avow* and justify in his plea, for what cause he took it, if he took it in his own right, and this is called an *avowry* if he took it in the right of another, then, when he hath shewed the cause, he must make *conusance* of the taking, as bailiff or servant to him, in whose right he took it. *Terms of the L.*

X. *Sale of the distress.*

Distress taken for an offence presented in the leet, may Sale of common right be sold, because it is a court of record, but otherwise it is, of distresses in courts that are not of record. 12 *Mod.* 330.

So a distress for an amercement in a court baron cannot be sold, but in such case a distress infinite shall go. 1 *Bulst.* 52, 53.

In like manner, before the statute of the 2 *W* sess. 1. c 5 distress for rent in arrear could not be sold, but only detained till payment of the rent. But by the said statute it is enacted, that *whereas the most ordinary and ready way for recovery of arrears of rent is by distress, yet such distresses not being to be sold, but only detained as pledges for enforcing the payment of such rent, the persons distraining have little benefit thereby therefore from henceforth, where any goods shall be distrained* (I) *for rent reserved and due upon any demise, lease, or contract whatsoever, and the tenant, or owner of the goods distrained, shall not within five days next after such distress taken, and notice* (K) *thereof (with the cause of such taking) left at the chief mansion house, or other most notorious place on the premisses, replevy the same, in such case the person distraining shall, with the sheriff or under-sheriff of the county, or with the constable of the hundred, parish, or place, where such distress shall be taken, cause the goods and chattels so distrained to be appraised by two sworn* (L) *appraisers (whom such sheriff, under-sheriff, or constable shall swear) to appraise* (M) *the same truly, according to the best of their understandings, and and after such appraisement, shall sell the same for the best price can be gotten for them, for satisfaction of the rent, and charges of the distress, appraisement, and sale, leaving the overplus (if any) with the sheriff, under-sheriff, or constable, for the owner's use.* 2 W sess 1 c 5 s 2

Shall not within five days] M 13 G. Griffin and Scott. Trespass for entring his house, and keeping possession of

his

his goods eight days   The defendant juſtifies under a diſtreſs for rent   But by the court   The defendant ought to have removed the goods at the five day's end, and for the other three he is a treſpaſſer, and there is no juſtification   *St 717*

The conſtable of the hundred, pariſh, or place, where ſuch diſtreſs ſhall be taken]   *7 W Walter* and *Rumbald*   The tenement whereupon the diſtreſs was made, lay part in the hundred of *Kinaſley* in *Wiltſhire*, and part in the hundred of *Andover* in the county of *Southampton*, and part of the diſtreſs was taken in *Kinaſley*, and part in *Andover*, and all impounded together in the hundred of *Kinaſley*, and the conſtable of *Kinaſley* adminiſtred the oath to the appraiſers for the whole, in the preſence of the conſtable of *Andover*   It was objected, that the goods which were taken in *Andover* ought to have been impounded, appraiſed, and ſold in *Andover*, and that the conſtable of *Andover*, tho' preſent in *Kinaſley* when the appraiſement was made, had no juriſdiction there, ſo that the whole was done ſolely by the conſtable of *Kinaſley*, which therefore as to the goods taken in *Andover* was void   But why the court, the chaſing the diſtreſs over into the other county, is a continuance of the taking the diſtreſs, and the party, ſince it was for one intire cauſe, cannot ſever the diſtreſs, but ought to chaſe them all together, and impound them in one pound.   *L. Raym 53*

By the *1 & 2 P & M. c 12*   No perſon ſhall take for keeping in pound, or impounding any diſtreſs, above 4 d for any one whole diſtreſs   and where leſs hath been uſed, there to take leſs, on pain of 5 l to the party grieved, beſides what he ſhall take above 4 d.   *ſ 2.*

XI. Irregularity in the proceedings.

Irregularity

Where any diſtreſs ſhall be made, for any kind of rent juſtly due, and any irregularity ſhall be afterwards done by the party diſtraining, or his agent, the diſtreſs ſhall not be deemed unlawful, nor the diſtrainer a treſpaſſer *ab initio*, but the party aggrieved may recover ſatisfaction for the ſpecial damage, in an action of treſpaſs or on the caſe, and if he recover, he ſhall have full coſts.   *11 G 2 c 19 ſ 19*

But no tenant ſhall recover on ſuch action, if tender of amends hath been made before the action brought   *ſ 20*

XII. Landlord re-entring on non-payment.

In caſe where an half year's rent ſhall be in arrear, and the landlord or leſſor hath right by law to re-enter for non-payment thereof, he may, without any formal demand or re-entry, ſerve a declaration in ejectment, and on recovering judgment and execution, ſhall hold the premiſſes diſcharged from the leaſe But this not to bar the right of any mortgagee And if the defendant files a bill in equity, he ſhall not have an injunction againſt the proceedings at law, unleſs he ſhall bring the arrears into court, and alſo the coſts taxed in the ſaid ſuit Provided, that if the tenant ſhall before the trial in ejectment, pay all the arrears and coſts, the proceedings on the ejectment ſhall thenceforth ceaſe. 4 G 2. 28 ſ 2, 3, 4.

Re-entring.

XIII. Caſe of tenant holding over.

1 By the 8 *Ann. c.* 14. Whereas tenants *pur autre vie* (that is, holding during the life of another perſon), and leſſees for years, or at will, frequently hold over after the determination of the leaſe, and whereas after the determination of ſuch, or any other leaſes, no diſtreſs can be made for arrears of rent that grew due on ſuch leaſes before the determination thereof, it is therefore enacted, that it ſhall be lawful to diſtrain after the determination of ſuch leaſe, in the ſame manner as if it had not been determined provided, that the diſtreſs be made within ſix kalendar months after the determination of the leaſe, and during the continuance of the landlord's title or intereſt, and during the poſſeſſion of the tenant from whom ſuch arrear became due ſ 6, 7

Holding over after the term expired.

And by the 4 G 2 c 28 If any tenant for life or years, or other perſon who ſhall come into poſſeſſion by, from, or under him, ſhall wilfully hold over any lands, after the determination of ſuch term, and after demand made, and notice in writing given for delivering the poſſeſſion thereof, he ſhall, for the time that he ſhall ſo hold over, pay double the yearly value thereof, to be recovered by action of debt, in any court of record ſ 1

After the determination of ſuch term, and after demand made, and notice in writing given] E. 16 G. 3. *Cutting* and *Derby*. On an action for double value of the farm, it appeared, that the plaintiff on the 30th of September, and again on the 7th of October, gave a written notice to the defendant to quit the premiſſes on the 10th of October then following,

lowing, being the day on which the leaſe would expire
It was objected, that by the ſtatute the notice ought to be
after and not *before* the expiration of the term. But by the
court, notwithſtanding the order in which the words are
placed in the act of parliament, it is evident that the notice
ought to be previous, otherwiſe it would be abſurd, and
impoſſible to be complied with, to require *after* the expiration of the term that the tenant ſhould quit *at* the expiration This ſtatute, and the 11 *G.* 2 *c* 19 being in *pari
materia* ought to have the ſame conſtruction, and where,
by the latter the tenant is to be bound by his own notice to
quit, that muſt be clearly previous *Black Rep.* 1075

E 6 *G* 3. *Taſker* and *Burr.* The landlord demiſed to
the tenant from year to year, commencing the 10th of
October, being old Michaelmaſs-day The tenant dies on
the 27th of Auguſt The landlord, on the 9th of September gives notice to the executor to quit, at the end of
the term The queſtion was, If this notice is ſufficient?
The court held clearly, that in a common caſe, it would
not be ſufficient notice, but in the caſe of an executor,
they doubted But lord *Mansfield* inclined ſtrongly, that
the nature of the contract being to hold from year to year,
unleſs reaſonable notice was given on either ſide, and notice
not having been given in reaſonable time, the executor
was bound to keep the farm, if required, another year
And therefore, on the other hand, is at liberty to keep it,
if he chuſes it. *Black. Rep* 596.

M. 19 *G.* 3 *Dagget* and *Snowden.* In the common
pleas. On the 5th of October 1769, a written memorandum was entred into, whereby the plaintiff agreed to
let to the defendant a farm, to hold the arable ground from
old Candlemaſs then next, the paſture from old Lady-day,
and the meadow from old May-day, for ſeven years from
the ſaid days and times, paying rent half yearly, at old
Michaelmaſs and Lady-day. In September 1777, the
plaintiff gave the defendant a written notice, to quit the
arable land at old Candlemaſs next, the paſture at old
Lady-day, and the meadow ground at old May-day The
queſtion was, whether this notice was ſufficient to intitle
the plaintiff to recover the whole or any part of the premiſſes ? For the defendant it was argued, that this was not
a ſufficient notice for any part, the whole being one intire tenancy, and therefore notice to quit ought to have
been given on the 13th of Auguſt, being ſix months previous to the time when the firſt part of the term expired
But by the court, The notice was ſufficient for the whole
It was ſettled by all the judges about ten years ago, to avoid

di-

diverſity of opinions, and for general convenience, that in tenancies from year to year (which theſe kinds of holding over are held to be) there muſt be ſix months notice on either ſide to quit, according to the ancient law, except where any ſpecial agreement, or the cuſtom of any particular places, intervenes   The true conſtruction of this agreement is, that it is a holding from Lady-day to Lady-day, the rent being payable at Michaelmaſs and Lady-day And tho' part of the farm is to be entred upon and quitted at old Candlemaſs, and other part not till old May-day, yet that is no more than the cuſtom of moſt countries would have directed, without any ſpecial words for that purpoſe, in a taking from old Lady-day *Black Rep* 1224

But after all, this remedy by action ſeemeth not altogether adequate to the evil, for three reaſons   1 Becauſe ſuch action is certainly tedious and expenſive   2 It is uncertain, when the action is over, whether the tenant will be able to pay   3 What is chiefly wanted, namely, putting the landlord into poſſeſſion, is not obtained by ſuch action, but for that he ſhall be ſtill to ſeek.   A more ſhort and eaſy method of ouſting the tenant of his poſſeſſion, ſeemeth more eligible in the like caſes

2 Whereas great inconveniencies have happened to landlords, whoſe tenants have power to determine their leaſes, by giving notice to quit the premiſſes, and yet refuſing to deliver up the poſſeſſion, when the landlord hath agreed with another tenant for the ſame, it is therefore enacted, that if any tenant ſhall give notice of his intention to quit the premiſſes at a time mentioned in ſuch notice, and ſhall not accordingly deliver up the poſſeſſion at the time in ſuch notice contained, he, his executors or adminiſtrators, ſhall from thence forward pay double rent, to be recovered in like manner as the ſingle rent   11 G 2 c 19 ſ 18

H 5 G 3 *Timmins* and *Rowhſon.*   In replevin, the landlord avows, that he demiſed the premiſſes to the tenant for one year from the 5th of April 1760, that the tenant gave notice that he would quit the 5th of April 1761, but held over till the 10th of October, wherefore he avows for double rent for half a year   The tenant pleads a demiſe from the landlord for one year from the 5th of April 1760, and ſo from year to year, as long as both parties pleaſed. That the demiſe was only by parol, and that the notice proved to be given by the tenant to the landlord to quit the 5th of April 1761, was only by parol likewiſe   The queſtion was, Whether the tenant was liable to pay double rent for not quitting after a parol notice, and further, as he he held under a parol demiſe, as tenant from year to year, whether this is a holding under the ſtatute, ſo as to ſubject the tenant to double rent for not quitting after notice —— It was argued for the tenant, that the act muſt be confined to leaſes, wherein an expreſs power is reſerved to determine the tenure by notice, and to notices in writing only, becauſe the ſtatute ſpeaks of the time in ſuch notice *mentioned* and *contained*, which words are not applicable to parol notices —— For the landlord it was inſiſted, that this being a remedial law, the words might be fairly extended to parol leaſes, which are the moſt common, and to parol notices, without which, the clauſe would be nugatory, and affect only ſuch tenants as were fooliſh enough, to give written inſtead of parol notices. —— By lord *Mansfield* chief juſtice Statutes *in pari materia* are to be taken all as one ſyſtem, to ſuppreſs the miſchief The miſchief is an act of vexation, inconvenience, and injuſtice, by the tenant, after notice given by himſelf, after the landlord has another tenant ready, to ſtop ſhort and ſay, I won't quit This is an univerſal ſort of holding, and therefore this practice might be a very extenſive evil The legiſlature, in the 4 *G* 2 made a proviſion, where the landlord gives notice, and afterwards in the 11 *G* 2. this additional proviſion, in caſe the notice comes from the tenant The two laws are only parts of the ſame proviſion It is ſaid, the notice muſt be in writing Why? Does the act ſay ſo? No But the act of 4 *G* 2 does That is the ſtrongeſt reaſon againſt it It is here purpoſely omitted The drawer of the act could not leave it out by accident, having the other act before him. As to the words *mentioned* and contained, may not that be in a parol notice? Certainly it may. I therefore think this is a caſe within the miſchief, the preamble, and the enacting words of the ſtatute —— *Wilmot* juſtice (the other two juſtices being abſent) As to the notice being in writing, the different penning of the acts furniſhes evidence of different intentions The 4 *G* 2. ſeems to reſpect chiefly leaſes for lives or for long terms of years; and if the tenant holds over, and the landlord gives notice in writing for him to quit, he ſhall recover not double rent (for that might not be an equivalent) but double the yearly value of the eſtate And for that reaſon it was neceſſary, that it ſhould be recovered by action, and not by diſtreſs There are two good reaſons why one ſhould be in writing, and the other not. Firſt, if the tenant gives ſuch notice as will juſtify his leaving the farm, and doth not leave it, that is the miſchief which the act meant to meet, and parol notice

tice is ſufficient for that   Secondly, landlords generally
can write tenants in the country very ſeldom can   This
caſe is within the preamble and the enacting words, but,
had the preamble been confined, I ſhould have been for
extending the remedy according to the enacting words.
Theſe tenancies are the moſt uſual of any   It hath almoſt extinguiſhed tenancy at will, which by reaſon of the
inconveniencies that would otherwiſe enſue to both parties,
is not now to be underſtood as determinable at pleaſure,
but for a year certain, which was better, but ſtill inconvenient, to turn out or quit at the end of the year, without notice   This produced the preſent rule, that landlords
and tenants ſhall mutually give reaſonable notice   What
is reaſonable, is matter of circumſtances   This brings
the preſent leaſe within the words of the act   They have
power to quit and determine, upon giving reaſonable
notice ——— And judgment was given for the landlord.
Black Rep 533 *Bar Manſf* 1603

But this remedy, in like manner as the former, ſeemeth
not oppoſite to the main purpoſe   The ſtatute proceeds
upon a ſuppoſition that the tenant is a man of ſubſtance.
Which probably may not be the caſe   It is moſt likely,
that if he were able to live elſewhere, he would not chuſe
to hold over under ſuch circumſtances, nor perhaps would
the landlord want to be rid of him   The putting him out
of poſſeſſion, by ſome expeditious and eaſy method,
ſeemeth the more adequate remedy in this caſe alſo, in like
manner as is provided in the caſe where the tenant de-
ſerteth the premiſſes, as hereafter followeth.

XIV Attorning to ſtrangers.

Whereas the poſſeſſion of eſtates is rendred precarious,
by tenants attorning to ſtrangers, it is enacted, that all
ſuch attornments ſhall be void, unleſs the ſame be made
purſuant to ſome judgment at law or decree in equity, or
be with the conſent of the landlord, or be to a mortgagee
after the mortgage is become forfeited   11 G 2 c. 19.
ſ 11.

And tenants to whom any declaration in ejectment
ſhall be delivered, ſhall forthwith give notice thereof to
the landlord, on pain of forfeiting to him three years
value of the rent, and the landlord may make himſelf defendant by joining with the tenant, or may appear by himſelf ſ. 12, 13

And if the tenant ſhall not give notice to the landlord,
and the plaintiff ſhall obtain judgment againſt him by de-

fault, the court, on application, will ſet aſide the judgment, and order the tenant to pay the coſts. *Bur. Man f* 1996

XV *Deſerting the premiſſes.*

Tenant deſerting

If any tenant at rack rent, or where the rent reſerved ſhall be full three fourths of the yearly value of the demiſed premiſſes, who ſhall be in arrear for one year's rent, ſhall deſert the premiſſes, and leave the ſame uncultivated or unoccupied, ſo is no ſufficient diſtreſs can be had, two juſtices (having no intereſt in the premiſſes) may, at the requeſt of the landlord, go upon and view the ſame, and affix on the moſt notorious part of the premiſſes, notice in writing, what day (at the diſtance of 14 days at the leaſt) they will return to take a ſecond view and if on ſuch ſecond view, the tenant ſhall not appear and pay the rent, or there ſhall not be ſufficient diſtreſs on the premiſſes, then the juſtices may put the landlord into poſſeſſion, and the leaſe as to ſuch demiſe ſhall from thence be void 11 G 2 c 19 f. 16

But the tenant may appeal to the next juſtice or juſtices of aſſize, who may award coſts to either party   f 17.

XVI *Rent in caſe of an extent or execution.*

Extent or execution

In the caſe of A and *Cotton, T* 1755, it was determined by the barons of the exchequer, and affirmed on a writ of error, that if a diſtreſs be made for rent, and before the five days given by act of parliament are expired an extent is iſſued, tho' it be not levied, for a debt due to the crown, the extent ſhall take place of the diſtreſs becauſe the diſtreſs doth not ouſt the property of the effects into the landlord, but is only a pledge for ſecurity in his hands for his rent

But by the 8 *An c* 14 No goods being on any meſſuage, lands, or tenements, leaſed for life, term of years, at will, or otherwiſe, ſhall be liable to be taken by execution, unleſs the party, at whoſe ſuit the execution is ſued out, ſhall before the removal of ſuch goods from off the premiſſes, pay to the landlord or his bailiff all ſuch rent as ſhall be then due for the premiſſes, provided that it amount not to more than one year's rent, and if the ſaid arrears ſhall exceed one year's rent, then the party paying ſuch landlord one year's rent, may proceed to execute his judgment. f 1

And in caſe of two executions, there ſhall not be two years rent paid to the landlord for the intent of the act was

was to reſerve to the landlord only the rent for one year, and it was his own fault if he let more run in arrear Therefore one year's rent to the landlord being paid to him on the firſt execution, the ſheriff is not to levy for him again any thing on a ſubſequent execution *Str* 1024

XVII. *Rent on the death of tenant for life*

Whereas where any leſſor or landlord, having only an eſtate for life, in the lands, tenements or hereditaments demiſed, happens to die before or on the day on which any rent is reſerved or made payable, ſuch rent or any part thereof is not by law recoverable by the executors or adminiſtrators of ſuch leſſor or landlord, nor is the perſon in reverſion intitled thereto, other than for the uſe and occupation from the death of the tenant for life, of which, advantage hath often been taken by the under-tenants, who thereby avoid paying any thing for the ſame for remedy thereof, where any tenant for life ſhall happen to die before or on the day, on which any rent was reſerved or made payable, upon any demiſe or leaſe of any lands, tenements or hereditaments, which determined on the death of ſuch tenant for life, the executors or adminiſtrators of ſuch tenant for life may, in an action on the caſe, recover of ſuch under-tenant, if ſuch tenant for life die on the day on which the ſame was made payable, the whole, or if before ſuch day then a proportion, of ſuch rent, according to the time ſuch tenant for life lived, of the laſt year, or quarter of a year, or other time in which the ſaid rent was growing due 11 *G* 2 *c* 19. ſ 15

Tenant for life dying

In the caſe of *Pagett* and *Gee*, Dec 4, 1753 Tenant in tail, remainder to the defendant in fee, leaſes for years, and dies without iſſue a week before the day of payment of the half year s rent The leſſee, at the day, pays all the half year's rent to the defendant The executor of the tenant in tail brings his bill for apportionment of the rent ————By the lord chancellor *Hardwicke* This point has never been determined, but this is ſo ſtrong a caſe, that I ſhall make it a precedent There are in it two grounds for relief in equity The firſt ariſes on the ſtatute of the 11 *G* 2 The ſecond ariſes on the tenant's having ſubmitted to pay the rent to the defendant ———— The relief ariſing upon the ſtatute, is, either from the ſtrict legal conſtruction, or equity formed upon the reaſon of it. And here it is proper to conſider, what the miſchief was before the act, and what remedy is provided t

com mon

common law If tenant for life, or any who had a determinable eſtate, died but a day before the rent reſerved on a leaſe of his became due, the rent was loſt. For no one was intitled to recover it. His repreſentatives could not, becauſe they could only bring an action for the uſe and occupation, and that would not lie where there was a leaſe, but debt or covenant. Nor could the remainderman, becauſe it did not accrue in his time. Now this act appoints the apportioning the rent, and gives the remedy. But there are two deſcriptions of the perſon, to whoſe executors the remedy is given In the preamble, it is one having only an eſtate for life. In the enacting part, it is, tenant for life Now tenant in tail comes expreſsly within the miſchief I do not know how the judges at common law would conſtrue it but I ſhould be inclined in this court to extend it to them I ſhould make no doubt, were this the caſe of tenant in tail after poſſibility of iſſue extinct, for he is conſidered in many reſpects as tenant for life only He cannot ſuffer a recovery He may be injoined from committing waſte, ſuch as hurts the inheritance, as felling timber, though not for committing common waſte, being conſidered as to that as tenant in tail Were it the caſe of tenant for years determinable on lives, he certainly muſt be included within the act, tho' it ſays only tenant for life It would be playing with the words to ſay otherwiſe. Theſe caſes ſhew the neceſſity of conſtruing this act beyond the words Tenant in tail has certainly a larger eſtate than a mere tenant for life, for he has the inheritance in him, and may when he pleaſes turn it into a fee but if he does not, at the inſtant of his death he has but an intereſt for life Such too is the caſe of a wife tenant in tail *ex proviſione mariti* Upon this point I give no abſolute opinion As to the equity ariſing from this ſtatute, I know no better rule than this, *equitas ſequitur legem.* Where equity finds a rule of law agreeable to conſcience, it purſues the ſenſe of it to analogous caſes. If it does ſo as to maxims of the common law, why not as to the reaſons of acts of parliament? Nay, it has actually done ſo, on the ſtatute of forcible entry, upon which, this court grounds bills, not only to remove the force, but to quiet the poſſeſſion That act requires a legal eſtate in poſſeſſion This court extends the reaſon to equitable intereſt ——But I ground my opinion in this caſe, upon the tenant's having ſubmitted to pay the rent He has held himſelf bound in conſcience to pay it, for the uſe and occupation of the land the laſt half year He paid it to the defendant, which

which he was not bound to do in law. And in such a case, the person he pays it to shall be accountable, and considered as receiving it for those who are in equity intitled to it   The division must be that prescribed by the statute, and then the plaintiff is intitled to such a proportion of the rent as accrued during the testator's life.——— And accordingly it was decreed.   M S

XVIII Rent how far recoverable by executors or administrators

By the 32 H 8 c 37. Forasmuch as by the order of the common law, the executors or administrators of tenants in fee simple, fee tail, and for term of life, of rents services, rent charges, rent secks, and fee farms, have no remedy to recover such arrearages of the said rents or fee farms as were due to their testators in their lives, and yet the heirs of such testator, nor any person having the reversion of his estate after his decease, may distrain or have action to levy the same, it is enacted, that the executors and administrators of every such person to whom any such rent or fee farm shall be due and not paid at the time of his death, may have an action of debt for the same, against the tenant who ought to have paid the same, or against his executors and administrators, or may distrain upon the premisses, so long as they continue in the possession of such tenant in demesne, who ought immediately to have paid the same to the testator in his life, or of any other person claiming the same only by and from such tenant by purchase, gift, or descent. ſ. 1.

In like manner the husband may have action, or distrain for arrears due in the life time and in the right of his wife. ſ 3

And if any person shall have any rents or fee farms for the life of any other person, which shall be behind and unpaid at the death of such other person, he, his executors or administrators, may have action of debt against the tenant in demesne that ought to have paid the same when it was first due, his executors and administrators, or may distrain for the same upon the premisses, in such like manner as he might have done, if the person by whose death the estate was determined had been in full life. ſ 4.

Note, fee farm is, when the lord, upon the creation of the tenancy, reserves to himself and his heirs, either the

(margin note: Rent recoverable by executors or administrators.)

rent for which it was before let to farm, or at leaſt a fourth part of the value, without homage, fealty, or other ſervices, beyond what are eſpecially comprized in the feoffment   and it is called a fee farm rent, becauſe a farm rent is reſerved upon a grant in fee   2 *Inſt* 44.

XIX Of diſtreſs by warrant of juſtices of the peace.

By the 27 G 2 c 20 It is enacted as follows   *In all caſes where any juſtice of the peace is or ſhall be required or impowered, any or of parliament, to iſſue a warrant of diſtreſs, for the levying of any penalty inflicted, or any ſum of money directed to be paid by ſuch act, it ſhall be lawful for the juſtice granting ſuch warrant, therein to order and direct the goods and chattels ſo to be diſtrained, to be ſold and diſpoſed of within a certain time to be limited in ſuch warrant, ſo as ſuch time be not leſs than four days, nor more than eight days, unleſs the penalty or ſum of money for which ſuch diſtreſs ſhall be made, together with the reaſonable charge of taking and keeping ſuch diſtreſs, be ſooner paid*

And the officer making ſuch diſtreſs, ſhall and may deduct the reaſonable charges of taking, keeping, and ſelling ſuch diſtreſs, out of the money ariſing by ſuch ſale, and the overplus (if any) after ſuch charges, and alſo the ſaid penalty or ſum of money, ſhall be firſt fully end paid, ſhall be returned on demand, to the owner of the goods ſo diſtrained   and the officer executing ſuch warrant, if required, ſhall ſhew the ſame to the perſon whoſe goods are diſtrained, and ſhall ſuffer a copy thereof to be taken

But this ſhall not extend, to alter or proviſions relating to diſtreſs to enact for the payment of tithe and church rates to reſp the other queſtion, contained in the acts of the 7 & 8 W c 30 and of 1 G 2 c 6

Order of the goods to be ſold] And in this caſe no replevy lies   the ſheriff having no power to examine the proceedings of the juſtices   1 *Barnardiſt* 110 *St* 1184

Officer may deduct the reaſonable charges] But here is no power given to the juſtices, to aſcertain ſuch charges, therefore it ſeemeth, that the officer executing the warrant ſhall be the ſole judge thereof in the firſt inſtance, and afterwards, if the owner of the goods diſtrained ſhall be aſſeſſed the reaſonableneſs thereof ſhall be determined by a judge and jury upon an action brought

But by fpecial ftatutes, this power of afcertaining the charges of diftrefs and fale, is fometimes given to the juftices, as is fet forth in this book under the refpective titles.   •

Tithes and church rates by the people called quakers] The abovefaid ftatutes of the 7 & 8 *IV c* 34 and 1 G *f* 2. *c* 6 relate not only to *tithes and church rates* (by which laft feemeth only to be underftood the churchwardens rate for the repair and other ufes of the church), but alfo to any cuftomary or other rights, dues, or payments, belonging to any church or chapel, which of right by law and cuftom ought to be paid for the ftipend or maintenance of any minifter or curate officiating in any church or chapel Therefore for any thing that appears from the words of this ftatute, unlefs it be in the cafe of *tithes* or *church rates*, the juftices may order the diftrefs for thofe other dues and payments to be detained for a certain time, and the officer may deduct the charges not only of *diftraining*, but alfo of *keeping* and *felling* the diftrefs, whereas by thofe former acts above mentioned, the officer was only allowed to deduct the neceffary charges of *diftraining*

The eight precedents next following, drawn and communicated to the author by a gentleman of great learning and judgment, acting in the commiffion of the peace, * are inferted, not only as ufeful in this place, but as patterns for our imitation in other like cafes

A Complaint to be exhibited in writing before two juftices, in the cafe of goods clandeftinely removed, on the 11 G 2 *c.* 19.

Weftmorland ⎰ BE *it remembred, that this —— day of —— A I of —— complaineth, that A O of —— hath fraudulently and clandeftinely removed and conveyed away certain goods and chattels of —— not exceeding the value of 50l, from —— at —— to prevent —— from diftraining the faid goods and chattels for arrears of rent due to the faid —— for the faid —— And that B O of—— yeoman, and C O of —— yeoman, wil-*

---

fully and knowingly aided and aſſiſted the ſaid A O in ſo fraudulently and clandeſtinely removing and conveying away the ſaid goods and chattels, and in concealing the ſame.

A I.

Exhibited at —— the —— day of ——
before us ——— juſtices of the peace
of —— reſiding near —— not being
intereſted in ———.

B Warrant thereupon to ſummon the parties concerned.

Weſtmorland. } To the conſtable of ———

WHEREAS *a complaint in writing hath been this —— day of —— exhibited before us —— juſtices of the peace —— reſiding near —— not being intereſted in —— by A I of —— gentleman, ſetting forth that A O. of —— yeoman, hath fraudulently and clandeſtinely removed and conveyed away certain goods and chattels of —— not exceeding the value of 50l, from —— to prevent —— from diſtraining the ſaid goods and chattels, for arrears of rent due to the ſaid —— for the ſaid —— And that B O of —— yeoman, and C. O of —— yeoman, wilfully and knowingly aided and aſſiſted the ſaid —— in ſo fraudulently and clandeſtinely removing and conveying away the ſaid goods and chattels, and in concealing the ſame Theſe are therefore to command you forthwith to ſummon the ſaid A O B. O and C O. to appear before us at —— on the —— day of ——, at the hour of —— to anſwer the matter of the ſaid complaint. Given under our hands and ſeals at —— the —— day of ——*

C. Order of two juſtices thereupon

Weſtmorland } The order and adjudication of —— and —— juſtices of the peace of ———

WHEREAS A O *of —— yeoman, hath been duly charged before us —— and —— juſtices of the peace of —— reſiding near —— not being intereſted in —— with having fraudulently and clandeſtinely removed*

and

and conveyed away certain goods and chattels of ———— *not exceeding the value of* 50l, *from* ———— *to prevent the said* ———— *from distraining the said goods and chattels, for arrears of rent due to the said* ———— *for the said* ————, *And whereas* B O *of* ———— *yeoman, and* C. O *of* ———— *yeoman, have been also duly charged before us, with having wilfully and knowingly aided and assisted the said* ———— *in so fraudulently and clandestinely removing and conveying away the said goods and chattels, and in concealing the same, And we the said justices having summoned the parties concerned, and examined the fact, and all proper witnesses upon oath* [*or in case of a quaker, upon affirmation required by law*] *And it appearing and being fully proved before us, that the said* A. O *did so fraudulently and clandestinely remove and convey away, as aforesaid,* ———— *being of the value of* ———— *and the goods and chattels of the said* ————, *And it also appearing and being fully proved before us, that the said* B O *and* C. O. *wilfully and knowingly aided and assisted the said* A. O *in so removing and conveying away, as aforesaid, the said* ———— *and in concealing the same We the said justices do therefore this* ———— *day of* ———— *determine and adjudge that the said* A O B O *and* C O *are guilty of the offences, with which they the said* A. O B. O. *and* C O *are charged as aforesaid, and they are convicted thereof, And we do hereby order and adjudge them the said* A O B. O *and* C. O. *to pay the sum of* ———— *being double the value of the said goods and chattels, to* ———— *or to his bailiff, servant or agent, on or before the* ———— *day of* ————. *Given under our hands and seals at* ———— *the* ———— *day of* ————.

D. Warrant of distress, in case the offenders having notice, refuse or neglect to pay, pursuant to the preceding order. 11 G. 2. *c* 19. 27 G. 2. *c* 20.

Westmorland, } To the constable of ————.

W HEREAS A O, *of* ———— *yeoman,* B. O. *of* ———— *yeoman, and* C. O, *of* ———— *yeoman, were by an order dated the* ———— *day of* ———— *under the hands and seals of us* ———— *and* ———— *justices of the peace of* ———— *residing near* ———— *not being interested in* ———— *ordered to pay the sum of* ———— *to* ———— *or his bailiff, servant, or agent, on or before the* ———— *day of* ———— *being double the value of certain goods and chattels of the said* ———— *which the said* A. O. *was before us duly convicted of having fraudulently and clandestinely*

rem ved

removed and conveyed away from ———— to prevent the said
———— from distraining the said goods and chattels for arrears of
rent due to the said ———— for the said ———— and which the said
B O and C O were also duly convicted before us, of having
wilfully and knowingly aided and assisted the said A O in so
fraudulently and clandestinely moving and conveying away, and
concealing the same, And whereas the said A O B O and
C O having notice of our said order, have refused or neglected
to pay, and have not paid, the said sum of ———— pursuant
thereunto, and the same hath been fully proved before us, These
are therefore to command you to levy the said sum of ———— by
distress and sale of the goods and chattels of the said A O B O
and C O and we do hereby order and direct the goods and
chattels so to be distrained, to be sold and disposed of, within
———— days, unless the said sum of ———— for which such distress shall be made, together with the reasonable charges of taking
and keeping such distress, shall be sooner paid And you are also
hereby commanded to certify to us, what you shall do by virtue of
this our warrant Given under our hands and seals at ————
the ———— day of

E   The constable's return thereupon of the want
of distress

Westmorland   I A C constable of ———— do hereby certify
———— and ———— justices of the peace of
———— that I have made diligent search for, but do not know of,
nor can find, any goods and chattels of ———— and ————
and ———— or of any of them, by distress and sale whereof I may
levy the sum of ———— pursuant to their warrant for that purpose dated the ———— day of ———— Given under my hand
this ———— day of ————,

F   Commitment thereupon to the house of cor
rection

Westmorland   ⎰ To the constable of ———— and also to
⎱ the keeper of the house of correction
at ————.

WHEREAS ———— and ———— and ———— were
by an order dated the ———— day of ———— und
the hands and seals of us ———— justices of the peace of————
residing ——— ———— not being interested in ———— ordered
to pay, the sum of ———— to ———— or to his bailiff, servant,
or agent, on or before the ———— day of ———— being double
the value of certain goods and chattels of the said ————
which

which the ſaid ———— was before us duly convicted of having fraudulently and clandeſtinely removed and conveyed away from ———— to prevent the ſaid ———— from diſtraining the ſaid goods and chattels, for arrears of rent due to the ſaid ———— for the ſaid ———— And which the ſaid ———— and ———— were alſo duly convicted before us of having wilfully and knowingly aided and aſſiſted the ſaid ———— in ſo fraudulently and clandeſtinely removing and conveying away, and in concealing the ſame, And whereas the ſaid ———— and ———— and ———— having notice of our ſaid order, have refuſed or neglected to pay, and have not paid, the ſaid ſum of ———— purſuant thereunto, and the ſame hath been duly proved before us, And whereas it appears to us, by the return of ———— conſtable of ———— dated the ———— day of ———— that he hath made diligent ſearch for, but doth not know of, nor can find, any goods and chattels of the ſaid ———— and ———— and ———— or any of them, by diſtreſs and ſale whereof the ſaid ſum of ———— may be levied, purſuant to our warrant duly made and iſſued for the levying the ſaid ſum of ———— by diſtreſs and ſale of the goods and chattels of the ſaid ———— and ———— and ———— Theſe are therefore to command you the ſaid conſtable of ———— to apprehend the ſaid ———— and ———— and ———— and convey them to the ſaid houſe of correction at ———— aforeſaid, and deliver them there to the ſaid keeper of the ſaid houſe of correction, And theſe are alſo to command you the ſaid keeper of the ſaid houſe of correction, to receive them the ſaid ———— and ———— and ———— into the ſaid houſe of correction, and there keep them to hard labour, without bail or mainprize, for the ſpace of ſix months, unleſs the ſaid ſum of ———— ſo ordered to be paid as aforeſaid, ſhall be ſooner ſatisfied. Given under our hands and ſeals at ———— the ———— day of ————

G Form of a complaint and oath to be made before a juſtice, in caſe of a dwelling houſe, where goods and chattels are fraudulently and clandeſtinely removed and conveyed away and ſecured, ſo as to prevent them from being taken and ſeized as a diſtreſs for arrears of rent

Weſtmorland BE it remembred, that this ———— day of ———— A I of ———— yeoman, complaineth, and maketh oath, that certain goods and chattels of A O of ———— yeoman, have been fraudulently and clandeſtinely conveyed and carried away from ———— by the ſaid A O his ſervant or ſervants, agent or agents, or other perſon or perſons, aiding or aſſiſting therein, to prevent ———— from diſ-

iſtraining the ſaid goods and chattels for arrears of rent due
to th. ſaid ——— for the ſaid ——— And that the ſaid good,
and chattels are put, placed, or kept, in the houſe, barn, ſtabʾ,
outhouſ , aud, cloſe or other place of ——— at ——— lock d
up, faſtened, or otherwiſe ſecured, ſo as to prevent the ſaid goon,
and chattels from being taken and ſeized as a diſtreſs for arrears
of rent, And that the ſaid A I hath a reaſonable ground t
ſuſpeƈt, and doth ſuſpeƈt, that the ſaid goods and chattels are in
the dwelling houſe of the ſaid ——— at ———.

A. I

Taken and ſworn at ——— the ———
day ,of ——— before ———

H Warrant upon the preceding complaint and oath.

Weſtmorland { To the conſtable, headborough, borſhol
der, or other peace officer of ——— and
to each, and every of them

W HEREAS A. I. *of* ——— *yeoman, hath this* ———
day of ——— *exhibited his complaint and made oath*
before ——— *juſtices of the peace of* ——— *that certain goods*
and chattels of A O of ——— *yeoman, have been fraudulentl,*
and clandeſtinely conveyed and carried away from ——— *by the*
ſaid A O his ſervant or ſervants, agent or agents, or other
perſon or perſons aiding or aſſiſting therein, to prevent ———
from diſtraining the ſaid goods and chattels for arrears of rent
due to the ſaid ——— *for the ſaid* ———*, And that the ſaid*
goods and chattels are put, placed, or kept in the houſe, barn,
ſtable, outhouſe, yard, cloſe, or other place of ——— *at ——*
locked up, faſtened, or otherwiſe ſecured, ſo as to prevent the
ſaid goods and chattels from being taken and ſeized as a diſtreſs
for arrears of rent, and that the ſaid A I hath a reaſonable
ground to ſuſpeƈt, and doth ſuſpeƈt, that the ſaid goods and
chattels are in the dwelling houſe of ——— *at* ——— *Theſe*
are therefore to command you, and each and every of you, to
aid and aſſiſt ——— *his ſteward, bailiff, receiver, or other perſon*
or perſons impowered to take and ſeize as a diſtreſs for rent the
ſaid goods and chattels, in the day time to break open and enter
into the ſaid dwelling houſe, barn, ſtable, outhouſe, yard, cloſe,
or other place of the ſaid ——— *at* ——— *and to take and*
ſeize the ſaid goods and chattels for the ſaid arrears of rent,
according to law Given under my hand and ſeal at ———
the ——— *day of* ———

I. The form of the inventory of the goods distrained may be this

AN inventory of the several goods and chattels, distrained by us whose names are under written, the ———— day of ———— in the year ———— in the houses, outhouses and lands, of A T in ———— by the authority and on the behalf of A L of ————for ———— pounds arrear of rent due to him the said A. L.

> In the dwelling house ·
> One table,
> Six chairs, &c.
> In the cow house ·
> Six cows,
> Two calves, &c.

K Notice.

A T

TAKE notice, that by the authority and on the behalf of your landlord A L I have this ———— day of ———— in the year of our Lord ———— distrained the several goods and chattels specified in the schedule hereunto annexed, in your houses, outhouses, and grounds, at ———— for ———— pounds arrear of rent due to him the said A L And if you shall not pay the said rent so due and in arrear as aforesaid, or replevy the said goods and chattels, I shall, after the expiration of five days from the date hereof, cause the said goods and chattels to be appraised and sold, according to the statute in that case made and provided. Given under my hand the day and year first above written

A D

Witness that a copy hereof was this day delivered to the said A T. (Or, left at the chief mansion house of the said A T.)
A. W.

L. Appraisers oath.

YOU and each of you shall well and truly appraise the goods and chattels mentioned in this inventory, according to the best of your understanding. So help you God.

M. Form

M. Form of the appraiſement.

THE appraiſement may be in the form of the inventory, ſpecifying the particulars, and their reſpective valuations And then add at the end,

Appraiſed by us, this —— day of —— in the year ——

A P
B P. } ſworn appraiſers

Diſtringas   See **Proceſs.**

Divine Service   See **Publick Worſhip.**

Dogs.

So far as Dogs fall under the conſideration of the Game laws, See title **Game.**

Dogs miſchievous

1. A *Maſtiff*, going in the ſtreet unmuzzled, from the ferocity of his nature being dangerous and cauſe of terror to his majeſty's ſubjects, ſeemeth to be a common nuſance, and conſequently the owner may be indicted for ſuffering him to go at large

If a man has a dog that *kills ſheep*, this is not a publick nuſance, but the owner of the dog (knowing thereof) is liable to an action, but if he is ignorant of ſuch quality, he ſhall not be puniſhed for this killing And in an action upon the caſe for ſuch killing, the plaintiff ſhall be required to prove in evidence, that the dog had uſed to kill ſheep *Dyer* 25 *Het* 171.

And in order to maintain an action for *biting* by the defendant's dog, it muſt be proved alſo that he knew his dog to be uſed to bite, but one inſtance is ſufficient in that caſe 12 *Mod* 555

And if a man keeps a dog accuſtomed to bite *ſheep*, and he knows it, and notwithſtanding he keeps the dog ſtill, and afterwards the dog bites an *horſe*, this ſhall be actionable, altho' he had been known before to bite ſheep only becauſe the owner, after notice of the firſt miſchief, ought to have deſtroyed or hindred him from doing any more hurt Ld *Raym* 110.

2 *M*

2 *M* 17 *G* 3 On an action of trover and converfion for a pointing dog, the plaintiff proved the dog to be his property, and that it was found at the defendant's houfe twelve months after it was loft   The defendant faid, the dog ftrayed there cafually, and demanded 20 s for 20 weeks keeping, before he would deliver up the dog   A verdict was given for the plaintiff, fubject to the opinion of the court, whether this refufal amounted to a converfion of the dog   But the counfel for the defendant declined arguing the queftion, and the plaintiff had judgment   *Black Rep* 1117

3 Stealing dogs is not felony, for however they may be valued by the owner, yet they fhall never be fo highly regarded by the law, that for the fake of them a man fhall die   1 *Haw* 93

But by the 10 *G* 3 *c* 18   If any perfon fhall fteal any dog or dogs, of any kind or fort whatfoever, from the owner thereof, or from any perfon intrufted by the owner therewith , or fhall fell, buy, or receive, harbour, detain, or keep any fuch dog or dogs, knowing the fame to have been ftolen , every fuch perfon fhall, on conviction upon the oath of one witnefs, or his or her own confeffion, before two juftices, forfeit for the firft offence any fum not exceeding 30 l, nor lefs than 20 l, as to fuch juftices fhall feem meet, together with the charges previous to and attending fuch conviction, to be afcertained by fuch juftice before whom the offender fhall be convicted, and if not forthwith paid, the faid juftices fhall commit the offender to the common gaol or houfe of correction, for any time not exceeding 12 calendar months, nor lefs than fix, or until the penalty and charges fhall be paid , and if any perfon, having been convicted as aforefaid, fhall afterwards be guilty of the like offence, and fhall be thereof convicted in like manner as aforefaid, every fuch perfon fhall forfeit not exceeding 50 l, nor lefs than 30 l, as to fuch juftices fhall feem meet, together with the charges previous to and attending fuch conviction, to be afcertained by fuch juftices before whom the offender fhall be convicted, which faid penalties, or any of them, when recovered, fhall be paid half to the informer, and half to the poor, and upon non-payment thereof, fuch juftices fhall commit the offender to the common gaol or houfe of correction, for any time not exceeding 18 months, nor lefs than 12, or until the penalty and charges fhall be paid, and fuch juftices fhall alfo order the offender to be publickly whipped, within 3 days after fuch commitment, in the town wherein fuch gaol or houfe of correction fhall be,

between

between the hours of twelve and one of the clock. *ſ* 1

And one juſtice, on information to him made, may grant a warrant to ſearch for any dog ſtolen as aforeſaid, and in caſe any ſuch dog or the ſkin thereof ſhall upon ſuch ſearch be found, the ſaid juſtice ſhall take and reſtore ſuch dog or ſkin to the owner thereof, and the perſon in whoſe cuſtody or poſſeſſion ſuch dog or ſkin ſhall be ſo found (in caſe it ſhall appear that ſuch perſon was privy to ſuch dog having been ſtolen, or that ſuch ſkin was the ſkin of any ſuch dog ſtolen as aforeſaid) ſhall reſpectively be ſubject and liable to the like penalties and puniſhments, as perſons convicted of ſtealing any dog or dogs are herein before made ſubject and liable to *ſ*. 2.

And for the more eaſy conviction of offenders, the juſtices may cauſe the conviction to be drawn up in the following form, or to the ſame effect, as the caſe may happen

Be it remembred, That on the ——— *day of* ——— *in the year of our Lord* ——— *A B is convicted before us* ——— *of his majeſty's juſtices of the peace for the* ——— *of* ——— (ſpecifying the offence, and the time and place when and where the ſame was committed, as the caſe ſhall be) *Given under our hands and ſeals, the day and year aforeſaid.* *ſ* 3

Provided, that if any perſon ſhall think himſelf or herſelf aggrieved by any thing done in purſuance of this act, ſuch perſon may appeal to the next general quarter ſeſſions, within four days after the cauſe of complaint ſhall ariſe, ſuch appellant giving 14 days notice at leaſt in writing of his intention to appeal, and of the matter thereof, to the perſon whoſe acts are complained againſt, and within two days after ſuch notice, entring into a recognizance before a juſtice, with two ſureties, conditioned to try ſuch appeal, and abide the order of, and to pay ſuch coſts as ſhall be awarded by the juſtices at ſuch quarter ſeſſion And the ſaid juſtices at ſuch ſeſſion, on proof of ſuch notice and recognizance, ſhall hear and determine the appeal in a ſummary way, and award ſuch coſts to the parties appealing or appealed againſt, as they ſhall think proper And their determination ſhall be final, and no order or other proceedings touching the conviction of any offender againſt this act ſhall be quaſhed for want of form, or be removed by *certiorari* or other writ into any of his majeſty's courts of record at *Weſtminſter.* *ſ* 4

[Here

[Here feem to be fome difficulties upon this act as,

(1) With regard to the *offence* *If any perfon fhall fleal any dog or dogs* It is not a mere cavil, in a cafe where a man's property or liberty is fo confiderably affected, to furmife, that it may be doubtful whether upon this act it is penal to fleal a *bitch* In the cafe of *horfe ftealing*, the act runs, *any horfe, mare, or gelding.* And it is not ufual, where a man has ftolen a *mare*, to indict him for ftealing a *horfe*. And fo tender is the law in thefe matters, that when by the 1 *Ed* 6 *c* 12 it was enacted, that no perfon or perfons convicted of ftealing horfes, mares, or geldings, fhould be admitted to the benefit of clergy, this was not thought fufficient to exclude from the faid benefit any perfon who fhould fleal only one horfe, mare, or gelding, but an explanatory act (2 & 3 *Ed* 6. *c* 33) was thought neceffary for that purpofe And the reafon is plain What a man has a right to (as his life, liberty, or eftate) by a clear and undoubted law, fhall not be taken from him by a law lefs clear and certain And in this very act before us, a diftinction of fexes is made throughout with refpect to the *offenders, (him or her, himfelf or herſelf,)* which diftinction being not obferved with refpect to the *offence*, it may poffibly be argued, that in a cafe fo penal, the ftatute fhall not be extended further than the words will ftrictly bear

(2) With refpect to the *penalties* As the claufe ftands, there may be a doubt concerning the application of the forfeitures for the firft offence, for tho' it is faid, that the faid forfeitures or *any of them* fhall be paid half to the informer and half to the poor, yet in the very next words following, it is faid, that on non-payment thereof the juftices fhall commit the offender for any time not exceeding 18 months nor lefs than 12, which words are only applicable to the penalty for a fecond or other fubfequent offence ——— In like manner, it feems doubtful, whether the *whipping* fhall be underftood for the firft, or only for a fubfequent offence Alfo the fpecial *time* of whipping is not clearly afcertained, being only *between the hours of twelve and one of the clock*, which may be either in the morning foon after midnight, or in the afternoon ——— There is alfo a fmall miftake, where it is faid, that the charges of conviction fhall be afcertained by the *juftice* before whom the offender fhall be convicted, whereas the conviction muft be by *two* juftices

(3) The claufe concerning the *appeal* feemeth inconfiftent, or otherwife unintelligible The appeal muft be to the next general quarter *feffion*, within ten days after the caufe of complaint fhall arife, and of this fourteen days notice

shall be given to the persons whose acts are complained against.
——— Whatever these words may signify, the imprisonment is still going on, for if the forfeiture is not *forthwith* paid, the offender shall be committed And at all events, the *whipping* will be over, before the appeal can commence]

Door breaking open. See **Arrest.**
Dower. See **Forfeiture.**
Drunkenness. See **Alehouses.**
Duelling. See **Homicide.**

Egyptians. See **Vagrants**
Embracery. See **Maintenance.**

Escape.

THIS is to be understood of escapes in *criminal* cases, and not in *civil* cases, as for debt, or the like

Escape what　　An escape is, where one that is arrested gaineth his liberty, before he is delivered by course of law. *Terms de la ley.*

Several kinds thereof　　Escapes are of three kinds   1 By a person who hath the offender in his custody, this is properly called an *escape* 2 Caused by a stranger, this is commonly called a *rescue* 3 By the party himself, either without force, which is simply an escape, or with force, which is *prison breaking* *Rescous* and *prison breaking* are treated of under their respective titles, and this title treats only of escapes properly so called   Concerning which we will treat in the following order.

I. *Of escape by the party himself.*
II. *Escape suffered by a private person.*
III. *Escape suffered by an officer.*
IV. *What is a voluntary, and what a negligent escape.*
V. *Concerning the retaking of a person escaped.*

VI.

I. *Of escape by the party himself.*

As all persons are bound to submit themselves to the Escape by judgment of the law, and to be ready to be justified by party himself. it, whoever in any case refuses to undergo that imprisonment which the law thinks fit to put upon him, and flees himself from it by any artifice, before such time as he is delivered by due course of law, is guilty of an high contempt, punishable with fine and imprisonment 2 *Haw* 122

But escape committed by the party himself, belongs more properly to the title *Prison breaking*

II *Escape suffered by a private person.*

It seems to be a good general rule, that wherever any Escape by a person hath another lawfully in his custody, whether up- private person, on an arrest made by himself or another, he is guilty of an escape, if he suffer him to go at large, before he hath discharged himself of him, by delivering him over to some other who by law ought to have the custody of him. 2 *Haw* 138.

And the law is generally the same, in relation to escapes suffered by private persons, as by officers 2 *Haw.* 138

III *Escape suffered by an officer.*

1 In order to make an escape, there must be an actual Escape by an arrest, and therefore if an officer having a warrant to ar- officer. rest a man, see him shut up in a house, and challenge him There must be a as his prisoner, but never actually have him in his custody, previous arrest and the party get free, the officer cannot be charged with an escape 2 *Haw* 129

2 And as there must be an actual arrest, such arrest And justifiable. must be also justifiable, for if it be either for a supposed crime, where no such crime was committed, and the party neither indicted nor appealed, or for such a slight suspicion of an actual crime, and by such an irregular mittimus as will neither justify the arrest nor imprisonment, the officer is not guilty of an escape, by suffering the prisoner to go at large. 2 *Haw* 129

And for a criminal offence

3 And as the imprisonment must be justifiable, so it must be also for a criminal offence   2 *Haw* 129

And not detained only for fees.

4 Also if a prisoner be acquitted, and detained only for his fees, it will not be criminal to suffer him to escape, tho' the judgment were, that *he be discharged paying his fees*, so that till they be payed, the first imprisonment continued lawful as before, for inasmuch as he is detained, not as a criminal, but only as a debtor, his escape cannot be more criminal than that of any other debtor   Yet if a person convicted of a crime, be condemned to imprisonment for a certain time, and also *till he pay his fees*, and he escape after such time is elapsed, without paying them, perhaps such escape may be criminal, for that it was part of the punishment that the imprisonment be continued till the fees should be paid, but it seems, that this is to be intended where the fees are due to others as well as to the gaoler, for otherwise the gaoler will be the only sufferer by the escape, and it will be hard to punish him for suffering an injury to himself only, in the non-payment of a debt in his power to release   2 *H* 129, 130

Too much liberty, an escape

5 Also, it is an escape in some cases, to suffer a prisoner to have greater liberty, than by the law he ought to have, as to admit a person to bail, who by law ought not to be bailed, but to be kept in close custody   2 *Haw* 130

So if a gaoler, or other officer, shall licence his prisoner to go abroad for a time, and to come again, this is an escape, because the prisoner is found out of the bounds of his prison, tho' the prisoner return again, according as he shall be prescribed   *D* &c. 159

Losing sight, an escape

6 If the gaoler so closely pursues the prisoner who flies from him, that he retakes him, without losing sight of him, the law looks on the prisoner so far in his power all the time, as not to adjudge such a flight to amount at all to an escape, but if the gaoler once lose sight of the prisoner, and afterwards retake him, he seems in strictness to be guilty of an escape   And if he kill him in the pursuit, he is in like manner guilty of an escape, tho' he never lost sight of him, and could not otherwise take him, not only because the king loses the benefit he might have had by the forfeiture on his attainder, but also because the publick justice is not so well satisfied by the killing him in such an extrajudicial manner.   2 *Haw* 130.

IV What is a voluntary, and what a negligent escape

Voluntary escape

1 Wherever an officer, who hath the custody of a prisoner, charged with and guilty of a capital offence,
doth

doth knowingly give him his liberty, with an intent to
fave him from his trial or execution, this is a voluntary
efcape 2 *Haw* 130

2 A negligent efcape is, when the party arrefted or imprifoned doth efcape againft the will of him that arrefted
or imprifoned him, and is not frefhly purfued and taken
again, before he hath loft the fight of him *Dalt c.* 159

3 If the conftable or other officer fhall voluntarily fuffer a thief, being in his cuftody, to go into the water to
drown himfelf, this efcape is felony in the conftable, and
the drowning is felony in the thief Otherwife if the thief
fhall fuddenly, without the affent of the conftable, kill,
hang, or drown himfelf, this is but a negligent efcape in
the conftable *Dalt c* 159

V Concerning the retaking of a perfon efcaped

1 If an officer hath arrefted a man by virtue of a warrant, and then taketh his promife that he will come again,
and fo letteth him go, the officer cannot, after arreft, take
him again by force of his former warrant, for that this was
by the confent of the officer But if he return, and put
himfelf again under the cuftody of the officer, it feems
that it may be probably argued, that the officer may lawfully detain him, and bring him before the juftice in purfuance of the warrant *Dalt c* 169 1 *Haw* 81

2 But if the party arrefted had efcaped of his own
wrong, without the confent of the officer, now upon frefh
fuit, the officer may take him again and again, fo often as
he efcapeth, although he were out of view, or that he fhall
fly into another town or county, and bring him before
the juftice, upon whofe warrant he was firft arrefted
Dalt c 169

And it is faid generally in fome books, that an officer who
hath negligently fuffered a prifoner to efcape, may retake
him wherever he finds him, without mentioning any frefh
purfuit, and indeed fince the liberty gained by the prifoner
is wholly owing to his own wrong, there feems to be no
reafon he fhould take any manner of advantage from it
2 *Haw* 131, 132.

3 And wherever a perfon is lawfully arrefted for any
caufe, and afterwards efcapes, and fhelters himfelf in an
houfe, the doors may be broke open to take him, on refufal
of admittance 2 *Haw* 87

4 It is perhaps the better opinion, that wherever a
prifoner, by the negligence of his keeper, gets loofe or out
of his power, that the keeper lofes fight of him, the keeper

is punishable for the escape, notwithstanding he retook him immediately after And it is clear, that he cannot excuse himself from an escape, by killing a prisoner in the pursuit, tho' he could not possibly retake him, but must in such case be content to submit to such punishment, as his negligence shall appear to deserve 2 *Haw* 132.

VI *Indictment for an escape*

Indictment. It seems clear, that every indictment (A) for an escape, whether negligent or voluntary, must expresly shew, that the prisoner was actually in the defendant's custody for such a crime, and that he went at large And if for a voluntary escape, that the defendant feloniously and voluntarily suffered him to go at large, and must set forth, not the felony in general, but the particular kind of felony But it seems questionable, whether such certainty, as to the nature of the crime, be necessary in an indictment for a negligent escape, for that it is not material in this case, whether the person who escaped were guilty or not 2 *Haw* 133, 229

VII *Trial and conviction for an escape.*

Gaoler not producing him, a conviction. 1. If the prisoner be of record in a court, and the gaoler being called, cannot give an account where he is, this is a conviction of an escape, but seems not a conviction of a voluntary escape, unless the gaoler confesseth it And the gaoler may be fined in such a case, but not convicted of felony, without indictment or presentment. 1 *H H* 599, 603

Felony to be tried before the escape. 2 And it seems to be clear, that a keeper who voluntarily suffers another to escape, who was in his custody for felony, cannot be arraigned for such escape as for felony, until the principal be attainted, for that the felony of the prisoner shall not be tried between the king and the keeper, because the prisoner is a stranger thereunto, yet he may be indicted and tried for it as a misprision, before the attainder of the principal offender. 2 *Haw* 135 2 *Inst* 591, 592

VIII.

VIII. Punishment of an escape

1 If a felon escapes before arrest, it is not punishable in him as felony, but for the flight he forfeits his goods when presented   *Hale's Pl* 111

2 If a private person arrest a felon, and he escape by force from him, the township shall be amerced, but it seems it excuseth the party, because he cannot raise power to assist him, but if a constable or other officer hath the custody of a prisoner, bringing him to the gaol, it seems that a simple escape by the rescue of the prisoner himself, doth not wholly excuse him, because he may take sufficient strength to his assistance   1 *H H* 601

3 Wherever a person is found guilty upon an indictment or presentment of a negligent escape of a criminal actually in his custody, he is punishable by fine and imprisonment, according to the quality of the offence   2 *Haw.* 136, 139   1 *H H* 600, 604

And it seems to be the better opinion, that the sheriff is as much liable to answer for a negligent escape suffered by his bailiff, as if he had actually suffered it himself, and that the court may charge either the sheriff or bailiff for such an escape, and if a deputy gaoler be not sufficient to answer a negligent escape, his principal must answer for him   2 *Haw* 135

Note, Mr *Hawkins,* altho' he is one of the most accurate of all writers, yet hath inserted in this place certain penalties for escapes, which were expired above 200 years before   2 *Haw* 137.

If a prisoner for felony break the gaol, this seems to be a negligent escape in the gaoler, because there wanted either that due strength in the gaol, that should have secured him, or that due vigilance in the gaoler or his officers to have prevented it, and therefore it is lawful for the gaoler to hamper them with irons to prevent their escape, for if gaolers might not be punished for this as a negligent escape, they would be careless either to secure their prisoners, or to retake them that escape.   1 *H. H.* 601

4. It seems to be generally agreed, that a voluntary escape suffered by an officer, amounts to the same kind of crime, and is punishable in the same degree, as the offence of which the party was guilty, and for which he was in custody, whether it be treason, felony, or trespass. 2 *Haw* 134

But yet a voluntary escape is no felony, if the act done were not felony at the time of the escape made, as in case

K k 4   of

Marginal notes:
Punishment of escape before arrest

Of escape by a private person

Of a negligent escape

Of a voluntary escape.

of a mortal wound given, and the party not dying till after the escape, but the officer may be fined to the value of his goods. *Dalt c* 159

Also, a voluntary escape suffered by one who wrongfully takes upon him the keeping of a gaol, seems to be punishable in the same manner, as if he was never so rightfully intitled to such custody, for that the crime is in both cases or the same ill consequence to the publick, and there seems to be no reason that a wrongful officer should have greater favour than a rightful, and that for no other reason but because he is a wrongful one. *2 Haw* 134

But it seemeth to be clear, that no one is punishable as for felony, for the voluntary escape of a felon, but the person only who is actually guilty of it, and therefore that the principal gaoler is only fineable for a voluntary escape suffered by his deputy, for that no one shall suffer capitally for the crime of another. *2 Haw* 135

And therefore, altho' in all civil causes, the sheriff is to be responsible for the gaoler, at election, yet if the gaoler do voluntarily suffer a felon in his custody to escape, this, inasmuch as it reacheth to life, is felony only in the gaoler, that was immediately trusted with the custody, and not in the sheriff. *1 H H* 597

For the escape must be voluntarily permitted in him that permitted it, which could not be in the high sheriff, tho' it were such in the gaoler, for he was not privy to it, and therefore could not do it feloniously, but it was a negligent escape in him, in trusting such a person with the custody of his prisoners, that would be false to his trust, and therefore the sheriff shall pay, but not corporally suffer for the misscarriage of his gaoler. *1 H H* 597, 598

But altho' the felony for which a man is committed be not within clergy, yet the person who voluntarily suffers him to escape, shall have the benefit of clergy. *1 H H* 599

IX. *Aiding in attempting to escape*

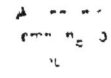

By the 16 *G* 2 *c* 31 If any person shall assist any prisoner to *attempt* his escape from any gaol, though no escape be actually made, if such prisoner was then attainted or convicted of treason or felony (except petty larceny) or lawfully committed to, or detained in any gaol, for treason or felony (except petty larceny) expressed in the warrant of commitment, he shall be guilty of felony, and be transported for seven years; and if such prisoner was then convicted of, or detained in gaol for petty larceny, or any other

other crime not being treafon or felony, expreffed in the warrant of commitment, or was then in gaol for debt amounting to 100l, he fhall be guilty of a mifdemeanor, and be liable to fine and imprifonment

And if any perfon fhall convey, or caufe to be conveyed, any *difguife, inftrument, or arms*, to any prifoner in gaol, or to any other perfon there for his ufe, without confent of the keeper, fuch perfon, although *no efcape or attempt* be actually made, fhall be deemed to have delivered fuch difguife, inftrument or arms, with an intent to affift fuch prifoner to efcape or attempt to efcape, and if fuch prifoner then was attainted or convicted of treafon or felony (except petty larceny), or lawfully detained in gaol for treafon or felony (except petty larceny) expreffed in the warrant of commitment,—he fhall be guilty of felony, and be tranfported for feven years but if the prifoner was then convicted or detained for petty larceny, or any other crime not being treafon or felony, expreffed in the warrant of commitment, or for debt amounting to 100l, he fhall be guilty of a mifdemeanor, and liable to fine and imprifonment

And if any perfon fhall affift any prifoner to attempt to efcape *from any conftable*, or other perfon, who fhall have the lawful charge of him, in order to carry him to gaol, by virtue of a warrant of commitment for treafon or felony, (except petty larceny), or if any perfon fhall affift any felon to attempt his efcape from on board any *boat or veffel carrying felons for tranfportation*, or from the *contractor* for the tranfportation of fuch felons, or his agents, he fhall be guilty of felony, and be tranfported for feven years

All profecutions on this act to be commenced within a year after the offence committed

A Indictment againft a conftable for an efcape.

Weftmorland   THE jurors for our lord the king upon
                their oath prefent, That on the ———
day of ——— in the ——— year of the reign of ——— at
in the county aforefaid, one A I of ——— came before J P
efquire, then and there one of our faid lord the king's
juffices of the faid county, and affigned to keep and
determine the affizes, &c.) and then and there was —— s
the f county, and in the ——— the A I of, th ———
there, on his oath before the faid juffice, charge, and
give information againft one A O of ——— upon ——
county aforefaid, yeoman, for a certain mifdemeanor, to be
                                 2

fish out of the pond of —— at —— in the said county [or, as the offence shall be] Whereupon he the said J P the justice aforesaid, did then and there, to wit, at —— aforesaid, in the county aforesaid, make a certain warrant, under his hand and seal, in due form of law, directed to the constable of —— aforesaid, in the county aforesaid, thereby requiring him the said constable to take the body of the said A. O and bring him before the said J P the justice aforesaid, to answer to such matters and things as should be alledged against him, touching the said misdemeanor Which said warrant, afterwards, to wit, on the same day and year abovementioned, at —— aforesaid, in the county aforesaid, was delivered to one A C. then being constable of —— aforesaid, in due form of law, to be executed, by virtue of which said warrant the said A C afterwards, to wit, on the said —— day of —— in the year aforesaid, at —— aforesaid, in the said county, did take and arrest the body of the said A O and him the said A O in his custody for the cause aforesaid, had Nevertheless, the said A C of —— aforesaid, in the county aforesaid, yeoman, afterward, to wit, on the said —— day of —— in the year aforesaid, the duty of his office in that part not regarding, at —— aforesaid, in the county aforesaid, unlawfully and negligently did permit the said A O to escape, and go at large, out of the custody of him the said A C to the great hindrance of justice, in contempt of our said lord the king, and of his laws, and against the peace of our said lord the king, his crown and dignity.

Escheat: See Forfeiture.

Estray.

And herein also of goods waived

Estray, &c. 2. 1. ESTRAY *is, where any horses, sheep, hogs, beasts, or swans, do come into a lordship, and are not owned by any man* Kitch 23

Where any horses, sheep, hogs, beasts, or swans] Bees, and other creatures of a wild nature, are not within this description, and therefore not to be reckoned amongst stray goods nevertheless it seemeth that a swarm of bees, of which the owner hath lost sight, and consequently can make out no property, may be seized for the use of the king, or of the lord of the manor, for it is a maxim of the com-

common law, that ſuch goods whereof no one can claim
property do belong to the king, and that which the king
hath he may grant to another, and conſequently another
may preſcribe to have the ſame, within ſuch a precinct or
lordſhip And therefore it is ſaid, that if any take honey
or ſwarms of bees within the demeſnes of the lord, it is
inquirable in the court baron. *Kitch* 114.

Swans] Swans that be unmarked and wild (being at
large and abroad) may be ſeized by the ſheriff for the uſe
of the king, by his prerogative *Dalt Sher* 80

Alſo ſwans marked and tame may be eſtrays *Kitch.*
86 But it ſeemeth that no other fowl can be eſtray.
Wood, b 2 c 2.

Do come into a lordſhip] That is, where the goods have
no right to be, and therefore an eſtray cannot be in ſuch
place, where the party hath a right of common *Dalt.*
Sher 79

And are not owned by any man] Whereupon (as hath
been ſaid) the property accrueth to the king, and the
cattle of the king cannot be eſtrays, nor forfeited as ſuch
to the lord of the manor *Kitch* 81

2. Waif is, where a felon in purſuit waiveth the goods, Waif, what.
or where the felon, for fear of being apprehended, thinking that a purſuit was made, having them with him in his
poſſeſſion, fleeth, and waiveth, caſteth away, or goeth
from the goods in theſe caſes, they ſhall be ſaid to be
waived in law. But if he hath not the goods with him,
when he fleeth being purſued, or for fear to be apprehended, they are not waived nor forfeited, but the owner
may take them when he will, without any freſh ſuit.
5 *Co* 109 *Dalt. Sher* 78.

But if the thief in his flight waive them, there the goods
are forfeited to the king or lord of the liberty by the common law, if the felon upon freſh ſuit was not attainted at
the ſuit of the owner of the goods And the reaſon why
waif is given to the king, and that the party ſhall loſe his
property in ſuch caſe, is for default in the owner that he
purſued not freſhly to apprehend the felon, for it concerneth the publick that crimes do not remain unpuniſhed And
therefore the law hath impoſed this penalty upon the owner,
that if the thief by his induſtry and freſh ſuit be not attainted at his ſuit, in an appeal of the ſame felony, he
ſhall loſe for his default all his goods which the thief at
the time of his flight waived But if the thief had them
not with him when he fled, having peradventure hid them,
there

there no default can be in the party, and therefore they shall not be forfeited, for if he maketh fresh suit after notice of the felony it sufficeth   5 Co 109

Seizure thereof by the lord.   3 Heretofore waifs and strays were the finder's, by the law of nature, and afterward, the king's, by the law of nations Dalt Sh. 79

Thus, one as a bailiff or servant to the sheriff seized a horse as an estray to the king's use, and proclaimed him according to law, and after the year and day sold him, and the sheriff accounted for him in the exchequer Dalt Sher 80

But now kings have granted this, and such like prerogatives, unto their subjects, within their liberties, so that waifs and strays are in many places the lord's of the franchise where they are found Dalt Sher 79

And therefore waived goods and estrays shall be *seized* by the officer of the king, to the use of the king, or by the officer or bailiff of the lord, who hath such things by grant of the king, or by prescription, to the use of the lord Dalt Sher 80

But if one have a waif, and it be taken out of his manor, he shall have *trespass* without seizing, and though he do not seize it Kitch 81

Proclaiming the goods seized   4 It seemeth to be agreed, that waifs and strays ought to be proclaimed in the two next market towns, and that if they are not proclaimed, the owner may take the stray goods again at any time And it seemeth to be the general tenor of the old books, that they ought also to be proclaimed in the church Which course it seemeth best to follow, to the end that the owner, who in this case is no wrong doer, may have a reasonable mean to come at his goods again, that is to say, that the goods be proclaimed at the least thrice, to wit, in the two market towns next adjoining to the place where they strayed, on the market days respectively, and at the church door on a Sunday, as the people come out of the church Kitch 23, 81, 105 Dalt Sher 79 Co Litz 716

How waifs or estrays are to be kept   5 And they ought to be wreathed, and to be put in some several ground in an open place, and not in any covert of wood, that the owner may have a view of them, for if they be in covert, the property is not changed, tho' they be there a year and a day Kitch 23

An estray is not to be used in any manner, except in case of necessity, as to milk a cow, or the like, but not to ride an horse, for within the year and day he hath not any property in him. Co Jac. 147, 8.

6 He who taketh an *eſtray*, may keep it until he be Owner claiming. ſatisfied for the finding, keeping, and proclaiming thereof *Dal. Sher* 79

But the owner (if it be within the year and day) may take it without telling any marks, or making any proof of property, but this may be done upon the trial, if conteſted. 2 *Salk* 686

And the lord ought to make a demand of what the amends ſhould be; and then if the party thinks the demand unreaſonable, he may tender ſufficient amends, and if the lord ſhall not accept it, this ſhall be ſettled by the jury upon trial

But it is ſufficient in this caſe to tender amends *generally*, without expreſſing any certain ſum. For there is a difference between this caſe, and that of a tender of amends for treſpaſs. In that of a treſpaſs, if the defendant pleads a tender of amends, he muſt ſhew what he tendred, for he muſt tender a certain ſum. And the law puts this difficulty upon him, becauſe he is the wrong doer. But the owner of the ſtray (as hath been ſaid) is no wrong doer, and it is impoſſible he ſhould know how long his beaſt hath been in the lord's cuſtody, nor how much will make a proper ſatisfaction. 2 *Salk* 686

In the caſe of goods waived, the owner may ſeize them twenty years after, if the lord of the franchiſe, nor the king ſeized before, but if they are ſeized, then they become forfeited to the king or lord of the liberty. *Kitch* 82

And this forfeiture is not like a ſtray, where tho' the lord may ſeize, yet the party who is the owner may retake them within the year and day, but here the true owner cannot ſeize his own goods, tho' upon freſh ſuit within the year and day. 1 *H H* 541

But this is not an abſolute loſs of the owner's goods, but rather an expedient ſettled by law, to drive the owner to convict the felon by proſecuting his appeal, and therefore if he make freſh ſuit, and proſecute his appeal, and the felon be thereupon convict or attaint, and the freſh ſuit be enquired and found by verdict or inqueſt of office, he ſhall have reſtitution of the goods ſo waived. 1 *H H* 541

7 Waifs and ſtrays, not claimed within the year and Property accroing to the lord, day, are the lord's. *Kitch* 23, 80, 81 on not claiming.

For where the lord hath by a year and a day a beaſt, and it be cried in the church and markets, the property is changed. *Kit.* 80.

That

That is to ſay, after he hath had the beaſt a year and day from the time of the proclamation, and not from the time of the ſeizure: for after the firſt proclamation it becometh an eſtray, but not ſooner. 11 *Mod* 89.

If the eſtray within the year eſtray out of the manor, the lord may chaſe back the eſtray unleſs it be ſeized by another lord who hath eſtrays, but if it be ſeized by ſuch other lord, then the firſt hath loſt all poſſibility of his gaining the property, and the other lord ought to proclaim it *de novo* Finch 177. Kitch. 81. Hutt. 67.

Eſtreat

Eſtreat, wha

1. E STREAT (*extractum*) is uſed for the true copy or note of ſome original writing or record, and eſpecially of fines and amerciaments, impoſed in the rolls of a court, to be levied by the bailiff or other officer.

Making out the eſtreats.

2. The juſtices and judges before whom fines or amerciaments ſhall be, ſhall charge the clerks of the eſtreats, by their oath to be made, that they make the rolls of ſuch eſtreats diſtinctly, by expreſs words, of the cauſe of the loſs, of the term of the year, and the nature of the writ, and betwixt what parties ſuch iſſues or amerciaments ſhall be loſt, as well in the king's ſuit, as in the ſuit of the party. 7 *H* 4 *c* 3.

Delivering the ſame to the ſheriff

3 All clerks of the peace, and town clerks, ſhall deliver to the ſheriff, within 20 days after *Sep* 29, yearly, a perfect eſtreat or ſchedule of all fines, iſſues, amerciaments, and other forfeitures whatſoever, forfeited in any ſeſſions before *Michaelmas*, on pain of 50 l, half to the king, and half to him that ſhall ſue. 22 & 23 *C* 2 *c* 22 ſ 7, 8.

And into the court of exchequer,

4 And ſhall alſo yearly, on or before the ſecond *Monday* after the morrow of *All Souls*, deliver into the court of exchequer, a duplicate, certificate, and eſtreat of ſuch eſtreats and ſchedules, ſo delivered to the ſheriff, on the like pain of 50 l *id* ſ 8. And likewiſe they may be further amerced by the barons of the exchequer 3 *G* c 15. ſ 12.

And upon delivery thereof, they ſhall take the following oath, to be adminiſtred by one of the barons.

" You ſhall ſwear, that theſe eſtreats now by you delivered, are truly and carefully made up and examined,
" and that all fines, iſſues, amerciaments, recognizances,
" and

" and forfeitures which were ſet, loſt, impoſed, or forfeit-
" ed, and in right and due courſe of law ought to be
" eſtreated in the court of exchequer, are, to the beſt of
" your knowledge and underſtanding, therein contained;
" and that in the ſame eſtreats are alſo contained and ex-
" preſſed all ſuch fines as have been paid into the court,
" from which the ſaid eſtreats are made, without any
" wilful or fraudulent diſcharge, omiſſion, miſnomer, or
" defect whatſoever So help you God " 4 & 5 W.
c 24 ſ 5.

5 And if he ſhall withhold, or miſcertify the ſame, he ^{Penalty of mak-}
ſhall forfeit treble, half to the king, and half to him ^{ing default}
that ſhall ſue, and ſhall alſo loſe his office, and be incapable to hold any office in the revenue   22 & 23 C 2
c 22 ſ 9

6 If recognizances be eſtreated into the exchequer, ^{Party coming in}
becauſe not punctually complied with, yet if the party ^{after the eſtreat,}
appears and takes his trial the next ſeſſions, or otherwiſe
performs what he was bound to by the recognizance as the
caſe ſhall be, he may compound for a very ſmall matter
in the court of exchequer becauſe the effect, tho' not
the exact form of the recognizance, is complied with.
10 Mod 278

7 Where any fine or forfeiture ſhall be paid to the ^{Proceſs for levy-}
ſheriff, clerk of the peace, or other officer, and ſo certi- ^{ing}
fied into the exchequer, proceſs ſhall be awarded to the
ſheriff againſt ſuch perſon for levying the ſame.   22 & 23
C 2 c 22. ſ 10

8 And in levying, the ſheriff ſhall ſhew the eſtreats ^{Sheriff's duty}
under the ſeal of the exchequer, to the party indebted, ^{in levying}
on pain of treble damages to the party, and fine to the
king, on conviction before the juſtices of the peace, or
other juſtices   42 Ed 3 c 9

9 And the ſheriff ſhall make no eſtreats to levy his own ^{Eſtreats in the}
amerciaments (that is to ſay, in the torn), till two juſtices ^{torn.}
(12) to be named at Michaelmas ſeſſions by the cuſtos rotulorum, or in his abſence by the eldeſt in the commiſſion,
have inſpected his books, and the ſaid eſtreats ſhall be
indented betwixt the ſaid juſtices and ſheriff, ſealed with
their ſeals, the one part to remain with the juſtices, and
the other with the ſheriff And the perſons who ſhall gather the ſaid amerciaments, ſhall be ſworn by the ſaid
juſtices, that they ſhall take no more than is forfeited, and
contained in the ſaid eſtreats. 11 H. 7 c. 15.

Form

Form of the estreat.

Westmorland *AN extract of all the issues, fines, amercia-*
ments and recognizances, set, lost, im-
posed, and forfeited to our sovereign lord the king, at the general
quarter sessions of the peace of our said lord the king, holden
at —— in and for the said county of —— on —— the ——
day of —— in the —— year of the reign of ——
before —— esquires, justices of our said lord the king,
assigned to keep the peace in the said county, and also to hear and
determine divers felonies, trespasses, and other misdemeanors in
the said county committed, Joshua Nicholson, gentleman, clerk
of the peace for the county aforesaid, then and there attending

Of A O late of —— in the said county, labour-
er, for a trespass and assault at —— aforesaid, in
the said county, whereof he is indicted and convicted,
his fine set at five shillings, which he paid to the sheriff   l. s. d.
in court   -   -   -   -   -   0 5 0

Of A O of —— in the said county, yeoman, be-
cause he came not now here to answer to such things as
against him, on the part of our said lord the king,
should be objected, as by a certain recognizance taken
before J P esquire, one of the justices of our said
lord the king, assigned to keep the peace in the said
county, he undertook   -   -   -   10 0 0

Of A S of —— in the said county, yeoman, one
of the pledges of the said A O. because he had him
not to answer as above   -   -   -   5 0 0

Of B S of —— in the said county, yeoman, the
other of the pledges of the said A O for the like   5 0 0

Evidence.

I Of evidence in general
II Of written evidence
III Of the evidence of witnesses.
IV Of process to cause witnesses to appear.
V. Of the manner of giving evidence.

I. Of evidence in general.

Evidence, what 1 EVIDENCE in legal understanding, doth not
only contain matters of record, as letters patents,
fines, recoveries, inrolments, and the like, and writings
under

under feal, as charters and deeds, and other writings without feal, as court rolls, accounts, and the like, but in a larger fenfe it containeth alfo the testimony of witnesses, and other proofs to be produced and given, for the finding of any issue joined between the parties. And it is called evidence, because hereby the point in issue is to be made evident to the jury. 1 Inst 283

2 But it is a general rule in all cases, civil and criminal, the best evidence that may be had, or that the nature of the thing will bear, is to be given, and it is upon this reason, that a copy of the record is admitted, because one cannot have the record itself, but a copy of a copy will not do. Law of Evid 280

The best evidence is required

3 Many times juries, together with other matter, are much induced by presumptions whereof there are three forts, violent, probable, and light or temerary. Violent presumption many times amounts to full proof, as if one be run through the body with a fword in a house, whereof he instantly dieth, and a man is seen to come out of that house, with a bloody fword, and no other man was at that time in the house. Probable presumption moveth little, but light or temerary presumption moveth not at all. 1 Inst 6

Presumptive evidence

If all the witnesses to a deed be dead (as no man can keep his witnesses alive, and time wearein out all men) then violent presumption, which stands for a proof, is continual and quiet possession, altho' the deed may receive credit from a comparing of hands, writing, and the like. 1 Inst 6

4 The common law did not require any certain number of witnesses, for the trial of any crime whatsoever 2 Haw 428

What number of witnesses are required

And before a justice of the peace in divers cases, one witness is sufficient to convict an offender, the same being directed by special statutes

But in case of high treason, whereby corruption of blood shall be made, no person shall be attained, but upon the oaths of two witnesses, either both to the same overt act, or one of them to one, and the other of them to another overt act of the same treason. 7 W c 3 f 2

In like manner, in those courts which proceed by the rules of the civil law, as the spiritual court, and the courts of equity, two witnesses are generally required. and the reason why the civil law requires two witnesses is, because their trial is by witnesses, and not by a jury of twelve men. But where the trial is by verdict of twelve men, there the judgment is not given upon witnesses, or other kind of evidence, but upon the verdict, and upon such evidence as is given to the jury, they give their verdict 1 *Inst* 6 *b*. *Plowd* 12 *a*

By 29 *C* 2 *c* 3 *s* 5 Devises of lands shall be attested by three witnesses at the least.

II. *Of written evidence.*

1. Acts of parliament relate either to the kingdom in general, and are therefore called *general* acts of parliament, or only to the concerns of private persons, and are thence called *private* acts of parliament *Theory of Evid* 2

A general act of parliament is taken notice of by the judges and jury, without being shewed, and hence it is that it hath been said, that the printed statute book is good evidence of general acts of parliament, not that the printed statutes are the perfect and authentic copies of the records themselves, but every person is supposed to know the law, and therefore the printed statutes are allowed to be evidence, because they are the hints of that which is supposed to be lodged in every man's mind already *id* 2, 8

But in the case of private acts of parliament, the printed statute book is not evidence, though reduced into the same volume with the general statutes, but the party ought to have a copy compared with the parliament roll, for they are not considered as already lodged in the minds of the people *id* 8

However, a private act of parliament, that is in print, which concerns a whole county (as the act of *Bedford Level*) or a large body of people (as the whole clergy in general) hath been allowed to be given in evidence, without comparing it with the record, and these things are the rather admitted, because they gain some authority from being printed by the king's printer, and besides, from the notoriety of the subject of them, they are supposed not to be wholly unknown *id* 8

2 Records of the king's courts prove themselves, and cannot be proved by witnesses But copies of them must be proved by witnesses, and then they are good evidence No razure or interlining shall be intended in them. But the surest way is, to exemplify a record under the great seal, or at least under the seal of the court 10 *Co* 92

And nothing shall be admitted as evidence of what was done at another trial, till the record of that trial be produced *Raa Evid*

But a record of a criminal conviction shall not be given in evidence in a civil action, because such conviction might

might have been upon the evidence of a party interested in the civil action. *Cafes in the time of lord Hardwicke*, 312

3 There are also other publick matters that are not re- Rolls of court not of record. cords, as court rolls, and tranfactions in chancery, and of thefe, copies may be given in evidence *Theory of Evid* 22, 23

The reafon why the proceedings in chancery are not re-cords is this, becaufe they are not the precedents of juftice, for the judgment there is, according to equity and good confcience, and not according to the laws and cuftoms. And the reafon why any record is of validity and authority is, becaufe it is a memorial of what is the law of the nation, now chancery proceedings are no memorials of the laws of *England*, becaufe the chancellor is not bound to proceed according to the laws. *id* 23

The rolls of a court baron are evidence, for they are the publick rolls, by which the inheritance of every te-nant is preferved, and they are the rolls of the manor court, which was anciently a court of juftice relating to all pro-perty within the diftrict *id* 43

4 Depofitions of witneffes may be read when the wit- Depofition nefs is dead, but not when the witnefs is living, for whilft the witnefs is living, they are not the beft evidence the nature of the thing is capable of *Theory of Evid* 30

Yet they may be read when a witnefs is fought and can-not be found, for then he is in the fame circumftances, as to the party that is to ufe him, as if he were dead *id*

So if it is proved that a witnefs was fubpœnaed, and fell fick by the way, for in this cafe likewife, the depofition is the beft evidence that can be had, and that anfwers what the law requires *id*

But a depofition cannot be given in evidence againft any perfon that was not party to the fuit, and the reafon is, becaufe he had not liberty to crofs-examine the witnefs, and it is againft natural juftice, that a man fhould be con-cluded by proofs in a caufe to which he was not a party For this reafon, depofitions in chancery fhall not be read for or againft the defendant upon an information or in-dictment, for the king was no party to the fuit *id*

Yet this rule admits of fome exceptions, as particu-larly, in all cafes where hearfay and reputation are evi-dence, for undoubtedly what a witnefs, who is dead, hath fworn in a court of juftice, is of more credit than what another perfon fwears he hath heard him fay So a depo-fition taken in a caufe between other parties, will be ad-mitted to be read, to contradict what the fame witnefs fwears at a trial. *id* 30, 31

It

It is a general rule, that depositions taken in a court not of record, shall not be allowed in evidence elsewhere So it hath been holden in regard to depositions in the ecclesiastical court, tho' the witnesses were dead So where there cannot be a cross-examination, as depositions taken before commissioners of bankrupts, they shall not be read in evidence *id* 33, 34

But it seems to be settled, that the examination of an informer taken upon oath, and subscribed by him, either before a coroner upon an inquisition of death, or before justices of the peace, in pursuance of the statutes of *Phil. & Mar* upon a bailment or commitment for any felony, may be given in evidence at the trial, if it be made out by oath to the satisfaction of the court, that such informer is dead, or unable to travel, or kept away by the means or procurement of the prisoner, and that the examination offered in evidence is the very same that was sworn before the coroner or justice, without any alteration whatsoever 2 *Haw* 429.

But it hath been adjudged, that it is not sufficient to authorize the reading of such examination, to make oath that the prosecutors have used all their endeavours to find the witness, but cannot find him. 2 *Haw* 430.

But it is said to have been adjudged, by the court of king's bench, in the 7 *W* (1 *Salk* 281) upon advice with the justices of the common pleas, on an indictment for a *libel*, that depositions taken before a justice of the peace, relating to the fact, could not be given in evidence, though the deponent were dead, and that the reason why such depositions may be given in evidence in *felony*, depends upon the statutes of *Phil & Mar* and that this cannot be extended further than the particular case of felony But in the report of this case, 5 *Mod* 165. it is said, that the reason why such depositions could not be read, was because the defendant was not present when they were taken, and therefore had not the benefit of a cross-examination 2 *Haw* 430

Anciently, depositions taken *in perpetuam rei memoriam* were not published till after the death of the witnesses, because they were no evidence while the witnesses were living, but this practise was found very inconvenient, because thereby witnesses became secure in swearing whatever they pleased, inasmuch as they never could be prosecuted for perjury. *Theory of Evid* 32

What a man himself, who is living, hath sworn at one trial, can never be given in evidence at another to support him, because it is no evidence of the truth, for if a man be be of that ill mind to fwear falfely at one trial, he may do the fame at another on the fame inducements, but what a man fays in difcourfe, without premeditation or expectation of the caufe in queftion, is good evidence to fupport him, becaufe that fhews that what he fwears is not from any undue influence   But if a man hath fworn at one trial different from what he hath fworn at another, this is good evidence as to his difcredit   *id* 35

5 No verdict fhall be given in evidence, but between fuch *Verdict* who were parties or privies to it, becaufe it otherwife, a man would be bound by a decifion, who had not the liberty to crofs-examine   and nothing can be more contrary to natural juftice, than that any body fhould be injured by a determination, that he, or thofe under whom he claims, was not at liberty to controvert   *Theory of Evid* 18, 19.

And a verdict will not be admitted in evidence, without likewife producing a copy of the judgment founded upon it, becaufe it may happen, that the judgment was arrefted upon a new trial granted   But this rule doth not hold, in the cafe of a verdict on an iffue directed out of chancery, becaufe it is not ufual to enter up judgment in fuch cafe, and the decree of the court of chancery is equally proof that the verdict was fatisfactory, and ftands in force *id* 21

6 A decree in chancery may be given in evidence be- *Sentence or* tween the fame parties, or all claiming under them, for *final judgment.* their judgments muft be of authority in thefe cafes, where the law gives them a jurifdiction   for it would be very abfurd, that the law fhould give them a jurifdiction, and yet not fuffer what is done by force of that jurifdiction to be full proof   *Theory of Evid* 36, 37

And note, wherever a matter comes to be tried in a collateral way, the decree, fentence, or judgment of any court, ecclefiaftical or civil, having competent jurifdiction, is conclufive evidence of fuch matter   and in cafe the determination is final in the court, of which it is a decree, fentence, or judgment, fuch decree, fentence, or judgment will be conclufive in any other court having concurrent jurifdiction   *id* 37

7 In the cafe of *Benfon* and *Olive* in the exchequer, *T.* *Ancient deed.* 3 G 2 a deed was offered to be produced, which bore date 38 years before, without proving that the witneffes were dead.   And allowed by the court   They faid that in general 40 years was allowed to be the rule, but the courts never tied themfelves up ftrictly to that rule, but 39, 38, nay 35, have been allowed the fame. 1 *Barnard* 348

And, *E.* 11 G 2 *Porter and Gordon*   Upon a trial at bar, a deed was offered in evidence, executed 36 years ago,

with-

without proving the hands, which was oppofed by the other fide, but admitted by the court, who faid, there was no fixed rule about it, but that it had often been allowed, where a deed was but 25 or 30 years old 12 *Viner* 57

Writings loft or concealed

8 In cafes where writings have been loft by burning of houfes, by rebellion, or when robbers have deftroyed them, or the like, the law, in fuch cafes of neceffity, allows them to be proved by witneffes *Jenk.* 19 *Wood, b* 4 *c* 4

If a man deftroys a thing that is defigned to be evidence againft himfelf, a fmall matter will fupply it, and therefore the defendant having torn his own note figned by him, a copy fworn was admitted to be good evidence to prove it L *Raym* 731

Where the defendant himfelf has the deed which concerns the land in queftion, and refufes (after notice) to produce it, a copy thereof will be permitted to be given in evidence, on its being proved to be a true copy And if the party has no copy, he may produce an abftract, nay even give parol evidence of the contents, becaufe in fuch cafe it may be impoffible to give better evidence In civil caufes, the court will fometimes oblige parties to produce evidence which may prove againft themfelves, or leave the refufal to do it (after proper notice) as a ftrong prefumption, to the jury The court will do it, in many cafes, under particular circumftances, by rule before the trial, efpecially, if the party, from whom the production is wanted applies for a favour But in a criminal or penal caufe, the defendant is never forced to produce any evidence, though he fhould hold it in his hands in court *Theory of Evid* 54 *Burr ru Mansf* 2489

Where an original note of hand is loft, and a copy of it is offered in evidence to ferve any particular purpofe in a caufe, fufficient probability muft be fhewed to fatisfy the court, that the original note was genuine, before the copy will be allowed to be read. 1 *Atk.* 446

But by lord *Hardwicke*, Ap 16, 1740 On exceptions to a mafter's report Where a rent charge is granted by deed, and the deed happens to be loft, the plaintiff cannot read a copy in evidence at law, but muft either fet up a prefcriptive title to the rent, from a conftant and uninterrupted payment, or he muft bring his bill in equity, to be relieved againft the accident of the original's being loft And the fame rule holds in cafe of a bond, for though an hundred witneffes could prove the fubftance of it, yet it is not fufficient at law, for the plaintiff muft declare

clare upon it, fetting forth that he produceth it in court.
2 *Atk.* 61.

9 An indenture to guide the ufes of a common reco- *Writing with*
very, was offered in evidence, but the feals were torn off, *the feal torn off.*
yet it being proved to have been done by a little boy, it was
allowed to be read *Palm* 402

To prove the taking of an oath, in the act of uniformity,
a certificate was produced that had only a fmall piece of
wax upon it. By *Twifden*, if it were fealed, tho' the
feal was broken off, yet it may be read, as we read recoveries after the feal broken off, and he faid, he had feen
an adminiftration given in evidence after the feal broken
off, and fo wills and deeds 11 *Mod* 11 *M* 21 *C* 2.
Clerk and *Heath.*

10 If upon collateral iffue, it is to be proved, that fuch *letters patent*
a one was juftice of the peace, baronet, or the like, common reputation is fufficient proof, without fhewing the
commiffion, or letters patent of the creation *Tr per pais*
347

11. The copy of the probate of a will is good evidence, *Copy of a will,*
where the will itfelf is of chattels, for there the probate *or of letters of*
is an original, taken by authority, and of a publick nature *adminiftration.*
otherwife, where the will is of things in the realty, be-
caufe in fuch cafe the ecclefiaftical courts have no authority to take probates, therefore fuch probate is but a copy,
and the copy of it is no more than the copy of a copy.
3 *Salk* 154

The ecclefiaftical court never grants an exemplification
of letters of adminiftration, but only a certificate that adminiftration was granted, therefore where a leffee pleads
an affignment of a term from an adminiftrator, fuch certificate is good evidence So would the book of the ecclefiaftical court, wherein was entered the order for granting
adminiftration. So would the copy of the probate of a
will, be evidence of fuch an one being an executor, but a
copy of the will would not be evidence of it *Kimbton* and
Crofs, E 8 G 2 *Buller's Law of N. fi pr*, 246

12 So the copy of the court roll of a manor, is good *Other copies*
evidence, as alfo the copy of a church-regifter, the copies
of town-books, and the like, for where the original itfelf
is good evidence, the immediate copy thereof is alfo good
evidence *Skin* 584 L *Raym* 154

And generally, wherever an original is of a public nature, and would be evidence if produced, an immediate
fworn copy thereof will be evidence, as a copy of a bargain
and fale, of a deed inrolled, and the like, but where an
original is of a private nature, a copy is not evidence,

unlefs

unless the original is lost or destroyed   3 *Salk* 154 *H 8 W Lynch and Clarke*

On a warrant to a constable to distrain goods by virtue of an act of parliament, the constable makes distress, and returns the overplus to the offender, but keeps the warrant   Resolved, that a copy of the warrant in this case will be good evidence   6 *Mod* 83   *M 2 Ann Morley and Staker*

So a copy of a conviction for killing game, was agreed to be evidence on an action brought for the same offence *T 5 G 3 B* and *Lutw Mansf* 1720

Inquisition post mortem   13 An inquisition *post mortem* is evidence, but not conclusive   2 *Term* 224   *M 34 C 2   Earl of Thanet v F.*

Parish register.   14 The entry of the names and titles of persons in a church-book, either for marriages or births is evidence, but not conclusive evidence of the marriage or birth of any persons, unless the identity of the person (by such entries intended) is fully proved, and also strengthened with circumstances, as cohabitation the allowance of the parties themselves, and the like   12 *Vin* 89

Heralds books   15 Rolls or ancient books in the heralds office, are evidence to prove a pedigree, but an extract of a pedigree, proved to be taken out of records, shall not, because such extract is not the best evidence in the nature of the thing, as a copy of such records might be had   *Theory of Evid* 45   3 *Black* 105

Founder roll   16 An old terrier, or survey of a manor, whether ecclesiastical or temporal, may be given in evidence, for there can be no other way of ascertaining the old tenures or boundaries   *Theory of Evid* 44

Terriers.   17 A terrier of glebe is not evidence for the parson, unless signed by the churchwardens, as well as the parson, nor then neither, if they be of his nomination   and tho' it be signed by them, yet it seems to deserve very little credit, unless it is likewise signed by the substantial inhabitants   But in all cases, it is certainly strong evidence against the parson   *Theory of Evid* 45

Indorsement of payment on a bond   18 *M 11 G Searle and lord Barrington*   The indorsement or a bond by the obligee, of payment of interest, was allowed to be given in evidence by his administrator, to take off the presumption from the length of time   *L Raym* 1371

Shop book   19 By the 7 *J* c 12   No tradesman nor handicraftman shall be allowed to give his shop-book in evidence, or an action for money due for wares delivered or for work done, above one year before the action brought. Put this not to extend to any trading between merchant and merchant, merchant and tradesman, or between tradesman and tradesman, for any thing directly falling within the compass of their mutual trades and merchandize

In the case of *Pitman* and *Maddox*, 11 *W*. A shop-book was allowed for evidence, it being proved that the servant that writ the book was dead, and this was his hand, and he accustomed to make the entries, and no proof was required of the delivery of the goods, and *Holt* Ch J said it was as good evidence as the proof of a witness's hand to an obligation, and he held, that tho' the statute of the 7 *J* says, a shop-book shall not be evidence after the year, yet it is not of itself evidence within the year 2 *Salk* 690.

20. A man's book of accounts is no evidence for the owner of the book, but for the adverse party, for his book cannot be of better credit than his oath, which would not serve in his own case *Tr per pais* 348. [Book of accounts]

21. In the case of the *Queen* and *Mead*, the defendant, and eight others, were incorporated under an act made 39 *El*. by the name of the surveyors of the highways at *Ailesbury* in the county of *Bucks*, and were trustees of a charity called *Bedford*'s gift An information was preferred against the defendant, for executing this office, being an office of trust, without having taken the oaths, contrary to the 25 *C* 2. *c*. 2 To which he pleaded not guilty And now it was moved for a rule, that the prosecutor might have two books produced, which these surveyors kept, in which they entered their elections, and also their receipts and disbursements, and that he might take copies of what he thought necessary, and that the books might be produced at the next assizes at the trial But it was denied by the court, because they are perfectly of a private nature, and it would be to make a man produce evidence against himself in a criminal prosecution *L. Raym* 927. [Private books of entries]

22 A copy of an inscription on a grave-stone, hath been allowed to be given in evidence [Inscription on a grave-stone.]

23 The examination of an almanack, that such a day of the month was *Sunday*, was ruled to be sufficient, and that a trial of this by a jury is not necessary, altho' it is a matter of fact *Cro Eliz* 227 [Almanack.]

And the reason why the kalendar in an almanack is allowed as evidence seemeth to be, because the said kalendar is part of the book of common prayer, which is established b a? of parliament

Father's entry of the child's birth.

24 An almanack wherein the father had writ the day of the nativity of his son, was allowed as evidence to prove the nonage of his son *Raym* 84

General history

25 *Camden's Britannia* was offered in evidence, to prove a particular custom, but refused, for the court held, that a general history might be given in evidence to prove a matter relating to the kingdom in general, because the nature of the thing requires it, but not to prove a particular right or custom So in the case of St *Katherine's* hospital, *Hale* Ch J allowed a chronicle to be evidence of a particular point of history in *Edward* the third's time So a year book may be evidence to prove the course of the court And in this case it was admitted, that heralds books are good evidence as to pedigrees, and parish registers as to births and marriages, upon the nature of the thing But in the exchequer, the question being whether the *Abbey de Fontibus* was an inferior abbey or not, *Dugdale's Monasticon* was refused for evidence, because the original records might be had in the augmentation office 1 *Said* 281 7 *W Stainer* and the *Burgesses of Droitwich*

So in the case of *Cockman* and *Mather*, E 13 G On a trial at bar, concerning the right of visiting university college in *Oxford*, one of the issues was, whether king *Alfred* was founder And the counsel for the plaintiff would have given in evidence several historians as to this point But the chief justice declared, that such evidence is never admitted, unless in proof of a point concerning the public government And the evidence was not allowed *Barnard* 14

Similitude of hand

26 It seems to have been generally holden, since the reversal of the attainder of *Algernon Sidney*, that similitude of hands is not evidence in any criminal case, whether capital or not capital 2 *Haw* 431 L *Raym* 39

And, generally, it is said, that similitude of hands is no evidence, but saying that he was well acquainted with his writing, and knew it to be the party's, is evidence 12 *Vin* 204

And in general cases, the witness should have gained his knowledge from having seen the party write, but under some circumstances that is not necessary, as where the hand-writing to be proved is of a person residing abroad, one who has frequently received letters from him in a course of correspondence, would be admitted to prove it, tho' he had never seen him write So where the antiquity of the writing makes it impossible for any living witness to swear he ever saw the party write, as where a parson's book was produced to prove a modus, the

parson

parfon having been long dead, a witnefs who had examined the parifh books, in which was the fame perfon's
name, was permitted to fwear to the fimilitude of the
hand-writing, for it was the beft evidence in the nature
of the thing, for the parifh books were not in the plaintiff's power to produce   *Theory of Evil* 25, 26

So in the cafe of *Gould* and *Jones*, *T* 2 *G* 3   On the
trial of an iffue out of chancery, before lord *Mansfield* at
the fittings in *Middlefex*, where it was difputed, whether
the name of one *William Jones*, fubfcribed to a declaration
of truft, was genuine, and, to prove the hand-writing
forged, a witnefs was produced, who had frequently cor-
refponded with *Jones*, but had never feen him write.
Lord *Mansfield*, upon debate, held him to be a good evidence, and his teftimony accordingly was admitted.
Black. Rep 384

III   *Of the evidence of witneffes.*

1 It feems that the confeffion of the defendant, whether **Confeffion**
taken on an examination before juftices of the peace, in
purfuance of the 1 & 2 *P. & M c.* 13 or 2 & 3 *P &
M. c.* 10 upon a bailment or commitment for felony, or
taken by the common law upon an examination for other
crimes not within thefe ftatutes, or in difcourfe with private perfons, hath always been allowed to be given in
evidence, againft the party confeffing, but not againft
others   2 *Haw* 429

2. It is to be obferved, that there be many circumftan- **Witnefs of kin**
ces that difable a juror, that are not fufficient exceptions **to the party.**
againft a witnefs   Thus the exception of kindred is a good
caufe of challenge againft a juror, but not againft a witnefs, therefore the father may be a competent witnefs for
or againft his fon, or the fon for or againft his father
Thefe and the like exceptions may be to the credit or credibility of the witnefs, but are not exceptions againft his
competency   2 *H H* 276

For, that I may obferve it once for all, the exceptions
to a witnefs are of two kinds   1. Exceptions to the credit of the witnefs, which do not at all difable him from
being fworn, but yet may blemifh the credibility of his
teftimony, and in fuch cafe the witnefs is to be allowed,
but the credit of his teftimony is left to the jury   2. Exceptions to the competency of the witnefs, which do exclude him from giving his teftimony, and of thefe exceptions the court is the judge   2 *H. H* 276, 277.

3 It

Witness infamous.

3 It seems agreed, that an attainder, judgment, or conviction of treason, felony, præmunire, perjury, or forgery on 5 *E.* and also a judgment in a *tales* for giving a false verdict, or in conspiracy at the suit of the king, and also judgment for any heinous crime to stand on the pillory, or to be whipped or branded, are good causes of exception against a witness, while they continue in force. 2 *Haw.* 432 *Treas. of Laws* 107

In the case of *Pearce* and *Maddock*, H 28 G 2 the question was, whether a person convicted and whipped for petit larceny shall be allowed to be a witness. And the court were clearly of opinion, that he shall not, and laid it down as a rule, that it is the crime that creates the infamy, and not the punishment for it. Petit larceny is felony, and there is no case where a person convicted thereof was ever admitted to be a witness. 2 *Hawp.* 18

But it is agreed, that no such conviction or judgment can be made use of to this purpose, unless the record be actually produced in court. 2 *Haw.* 433

Also, it is a general rule, that a witness shall not be asked any question, the answering to which might oblige him to accuse himself of a crime, and that his credit is to be impeached only by general accounts of his character and reputation, and not by proofs of particular crimes, whereof he never was convicted. 2 *Haw.* 433

And a man shall not be permitted to swear, that he was suborned and perjured. *St Tr V* 3 427

And lord *Coke* says, a witness alledging his own infamy or turpitude, is not to be heard. 4 *Inst.* 279

Thus a wife was disallowed to be a witness to prove her husband had no access to her in a case of bastardy. *Sess. Cases, V* 2 175 *K* and *Reading*, M 8 G 2

It seems clear at this day, that outlawry in a personal action is not a good exception against a witness, as it is against a juror. 2 *Haw.* 433

A person convicted of felony, who is admitted to his clergy, and burnt in the hand, is thereby re-enabled to be a witness. 2 *Haw.* 433

And it seems agreed, that the king's pardon of treason, or felony, after a conviction or attainder, restores the party to his credit. 2 *Haw.* 433

Witness, an infidel.

4 It seems agreed to be a good exception, that a witness is an infidel, that is, as it seemeth, that he believes neither the Old nor New Testament to be the word of God, on one of which our laws require the oath should be administred. 2 *Haw.* 434 But Mahomet is a

P a

Pagans have been admitted to be sworn in their own country way.

5 Want of discretion is a good exception against a witness, on which account alone it seems, that an infant may be excepted against 2 *Haw* 434

But if an infant be of the age of 14 years, he is as to this purpose of the age of discretion, to be sworn as a witness, but if under that age, yet if it appear that he hath a competent discretion, he may be sworn. 2 *H. H* 278

And in many cases an infant of tender years may be examined, where the exigence of the case requires it, which possibly, being fortified with concurrent evidences, may be of some weight, especially in cases of rape, buggery, and such crimes as are practised upon children. 2 *H H* 279, 284

But in no case shall an infant be admitted as evidence, without oath *Sir* 700 1 *Sbk* 29

6 It seems an uncontested rule in all cases, that it is a good exception against a witness that he is either to be a gainer or loser by the event of the cause, whether such advantage be direct and immediate, or consequential only 2 *Haw* 433

Thus in an information upon the statute of usury, the party to the usurious contract shall not be admitted to be a witness against the usurer, for in effect he should be witness in his own cause, and should avoid his own bonds and assurances, and discharge himself of the money borrowed 1 *Inst* 6.

Thus also an attorney ought not to be examined against his client, because he is obliged to keep his secrets but of his own knowledge before retainer, he may be examined as a witness, if served with a subpœna *Wood*, *b.* 4. *c.* 4

But upon an indictment for battery, or the like, the party grieved may be a witness against the defendant, because the prosecution is at the suit of the king *H w l*, *b.* 4 *c* 5

And in many criminal cases, from the necessity of the thing, interested persons are allowed as witnesses As where the owner prosecutes an indictment of felony for stolen goods, he is concerned in interest, for he will be intitled to restitution and yet his evidence is admitted So in removing an indictment by certiorari from the sessions to the king's bench, tho' the prosecutor in that case, if the defendant be convicted, is entitled to his costs, yet he is allowed as a witness. So where a man, in case of conviction

viction of the offender for a robbery, will be entitled to a
40 l reward, yet his evidence shall be received. And by
Parker chief justice. As to the cases where a 40 l reward
is given, they admit of this answer, that the intention of
those acts would be quite defeated, if so be the reward
should take off the evidence. The same answer may serve
to the cases put upon an indictment of felony for stolen
goods, and where the indictment is removed by certiorari:
for none in the first case but the owner can prove the property of the goods, and in the second, if the giving of
costs should take off the evidence of the prosecutor, the
act of parliament designed to discountenance the removing
of suits by certiorari, would give the greatest encouragement to them that is possible. 10 *Mod* 193 *M* 12 *An*
Q. and *Muscot.*

Also it seems agreed, that it is no good exception
against a witness, that he has a maintenance from the
king, for every one may maintain his own witnesses
2 *Haw* 434.

Thus also, one commoner may be a witness for another
claiming common, because in effect it charges himself,
that is to say, he admits another to have common with
himself. But if the prescription be, that all the inhabitants of such a place ought to have common there, one
of the inhabitants cannot be a witness, to prove that another of the said inhabitants ought to have common there,
because in effect he would swear to give himself right of
common there. *L Raym.* 731.

A trustee may be a witness, if he hath released his trust,
but not if he hath conveyed it over. *Sid* 315 *M* 18 *C* 2
Stevens and *Gerrard*

An heir at law may be a witness concerning the title to
the land, but the remainder-man cannot, for he hath a
present interest, but the heirship is a mere contingency
1 *Salk* 283 *M* 10 *W.* *Smith* and *Blackham*

In evidence to a jury at bar, a special issue by rule of
court was directed to try the custom of lady *Pierce*'s manor
of *Westward* in *Cumberland*, whether fines on the tenants
on their lord's death, be due to the heirs or successors of
the lord, during his minority, the defendant excepted to
the steward, because he had a fee on admission, but it was
not allowed, and he was sworn. 3 *Keb* 90.

A witness laying a wager in the cause, is no hindrance
to his being a witness, for the other has an interest in his
evidence which he cannot deprive him of. *Finch* 31.
Sir 652.

If

If a person *apprehends* himself to be interested, tho' in strictness of law he is not, yet he ought not to be sworn: as where the witness for the plaintiff apprehended that if the plaintiff should recover, he would remit a claim of some money which he (the plaintiff) had upon this witness, but if he should not recover, he would not remit it, although in strictness of law, his recovering or not recovering in that case would not alter the claim or as in case where the witness owned himself to be under an honorary, though not under a binding engagement, to pay the costs. *Str* 129

If a man hath been examined on interrogatories, being at that time disinterested, and afterwards becomes interested, his deposition may be given in evidence, because his evidence must be taken as it stood at the time of his examination So if a witness to a bond becomes afterwards representative of the obligee, his hand must be proved in like manner as if he were dead 2 *Atk* 615 2 *Vezey* 44

7 It seems agreed, that the husband and wife being as one and the same person in affection and interest, can no more give evidence for one another, in any case whatsoever, than for themselves, and that regularly the one shall not be admitted to give evidence *against* the other, nor the examination of the one be made use of against the other, by reason of the implacable dissension which might be caused by it, and the great danger of perjury from taking the oaths of persons under so great bias, and the extreme hardship of the case Yet some exceptions have been allowed in cases of evident necessity; as in the lord *Audley*'s case, who held his wife, while his servant by his command ravished her, or where a man is indicted for a forcible marriage on the statute of the 3 *H* 7 or where either a husband or wife have cause to demand sureties of the peace against the other 2 *Haw* 431, 432 *[margin: Husband and wife.]*

8 It seems agreed, that it is no exception against a person's giving evidence either for or against a prisoner, that he is one of the judges or jurors who are to try him. 2 *Haw* 432. *[margin: Judge or juror, being a witness.]*

But where a juror is called upon to give his evidence, he ought to give it upon oath openly in court, and not be examined privately by his companions. *Bac. Abr* Evid. A 2

9 It hath been long settled, that it is no exception against a witness, that he hath confessed himself guilty of the same crime, if he hath not been indicted for it, for if no accomplices were to be admitted as witnesses, it would be *[margin: Witness being an accomplice.]*

be generally impossible to find evidence to convict the greatest offenders 2 *Haw* 432.

Also it hath been often ruled, that accomplices who are indicted, are good witnesses for the king, until they be convicted 2 *Haw* 432

Also it hath often been adjudged, that such of the defendants in an information, against whom no evidence is given, may be witnesses for the others 2 *Haw* 432

It hath been also adjudged, that where three persons are sued in three several actions on the statute for a supposed perjury in their evidence concerning the same thing, they may be good witnesses in such actions for one another 2 *Haw* 432

Witness an alien or bondman
10 It seems agreed, that it is no good exception against a witness, that he is an alien, or villein, or bondman 2 *Haw* 434.

Witness blind
11 There were two witnesses to a deed, and one of them was blind It was ruled by *Holt* chief justice, that such deed might be proved by the other witness, and it is, or might be proved, without proving that this blind witness is dead, or without having him at the trial, proving only his hand L *Raym* 734 Wood *and* Drury

Witness over sea
12 If a witness is beyond the sea, it is usual to prove his hand, and that he is beyond the sea 12 *Viner* 224

Witness become insane
13. There were two witnesses to a bond, one in *Africa*, and the other in Bedlam, mad On an order to prove an exhibit *viva voce* in chancery, a witness proved their facts, and their hands to the bond as if dead. *T.* 5 & 6 G 2 12 *Viner* 224

Witness dead.
14 If a witness to a deed is dead, it is not sufficient to prove his hand-writing, but it must be proved also that he is dead 2 *Atk* 48

And where a person has lived abroad for some years, after attesting a deed, there must be strict proof of his death Otherwise it is, where the witness has lived constantly in *England*, from the time of subscribing his name to the day of his death, for in that case, a slight evidence of his death is sufficient, especially where the person who proves his hand knew him intimately, and swears that he believes him dead. *Id*

But where the witness is dead, it is sufficient to prove the witness's hand, without proving the hand of the party. 12 *Viner*. 224

The sayings of a dead man are not to be given in evidence to prove a particular fact, they are only to be admitted in proof of general usages and customs, but as for a particular fact, lying in the knowledge of a particular person, by his death the evidence is lost *St Tr V* 5 456

And

And it hath been agreed, that the evidence given by a witnefs at one trial, cannot in the ordinary courfe of juftice be made ufe againft a defendant, on the death of fuch witnefs at another trial   2 *Haw* 430

In the cafe of murder, what the deceafed declared after the wound given, may be given in evidence   12 *Viner.* 118

But where fuch declaration is reduced into writing, the writing itfelf muft be produced, and not evidence thereof given *viva voce*   *id* 119

15 It is a general rule that herefay is no evidence, for no evidence is to be admitted but what is upon oath, for if the firft fpeech was without oath, another oath that there was fuch fpeech, makes it no more than a bare fpeaking, and fo of no value in a court of juftice, and befides, the adverfe party had no opportunity of a crofs examination, and if the witnefs is living, what he has been heard to fay is not the beft evidence that the nature of the thing will admit   But tho' hearfay ought not to be allowed as direct evidence, yet it may be allowed in corroboration of a witnefs's teftimony, to fhew that he affirmed the fame thing before on other occafions, and that he is ftill conftant to himfelf.   So where the iffue is on the legitimacy of a perfon, it feems the practice to admit evidence of what the parents have been heard to fay, either as to their being or not being married, for the prefumption arifing from the cohabitation is either ftrengthened or deftroyed by fuch declarations, which altho' not to be given in evidence directly, yet they may be affigned by the witnefs as a reafon for his belief one way or other   So hearfay is good evidence to prove who was a man's grandfather, when he married, what children he had, and the like, of which it is not reafonable to prefume that there is better evidence   So to prove that a man's father or other kinfman beyond the fea is dead, the common reputation and belief of it in the family gives credit to fuch evidence, and for a ftranger it would be good evidence, if a perfon fwore that a brother or other near relation had told him fo, which relation is dead   So in queftions of prefcription, it is allowable to give hearfay evidence, in order to prove general reputation   and where the iffue was of a right to a way over the plaintiff's clofe, the defendants were admitted to give evidence of a converfation between perfons not interefted, then dead, wherein the right to the way was agreed   *Theory of Evid.* 111, 112.

So in eftablifhing a title to an eftate upon a pedigree, evidence that a man has not been heard of for many years,

Hearfay.

is fufficient evidence *prima facie* to prove him dead without iffue, fo as to put the oppofite party upon proof that he ftill exifts Many perfons go to the Eaft and Weft Indies, and are never heard of more. In the mean time what is done upon fuch a trial is no injury to the man or his iffue, if he or they fhall afterwards appear and claim the eftate. *Black. Rep* 404

IV. *Of procefs to caufe witneffes to appear.*

Two ways of caufing witneffes to appear.

1 The compulfory means to bring in witneffes, are of two kinds. 1 By procefs of *fubpœna* (A) iffued in the king's name, by the juftices, or others, where the trial is to be. 2 Which is the more ordinary and more effectual means (in criminal cafes), the juftices that take the examination of the perfon accufed, and the information of the witneffes, may at that time, or at any time after, and before the trial, bind over (B) the witneffes to appear at the feffions, and in cafe of their refufal either to come, or to be bound over, may commit them for their contempt in fuch refufal 2 H H 282.

Charges of witneffes.

2 By the 27 G 2 c 3 When any poor perfon fhall appear on recognizance in any court to give evidence againft another accufed of grand or petit larceny or other felony, the court may, at the prayer, and on the oath of fuch perfon, and on confideration of his circumftances, order the treafurer to pay him fuch fum as they fhall think reafonable for his time, trouble, and expence, which order the proper officer fhall make out for the fee of 6 d, except in *Middlefex*, where the fame fhall be paid by the overfeers of the poor where the perfon was apprehended

And by the 18 G 3 c. 19. The court where any perfon fhall appear on recognizance or *fubpœna* to give evidence as to any grand or petit larceny or other felony, whether any bill of indictment be preferred or not, may order the treafurer to pay to him fuch fum as they fhall think reafonable, not exceeding the expences he was *bona fide* put unto, making alfo, if he fhall appear to be in poor circumftances, a reafonable allowance for his trouble and lofs of time, which order the clerk of affize or of the peace refpectively fhall forthwith make out and deliver to him, on being paid for the fame 6 d and no more, and the treafurer upon fight of the order fhall forthwith pay the fame ſ 8 ———— And the juftices in feffions from time to time may lay down or alter fuch rules and regulations concerning any cofts or charges to be allowed to any perfon by virtue of this act, as to them fhall feem juft which rules and regulations,

gulations, having received the approbation and fignature of one or more of the judges of affize, fhall be binding on all perfons whatfoever ƒ 9

3. Where a witnefs is a prifoner in execution for debt, he muft be brought up by *habeas corpus ad teſtiſicandum*, to give his evidence *St Tr V* 2 580 *V* 4 37

Where a witneſs is a priſoner in execution.

4 One was fubpœnaed *ad teſtiſicandum*, and prayed a privilege from being arrefted, which was granted , and by the court, it will fuperfede an arreft upon *meſne* procefs, but not upon an execution , yet the fheriff in that cafe may be committed for his contempt *Nevil*'s cafe, 15 C 2 *Tr per p* 310

Witneſs how far privileged againſt an arreſt.

5 By the 5 *El c* 9 ƒ 12 If any perfon upon whom any procefs out of any of the courts of record within this realm fhall be ferved, to teftify or depofe concerning any matter depending therein, and having tendred unto him, according to his countenance or calling, fuch reafonable fum for his cofts and charges, as (having regard to the diftance of the places) is neceffary to be allowed in that behalf, do not appear according to the tenor of the procefs, having not a lawful and reafonable impediment , he fhall forfeit 10 l, and fhall yield fuch further recompence to the party grieved, as to the judge of the court, out of which the procefs was awarded, fhall feem meet, according to the lofs that the party which procured the procefs fhall fuftain , to be recovered by the party grieved, in any court of record

Penalty of a witneſs not appearing.

In the cafe of *Wyat* and *Winkford*, 2 *G* 2 A motion was made for an attachment againft a perfon for not attending at the affizes to give his evidence, being fubpœnaed, and having received one guinea for his charges, and being promifed to have one guinea a day while there, and his charges paid And a rule was made to fhew caufe. And afterwards caufe was fhewed, that an attachment ought not to go, but the party injured had his action upon the ftatute of *Eliz* but the court thought, that it was a good foundation for an attachment, the difobedience to the fubpœna being a contempt of the court; and though an action might be brought on the ftatute, yet that was a more dilatory method, and more difficult to proceed in, which encouraged witneffes not attending frequently upon trials, at which they were fubpœnaed to appear and give evidence And therefore the rule was made abfolute *L Raym.* 1529.

In the cafe of *Small* and *Whitmill*, *M* 10 *G*. 2. It was moved for an attachment againft one *Wakefield*, for not attending to give evidence, being ferved with a fubpœna.

The

The ticket and subpœna were not sworn to have been served personally, but delivered to a servant at the witness's house, who carried it up to his master, and brought down word, that he delivered it to his master, who said he would attend. By Lord *Hardwicke* Ch J. This way of proceeding by attachment is a new method. I do not know that it has been determined, that serving a subpœna on a servant, would be a sufficient service to maintain an *action*, but however, to be sure, it is not a sufficient ground for an *attachment*. And *Lee* J said, It hath been solemnly determined, that you must not only have an affidavit of tendring the shilling, but likewise of a tender of reasonable charges, to ground an attachment. And the attachment was denied. *Caf Hardw* 313. *Str* 1054.

E 14 *G* 2 *Chapman* and *Poynton*. A witness was served with a subpœna at *Chester*, to attend the sittings at *Guildhall*, and two guineas were tendred by the person who served it, and being objected to as too little, he declared he would give no more. The witness not coming up, an attachment was moved for, but on shewing cause was discharged. the court saying it was too little, and that the witness is not obliged to trust to the court's allowing him more when he comes to the book, for perhaps the party may not call him, and then it may be difficult for him to get home again. that this way of punishing as for a contempt was new, and practised only in this court. the common pleas not doing it to this day, but leaving the party to his remedy on the 5 *El* o and therefore they would not enter into any nice calculations of the expence, but confined their inquiry to the question, whether the non-attendance was thro' obstinacy or not. *Str* 1150.

M. 22 *G* 2. *Bowles* and *Johnson*. It was moved for an attachment against one *Yerburgh*, for not giving evidence at the assizes. He was subpœnaed, but had no offer to have his expences born; but came to the assizes, where money was tendred to him for that purpose, but he refused to be sworn. By *Lee* chief justice. Attachments are a new practice. I remember the first motion for them. It was then agreed, that the same restrictions should be used in attachments as in actions on the 5 *Eliz* one of which is, that a tender of expences should be made at the service of the subpœna. In this case, *Yerburgh* has not been subpœnaed regularly, so as to subject him to the 5 *Eliz*. In order to be subject to an attachment, you must shew him guilty of a contempt of this court. By *Wright* justice. A person not properly subpœnaed is to looked upon only as a stander-by, and it is no contempt of the court of *Nisi Prius*,

for

for a ftander-by to refufe to be examined, much lefs is it a contempt of this court   And the attachment was denied   *Black Rep* 36

And, by the court, in the cafe of *Hammond* and *Stewart*, *H 8 G* the witnefles ought to have a reafonable time to put their affairs in order, that their attendance upon the court may be as little prejudice to themfelves as poffible. *Str* 510

In criminal cafes, if a witnefs hath been bound over, and do not appear, he fhall forfeit his recognizance.

V Of the manner of giving evidence.

1   He who affirms the matter in iffue, whether plaintiff or defendant, ought to begin to give evidence   *Lit* 36.

2   The evidence both for and againft a prifoner, ought to be upon oath

And if a peer is produced as a witnefs, he ought to be fworn.   3 *Keb* 61.

Lord *Prefton* was committed by the court of quarter feffions, for refufing to be fworn to give evidence to the grand jury on an indictment of high treafon, and on his being brought by *habeas corpus* into the king's bench, *Holt*, Ch J. faid, it was a great contempt, and that had he been there, he would have fined him, and committed him till he paid the fine, but being otherwife, he was bailed   1 *Salk* 278.

But a quaker's affirmation, in all cafes not being criminal, fhall be allowed as evidence, without an oath, but in criminal cafes his affirmation fhall not be allowed.   7 & 8 *W c* 34.

3   It is no fatisfaction for a witnefs to fay, that he thinks or perfuades himfelf, and this for two reafons, by *Coke* chief juftice   1 Becaufe the judge is to give abfolute fentence, and ought to have more ground than thinking. 2. Becaufe judges, as judges, are always to give judgment *fecundum allegata et probata*, notwithftanding that private perfons think otherwife   *Dyer* 53.

4   The court may indulge a prifoner in examining the witnefles apart, but he cannot demand it of right   *St Tr* *V.* 4 9

5.   In cafes of life, no evidence is to be given againft a prifoner, but in his prefence   2 *Haw.* 428

6   In every iffue, the affirmative is to be proved. A negative cannot regularly be proved, and therefore it is fufficient to deny what is affirmed, until it be proved, but when the affirmative is proved, the other fide may conteft it with oppofite proofs, for this is not properly the proof

of

Side notes:
Which party fhall begin the evidence.

Evidence to be upon oath

Muft be pofitive.

Witneffes maybe examined apart.

Evidence to be given in the prifoner's prefence.

Witneffes cannot teftify a negative

of a negative, but the proof of some proposition totally inconsistent with what is affirmed as if the defendant be charged with a trespass, he need only make a general denial of the fact, and if the fact be proved, then he may prove a proposition inconsistent with the charge, as that he was at another place at the time, or the like. *Theory of Evid* 116, 117.

But to this rule there is an exception of such cases, where the law presumes the affirmative contained in the issue Therefore, in an information against lord *Halifax* for refusing to deliver up the rolls of the auditor of the exchequer the court of exchequer put the plaintiff upon proving the negative, namely, that he did not deliver them, for a person shall be presumed duly to execute his office, till the contrary appear *id* 117

A man shall not disprove his own witnesses

7 A prisoner may not call witnesses to disprove what his own witnesses have sworn *St Tr V* 2 764, 792

Whether a witness may read his evidence

8 A witness shall not be permitted to read his evidence, but he may look upon his notes to refresh his memory. *St. Tr. V* 445

When he may be cross examined

9 A witness shall not be cross examined, till he has gone thro' the evidence for the party on whose side he was produced *St Tr V* 2792

Variance.

10 It hath been admitted, that in order to shew a variance in the evidence, a deposition taken by a witness before a justice of the peace, may at the prisoner's desire be read at the trial, in order to take off the credit of the witness, by shewing a variance between such depositions, and the evidence given in court. And for the same reason it seems agreed, that where a witness at one trial varies from his own evidence at another, in relation to the same matter, such variance may also be given in evidence to invalidate his testimony at the second trial. 2 *Haw* 430.

Which party shall conclude

11. The counsel of that party which doth begin to maintain the issue, ought to conclude *Tri p pais* 220.

A. Subpœna to give evidence

GEORGE *the third, by the grace of God, of Great Britain, France, and Ireland, king, defender of the faith, and so forth To A. B. C D and E F greeting We command you, and every of you, that all business being laid aside, and all excuses whatsoever ceasing, you do in your proper persons appear before our justices assigned to keep the peace in our county of ———— and also to hear and determine divers felonies, trespasses, and other misdemeanors in the said county* com-

committed, at the general quarter *seffions of the peace, to be holden at* ———— *in and for the faid county, on* ——— *the* ———— *day of* ———— *at the hour of ten in the forenoon of the fame day, to teftify the truth, and give evidence on behalf of the inhabitants of the parifh of* ——— *in the faid county, againft* A. O *in a cafe of baftardy. And this you are in no wife to omit, nor any of you to omit, on pain of one hundred pounds Witnefs Sir* James Lowther, *baronet, the* ———— *day of* ———— *in the* ———— *year of our reign.*

C.

Note ; There may be four witneffes put in one *fubpœna.*

A fubpœna ticket.

To Mr. A. W.

BY *virtue of his majefty's writ of fubpœna to you directed, and herewith fhewn to you, you are perfonally to be before his majefty's juftices of the peace for the county of* ——— *at the general quarter feffions of the peace to be holden for the faid county, at* ——— *in the faid county, on* ——— *the* ———— *day of* ———— *next, to teftify the truth, and give evidence on behalf of the inhabitants of the parifh of* ——— *in the faid county, againft* A O *in a cafe of baftardy. And this you are not to omit, upon pain of one hundred pounds Dated this* ———— *day of* ———— *in the year* ————

By the court,
C

B. Condition of a recognizance to appear and give evidence

THE *condition of this recognizance is fuch, that if the above-bound* A W *fhall perfonally appear at the next general quarter feffions of the peace to be holden at* — *in and for the faid county, and then and there give fuch evidence as he knoweth, upon a bill of indictment to be exhibited by* A I *of* ——— *yeoman, to the grand jury, againft* A O *late of* ——— *in the faid county, yeoman, for the feloniously taking and carrying away* ———— *the property of* ———— *and in cafe the faid bill be found a true bill, then if the faid* A W. *fhall then and there give evidence to the jurors that fhall pafs on the trial of the faid* A. O *upon the faid bill of indictment, and not depart thence without leave of the court, then this recognizance to be void, otherwife of force.*

Exa-

Examination.

IF a felony is committed, and one is brought before a justice upon suspicion thereof, and the justice finds upon examination that the prisoner is not guilty, yet the justice shall not discharge him, but he must either be bailed or committed for it is not fit that a man once arrested and charged with felony, or suspicion thereof, should be delivered upon any man's discretion, without farther trial. *Dalt. c* 164

In order to which bail or commitment, the examination and information of the parties must first be taken, according to the following statutes

Two or more justices (1 Q) or one of the said justices, before they bail a person apprehended for felony (if the offence is bailable) shall take his examination (A) and the information (B) of them that bring him, of the fact and circumstances thereof, and the same, or as much thereof as shall be material to prove the felony, shall put in writing, which examination they shall certify (together with the bailment) at the next general gaol delivery, to be holden within the limits of their commission 1 & 2 P & M c. 13 f 4

And they shall have power to bind by recognizance (C) all such as do declare any thing material to prove the offence, to appear at the next general gaol delivery, to be holden within the county where the trial shall be, then and there to give evidence against the party, and shall certify such recognizance in like manner. f. 5

And if they offend in any thing herein, they shall be fined by the justices of gaol delivery id

In like manner, where the person is not bailed, but committed to ward, the justice or justices who commit him, shall before such commitment, take the like examination and information, and shall put the same in writing within two days after the said examination, and shall in like manner bind over the witnesses, and certify the whole as above. 2 & 3 P. & M. c. 10

Shall take his examination] And in order thereunto, if by some reasonable occasion, the justice cannot at the return of the warrant take the examination, he may by word of mouth command the constable or any other person, to detain in custody the prisoner till the next day, and then to bring him before the justice, for farther examination And this detainer is justifiable by the constable or any

other

other perſon, without ſhewing the particular cauſe for which he was to be examined, or any warrant in writing 1 *H H* 585.

But the time of the detainer muſt be no longer than is neceſſary for ſuch purpoſe, for which it is ſaid, that the ſpace of three days is a reaſonable time 2 *Haw* 119

The examination of the perſon accuſed, ought not to be upon oath 1 *H H* 585

But if upon his examination he ſhall confeſs the matter, it ſhall not be amiſs that he ſubſcribe his name, or mark to it *Dalt c* 164

Which examination being voluntary, and ſworn by the juſtice or his clerk to be truly taken, may be given in evidence againſt the party confeſſing, but not againſt others 1 *H. H* 585 2 *Haw.* 429

Information of them that bring him] Or of other witneſſes, whom the juſtice may bring before him by his warrant (D) for that purpoſe. 1 *H H* 586 *Dalt* 164

And this information muſt be upon oath *Dalt c* 164 1 *H H* 586

And therefore if a quaker is witneſs, his affirmation muſt not be taken in this caſe, for by the 7 & 8 *W c* 34 ſ 36. it is provided, that no quaker ſhall be examined for or againſt any perſon in any criminal cauſe, unleſs it be upon oath

And the ſaid information being upon the trial ſworn to be truly taken, by the juſtice or his clerk, may be given in evidence againſt the priſoner, if the witneſſes be dead or not able to travel. 1 *H H* 586

Or as much thereof as ſhall be material to prove the felony] Yet it ſeemeth alſo juſt and right, that the juſtices who take information againſt a felon, or perſon ſuſpected of felony, ſhould take and certify as well ſuch information, proof, and evidence, as goeth to the acquittal or clearing of the priſoner, as ſuch as maketh againſt the priſoner for ſuch information, evidence, or proof ſo taken, is only to inform the king and his juſtices of the truth of the matter *Dalt. c.* 165.

Shall certify at the next gaol delivery] And yet for petty larcenies, and ſmall felonies, the offenders may be tried at the quarter ſeſſions, and the examinations and informations may be certified thither *Dalt. c* 104

To be holden within the limits of their commiſſion] And yet examinations taken by juſtices of the peace in one county, may be by them certified in another county, and there read, and given in evidence against the prisoner. *Dalt. c* 164.

To bind by recognizance] And upon refusal may commit the person refusing   1 *H H.* 586.

And the parties grieved ought to be bound, not only to give evidence, but also to prefer a bill of indictment against the prisoner *Dalt. c* 164.

A. Examination of a felon.

Westmorland. THE *examination of* A O *of* ——— *yeoman, taken before me* Henry Chaytor, *doctor of laws, one of his majesty's justices of the peace for the said county* [or, in the case of bail, — *taken before us* ——— *two of his majesty's justices of the peace for the said county, and one of us of the* quorum] *the* —— *day of* —— *in the* —— *year of the reign of* ——— ———

The said A.O *being charged before me* [or, *us*] *by* A. I *of* ——— ——— *yeoman, with the felonious stealing out of the house of the said* A I *at* —— *on the* —— *day of* —— *the following goods, to wit* —— *of the value of* —— *he the said* A O *upon his examination now taken before me* [or, *us*] *confesseth that* —— [or, *saith that* ——] &c

B Information of a witness.

Westmorland THE *information of* A I *of* ——— ——— *yeoman, taken upon oath before me* [as before]

C Recognizance to give evidence.

Westmorland BE it remembered, *that on the* ——— *day of* ——— *in the* ——— *year of the reign of* ——— A I *of* ——— *in the said county, yeoman, did come before me* Henry Chaytor, *doctor of laws, one of the justices of our said lord the king, assigned to keep the peace in the said county, and did acknowledge himself to owe to our said lord the king ten pounds of lawful money of* Great Britain, *under condition, that if he shall personally appear before the justice of our said lord the king, at the next general quarter sessions of the peace* [or, *gaol delivery*] *to be holden in and for the said county,*

then

then and there to give evidence in behalf of our said lord the king, against A O late of —— —— who being attacked, and suspected of felony, is now committed to the gaol of our said lord the king in the said county, then this recognizance to be void, otherwise of force.

Or thus, to prefer a bill of indictment, and give evidence.

Westmorland BE it remembered, that on the —— day of —— in the —— year of the reign of —— —— A I of —— in the said county, yeoman, personally came before me Henry Chaytor, doctor of laws, one of the justices of our said lord the king, assigned to keep the peace in the said county, and acknowledged himself to owe to our said lord the king, the sum of —— of good and lawful money of Great Britain, to be made and levied of his goods and chattels, lands and tenements, to the use of our said lord the king, his heirs and successors, if he the said A. I. shall fail in the condition indorsed

               H. C.

The condition of the within written recognizance is such, that whereas one A O. late of —— was this present day brought before the justice within mentioned by the within bounden A I. and was by him charged with the felonious taking and carrying away —— of the goods of him the said A I and thereupon was committed by the said justice to the common gaol in and for the said county if therefore he the said A I shall and do at the next general quarter sessions of the peace [or, gaol delivery] to be holden in and for the said county, prefer or cause to be preferred, one bill of indictment of the said felony against the said A O and shall then also give evidence there concerning the same, as well to the jurors, that shall then inquire of the said felony, as also to them that shall pass upon the trial of the said A O that then the said recognizance to be void, or else to stand in full force for the king

D. Warrant for a witness.

Westmorland { To the constable of ——

WHEREAS *oath hath been made before me ——* *one of his majesty's justices of the peace in and for the said county, by A I. of —— yeoman, that he the said A I.*

was

was lately robbed at ——— and that he hath good cause to believe that A W. of ——— is a material witness to prove by whom the said robbery was committed   these are therefore to require you to cause the said A I forthwith to come before me, to give such information and evidence as he knoweth concerning the said offence, that such further proceeding may be had therein, as to the law doth appertain   Given under my hand and seal at ——— in the said county, the ——— day of———.

Here endeth the First Volume.

FOLIO.

A NEW Law Dictionary, containing the Interpretation and Definition of Words and Terms used in the Law, as also the Law and Practice, under the proper Heads and Titles. Together with such Learning as explains The History and Antiquity of the Law, our Manners, Customs, and original Government. Originally compiled by *Giles Jacob*, and now corrected and greatly enlarged by *John Morgan*, Esq. Tenth Edition. 2l 2s.

Lex Mercatoria Rediviva: or, the Merchant's Directory. Being a complete Guide to all Men in Business, whether as Traders, Remitters, Owners, Freighters, Captains, Insurers, Brokers, Factors, Supercargoes or Agents: containing an Account of our Mercantile Companies, of our Colonies and Factories Abroad, of our commercial Treaties with Foreign Powers, of the Duty of Consuls, and of the Laws concerning Aliens, Naturalizations, and Denization. To which is added, A Sketch of the present State of the Commerce of the whole World, describing the Manufactures and Produce of each particular Nation, with Tables of the Correspondence and Agreement of their respective Coins, Weights, and Measures. By the late *Wyndham Beawes*, Esq. and now considerably improved and corrected to the present Time. By *Thomas Mortimer*, Esq. 2l 2s.

QUARTO.

The History and Antiquities of the Counties of *Westmoreland* and *Cumberland*. By *Joseph Nicholson*, Esq. and *Richard Burn*, LL. D. 2 Vols. 2l 10s.

The History of the Legal Polity of the Roman State, of the Rise, Progress, and Extent of the Roman Laws. By *Thomas Bever*, LL. D. 18s. in boards.

An Inquiry into the Principles of Political Oeconomy; being an Essay on the Science of Domestic Policy in Free Nations,

BOOKS.

Nations, in which are particularly confidered, Population, Agriculture, Trade, Induſtry, Money, Coin, Intereſt, Circulation, Banks, Exchange, Public Credit,
Taxes, &c. By Sir *James Stuart*, Bart, 2 Vols Royal
Paper, 2l 2s. *boards*

Lectures on Rhetoric and Belles Letters By *Hugh
Blair*, D D one of the Miniſters of the High Church,
and Profeſſor of Rhetoric and Belles Lettres, in the Univerſity of *Edinburgh*. With a Head of the Author.
2 Vols. 2l 2s.

OCTAVOS and TWELVES.

An Inquiry into the Nature and Cauſes of the Wealth
of Nations By *Adam Smith*, LL D F R S formerly
Profeſſor of Moral Philoſophy, in the Univerſity of
Glaſgow 3 Vols 1l 1s. 3d Edition.

The Hiſtory of *England*, from the earlieſt Accounts of
Time, to the Death of *George* the Second, adorned with
Heads elegantly engraved. By Dr. *Goldſmith*. 4 Vols.
1l 4s;

An Abridgment of the above Book, by Dr *Goldſmith*
Adorned with Cuts, for the Uſe of Schools. 3s 6d

The Parliamentary or Conſtitutional Hiſtory of *England*, from the earlieſt Times to the Reſtoration of King
Charles II Collected from the Records, the Rolls of Parliament, the Journals of both Houſes, the public Libraries, original Manuſcripts, ſcarce Speeches and Tracts.
All compared with the ſeveral cotemporary Writers, and
connected throughout with the Hiſtory of the Times.
With a good Index, by ſeveral Hands. 24 Vols 8vo.
7l 7s

Grey's Debates, being a Continuation of the above In
10 Vols. 3l. 3s

The Hiſtory of the Decline and Fall of the Roman
Empire. By *Edward Gibbon*, Eſq which completes a Period of Hiſtory from the Age of Trajan and the Antonines,
to the total Deſtruction of the Roman Empire in the
Weſt, adorned with a Head of the Author, and Maps
adapted to the Work. 6 Vols. 1l 16s.

The Hiſtory of *England*, from the Invaſion of *Julius
Cæſar* to the Revolution in 1688 By *David Hume*, Eſq.
8 Vols 2l 8s A new Edition, to which is now pre-
fixed his Life, written by himſelf.

One Hundred BLANK PRECEDENTS relating to the Office
of Juſtices of the Peace, ſettled by Dr. BURN.